The Authority and Interpretation of the Bible

Books by Jack Rogers:

The Authority and Interpretation of the Bible: An Historical Approach

Biblical Authority, editor and contributor

Case Studies in Christ and Salvation, with Ross Mackenzie and Louis Weeks

The Family Together, with Sharee Rogers

Confessions of a Conservative Evangelical

Scripture in the Westminster Confession

Books by Donald McKim:

The Authority and Interpretation of the Bible: An Historical Approach

The Church: Its Early Life

The Authority and Interpretation of the Bible

An Historical Approach

by
Jack B. Rogers
& Donald K. McKim

Published in San Francisco by

HARPER & ROW, PUBLISHERS

New York   Hagerstown   San Francisco   London

To Sharee,

Still a "Wife in Deed," whose love has made this possible

—Jack

To LindaJo,

Whose love and support made this writing a joy

—Don

The Authority and Interpretation of the Bible: An Historical Approach. Copyright ©
1979 by Jack Bartlett Rogers and Donald Keith McKim.

FIRST EDITION

Designed by Leigh McLellan

Library of Congress Cataloging in Publication Data

Rogers, Jack Bartlett.
  The authority and interpretation of the
Bible.

  Includes bibliographies and index.
  1. Bible—Criticism, interpretation, etc.—History.
2. Bible—Evidences, authority, etc.—History. 3. Theology, Reformed Church—History. I, McKim, Donald K., joint author. II. Title.
BS500.R63 1979   220.6′09   78-20584
ISBN 0-06-066696-X

79 80 81 82 83 10 9 8 7 6 5 4 3 2 1

Contents

Abbreviations
Used in Notes

IP	Reid, *Essays on the Intellectual Powers of Man*
ISBE	*International Standard Bible Encyclopedia,* ed. Orr
JPH	*Journal of Presbyterian History*
LAA	J. W. Alexander, *Life of Archibald Alexander*
LCC	Library of Christian Classics
LCH	A. A. Hodge, *Life of Charles Hodge, D.D. LL.D*
LW	*Luther's Works,* ed. Pelikan and Lehmann
M&S	M'Clintock & Strong, *Cyclopedia of Biblical, Theological & Ecclesiastical Literature*
NEBM	*New Encyclopaedia Britannica: Micropaedia*
NIDCC	*New International Dictionary of the Christian Church,* ed. Douglas (1974)
NPNF	*Nicene and Post-Nicene Fathers,* ed. Schaff
NSH	*The New Schaff-Herzog Encyclopedia of Religious Knowledge,* ed. Jackson
ODC	*Oxford Dictionary of the Christian Church,* ed. Cross and Livingstone (2d ed.)
O	Daniélou, *Origen*
PE	*Works of Martin Luther,* Philadelphia edition
PAS	Bozeman, *Protestants in an Age of Science*
PG	*Patrologia Series Graeca,* ed. Migne
PL	*Patrologia Series Latina,* ed. Migne
PR	*Princeton Review*
PRR	*Presbyterian & Reformed Review*
PST	Kuyper, *Principles of Sacred Theology*
PTR	*Princeton Theological Review*
SB	Smalley, *The Study of the Bible in the Middle Ages*
SCG	Aquinas, *Summa Contra Gentiles*
SH	Grant, *A Short History of the Interpretation of the Bible*
SJT	*Scottish Journal of Theology*
SL	*D. Martin Luthers Sämtliche Schriften,* ed. Walch
SM	*Sacramentum Mundi: An Encyclopedia of Theology,* ed. Rahner et al.
ST	Aquinas, *Summa Theologiae*
SWC	Rogers, *Scripture in the Westminster Confession*
SWW—I	*Selected Shorter Writings of Benjamin B. Warfield—I,* ed. Meeter
SWW—II	*Selected Shorter Writings of Benjamin B. Warfield—II,* ed. Meeter
WA	Luther, *Weimarer Ausgabe,* ed. Knaake
WATR	*D. Martin Luthers Werke Tischreden,* ed. Drescher
WDCH	*The Westminster Dictionary of Church History,* ed. Brauer
WGWM	Barth, *The Word of God & the Word of Man*

Preface

For two relatively young scholars to present a book under the title *The Authority and Interpretation of the Bible: An Historical Approach* might seem presumptuous. We do not intend it to be. We have no illusions that we have provided a definitive statement. We did not set out to do so. Our fondest hope is that this book might not close, but open discussion. Our own life experience and study, especially in the last ten years, has convinced us that a new approach to the subject of biblical authority and interpretation is needed. Some peculiar twists of American history have conspired to distort our perception of the central Christian tradition regarding the status and use of Scripture. We need a new model, perspective, or paradigm by which to view the Bible. We believe that such a model is available in the central Christian tradition, especially as it came to expression at the time of the Reformation. A particular post-Reformation scholastic tradition that has prevailed in much of American Protestant thought and church life has succeeded in obscuring our awareness of the central church tradition and its Reformation expression.

Doing this investigation and interpretation has been for us an experience of further defining and deepening our own theological and ecclesiastical roots. Both of us are ordained ministers in the United Presbyterian Church in the United States of America. We appreciate and honor the ethos and experience of our ecclesiastical tradition. At the same time, we both gratefully acknowledge that we have been nurtured as well by that somewhat amorphous and often overlapping tradition known in America as "evangelicalism." Indeed, we are both in part products of that particular branch of evangelicalism that came to full expression in the late nineteenth and early twentieth centuries in the post-Reformation scholastic theology of old Princeton Seminary. For many Americans, as for us in our youth, that Reformed scholasticism was identified with the approach to the Bible of the Reformers and the theologians of the early church. To discover that what we had been taught by respected pastors and professors was not historically correct has been an often painful experience. We intend to continue to respect and honor our foreparents in the faith by following their intention to seek the truth rather than by simply accepting the tradition they passed on to us.

Both of us came to a new understanding of the Reformed tradition through the study of primary source documents. In the case of Rogers it was especially the Westminster Divines and nineteenth-century Dutch Calvinism. In the case of McKim, it was Calvin and John Owen. We each found our studies leading us to the old Princeton theology in order to account for the discrepancies between what we had been taught as Reformed theology and the testimony of the primary sources. It is for this reason that we have placed such emphasis on the scholastic tradition culminating in old Princeton. By setting that especially influential American theology in the context of the older traditions of the Reformation and the early church we hope to enable readers to make a fresh evaluation of our American theological heritage.

It has not been our basic purpose to add data from previously unpublished primary documents although in each period some primary sources are probed. Rather, we have concentrated on gathering the ample testimony from already existing studies, often known primarily to specialists. We are well aware that experts in each area we touch in this broad survey can raise questions and point to lacunae in our treatment of their terrain. We will be grateful for every further contribution to our understanding of this extensive and essential topic. We ask that our own endeavor be viewed as the attempt to suggest a new paradigm, an alternative viewpoint, a more historically sound perspective, from which further discussion can proceed.

To further our purpose, we have cited in the text only the historical personages whose views we seek to expound, such as Augustine, Calvin, Hodge. In the footnotes we point to the diverse opinions of scholars in interpreting the primary personages. We sometimes engage in extensive excursuses that are intended to carry on the scholarly debate and to indicate why we take the particular interpretative position we do. Over 760 works are cited in the footnotes. We are indebted to Kenneth A. Ross, III, who compiled a full bibliography of these sources. Since all of these works are cited in full at their first use in each chapter, we have reproduced at the end of each chapter only a selected bibliography to guide additional study of the historical period treated. These works generally are intended to acknowledge scholars whose studies have guided us in our understanding of the period. A list of standard abbreviations has been included of works, both primary and secondary, to which we have made frequent reference.

It would of course be impossible to acknowledge all the persons who have contributed to our thinking on this subject. But we do wish to thank some groups and individuals whose input has been especially significant.

We benefited from the response to our material as presented in successive stages by Jack Rogers in the E. C. Westervelt Lectures at Austin Presbyterian Seminary in 1977 and later that year in lectures to Presbyterian ministers in Wabash Valley Presbytery (Indiana) and to faculty, students, and guests at Western Theological Seminary, Holland, Michigan. In 1978 Rogers was able to test our materials in lectures at the Colonial Church (Congregational) and at Christ's Church (Presbyterian) both in Edina, Minnesota. We benefited as well from interaction with students and faculty at Westminster College in Pennsylvania and at Bethel College and Seminary in St. Paul, Minnesota. A special word of thanks is due to the class of sixteen students at Fuller Seminary who worked through the manuscript with Jack Rogers upon its completion in first draft.

Three institutions have given major support and encouragement to us in carrying out this project. Jack Rogers is grateful to the Board of Trustees and Administration of Fuller Theological Seminary for granting him a sabbatical leave for the academic year 1977–78, during which time the final writing of the manuscript was completed. The continuing moral and substantive support by colleagues and staff at Fuller have enabled him to progress. Beverly May, secretary in the graduate office, typed the last two-thirds of the manuscript.

Rogers benefited greatly by the opportunity to be in residence as a Fellow of the Institute for Ecumenical and Cultural Research in Collegeville, Minnesota, from September 1977, until June 1978. Not only the facilities for living and study but also the friendship and lively interaction of the ecumenical community at the Institute and adjacent St. John's University and Benedictine Abbey contributed importantly to the development of this work. Sister Romaine Thiessen of the Convent of St. Benedict in St. Joseph, Minnesota, typed the first third of the manuscript.

Donald McKim wishes to thank the members of his dissertation committee at both the University of Pittsburgh and Pittsburgh Theological Seminary for their indulgence and support of his taking time from his dissertation to complete this project: Dr. Richard H. Wilmer, Jr.; Dr. Hugh F. Kearney; Dr. Charles B. Partee; Dr. Robert S. Paul (now of Austin Presbyterian Theological Seminary); and Dr. Ford L. Battles (now of Calvin Theological Seminary). Dr. Battles, in addition, most graciously provided a foreword.

Finally, we are grateful to our families for their love and affirmation and especially to our wives to whom this book is affectionately dedicated.

Jack Rogers and Donald McKim, Advent, 1978.

Foreword

The writings of most Calvinists of the seventeenth and eighteenth centuries seldom if ever make reference to John Calvin, their avowed progenitor. As one who has come to cherish the *Institutes of the Christian Reglion* next only to the Scripture, I remember eagerly searching the pages of his spiritual sons for a mention of his name, only to find it absent. Why? Could it be that so powerfully did Calvin's mind turn his readers to Scripture, so self-effacedly did he set forth a scriptural method of theologizing that, like his self-chosen unmarked grave, his theological masterpiece became a memorial not to himself but to his Master? Calvin would not have been unhappy for his name to go thus unmentioned.

But perhaps he would have sorrowed much to see the positions, so eloquently and prayerfully taken by him, forgotten, disregarded, even gainsaid or repudiated. It would have been unendurable for him to see his theology recast into an Aquinian mold in order to preserve in truncated form both it and the branch of the church to which it had given existence, from the renewed papalism that followed the Council of Trent, and from other perils, religious and secular, that marked the two centuries after his death. The growing crisis in religion brought on by the advance of science in that epoch was not the least of these perils. For his theology, steering a middle course of truth between the Scylla of the falsity of defect and the Charybdis of the falsity of excess, was not the faith of a Christian philosopher with reason virtually intact, but the faith of a scriptural exegete, resting his ever-growing rational insight into divine truth upon the grace of God in Christ, given by the Holy Spirit.

My personal question—why no mention of Calvin by Calvinists?—is thoroughly answered here by Jack Rogers and Donald McKim. But this was not their chief goal. Theirs rather was to answer the question: How did the defensive, intransigent position of inerrancy that marks the handling of Scripture among certain twentieth-century children of the Protestant Reformation come into existence? Our authors have read the early church fathers, the medieval exegetes, and especially the magistral Reformers, and have found no such teaching about Scripture and its inspiration in those authors. Building on the growing monographic literature on Protestant scholasticism, they have traced this scholasticizing, philosophizing phenomenon from its roots in Calvin's immediate theological successors through the perilous passage from the seventeenth to the twentieth centuries. They have especially concentrated on the elaboration of the Princeton theology—that *Turretinus Redivivus*—of the nineteenth century, and its aftermath. While their chief concern is the disarray of scriptural understanding in contemporary American Presbyterianism, their diagnosis of the patient and their proposed therapy may be applied, with slight adaptations, to all ailing evangelicals.

To take seriously once more Calvin's teaching on the Holy Scripture and its roots in Christian history and in the Bible itself means to restore the place of the Holy Spirit, not only as the inspirer of real, living human authors, but as the inspirer too of real, living human interpreters. It is to heed the long history of scriptural exegesis in the Church. But it is supremely to see the fatherly care with which God in Christ has made and is making his will known to us his children in language commensurate with our capacity, the language of his Holy Word, ever old, ever new.

Ford Lewis Battles
Calvin Theological Seminary

Introduction*

One of the most important and least known facts of American church history is that the principal textbook in systematic theology at Princeton Seminary from its founding in 1812 until 1872 was the *Institutio Theologiae Elencticae* of Francis Turretin. In 1872 Charles Hodge's famous *Systematic Theology* replaced Turretin's Latin tome as the text, but continued Turretin's theological method. For over one hundred years professors at Princeton vowed to "receive and subscribe" the Westminster Confession of Faith and Catechisms. They thought of themselves as followers of Calvin. But in actuality they believed and taught a theological method regarding the authority and interpretation of the Bible that was rooted in a post-Reformation scholasticism, an approach almost the exact opposite of Calvin's own. More importantly, certain features of the central church tradition regarding the authority and interpretation of Scripture, which had been retained from the early church down through the Reformation, were lost in the post-Reformation reaction to the rise of scientific criticism of the Bible.

Calvin, in common with the early church fathers, held that the authority of Scripture resided in its function of bringing people into a saving relationship with God through Jesus Christ. The Bible was to be interpreted as a document in which God had accommodated his ways and thoughts to our limited, human ways of thinking and speaking. Thus the historical, cultural period in which the writing occurred had to be taken seriously into account in order to arrive at the natural meaning of the author. It was this natural meaning, the gospel message—not the cultural context—that was normative for contemporary hearers of the Word.

Turretin, on the other hand, held that the authority of Scripture was based on its form of inerrant words. The Bible was a repository of information about all manner of things, including science and history, which had to be proven accurate by then-current standards. There was no trace of the central Christian tradition of accommodation. Rather, it

*Notes indicated by a number in bold typeface (e.g.,[12]) contain further discussion; those indicated by a number in the regular typeface (e.g.,[13]) are bibliographic citations—Editor's note.

was assumed that what the Bible told us was what God told us, down to the details. Inspired men thought God's thoughts after him and transmitted them in writing. The historical and cultural context faded in importance for the interpreter. It was assumed that all persons in all places thought alike and that Western logic was the clue to reality. Therefore, statements in the Bible were treated like logical propositions that could be interpreted quite literally according to contemporary standards.

These notions about language and culture were reinforced in the Princeton theologians by their uncritical acceptance of Scottish common sense philosophy brought to America in 1768 by John Witherspoon. Such views quite naturally brought the Princeton theologians into violent conflict with the rising tide of biblical criticism. The scholarly debate gave way to an ecclesiastical trial in the late nineteenth century. Professor Charles Augustus Briggs of Union Seminary introduced biblical criticism into the Presbyterian Church. He also attacked the Princeton theologians for departing from the theology of Calvin and the Westminster Confession and substituting the theology of Francis Turretin. Briggs's principal opponent was Benjamin Breckinridge Warfield, who held that the theology of Charles Hodge was a normative example of all Reformed theology.

Although Briggs was historically correct, Warfield's views prevailed since the majority of ministers, and through them members, of the Presbyterian Church had been trained in the scholastic views that Warfield espoused. In 1893 Briggs was suspended from the Presbyterian ministry. Furthermore, the General Assembly of the Presbyterian Church in that year adopted a statement that the "original Scriptures of the Old and New Testaments, being immediately inspired by God were without error."[1] The statement went on to assert that this view "has always been the belief of the Church." Thus the position taken in an 1881 article by A. A. Hodge and B. B. Warfield asserting the inerrancy of the (lost) autographs of the Bible was declared the official teaching of the Presbyterian Church and read back into its history as the confessional position of the church.

Such matters were front page news in the late nineteenth and early twentieth centuries. The inerrancy of the Scriptures along with the evolution of the species formed the central core of the famous fundamentalist-modernist controversy in American Protestantism. The conflict in the Presbyterian Church had importance far beyond that denomination. In other denominations people tended to take sides with the critics or with the Princeton theologians and to incorporate that controversy into the categories of their own ecclesiastical traditions.

The effects of that controversy are still with us. They are particularly poignant for two groups of people: those concerned to define their own denominational heritage and those who call themselves "evangelicals" because they hold strongly to the authority of the Bible. Because the historically false dichotomy posed by the liberal-fundamentalist controversy was never resolved, many Americans still have a distorted picture of their theological options. They assume that one must hold a rationalistic conservatism or open the door to a subjective liberalism. In the United Presbyterian Church and the Missouri Synod Lutheran Church, for example, the polarities are plain. Other denominations, whose own theological orientation is quite distinct from the Presbyterian or Lutheran—for example, the Assemblies of God—have accepted the old Princeton approach to Scripture with resulting conflicts among their members.

The Presbyterian Church was so traumatized in the 1920s by the conflict over the inerrancy of the Bible that, in 1927, it adopted a report which declared that the General Assembly did not have the constitutional power to issue binding definitions of "essential and necessary doctrines."[2] The Westminster Confession practically ceased to function and the church was left without a clear confessional position. It was hoped by many that the introduction of the Confession of 1967 would return the church to a centrist position. Theological pluralism was so extensive in the denomination, however, that C'67 was not accepted as providing a normative standard regarding the authority and interpretation of the Bible. Almost annually the church has been torn by controversies that are replayed in the terms of the fundamentalist-liberal dichotomy. Many in the church still hold to the literalism inculcated by the old Princeton theology. Others, in reaction, seem to hold that any subjective view, sincerely held, must be granted legitimacy.

In the Missouri Synod Lutheran Church, since the ascendancy of Jacob Preus to the presidency, a scholastic view of the inerrancy of the Bible has been enforced. The Lutheran*ism* of the seventeenth-century post-Reformation scholastics has been made normative.[3] That attitude in the American situation is reinforced by the powerful alliance of the old Princeton scholasticism with a popular fundamentalism. In the Missouri Synod, one consequence has been a tragic split in which many of that denomination's finest scholars finally were forced to leave rather than submit to an historically false definition of their denominational heritage.

The other group of people deeply affected by the continuing grip of post-Reformation scholasticism are those who call themselves "evangelicals." The secular media estimate that self-styled "evangelicals" may number as many as forty million Americans. Their common defining characteristics are that they hold to the authority of the Bible and the validity of a personal relationship with God in Jesus Christ. These evangelicals include people from a wide variety of theological traditions—

Pentecostal (such as the Assemblies of God), Wesleyan, Anabaptist, Roman Catholic—in addition to those with a post-Reformation scholastic heritage such as the Presbyterians and Lutherans.[4] But because of the powerful image projected by the old Princeton theologians as defenders of the authority of the Bible, groups with otherwise antithetical theological backgrounds, such as neo-Pentecostals have adopted the old Princeton definition of inerrancy as part of their dogma. In 1978 the Melodyland School of Theology (now Anaheim Christian Theological Seminary), founded to train ministers with a charismatic orientation, was rent internally, in part by the imposition on its faculty of a doctrinal statement claiming the inerrancy of Scripture in matters of science and history. A post-Reformation scholastic approach toward Scripture similar to that currently enforced in the Lutheran Church, Missouri Synod, was injected into a setting where it had no theological precedent or historically appropriate place. The result was strife.

Harold Lindsell, formerly editor of the largest circulation evangelical magazine, *Christianity Today*, in 1976 published a book entitled *The Battle for the Bible*.[5] Lindsell, a Southern Baptist, set forth the old Princeton position of Hodge and Warfield that the Bible is inerrant by modern standards in all matters that it mentions, including "chemistry, astronomy, philosophy, or medicine."[6] Lindsell further asserted that this was the central Christian tradition, held by the church for two thousand years. He attempted to demonstrate his thesis by quoting theologians throughout history, saying that they believed in the inspiration and authority of the Bible. He assumed that their statements entailed the Hodge-Warfield view of inerrancy. The book was written for lay people and urged them to bring pressure to bear on Southern Baptist churches and institutions and other denominations, schools, and parachurch organizations to adhere to Lindsell's notion of inerrancy. Such a view, according to Lindsell, was the badge that determined whether one was truly evangelical. He alleged that ethical deceit and moral failure always accompanied the abandonment of such a view. And he avowed that "godly men through the ages have come to the Scriptures without advanced theological training and have been better interpreters and more spiritual leaders than many who have undergone the most rigorous theological training."[7] This last statement illustrates a pervasive coupling of the rationalistic scholasticism of the old Princeton school with the anti-intellectualism of American fundamentalism.

More recently a group has been formed under the name "The International Council on Biblical Inerrancy." This group has initiated a ten-year drive in which it will "attempt to win back that portion of the church which has drifted away from this historic position" of inerrancy.[8] While distancing themselves from some of Lindsell's attitudes and tactics, this group shares his view that the Hodge-Warfield definition of inerrancy is the historic position of the Christian church and particularly of that tradition known as Reformed theology.

The ICBI sponsored a summit meeting in Chicago, on October 26–29, 1978. Approximately 300 persons already committed to the doctrine of inerrancy were invited. Fourteen papers were read and discussed and a 4,000-word "Chicago Statement on Biblical Inerrancy" was drafted and later signed by a majority of the participants. The IBCI statement contained numerous qualifications designed to acknowledge phenomena of Scripture that could be considered at variance with the inerrancy position. The stance of the participants was largely irenic, and they were open to dialogue with those who differed with them. But the theory about the Bible espoused by the ICBI leadership self-consciously adhered to the old Princeton position. This was evident in its emphases on the inerrancy of Scripture in the areas of science and history, and in its explicit denial that inerrancy was a doctrine invented by scholastic Protestantism or a reactionary position postulated in response to negative higher criticism.[9]

An aggressive program to propagate its position was outlined by the ICBI leadership. A congress for lay people, traveling seminars, and extensive publishing endeavors were approved. A first book, *The Foundation of Biblical Authority*, edited by ICBI chairman James M. Boice, was issued at the time of the Chicago meeting. The foreword to the book, which was written by Francis A. Schaeffer, put the discussion into the context of the American fundamentalist-modernist controversy. He contended that the task of the inerrantists was a "going back to the 1930s and picking up the pieces from the mistakes that were made then."[10] John H. Gerstner, writing the historical chapter, affirmed that the old Princeton position on inerrancy was his own and acknowledged that he taught that it was the only *sound* tradition.[11] The groundwork was thereby laid, at the Chicago meeting of the ICBI and in its literature, for a continued insistence on the Hodge-Warfield theory of the inerrancy of Scripture and the ahistorical assertion that this had always been the stance of the Christian church.

Thus, for many American Protestants the false dichotomy of the fundamentalist-modernist controversy may continue to define the available theological options. Warfield's fear of "mysticism" is carried on in the current preoccupation of conservatives with refuting existentialism. The only alternative offered is to adopt the scholastic rationalism of the nineteenth-century Hodge-Warfield tradition. A particular form of scholastic Aristotelian thinking is labeled "logic." Persons who reason, for example, from Augustinian premises are wrongly branded as irrational since the post-Reformation scholastic tradition recognized only two extreme alternatives.

It is the burden of this book to document the fact that rationalism and mysticism are not the only available alternatives. Our hypothesis is that the peculiar twists of American history have served to distort our view of both the central Christian tradition and especially of its Reformed branch. The early church fathers shared a common foundation that has been lost in the scholastic overreaction to biblical criticism. The central Christian tradition affirmed that Scripture was inspired by God and authoritative for human beings. Not rational proofs, but the Holy Spirit persuaded people of the Bible's authority. As biblical truth was interpreted and applied, faith in Scripture led to understanding of life. Theology was a practical, not a theoretical discipline. The function, or purpose, of the Bible was to bring people into a saving relationship with God through Jesus Christ.[12] The Bible was not used as an encyclopedia of information on all subjects. The principal theological teachers of the church urged that the Bible not be used to judge matters of science, for example, astronomy. Scripture's use was clearly for salvation, not science. The forms of the Bible's language and its cultural context were open to scholarly investigation. The central Christian tradition included the concept of accommodation. This was a grateful acknowledgement that God had condescended and adapted himself in Scripture to our human ways of thinking and speaking. God's ways are not our ways and his thoughts are not our thoughts.[13] But for our sakes, God became intelligible to us in the incarnation, the person of Christ, as well as in the normal language and experiences of human beings recorded in the Bible. Through both of these very human means, the Good News of God's salvation is clearly shown. To erect a standard of modern, technical precision in language as the hallmark of biblical authority was totally foreign to the foundation shared by the early church.

In the Middle Ages, certain shifts in theological method occurred that led to the development of scholasticism. At one extreme were those who, like the twelfth-century Peter Abelard, contended that "nothing could be believed unless it was first understood."[14] Thomas Aquinas produced a *Summa Theologica* which attempted to synthesize Aristotelian philosophy and Augustinian theology. In reaction to the academic scholasticizing of theology, some monks, like Bernard of Clairvaux, turned away from study to mystical experience. For Bernard, faith and devotional reading of the Bible should lead ideally to a rapturous ecstatic union with God. But between these two extremes the central theological tradition inherited from the early church continued. Its medieval exemplar was Anselm of Canterbury. Anselm gave faith priority over reason in his famous declaration: "I do not seek to understand so that I can believe, but rather believe that I might understand."[15] It was to this tradition that the Protestant Reformers, Luther and Calvin, returned. They accepted the authority of the Bible in faith, persuaded by the Holy Spirit of its saving message. Then they applied all the tools of scholarship to understanding, interpreting, and applying Scripture to the life of faith.

The intent of this study is to describe the central church tradition regarding the authority and interpretation of the Bible, especially as it has influenced the Reformed tradition of theology. The Reformers reacted equally to the extremes of Counter-Reformation Roman Catholic and Socinian rationalism on the one hand, and Anabaptist and sectarian spiritualism on the other. But their followers in the post-Reformation period shifted to the rationalistic side in their desire for objective certainty. In this century both fundamentalism and modernism sometimes took extreme positions regarding the Bible. This study will be most concerned with the rationalistic extreme because of the dominant influence it has had on the Reformed tradition in the United States. This is especially important because at the present time a resurgent Protestant scholasticism is again forcing discussion about the Bible into the categories developed by the nineteenth-century Princeton theology.[16]

Significant questions remain to be discussed regarding the role of the Bible in churches today. But we must first set the historical record straight. We cannot grapple seriously with contemporary issues until we know that the central church tradition was much richer and more flexible than seventeenth-century scholasticism or nineteenth-century fundamentalism. The authors are convinced that the central church tradition carried on in Reformation theology has a contribution to make to contemporary church life. Every age must do its own theology in relationship to the particular problems facing it. But we can be oriented and informed by the rich heritage left to us by Origen and Chrysostom, Augustine and Anselm, Calvin and the Westminster Divines, as well as their more recent critics and interpreters.[17]

Notes

1. Lefferts A. Loetscher, *The Broadening Church* (Philadelphia: University of Pennsylvania, 1954), p. 61. (Hereafter cited as *BC*.)
2. *BC*, p. 135.
3. See Martin E. Marty, "Showdown in the Missouri Synod," *The Christian Century* (September 27, 1972), pp. 943–946. A thorough historical discussion is found in David Arnold Owren, "The Doctrine of the Inerrancy of Scripture in the Theology of the Lutheran Church—Missouri Synod: An Historical Analysis of the Hermeneutical Shift within The Lutheran Church—Missouri Synod with Respect to the Term 'Inerrancy' and Its Ramifications for Biblical Authority, 1932–1969" (Th.M. thesis, Pacific Lutheran Theological Seminary, 1977).
4. Timothy L. Smith, "Determining Biblical Authority's Base," *The Christian Century* (March 2, 1977), p. 198. In a lengthy letter to the editor, Johns Hopkins University historian Smith, a Wesleyan, points out that "evangelicals who reject the verbal inerrancy of the Scriptures on matters of history

and cosmology" are *not* "taking their cues from modern biblical scholarship" but are recovering their own evangelical heritage. Recent articles that document the intrusion of an old Princeton scholastic doctrine of Scripture into American theological traditions that are not scholastic in orientation include: Paul Merritt Bassett, "The Fundamentalist Leavening of the Holiness Movement, 1914–1940, The Church of the Nazarene: A Case Study," *Wesleyan Theological Journal* 13 (Spring 1978): 65–91; and Gerald T. Sheppard, "Word and Spirit: Scripture in the Pentecostal Tradition," part 1, *Agora* 1, no. 4 (Spring 1978): 4–5, 17–22, and part 2, *Agora* 2, no. 1 (Summer 1978): 14–19.

5. Harold Lindsell, *The Battle for the Bible* (Grand Rapids, Mich.: Zondervan, 1976).

6. Ibid., p. 18.

7. Ibid., p. 210.

8. "Taking a Stand on Scripture," advertisement in *Christianity Today* (December 30, 1977), p. 25.

9. For news reports see "Proinerrancy Forces Draft Their Platform," *Christianity Today* (November 17, 1978), pp. 36–37; "Scholars Consider Inerrancy in Chicago," *Presbyterian Journal* (November 8, 1978): 4–5; "Inerrancy on the March," *Christian Century* (November 22, 1978), p. 1126. The present manuscript was already at the publisher when these events took place leaving opportunity only for acknowledgement of their relevance but not for extensive interaction with the materials produced.

10. Francis A. Schaeffer, "God Gives His People a Second Opportunity," the foreword to *The Foundation of Biblical Authority* (hereafter cited as *Foundation*), ed. James Montgomery Boice (Grand Rapids, Mich.: Zondervan, 1978), p. 18.

11. John H. Gerstner, "The Church's Doctrine of Biblical Inspiration" in *Foundation*, pp. 51–52. It should be noted that *Foundation* was designed as a chapter-by-chapter refutation of the book *Biblical Authority*, ed. Jack Rogers (Waco, Texas: Word Books, 1977). The completion of the present manuscript prior to the issuance of *Founda-*

tion has precluded a thorough correlation of the two.

12. The use of "salvation" to designate the primary purpose of Scripture in this study should not be taken to exclude, for example, social and ethical concerns. It is not meant to make the Bible only a book of personal piety. Scripture certainly deals with the relationships of persons to God, to themselves, and to their neighbors. What "salvation" is meant to exclude is the post-Reformation scholastic notion that the Bible is a competing and superior source of technical information in the various sciences. Our view is akin to that of Herman Ridderbos, *Studies in Scripture and Its Authority* (Grand Rapids, Mich.: Wm. B. Eerdmans, 1978), who says on p. 24: "What Scripture does intend is to place us as humans in a right position to God, even in our scientific studies and efforts. . . . But it is the book of history of salvation; and it is this point of view that represents and defines the authority of Scripture."

13. Isa. 55:8.

14. Quoted in Jack Rogers, Ross Mackenzie, and Louis Weeks, *Case Studies in Christ and Salvation* (Philadelphia: Westminster Press, 1977), p. 56.

15. Quoted in Rogers et al., p. 53.

16. The authors have left untouched undoubtedly instructive parallels in nineteenth- and twentieth-century Roman Catholicism.

17. The authors are not simply antiquarians. They desire to do theology in the context of our present time and culture. And they seek to do so in the spirit of the ordination vows taken by officebearers in the United Presbyterian Church in the United States of America: "In obedience to Jesus Christ, under the authority of the Scriptures, and under the continuing instruction and guidance of the confessions of this Church." See *The Constitution of the United Presbyterian Church in the United States of America, Part II: Book of Order* (Philadelphia: General Assembly of the United Presbyterian Church in the United States of America, 1967), Chapter 19, 49.043.

PART I

Classical Roots:

Developing Understandings of the Foundation, Form, and Function of Scripture

CHAPTER 1

Common Theological Foundations in the Early Church and the Middle Ages

a. Faith and Reason: Clement

Hebrew Origins and Greek Adaptations

Christianity appeared in a Jewish environment. Its first Scriptures were the holy books of the Jews, which we now call the Old Testament. The writers of the New Testament all lived in this Jewish context, and thought in its categories. Until the middle of the second century, Christianity was primarily an offshoot of Judaism, from which it originated. The Old Testament was authoritative. The principal interpretative task that early Christians faced was to demonstrate that the historical and literary types and figures used in the Old Testament pointed to their fulfillment in Jesus Christ as the Messiah.[1]

This Jewish environment was immersed in a larger world whose rulers were Roman and whose language and culture were Greek. Early Christian thought had to adapt to this Hellenistic culture in order to survive and, in the effort, to win converts. Communicating the Christian message in the Greek environment demanded different elements than had been required in relating it to Judaism. Rather than showing Christianity to be the fulfillment of the Old Testament faith, it now had to be presented in relation to the religious philosophies of the pagan world. Some of the New Testament writers, especially Paul, labored to translate the Christian message from its original Jewish milieu to its new Greek missionary setting.

In the second to the fourth centuries of the Christian era, a number of Christian teachers wrestled with the problems posed by their twofold environment. We now call them the Apologists. Their answer was a dual and daring one. They proclaimed Christianity as the legitimate heir of Jewish faith and the appropriate response to Hellenistic reason.[2]

These early Christian theologians relied on the Old Testament as a revelation of God's saving mercy in Jesus Christ and as a guide in living the life of faith. The influence of their Hellenistic environment is seen in the fact that most early Christians did not read the Old Testament in Hebrew but in a Greek translation, the Septuagint.[3] The canon, setting the limits of the New Testament, was not officially fixed by the church until late in the fourth century. But the documents that eventually made up the New Testament seem to have been in general circulation by A.D. 200.[4] They focused the Old Testament message on its fulfillment in Jesus Christ. But, for the main body of the early church, both testaments were part of one whole, and harmonious in their teachings.

Problems arose when individuals or groups interpreted the Old Testament in ways that were at variance with the New Testament. Four styles of interpretation particularly caused problems in the early church. Three of these were literalistic and one was spiritualistic. First, the Jews insisted on a literal interpretation of the Old Testament. They refused to see Jesus Christ as the center and message of Scripture. Against Jewish literalism, Christians insisted on a spiritual meaning in the Old Testament. Second, the Marcionites were an anti-Semitic sect in early Christianity. They adopted a literalistic interpretation of the Old Testament and then rejected it as not a Christian book. To hold onto the Old Testament other Christians insisted on interpreting it by typology or allegory in order to see the message concerning Jesus in it. Third, the Gnostics were another sect who interpreted the Old Testament literally and found in it "evil sayings." They taught instead a "secret tradition" that they passed on orally to their initiates. Against them, the early Christians insisted on the written, public tradition contained in the Old and New Testament Scriptures. Fourth, yet another sect, the Montanists, claimed to have individual, private revelations from God that they received in experiences of ecstasy. Against them, the early church stressed that only the written Scriptures were inspired. The main body also stressed the need for the Bible to be interpreted by the church, not by charismatic individuals.[5]

From the beginning the church had to struggle with literalism and legalism on the one side and with spiritualism and sectarianism on the other. But the heaviest problems for the Apologists of the early church came from those who employed a kind of surface literalism in interpreting the Bible. The Apologists necessarily employed interpretations that enabled them to expound Scripture in its Christian meaning. They drew on both Jewish typology and Greek philosophy in understanding the Bible as a revelation of salvation in Christ and a guide for life as a Christian.

The Apologists were missionary statesmen concerned with forming a favorable public opinion. They published "open letters" to their rulers defending Christianity from false charges of godlessness and immorality. They pleaded for parity of treatment with other inhabitants of the empire.[6]

Because of their task, the Apologists had to come to terms with the public opinion formers, the dominant philosophies of the day. Most of the Apologists adopted a cautious but not condemning approach to Greek philosophy. Philosophy had elements of worth. The Apologists generally attributed these valuable aspects to borrowings from Scripture, revelations of angels to the philosophers, or the common human ability to reason.[7] The Apologists urged an attitude of discrimination: Philosophy gave partial knowledge; Christianity gave perfect knowledge. Philosophy was confused; Christianity was clear. Philosophy was preparation; Christianity was completion. Philosophy could be of use, even for the Christian person; but it could be misused, as the various Christian heresies demonstrated.

The Apologists co-opted philosophy in the service of their cause. At the same time, through their work, theology was cast into a philosophical mold that in some measure shaped Christian thought. It is, therefore, important to understand something of the central philosophical influences on the Apologists.

Plato and Aristotle

Greek philosophy came to maturity in the fourth and fifth centuries B.C. The two principal schools were those of Plato and Aristotle, which, taken together, formed what is now known as "classical realism." Both schools believed there was a real world, independent of humanity, that could nevertheless, be known by the human mind. The schools differed, however, on the *nature* of that real world and on *how* it could be known.[8]

Plato was disturbed by the problem of change. He despaired of finding anything real in a world of instability and impermanence, and concluded that reality was not made of changing things. Reality was composed of unchanging ideas or ideals that Plato called "forms." It was not the changing rose on earth that was real, but the unchanging idea of Beauty. Those original realities, like Beauty, existed in heaven. Things on this earth, like the rose, were only shadowy reflections of them. Human beings (primarily philosophers) could know the absolute ideas by memory and deduction, since we all once existed in heaven. But when we were born into this world, we retained only a dim memory of those ideals we had known. Plato taught that philosophers (lovers of wisdom) should not be attached to the things of this world. They should see through earthly things to the heavenly ideals these things imperfectly represented. From the great ideas they had in their minds from birth they could deduce all they needed to know. Knowledge of true reality came by deduction from the general to the particular.

Aristotle was Plato's greatest pupil. Aristotle developed Plato's concept of deduction from axioms into a system of logic. The central feature of this system was the syllogism. This logical form involved two premises, already known, from which a new and previously unknown proposition could be deduced as the conclusion. Aristotle's logical writings were gathered in a collection known as the *Organon*—the "tool." Logic was regarded as the tool, or instrument of philosophy.[9]

In addition, Aristotle developed his own ideas which in many ways diverged from those of his master. Aristotle grew up in the family of a medical doctor. He was accustomed to careful observation of worldly things. Aristotle recognized the problem of change. But he believed that by close observation and reasoning the philosopher could perceive not only change but patterns of continuity within the changing world. For Aristotle reality consisted not of ideas in heaven, but of concrete, particular things in this world. Each thing, or entity, Aristotle called a "substance." Each substance was understood by the application of principles that Aristotle developed regarding form and matter. Form was the purpose or objective the entity served in the scheme of reality. Matter was the stuff of which it was made. Substances were encountered by our five natural senses. General principles were derived by induction for Aristotle. He taught that one should examine a great many particular things in the world and then draw a general conclusion based on perceived similarities.

The ideas of this Golden Age of Greek philosophy were not taught in pure form in the first several centuries of the Christian era. There had been an eclectic trend in philosophy since the first century B.C. that had resulted in a partial harmonization of Platonic, Aristotelian, and Stoic thought. The dominant philosophy of the second century A.D. was Middle Platonism, which carried on this synthetic tendency and yielded to Neo-platonism from the third century on into the Middle Ages.[10]

Platonism then was the dominant influence on Christian theologians of the early church, and especially the Apologists.[11] Christian philosophical theologians were not interested in the fine points of the different schools of philosophy. They were simply responding to, trying to make use of, and in turn being influenced by the contemporary intellectual currents of their times. Thus, the forms of thought they used in interpreting Scripture and through which they communicated its meaning were Platonic. However, they did not hesitate to criticize or depart from that preferred philosophical tradition when they perceived that it contradicted the Christian gospel.

Aristotelian influence was much less significant. No eminent philosophers identified themselves as adherents of Aristotle in the second century.[12] There were several reasons for this situation. Much of Aristotle's most significant writing was unknown in the period of the early church. Only his logic was available, and this was considered a common tool of philosophers. Artistotle's inductive philosophy was rediscovered and adapted for use in theology only during the Middle Ages. In the early church, what was known of Aristotle's religious notions was considered incompatible with Christianity. Aristotelians and Epicureans were regarded as atheists because they denied Providence and the immortality of the soul. Platonists and Stoics, on the other hand, defended Providence in various ways. Aristotle was more interested in experience in this world. Plato concentrated on ideal realities found in heaven.[13]

Alexandria in North Africa was a center of Platonizing philosophy. Two of the most important Christian Platonists learned and taught there. They were Clement (150?–?213) and Origen (185?–?254). A precedent for expounding the Old Testament in Platonic categories had been established by the great Hellenistic Jewish scholar, Philo of Alexandria, who died around A.D. 40.[14] Clement helps us to understand how faith and reason are related with reference to the Bible. Origen illustrates how these philosophical categories influence biblical interpretation.

Faith and Philosophy

Clement of Alexandria was one of the first Christian teachers to struggle seriously and systematically with the interrelationship of faith, reason, and the Bible. Many Christians opposed any use of philosophy, arguing that philosophy was harmful or simply unnecessary since persons needed only faith to become perfect. Clement, therefore, wrote to justify his position. He commented that Christians in general

> fear Greek philosophy as children fear ogres—they are frightened of being carried off by them. If our faith (I will not say, our *gnosis*) is such that it is destroyed by force of argument, then let it be destroyed; for it will have been proved that we do not possess the truth.[15]

Clement had to clarify the nature of faith, its relationship to knowledge, and the relationship of both to the Bible.

Faith was the one essential factor in becoming a Christian, according to Clement. Before the coming of Christ, philosophy was a means of salvation for pagans, but after Christ, philosophy became secondary and not essential to salvation. Clement referred to Greek philosophy as "a preparatory training for the truth," which came fully and perfectly in Christ. He wrote: "This partial philosophy is rudimentary in contrast to the perfect knowledge unveiled in Christ."[16]

For Clement, faith was knowledge given directly to persons by God. This belief fit neatly with the Platonic notion of innate ideas. For Plato, all persons at birth possessed a dim knowledge of the great ideals and principles of reality and to Clement there was "a dim knowledge of God even among the heathen."[17] Clement used the Platonic terminology of innate ideas to express his belief that God had implanted a partial and imperfect, but nonetheless authentic, knowledge of Himself within every person. "A reflection of the one omnipotent God is natural among all men everywhere who think rightly," according to Clement. It was by reflection on this innate knowledge that "the most penetrating of the Greek philosophers see God."[18]

Clement developed his own coherent set of concepts. They fit generally within a Middle Platonic framework, but he felt under no constraint to conform to the philosophers. Rather, he was compelled to express what to him was the faith of the gospel and to communicate it in philosophical terminology.

Biblical Interpretation

The Bible, for Clement, was a resource of primary data, accepted in faith, from which persons could then draw reasoned conclusions. He said: "*Gnosis* [knowledge] is clear demonstration starting from the testimony of Scripture."[19] Clement deliberately used the word *gnosis* to contrast Christian knowledge with the claims to knowledge of the heretical Gnostic sects which were particularly strong in Alexandria. The Christian had true *gnosis,* or knowledge, because it developed out of faith.[20] The Bible itself, for Clement, was accepted on faith. It did not need to be proved to be authentic. The Bible held the same place in Clement's Christian proof that the basic premises of logic held in philosophical reasoning. For Clement faith preceded and led to understanding. God had given humans the Bible and had implanted within them a knowledge of God that was confirmed by Scripture. People, therefore, should accept the Bible in faith and allow it to provide the premises from which to reason to further knowledge.

Only faith was needed for salvation, according to Clement. But it was important that people go on from mere saving faith to Christian maturity in knowledge. The difference between the simple believer and the true "Gnostic," or mature Christian, was the difference between a person with a rudimentary and one with a rich knowledge of Scripture.[21]

Clement held that Christian maturity was a matter of faith seeking understanding. And the entire seeking process remained rooted in Scripture. No "theological proofs" like those found in the Middle Ages were derived from the unaided reason. The arguments were provided by the Bible itself. The convergence of many biblical texts on one point served to awaken people to the truth of that point. To be really "scientific," for Clement, was to stick close to Scripture. He said: "We do not rely on human testimony, but we believe in the object of our investigation on the word of the Lord."[22]

Typology

The primary orientation to biblical categories of Clement and the other Apologists is seen in their principles of interpretation. They felt the central Christian task to be to show the unity of the Old and the New Testaments, and they argued that Christ fulfilled the predictions of the Old Covenant and thus provided its unity with the New. The basic interpretative tool the Apologists used was *typology*. They had inherited that tradition from rabbinic Judaism. For the rabbis, Israel's redemption in the messianic age was foreshadowed in every detail by Israel's redemption from Egypt.[23] The early Christians read in the New Testament Gospels Christ's presentation of himself as the fulfillment of events predicted by the prophets, and purposes foreshadowed by Jewish institutions. Typology was thus neither literal exegesis concerned only with the past historical events themselves, nor allegorical exegesis which treated past happenings only as symbols to be spiritually interpreted. Rather, typology stressed the historical interrelationship of a past event as promise and a later event as fulfillment. The underlying assumption was that God had deliberately designed this relatedness as part of the Divine plan. This kind of typological interpretation of the Bible was a common factor in all early Christian exegesis. It was used by all biblical interpreters, including the Apologists, and was not confined to any one school of thought.[24]

Accommodation

In addition to typology, the concept of accommodation was another common factor influencing all early Christian biblical interpretation. The early Christian theologians were quite conscious of the limited capacity of the human mind. Humans were, first of all, creatures who were not on the same level as their creator. Secondly, human minds had been adversely affected by the Fall. Sin affected the total human person. This meant that the mind now had a perverted perspective. Human intelligence was not less, but it was not favorably disposed to see things from the perspective of a child of God.

In order to communicate effectively with human beings, God condescended, humbled, and accommodated himself to human categories of thought and speech. This was not a matter of deception, but of necessary adaptation on God's part if humans were to be able to understand His will for them. In the incarnation, God humbled himself and became a weak and helpless baby in order to identify with and communicate with human beings. This incarnational principle had always been God's style according to the early Christian theologians. In revealing himself God had always accommodated himself to humans' limited and sinful capacities. Clement expressed both the concept and its merciful purpose:

> But in as far as it was possible for us to hear, burdened as we were with flesh, so did the prophets speak to us, as the Lord accommodated himself to human weakness for our salvation.[25]

The early Christians were quite ready to acknowledge that in relation to their heavenly Father they were like children. They were grateful that God adapted himself, like a good parent, to their weak condition. The implication for biblical interpretation was that the human context of God's divine revelation had to be taken with full seriousness. God did not impose a divine literature on human beings. God used the very human literature the biblical writers created in order to communicate His Divine message. It was a mark of God's greatness, for which the early Christian theologians praised him, that God could use weak, human instruments to accomplish his perfect, Divine purpose. God did not need to correct bad spelling or poor syntax. God did not require persons to have knowledge of the universe beyond that of their contemporaries. God was not concerned with inculcating a perfect philosophy or a perfect physics. God wanted to bring persons into a harmonious relationship to Himself. He wanted to guide them in living a life of obedient faith. God was able to accomplish that purpose adequately by using the normal modes of thought and forms of speech of ordinary persons.

The concept of accommodation was central to the common foundation of biblical interpretation in the early church. It enabled theologians to take seriously both the human textual matrix and the divine theological meaning. It functioned to modify the prevailing philosophical forms of thought that early Christian theologians had adopted from their Greek environment. When either the human context or the Divine saving purpose were forgotten or pushed into the background, then philosophical speculation or human systematizing sometimes took over and distorted the biblical message. The early Christian theologians had faith in the Divine message of the Bible. They used reason to understand the human linguistic and cultural matrix in which the Divine message came.

b. Allegorical Interpretation: Origen

The person who best exemplified the blending of Greek culture and biblical thought was Origen of Alexandria (185?–?254). Origen has been called the first great preacher, devotional writer, biblical commentator and systematic theologian of Christianity.[26] It was Origen who laid the foundation and built much of the framework of later biblical interpretation.[27]

Origen was a Platonist. He asked the same questions and used the same concepts as his most learned non-Christian contemporaries.[28] But because of his interaction with the Bible, his answers were consciously different.

The Bible was authoritative for Origen.[29] A modern reader who looked only at Origen's views on the Bible's authority and did not also attend to his understanding of the purpose and character of Scripture could easily draw inaccurate implications. To Origen the Bible was entirely the work of God. Indeed, Origen declared that "the Sacred Books are not the works of men," but "were written by inspiration of the Holy Spirit at the will of the Father of All, through Jesus Christ."[30] The background of such statements was Origen's conviction that the basic purpose of Scripture was to bring persons to salvation, and that to accomplish that purpose God had accommodated himself to human forms of thought and speech. It was the saving message, not the form of the words, that was wholly from God.

Accommodation

Origen was completely conscious of the human character of the holy writings. He rejected any idea of a mechanical mode of inspiration, whether that of the prophets or of the biblical writers. He acknowledged that the New Testament evangelists and Paul expressed their own opinions, and that they could have erred when speaking on their own authority. Origen distinguished between the communication of the revealed message and the commentary on it by the scriptural authors. He was concerned to investigate the context of a biblical utterance in order to discover the understanding and intention of the author.[31] He was aware that the New Testament was not written in the best Greek, but held that to be unimportant. Revelation, for Origen, did not consist in the human words used, but in the divine meaning expressed. Indeed, it was at the times when he focused on the divine meaning in each word that some of his most heterodox ideas appeared.[32]

Origen usually was able to distinguish and yet hold in harmony the divine and the human, the message and the medium of Scripture. The basis for this balance was Origen's concept of accommodation. His model was the incarnation, God coming into lowly human form. For Origen, the very reason that human beings could know the revelation of God was that God had "condescended" or "accommodated" himself to human understanding. God's infinite mysteries were beyond the powers of human minds to grasp. So God adapted and adjusted to human ways of thinking and speaking so that human beings could understand and be saved.

Origen inherited the principle of accommodation from the Alexandrian school of exegetical work. Philo, his Jewish predecessor, had applied the concept of accommodation to anthropomorphisms in the Old Testament. For Origen, accommodation (Greek, *symperiphora*) could work in two opposing ways: To the godly it could reveal the truths of God; to the ungodly it could conceal those truths. The primary purpose of accommodation was pastoral, however. God acted as a kindly adult, condescending to adopt the ways of children, for their sakes. Origen used the biblical images of God as teacher and father saying:

> He condescends and lowers himself, accommodating himself to our weakness, like a schoolmaster talking a "little language" to his children, like a father caring for his own children and adopting their ways.[33]

The central purpose of Scripture for Origen was to communicate the message of God's salvation in Jesus Christ and guide people in living the Christian life. The appropriate means for achieving this purpose was "baby-talk," since human beings had the understanding of children relative to God their Father. So God graciously condescended to communicate in human terms so that human beings might "attain a clear knowledge of him."[34] The Bible was a book of salvation, not of human science. And its mode of communication was not the exalted language of which God is capable but the lowly language that met human beings at their level of need. The concept that expressed the harmony between the purpose of Scripture and the character of its communication was "accommodation." It began with the Alexandrian school and became the common property of the central Christian tradition from Origen through Augustine and on to Luther and Calvin.

Allegory

Origen was concerned not only for the authority of Scripture and its accommodated character of communication. He needed to interpret the Word of God so that it could serve as a guide to salvation and to living the Christian life. Origen wrote his major theological work, *On First Principles,* to refute those who interpreted the Bible literally and thus denied its saving message. Origen challenged three groups: the heretics, the Jews, and the "simple." Heretical sects (particularly the Gnostics and Marcionites) had arisen that read the Old Testament literally and rejected it as a revelation of God because of its "evil sayings." These sects explained texts such as: "I repent of having anointed Saul to be King" (1 Sam. 15:11) as being the words of the Demiurge, an "imperfect and unbenevolent God." To them the Saviour had come to "announce a more perfect Diety" (IV.8). In Book IV, section 8, he criticized the Jews for being "over-literal" in their expectations of messianic prophecy. The "simple" (*polloi*) of the early church he chastised for taking the Old Testament literally and arriving at a picture of God that "would not be believed of the most savage and unjust of mankind." All of these wrong understandings resulted from interpreting the Bible according to the "bare letter" and not according to its "spiritual meaning" (IV.9).[35]

In order to avoid these literalistic errors, Origen put forth "the way then, as it appears to us, in which we ought to deal with the Scriptures, and extract from them their meaning" (IV.11). The resulting hermeneutic, or theory of interpretation, was the allegorical method.[36]

Origen recognized that even though the Bible was inspired, and God had accommodated himself to human thought, there were still parts of Scripture that were obscure or unclear. He concluded that this was partly due to God's providence, in order to stir us to study Scripture. It was also partly due to the "inability of our weakness to discover in every expression the hidden splendour of the doctrines veiled in common and unattractive phraseology" (I.7). By allowing various levels of clarity in Scripture, God took into account the differing abilities of human beings and also set traps for the wise who would rely on their own logic and reasoning to discover God's great teachings. The task of the exegete was to peel off the husk of the letter and get at the kernel of the spiritual meaning, in order to share it with others.[37] In his *Commentary on John,* Origen asked in piety:

> For how can anyone be said in the full sense to believe the Scripture when he does not see in it the mind of the Holy Spirit which God would have us to believe rather than the literal meaning?[38]

Since the Bible's purpose was to show us Christ, Origen assumed that the Divine Author intended that the words of Scripture be expounded in more than one sense. In Book IV, section II of *Commentary on John*, Origen pointed to three senses that any Scripture passage might have: the literal (fleshly); the moral (psychic); and the anagogical (intellectual). These corresponded to the three elements Origen thought constituted a human being: the body (*sōma*); soul (*psychē*); and the spirit (*pneuma*). This three-fold division was based biblically on the Septuagint's incorrect rendering of Proverbs 22:20, "Have I not written unto thee in a triple way (*triss-ōs*)?"[39] The philosophical basis was the Platonic trichotomy of body, soul, and spirit, which probably came to Origen through Philo.[40] These three senses of a Scripture passage made it available to three types of readers. The literal or fleshly sense was related to the human body and was for the simple believer. The moral or psychic sense of Scripture appealed to the human soul and was for one making spiritual progress. The anagogical or intellectual sense was directed to the human spirit and was beneficial to the perfected believer. Origen did not believe that all passages of Scripture had all three senses. Sometimes he wrote as if there were only the literal and spiritual senses. Occasionally he declared that the literal sense of a passage was not true at all and that the text had to be taken as completely spiritual.[41]

By focusing on the spiritual meaning, Origen could not only maintain the unity of the Old and New Testaments, but could face problems in the biblical records without being baffled by them. For example, there were passages in the Bible that Origen felt could not be literally true, such as the statement in Genesis that light was created before the sun or moon existed. Some predictions in Scripture had not yet been fulfilled. Sometimes Scripture made demands that were impossible for humans to fulfill. At other times passages were inconsistent with each other. Origen's method for dealing with all of these problems was to allegorize. He was always glad to discover a difficulty or contradiction, since that demonstrated that one needed to interpret allegorically.[42]

By allegorical interpretation, Origen attempted to bring together the strengths of his dual environment. He attempted to reconcile the Jewish philosophy of historical fulfillment and the Platonic philosophy of eternal ideas.[43] When charged with subjective speculation, he appealed to the precedent of Paul and the symbolism in John's Gospel. At the very least he strove to give the ancient Jewish Book a contemporary Christian meaning.[44]

Systematic Speculation

The strengths and weaknesses of most people are opposite sides of the same coin. That was certainly true of Origen. He was a "man of the

Book," who studied the Bible more thoroughly than any theologian of his time. He was at the same time a "man of his age." He imbibed the reigning philosophy and did his best to make Christianity credible in Platonic categories. He was a great speculative genius, who moved beyond the common typological interpretations of other Apologists to solve difficult problems through allegorical exegesis. What set Origen apart in many places from other Apologists was that they exegeted typologically in the context of the *kerygma,* the central gospel message, the pattern of Christian truth recognized by the church, whereas Origen erected his own systematic theology on the speculation that every verse had a specific spiritual meaning.[45] Origen thus focused on the parts rather than the whole. In allegorizing he concentrated on the forms, the individual words of the Bible, which he took to be inspired, as well as the function, the central saving content of Scripture.

Origen produced the first systematic theology of the Christian era by looking for spiritual meaning in every single word. At the same time this method allowed him, consciously or unconsciously, to incorporate many elements into his system that did not derive from biblical revelation. When the requirements of the system became the norm, Origen sometimes changed the meaning of the biblical message in order to make it fit his reason.[46] For those lapses from adherence to the biblical faith, he was posthumously declared a heretic. Origen's allegorical method defended the authority of the Bible by defining all of its material as pointing to Jesus Christ. His emphasis on accommodation helped to keep him in touch with the *kerygma,* the proclamation, the central saving message of the Bible. But when he allowed himself to speculate on the meaning of each verse in a philosophical vein, he created methodological problems that continued to plague the church for centuries.

At his best, Origen held in balance the divine authority of the Bible, its human-accommodated form and the difficult task of the theologian who must responsibly interpret all of Scripture. The wholesome blend of piety and scholarship Origen often displayed is illustrated by his statement in *On First Principles:*

> But just as providence is not abolished because of our ignorance, at least not for those who have once rightly believed in it, so neither is the divine character of scripture, which extends through all of it, abolished because our weakness cannot discern in every sentence the hidden splendour of its teachings, concealed under a poor and humble style.[47]

When Origen approached Scripture as a person of faith, he usually proceeded to a helpful understanding of it. When he used the Bible as a resource for his own reason, and tried to make Scripture fit his system, he often distorted its meaning. Both the progress Origen made and the problems he created as an interpreter of Scripture were bequeathed to Augustine and through him to the Middle Ages.

c. Grammatical-Historical Interpretation: Chrysostom

Although the tradition of allegorical exegesis became firmly established in the church in the years after Origen, it did not remain unchallenged. In the fourth and fifth centuries, a vigorous alternative arose at Antioch in Syria. Antioch contained the oldest Christian community after Jerusalem. It was in Antioch that the followers of Jesus were first called Christians. It was a great capital city with a long tradition of learning and culture.[48] The Antiochene school of theology and exegesis represented the eastern Mediterranean world. It vied with the Alexandrian school in the West for dominance in the Christian Church.

Antioch favored the minor Aristotelian philosophical orientation. Aristotle seemed more down-to-earth compared to Plato's more other-worldly views.[49] In Antioch there was a stronger feeling for the human element in the biblical writings and for the historical reality of biblical revelation.[50] The result in Antiochene exegesis was a search for the natural sense of the author in the historical setting, rather than, as in the Alexandrian school, interest in a hidden spiritual meaning of the text. The Antiochene exegesis was also critical, perceiving that some parts of the Bible were of more value than others.[51]

From this eastern school grew the grammatical-historical method of biblical interpretation. Antiochenes preferred to begin with the natural historical meaning of the biblical text. In this they followed the Jewish rabbis and Aristotle, rather than Philo and Plato. They were not reacting to the literalism of the Jews and heretics. Rather, they were rejecting the excesses of Alexandrian allegorism. They did consent to use the common tradition of typology, which they felt had been created by God, to find fulfillment of Old Testament texts in Christ. However, the commitment to Aristotelian logic sometimes led the Antiochenes to very rationalistic interpretations in order to make sense of the literal meanings. When reason was given precedence over faith, just as with Origen, they often went to speculative excesses.[52]

Between the periods of struggle in the church occasioned by the heresies of Arianism and Nestorianism, the Antiochene school produced perhaps the most beloved preacher of early Christianity, John Chrysostom (347?–407). Chrysostom was trained by a representative of the orthodox party, Diodorus, who with Flavian and Meletius had opposed the Arian or semi-Arian bishops of Antioch patronized by the Emperor Constantius during his reign (350–361). In addition, Chrysostom knew the writings of the Cappadocian fathers, Gregory of Nazianzus, Basil the Great, and perhaps Gregory of Nyssa. From them, and from the writings of Eusebius, Bishop of Emesa, John Chrysostom learned a love for the Bible and the method of grammatical-historical interpretation.[53] In part because of charges of heresy, most of the writings of others from the Antiochene school of biblical interpretation were destroyed. John Chrysostom, therefore, is now regarded as the finest representative of the school and most of what we know of its actual exegetical practice has come from his sermons.[54]

Faith, Reason, and Rhetoric

John Chrysostom apparently possessed a natural gift for language, and had also thoroughly trained himself in the Greek classics. He wrote the purest Greek of all the ecclesiastical authors.[55] Greek was his native language, and he had read the Bible in it from childhood. He knew no Hebrew. He read the Old Testament in the Septuagint and occasionally quoted from Origen's *Hexapla,* a Hebrew text written in Greek letters.[56]

Philosophically, Chrysostom held to the major tradition and regarded Plato as the "most outstanding" among the philosophers. Although he knew and cited a wide variety of Greek philosophers, poets, scientists, and historians, he cited Plato most often, at least thirty times in his writings.[57]

At the same time, Chrysostom was not himself a philosopher, but a preacher and moralist. During the time in which he lived, people were experiencing a resurgence of interest in the old pagan gods. Tens of thousands of temples to these ancient deities still stood in the Roman empire and people adhered to them out of loyalty to tradition and patriotism to Roman rule. There were no first-rate philosophers in the fourth century. Rather, the philosophers acted as spokesmen for the pagan status quo and poured scorn and suspicion on the Christians.[58] Chrysostom praised Christianity as the highest and most noble "philosophy," and he declared that monks and martyrs were the best "philosophers."[59] He noted that Plato's teaching had failed to regenerate people while St. Paul's preaching had led to changed lives.[60]

Chrysostom affirmed that "Faith stands as an enemy of rationalism."[61] He reacted against the Arians who placed reason before faith, and who claimed that the existence of God could be known by reason alone.[62] For him, heretics were those who did not found their teaching on Scripture as interpreted by the *kerygma,* the central saving message, as embodied in the early creeds. After his elevation to the bishopric of Constantinople, Chrysostom dealt with the question raised by a pagan as to how to choose among the competing Christian sects. His answer was twofold. First, he declared that one should simply read the Bible.

> To such a one I answer: If we say that you should listen to proofs founded on reason, you would rightly be confused: but instead, we say that you should believe the Scriptures, which are so simple and true, that the decision is made easy. He who is a Christian, agrees with the Holy Scripture, and he who does not agree with it, has deviated from the true faith.[63]

Second, to those who complained of diverse interpretations of the Bible, Chrysostom pointed to the central Christian tradition, handed down since the time of the apostles.[64]

Chrysostom not only objected to the pagan content of the philosopher's teachings, but he was offended by the artificial and unnatural form of their rhetoric. For him, theology was a practical discipline, not a theoretical one. The final judge of any teaching was its effect on human life. Chrysostom asked his philosophical opponents:

> Why do you flatter yourself so much? On the wisdom of your teaching? But it is no art to philosophize with words. Show me your wisdom in your deeds and in practical life; that is the best method of teaching.[65]

Chrysostom rejoiced that the apostles had been unlettered men and yet had conquered the land of Greece.

At the same time, Chrysostom had been formed as a preacher by his early study under Libanius, the last great rhetorician of pagan antiquity. Libanius (314–393) returned to Antioch about A.D. 354 and served there as city rhetorician for about forty years. As the most celebrated orator of his time, Libanius counted among his pupils both the "apostate" emperor Julian and the Christian theologians Basil the Great, Gregory of Nazianzus, and John Chrysostom. Chrysostom's training therefore paralleled that of Augustine. Chrysostom, the orator of Greek Christianity, was the heir of Demosthenes, while Augustine, the orator of Latin Christianity, was the heir of Cicero.[66] For both of them, their rhetorical training in adapting to the needs of the audience harmonized well with the theological concept of God's accommodation to human ways of thought and speech.

Accommodation

Despite the differences in exegetical method between the Alexandrian school of Origen and the Antiochene school of Chrysostom, both schools shared the common view of the early church that God had accommodated his teaching to our capacities for understanding. For Chrysostom, God had condescended to our human ways of thought and speech in order that we might understand mysteries otherwise beyond us and thus be saved in a manner worthy of God and commensurate with our weakness. God could have spoken in lofty phrases and with exacting technical accuracy, but Chrysostom's study of Scripture convinced him that God utilized completely human ways of thinking and turned them to our benefit. Chrysostom wrote in imagery almost exactly paralleling that of Origen:

> And if a father considers not his own dignity, but talks lispingly with his children and calls their meat and drink not by their Greek names, but by some childish and barbarous words, much more doth God . . . in every part of Scripture there are instances of His condescension both in words and actions.[67]

The supreme instance of God condescending to the human condition was his incarnation in Jesus Christ to accomplish our salvation. Chrysostom asserted:

> Christ often checked himself for the sake of the weakness of his hearers when he dealt with lofty doctrines and that he usually did not choose such words as were in accord with his glory but rather those which agreed with the capability of men.[68]

The awareness that God did not stand on his dignity but rather humbled himself for our benefit was central to Chrysostom.[69]

Although committed to grammatical-historical exegesis of both the Old and New Testaments, Chrysostom, nevertheless, recognized anthropomorphism, the speaking of God in human terms, as a necessary accommodation to human weakness. Accordingly, when he came to the statement in Genesis that "God walked in the garden in the cool of the day," he commented:

> We should not take these words too lightly, but neither should we interpret them as they stand. We ought rather to reflect that such simple speech is used because of our weakness, and in order that our salvation be brought about in a manner worthy of God. For if we wish to take words just as they are, and not explain them in a way which befits God, will not the result be utter absurdity?[70]

The twin concerns expressed by Chrysostom in his concept of accommodation are our weakness and God's worthiness. Language must be understood in a way that is effective for our salvation and which "befits God." An exegete who failed to heed those principles of interpretation would descend to mere literalism and the result would be "utter absurdity."[71] The "style" or form (Gr., *lezis*) of God's communication was admirably adapted to our need to understand "ineffable mysteries." We should, accordingly, interpret Scripture in a way that appreciates God's condescension and thus is "worthy of God."

Biblical Interpretation

First and foremost, Chrysostom urged people to read the Bible. It was said that during his time as a hermit he memorized the "Testamente Christi" by heart. His printed treatises and 600 sermons contain about 18,000 Scripture citations. About 7,000 are from the Old Testament, and 11,000 from the New Testament.[72] Chrysostom's quotations often differ from contemporary texts both because of the different textual sources he used and because of his habit of citing from memory, weaving together passages from various places, and expanding and improvising as his rhetoric carried him along.[73]

Although he attributed the content or message of Scripture to God, Chrysostom understood the form of writing to be human, in accordance with his doctrine of accommodation.[74] He recognized differences in the Gospel accounts of the same events, but regarded the fact that they agreed in essentials, while differing in details, as powerful evidence of their veracity. An exact verbal coincidence in all particulars would have caused opponents of Christianity to suspect collusion among the biblical writers.[75] Further, he explained an enigmatic saying of Jesus by asserting that "he hath put the thing hyperbolically"—another evidence of his concentration on the message rather than the words.[76]

In common with the chief theologians of the early church, Chrysostom fully accepted the authority of Scripture and attributed its saving message to God. At the same time he clearly acknowledged the imperfect human character of the language and thought through which God's message was communicated.[77] The link between these two notions was the idea of accommodation, which was commonly held in the early church.

Chrysostom preferred the natural, grammatical-historical sense of the Bible; he also recognized that, at times, figurative meanings were intended. But he saw a real peril in allegorical speculations. He declared:

> The practice of importing into Holy Scripture alien ideas of one's own imagination instead of accepting what stands written in the text, in my opinion, carries great danger for those who have the hardihood to follow it.[78]

Accordingly, Chrysostom felt free to correct the Apostle Paul who concluded his comments in Galatians 4:23–24 by stating, "Now this is an allegory." Chrysostom countered:

By a misuse of language he called the type allegory. What he means is this: The history itself not only has the apparent meaning but also proclaims other matters; therefore it is called allegory. But what did it proclaim? Nothing other than everything that now is.[79]

When the nature of the text required more than a mere historical exposition, Chrysostom preferred a cautious typology as an exegetical method. What Chrysostom meant by a "type" was a kind of outline sketch such as an artist might make for a portrait before filling in the colors. There had to be a resemblance to that which was "typified." The historical meaning gave the outline; but only the typological meaning gave the final form of the portrait.[80] If an historical passage declared not only the obvious fact, but proclaimed some other meaning as well, Chrysostom required that the "other meaning" be tied firmly to the historical sense of Scripture.[81]

A rootedness in the text and a flexibility of understanding characterized Chrysostom's interpretation of the Bible. He began with the natural, grammatical-historical meaning of the text. And he admitted other meanings that went beyond the strict literal interpretation of the passage. He recognized (as Origen did) that literal readings could produce interpretations that would be "downright inhuman." So, he allowed his understanding of the central, saving message of the whole of Scripture to govern his interpretation of any part. This did not mean that Chrysostom at times gave way to his own subjective desires or relied on mystical intuitions. Rather, he treated the context as part of the text. And the widest context was the Bible as a whole with its saving message. Chrysostom was not wedded to the words alone, but to their meaning as well. He was not focused on form alone, but on function as well. He took both words and meaning seriously and attempted to "accept both the sense of the words as they stand and the meaning that plainly arises from them." It was this balance that commended Chrysostom as an exegetical mentor to the greatest of the medieval theologians, Thomas Aquinas, and to the leading Protestant Reformers, Martin Luther and John Calvin.[82]

The name Chrysostom meant "golden-mouthed." He used all of his oratorical skills to proclaim Scripture's saving and life-directing sense. For Chrysostom, theology was a practical, not a theoretical calling. The biblical message made a difference in people's lives. He declared that "more powerful than fire to melt the heart is the good word which resounds from the divine Scriptures and prepared a man for any good work."[83]

Chrysostom continually urged people to accept Scripture in faith and to seek its saving message. He also urged that those who were Christians should go on to understanding. The obscure parts of the Bible required not only an attentive listener or reader, but also a good and wise interpreter. He affirmed that

> God in His goodness and solicitude has so directed that we, besides the reading of the Holy Scriptures, have also the guidance (spiritual leadership), on the part of our teachers.[84]

All could understand the saving message of the Bible. But to understand all of its context and the nuances of its meaning required skill and scholarship. The study of Scripture was a main ministry of the Christian community. For Chrysostom, "to attain understanding of the Scriptures one must have not only a wise teacher, but also an intelligent listener."[85] Chrysostom had no developed theory about the teaching authority of the church. He simply accepted the importance of laity and clergy, the untrained and the exegetically trained, learning together. It remained for Augustine to develop further the relationship of faith to understanding.

d. Authority and Accommodation: Augustine

Aurelius Augustinus (354–430) served as a bridge between the early church and the Middle Ages. The facts of his early life are well known. His father was a pagan and his mother Monica was a devout Christian. He was educated at the University of Carthage and became a teacher of rhetoric. Reading Cicero's "Hortensius" aroused his interest in philosophy. And for nine years he was a devotee of the Manichaean sect.[86]

Augustine's conversion to Christianity was preceded by a conversion to Neoplatonism. Disillusioned by the failure of a celebrated Manichaean, Faustus, to answer many of the questions plaguing him, Augustine sailed for Rome in 383. Within a year he moved to Milan as a professor of rhetoric. There he joined a group of young intellectuals who were Neoplatonists, and with them he heard the preaching of Bishop Ambrose, whose sermons were often a synthesis of Scripture and Neoplatonic ideas. Ambrose captivated Augustine with his able defense of the Old Testament against the objections of the Manichaeans.[87] Augustine began to read the Neoplatonists Plotinus (205?–270) and Porphyry (232?–303); their thought emancipated him from the Manichaean philosophy.[88] Near the end of August 386, Augustine experienced a dramatic conversion to Christianity. He was baptized by Ambrose on Easter Eve 387.[89] Ordained a priest in 391, Augustine served as the Bishop of Hippo in North Africa from 396 until his death on August 28, 430.

I Believe in Order that I May Understand

Augustine was perhaps the greatest of the Christian Platonists.[90] The integration of biblical data and Platonic philosophy can be seen particularly in the famous maxim of Augustine's theological method: "I believe in order that I may understand" (*Credo ut intelligam*). Augustine derived the biblical foundation of this principle from the Latin version of the Septuagint translation of Isaiah 7:9, "Unless you believe, you shall not understand" (*nisi credideritis non intelligetis*). The philosophical foundation came from the Platonic notion of innate first principles, which enabled persons to understand particulars in this world. In Augustine's treatise *On Free Will* he declared:

> You remember the position we adopted at the beginning of our former discussion. We cannot deny that believing and knowing are different things, and that in matters of great importance, pertaining to divinity, we must first believe before we seek to know. Otherwise the words of the prophet would be vain, where he says: 'Except ye believe ye shall not understand' (Isa. 7:9 LXX). Our Lord himself, both in his words and by his deeds, exhorted those whom he called to salvation first of all to believe. And no one is fit to find God who does not first believe what he will afterwards learn to know.[91]

The relationship between faith and reason is complex. Augustine certainly did not develop a precise epistemology comparable to that of philosophers in later centuries.[92] This issue is especially difficult to deal with because the problems and proposed solutions of later schools of thought are often read back into Augustine. Since Aristotle replaced Plato as *the* philosopher in the church in the Middle Ages, there have been strenuous efforts to rework Augustine's thought in order to make it compatible with Thomas Aquinas's Aristotelian-based theology.[93] Augustine, however, must be allowed to be a person of his own time, a time in which Platonism dominated. He did not believe that all knowledge begins with sense experience, as the Aristotelians (and most modern people) do. For Augustine, things in this world could indeed be known by the senses, but the truly important realities—the knowledge of God, and of virtue, and eternal principles—were implanted in the mind by God from our birth. These realities could be known by intellectual vision, by contemplation, by memory. And the knowledge they produced was *sapientia*, wisdom, as opposed to *scientia*, the knowledge, or science, of temporal things. The realm of the eternal and the realm of the temporal were different and were known differently. And for Augustine the realm of the eternal was the most important. The knowledge of the eternal preceded and helped to illumine the realm of the temporal. Knowledge from the realm of the eternal was accepted in faith and led to understanding of both the eternal and the temporal realm.

The twin facts that God was known differently from things and that the knowledge of God preceded and enabled people to understand other things were fundamental for Augustine. Augustine prayed to God in his *Confessions:* "No one can call upon Thee without knowing Thee."[94] In expounding the Fourth Gospel, Augustine declared: "For we believe in order that we may know, we do not know in order that we may believe."[95]

Augustine spoke of faith in two senses. In some places faith referred to the content of Christianity, the revelation of God implanted in the heart and elaborated in the Bible. In other places Augustine used faith to refer to the relationship of people to that content and to God who gave it. In both instances Augustine accepted the knowledge of God and relationship to God as true and trustworthy and allowed them to guide him in understanding and living life.[96] For Augustine, the precedence of faith to understanding corresponded to the biblical distinction between "walking by faith" or by "sight." Augustine wrote:

> When the mind has been imbued with the first elements of that faith which worketh by love (Galatians 5:6), it endeavors by purity of life to attain unto sight, where the pure and perfect in heart know that unspeakable beauty, the full vision of which is supreme happiness. Here surely is an answer to your question as to what is the starting-point, and what the goal: We begin in faith, and are made perfect by sight. This also is the sum of the whole body of doctrine.[97]

For those who, in faith, had embraced the God-given revelation in their hearts and in the Bible, reason could help them in the quest for a full understanding of the transcendent truths of God. According to Augustine, the "things below" were aids for coming to a full knowledge of "things above."[98] Things in the created world could function as "signs" or "symbols" through which God was understood. This was not a "natural theology" grounded on the unaided human reason, however. According to Augustine, all understanding was possible because of the illumination afforded by the Uncreated Light of God.[99] Augustine asserted that "for the mind to see God it must be illuminated by God Himself."[100] He agreed with the Platonists that God "the creator of all things, is the light of the mind, which makes possible every acquisition of knowledge."[101]

For Augustine the function of reason in religious matters was to provide analogies that would help people assimilate and accept divine truths. Augustine averred that, for believers, reason could

> let you see God with your mind as the sun is seen with the eye. The mind has, as it were, eyes of its own, analogous to the soul's senses. The certain truths of the sciences are analogous to the objects which the sun's rays make visible, such as the earth and earthly things. And it is God Himself who illumines all. I, Reason, am in minds as the power of looking is in the eyes.[102]

Augustine offered arguments for the existence of God even though he knew that a commitment to God required the act of God's grace on the person.[103] These human arguments did not demonstrate the content of the Christian faith, but only afforded analogies that made that content more understandable, through comparison with things in human experience. Augustine, for example, did not start from human evidence and then reason to the doctrine of the Trinity. Rather, he started with the doctrine of the Trinity and attempted through a reflective analysis of human experience to show the intelligibility of speaking of God as a trinity or community of persons.[104]

In *no* passages did Augustine put reason before faith as a method of knowing God.[105] He acknowledged human beings as creatures to whom God had given rational capacities. God had also implanted in the hearts of those same people the knowledge of himself. Theologically, therefore, faith preceded and led to understanding for Augustine. Understanding was the fruit of faith. Faith itself was the starting point for accepting the knowledge of God, which became more clear and intelligible through the activities of human reason and experience.[106] Augustine's response to those who sought to know God by reason without faith was quite sharp: "But, if they say that we are not even to believe in Christ, unless they can give a reason that cannot be doubted, then they are not Christians."[107] The need for exalting reason to protect against irrationalism was foreign to Augustine. His theological method, true to his roots in Plato and Scripture, stood squarely between those false extremes. God implanted a knowledge of himself in the human heart. The Holy Spirit enabled people to accept that in faith. From that divinely implanted knowledge the human mind could proceed to a greater understanding of God and of God's world.

Authority

Augustine's understanding of the authority of Scripture flowed from his general method: "I believe in order to understand." The Bible was accepted in faith as the guide to salvation and life. Then Augustine used all of the talent and training available to him to arrive at a clearer understanding of that which he believed.

For Augustine, the Bible was "holy Scripture," "divine Scripture," the "word of God," the "divine oracles."[108] He urged that "all that is in these Scriptures, believe me, is profound and divine."[109] These Scriptures were inspired by God.

Augustine very rarely tried to prove the inspiration of the Bible. He took the inspiration for granted because of the effect the Bible had on people.[110] For Augustine, the Holy Spirit was also at work in the present-day reading of Scripture and in hearing it preached. According to him, the Spirit worked, so that "what was hidden may come to light and what was unpleasant may be made agreeable."[111] Indeed, "His grace works within us our illumination and justification."[112] It was the mutual working of the Word and the Spirit which gave the written and the preached Word ultimate authority.[113] The proclaimed Word had authority because it carried with it the power to persuade and to change lives.[114]

The function of this inspired Scripture was to bring people to salvation in Jesus Christ. Augustine declared: "All the passages of the Scripture speak of Christ. The head now ascended into heaven along with the body still suffering on earth is the full development of the whole purpose of the authors of Scripture, which is well called Sacred Scripture."[115] Against the Manichaeans, Augustine argued that the agreement between the Old and New Testaments in setting forth Christ as savior showed decisively that the two were the work of one God.[116] The authority of Scripture for Augustine was firmly related to the saving purpose of Scripture. He announced that since humans were "too weak by unaided reason to find out truth . . . we need the authority of the Holy Writings . . . [since] through them thy will may be believed in and . . . thou mightest be sought."[117] It was God's purpose to give us an authoritative record of his will "for our good."[118]

According to Augustine, the purpose of Scripture was not to bring people information in general, but to bring the Good News of salvation and guidance in the Christian way of life. The Bible was not a textbook of science or an academic tract. It was the Book of Life, written in the language of life. When Felix the Manichaean claimed that the Holy Spirit had revealed to Manichaeus the orbits of the heavenly bodies, Augustine replied that God desired us to become Christians, not astronomers.[119] Such talk, Augustine said:

> takes up much of our valuable time and thus distracts our attention from more wholesome matters. Although our authors knew the truth about the shape of the heavens, the Spirit of God who spoke by them did not intend to teach men these things, in no way profitable for salvation.[120]

Augustine warned Christians not to take their "science" from the Bible. He felt that such appeals to Scripture for ammunition in waging war with unbelievers would expose the Bible to ridicule and inhibit non-Christians from hearing the saving truths that Scripture proclaimed with authority. Augustine declared:

> Many non-Christians happen to be well-versed in knowledge of the earth, the heaven, of all the other elements of the world, of the motion, the revolutions, the size and distance of the stars, of eclipses of the sun and the moon,

of such periodic events as the years and the tides, of the nature of animals, plants, stones and of other things which can all be understood by keen reasoning or experience. It is therefore deplorable that Christians, even though they ostensibly base their dicta on the Bible, should utter so much nonsense that they expose themselves to ridicule. While ridicule is all they deserve, they also give the impression that the Biblical authors are responsible for their mutterings, thus discrediting Christianity before the world, which is led to assume that the authors of the Scriptures were ignorant fools also. Whenever any Christian is confounded and shown to be an idle chatterer, his chatter is attributed to our Holy Books. No wonder that the critics refuse to believe what Scripture has to say on the resurrection, on life eternal and the kingdom of heaven, when they can point out that the Bible is ostensibly wrong about facts which they can see or determine for themselves. Hence these idle boasters cause untold grief to our more thoughtful brethren.[121]

Accommodation

God's style of condescension or accommodation in the Bible was as apparent to Augustine as it had been to Clement and Origen and Chrysostom. Augustine knew that the primary purpose of Scripture was to bring us as children into a right relationship with God our parent. Augustine declared, in a quotation used and affirmed by Calvin centuries later; "We can safely follow Scripture, which proceeds at the pace of a mother stooping to her child, so to speak, so as not to leave us behind in our weakness.[122] The source of Augustine's statement was his book *Genesis according to the Literal Sense*. To free himself from the Manichaeans, Augustine had to come to terms with the Christian notion of creation and thus with the Book of Genesis. Augustine used the concept of accommodation to resolve the antitheses between the Old and New Testaments which the Manichaeans, the Gnostics, and the Marcionites had created by reading the Bible literally.

Earlier, as a teacher of rhetoric, Augustine had been put off by what seemed to him the crude and even barbarous style of Scripture. In his *Confessions*, Augustine acknowledged that he did not feel comfortable in his Christian faith until he accepted the fact that depth of truth and sublimity of style did not necessarily go together. The concept of accommodation helped him to resolve that seeming contradiction. His insight was developed at length in *On Christian Doctrine*, which was the first full-scale Christian rhetoric.[123] The form of God's message he realized was adapted to its function of bringing all people into a living relationship with God.

Augustine spoke about "the Holy Scripture, which suits itself to babes."[124] Commenting on the Apostle John, Augustine said:

> I venture to say, brethren, that not even John himself has presented these things just as they are, but only as best he could, since he was a man who spoke of God—inspired, of course, but still a man. Because he was inspired he was able to say something; but because he who was inspired remained a man, he could not present the full reality, but only what a man could say about it.[125]

That God adapted to our human forms of thought and speech did not imply a hindrance, but an enhancement of God's ability to accomplish his saving purpose. As Augustine put it: "God speaks through a man, in a human way, because in thus speaking he is looking for us."[126]

Augustine's views of the divine authority of the Bible and its humanly accommodated form are brought together in his discussion of the language used in Scripture. The actual outworking of his theological method, "I believe in order to understand," is well illustrated. Scripture was a divine unity for Augustine. He did not allow that discordancy of any kind could exist.[127] Yet the unity of Scripture was in the consistency of its message, not in a formal harmony of all its verbal forms, in which God's message was expressed. Augustine had many ways of handling apparent disharmonies. He pointed to various possible difficulties:

> If we are perplexed by an apparent contradiction in Scripture, it is not permissible to say, the author of this book is mistaken; instead, the manuscript is faulty, or the translation is wrong, or you have not understood.... Scripture has a sacredness peculiar to itself. In other books the reader may form his own opinion and perhaps, from not understanding the writer, may differ from him.... We are bound to receive as true whatever the canon shows to have been said by even one prophet or apostle or evangelist.[128]

Augustine never wavered in his belief that the message conveyed in the Bible was true. But he was quite aware of disagreements in form between the accounts offered by different biblical writers. When discussing the order in which a narrative about Peter's mother-in-law was introduced, Augustine wrote:

> It is quite probable that each evangelist believed it to have been his duty to recount what he had to in that order in which it pleased God to suggest it to his memory—in those things at least in which the order, whether it be this or that, detracts in nothing from the truth and authority of the Gospel. But why the Holy Spirit, who apportions individually to each one as he wills (I Cor. 12:11), and who therefore undoubtedly also governed and ruled the minds of the holy writers in recalling what they were to write because of the preeminent authority which the books were to enjoy, permitted one to compile his narrative in this way, and another in that, anyone with pious diligence may seek the reason and with divine aid will be able to find it.[129]

For Augustine, God "permitted" variant forms in order to accomplish his single saving purpose. Augustine therefore focused on the meaning expressed, not the mechanics of expression. He stated that the one "requisite" or goal "in order to get at the knowledge of the truth is just to make sure of the things really meant, whatever may be the precise words in which they happen to be expressed.[130] The authority of the Bible remained constant through its expression in humanly accommodated forms. Augustine declared that the authority of the Bible forbade supposing that "any one of the writers is giving an unreliable account, if, when several persons are recalling some matter either heard or seen by them, they fail to follow the very same plan, or to use the very same words, while describing, nevertheless, the self-same fact.[131] One must not suppose that "the most literal accuracy" (Augustine's phrase) is required or that the evangelists must have been instructed by the Holy Spirit in their choice of words. The harmony of biblical authority and accommodation in its application to the actual text of Scripture is evidenced in the following statement by Augustine:

> If anyone should claim that the power of the Holy Spirit ought to have helped the evangelists not to differ in their choices of words, the ordering of the words, or the numbers of their words, then he simply does not understand that this procedure of the evangelists was quite necessary if they were to persuade other men of their veracity. There can be no question of lying where many people describe the same event but differ from one another in their manner of expression. In other words, the truth is in no wise violated if the same events are narrated in different ways and with different words. It follows from what we have said above about the divine 'condescension' that this procedure is quite admissible in Sacred Scripture, and thus in the Gospels.[132]

The activity of the Holy Spirit governed the outcome, but not the methods of the biblical writers, according to Augustine. When dealing with the actual words spoken by John the Baptist at the baptism of Jesus (Matt. 3:7–12; Luke 3:7–9), Augustine said: "It is clear that each of them [the evangelists] has given an account according to his recollection of the event, and according to his judgment as to how it should be proposed, either briefly or in detail; but there is always the same thought.[133] The Holy Spirit allowed each of the Gospel writers "to dispose the events in his narration, one man this way, another that, as it was given to each to view things with the aid of the divine light.[134] Augustine could take account of all the human techniques used by the writers of Scripture while affirming the divine truth of what they said.[135] Variant readings concerning the same event were not an ultimate problem for Augustine because he saw them as the work of the Holy Spirit who permitted this pluriformity of perspectives in order to whet people's spiritual appetites for understanding.[136]

The problems in the biblical text were problems for human understanding. They were not problems for Christian faith. Augustine knew that the truth of Scripture resided finally in the thought of the biblical writers and not in the form of their words. He commented:

> In any man's words the thing which we ought narrowly to regard is only the writer's thought which was meant to be expressed, and to which the words ought to be subservient.... And we ought not to let the wretched cavillers at words fancy that truth must be tied somehow or other to the jots and tittles of letters; whereas the fact is, that not in the matter of words only, but equally in all other methods by which sentiments are indicated, the sentiment itself, and nothing else, is what ought to be looked at.[137]

Augustine commended the function, the saving purpose, of Scripture as the focus of human concern rather than the form of writing. He asserted: "We have the wholesome lesson inculcated upon us, that what we have to look to in studying a person's words is nothing less than the intention of the speakers.[138]

Concept of Error

Augustine's concentration on the meaning of a biblical text rather than on its form of words is well illustrated by the famous passage in his letter 82 to Jerome in which Augustine declared: "For I confess to your charity that I have learned to yield this respect and honour only to the canonical books of Scripture: of these alone do I most firmly believe that the authors were completely free from error."[139] This was a follow-up letter, replacing Augustine's first letter to Jerome, which had been lost and never delivered. Both letters dealt with the same issues. In the first letter (28) Augustine chided Jerome for translating the Old Testament directly from the Hebrew rather than sticking to the Septuagint, which Augustine regarded as inspired and authoritative. In letter 82, Augustine conceded the usefulness of Jerome's translation of the Old Testament from Hebrew into Latin but stated his preference that it not be used in public worship lest the faithful, used to the Septuagint, should be upset. The main substance of both letters was Augustine's shocked dismay that Jerome in his *Commentary on Galatians* represented Paul as having deliberately lied about his confrontation with Peter for the sake of expediency.[140] In the original letter (28) Augustine made clear his concern when he wrote:

It is one question whether it may be at any time the duty of a good man to deceive; but it is another question whether it can have been the duty of a writer of Holy Scripture to deceive: nay, it is not another question—it is no question at all. For if you once admit into such a high sanctuary of authority one false statement as made in the way of duty, there will not be left a single sentence of those books which, if appearing to any one difficult in practice or hard to believe, may not by the same fatal rule be explained away, as a statement in which, intentionally, and under a sense of duty, the author declared what was not true.[141]

Jerome averred that he had been following Origen and a long line of Greek commentators who viewed Peter and Paul as both acting parts at Antioch when one seemed to revert to Jewish food laws and the other appeared to censure him. This tack had apparently been taken to silence Porphyry who had made much of the quarrel between the apostles. Augustine replied that it was better to believe that Peter had done what was not right, and that the Scripture had honestly told it, than to assume that Paul had deliberately written what was not true. Augustine concluded:

Better far that I should read with certainty and persuasion of its truth the Holy Scripture, placed on the highest (even the heavenly) pinnacle of authority, and should without questioning the trustworthiness of its statements, learn from it that men have been either commended, or corrected, or condemned, than that through fear of believing that by men, who though of most praiseworthy excellence, were no more than men, actions deserving rebuke might sometimes be done, I should admit suspicions affecting the trustworthiness of the whole "oracles of God."[142]

Error, for Augustine, had to do with deliberate and deceitful telling of that which the author knew to be untrue. It was in that context of ethical seriousness that he declared that the biblical "authors were completely free from error." He did not apply the concept of error to problems that arose from the human limitations of knowledge, various perspectives in reporting events, or historical or cultural conditioning of the writers. Those problems belonged to the area of understanding Scripture with the tools of research. But the integrity of the biblical authors' intentions was for Augustine a matter of faith.[143]

It is wholesome for those of us who live in the age of the computer printout to recall that Augustine, like the biblical writers, lived before the age of complete technical accuracy in verbal communication. Words like *dictation* and *error* did not then have the technological overtones they now carry. A rhetorician like Augustine knew that truth could be conveyed by a great variety of words, and he did not expect the biblical writers always to give a literal, technical reproduction of events.[144]

Allegorical Interpretation

Augustine's desire to get at the meaning in accordance with the purpose of the Bible comes out in his method of biblical interpretation. The goal of Bible study for Augustine was to increase love for God and for one's neighbor. Augustine urged: "What is read should be subjected to diligent scrutiny until an interpretation contributing to the reign of charity is produced."[145] This interest in the practical fruits of Scripture study gave Augustine a principle of interpretation. He asserted that "whatever there is in the word of God that cannot when taken literally be referred to purity of life or soundness of doctrine, you may set down as figurative."[146]

As with Origen, some of whose works he knew in translation, Augustine was concerned to protect the message of Scripture from charges of crudity and impurity.[147] Furthermore, as a Neoplatonist, it was natural for Augustine to value the spiritual sense above the literal one. When he began the exposition of a passage of Scripture, Augustine looked primarily not for what the historical author intended to say, but for what God intended to teach through the literal or any one of a number of attached senses.[148] The direction in which these desires for deeper meaning took Augustine was into allegorical exegesis.

As Augustine told it, it was his bishop, Ambrose, who opened the method of allegorical exegesis for him:

> I listened with delight to Ambrose, in his sermons to the people, often recommending this text most diligently as a rule: 'The letter kills, but the spirit gives life' (II Cor. 3:6), while at the same time he drew aside the mystic veil and opened to view the spiritual meaning of what seemed to teach perverse doctrine if it were taken according to the letter.[149]

The Manichaeans insisted on reading the Old Testament literally. They used this literalism to discredit the Patriarchs by pointing to the immoralities that Scripture recorded about them. An allegorical exegesis of these texts became of critical importance to Augustine. He declared that it was only after he discovered the allegorical method of interpreting the Bible that he was able to become a Christian.[150]

Augustine was well aware that there was a root historical meaning in each text, and he wished to acknowledge that sense even as he probed for an allegorical one. He defended his allegorism by saying: "There is no prohibition against such exegesis, provided that we also believe in the truth of the story as a faithful record of historical fact."[151]

Some guidelines were needed, both to discern the texts to be taken figuratively and to ensure that such interpretations were properly attained and controlled. Augustine accordingly adopted and modified the

"Seven Rules of Tyconius," which Tyconius, the Donatist theologian (d. ?400), had formulated as hermeneutical "keys."[152] Augustine designated four "senses" of Scripture: historical (*historia*), aetiological (*aetiologia*), analogical (*analogia*), and allegorical (*allegoria*).[153] Augustine asserted: "In every sacred book one should note the things of eternity which are communicated, the facts of history which are recounted, future events which are foretold, moral precepts which are enjoined or counseled.[154] This fourfold division was later elaborated on by the theologians of the Middle Ages.

Augustine preferred to give both a literal and a spiritual interpretation of the same text to indicate that the one signified or prefigured the other. This was made possible by one of his interpretative axioms: "In the Old Testament the New is concealed; in the New, the Old is revealed."[155] Augustine usually was able to deal with these dual senses in an edifying manner. He asserted, for example, that certain customs cited in the Old Testament, such as polygamy, were permitted to primitive people; sins of righteous persons, such as David's adultery, were recorded to warn us against pride. But at times, his spiritualizing exegesis was severely strained, as when he explained that Jacob set up the rods before the flocks as a prophecy of Christ, not in order to cheat his father-in-law.[156]

Like Origen, Augustine wandered farthest afield when he treated each text as having an individual, spiritual meaning instead of seeing them as part of the whole *kerygma*. His sensitivity to the spiritual sense enabled him to render the Hebrew Scriptures as a wholly Christian literature. But his atomistic reading of each text for its spiritual meaning tended to suppress the intrinsic historical significance of Scripture.[157] We must remember that for Augustine, literalism was the enemy. For him, there was sufficient evidence that too much literalism led to heresy. He was conscious that Satan used Scripture to tempt Christ. Therefore, while the literal, historical sense was to be treated as foundational, one was as soon as possible to move beyond it to the spiritual.[158]

Church and Creed

Augustine's more atomistic allegorism was modified by his adherence to the authority of the church and the creed. Augustine acknowledged the church as the means that had brought him to Christ. He wrote: "I should not believe the gospel except as moved by the authority of the Catholic Church."[159] Augustine loved to say, as when discussing the Trinity: "This is also my faith, since it is the Catholic faith."[160] For him the goal of Scripture was to induce love for God and neighbor, but he felt that these were found in their true form only in the church, which was the body knit together in love to Christ the head.[161] Against various heretical sects who went to extremes following their own private interpretations, Augustine stressed the need for the authority of the Catholic Church in interpreting the Scriptures.

An outgrowth of the interaction of church and Scripture was the *regula fidei,* the rule of faith. There was in circulation in the church a brief creedal formula. It was probably originally a baptismal formula that had been elaborated for use in instructing new members of the church.[162] Around this core statement of faith were grouped a series of fundamental doctrines of the Christian faith acknowledged as essential by the church. This creedal statement and these doctrines were traditionally attributed to Christ himself, as communicated through the apostles. Rufinus of Aquileia (345?–?410) in his *Exposition of the Creed* (c. 404) asserted that the apostles, before they departed after Pentecost, gathered to establish a common basis for their preaching. According to the legend, each apostle contributed an article, and this became the Apostles' Creed.[163]

Through his appeal to the *regula fidei* as an interpreting principle, Augustine was kept in touch with the *kerygma,* the central saving message of the church. That helped to modify the excesses of allegorism to which he might otherwise have been led. By accepting the tradition as normative, Augustine also assisted in strengthening the authority of the church.

Augustine was great, in part, because he held together in tension many essential realities he could not press into a system: faith and reason, divine and human, practical and theoretical, Bible and church. He knew that all were true and necessary. He had orders of priority and methods of interpretation by which he usually related them. At times, he went to one or the other extreme in violation of his own principles when responding to particular pressures. Because he began in faith but sought through reason to understand the implications of that faith, the Roman Catholic Church later called him a Doctor of Grace and Protestants saw him as a forerunner of the Reformation. Those who followed him in the Middle Ages were not flexible enough to keep his balance and live with its tensions. They reduced complex truths to simpler systems at the expense of keeping the breadth and richness of biblical revelation.

e. Developing Scholasticism: Anselm to Abelard

Transition from Ancient to Medieval Period

The Middle Ages is a conventional name for that period of Western history that lasted for a thousand years—from the fifth to the fifteenth centuries.[164] Politically, the Middle Ages marked the end of the Roman Empire and the coming into being of Europe as a political entity. Peace and order under Roman law were replaced by struggle among the relatively isolated, largely agrarian, units of a feudal society.[165] This breakdown of centralized authority was a challenge to Christians as well as to others. Augustine's work, *Concerning the City of God against the Pagans,* was an apologetic designed to refute charges that the sack of Rome in A.D. 410 by Alaric the Goth was punishment for unfaithfulness to the ancient Roman gods.[166]

Ecclesiastically, the Middle Ages was that period when the Roman church claimed to be the one true state.[167] The strength of the Roman pontiff increased enormously beginning with Gregory I (pope from 590 to 604). The church subjected the whole of the human enterprise to its understanding of the will of God. It was an "ark of salvation" in a "sea of destruction." Whether there could be any rational social order outside the church was disputed. Certainly membership in the church was intended to give intelligible purpose and place to people in this world as well as the next.[168]

Especially during those early years of the Middle Ages, sometimes called the "Dark Ages," the church kept alive something of ancient culture. The Latin language was the church's link with the past. Scribes in monasteries spent incalculable amounts of time and energy copying manuscripts and thus preserving some of the learning of antiquity.[169] Not all was rescued, of course. For example, of the works of Plato, only the *Timaeus* was known. Of Aristotle, only parts of the works on logic survived.[170]

The High Middle Ages (700–1300) saw internal conflicts in the church between competing popes and antipopes. In the Late Middle Ages (1300 –1500), popular reaction was aroused against the papacy, in part by the ill-fated Crusades to rescue the Holy Land from the Muslims. Renaissance humanists rediscovered richer sources of ancient learning than those transmitted by the church. And Protestant Reformers went back to Scripture as a source of authority more sure than the medieval papacy.

Foundations of Scholasticism

Both of the major ancient philosophical schools, that of Plato and that of Aristotle, were carried on into the Middle Ages. Until the revival of Aristotelian studies in the thirteenth century, Platonism, of some form, dominated. This philosophical tradition was transmitted largely through the theology of Augustine.[171] Another channel was the writings of the "Pseudo-Dionysius." Supposedly this was the work of Dionysius the Areopagite who was converted by Paul at Athens (Acts 17:34)[172] Actually, this theological writer probably lived sometime in the fifth century, probably in Syria. These Pseudo-Dionysian writings became a charter for subsequent Christian mysticism. They stressed the hierarchical pattern of the universe, the intimate union between the soul and God, and the eventual deification of human beings.[173]

In the Eastern Church the Pseudo-Dionysian writings became a standard theological authority because of their alleged authenticity and their mystical message. In the West, the Lateran Council of 649 quoted them as an authority against the Monothelitists—those who confessed Christ to have but one will. The Pseudo-Dionysian writings became widely known in the West through their translation into Latin by John Scotus Erigena (810?–?877). Their importance was enhanced by incorporation in the work of medieval theologians who leaned to mysticism, such as Hugh of St. Victor (d. 1142), Bonaventure (1217?–1274) and Meister Eckhart (1260?–?1327). Aristotelian scholastics, such as Albert the Great (1200?–1280), and Thomas Aquinas (1225–1274), also knew and used the Pseudo-Dionysius.

Aristotelian logic came to the Middle Ages through translations and commentaries by Boethius (480?–?524)[174] Boethius began the shift from an Augustinian to a scholastic approach in medieval philosophy and theology. He consciously applied the procedure of Augustine to theological issues. However, he was more technical and dialectic in his method. He regarded the power of human reason to explain the doctrines of the Christian faith and to support their authority as the principal means of clarifying revealed truth. Boethius's influence on thinkers of the Early Scholastic period was great. His commentary on Porphyry initiated the controversy about universals in the eleventh and twelfth centuries. His translations and commentaries on both Aristotle and Porphyry emphasized logic; this tended to direct the attention of medieval thinkers to matters of method rather than content. It shaped the style of academic teaching by placing a premium on accuracy of form and subtlety of expression rather than on practical consequences in life. Logic became a substitute for discovery.

Scholasticism is a word used to describe philosophy, theology, and the teaching of law and the liberal arts in the medieval period.[175] The word comes from the Latin *schola* meaning "school." A *scholasticus* was a lecturer or teacher (and later a student) in a recognized school. The word *scholastic* was later applied to the method of teaching in the medieval schools and to the mentality that informed it. It is difficult to define scholasticism with precision. We can, however, point to certain trends and tendencies, methods and mentalities that characterized this development in the Middle Ages.

Not everything medieval was Scholastic—there were countertrends and reactions. Scholasticism represented a movement away from the early church's common foundations of theological method and its approach to the Bible, which we described in preceding sections. In the following sections is a sketch of elements important for understanding the Scholastic treatment of the Bible. The development proceeded in several stages: Pre-Scholasticism from about the seventh to the eleventh centuries; Early Scholasticism from the eleventh to the thirteenth centuries; Classical Scholasticism in the thirteenth century; and, the period of criticism in Late Scholasticism, the fourteenth and fifteenth centuries. The developments were uneven, but the direction is discernible. Christian doctrine was organized, sorted out, and classified as a body of knowledge to be analyzed and expounded by human reason.[176]

Pre-Scholasticism: John Scotus Erigena

Augustine was the transitional figure between the early church and the Middle Ages. Some scholars assert that Augustine was the first Scholastic, while most assign him the title of last of the church fathers.[177] For several centuries after Augustine, scholars generally followed his method without new departures. The movement toward Scholasticism really did not begin, even as Pre-Scholasticism, however, until the seventh to the eleventh centuries.[178]

The seventh and eighth centuries were dark ages for culture in Western Europe. The Roman school system had almost vanished. Monasteries alone were preserving and transmitting learning. The theologians of this period continued the Augustinian attitude toward the authority of the Bible and its allegorical interpretation. Pope Gregory I (d. 604) laid down much of the structure of the medieval Catholic Church. In interpreting the Bible, he became so absorbed in the spiritual and moral sense of Scripture that the literal sense was almost ignored.[179] The most important scholar of this time was the Venerable Bede (d. 735). He continued the trend of moralizing and allegorizing, complaining: "If we seek to follow the letter of Scripture only, in the Jewish way, what shall we find to correct our sins, to console or instruct us?"[180]

Cassiodorus (485?–?580), a follower of Boethius, instituted a plan at his monastery in Vivarium that put the seven liberal arts at the basis of all secular and sacred learning. The *Trivium* (Grammar, Rhetoric, and Dialectic), and the *Quadrivium* (Arithmetic, Geometry, Astronomy, and Music) were thought to encompass all human knowledge. The liberal arts were esteemed for the aid they gave in interpreting Scripture. The study of these subjects led to a modest revival of learning, known as the Carolingian Renaissance (accomplished during the reign of Charles the

Great).[181] Alcuin, one of the important early organizers of studies in France, introduced scholastic exercises into these studies. After the *lectio,* the reading of texts, from Scripture and the church fathers, and the teacher's lecture on them, came the *disputatio,* the argument, at first to clear away linguistic and grammatical difficulties, and later to harmonize authorities. This argumentation took the form of dialectic, the *sic et non,* or yes and no; The approach balanced possible answers on both sides of a question until some harmonization was reached. This study and interpretation of texts later took on a standardized four-step form: question (*utrum*), provisional answer (*videtur quod*), objection (*sed contra*), and definitive answer by the professor (*respondeo*). The methodology shifted the focus of the student from faith in the authority to the reasons why an opinion was held. Alcuin asserted that even the contents of revelation should be discussed dialectically. He presented the doctrines of the Trinity, incarnation, creation, and last things by the dialectical method although in substance his approach did not depart significantly from that of Augustine and Boethius.[182]

The Irish monk, John Scotus Erigena (810?–?877), was the most influential philosophical thinker between Augustine and Anselm of Canterbury.[183] He directed and developed the move toward Scholasticism through his translations and expositions of the Neoplatonic Pseudo-Dionysius and the Aristotelian logic of Boethius.

In Erigena's system, philosophical and theological elements were inextricably mixed.[184] His aim was to provide a complete, rational explanation of Christian doctrine as found in the Bible and the church fathers.[185] He did not question the authority of Scripture or the creeds, but he did demand that the theologian's interpretation of the Bible be that which best accorded with reason. He wrote: "Reason and authority come alike from the one source of divine wisdom, and cannot contradict each other."[186]

Some later writers have named Erigena the father of scholasticism.[187] Although this title is not wholly appropriate, Erigena did begin the philosophical shift that finally led to Platonic thought being replaced by Aristotelian reasoning. Erigena had absorbed Augustine's Neoplatonic "faith seeking understanding" methodology, but his concern was different from Augustine's. Erigena wanted clearly to distinguish between *auctoritas* (Holy Scripture) and *ratio* (reason). The Bible was still the main source of our knowledge of God. But, it was the duty of reason, illuminated by God, to investigate and explain the biblical data.[188] Erigena was not yet a full Scholastic, giving reason priority over Scripture. But his emphasis had shifted in that direction and influenced later medieval theologians in that manner.

Transitional Period: Anselm of Canterbury

Anselm (1033?–1109) exemplified a balance between the ancient tradition and the new thought that was soon to be broken up. He was a monk and a scholar as well as an able administrator and reformer. At the age of 26 he entered the Abbey of Bec. Two decades later he was elected its abbot. Under his leadership, Bec gained renown as a center of philosophical and theological studies. In 1093, Anselm was appointed Archbishop of Canterbury. He spent the rest of his life struggling for the freedom of the church against the power of successive English kings.[189]

Anselm intended to continue the Augustinian tradition. He began his *Monologion* (1076) by stating that he did not wish to hold any doctrine or make any statement "which is inconsistent with the writings of the Catholic Fathers, or especially with those of St. Augustine."[190] At the same time, Anselm imbibed a logical and rationalist strain of thought from Boethius and Aristotle.[191]

It is evident that Anselm fully accepted and wished to further Augustine's theological method of "faith seeking understanding." In the preface to his *Proslogion* (1077–1078) Anselm mentioned the titles he had originally proposed for his works: "So I have given to each its title, the first being called *An Example of Meditation on the Meaning of Faith,* and the sequel, *Faith in Quest of Understanding.*"[192] The Augustinian stamp was plain in the first chapter of the *Proslogion*:

> I do not try, Lord, to attain Your Lofty heights, because my understanding is in no way equal to it. But I do desire to understand Your truth a little, that truth that my heart believes and loves. For I do not seek to understand so that I may believe; but I believe so that I may understand. For I believe this also, that 'unless I believe, I shall not understand.'[193]

In *Cur Deus Homo* (1097–1098) Anselm's agreement with Augustine was again apparent:

> As the right order requires us to believe the deep things of Christian faith before we undertake to discuss them by reason; so to my mind it appears a neglect if, after we are established in the faith, we do not seek to understand what we believe.[194]

Anselm, however, expanded on Augustine with regard to the powers assigned to reason. For believers, Anselm followed the Augustinian pattern. Reason enabled people to penetrate more deeply into their beliefs. In this way, the faith of believers was strengthened. They were enabled to make intelligible their own experience of faith and to expound it according to human reason. This was designed to help believers defend their faith against attack. Anselm wrote in this vein in *Cur Deus Homo*:

I have been often and most earnestly requested by many, both personally and by letter, that I would hand down in writing the proofs of a certain doctrine of our faith, which I am accustomed to give to inquirers; for they say that these proofs gratify them, and are considered sufficient. This they ask, not for the sake of attaining to faith by means of reason, but that they may be gladdened by understanding and meditating on those things which they believe; and that, as far as possible, they may be always ready to convince any one who demands of them a reason of that hope which is in us.[195]

The shift in the direction of Scholasticism came when Anselm addressed nonbelievers. He hoped to set forth his arguments in such a way as to convince them of the truth of the Christian faith. Rather than depending on the Holy Spirit illuminating the mind as Augustine did, Anselm relied on the power of reason appealing to the mind. Augustine's Neoplatonist notion of innate ideas and his strong sense of human inability due to original sin was beginning to slip into the background as Anselm relied on human reason to appeal to an open mind. In the *Cur Deus Homo,* Anselm sought to show why God had become Man and to prove "by absolute reasons, the impossibility that any man should be saved without him." The first section of this work was addressed to the objections of "infidels, who despise the Christian faith because they deem it contrary to reason." Anselm appealed to "plain reasoning" to prove his arguments. He believed that he could make his case even by "leaving Christ out of view (as if nothing had ever been known of him)."[196]

The claims that Anselm made for human reason outside the realm of a faith commitment went beyond those advocated by Augustine. The appeal to logic, on the hypothetical supposition that nothing need be known of Christ, set in motion the way of thinking that gave reason priority over faith and finally led to the separation of faith and reason. Attention ultimately shifted in Scholasticism from the biblical message accepted in faith to interest in what reason could erect on its own apart from Scripture.[197]

Anselm did not develop as fully as did later Scholastics the function of reason apart from the act of faith. For him, reason in the believer confirmed faith, but did not replace faith.[198] For nonbelievers, reason showed the credibility of Christian claims. It was the increasing priority given to the latter, apologetic approach that marked theologians in the next century.[199] Anselm lived at a time before the whole Aristotelian philosophical corpus was known. He did not possess the philosophical support that later Scholastics had for asserting the extensive powers of natural reason. Reason did not have the same unquestioned superiority for Anselm that it came to have in the thirteenth century.[200] Anselm suggested tentatively what later was asserted as obvious, namely, that theological understanding could draw on knowledge and experience in the world that was not related to the deposit of Christian faith.[201] For Anselm, faith and reason were still opposite sides of the same coin. They remained inseparable. And faith still had priority.

Early Scholasticism: Peter Abelard

The twelfth century exemplified the shortcomings of a feudal age. Regional princes and robber barons struggled for power through constant warfare. Rival popes excommunicated each other and left the church without clear authority. Corruption and disorder disturbed life in the monasteries.

One movement of reform that brought some promise of progress and order into this confused situation was intellectual. It grew from a fresh study of Roman law and further discoveries in Aristotelian logic. It coincided with a change in the location of higher education from the monasteries in the countryside to the cathedral schools in the urban centers. These cathedral schools became the foundation of modern universities. The University of Paris came to be acknowledged in the twelfth century as the center of learning in the world.

Peter Abelard (1079–1142) symbolized the intellectual movement for reform. He was a "peripatetic philosopher." From the age of fifteen he traveled to any place in Europe where he could learn, and later teach, logic. By his mid-thirties, Abelard was appointed master scholar at Notre Dame in Paris. His theological method was the opposite of Anselm's *Credo ut intelligam* (I believe in order that I may know). Abelard's attitude was *Intelligo ut credam* (I know in order that I may believe). Abelard declared:

> I . . . set out to develop the actual foundation of our belief by means of analogies taken from human reason. . . . Nothing could be believed unless it was first understood, and it was ridiculous for some to preach to others on matters neither they nor their listeners could understand.[202]

Anselm held together piety and learning, faith and reason, the Word and the Spirit. Abelard separated them.[203] Anselm had been a monk, a scholar, and a church administrator. Abelard was interested only in scholarship. He became a monk only late in life because of personal tragedy and public shame.

Abelard's book, *Theologia Christiana*, introduced the word *theology* in the sense it was subsequently used: as a body of doctrine that could be analyzed. The church fathers had never used "theology" in that sense to refer to Christian doctrine, but only to Greco-Roman mythology. Abelard was also the first to achieve a synthesis of the whole of theology by grouping all doctrines under the three headings of *fides* (faith), *caritas* (love), and *sacramentum* (sacrament).[204]

Despite all his questioning of authorities, Abelard was committed to the authority of the Bible. He considered that statements from the church fathers, the decrees or canons of the church, might be false or historically spurious. But statements in the Bible he considered absolutely inviolable.[205] Like the theologians of the early church, Abelard believed that biblical writers never deceived in communicating their divine religious message. This confidence in the saving and guiding function of Scripture did not preclude him, however, from a scholarly examination of its linguistic forms. He admitted that, at this level, even the prophets and apostles were not wholly free from error in the sense that they necessarily spoke in popular language. He also distinguished between important and unimportant elements in Scripture.[206]

A further advance in Abelard's attempt at a systematic organization of theology was made by Peter Lombard (1095?–1160). In the Early Scholastic period, annotations and commentaries on texts of Scripture and the church fathers were called *sententiae*. These were often combined into collections of "sentences." Peter Lombard produced a formative work entitled *Four Books of Sentences*. The texts and commentaries were organized into four books on the plan of the chronological order of the history of salvation: (1) God, (2) creation, (3) redemption, and (4) the sacraments and eschatology. Peter provided a balanced selection from the opinions of various schools of thought as well as his own thoughts. Because of the nonpolemical manner in which this was done, the adherents of various theological persuasions found the work helpful. The *Four Books of Sentences* became the standard theological textbook until the time of the Protestant Reformation. Its style and plan of organization influenced the subsequent *Summas* by Thomas Aquinas and others.[207]

These theological texts were studied and expounded far more than the Scriptures during the Scholastic era.[208] They focused the attention of theologians on traditions and the opinions of theological schools. The logical method of dialectic was the means of analyzing and harmonizing traditions and opinions into a working theological perspective. Peter Lombard, along with most Scholastics, asserted that Scripture was the highest authority. Aristotelian logic, as a means of resolving contradictions among traditional opinions, was, however, the operative norm by which theological decisions were made.

f. Classical Scholasticism: Thomas Aquinas

The Rediscovery of Aristotle

The Crusades of the eleventh and twelfth centuries had brought Europe into contact with Islamic culture. Through the Arabs, the complete philosophical works of Aristotle arrived in Western Europe in the thirteenth century. It was this infusion of a fresh philosophical perspective that made possible the development of Classical Scholasticism.

A new group of Aristotle's logical works had appeared in the mid-twelfth century. This made the *Organum* (of logical treatises) complete and gave impetus to fresh efforts in dialectics. Then, in the thirteenth century, Aristotle's works in metaphysics, natural history, and inductive philosophy appeared. Now, for the first time, theologians discovered the presuppositions, the world view, the complete system of thought that Aristotle offered. This situation created the conditions for the revolution in theology wrought by Classical Scholasticism.

The Christianized Neoplatonism of the early church formulated by Augustine had dominated theology for eight hundred years. Now it was gradually replaced by a theological system built on Aristotle that was to become normative for both Roman Catholic and later Protestant scholasticism. The assumption of Aristotle's empirical philosophy that all knowledge begins in human sense impressions reversed the Augustinian priority of faith over reason. Reason now came first and was thought to lead to faith. The deductive method of Aristotle's logic determined the style by which theological conclusions were derived.

The newly discovered works of Aristotle came in rather bad Latin translations that had been mediated through Syriac, Arabic, and Spanish. So in the mid-thirteenth century fresh Latin translations were made from the original Greek by William of Moerbeke. The work of this Hellenist scholar was done under the sponsorship of the papal court. William was joined in this project by Albert the Great and Thomas Aquinas (although Thomas had only a scanty knowledge of Greek—and no knowledge of Hebrew). But using William's translations, Albert and Thomas wrote commentaries on Aristotle's works, as well as their own theological syntheses based on Aristotle's philosophy.[209]

Further complicating the reception of Aristotle in the West were the interpretative commentaries of Arabic and Jewish thinkers which accompanied it. Important among these commentators were the Arabs, Avicenna (980–1037) and Averroes (1126–1198), and the Jew, Moses Maimonides (1135–1204). Skepticism concerning the mixing of their heretical doctrines with those of Aristotle caused the church at first to prohibit the teaching of the "new philosophy." By 1231, however, study of Aristotle was permitted insofar as his work was purified from the suspicion of Arabic and Jewish influence. By 1255, the study of Aristotle was made obligatory at the University of Paris, then the leading university of Europe. Soon Aristotle was spoken of as a precursor of Christ in nature just as John the Baptist was the Lord's precursor in grace.

Albert the Great (1200?–1280) declared Aristotle's philosophy to be the rule of truth and the highest perfection of human reason.[210] Albert was a Dominican and taught for his order in Cologne, Hildersheim, Freiburg, Regensburg, Strasbourg, and Paris. His most influential role was as head of the Dominican House of Studies in Cologne. There Thomas Aquinas was his pupil from 1248 to 1252. Albert embodied most of the knowledge of his age in philosophy, theology, natural science, and medicine. His aim was to penetrate all the fields of knowledge with religious insight.[211]

Faith and Reason

Thomas Aquinas (1225?–1274) first became acquainted with the philosophy of Aristotle as a young man at the University of Naples. He also encountered members of the Dominican Order there. Despite the strenuous objections of his parents, Thomas became a Dominican in 1243–44. He studied with Albert the Great in Paris and Cologne. As a pupil Thomas did more than receive and repeat the Aristotelian paraphrases of his master. He incorporated the Aristotelian scheme into his own thought and brought it to theological expression in a comprehensive system. Just as Augustine had been the culmination of Christian Platonism, so Thomas became the epitome of Christian Aristotelianism.[212]

The goal of theology for Aristotle was the knowledge of God. He said that the whole theological and philosophical enterprise was wholly directed to the knowledge of God as its last end. Indeed, for Aquinas, following Aristotle, "the knowledge of God is the last end of all human knowledge and activity."[213]

The form in which theology was done by Thomas was distinctly philosophical. Thomas responded to the intellectual, political, and even military pressure on Europe from the Arabs by seeking common ground with them. His motive was apologetical. Since the Arabs accepted the authority of Aristotle, Thomas concluded that it would be appropriate to present the Gospel to them in Aristotelian terms. This approach was a compatible one for Thomas because he viewed Aristotle's philosophy as simply a clear expression of the way in which every uncluttered human mind worked.[214]

Thomas's apologetic work was presented in his *Summa contra Gentiles*. He had previously written a *Commentary on the Sentences* and *Commentaries on Pseudo-Dionysius and Boethius*, as well as several philosophical works. He completed his apologetic work while attached to the papal court in Italy. There he collaborated with William of Moerbeke and his former teacher Albert the Great. He also wrote commentaries on Scripture and began a commentary on Aristotle's *Metaphysics*. His greatest work was the *Summa Theologiae*, the first part of which he wrote at this time. He continued to work on the *Summa* with many interruptions for the rest of his life.[215]

At the very beginning of the *Summa Theologiae* (Ia, I, I) Thomas asked: "Is another teaching required apart from philosophical studies?" As a first point he noted that "the things lying within range of reason yield well enough to scientific and philosophical treatment." Furthermore, he noted that "the philosophical sciences deal with all parts of reality, even with God; hence Aristotle refers to one department of philosophy as theology or the divine science." On the other hand, Thomas took note of 2 Timothy 3:16 which said, "All Scripture inspired of God is profitable to teach, to reprove, to correct, to instruct in righteousness." Thomas asserted therefore: "Divinely inspired Scripture, however, is no part of the branches of philosophy traced by reasoning." His reply, then, to all of these considerations was: "It should be urged that human well-being called for schooling in what God has revealed, in addition to the philosophical researches pursued by human reasoning." There are, for Thomas, "divine truths surpassing reason." These truths are "signified to us through divine revelation."

The reasons why human beings needed these divine truths in revelation were basically two: (1) God destined us for an end, or goal beyond the grasp of reason; (2) the rational truth about God would have been known to only a few and would be "mixed with many mistakes." Thomas concluded that "it was to prosper the salvation of human beings" that "they were provided for by divine revelation about divine things." He then added as implications of the above: (1) that humans "should not pry into things too high for human knowledge" but welcome them in faith when they are revealed by God; and (2) that some divine truths could be known by both reason and revelation. Thomas said regarding the latter point:

> Accordingly, there is nothing to stop the same things from being treated by the philosophical sciences when they can be looked at in the light of natural reason and by another science when they are looked at in the light of divine revelation. Consequently the theology of holy teaching differs in kind from that theology which is ranked as a part of philosophy.[216]

Thomas indicated that, in some sense, reason and revelation were given for two groups of people—the learned and the simple. Since only a few would come to the knowledge of God through reason, it was important to have revelation, in which all could have faith.[217]

For Thomas, the fact that humans could know or say anything about God at all in this life was because they could speak "analogically."[218] Thomas asserted:

> Sensible things, from which the human reason takes the origin of its knowledge, retain within themselves some sort of trace of a likeness to God.[219]

This "analogy of being" lay at the heart of Thomas's thought. At its simplest it meant that all things that exist have a fundamental commonness at root—they exist, or "have being." All beings, whether a gourd growing in the garden, or God reigning in heaven, function according to certain laws such as cause and effect. Therefore, one could reason back from effects in the world, for example, to God as their First Cause.

This did not mean that humans knew God's essence, according to Thomas. But *that* God exists, and something of God's character and attributes, *could* be known by analogy from God's effects in this world.[220] The "Five Ways" or five proofs for the existence of God utilized the concept of analogy and were built on the ability of the human mind to reason accurately from valid sense perceptions. They were designed to be persuasive to Arabs and Christians alike.

Biblical Interpretation

In Thomas's teaching, the concept of error shifted somewhat. The early church theologians like Augustine had understood error in the biblical sense of willful intent to deceive, and they were quick to affirm that the Bible never erred in that sense. But Augustine did not apply the concept of error to limited scientific knowledge on the part of the biblical writers. Thomas moved in a different direction when he introduced the quote from Augustine: "Only to those books or writings which are called canonical have I learnt to pay such honour that I firmly believe that none of their authors have erred in composing them."[221] The context in which Thomas was speaking was his assertion that human reason could validly deduce or infer truths from authorities. Arguments from the church fathers, for example, would only carry the weight of probability. He cited Augustine to buttress his assertion that reasoning from the premises of Scripture would produce certain conclusions. The context in which Thomas used the concept of error was one of logical science rather than Augustine's own context of ethical Christian living.

Thomas exerted a significant influence on biblical interpretation. In his concern to be scientific he turned attention away from allegorical speculation to the grammatical-historical, literal sense of the biblical text. Thomas did not deny the Augustinian tradition which held that Scripture had several senses. But, he leaned to Chrysostom and the Antiochean tradition, which began with the literal sense. He held that the natural sense, that intended by the human author, was the basis for the other senses.[222] Thomas felt that scholars should deal primarily with the literal sense because it could be more definitely ascertained and more easily controlled, not because it was necessarily more true.[223] Thomas focused on the words of Scripture. He remarked that the literal sense developed the meaning of the words whereas the spiritual sense developed the meaning of the things the words signified.[224]

Thomas's thought was subtle and complex. Counter-Reformation Catholics and post-Reformation Protestant scholastics accented the Aristotelian apologetic elements in Thomas's thought at the expense of his continuing adherence to Augustine in matters of faith. Textbook Thomism in the seventeenth century put reason prior to faith, emphasized proofs for the existence of God, and accented the words of the Bible interpreted according to a logical system rather than the meaning of Scripture interpreted in its historical context.[225]

Thomas had written commentaries on Scripture during the early part of his teaching career in Paris and Italy. In 1272, he organized a seminary for his Dominican Order in Naples, where he taught for the last time. Two years before his death he was at work on the third part of his *Summa*, on commentaries on the Psalms and Pauline Epistles, and on Aristotle. Without warning, Thomas fell into a trance on the feast of St. Nicholas in 1273. He had a vision of heaven, and afterwards declared that his writings appeared to him as so much chaff. He ceased to write and became increasingly remote from the world. Nonetheless, he obeyed a summons from the pope to attend the Council of Lyons in 1274. On the way he fell ill and was taken to the Cistercian Abbey at Fossanova. On his deathbed, he expounded to the monks the Song of Songs. At the end, the greatest of the Scholastic theologians turned to mysticism.[226]

g. Declining Scholasticism: Neoplatonists and Mystics

The Dominican theology of Albert the Great and Thomas Aquinas crystallized the synthesis of Aristotelian philosophy and Christian theology in Classical Scholasticism. During this period the order of St. Francis produced theologians who were affected by the Scholastic trends, but who held largely to the older Neoplatonic-Augustinian synthesis in theology. Thus, the Franciscans functioned often as the critics of Aristotelian Scholasticism. They nurtured alternative movements such as nominalism and mysticism.

Neoplatonic Franciscans: Duns Scotus and William of Occam

The synthesis of reason and faith, which was created by Classical Scholasticism, began to disintegrate in the late thirteenth and fourteenth centuries. Two British Franciscans, John Duns Scotus (1265?–?1308) and William of Occam (1285?–1347) became very skeptical of the Aristotelian-Thomist claims to certain knowledge. They proceeded from Neoplatonic-Augustinian premises and probed the philosophical assertions of Thomism with negative results.

Duns Scotus was known as the "Subtle Doctor." His teaching marked a turning point in medieval Scholasticism.[227] Scotus distinguished between a religious and a philosophical approach to reality. For him, God was not an appropriate object for metaphysical thought. God was properly approached only by theological thought. Scotus said that "by our natural power we can know some truths concerning God." But he, nevertheless, considered philosophical arguments for God's existence (including Anselm's ontological argument) as offering only "probable persuasion."[228] Despite his Scholastic skills and "subtleties," Duns Scotus was an Augustinian who believed that theology was a practical and not a theoretical science.[229]

In Scotus's thought, theology presupposed revelation. Those truths essential for salvation were revealed in the Bible. Scripture was wholly trustworthy in accomplishing its saving purpose. Scotus believed that "the doctrine of the canon is true," and "that the Sacred Scriptures sufficiently contain the doctrine necessary to the pilgrim."[230] For him, the Apostles' Creed and the teachings of "the authentic Fathers" also held authority along with the teachings of the "Romish Church."[231] Scripture and church were the main authorities for his faith.

Scotus worked in the heyday of Classical Scholasticism. He introduced critical elements that would be expanded in the next century, especially the primacy of the will over the intellect and skepticism regarding the ability of reason to prove God's existence.[232] The primary authorities for Scotus became Scripture and church rather than rational demonstration. Scotus considerably increased the list of revealed truths a Christian ought to believe but could not prove.[233]

The structure of Classical Scholasticism was further weakened in the mid-fourteenth century through the nominalism developed by another British Franciscan, William of Occam. The word nominalism represents one position in the Scholastic dispute over the reality of universals. An extreme realism, such as that of William of Champeaux (1070?–1121) held that universals such as Beauty and Justice were ultimately real things and existed independently of objects in the world. The opposite extreme, held in an early form by, for example, Roscelin of Compiègne (d. 1120?) contended that universals had no objective reference. They were only names used arbitrarily and for convenience's sake. This is the position most often called nominalism. Both William of Champeaux and Roscelin of Compiègne had been teachers of Abelard, who attempted a middle position known as conceptualism. For Abelard, universals were not ultimate realities in themselves. But neither were they merely names of attributes or qualities that people assigned to things. Universals had a reality as concepts in the mind. They corresponded to the conceptual reality that individual objects shared in common.

In the fourteenth century Duns Scotus developed a moderate and refined realism. His follower Occam responded by reviving a form of Abelard's conceptualism. Occam believed that only particular things existed. Universals were strictly mental facts formed by the activity of the mind in synthesizing the common elements in particulars. Thus, universal concepts such as Beauty and Justice were real, not in themselves, but as ideas composed in the mind, which represented the common elements of particular things in the world, such as beautiful objects and just actions. This is what was known as nominalism in Late Scholasticism. In later philosophy nominalism sometimes identified any theory that denied absolute value to human concepts.[234]

Occam's critique of the Aristotelian-Thomist synthesis was so radical that his thought is used to mark Late Scholasticism, the period of criticism and decline. Though Scotus had opened the way, Occam is considered the father of late medieval nominalism.[235]

For Occam, science and theology were separate realms, each with its own validations. Evidence was used to validate science, and faith was used to validate theology. Neither God's existence, nor unity, nor infinity could be rationally demonstrated. Faith, for Occam, did not supplement and perfect reason. The spheres of faith and reason were absolutely separate. The radical character of his approach was manifested in his assertion that reason could, on occasion, contradict faith. It was possible that something contradictory to certain dogmas might be demonstrated by reason. According to Occam, when that happened, the Christian was bound to follow faith even if it seemed to be irrational. In theology, faith was supreme and reason was irrelevant.[236]

The Bible had credibility for Occam since it was inspired.[237] He contended that Scripture "has been written and asserted by suggestion (*instinctu*) of the Holy Spirit."[238] One could therefore believe theological truths derived from Scripture that could not be rationally proved and might even be contradictory to reason. Occam declared: "Whoever is a Catholic and believing Christian can easily believe anything to which he could by no means by his natural powers assent." This was possible because God came to the person's aid. Occam asserted: "God, out of his grace, infuses into him a *habitus,* through the medium of which he is able to assent to any article of faith whatsoever.[239]

Occam's thought represented such a drastic departure from the directions taken by Classical Scholasticism that it came to be known as the *via moderna,* the modern way. The thirteenth century work of Thomas and Scotus was classified as the *via antiqua,* the ancient way, by subsequent generations of Scholastic teachers.[240]

Occam's follower Gabriel Biel (1420?–1495) taught nominalism at Tübingen in Germany and faithfully preserved the coherent structure of the Occamist system of thought.[241] In addition to maintaining the philosophical tradition, Biel affirmed Occam's views on Scripture and tradition. He repeatedly stressed "Scripture alone" against the opinion of an individual, even if that individual were a doctor of the church. Since the contents of Scripture were canonical, they were reliable and self-authenticating. According to Biel:

> Only Holy Scripture teaches all that is to be believed and hoped and all other things necessary for salvation. Scripture is the Word of God, the very mouth of God, the standard by which we can measure the distance by which we are removed from God or our nearness to Him. This word is instruction, consolation, and exhortation which reaches us through listening, reading, meditation, and contemplation. It is sufficient for salvation to believe in general that everything revealed by God is true in the sense intended by the Holy Spirit. All these truths of revelation are contained in Holy Scripture.[242]

Nominalism, both in its biblical and philosophical affirmations, planted seeds that were to germinate later in Protestant theology. Martin Luther's philosophy professors at Erfurt were Occamists, and his first theology professors were followers of Biel. Luther, in turn, called Occam, "beloved master," and "the most eminent and the most brilliant of the Scholastic doctors."[243] Even after Luther turned against nominalist theology, he retained his respect for the anti-Scholastic aspect of Occamist philosophy.[244]

Monastic Mysticism: Bernard of Clairvaux

What has been called "monastic theology" emerged with all of its distinguishing characteristics in the twelfth century.[245] It was an experiential movement for reform just as Scholasticism had been an intellectual movement for reform in the Middle Ages. A new surge of piety linked with a strong desire for subjective experience of redemption and union with God led to sweeping changes in the monasteries. General education ceased to be part of the business of the cloisters. They used their relative rural isolation to further their central purpose as places of contemplation.

Bernard of Clairvaux (1090-1153) was a leader in monastic reform, and gave impetus to the development of an experiential, mystical theology. His motto was: "I believe in order that I may experience." Reason was disdained and de-emphasized in religion. Experience, especially mystical experience, became the goal of theological endeavor. Bernard and his followers emphasized contemplation of Scripture's mystical and devotional significance. Bernard declared:

> As for us, in the commentary of mystical and sacred words, let us proceed with caution and simplicity. Let us model ourselves on Scripture which expresses the wisdom hidden in mystery in our own words: when Scripture portrays God for us it suggests Him in terms of our own feelings. The invisible and hidden realities of God which are of such great price are rendered accessible to human minds, vessels, as it were, of little worth, by means of comparisons taken from the realities we know through our senses.[246]

The Holy Spirit, in monastic theology, was expected not only to assure the believer of the authority of Scripture, as was the case in the early church theology, but to work directly upon the feelings of the contemplative person and provide both knowledge and volition. All of the graces were known immediately in experience in such a way that they could not be doubted or thought in error. Such an experiential theology provided strong confidence to a person like Bernard, who was sure that he understood and acted in accordance with God's mind and will.

Monastic theology was oriented toward preserving tradition rather than pursuing new problems or solutions. This unquestioning attachment to tradition was considered a form of humility, that humility which St. Benedict (480?-?550), the father of Western monasticism, had established as the first degree of obedience. Benedict was himself said to have been "learnedly ignorant and wisely unlearned."[247] It was understandable, therefore, that when Scholasticism threatened to turn the Christian life into a pursuit of logic and speculation, monasticism reacted by exalting tradition and experience.

When the Schoolmen became preoccupied with reason rather than revelation, the monks tended to put all their confidence in prayer and subjective experience. Bernard stated: "We search in a worthier manner, we discover with greater facility through prayer than through disputation."[248] In his famous commentary on the Song of Songs, Bernard exhorted his readers: "Lend your inner ear, gaze with the eyes of your heart and you will grasp by your own experience what is meant here."[249] Commenting in another work on St. Paul's words, *joyous in hope*, Bernard wrote: "Whosoever among you feels that (joy in hope) come about within him, knows what the Spirit says, he whose voice is hand in glove with his action. He understands what is said because what he hears without, he feels within.[250] When Bernard was confronted with the question of how religious experience could be validated, he concluded that for the experiencing subject the validation came in yet another experience. There was no escape from subjectivity and none was to be sought. Bernard wrote: "We who have passed from death to life by the Spirit who quickens know by a certain and daily experience—he himself by his enlightening gives us proof—that our vows and our groanings do come from him and do go to God, and there find mercy in his sight."[251]

There were, and are, differences of emphasis, even within monastic theology. The older Benedictine tradition, the "black monks," stayed closer to the whole of Augustinian theology. They emphasized the history of salvation as found in Scripture. The new, reforming monks, such as Bernard's Cistercians, emphasized the presence of God within persons and the possibility of human union with God. The mystery of salvation versus the mystery of union with God represented the differing emphases on the objective revelation in Holy Scripture and the subjective revelation within the contemplative person.[252]

The Middle Ages witnessed a division of the two aspects of the theology of the early church, which had been held together in the Augustinian motto: "I believe in order that I may understand." Some Scholastic theology went to an extreme in emphasizing understanding. Reason was given precedence over faith. Finally reason was separated from faith and placed in an autonomous sphere. Some monastic theology went to an extreme in emphasizing believing. Faith was made more important than learning. Finally, mystical experience became an end in itself. One concern of the Protestant Reformers was to put back together the lost Augustinian balance and to restore the early church consensus that faith should lead to understanding.

Mysticism, nonetheless, continued to be an important alternative force in Christendom.[253] An outgrowth of mysticism known as the *devotio moderna*, modern devotion, which emphasized the pursuit of personal religious experience with evangelical earnestness, later influenced Calvin.[254] This more moderate form of personal piety was promoted widely in the fourteenth and fifteenth centuries by a loose association of clerics and laypersons known as the Brethren of the Common Life. They urged reform in the church and founded schools of high quality. Among the "Brethren" were Gabriel Biel and Thomas à Kempis (1380?–1471).[255]

h. Summary

Early Christians had to cope with a dual environment. They accepted the Hebrew Scriptures as authoritative, but they had to interpret them to teach that Jesus was the Messiah. At the same time they had to communicate their faith in a way compatible with the Greek culture in which most Christians lived. That meant using the categories of Greek philosophy.

Christian teachers struggled for balance between these twin forces. They fought against attacks from without and excesses from within caused by literalism and legalism on the one side and spiritualism and sectarianism on the other. Literalists posed the heaviest threat in the early church. For this reason, the dominant Platonic philosophy, which stressed a spiritual perspective, became an ally. The Apologists, like Clement of Alexandria and Origen, made use of and to some extent were molded by this philosophical medium. Platonism, modified by biblical meanings, afforded a framework in which theology could be communicated in their culture.

Theologians of the early church had a fund of common concepts that formed the foundation of a Christian acceptance and interpretation of the Bible. Scripture—Old and New Testament alike—was completely authoritative. The Bible was accepted in faith by the working of the Holy Spirit in human hearts. Faith that Scripture was authoritative freed Christians to proceed to a scholarly understanding of it using the tools and techniques available to them. "Faith leads to understanding" was both a theological method and a call to Christian maturity. The theology that resulted was viewed as primarily a practical rather than a theoretical discipline. Its purpose, like that of Scripture, was to instruct people concerning God's salvation and guide them in living the life of faith. The Bible was not to be used as a book of science. Its focus was rather on that saving wholeness which encompassed love of God and love of neighbor as well. Awareness of that goal also yielded principles of interpretation.

The early theologians affirmed God's accommodated style of communication. The incarnation modeled God's willingness to humble himself in seeking to bring people salvation. Christians likened God's speaking in Scripture to that of a parent or teacher who condescended to think in the concepts and speak in the language of children for the children's benefit. The notion of accommodation enabled theologians to exegete Scripture in a way that upheld God's worthiness and accepted human limitations.

Interpreters of the Bible shared the common tradition of typology inherited from rabbinic Judaism. Promises in the Old Testament were linked historically to fulfillments in the New. Beyond that, two divergent methods of interpretation developed. The principal one was allegory, flowing from the Platonic center in Alexandria. It sought spiritual meanings to solve the problems posed by literalism. Augustine exemplified this approach and passed it on to the Middle Ages. The lesser known school of interpretation was the grammatical-historical one situated in the more Aristotelian center at Antioch. It reacted against allegorism and sought the natural meaning of the author in its historical context. Chrysostom commended this method by his use of it in preaching. Whereas the Protestant Reformers followed Augustine's theological method, they focused on Chrysostom as their exegetical mentor.

Despite differences in their method of biblical interpretation, Augustine and Chrysostom exemplified the consensus of the early church regarding the Bible as God's accommodated message. Their common rhetorical training helped them separate the depth of truth contained in Scripture from its lowly accommodated style. They sought the intention of the author and the meaning of his thought. Error was a matter of deliberate deception from which the Bible was free. Human limitations of thought and speech were matters for scholarly study.

Misuses of both the allegorical and the grammatical-historical methods occurred when theologians concentrated too much on the single words and sentences of the Bible and not enough on the whole story of Scripture. A consciousness of the *kerygma*, the central saving message of Scripture, preached in the church and summarized in the creed, helped to modify these excesses.

The Augustinian tradition, rooted in Neoplatonism, was carried on down to the twelfth century. Its chief exponents were John Scotus Erigena and Anselm of Canterbury. They maintained the theological method expressed in the motto: "I believe in order that I may understand." In their work, however, a subtle shift of accent occurred as the emphasis moved from believing to understanding.

In the Early Scholastic period of the twelfth century a further shift in theological priorities occurred. Beginning with Peter Abelard, theological method became predicated on Aristotelian logic. The motto of this approach was "I know in order that I may believe." The rediscovery of the metaphysical works of Aristotle stimulated the sweep of rationalism into theology. By the thirteenth century, Scholasticism entered what is now known as its classical period. During this time, Thomas Aquinas produced a *Summa Theologiae*, which gave comprehensive and systematic expression to medieval Scholasticism. Many of Aquinas's followers shifted their attention from exegesis of the biblical text to philosophical speculation. Nonetheless, one benefit of Scholasticism was a return to the grammatical-historical interpretation of Scripture that was more scientifically controllable than the allegorical search for spiritual senses.

Franciscan theology continued the Neoplatonic-Augustinian tradition through medieval Scholasticism in opposition to the Aristotelian innovations of the Dominicans. The Franciscan thinkers moved in several directions by way of critique and correction of the dominant Scholastic synthesis. Duns Scotus and Occam denied that the truth of Christianity could be rationally demonstrated. The will, rather than the intellect, was given primacy in human actions. Theology was understood as a practical, not a theoretical, discipline. Authority was to be found in Scripture and in church, not in the demonstrations of reason.

The most extreme reaction to Scholasticism, however, was expressed in monastic theology. Some monks, influenced by Bernard of Clairvaux, distrusted all academic approaches to theology and developed the mystical tradition. Bernard's theological method was expressed in the notion: "I believe in order to experience." Monastic theology called for faith alone, and contended that the result of devotional reading of Scripture and prayer should be the experience of union with God.

The anti-Aristotelian-Scholastic movements of the Middle Ages, including a moderate mysticism and philosophical nominalism, helped to direct the Protestant Reformers back to the Augustinian approach to the Bible.

i. Notes

1. Jean Daniélou, *The Theology of Jewish Christianity*, trans. and ed. John A. Baker, A History of Early Christian Doctrine before the Council of Nicea, Vol. I (Philadelphia: Westminster Press, 1964), pp. 9, 10, and 87. The immense implications of this ancient, Near Eastern environment for biblical interpretation are the proper subject for another study. The issues of biblical authority and interpretation inherited by those in the Reformed tradition come from the Western world with its Greek and Latin roots; it is on this history that we concentrate here.
2. Jean Daniélou, *Gospel Message and Hellenistic Culture*, trans. and ed. with a postscript by John Austin Baker, A History of Early Christian Doctrine before the Council of Nicea, Vol. II (Philadelphia: Westminster Press, 1973), p. 197. (Hereafter cited as *C*.)

3. J. N. D. Kelly, *Early Christian Doctrines*, 2d ed. (New York: Harper & Row, 1960), pp. 52–53. (Hereafter cited as Kelly, *Doctrines*.)
4. Bernhard Lohse, *A Short History of Christian Doctrine*, trans. F. Ernest Stoeffler (Philadelphia: Fortress Press, 1966), p. 28.
5. Geoffrey W. Bromiley, "The Church Doctrine of Inspiration," in *Revelation and the Bible*, ed. Carl F. H. Henry (Grand Rapids, Mich.: Baker Book House, 1958), p. 206. This article is still perhaps the best brief overview of the history of the doctrine of inspiration. (Hereafter cited as Bromiley, "Doctrine of Inspiration.")
6. *The Encyclopedia of Philosophy*, ed. Paul Edwards (New York: Macmillan and The Free Press, 1967), s.v. "Apologists." (Hereafter cited as *EP*.) See C, pp. 7–9.
7. *C*, p. 73.

8. A helpful text that organizes readings from philosophers by schools of thought is Robert N. Beck, *Perspectives in Philosophy*, 2d ed. (New York: Holt, Rinehart and Winston, 1969). See part 2, "Classical Realism."

9. *EP*, s.v. "Logic, History of."

10. *EP*, s.v. "Platonism and the Platonic Tradition."

11. *EP*, s.v. "Apologists"; see *C*, pp. 39, 107, 129.

12. Jean Daniélou, *Origen*, trans. Walter Mitchell (New York: Sheed and Ward, 1955), p. 80. (Hereafter cited as *O*.)

13. *O*, pp. 74, 80.

14. *EP*, s.v. "Philo Judaeus."

15. *Stromateis*, VI, 10:30, 5–81, I, cited in *C*, p. 304.

16. *Strom.*, VI, 7:62, I; *Strom.*, VI, 8:68, I, cited in *C*, p. 68; See also *Strom.*, I, 20:99, I, cited in *C*, p. 305.

17. *Strom.*, VI, 8:64, 6, cited in *C*, p. 50.

18. *Strom.*, V, 13:87, 2; *Strom.*, I, 19:94, 7, cited in *C*, p. 50; see also *Strom.*, VIII, 3:7 I; VIII, 3:8, 6–4:9, I, cited in *C*, p. 311, and *Strom.*, I, 6:37, 6, cited in *C*, p. 309.

19. *Strom.*, VII, 16:102, I, cited in *C*, p. 316.

20. *EP*, s.v. "Clement of Alexandria."

21. See *Strom.*, VII, 16:95, 9–96, I, cited in *C*, p. 321.

22. *Strom.*, VII, 16:93, 8, cited in *C*, p. 320; see also pp. 308 and 322.

23. R. P. C. Hanson, *Allegory and Event* (Richmond: John Knox Press, 1959), p. 7. (Hereafter cited as *AE*.)

24. *C*, p. 198.

25. See *Strom.*, II, 16:22, as cited in Ford Lewis Battles, "God Was Accommodating Himself to Human Capacity" (hereafter cited as Battles, "Accommodating"), *Interpretation* (hereafter cited as *Itpn.*) 31, no. 1 (January 1977):-23; see also his *Calculus Fidei: Some Ruminations on the Structure of the Theology of John Calvin* (Grand Rapids, Mich.: Calvin Theological Seminary, 1978), p. 45; see also C. S. Lewis, *Reflections on the Psalms* (London: Collins, 1967; rep, 1958), p. 94.

26. Charles Bigg, *The Christian Platonists of Alexandria* (Oxford: Clarendon Press, 1886), p. 115. Raymond E. Brown contends that Origen "probably had more influence on Scripture than any other scholar since St. Paul" in *The 'Sensus Plenior' of Sacred Scripture* (Baltimore: St. Mary's University, 1955), p. 40. (Hereafter cited as R. E. Brown, 'Sensus Plenior'.)

27. Frederic W. Farrar writes: "His exegetical writings were the model and sources for all succeeding Greek commentators . . . and for most of the Latin ones also," in *History of Interpretation* (London: MacMillan, 1886), p. 201. (Hereafter cited as *HI*.)

28. It is certain that Origen espoused some form of Platonism, as an early work (*Stromateis*) "sought to translate into Platonic language some basic New Testament ideas like 'eternal life' and to show the harmony of Jesus and Plato," writes Henry Chadwick in *Early Christian Thought and the Classical Tradition* (New York: Oxford University Press, 1966), pp. 71–72; see also Karl Otto Weber, *Origenes Der Neuplatoniker* (Munich: C. N. Beck, 1962).

29. See *Homily on Jeremiah 21, 2, Patrologia Series Graeca*, ed. J. P. Migne, 161 vols. (Paris, 1857–1866), 13, 536 (hereafter cited as *PG*); also *Contra Celsum*, Book 8 in The Ante-Nicene Fathers, eds. Alexander, Roberts and James Donaldson, 10 Vols. (Grand Rapids, Mich.: Wm. B. Eerdmans, 1972), IV, 399 (hereafter cited as *ANF*). These are originally cited by F. A. D. Tholuck, "The Doctrine of Inspiration," *Journal of Sacred Literature* (July 1854): 335; Origen, *De Principiis (On First Principles)* (hereafter cited as *De Princ.*), see also Book IV, 9 and IV, 8, pp. 356–57; "Origen Against Celsus," Book VII, 42 (ANF, IV, 628) and Book V, 60 (ANF IV, 569). Scripture presented an inseparable unity in Origen's view; see *AE*, pp. 198ff.; *HI*, p. 190; and the fragment from Book II of Origen's *Commentary on Matthew* preserved in *The Philocalia of Origen*, ed. J. A. Robinson (Cambridge: Cambridge University Press, 1893), p. vi, and in *PG* 13, 832. In Origen's *Commentary on John* (hereafter cited as *Jn*) X.13 his commentary reads: "We must approach the whole of Scripture as one body, we must not lacerate nor break through the strong and well-knit connections which exist in the harmony of its whole composition, as those do who lacerate, so far as they can, the unity of the Spirit that is in all the Scriptures" (*ANF*, X, 390). Also see *Philocalia*, VI (*PG* 13, 832).

30. *De Princ.* 4.9, cited in Bruce Vawter, *Biblical Inspiration*, Theological Resources, eds. J. P. Whalen and J. Pelikan (Philadelphia: Westminster Press, 1972), p. 27. See also his *Homily 26* on the Book of Numbers (*PG* 12, 774) where he writes of God speaking as "The Holy Spirit relates this." See also the section: "God the Author of Scripture" in

Luis Alonso Schökel, *The Inspired Word*, trans. Francis Martin (New York: Herder and Herder, 1972; rep, 1965), pp. 77ff, esp. p. 83.

31. Vawter, p. 26; see also *AE*, p. 194. This summary is seen in light of Origen's statements: "Those who are truly wise in Christ are of opinion that the Apostolical writings have indeed been disposed wisely, credibly, and with reverence for God; but, nevertheless, not to be compared with such declarations as—'Thus saith the Lord Almighty.' And on this account we must consider whether, when Paul says, 'All Scripture is inspired by God and useful,' he includes his own Epistles, and whether he would exclude some parts of them, such as those where it is said, 'That which I speak, I speak not after the Lord;' and this—'As I teach everywhere in every Church'; and again, 'At Antioch, at Iconium, at Lystra, what persecutions I endured'; and other like things which here and there he has written of his own knowledge, and by authority (*kata exousian*), but yet which have not flowed forth purely and entirely from divine inspiration," quoted in Tholuck, p. 337, from *In Johann.* tome 1, p. 4, ed. 1668. See also Rolf Gögler, *Zur Theologie des Biblischen Wortes bei Origenes* (Düsseldorf: Patmos-Verlag, 1963), chap. 5.

32. *HI*, p. 190.

33. *Fragment on Deuteronomy* 1:21 (*PG*, 17.24), quoted in *AE*, p. 226; see also *PG* 13.1244; see also Vawter, p. 41, and other instances in Origen—*Fragment on 1 Samuel* 15:11 (*PG*, 12. 992); *Commentary on Romans* VII. 6 (*PG*, 11. 101); *Homily on Jeremiah* 19.15 and 20.3; *Commentary on Matthew* XVII.15–17; *Contra Celsum* IV. 71, V. 16, cited in *AE*, p. 226; and *Homily on Jeremiah* 18.6, cited in *AE*, p. 227. See too K. R. Hagenbach, *A Text-Book of the History of Doctrines*, trans. C. W. Buch and Henry B. Smith, 2 vols. (New York: Sheldon & Co.: 1861), 1:90, 91. Origen's most extreme usage is perhaps *Homilies on Jeremiah* 29. 3 (*PG*, 13. 504f.) where he writes: "God can so accommodate himself to human ways as to deceive men for their own good." This seems to represent a shift from Origen's earlier *Stromateis* where he wrote: "It is not to be thought that God sometimes tells a lie as a matter of accommodation. But if it is to benefit his hearers, he will sometimes use ambiguous words and cover with a veil what might do hurt if it were openly stated" (*PG*, 11. 104), cited in *AE*, p. 229.

34. *Contra Celsum* VII. 42. We are indebted for an historical overview of the use of accommodation to Arthur W. Lindsley, Jr., "The Principle of Accommodation" (Pittsburgh Theological Seminary, 1975).

35. Origen warns in *De Princ.* II. 4.4 that "when we read either in the Old Testament or in the New of the anger of God, we do not take such expressions literally, but seek in them a spiritual meaning, that we may think of God as he deserves to be thought of." See also *Jn.* I. 42, which speaks of God's hands, arms, and fingers.

36. Caution must be taken with the terms used in describing the various facets of Origen's method. Hanson distinguishes between "typology" and "allegory"; "Typology is the interpreting of an event belonging to the present or the recent past as the fulfillment of a similar situation recorded or prophesied in Scripture. Allegory is the interpretation of an object or person or a number of objects or persons as in reality meaning some object or person of a later time, with no attempt made to trace a relationship of 'similar situation' between them," *AE*, p. 7; see also M. F. Wiles, "Origen," *Cambridge History of the Bible*, 3 vols. (Cambridge: Cambridge University Press, 1970), 1:481. (Hereafter cited as *CHB*.) See also the citation from Origen's *Eleventh Homily on Numbers* in K. J. Woollcombe, "The Biblical Origins and Patristic Development of Typology," in G. W. H. Lampe and K. J. Woollcombe, *Essays on Typology* (Naperville, Ill.: Alex R. Allenson, 1957), p. 58.

37. *O*, p. 139. See *Jn.* 5.4, which speaks of the meaning that is "obvious" and the other that is "spiritual." R. M. Grant writes: "This analysis (in Origen's fourth book [*De Princ.*] shows that while, like other allegorizers, he can admit the historical reality of much of his text, his ultimate concern is not with history at all," in *The Letter and the Spirit* (New York: Macmillan, 1957), p. 96. (Hereafter cited as Grant, *Letter.*)

38. *Jn.* X. 27 (*ANF*, X, 407). Origen's use of Scripture in the John commentary is explored more thoroughly by Donald K. McKim, "The Doctrine of Scripture in Origen and Its Use in the *Commentary on John*" (Pittsburgh Theological Seminary, 1972) and H. J. Mumm, "Origen as an Exegete of the Fourth Gospel" (Ph.D. thesis, Hartford Seminary Foundation, 1952).

39. See *AE*, p. 235. The correct reading is:

"Have I not written unto thee excellent things?"; see also *De Princ.* IV. 20.

40. R. E. Brown, '*Sensus Plenior*', p. 42. He points out, however, that in his review of Daniélou's, *Origène*, in *Theological Studies* 10 (1949), John L. McKenzie warns that we are not sure of the source of his Platonism; see also Weber.

41. See *AE*, p. 239. This is the case with some of the legislation of the Pentateuch and in the Fragment of Book XXXII dealing with John 13:2–33, the account of Christ's last meal with his disciples, Origen gives no literal meaning, only a spiritual one. See Mumm, pp. 171ff. In *De Princ.* IV. 20, he writes that the whole of Holy Scripture has a "'spiritual,' but not the whole a bodily meaning, because the bodily meaning is in many places proved to be impossible." Origen followed Paul for his spiritual exegesis of the Old Testament. See *Selections from the Commentaries and Homilies of Origen*, ed. R. B. Tollinton. (London: S.P.C.K., 1929), p. 72; see also *Homilies on Exodus*, V.1.; *Jn.* VI. 26 where "the story of Israel's crossing the Jordan is typical of Christian things and is written for our instruction," and *AE*, p. 65. For Origen, Christ was prefigured in the Old Testament in all his fullness. See *O*, p. 148. Christ is the key to interpreting both the Old and New Testaments: "Christ is written about even in the Pentateuch; He is spoken of in each of the prophets, and in the Psalms, and, in a word, as the Saviour Himself says, 'Search the Scriptures, for in them ye think ye have eternal life, and these are they which testify of me.' And if He refers us to the Scriptures as testifying of Him, it is not to one that He sends us, to the exclusion of another, but to all that speak of Him," *Jn.* V. 4.

42. Henry Chadwick, "The Bible and the Greek Fathers," in *The Church's Use of the Bible*, ed. D. E. Nineham (London: S.P.C.K., 1963), p. 38. (Hereafter cited as Chadwick, "Bible.")

43. W. R. Inge, *The Philosophy of Plotinus*, 3d ed., 2 vols. (London: Longmans, Green and Co., 1929), 2:19.

44. Chadwick, "Bible," p. 38.

45. *C*, pp. 257, 274, 281; see also *HI*, p. 190.

46. Baker, postscript in *C*, p. 504.

47. *De Princ.* IV. 1, cited in *Origen on First Principles*, trans. G. W. Butterworth (London: S.P.C.K., 1936), p. 267.

48. Chrysostomus Baur, O.S.B., *John Chrysostom and His Time*, Vol. 1, *Antioch* (London: Sands & Co., Ltd., 1959), p. 45; see also Stephen Neill, *Chrysostom and His Message*, World Christian Books, no. 44 (London: Lutterworth Press, 1962), p. 8.

49. *New International Dictionary of the Christian Church*, ed. J. D. Douglas (Grand Rapids, Mich.: Zondavan, 1974), s.v. "Antiochene Theology." (Hereafter cited as *NIDCC*.)

50. Grant, *Letter*, p. 105.

51. *Oxford Dictionary of the Christian Church*, eds. F. L. Cross and E. A. Livingstone, 2d rev. ed. (London: Oxford University Press, 1974), s.v. "Antiochene Theology." (Hereafter cited as *ODC*.)

52. See Adolf Harnack, *History of Dogma*, trans. Neil Buchanan, 7 vols. (New York: Dover Publications, 1961), 3:202. (Hereafter cited as *HD*.)

53. Baur, pp. 90–91, 96. See also Jaroslav Pelikan, *The Preaching of Chrysostom: Homilies on the Sermon on the Mount*, Preacher's Paperback Library (Philadelphia: Fortress Press, 1967), pp. 14–15, on the exegetical struggle between Alexandria and Antioch during this period. (Hereafter cited as Pelikan, *Chrysostom*.)

54. Pelikan, *Chrysostom*, p. 12. See also Donald Attwater, *St. John Chrysostom: The Voice of Gold* (Milwaukee: Bruce Publishing, 1939), p. 186.

55. Baur, pp. 305–306.

56. Ibid., p. 97.

57. Ibid., p. 306.

58. Ibid., pp. 309–311.

59. Baur, p. 310.

60. W. R. W. Stephens, *Saint Chrysostom: His Life and Times* (London: John Murray, 1872), p. 448.

61. Homily 33, 3 in *Hebrews* (63, 229).

62. See *Homily 5, 3 in Colossians* (62, 335), cited in Baur, p. 338. Baur, himself an Aristotelian-Thomist, is forced to demur, commenting: "Here, however Chrysostom errs, for the omnipresence of God and His incorporeality can be known by the intellect alone."

63. Homily 34, 4 in *Acts of the Apostles* (60, 243–45), cited in Baur, pp. 242–243.

64. See *Homily 4, 14 in 2 Thessalonians* (62, 488), cited in Baur, pp. 341–342.

65. Homily 30, 3 in *Acts of the Apostles* (60, 225), cited in Baur, p. 311.

66. Pelikan, *Chrysostom*, pp. 19–28; see also Baur, pp. 16–21, and Thomas E. Ameringen, O.F.M., *The Stylistic Influence of the Second Sophistic on the Panegyrical Sermons of St. John*

Chrysostom: A Study in Greek Rhetoric (Washington, D.C.: Catholic University of America, 1921), p. 101.
67. Homily *on Titus*, III in *Nicene and Post-Nicene Fathers*, ed. Philip Schaff, 1st series, 14 vols. (Grand Rapids, Mich.: Wm. B. Eerdmans, 1969), 13:529. (Hereafter cited as *NPNF*.)
68. Cited in G. C. Berkouwer, *Holy Scripture*, ed. and trans. Jack B. Rogers (Grand Rapids, Mich.: Wm. B. Eerdmans, 1975), pp. 175–176. (Hereafter cited as *HS.*)
69. See *Homily on Titus*, III (*NPNF*, 13:529). Here on Titus 1:12, Chrysostom commented: "Thus he everywhere condescends" (p. 529). See Vawter's discussion of "Condescension," where he contends that Chrysostom's view of revelation made it possible for him "to distinguish the divine word in accordance with its human speakers in their distinct circumstances, and not simply to meld out OT and NT into a homogeneous and synchronous pronouncement of the Eternal." This, he suggests, is an advancement over Origen (and the extreme in Origen, that God may accommodate so as to deceive people [see above] as doctors must sometimes do to save a life). Chrysostom's notion of accommodation includes "the very fact of human authorship itself, the human condition of mind, heart, and circumstances from which would emerge metaphor, deliberate overstatement, or *captatio benevolentiae*," p. 41; see pp. 40–42.
70. *Homily 17 on Genesis* 3 (*PG* 53, 135), cited in Schökel, p. 43.
71. *Homily 15 on Genesis* 2 (*PG* 53, 121), cited in Schökel, p. 44.
72. Baur, pp. 315–316.
73. Pelikan, *Chrysostom*, pp. 35–36.
74. See Chrysostom, *Homily XLVII*, 1 *in John* (on John 6:53–54) in *NPNF*, 14:168; *Homily 15 on Genesis*, (*PG* 53, 119), cited in Schökel, p. 137; Kelly, *Doctrines*, pp. 42–43, citing *In Colossian homily* 9, 1; in *2 Thessalonians homily* 3, 4 (*PG* 62, 361; 485); John Robert Walchenbach, "John Calvin as Biblical Commentator: An Investigation into Calvin's Use of John Chrysostom as an Exegetical Tutor" (Ph.D. thesis, University of Pittsburgh, 1974), p. 199 (hereafter cited as Walchenbach, "Calvin as Commentator"); and Pelikan, *Chrysostom*, pp. 31–32.
Chrysostom's stress on Scripture's message as coming from God is seen in places such as *On 1 Thessalonians* 4:15, (*PG* 62, 439) quoted in Schökel, p. 70 and his comments

on Heb. 1:3–4: "Here we must admire not the intelligence of Paul, but the grace of the Spirit. For not of his own mind did he say this, nor did he acquire the wisdom of himself. Whence, then? ... By the grace of the Spirit who shows his power by whomever he wills" (*In Heb. homily* 1.2; *PG* 63:15–16), cited in Vawter, p. 38. Kelly points out that "Chrysostom speaks of St. John and St. Paul as musical instruments played upon by the Holy Spirit" (*In Ioh. homily* I, 1f; *de Lazaro concio*, 6,9), cited in *Doctrines*, p. 62; see also *Homily on Romans* 16:3 (*PG* 51, 187), cited in Schökel, p. 81. Yet words like *literally* and *dictates* were not inconsistent for Chrysostom with a frank recognition of the human elements in Scripture. The content came from God, the form came from the human writer. See *NPNF*, 12:169; see also his notes on Ps. LXIV mentioned in *HI*, p. 221, and Kelly, *Doctrines*, p. 63, citing Chrysostom's *In Gen. homily* 7, 4; 12, 1; 20, 4, where he says that he, along with Cyril of Alexandria, "make much of the personal contribution of Moses, St. John, and St. Paul in the actual composition of their works." See also the comments by Baur, pp. 318–19, who cites S. Haidacher, *Die Lehre des heiligen Joh. Chrysostomus über die Schriftinspiration* (Salzburg, 1897).
75. Stephens, pp. 442–443. See Chrysostom's *Homilies on the Gospel of Matthew*, *ANF*, X, 3 (*PG* 57, 16). He writes: "But if there be anything touching times or places, which they have related differently, this nothing [in no respect] injures the truth of what they have said." See also Hagenbach, 1:320, 321.
76. Pelikan, *Chrysostom*, p. 27.
77. In *I Thessalonian homily* 8, 1 (*PG* 62, 439). See Johannes Beumer, *Die Inspiration der Heiligen Schrift* (Freiburg: Herder, 1968), p. 24. Tholuck points to Chrysostom's comments on the words of Paul in Acts 26:6: "He speaks humanly, and does not throughout enjoy grace, but it is permitted him even to intermix his own materials," p. 338; Baur, p. 318; and, Kelly, *Doctrines*, p. 64; cf. Beumer, p. 24. Tholuck sums up Patristic teaching: "We see, then, that even amongst the ancient Church fathers, although they had a general impression of the divinely inspired character of Scripture, the opinion that its language was human and imperfect was held to be unmistakable; that verbal contradictions, nay contradictions even in matters of fact, were ascribed to it without hesitation; and that the authority of the Ap-

ostolical writings was regarded as secondary to those which were said to have proceeded immediately from God himself," pp.
338–339.
78. *Homily in Genesis* (*PG* 53, 109), cited in
Walchenbach, "Calvin as Commentator," p.
53.
79. In *Epistle to Galatians* IV (*PG* 61, 662),
cited in Robert M. Grant, *A Short History of
the Interpretation of the Bible*, rev. ed. (New
York: Macmillan, 1966), p. 96. (Hereafter
cited as *SH*.)
80. *Epistle to Philippians homily* 10 (*PG* 62,
257), cited in *SH*, pp. 96–97; see also Lampe
and Woollcombe, pp. 39–40. As distinguished from allegorism, K. J. Woollcombe
writes that "typological exegesis is the
search for linkages between events, persons
or things *within the historical framework of revelation*, whereas allegorism is the search for
a secondary and hidden meaning underlying the primary and obvious meaning of a
narrative. This secondary sense of a narrative, discovered by allegorism, does not
necessarily have any connexion at all with
the historical framework of revelation," p.
40. See also John H. McIndoe, "Chrysostom on St. Matthew, A Study in Antiochene
Exegesis" (S.T.M. thesis, Hartford Seminary Foundation, 1960), p. 62, cited in Walchenbach," Calvin as Commentator," p. 51.
81. See *In Isaiam*, V (*PG* 56, 60), cited in
Walchenbach, "Calvin as Commentator," p.
51. In other places "Chrysostom admonished Biblical students that they were not to
act as if they were the lords of Scripture;
their task was not to adapt passages such as
Isa. 5:1–7 to suit their own preconceived
ideas of what the allegory meant, but rather
to follow the guidance of the context, and
accept the interpretation given therein; for
wherever allegories occurred in the Bible,
they were invariably accompanied by their
interpretations (*Isa. interp.* 5:3), Lampe and
Woollcombe, p. 56; see also *Expositio in Psal-
mum*, IX (*PG* 55, 126–27), cited in Walchenbach, "Calvin as Commentator," p. 52.
82. *SH*, p. 97; see also Frederick Henry
Chase, *Chrysostom: A Study in the History of
Biblical Interpretation* (Cambridge: Cambridge University Press, 1887), chap. 1; and
HI, p. 222.
83. *Homily 2, 10 on Mt.* (*PG* 57, 31), cited in
Schökel, pp. 351–352; see also *Homily 21 on
Gn.* (*PG* 53, 183), cited in Schökel, p. 384;
and *Homily on Ps. 48* (*PG* 55, 513), cited in
Schökel, p. 384.

84. *Homily 54, 1 in Gen.* (*PG* 54, 472); see
also *Hom.* 8, 4 *in Hebr.* (*PG* 63, 73), cited in
Baur, p. 326.
85. *In Ps. 48, 17* (*PG* 55, 499), cited in Baur,
p. 326.
86. On the life of Augustine see Peter
Brown, *Augustine of Hippo* (Berkeley and Los
Angeles: University of California Press,
1969); Gerald Bonner, *St. Augustine of Hippo
—Life and Controversies* (Philadelphia: Westminster Press, 1963); John J. O'Meara, *The
Young Augustine: The Growth of St. Augustine's
Mind up to His Conversion* (London: Longmans, Green, 1954); and Eugene TeSelle,
Augustine the Theologian (New York: Herder
and Herder, 1970). (Hereafter cited as Te-
Selle, *Augustine.*) On the Manichaean phase,
see Brown, chap. 5; Bonner, chap. 4; and
O'Meara, chap. 4; and several of Augustine's works devoted to this sect. On the
"wisdom," of philosophy (Gr. *philo-sophia:*
"love of wisdom"), see Brown, chap. 4.
87. See P. Brown, chap. 8. On Ambrose see
F. Homes Dudden, *The Life and Times of St.
Ambrose*, 2 vols. (Oxford: The Clarendon
Press, 1935).
88. For the philosophy of Plotinus see
Émile Bréhier, *The Philosophy of Plotinus*,
trans. Joseph Thomas (Chicago: University
of Chicago Press, 1958); Philip Merlan,
"Plotinus," in *EP*, VI, 351–359; Frederick
Copleston, *A History of Philosophy*, 8 vols.
(New York: Doubleday, 1962) (hereafter cit-
ed as *HP*), I/2, 207–218. For Porphyry's
philosophy see Andrew Smith, *Porphyry's
Place in the Neo-Platonic Tradition: A Study in
Post-Plotinian Neoplatonism* (The Hague: Mar-
tinus Nijhoff, 1974); A. C. Lloyd, "Porphy-
ry," in *EP*, VI, 411–412. On the
Neo-platonic tradition see particularly D. A.
Rees, "Platonism and the Platonic Tradi-
tion," in *EP*, VI, esp. 337ff.; Philip Merlan,
"Neoplatonism," in *EP*, VI, 473–476; and
Thomas Whittaker, *The Neo-Platonists: A
Study in the History of Hellenism*, 2d ed. (Cam-
bridge: Cambridge University Press, 1918).
Victorinus (see *ODC*, s.v. "Victorinus"),
the Latin translator of the Neoplatonists,
was converted to Christianity by Sim-
plicianus (d. 400). See *ODC*, s.v. "Sim-
plicianus" and *Augustine: Confessions and
Enchiridion* (hereafter cited as *Conf.*), trans.
and ed. Albert C. Outler, Library of Chris-
tian Classics (hereafter cited as *LCC*)
(Philadelphia; Westminster Press, 1955),
VIII. I–V. Simplicianus became Bishop of
Milan and was the tutor and spiritual father

of Ambrose. For these men, both Platonism and Christianity were otherworldly. See P. Brown, p. 93, quoting Ambrose, Epistle 34, 1, in *Patrologia Series Latina,* ed. J. P. Migne, 221 vols. (Paris, 1844–1904), 16, 1119. (Hereafter cited as *PL.*) Plotinus provided Augustine, however, with philosophical arguments for a spiritual world that was related to the world of time and space and yet distinct from it. This enabled him to see that God was separate from his creatures and that humans had to be changed to conform to God. See P. Brown, p. 98, citing R. J. O'Connell, "Ennead VI, 4 and 5 in the Works of St. Augustine," *Revue des études augustiniennes* IX (1963), pp. 13–14; and O'-Meara, chaps. IX and X; as well as *Conf.* VII. X. 16. After he became a Christian, Augustine's appreciation for Platonism continued, although modified by biblical meanings. See P. Brown, p. 111, citing *Contra Acad. (Against the Academics),* II. iii. 9. Christianity did not conflict with Augustine's search for and "love of wisdom." He sought to develop his intellect fully within the Catholic Church and wrote approvingly of Plato: "Plato has no hesitation in asserting that to be a philosopher is to love God." See Augustine, *City of God,* trans. Henry Bettenson (Baltimore: Penguin Books, 1972), VIII, 8. See also R. A. Markus, "St. Augustine," in *EP,* I, 198–199, who comments: "He shared with all his contemporaries the belief that it was the business of philosophy to discover the way to wisdom and thereby to show men the way to happiness or blessedness (*beatitudo*). The chief difference between Christianity and the pagan philosophies was that Christianity considered this way as having been provided for men in Jesus Christ. Christianity could still be thought of as a philosophy, however, in that its aim was the same as that of other philosophic schools." Christians lived out their knowledge of God better than other philosophers, according to Augustine. See P. Brown, p. 112. Since theology had as its purpose to bring salvation to people, Augustine viewed theology as a practical rather than a theoretical discipline. See TeSelle, *Augustine,* who writes that for Augustine, "Christianity, then, is the true fulfillment of Platonism, proclaiming those same truths about God which the Platonists had already glimpsed, now purged of the superstitions of pagan religion. What Augustine treasures most about the true

religion is not that it gives a more certain knowledge of God ... but that in it men have *lived out* their knowledge of God in such a way as to convince others, even the unphilosophical, of its truth and to inspire them to follow the same way of life. What the Platonists only intimated, the true religion has actualized and made available to all" (p. 124) and that "the Scriptural record is important chiefly because of what it says about the work of salvation, both as it affects each individual (and Augustine in his interpretation of Scripture always attempts to bring it into relation with existential problems) and on the broad stage of world history" (pp. 129–130).

89. See his famous account in *Conf.,* book VIII.

90. A Hilary Armstrong *St. Augustine and Christian Platonism* (Villanova, Pa.: Villanova University Press, 1967), p. 1. Augustine spoke Latin but knew no Greek. See Appendix A in Bonner, pp. 394–395. He read the Neoplatonists through the Latin translations of Victorinus.

91. Bk. II, 4, 6 in *Augustine: Earlier Writings,* trans. John H. S. Burleigh, LCC, vol. 6 (Philadelphia: Westminster Press, 1953), p. 137.

92. *HP,* II/1, 65; see also Ronald H. Nash, *The Light of the Mind: St. Augustine's Theory of Knowledge* (Lexington: University Press of Kentucky, 1969), pp. 1–3.

93. See John E. Smith, *The Analogy of Experience* (New York: Harper & Row, 1973), pp. 2ff., for his discussion of this problem with relation to interpreting Anselm's (1033?–1109) *fides quaerens intellectum* ("faith seeking understanding"). According to Smith, by the time of Anselm, "reason" was confined to the sphere of the "natural" while "faith" had its domain in the "supernatural." In Augustine, Smith maintains, faith and reason interpenetrated and were held in a "dynamic relation." Cf. Nash, chap. 1, for example, who rejects the Thomist interpretations of Augustine but tries himself to reconcile Augustine with Warfield and the American old Princeton tradition (also influenced by Aristotle) and thus is left with seeming inconsistencies in Augustine. See, e.g., p. 5 and the qualification in fn. 9.

94. *Conf.* I. 1, as cited in J. E. Smith, p. 8.

95. *Tractates on the Gospel of St. John* XL. 9 (*NPNF,* 7:228).

96. J. E. Smith, p. 5.

97. *Enchiridion, I,* 5 (*LCC,* VII, 338). This

translation is from *NPNF*, 3:238; see also *Sermons on New Testament Lessons* LXXXIX 1 (on John 10:30) (*NPNF*, 6:527); *Sermons on New Testament Lessons* LXVIII. 1 (on John 1) (*NPNF*, 6:465); *Sermons on New Testament Lessons* LXXVI. 1 (on John 5:19) (*NPNF*, 6:481); and *Tract. on the Gospel of John* XXIX. 6 (*NPNF*, 7:184). Other examples: "But before we can understand, we have to believe," *De Trinitate* (*The Trinity*) VIII. 8, from *Augustine: Later Works*, trans. John Burnaby, LCC, p. 45. From the same work: "A sure faith is itself a beginning of knowledge," IX. 1 (LCC, VIII, 57).

The faith that preceded understanding for Augustine was both intellectual (cognitive) in that it required the mind to be used; and emotional (volitional) in that it involved one's emotions and will. See *De Spiritu et littera* (*The Spirit and the Letter*), 54 (LCC, VIII, 237); *De praedestinatione sanctorum* (*The Predestination of the Saints*), 2.5 as translated in Reinhold Seeberg, *Text-Book of the History of Doctrines*, trans. Charles E. Hay, 2 vols. (Grand Rapids, Mich.: Baker Book House, 1966), 1:347; (*PL* 44, 962); (*NPNF*, 5:499) "To think with assent"; *Enchiridion*, VII. 20 (LCC, VII, 351). In the context of his Platonic orientation, Augustine viewed assent not just as a theoretical act of the mind, but as a commitment of the total person. See M. J. Charlesworth, *St. Anselm's Proslogion* (Oxford: The Clarendon Press, 1965), p. 27, quoting A. A. Cayré, *La Contemplation augustinienne* (Paris, 1954), p. 223. Knowing, loving, and trusting were all aspects of faith for Augustine. Faith involved commitment to the form of life, which Christianity commended. Living out that life led to understanding the faith more fully. See J. E. Smith, p. 5.

98. See *On the Trinity*, I. 1 (*NPNF*, 3:17).
99. J. E. Smith, p. 6.
100. Avery Dulles, *A History of Apologetics*, Theological Resources, ed. Jaroslav Pelikan and John P. Whalen (New York: Corpus Publications, 1971), p. 61, citing Augustine's *Soliloquiae* (*Soliloquies*) I. VI. 13 where Augustine writes: "But even looking cannot turn eyes already healed to the light unless these three things are present: faith that believes that the object to which our looking ought to be directed can, when seen, make us blessed; hope which is assured that vision will follow right looking; love which longs to see and to enjoy" (LCC, VI, 31).
101. *City of God*, VIII. 8.

102. *Soliloquiae* I. VI. 12; see also Robert E Cushman, "Faith and Reason," in *A Companion to the Study of St. Augustine*, ed. Roy W. Battenhouse (New York: Oxford University Press, 1955), pp. 291–293, "Illumination." In *Sermon 126* (*PL* 38, 699) Augustine wrote: "God made you a rational animal . . . and formed you in His own image. . . . Therefore lift up your mind, use your eyes like a man, look at heaven and earth, look at the things that are made and look for the Maker; look at the things you see, and look for Him whom you do not see" (as translated in Charlesworth, p. 27, note 2).
103. *HP*, II/1, 63.
104. J. E. Smith, p. 7.
105. Theologians who have been concerned to defend reason against a feared irrationalism have seized upon any evidence in Augustine that would make reason prior to faith. See B. B. Warfield, "Augustine's Doctrine of Knowledge" (hereafter cited as Warfield, "Doctrine of Knowledge") in *Calvin and Augustine* (hereafter cited as *CA*), ed. Samuel G. Craig (Nutley, N.J.: Presbyterian and Reformed, 1974; rep. 1956), pp. 422ff. and John H. Gerstner, "The Church's Doctrine of Biblical Inspiration," in *The Foundation of Biblical Authority*, ed. James Montgomery Boice (Grand Rapids, Mich.: Zondervan, 1978), pp. 29ff. There are two citations in Augustine's work that seem to give reason priority over faith. In an early work, Augustine writes "In point of time, authority is first; but in the order of reality, reason is prior," *De ordine* (*On Order*) II. 9. 26 (*Tempore auctoritas, re autem ratio prior est*), translated in J. E. Smith, p. 9. Again, in *Epistle* 120, 3, Augustine says, "So therefore, if it is rational that faith precedes reason in the case of certain great matters that cannot be grasped, there cannot be the least doubt that reason which persuades us of this precept—that faith precedes reason—itself precedes faith." See this translation in Charlesworth, p. 27 (*PL* 33, 453). In both instances, Augustine's concern was not with theological method as such. In these citations "reason" has to do with a human being's capacity for thought. Reason was, for Augustine, the ability to use language, form concepts, and do all of the intentional acts of the mind. See J. E. Smith, p. 9. Charles Norris Cochrane writes: "While, therefore, authority is prior in time to reason, reason is prior to authority in fact. Such is the constitution of human nature that, when we un-

dertake to learn anything, authority must precede reason (*De moribus ecclesiae catholicae, de moribus Manichaeorum—On the Morals of the Catholic Church and of the Manichaeans*, I. 2. 3; *NPNF*, 4:70). But this authority is accepted only as a means to understanding. 'Believe,' he says, 'in order that you may understand,'" *Christianity and Classical Culture* (New York: Oxford University Press, 1972), p. 402. Both Warfield and Gerstner too severely limit Augustine's concept of "reason" to mean only (intellectual) knowledge of some sort. In the citations mentioned, "reason" has a broader dimension. Of the first, J. E. Smith writes: "It is clear from the context that he [Augustine] refers to progress in the quest for the understanding of faith which stems from rational analysis and reflection"; of the second: "In short, if man were not a rational being to begin with he could not grasp either the meaning of *credo ut intelligam* [I believe in order that I may understand] and *fides quaerens intellectum* [faith seeking understanding], or see the superiority of these principles over other alternatives. And Augustine, as is evident in *De utilitate credendi*, argued the case against those who rejected his own formula that one must believe in order to understand," pp. 9–10. "Reason" in this sense—of the ability to use language, form concepts, and so on —was predicated on the functioning of the mind. It was this kind of reasoning ability that for Augustine distinguished human beings from other creatures. See *De libero arbitrio* (*The Freedom of the Will*) II. iii. 7–vi. 13 (LCC, VI, 138–143); see also Cushman, p. 292f.

106. J. E. Smith, p. 10. Dulles points out (p. 62) the difficulty with having to have "reasons" for accepting an authority: "But this brings one face to face with a grave difficulty. How can one know who is wise unless he himself is wise? Wisdom, unlike material things, is of such a nature that it cannot be known except by those who possess it; and if one is seeking it, he does not possess it. Hence he is in no position to judge what teacher is or is not wise." He cites Augustine's *De utilitate credendi* (*The Usefulness of Belief*) where he argues: "But wisdom cannot be seen by the mental eye of anyone who lacks it . . . no one can with absolute certainty discover a wise man, by obeying whom he may be delivered from the evil of his folly" (XIII, 280) (LCC, VI, 315).

107. "The Advantage of Believing," in *The Writings of St. Augustine*, trans. Luanne Meagher, II, *Fathers of the Church* (New York: Cima, 1947), cited in *Classical Statements on Faith and Reason*, ed. Ed. L. Miller (New York: Random House, 1970), p. 36.

108. "Holy Scripture": *City of God*, XV. 8; "divine Scripture": *Ench. I*, 4 (*divina;* LCC, VII, 338; *PL* 40, 233). See also "divine Scriptures": *City of God*, IX. 20; "words of God": *City of God*, X, 1; "God's Word": *Enarrationes in Psalmos* (*Expositions on the Book of Psalms*) 146, 12 (*NPNF*, 8:667; On Psalm 147:10, a commentary on Psalm 147:6:); "divine oracles": *Epistle* 55, 37; 147, 40.

109. *The Usefulness of Belief*, vi. 13 (LCC, VI, 302). Cf. other descriptions in *Ep.* 82, 1, 3 and so on, cited in Seeberg, 1:358, note 1. In *On Christian Doctrine* Augustine writes: "In the plain teaching of Scripture we find all that concerns our belief and moral conduct," translated in Kelly, *Doctrines*, p. 43. The citation is from *On Christian Doctrine*, II. IX. 14; see also *City of God*, XVIII. 41; *Enarr. in Ps.* 8. 7 (*NPNF*, 8:29).

110. A. D. R. Polman, *The Word of God According to St. Augustine*, trans. A. J. Pomerans (Grand Rapids, Mich.: Wm. B. Eerdmans, 1961), p. 41.

111. *De peccatorum meritis et remissione* (*On the Merits and Remission of Sins*, II, 26, 27 (*NPNF*, 5:55); cf. *The Spirit and the Letter*, 5 (iii.) (LCC, VIII, 197).

112. *On the Merits and Remission of Sins*, I, 7, 10 (*NPNF*, 5:18).

113. For an interpretation of Augustine's view of "The Word of God as Proclamation," see Polman, pp. 123–176.

114. Eugene TeSelle, *Augustine's Strategy as an Apologist* (Villanova, Pa.: Villanova University Press, 1974), p. 12.

115. *Contra Faustum Manichaeum* (*Reply to Faustus the Manichaean*), XXII, 94 (*NPNF*, 4:-310). On the Christocentric character of the Scriptures, see Maurice Pontet, *L'Exegese de Saint-Augustin Prédicateur* (Paris, 1945), pp. 149ff. and 305ff. Exegetically this theological belief worked itself out in Augustine's use of allegory and his view of the relationship of the Testaments. This view was developed with particular regard to the Manichaean attacks on the Old Testament. See Polman, pp. 75ff.

116. *Contra Adimantum Manichaeum*, III, 3; VII, 5 (*PL* 42, 133; 138).

117. *Conf.* VI, v. 8.

118. *City of God*, XI, 3 (*PL* 41, 318) and *De Doctrina Christiana* (*On Christian Doctrine*) II.

viii. 12–13 and II. v. 6. See the translation by
D. W. Robertson, Jr., Library of Liberal
Arts, ed. Oskar Piest (New York: Liberal
Arts Press, 1958), pp. 40–42.
119. *De actis com Felice Manichaeo* (*Proceedings
with Felix the Manichee*), I, 10, cited in Polman, p. 59.
120. *De Genesi ad litteram* (*On Genesis according
to the Literal Sense*), II, 20, cited in Polman, p.
60.
121. Polman, p. 61, citing *On Genesis according to the Literal Sense*, I, 39.
122. *Calvin: Institutes of the Christian Religion*,
ed. John T. McNeill, trans. Ford Lewis Battles, 2 vols., LCC (1960) (hereafter cited as
Inst.), III. xxi. 4; cf. Battles, "Accommodating," pp. 25–26.
123. Battles, "Accommodating," p. 25.
124. *On the Trinity*, I. i. 2 (*NPNF*, 3:18).
125. *Tract. on John I.* 1 (*PL* 35, 1379–1380;
NPNF, 7:7), as translated in Augustin Bea,
The Study of the Synoptic Gospels, ed. Joseph A.
Fitzmeyer (New York: Harper & Row,
1965), p. 59, n. 2.
126. *"Sed per hominem more hominum loquitur;
quia et sic loquendo nos quaerit,"* City of God,
XVII, 6 (*PL* 41, 537). This implied the need
for scholarly study to understand the human forms of God's communication.
Augustine was fully conscious that the Bible
was written in foreign languages and that it
introduced cultures different from his own.
See *On Christian Doctrine*, II, XI. 16ff., from
The Works of Aurelius Augustinus, ed. Marcus
Dods, 15 vols. (Edinburgh: T & T Clark,
1871–1876), 9:44.
127. *Sermon* 82:9 (Benedictine edition);
"Scriptura sancta in nulla parte discordat," Sermons on New Testament Lessons, XXXII. 9 (on
Matthew 18:15: "Holy Scripture will in no
part disagree with itself" (*NPNF*, 6:360);
(*PL* 38, 510).
128. *Reply to Faustus the Manichaean*, XI, 5
(*NPNF*, 4:180). Cf. *Epistle* 82 to Jerome: "If
I do find anything in those books which
seems contrary to truth, I decide that either
the text is corrupt, or the translator did not
follow what was really said, or that I failed to
understand it" (from *The Fathers of the
Church*, ed. Bernard M. Peebles et al., 67
vols. (Washington D.C.: The Catholic University of America Press, 1947–1974),
12:392. (Hereafter cited as *FC*.) See William
Sanday, *Inspiration* (London: Longmans,
Green, 1893), pp. 36–38 for additional examples.
129. *De consensu evangelistarum* (*The Harmony

of the Gospels), II, xxi, 51–52, as translated in
Bea, p. 42. See also Schökel, pp. 115–116;
and the translation in *NPNF*, 6:127. (Hereafter cited as *Harmony*.)
130. *Harmony*, II, xii, 27 (*NPNF*, 6:117).
131. *Harmony*, *II*, xii, 28 (*NPNF*, 6:118).
132. *Harmony*, II, xii, 28, as translated in
Bea, p. 55, note 1. Augustine spoke quite
strongly of the work of the Holy Spirit in
inspiring the biblical authors. He maintained with equal strength (as did Origen
and Chrysostom) that the writers used
freely the forms of expression available to
them, and at the same time the divine function or purpose was achieved. Augustine
combined both elements when he wrote:

> He is the Head of all His disciples,
> who are as members of His body
> through that human nature which He has
> assumed. Thus, when they write what He
> has taught and said, it should not be as-
> serted that He did not write it, since the
> members only put down what they had
> come to know at the dictation [*dictis*] of
> the Head. Therefore, whatever He want-
> ed us to read concerning His words and
> deeds, He commanded the disciples, His
> hands, to write. Whoever understands
> this shared unity and the convergence in
> divine functions of many members un-
> der one Head, cannot but receive what
> he reads in the Gospels, though written
> by the disciples, as though it were writ-
> ten by the very hand of the Lord Him-
> self.

See *Harmony*, I, xxxv, 54, as translated in
Schökel, p. 60 (see also *NPNF*, 6:101). This
is cited by Karl Barth who writes: "If I am
right, it was Augustine who first spoke
clearly about a divine dictation, or the encountering of it throughout the biblical
writers," *Church Dogmatics*, trans. G. T.
Thomson and Harold Knight (Edinburgh:
T & T Clark, 1963, I/2, 518. (Hereafter cited
as *CD*.) But we are on safer ground to agree
with the major English translator of Barth,
G. W. Bromiley, who writes: "Although in
this context this does not mean more than
that the members of Christ's body act in
behalf of Christ himself as the Head." See
Bromiley, "Doctrine of Inspiration," p. 208.
See also Schökel, p. 66f. Polman points out
the different words Augustine uses for "inspiration," p. 44ff. Other, similar statements by Augustine include this one from a
sermon: "We read that the law was written

with the finger of God and given through Moses, his holy servant" and this: "The Scriptures, by the operation of the Holy Ghost, are written by the ministers," from *Sermon on Psalm 5.* His words are: *"Legimus digito Dei scriptum legem et datum per Moysen,"* and *"Operante Spiritu sancto per ministros."* Cited in Polman, p. 51.

133. *Harmony*, II, xii, 27, as translated in Bea, p. 54 (*PL* 34, 1090–1091; *NPNF*, 6:117). Cf. Kelly, *Doctrines*, p. 63, who mentions *Sermon* 246, 1 (*PL* 38, 1153).

134. *Harmony*, II, xxi, 52, as translated in Schökel, p. 116. See note 129 above. See Polman, p. 50, for other examples.

135. Schökel, p. 116. Cf. Polman, pp. 50–51, quoting Paul Schanz, *Apologie des Christentums* 3d. ed. (Freiburg, 1906), II, 636. Polman also writes: "Thus the difference between the Gospels must be attributed both to what it pleased the Holy Ghost to put in them and also to the spiritual tendencies of the Evangelists." To Polman, "St. Augustine fully appreciated what Bavinck has called 'organic inspiration,' at least in his total approach, though not perhaps in some of his more equivocal utterances." p. 51.

136. Vawter, pp. 38–39.

137. *Harmony*, II, xxviii, 67 (*NPNF*, 6:135). He also writes: "Let us not think [that it is an advantage for our faith to know all these things], as if the truth were somehow bolstered up by a set and consecrated words (*consecratis sonis*), or as if God were entrusting to us not only the thing itself, but also the words which were used about it. Rather, the thing which in itself is so much more to be preferred that we should not seek after those words (*istos* [*sonos*]) at all, if we could know it without them, as God knows it, and as his angels know it in him," *Harmony*, II, lxvi, 128 (*PL* 34, 1139; *NPNF*, 6:160). He speaks of the "harmonious diversity which marks the four evangelists." The translation is in Bea, p. 69.

138. *Harmony*, II, xlvii, 97 (*NPNF*, 6:149); See also II, lxvi, 128 (*NPNF*, 6:160).

139. *Epistle LXXXII*, 3 (*NPNF*, 1:350).

140. For the context of the correspondence see J. N. D. Kelly, *Jerome: His Life, Writings and Controversies* (New York: Harper & Row, 1975), pp. 217–220 and 268–273.

141. *Epistle XXVIII*, 3 (*NPNF*, 1:252).

142. *Epistle LXXXII*, 3 (*NPNF*, 1:351).

143. It is unfortunate that some contemporary writers continue the old Princeton tradition by taking the utterances of Augustine regarding the freedom of the biblical writers from deliberate ethical deceit and ascribing to them a claim of technical precision of the words of Scripture in matters of science, history, and so on—a position Augustine specifically disclaimed. See, for example, David W. Kerr, "Augustine of Hippo," in *Inspiration and Interpretation*, ed. John F. Walvoord (Grand Rapids, Mich.: Wm. B. Eerdmans, 1957), p. 73; and John Warwick Montgomery in *God's Inerrant Word: An International Symposium on the Trustworthiness of Scripture*, ed. John Warwick Montgomery (Minneapolis: Bethany Fellowship, 1974), p. 64, "unqualified accuracy," and p. 9, n. 26, "inerrancy."

144. See *Harmony*, II, xii, 29 (*NPNF*, 6:118–119).

145. *On Christian Doctrine*, III. XV. 23.

146. *On Christian Doctrine*, III. X. 14 (Dods translation); See also Beryl Smalley, *The Study of the Bible in the Middle Ages* (Notre Dame, Ind.: University of Notre Dame Press, 1970), p. 23. (Hereafter cited as *SB.*) God, for Augustine (and Origen) was not limited to just one sense of Scripture. When he approached the Bible, he first asked theological rather than historical questions. See P. Brown, p. 253.

147. It was P. Courcelle in *Les Lettres grecques en Occident de Macrobe à Cassiodore*, 2d ed. (Paris, 1938), pp. 185–193, who showed that Augustine knew and used the works of some of the Greek Fathers, including Origen. See also *SB*, pp. 22–3, n. 4.

148. Vawter, p. 173 (n. 7, chap. 2). For a thorough examination of Augustine's exegesis, see Pontet.

149. *Conf.* VI. iv. 6 (LCC, VII, 117–118); See also *Conf.* V. xiv. 24 (LCC, VII, 111).

150. *SH*, p. 109.

151. *City of God*, XIII. 22. Augustine made this comment after giving a highly symbolic interpretation of the Paradise story in Genesis. Perhaps Augustine's most famous allegory was his interpretation of the parable of the Good Samaritan. See *Quaestiones Evangeliorum*, 2. 19 (*PL*, 35, 1340), as summarized in A. M. Hunter, *Interpreting the Parables* (London: SCM Press, 1960), p. 26.

152. For a discussion of Augustine's use of Tyconius, see James Samuel Preus, *From Shadow to Promise: Old Testament Interpretation from Augustine to the Young Luther* (Cambridge, Mass.: Harvard University Press, 1969), chap. 1. See also *HI*, p. 239. Augus-

tine takes up these rules in *On Christian Doctrine*, III. xxx. 42ff.

153. These are given in *Genesis According to the Literal Sense*, c. 2, n. 5 (*PL* 34, 222) and in *On the Usefulness of Belief*, iii, 5 (LCC, VI, 294–295). He writes there: "In Scripture, according to the historical sense, we are told what has been written or done.... According to the aetiological sense we are told for what cause something has been done or said. According to the analogical sense we are shown that the Old and New Testaments do not conflict. According to the allegorical sense we are taught that everything in Scripture is not to be taken literally but must be understood figuratively." See also J. Preus, p. 21.

154. *Genesis According to the Literal Sense*, I, 1, as cited in Robert E. McNally, *The Bible in the Early Middle Ages* (Westminster, Md.: Newman Press, 1959), p. 54 (*PL* 34, 247).

155. " ... *quamquam et in Vetere Novum lateat, et in Novo Vetus pateat.*" This translation is from Jan H. Walgrave, *Unfolding Revelation*, Theological Resources, ed. Jaroslav Pelikan and John P. Whalen (Philadelphia: Westminster Press, 1972), p. 59. See also R. E. Brown, '*Sensus Plenior*', p. 55, who translates it: "The New Testament lies hidden in the Old; the Old Testament is enlightened through the New."

156. *SB*, p. 24, citing *Quaestiones in Heptateuchum*, i. 93.

157. Vawter, p. 173, quoting Pontet, pp. 162–163: "*Il va sembler que tous les textes, écrits de la même encre et de la même main, sont datés de la même époque.*"

158. R. E. Brown, '*Sensus Plenior,*' pp. 53–54, quoting Pontet, p. 173.

159. *Contra Epistolam Manichaei Fundamenti* (*Against the Epistle of Manichaeus Called Fundamental*), V. 6 (*NPNF*, 4:131). His words are: "*Ego vero evangelio non crederem, nisi me catholicae Ecclesiae commoveret auctoritas.*" (*PL*, 42, 176).

160. *On the Trinity*, I. iv. 7 (*NPNF*, 3:20). See also discussions of this statement in Warfield, "Doctrine of Knowledge," pp. 430ff. and Harnack, "Augustine as Reformer of Piety," in *HD*, 5:61ff.

161. Kerr, p. 77, citing *De Unitate Ecclesiae* (*On the Unity of the Church*), ii. 2.

162. Lohse, pp. 34–35. Cf. J. N. D. Kelly, *Early Christian Creeds*, 3d ed. (London: Longman, 1972); Kelly, *Doctrines*, p. 43: "According to Origen, the rule of faith, or canon, was the body of beliefs currently ac-

cepted by ordinary Christians; or again it could stand for the whole content of the faith. In his usage it was equivalent to what he called 'the ecclesiastical preaching' (*kerygma*), and he meant by it the Christian faith as taught in the Church of his day and handed down from the apostles. Though its contents coincided with those of the Bible, it was formally independent of the Bible, and indeed included the principles of Biblical interpretation."

163. Lohse, pp. 35–6. Augustine used the *regula fidei* as a tool for interpreting Scripture. His *On Christian Doctrine* was an introductory manual for the interpretation of the Bible. For a discussion of the nature and purpose of this work, as well as of its influence, see D. W. Robertson, Jr.'s translator's introduction, ix–xxi. In the work, Augustine resorted to the "rule of faith" as an authority for resolving ambiguities in Scripture. See *On Christian Doctrine*, III. ii. 2, 5.

164. See *The New Encyclopaedia Britannica: Micropaedia* (hereafter cited as *NEBM*), *s.v.* "Middle Ages (c. 395–1500)"; *NIDCC*, *s.v.* "Middle Ages"; *ODC*, *s.v.* "Middle Ages, The"; *EP*, *s.v.* "Medieval Philosophy."

165. W. T. Jones, *The Medieval Mind*, 2d ed., A History of Western Philosophy, (New York: Harcourt, Brace & World, 1969), p. 141.

166. See *Retractiones* 2, 43, 1, 2 (*PL* 32, 647; *FC* 60, 209), cited in *City of God*, trans. Bettenson, Introduction, xv–xvi. For the psychological shock Rome's fall had on Jerome, see F. A. Wright, *Fathers of the Church* (London: Routledge, 1928), p. 213.

167. R. W. Southern, *Western Society and the Church in the Middle Ages*, Pelican History of the Church (Middlesex, England: Penguin Books, 1970), p. 24.

168. Southern, p. 22.

169. See Jones, pp. 141–142 and *SB*.

170. See Jones, p. 141.

171. *EP*, VI, 338.

172. See *ODC*, 406. Cf. Maurice de Wulf, *History of Medieval Philosophy*, trans. Ernest C. Messenger, 2 vols. (New York: Dover Publications, 1952), 1:101ff., and E. Gilson, *History of Christian Philosophy in the Middle Ages* (London: Sheed and Ward, 1972), pp. 81–85. (Hereafter cited as *H*.)

173. For a more detailed study, see *HP*, II/1, chap. 9. Cf. *EP*, *s.v.* "Pseudo-Dionysius," and Justo L. González, *A History of Christian Thought*, 3 vols. (Nashville: Abingdon Press, 1971), 2:91–94. (Hereafter cited as *HCT*.)

174. See *ODC*, 183–184. See also *H*, pp. 97–106 and de Wulf, 1:106ff; *EP*, s.v. "Boethius, Anicius Manlius Severinus," and "Porphyry"; and *HP*, II/1, 116–119.

175. For a thorough survey with sections by several scholars, see the article, "Scholasticism," in Karl Rahner et al., eds., *Sacramentum Mundi: An Encyclopedia of Theology* (New York: Herder and Herder, 1970). (Hereafter cited as *SM*.) See also *NIDCC*, s.v. "Scholasticism"; *ODC*, s.v. "Scholasticism"; *The Encyclopaedia Britannica* (Chicago: Encyclopaedia Britannica, 1971) (hereafter cited as *EB*), s.v. "Scholasticism"; *NEBM*, s.v. "Scholasticism"; *EP*, s.v. "Medieval Philosophy."

176. For a discussion of the legitimacy of speaking of "medieval philosophy" as distinct from "medieval theology," see *HP*, II/1, 18ff.

177. Compare *ODC* and *NIDCC* articles on "Scholasticism," for example.

178. *SM*, s.v. "Scholasticism."

179. McNally, p. 55.

180. *SB*, p. 36.

181. *ODC*, s.v. "Scholasticism."

182. *SM*, s.v. "Scholasticism,"

183. On Erigena's life and work see *ODC*, 468; *HP*, II/1, chaps. 12 and 13; *HCT*, 2:128–135; *H*, 113–128; and *EP*, s.v. "Erigena, John Scotus."

184. He writes that "True philosophy is true religion and, inversely, the true religion is true philosophy." Also, "no one enters into heaven save through philosophy." Cited in Charlesworth, pp. 23–24, from M. Cappuyns, *Jean Scot Erigène, sa vie, son oeuvre, sa pensée* (Paris: Louvain, 1933), pp. 303–305 from *De Praedestinatione*, I. i; *Annotationes in Martianum, 38, ii.*

185. *EP*, s.v. "Erigena." Cf. de Wulf, 1:123–124.

186. Raymond Larry Shelton, "Martin Luther's Concept of Biblical Interpretation in Historical Perspective" (Ph.D. dissertation, Fuller Theological Seminary, 1974), p. 109, citing Erigena, *De Divisione Naturae* I, 66, 68; IV, 9, 16. See also *HP*, II/1, p. 149; *H*, pp. 113–114; and Jones, p. 197.

187. See Alfred Weber, *History of Philosophy*, trans. Frank Thilly (New York: Charles Scribners' Sons, 1896), p. 202. For a denial, see *HCT*, 2:135, and *NIDCC*, 885. For the claim that the true "father" is Anselm, see *EP*, V, 253, and Jasper Hopkins' and Herbert Richardson's editor's introduction to their *Anselm of Canterbury, Truth, Freedom, and*

Evil: Three Philosophical Dialogues (New York: Harper & Row, 1967), p. 10.

188. *ODC*, 1245.

189. For more on Anselm, especially in relation to Abelard and Bernard, see Jack Rogers et al., *Case Studies in Christ and Salvation* (Philadelphia: Westminster Press, 1977), pp. 51–64.

190. Anselm, "Monologium," in St. Anselm, *Basic Writings*, trans. S. N. Deane, 2d ed. (LaSalle, Ill.: Open Court, 1974), p. 36. On Anselm see also *H*, pp. 129–139; and *HP*, II/1, chap. 15.

191. Charlesworth, p. 23. Anselm seeks the inner intelligibility of the truths of faith. Dulles writes: "Authorities can correct the theologian when he goes astray, but they do not take the place of cogent reasons. Theology, as Anselm conceives it, must necessarily be conducted *sola ratione* ("Monologium," 1.1, p. 38). In the *Monologion* he [Anselm] agrees to write in such wise 'that nothing from Scripture should be urged on the authority of Scripture itself, but that whatever the conclusion of independent investigation should declare to be true, should, in an unadorned style, with common proofs and with a simple argument, be briefly enforced by the cogency of reason, and plainly expounded in the light of truth' " (from preface to *Monologium*, p. 35), in Dulles, p. 78.

192. As rendered in Charlesworth, p. 105 (*PL* 158, 225).

193. Charlesworth, p. 115 (*PL* 158, 225): *nisi credidero, non intelligam.*

194. *Cur Deus Homo* I, ch. 2 (*PL* 158, 362) (Deane translation, p. 179).

195. I ch. 1 (*PL* 158, 361) (Deane translation, p. 178).

196. *Cur Deus Homo*, "Preface," (*PL* 158, 359) (Deane translation, p. 177). See also *HP*, II/1, 178–179.

197. J. E. Smith, p. 15. Anselm's dialectic between faith and reasoning was evident when he wrote on the Trinity. He wished to penetrate the mystery of faith by faith-enlightened reason without rationalizing away the mystery, See "Monologium," chap. LXIV (*PL* 158, 210) (Dean translation, p. 128). See also David Knowles, *The Evolution of Medieval Thought* (London: Longmans, 1962), p. 101 (hereafter cited as Knowles, *(Medieval Thought,)* and de Wulf, 1:168. Anselm concluded: "We can explain *that* there are three persons in God even if we cannot

explain *how* this can be." See Charlesworth, p. 38.

198. J. E. Smith, p. 14. The leading interpretation of Anselm as a fideist, that is, as one to whom nothing can be known except on the basis of faith, is that of Karl Barth in his *Anselm: Fides quaerens intellectum*, trans. I. W. Robertson (Cleveland: World Publishing, 1962). For a discussion of his view, see J. E. Smith, p. 13, and Charlesworth, pp. 40ff.

199. J. E. Smith, p. 16; See also Charlesworth, p. 37.

200. Charlesworth, p. 39.

201. J. E. Smith, p. 17.

202. Cited in Rogers et al., p. 56.

203. See Dulles, p. 83. He cites H. Ligeard, "Le Rationalisme de Pierre Abelard," *Revue des sciences religieuses* 2 (1911):384–396. Abelard assumed that reason would not contradict revelation. He believed that greater understanding would open the gateway to faith. See Otto W. Heick, *A History of Christian Thought*, 2 vols. (Philadelphia: Fortress Press, 1976), 1:268. He was not, however, a "rationalist" in the eighteenth-century sense of the term. As Paul Tillich puts it: "He did not wish to derive the mysteries from reason, but to make them understandable to reason." See Paul Tillich, *A Complete History of Christian Thought*, ed. Carl E. Braaten (New York: Harper & Row, 1968), p. 167 (from his *A History of Christian Thought*); cf. Knowles, *Medieval Thought*, p. 122. Abelard's attitude toward "philosophy," negatively expressed, is seen in his statement: "I do not wish to be a philosopher in order to contradict Paul, nor an Aristotle in order to be cut off from Christ," *Letter 17* (*PL* 178, 375), cited in Julius R. Weinberg, *A Short History of Medieval Philosophy* (Princeton: Princeton University Press, 1964), p. 74. Abelard tested each of the Christian doctrines by reason (Heick, 1:269). His program is expressed in his *Introduction to Theology:* "Now therefore it remains for us, after having laid down the foundation of authority, to place upon it the buttresses of reasoning" (*lib.* 2; *PL* 178, 980), cited in Knowles, *Medieval Thought*, p. 123.

This method that Abelard developed was "dialectic"—the art of proving something through logic. See Heick, 1:265. On the meaning of "Dialectic," see *EP*, II, 385ff. Abelard produced a book, *Sic et Non* (*Yes and No*) that was a collection of opinions from Scripture and the church fathers for and against various propositions. The title refers back to the basic meaning of the Greek term *dialektikē technē* as "the art of conversation." As it developed in the schools, dialectic was one of the seven basic liberal arts thought to encompass all knowledge. These arts were the standard fare for students' studies. They were studied before one could go on to specialize in theology, medicine, or law. For background, see Walter J. Ong, *Ramus: Method, and the Decay of Dialogue*, rep. 1958 (New York: Octagon Books, 1974). In *Sic et Non* Abelard used the dialectical method for theology. He gave a series of 158 questions, with quotations arranged to support both the yes side and the no side. Abelard weighed the value of each of the authorities through logical investigation. For a discussion of his method see Jaroslav Pelikan, *Historical Theology*, Theological Resources, ed. Jaroslav Pelikan and John P. Whalen (New York: Corpus Publications, 1971), pp. 12–14. Later theologians gave definite answers to the questions. Hence the Scholastic method of inquiry was eventually reduced to a repetition of textbook answers.

204. *ODC*, s.v. "Scholasticism." See Rogers et al., pp. 56–57.

205. Heick, 1:269. Abelard was not out to cast doubt on the church or its authorities by using his method. As Tillich writes: "When Abelard wrote his book, he tried to harmonize the doctrines, not to show dogmatic differences in order to arouse doubt and skepticism. On the contrary, he wanted to show that a unity is maintained in the tradition which can be proved by methods of harmonization," I, 169.

206. See *HI*, pp. 260–261, citing *Sic et Non*, Prologue: *Constat et prophetas ipsos quandoque prophetiae gratia caruisse.* For Abelard "the writings of the fathers are to be read 'not with the necessity of believing, but with the liberty of judging.' Inquiry is the chief key of knowledge, 'for by doubting we come to inquiry, and by inquiring we discover the truth,'" Seeberg, 2:58.

207. *SM*, s.v. "Scholasticism"; *ODC*, s.v. "Scholasticism."

208. *HI*, p. 263. On Peter Lombard see *ODC*, 1073; LCC, X, 226–228; Knowles, *Medieval Thought*, pp. 179–184; and *HCT*, 2:177–180. The Schools of Chartres, St. Victor, Hugh of St. Victor, and Gilbert de la Porrée all made contributions toward the molding of Scholasticism. On them see *H; HP*, II/1, chaps. 16 and 17; and Knowles, *Medieval Thought*, chap. 11.

209. See *HP*, II/1, chap. 21: "The Translations" and F. van Steenberghen, *Aristotle in the West: The Origins of Latin Aristotelianism*, trans. Leonard Johnston (Louvain: E. Nauwelaerts, 1955), pp. 62–63. Cf. *H*, pp. 235–246.

210. Heick, 1:282; cf. 281. On the Arab and Jewish philosophy see *H*, pp. 181–231 and Knowles, *Medieval Thought*, chap. 16.

211. On Albert, see *EP*, I, 65–66; *HCT*, 2:-256–258; *HP*, II/2, 11–19; *H*, pp. 227–294; *SM*, s.v. "Scholasticism." See L. A. Kennedy, "The Nature of the Human Intellect According to St. Albert the Great," *Modern Schoolman* 37 (1960):121–137. *SM*, s.v. "Scholasticism." Albert attempted to comment on all the Aristotelian corpus. See *HP*, II/2, 16–17.

212. Heick, 1:284. The literature on Aquinas is enormous. See the works cited in *HP*, II/2, 294ff.; *EP*, VIII, 114–116; and *H*, pp. 709ff.

213. *The Summa Contra Gentiles*, III, 25 in *Introduction to St. Thomas Aquinas*, ed. Anton C. Pegis (New York: Random House, 1948), p. 445.

214. David Knowles, *The Historical Context of the Philosophical Works of St. Thomas Aquinas* (London: Aquinas Press, 1958), p. 8. See also Knowles, *Medieval Thought*, p. 257: "As a follower of Albert who outran his master he accepted human reason as an adequate and self-sufficient instrument for attaining truth within the realm of man's natural experience, and in so doing gave, not only to abstract thought but to all scientific knowledge, rights of citizenship in a Christian world."

215. *SM*, s.v. "Scholasticism."

216. The edition cited is the recent Dominican publication: St. Thomas Aquinas, *Summa Theologiae*, Vol. I, *Christian Theology* (Ia.I), ed. Thomas Gilby, O.P. (Cambridge: Blackfriars, in conjunction with McGraw-Hill, New York, 1963), pp. 59. (Hereafter cited as *ST*.)

217. For Thomas, reason was always based on sense experience. See *ST*, I.ii.2. Thomas also developed "Five Ways" or "Five Proofs" for the existence of God. They all depended on the principle of cause and effect and began with empirical knowledge of the physical world and reasoned back to God as the cause of these effects. See *EP*, VIII, 110: "They [the five ways] are not entirely original with Aquinas, depending not only on Plato, Aristotle, and Avicenna but also on Augustine and especially on Moses Maimonides."

218. There are many studies of Thomas's doctrine of analogy. But see the collection of texts in G. P. Klubertanz, *St. Thomas Aquinas on Analogy: A Textual Analysis and Systematic Synthesis* (Chicago: Loyola University Press, 1960) and Hampus Lyttkens, *The Analogy Between God and the World: An Investigation of Its Background and Interpretation of Its Use by Thomas of Aquino* (Uppsala, Sweden: A. B. Lundequistska, 1953).

219. Cited in E. L. Miller, ed. *Classical Statements on Faith and Reason* (New York: Random House, 1970), p. 51, citing Thomas Aquinas, *Summa Contra Gentiles*, I, viii, 1. (Hereafter cited as *SCG*.) See also *ST*, I. xiii. 5 and *HP*, II/2, 72–78.

220. *HP*, II/2, 74–75. For Aquinas, "it was from contact with external reality, not from a divine illumination or contact with the divine ideas, that a knowledge of truth came. This was in harmony with a key proposition of Aquinas: *quicquid recipitur, secundum modum recipientis recipitur*, which in the field of epistemology became: *cognitum est in cognoscente per modum cognoscentis* ('Whatever is received, is received according to the mode of being of the receiver,' as for example, the sound of a clock striking is heard merely as a sound by an animal, but as a time-signal by a man. 'What is known is in the mind of the knower according to his mode of being'). God is known from His works not in Himself. . . ," Knowles, *Medieval Thought*, p. 261. Thomas saw man (following Aristotle) as essentially a rational animal. Intellect distinguished humans from animals and was the primary characteristic of God. See *ST*, I, xiv, 1. "Hence since God is immaterial in the highest degree . . . it follows that he has knowledge in the highest degree." Reason (nature) preceded and led to faith (grace) for Thomas. See the citation in Miller, p. 41, from *SCG*, I, iii, 2. Reason could perceive all of the truth in the material world and move beyond it into the spiritual world by arguments from analogy. See Knowles, *Medieval Thought*, p. 261. The purpose of revelation was to supplement reason. Some truths, such as the Trinity, were beyond reason's power to discover on its own. See *ST*, I. ii, 2. But truths such as the existence of God could be known by reason and also accepted in faith.

This delineation is in the form of a "double distinction. First, he distinguished between philosophy and theology: Philosophy is what can be proved by the natural light of reason; theology is whatever rests on faith. Second, he distinguished between revealed and natural theology: The latter is the part of the former that is susceptible of proof. Thus, philosophy and theology overlap. Some of the truths that rest on faith (and so belong in the field of theology) are demonstrable (and so belong in the field of philosophy). Natural theology is the name Thomas gave to the set of propositions that constitute the field of knowledge in which faith and reason overlap," Jones, pp. 213–214. Gilson writes: "Although the relationship established between faith and reason is so intimate, they still constitute two formally distinct types of knowledge, and the same can be said of philosophy and theology," in *The Christian Philosophy of St. Thomas Aquinas,* trans. L. K. Shook (London: Victor Gollancz, 1957), pp. 20–21. See *ST,* I. ii. 2. Basically, to Thomas, "Grace does not scrap nature, but brings it to perfection." See *ST,* I.i.8: *Gratia non tollit sed perficit naturam.* The assertion to which he was objecting came from Gregory the Great, *In Evang.* II, homily 26 (PL 76, 1197).

221. Cited in *ST,* I, i, 8.

222. Vawter, p. 46.

223. Berndt, Moeller, "Scripture, Tradition and Sacrament in the Middle Ages and in Luther," *Holy Book and Holy Tradition,* ed. F. F. Bruce and E. G. Rupp (Manchester, England: Manchester University Press, 1968), p. 122.

224. *ST,* I, i, 10. See also *HI,* p. 276.

225. See Gerald A. McCool, "Twentieth-Century Scholasticism" in *Celebrating the Medieval Heritage,* ed. David Tracy, a supplement to *The Journal of Religion* vol. 58 (Chicago: University of Chicago Press, 1978), pp. S198–S221. See also Geoffrey W. Bromiley, *Historical Theology: An Introduction* (Grand Rapids, Mich.: Wm. B. Eerdmans, 1978), pp. 200–201 and 208–209.

226. *SM,* s.v. "Scholasticism;" "Introduction" to *ST* (Blackfriars edition, p. xxiii).

227. On Duns Scotus, see: *EP,* II, 427–36; Seeberg, 2:147–165; Knowles, *Medieval Thought,* pp. 303–310; *HP,* II/2, chaps. 45–50; *H,* pp. 454ff.; and Jones, pp. 299–316.

228. See *HP,* II/2, 241, 250. See also *H,* pp. 457–459; and *EP,* II, 429–430.

229. See his *Ordinatio* (his Commentary on Lombard's *Sentences*), "Prologue," pars 5, q.

1–2 (1; 217 of the edition of his works edited by the Scotist Commission). For Scotus, theology presupposed revelation. Scripture and Church were the main authorities for his faith.

230. *Ord.* prol. q. 2.14, cited in Seeberg, 2:149.

231. *Ord.* prol. III. d. 25, q. 1.4; i. d. 26, cited in Seeberg, 2:149. *Ord.* d. 11, q. 3.5, cited in Seeberg, 2:149. Scotus criticized Thomism for teaching the primacy of the intellect over the will. Scotus, in the Augustinian tradition, insisted on the primacy of the will over the reason. See *Ord.* prol. q. 1 and *H,* p. 463: "It is the will alone, Scotus says in a striking formula, which is the total cause of volition in the will: *nihil aliud a voluntate est causa totalis volitionis in voluntate.* It is true that we have to know an object to will it and that it is the good that we know to be in that object that makes us will it; but it is equally true that if we know that object rather than another, it is because we will to know it."

232. *HP,* II/2, 209.

233. Etienne Gilson, *Reason and Revelation in the Middle Ages* (New York: Charles Scribners' Sons, 1948), p. 85.

234. On Nominalism see: *EP,* viii, 203f.; *HP* II/1, chap. 14; *H,* pp. 449ff.; Meyrick H. Carré, *Realists and Nominalists* (Oxford: Oxford University Press, 1949), p. 38f.; Knowles, *Medieval Thought,* chap. 9 and Heiko A. Oberman, *The Harvest of Medieval Theology,* rev. ed. (Grand Rapids, Mich.: Wm. B. Eerdmans, 1967). (Hereafter cited as Oberman, *Harvest.*)

235. On Occam, see, Gordon Leff, *William of Ockham: The Metamorphosis of Scholastic Doctrine* (Manchester, England: Manchester University Press, 1975); *HP,* III/1, 56–133; *EP,* VIII, 306–317; *H,* pp. 489–497; *HCT,* 2:316ff; and Jones, pp. 316–326.

236. Jones, p. 317.

237. See citation in Seeberg 2:192; from *De Sacr. alt.* I. 16; *quodlib.* iv. 35. On the relation of church tradition to biblical authority for Occam and his followers, see Oberman, *Harvest,* pp. 378ff. Also see Seeberg, 2:192, citing Occam, *Dial,* p. 411, 769f. (Goldast, *Monarchia,* Frankfurt, 1614). Occam does, however, also seem to believe that there are extra-scriptural truths, that is, truths coming from the tradition of the church. See Oberman, *Harvest,* p. 382.

238. In Seeberg, 2:192, citing Occam, p. 822, 834 (Goldast).

239. In Seeberg, 2:195, citing Occam, *Centiloquium theologicum*. 60.

240. *EB*, s.v. "Scholasticism"; *SM*, s.v. "Scholasticism."

241. Oberman, *Harvest*, p. 424.

242. Oberman, *Harvest*, p. 394, quoting *Lect.* 71 G. and I *Sent.* Prol. q. 1, a 1, nota 3D. Philosophically Nominalism strengthened the movement in the Roman Catholic Church that lodged authority in Church Councils rather than in the Papacy. If the Pope ceased to serve the real Church—the body of believers—he should be deposed. See *HCT*, 2:320, citing Seeberg, 2:169.

243. *D. Martin Luther Werke. Kritische Gesamtaussabe*, ed. J. F. K. Knaake (Weimar: H. Böhlav, 1883—). (Hereafter cited as *WA* [Weimarer Ausgabe]). See *WA* 30. ii. 300 and *WA* 6. 183; See also *WA* 39. i. 420, 38, 160. In his *Luther's Progress to the Diet of Worms* (London: SCM Press, 1951), E. Gordon Rupp asserts that many of the deferential remarks made by Luther about Occam turn out to be ironical (see p. 17). See also Gerhard Ebeling, *Luther: An Introduction to His Thought*, trans. R. A. Wilson (Philadelphia: Fortress Press, 1972), p. 37, who writes that "Luther's Ockhamist training continued to be the decisive influence upon his theological studies" at Erfurt. Biel's *Collectorium* (1495; his Commentary on *The Sentences*) "was one of the most important textbooks studied by the young Luther." See M. Reu, *Luther and the Scriptures* (Columbus, Ohio: Wartburg Press, 1944), p. 13.

244. Heiko A. Oberman, "Headwaters of the Reformation" in *Luther and the Dawn of the Modern Era*, ed. Heiko A. Oberman (Leiden: E. J. Brill, 1974), pp. 69, 82, 88.

245. The understanding of monastic as distinguished from scholastic theology has especially been developed by Jean Leclerq, O.S.B. See his *The Love of Learning and the Desire for God: A Study of Monastic Culture*, trans. Catherine Misrahi (New York: Fordham University Press, 1961). See also an excellent interpretative article by Kilian McDonnell, O.S.B., "I Believe That I Might Experience," *Continuum*, 5, no. 4 (Winter 1968):673–685. (Hereafter cited as McDonnell, "I Believe.")

246. Serm. sup. Cant., 74.2 cited in Leclerq. p. 246.

247. Leclerq, pp. 248 and 257; *ODC*, s.v. "Benedict, St."

248. *De consideratione* V, 32 (*PL* 182.808), cited in Leclerq, p. 262.

249. *Sancti Bernardi Claravallensis Abbatis Operum* (Venetiis, 1781), vol. 2, 415 (*De Conversione*, 3), cited in McDonnell, "I Believe," p. 683.

250. *S. Bernardi Opera*, Editiones Cistercienses, vol. 2, 11 (*Super Cantica*, 37:3), cited in McDonnell, "I Believe," p. 683.

251. *Super Cantica*, 59:6, cited in McDonnell, "I Believe," p. 683.

252. Leclerq, p. 271. Kilian McDonnell, himself a modern "black monk," offers a wise word regarding balance in theology: "Even with this biblical and patristic evidence the history of enthusiasm, both its presence and its absence, gives one pause. There are two extremes to be avoided, either erecting religious experience into an ultimate so that it becomes the definitive norm, or rejecting the whole experimental dimension of grace, reducing the spiritual life to a syllogistic gnosticism," "I Believe," pp. 683–684.

253. After Bernard, the most influential medieval mystic was John Eckhart—(1260?–1327), known as Meister Eckhart. On Eckhart, see *EP*, II, 449–451; *H*, pp. 438–442. Copleston (*HP*, III/1, 194) writes: "One might reasonably be inclined to see in the flowering of mystical writing in the fourteenth century a reaction against logical and abstract metaphysical studies, against what some people call 'objective thinking,' in favour of the one thing needful, salvation through union with God. And that there was such a reaction seems to be true enough. On the one hand, there were the older philosophical traditions and schools; on the other hand, there was the *via moderna*, the nominalist movement. The wranglings of the schools could not transform the heart; nor did they bring a man nearer to God. What more natural, then, than that the religious consciousness should turn to a 'philosophy' or pursuit of wisdom which was truly Christian and which looked to the work of divine grace rather than to the arid play of the natural intellect?"

254. Kilian McDonnell, O.S.B., *John Calvin, the Church, and the Eucharist* (Princeton, N.J.: Princeton University Press, 1967), pp. 25–26. Luther also was influenced by the mystics. See Heick, 1:316 and B. R. Hoffmann, *Luther and the Mystics* (Minneapolis: Augsburg Publishing, 1976).

255. *ODC*, s.v. "Brethren of the Common Life"; "Devotio Moderna"; "Thomas à Kempis."

j. Selected Bibliography

Baur, Chrysostomus. *John Chrysostom and His Time.* Vol. 1. Sands & Co., Ltd., 1959.

Brown, Peter. *Augustine of Hippo.* University of California Press, 1969.

Copleston, Frederick. *A History of Philosophy* Vols. 1–3. Doubleday, 1962–1963.

Daniélou, Jean. *Gospel Message and Hellenistic Culture.* Translated by John Austin Baker. Westminster Press, 1973.

Daniélou, Jean. *Origen.* Translated by Walter Mitchell. Sheed and Ward, 1955.

Farrar, Frederic W. *History of Interpretation.* MacMillan, 1886.

Gilson, Etienne. *History of Christian Philosophy in the Middle Ages.* Sheed and Ward, 1972.

González, Justo L. *A History of Christian Thought* Vols. 1, 2. Abingdon Press, 1970, 1971.

Grant, Robert M. *A Short History of the Interpretation of the Bible.* Rev. ed. Macmillan, 1966.

Hanson, R. P. C. *Allegory and Event.* John Knox Press, 1959.

Kelly, J. N. D. *Early Christian Doctrines.* 2d ed. Harper & Row, 1960.

Knowles, David. *The Evolution of Medieval Thought.* Longmans, 1962.

McNally, Robert E. *The Bible in the Early Middle Ages.* Newman Press, 1959.

Oberman, Heiko A. *The Harvest of Medieval Theology.* Rev. ed. Wm. B. Eerdmans, 1967.

Polman, A.D.R. *The Word of God According to St. Augustine.* Translated by A. J. Pomerans. Wm. B. Eerdmans, 1961.

Schökel, Luis Alonso. *The Inspired Word.* Translated by Francis Martin. Herder and Herder, 1972, rep. 1965.

Smalley, Beryl. *The Study of the Bible in the Middle Ages.* Notre Dame Press, 1970.

Vawter, Bruce. *Biblical Inspiration.* Westminster Press, 1972.

CHAPTER 2

Concentration on the Bible's Saving Function during the Reformation

a. Pre-Reformers: Wycliffe and Huss

The late fourteenth and early fifteenth centuries saw a reaction by some theologians to both the Scholasticism of Thomas Aquinas and the extreme forms of skepticism arising from nominalism. The search for meaningful, personal religious experience fostered by the mystics also helped to pave the way for a return to Neoplatonic Augustinianism.[1]

John Wycliffe

John Wycliffe (1330?–1384) was educated at Merton College, Oxford.[2] He reacted against the skepticism there that separated the realms of natural and supernatural knowledge.[3] Wycliffe returned to a Neoplatonic realism under the influence of Thomas Bradwardine's reading of Augustine. Thomas Bradwardine (1290?–1349) at Oxford opposed Occam philosophically and returned to Augustine's ideas on grace and predestination.[4] Wycliffe thus opposed the prevailing Aristotelianism of his day.[5] His philosophical works, particularly *Summa de Ente* (c. 1365–1372), were nurtured by his religious concerns and especially an impatience with the spiritual sterility of skepticism.[6]

Wycliffe attacked what he believed were unbiblical aspects of the Roman Church and incurred its ire. He declared that the authority of the pope was not scriptural, and he attacked the doctrine of transubstantiation in the Eucharist. Wycliffe was denounced by the Roman hierarchy and posthumously condemned by the Council of Constance in 1415. The "poor preachers" (called "Lollards") whom Wycliffe sent out were severely persecuted.[7]

Wycliffe's debt to Bradwardine was great. Thomas Bradwardine was one of the first men in the fourteenth century to speak out for a tradition that held to the sufficiency of Holy Scripture as understood by the fathers and doctors of the church. In the case of disagreement between these authorities, Scripture had the final authority.[8] This view stood in opposition to a second concept of tradition, which held to both a written *and* unwritten apostolic message approved by the church. This second concept of tradition had the bishops, rather than the Scripture scholars, as its interpreters. The hierarchy claimed its own oral tradition which, to a certain undefined extent, became independent of the canonical books. Ecclesiastical traditions, including canon law, came to be invested with the same degree of authority as that of Holy Scripture.[9]

Wycliffe followed Bradwardine in opposing this second concept of tradition. At first, Wycliffe conceded that the church and ecclesiastical tradition were to serve as guides in the interpretation of Scripture. But he grew increasingly convinced that much of so-called Christian tradition contradicted the teachings of the Bible.[10] In the end, he came more emphatically than any prior medieval schoolman to a position that Scripture alone was the final religious authority.[11]

Wycliffe expounded his views regarding the Bible in *De Veritate Sacrae Scripturae* (*The Truth of Holy Scripture,* 1377). In it he held that the Bible was the only authority for the church's health and people's salvation. Wycliffe declared: "The Bible is therefore the only source of doctrine that will insure the health of the Church and the salvation of the faithful."[12] With this understanding that the purpose of Scripture was salvation and guidance for the life of faith, Wycliffe could say "any part of Holy Scripture is true according to the excellence of the Divine Word."[13]

In accepting the authority of Scripture, Wycliffe was guided by Augustine's formula that faith leads to understanding. Wycliffe cited Augustine often and relied on Augustine's judgment regarding the place of reason: "If reason is set against the authority of the Divine Scriptures, no matter how keen it may be, it fails of accuracy, for it cannot be true."[14]

In interpreting Scripture, Wycliffe also followed the Augustinian pattern. He trusted the leading of the Holy Spirit and then used his regenerated reason. Wycliffe proclaimed that the Bible's meaning was plain for anyone who prayerfully sought it, apart from interpretations the church had made. Wycliffe then added several rules for reading the Scriptures: Obtain a reliable text; understand Scripture's logic; compare parts of Scripture with each other; and maintain a humble, seeking attitude so that the Spirit can instruct.[15] Finally, Wycliffe utilized the Augustinian principle that the rule of love was a guide in interpreting the Bible. He desired that the spirit of love and humility should guide the reader of Scripture. Wycliffe's Augustinianism was so pronounced that he was sometimes called, "John, Son of Augustine."[16]

Theology for Wycliffe was not a theoretical, but a practical matter. His burning passion was for the reform of the church. For him, the Bible was the sole authority for religious teaching and guidance in the life of faith. To this end, he interpreted the Bible both in its grammatical-historical and its allegorical senses. Allegorizing enabled Wycliffe to apply the sense of Scripture to preaching, theology, and to the areas of civil and ecclesiastical law.[17]

Wycliffe's allegorizing was guided by his awareness of the *kerygma*, the central saving message of Scripture. He contended: "The Holy Spirit teaches us the sense of Scripture as Christ opened the Scriptures to His apostles."[18] The allegorical interpretations were built on the grammatical-historical sense of Scripture. He maintained that "all things necessary in Scripture are contained in its proper literal and historical senses."[19] On this foundation, Wycliffe felt free to expand the meaning of Scripture allegorically.[20] Where the Christian sense was not explicitly stated, for example, he felt free to present it allegorically.[21] However, Wycliffe had no use for those who subverted the message of Scripture by fanciful allegories.[22]

John Huss

The Bohemian reformer, John Huss (1372?–1415) was deeply influenced by Wycliffe's teachings. In fact, many of Wycliffe's writings have survived only in Czech manuscripts.[23] Huss adopted Wycliffe's views on tradition in his own battles with the Roman hierarchy. Huss's opposition to the pope centered in any addition of the pope's own laws to the law of God, Holy Scripture.[24] Huss rejected the charge that he was arbitrary in his interpretations of the Bible. He stressed the role of the Holy Spirit in illuminating believers. Huss also believed that the Spirit had provided the doctors of the church with a gift of understanding, and he did not intend to deviate from them. His exegesis won Luther's praise; he said that Huss was "skillful and weighty in the treatment of Scripture."[25]

b. The German Reformation: Martin Luther

Martin Luther (1483–1546) had an original mind. In the providence of God he began a new movement—the Protestant Reformation. At the same time, by his own admission, he learned from and was helped by many traditions that preceded him.[26]

It is important to sense in what ways Luther's views on Scripture were an extension of medieval views, in what ways he was going back to earlier traditions, and in what ways he contributed something distinctively new. Luther certainly was in continuity with the medieval church in his belief in the inspiration and authority of the Bible. As we have seen, however, people can agree on the inspiration and authority of the Bible, yet have decisive differences regarding the nature and purpose of the Bible and the manner in which it is to be interpreted.

One way in which the Reformation can be understood is as a rejection of an Aristotelian-Scholastic method of understanding and interpreting the Bible during the Middle Ages. Luther reached back to the attitudes of the early church by regarding the Bible's purpose as salvation and guidance in the life of faith. He also accepted its accommodated, incarnational form by which God had lowered himself to speak in human language and patterns of thought. Thus, Luther reunited two elements of the early church theological tradition; a Neoplatonic-Augustinian acceptance of the Bible in faith, and a scholarly and critical appraisal of the natural, grammatical sense of the biblical text in its historical context. The faith of simple believers and the scholarship of trained theologians were to be united. Faith was the beginning and basis of sound theology, and careful study was the means of growing into Christian maturity. The pastor-teacher rather than the ecclesiastical authority was to be looked to for guidance in interpreting the Bible.

What made Luther's speech at Worms revolutionary was not that he affirmed the authority of Scripture. It was rather that he denied the authority of popes and councils as the exclusive interpreters of the Bible.[27] Luther's *Sola Scriptura* (Scripture Alone) principle had been enunciated in his 1519 Leipzig debate with Johann Eck (1486–1543). Luther stated flatly: "It is not in the power of the Roman pontiff or of the Inquisition to construct new articles of faith. No believing Christian can be coerced beyond Holy Writ. By divine law we are forbidden to believe anything which is not established by divine Scripture or manifest revelation."[28] Luther thus parted company with both the Aristotelian Scholastics and the nominalists in denying the ultimate authority of pope and hierarchy.[29]

For Luther, the Bible's authority took priority over the authority of the church. He said: "The Scripture is the womb from which are born theological truth and the Church" and "The Word of God preserves the Church of God."[30] For him, the Bible was the "touchstone," "ruler," "plumb line" or "Lydian stone by which I can tell black from white and evil from good."[31]

Luther accepted the ancient creeds, not because the councils of the church had ratified them, but because their content conformed to Scripture. Because he felt that the creeds did incorporate the *kerygma*, the central saving message of Scripture, he often linked the creeds with the Bible as his authorities. Thus Luther showed that he was not a rebel against the universal church, but only against errors and abuses of the papal organization.[32] Luther subjected all authorities, including the church fathers, to the test of fidelity to Scripture. He announced: "I will not listen to the Church or the fathers or the apostles unless they bring and teach the pure Word of God" and "Their authority is worth most when it has clear scriptural support."[33] Luther was influenced by the Augustinians, the nominalists, the humanists, and even the mystics. All of these affected the way he read the Bible. But, for Luther, it was primarily Scripture itself that showed him the way. Most important of all is to understand Luther's motivation for turning to Scripture—his personal search for salvation. Luther's question was: "How may I find a gracious God?" and it was in the Bible that Luther found a God who justified the ungodly. Jesus Christ was the manifestation of that gracious God. And Jesus Christ was at the center of Scripture.

Accommodation

There was no conflict, for Luther, between the authority of the Bible and its accommodated, incarnational form. God humbled himself to communicate with us through a person, Jesus Christ. Scripture was a fully human record of that divine communication. The purpose of Scripture was not to construct a theoretical science. The function of the Bible was to speak to us of Jesus Christ and his salvation. Luther spoke of the truth of Scripture as "a perfect, seamless ring of gold; it comprises only one doctrine, Christ."[34] On one occasion he asked Erasmus: "When you take Christ out of the Bible, what have you left?"[35] In a favorite figure of speech, he spoke of Christ as the " 'central point of the circle,' around which everything else in the Bible revolves."[36] This was true of the Old Testament as well as of the New. Both the distinction and the harmony between the divine saving message and the human surrounding milieu were evident in Luther's words: "Here you will find the swaddling-clothes and the mangers in which Christ lies. Simple and little are the swaddling clothes, but dear is the treasure, Christ, that lies in them."[37] The subject matter of Scripture, by which all of its parts were rightly interpreted, was nothing but the message of Christ.[38] Luther declared:

The Gospel, then is nothing but the preaching about Christ, Son of God and of David, true God and man, who by His death and resurrection has overcome all men's sin, and death and hell, for us who believe in Him.[39]

For Luther, the Bible was not a source book of Christian wisdom about all sorts of topics. It was a book to lead people to Christ whose preparation and appearance was its theme.[40]

For Luther, the Bible's authority was in its content—Christ—and its function—bringing salvation. The Bible's imperfect form of human words was, for Luther, an example of God's gracious condescension. God was willing and able to clothe his Word in an adequate, though earthly form. Luther mused:

> Holy Scripture possesses no external glory, attracts no attention, lacks all beauty and adornment. You can scarcely imagine that anyone would attach faith to such a divine Word, because it is without any glory or charm. Yet faith comes from this divine Word, through its inner power without any external loveliness.[41]

This led Luther to conclude: "It is only the internal working of the Holy Spirit that causes us to place our trust in this Word of God, which is without form or comeliness."[42]

What the early church theologians had called God's accommodation, Luther understood as an incarnational style of communication. Luther saw a divine and a human nature of the Bible just as there was a divine and human nature in Christ. The Bible was the Word of God in the words of human beings. Luther contended that just as

> the divinity and power of God are embedded in the vessel of Christ's incarnate body, so the same divinity and power of God are embedded in Scripture, a vessel made of letters, composed of paper and printer's ink. In order to grasp the biblical revelation in its fulness it is necessary to conceive of Scripture in terms of the divine-human nature of Christ.[43]

Luther could boldly say: "Sacred Scripture is God incarnate." He deliberately drew the analogy between the Bible and the person of Christ.[44] "And the Word," he said, "is just like the Son of God."[45] He spelled it out explicitly:

> The Holy Scripture is God's Word, written, and so to say 'in-lettered', just as Christ is the eternal Word of God incarnate in the garment of his humanity. And just as it is with Christ in the world, as he is viewed and dealt with, so it is also with the written Word of God.[46]

Luther's Christology strongly stressed the real humanity of Christ. Similarly, he accepted fully the genuine humanity of Scripture. The mystery was not that God had created some perfect and flawless form of words.

The wonder was that God had chosen to use weak and imperfect human speech adequately to communicate his divine message. Luther thought in biblical and human images. He was far from attributing scientific and technical accuracy to the Bible. He knew that the writers were human and that what they wrote had been recorded in normal human fashion.[47] And yet through this accommodated, incarnational medium, human beings received God's saving message.

All of Luther's statements about the authority of Scripture must be understood in the context of his commitment to an accommodated, incarnational Word in which God had condescended to use our lowly human means of communication. Luther's understanding of both the authority and interpretation of the Bible also must be seen against the background of his Augustinian reliance on the Holy Spirit as the authenticator and interpreter of the Word.

Luther announced: "When you read the words of Holy Scripture, you must realize that God is speaking in them."[48] The Bible is the Book of Christ.[49] It is also "the book of the Holy Spirit" since it was written through the Spirit.[50] But Luther did not draw the implication that the words of Scripture had meaning as isolated units. It was rather the saving story they told as a unified whole that mattered. And they did not speak about technical, scientific, or philosophic questions. Rather, the Scriptures spoke with clarity about salvation and the life of faith. Luther said that "the Holy Scriptures are a spiritual light far brighter even than the sun, especially in what relates to salvation and all essential matters."[51] Scripture authenticated itself. Luther announced: "Believing and reading Scripture means that we hear the Word from Christ's mouth. When that happens to you, you know that this is no mere human word, but truly God's."[52] The authority of Scripture, for Luther, was in its saving function, which the Holy Spirit accomplished in persons.[53]

For Luther, the Holy Spirit was both the inspirer of Scripture in the past and the interpreter of Scripture in the present. The Holy Spirit was at work to make the Scriptures "for us."[54] Word and Spirit were bound inextricably together. It was the Spirit who "speaks to the heart" and "impresses" the Word upon the heart of the hearers. The Spirit "touches and moves the heart."[55] The Spirit "enlightens 'with and through the word.' "[56] Thus, for Luther, more than a knowledge of words and grammar was required when reading the Bible. As Luther put it, "The Bible cannot be mastered by study or talent; you must rely solely on the influx of the Spirit."[57] This inner testimony of the Holy Spirit testified to Christ and thus gave authority to the Word. Luther asked "How can we know what is God's Word, and what is right or wrong? . . . You must determine this matter yourself, for your very life depends upon it. Therefore God must speak to your heart."[58]

Faith and Reason

Luther's attitudes toward the Bible were born out of his personal search and struggle to find salvation. At the same time, his academic training and the intellectual movements for change around him prepared and enabled him to receive the authoritative message, which he discovered in its accommodated form.

Luther was an Augustinian monk. He was nurtured in the Neoplatonic philosophical milieu of Augustinianism that put faith before reason. It enabled him to go directly to the Bible, trusting in the guidance of the Holy Spirit, rather than having to accept some philosophical system as a prior guarantee or guide. Luther said he learned more from Augustine and the Bible than from all other books.[59] He wrote: "For Isaiah vii makes reason subject to faith, when it says: 'Except ye believe, ye shall not have understanding or reason.' It does not say, "Except ye have reason, ye shall not believe.' "[60] God's existence could not be proved, as was attempted in the Thomist system. God was known by faith on the basis of the revelation of Himself in Scripture.[61] This was a "spiritual matter" in which "human reasoning certainly is not in order."[62]

Luther's training in the university by Occamist philosophers provided him with a philosophical rationale to support his Augustinian attitude. Luther had studied at Erfurt from 1501 to 1505 where the *via moderna*, the nominalism of Occam, was the reigning philosophy. Against Aquinas and Classical Scholasticism, Luther held, with the nominalists, that theology could not properly be classed as a science since its assertions rested on statements of faith. The invisible world with which theology dealt, and which could be known only through faith, stood in marked contrast to the visible world that was accessible to reason. This latter realm, which embraced all rational knowledge and science, was "philosophy."[63]

Luther made many disparaging statements about "philosophy" and the "reason" that was its tool. Vehemently he cried out against reason as a "beast" and "enemy of God," "the Devil's Whore," and a "source of mischief."[64] Aristotle, whose name to Luther *meant* philosophy, was to him "a destroyer of pious doctrine," a "mere Sophist and quibbler," and "inventor of fable," and an "ungodly public enemy of the truth." Without exhausting all of Luther's epithets, Aristotle was "the stinking philosopher," "the pagan beast," "lazy-ass," "billy-goat" and many more.[65]

Luther, with Occam, rejected reason as the basis for faith. He did not believe, as the Thomists, did, that all knowledge began with the knowledge of the world. As an Augustinian, he believed that God had implanted the knowledge of Himself in human hearts from which faith their reasonings could begin when awakened by the Spirit. Luther made a clear distinction between philosophy and theology:

> Philosophy is concerned with the objects of sensory perception, things which can be experienced and conceptualized; whereas the Christian's concern is with invisible things, the "things which are not," that is, things whose existence men question because they cannot see them. It is the Gospel that teaches us about the nature of God and of ourselves, "whence we came and whither we are going." In these matters the philosophers are totally ignorant.[66]

According to Luther, philosophy must not be mixed up with theology because "philosophy does not understand sacred things." Philosophy could never be used as the "substance of theology"[67] (*ipsam rem theologiae*). Luther was willing to use philosophy to substantiate a point, but he was totally averse to building upon its foundations. He inveighed: "Philosophy is *the heathen's* theology."[68] Luther was arguing that reason should be kept in its proper place (*in suo loco*). It did have an area of competence in worldly matters but reason's philosophical judgments and categories should not be allowed to invade the realm of theology.[69]

Luther did not look to the Bible for answers to questions about this world. In a lengthy passage, Luther had an objector point out that Christ praised the wisdom of the man who built his house upon a rock, which seemed to indicate that the use of one's natural reason could draw merit from God. Luther replied "That is all true; but you must here distinguish God and men, things eternal and things temporal." He then proceeded to explain his meaning:

> In godly affairs, that is, in those which have to do with God, where man must do what is acceptable with God and be saved thereby—*here*, however, nature is absolutely stone-blind, so that it cannot even catch a glimpse (*eyn harbreytt anzeygen*) of what those things are.[70]

For Luther, reason was able to do many things in "mundane" affairs. But when it overstepped its bounds and attempted to dictate in theology it became demonic.[71]

Reason did have a legitimate place in the life of the believer when it came after faith and was regenerated by the Holy Spirit. Luther knew that "although the Gospel is a higher gift and wisdom than human reason, it does not alter or tear up man's understanding: for it was God Himself who implanted reason in man."[72] But, to be useful, reason had to be transformed. Thus, for Luther, reason's "presumptuousness" could be tamed by the Holy Spirit and then reason could become a servant of faith. It is in this light that his famous statement at Worms (1521) must be understood: "Unless I am convicted by Scripture or plain reason . . ."[73]

Luther was not setting up reason as an independent source of knowledge apart from Scripture. He was affirming rather that he must be persuaded either by scriptural citations themselves, or from the inferences a regenerated reason could draw from Scripture.[74]

Luther's views regarding reason were therefore based on three careful distinctions: (1) Natural reason had as its proper realm philosophical inquiries about this world; (2) arrogant reason was reason that misguidedly attempted to invade the realm of faith; and (3) regenerate reason served to heighten Christian understanding that proceeded from faith.[75]

While Luther followed Occam philosophically, he opposed nominalism theologically. Luther accepted the nominalist distinction between the spheres of faith and reason and its stress on the priority of faith. But Luther could not go along with what appeared to him the semi-Pelagianism of the movement. Occam's optimism regarding the powers of the human will seemed to Luther to be unwarranted from Scripture and thus to be rejected.[76]

For Luther, the epistemological issue of "How do I know God?" was subordinated to the soterological issue of "What must I do to be saved?" Human reason became identified, for him, with human autonomy and with the desire to elevate the religious and moral abilities of the human will for salvation. Luther thus attacked reason in true nominalist style, not only to refute Thomism, but also to destroy nominalism's optimism about the power of the human will.[77] The order of priority—soteriology over epistemology (salvation over theoretical knowledge)—was the distinctive element that made Reformation methodologically different from the medieval Scholasticism that preceded it and from the post-Reformation scholasticism that followed it.

Christian Humanism

Erasmus (1469–1536) and Renaissance humanism also influenced Luther and paved the way for his reforms.[78] In his theological work, Luther presupposed the scholarly achievements of humanism.[79] Renaissance humanists with religious convictions attacked scholastic theology and urged a return to the sources of Christianity in the Bible and the early church fathers. These sources were considered Christian classics that shared the prestige of the Greek and Roman literary classics of antiquity. It was assumed that the same methods of historical and linguistic scholarship should be applied to the Bible as applied to other ancient sources.[80]

Erasmus was the outstanding example of a Christian humanist. He rejected scholastic reasoning and demanded a return to the sources of the faith with the Bible as primary. He emphasized that the early Christian writers were grammarians, but not dialecticians.[81] Erasmus used critical methods to evaluate ecclesiastical dogma, and demanded reform. He made textual criticism and a mastery of biblical languages necessary for exegesis and said: "Indeed the whole task of translating Scripture is the task of the grammarian."[82]

Erasmus was also influenced by the rhetorical tradition and by pastoral considerations. Erasmus felt the Bible should be interpreted with the needs of the hearers or readers kept in mind. He said:

> The Scriptures, since now they compel these, now compel those, should be interpreted according to the quality of those to whom one speaks.[83]

Otherwise, Erasmus felt that Scripture would seem to fight with itself in many places, when nothing fights less with itself than Scripture with Scripture.

These scholarly and pastoral considerations led, during the period of the Renaissance and Reformation, to new interpretations of early Christian thought. Scholars such as Marsilio Ficino (1433–1499), John Colet (1466?–1519), and Erasmus attempted to interpret the Pauline Epistles without the context and superstructure of the dominant scholastic theology.[84]

Although he differed theologically from Erasmus, Luther accepted and implemented his scholarly methods. Luther's concern for philological studies was evidenced in his statement: "We shall not long preserve the Gospel without the languages. The languages are the sheath in which this sword of the Spirit is contained."[85] Luther's humanistic orientation and approach to theological study represented a shift away from the marriage of philosophy and theology. Luther grounded theology rather in the fruits of biblical exegesis. He said:

> I believe that I am obligated to the Lord to raise my voice against (Scholastic) philosophy and to bring men back to the Holy Scriptures. If someone else were to do it, he would not be believed. But I have occupied myself with this philosophy for so many years and have myself experienced what I now hear from many others, that it is a useless study, doomed to destruction. . . . It is high time to let go of this theology and to hold fast instead to Christ and him crucified."[86]

Biblical Interpretation

One positive influence from the Middle Ages that Luther carried over was the increased emphasis on the literal, or natural, historical sense of Scripture. Certain medieval theologians picked up the Antiochene approach to the Bible typified by John Chrysostom and departed from the previously dominant Alexandrian emphasis on allegory. Hugo of St.

Victor, his pupil, Andrew of St. Victor, and Thomas Aquinas himself all emphasized that the spiritual sense of Scripture should be based on a study of the grammatical-historical sense of the biblical text.[87]

Luther knew of these developments and was influenced by them. He was particularly guided by the exegetical practice of Nicholas of Lyra, a contemporary of Huss who had significantly influenced the Czech pre-Reformer. Lyra often followed the conclusions of Rashi and other Jewish scholars rather than those of the church fathers. At other times, Lyra set aside all previous interpretations in favor of his own. He began thereby to break the iron grip that ecclesiastical tradition had on exegesis. Lyra contended, for example, that:

> Nothing can be subsumed under the spiritual sense as necessary for the faith which the Scripture does not somewhere plainly hand down through its literal meaning.[88]

Luther was strongly influenced by Lyra as well as Huss. At first, Luther was repelled by literalism. And he continued to fault Lyra and other scholastics for deferring too much to ecclesiastical tradition. But he came to appreciate and emulate Lyra's emphasis on studying the natural, historical sense of the biblical text.[89]

Through his own study of Scripture and these medieval influences Luther moved away from Alexandrian allegorizing. He began to follow the Antiochene stream of grammatical-historical exegesis from the early church.

Another exegetical principle of Luther's, in which he followed the early fathers, was that Holy Scripture is its own interpreter (*sui ipsius interpres*). The emphasis on the natural, grammatical-historical setting of the text did not lead in Luther to an atomism whereby each text was treated independently. Quite in contrast, Luther stressed the unity of the Bible, which was manifested in its concentration on Christ and his saving work. Each Scripture passage was to be interpreted in the light of the whole message of the Bible. The hermeneutical principle was that a doubtful and obscure passage should be explained by a clear and certain passage.[90] Luther stated that "One passage of Scripture must be clarified by other passages."[91] For Luther, this was simply allowing the Holy Spirit to do his work of guiding the believer into a growing awareness of Scripture's message and its implications. At one point, after shedding light on Deuteronomy 1:20 by reference to Numbers 13:2, Luther observed:

> Such is the way of the whole Scripture: it wants to be interpreted by a comparison of passages from everywhere, and understood under its own discretion. The safest of all methods for discerning the meaning of Scripture is to work for it by drawing together and scrutinizing passages.[92]

The authority of the Bible for Luther was in its content, clearly expressed in its central saving theme, by which all its parts could be understood.[93]

Luther's concern to deal seriously with the historical context and to stay consistent with the *kerygma* led him to abandon the fourfold meaning of Scripture that had been popular before and during the Middle Ages.[94] Luther's development away from allegorizing was gradual. His *Lectures on the Psalms* in 1518–21 evidence this.[95] He confessed:

> It was very difficult for me to break away from my habitual zeal for allegory. And yet I was aware that allegories were empty speculations and the froth, as it were, of the Holy Scriptures. It is the historical sense alone which supplies the true and sound doctrine.[96]

Luther's recognition of the human element in Scripture led him to a fundamental dictum: "Faith rests upon history."[97] Luther's exegetical goal was to make Christ, the content of Scripture, present to the individual in both judgment and grace. But Luther found that he did not have to invoke the traditional fourfold method with its arbitrary allusions to the text in order for the Bible to yield hope and help for people's spiritual needs. Luther's great breakthrough was to deny the equation of a spiritual understanding of the text with its allegorical explanation.[98] Luther returned to the prophetic and the typological senses of Scripture and found in them a spiritual meaning that pointed toward Christ as judge and savior. He used this "spiritual" criterion rather than false allegorizing henceforth.[99]

The Old Testament came alive for Luther when he realized that there was a "Gospel" there, in the sense that God was at work in the history of His people for their good. One therefore did not need to allegorize in order to find a "spiritual" meaning.

Luther felt that one would come to appreciate this Good News in history only when one followed the literal sense and refused to be knocked off one's feet by allegories. Otherwise Scripture became what Luther called a "torn net." Luther exclaimed: "Everyone poked a hole in it wherever his snout pointed, and followed his own opinions, interpreting and twisting it any way he pleased."[100] For Luther, it was the literal sense, when properly understood Christologically, which was "the whole basis of faith and Christian theology." This natural and intended sense alone would provide help in time of trouble. Luther expounded:

> [The literal sense] alone holds the ground in trouble and trial, conquers the gates of hell (Matt. 16:18) along with sin and death, and triumphs for the praise and glory of God. Allegory, however, is too often uncertain, unreliable, and by no means safe for supporting faith. Too frequently it depends upon human guess-work and opinion; and if one leans on it, one will lean on a staff made of Egyptian reed (Ezek. 29:6).[101]

Luther's concern was not to be simplistic, but serious with the scriptural text. He said: "If we want to treat Holy Scripture skillfully, our effort must be concentrated on arriving at one simple, pertinent, and sure literal sense."[102]

It is very instructive to note that in spite of Luther's continuing warnings to "beware of allegories," he did in fact often use them.[103] He acknowledged that they could serve a useful purpose provided (1) that they were based on the historical sense of the text and (2) that they were employed *after* the "literal" meaning had been determined. He wrote:

> The historical account is like logic in that it teaches what is certainly true; the allegory, on the other hand, is like rhetoric in that it ought to illustrate the historical account but has no value at all for giving proof.[104]

Luther's basic criteria for the use of allegories were that they should be used according to the analogy of faith (in harmony with the *kerygma*) and that they should be directed toward a goal that was clearly and unequivocally determined by the literal sense of other Scripture passages.[105] His 1525 Lectures on Deuteronomy showed sharp distinctions between "Law" and "Grace" when the mysteries of the book were explained in allegorical terms of Christ and His kingdom. That Moses no longer crossed the Jordan (Deut. 3) meant that law does not lead to the kingdom of God; Joshua represented Christ; the golden calf (Deut. 9:16) referred to the doctrine of works-righteousness, which the priests invented to their advantage; splitting hooves (Deut. 14:6) meant differentiating law and gospel; wars of nations (Deut. 20) meant spiritual wars; not to fell fruit trees (Deut. 20:19) meant not to deny the bit of truth contained in every heresy.[106] While Luther continued to use allegory at all periods of his life, he became more cautious in its use after 1525 and used it less and less after 1529.[107]

The fundamental hermeneutical principle that Luther attempted to practice was this: A text of Scripture should be taken as it stood unless there were compelling reasons for taking it otherwise.[108] While Luther never suppressed the literal sense in favor of the allegorical, he did frequently add a spiritual interpretation, pertaining to Christ and His kingdom, to the literal exegesis. Luther classed allegory as an artistic device used by the biblical writers themselves. Luther's examples included Paul's use of the veil over the face of Moses (2 Cor. 3:13), Paul's discussion of Sarah and Hagar (Gal. 4:22ff.), and the allegories in the Book of Hebrews. But once Luther had clearly broken with the scholastic methods of exegesis, he always strove to expound the clear sense of Holy Scripture.[109]

Concept of Error

Luther's release from bondage to medieval interpretative schemes and the necessity of slavishly following the early fathers had two results. One was a greater reliance on Scripture alone as the source of authority. The other was an openness to historical-critical methods of biblical interpretation.[110] Luther's stress on the natural, historical sense stimulated scientific study of the historical context of biblical writings.[111] Luther himself held some "critical opinions" regarding textual matters including his statements regarding the authorship of Genesis, Ecclesiastes, and Jude; the propriety of the canonicity of Esther, Hebrews, James, and Revelation; the "errors" of the prophets, the trustworthiness of Kings vis-à-vis Chronicles; and the value of the Gospel accounts.[112]

It is important, however, not to remove Luther from his historical setting and attribute to him attitudes from later periods. Luther acknowledged difficulties in the biblical text, and he attempted to resolve them. He was, however, neither a biblical critic in the modern sense, nor did he hold to the theory of the scientific and historical inerrancy of the original manuscripts of Scripture that began to develop in the post-Reformation period.

With the Platonic-Augustinian tradition from the early church, Luther found the authority of Scripture in its content, the message of Christ and his salvation. That content had the function of bringing people into a right relationship with God, which for Luther was the greatest argument for the Bible's authority. He declared: "When a man hears the Word, God must put into his heart the conviction that this is surely the Father's Word. And when he hears the Word of this Man Christ, he is persuaded that he is hearing the Word of God the Father."[113] For Luther, the Bible was infallible in accomplishing its purpose of proclaiming the salvation which the Father had wrought in His Son Jesus Christ.

Luther held firmly to the authority of Scripture and at the same time exercised scholarly criticism of the human forms of the words in which the divine message came. Luther had fully accepted the incarnational, accommodated style of Scripture as adequate to communicate God's saving message. He therefore could deal with scholarly problems without their becoming barriers to faith in the Bible's authority. Luther's basic attitude was: "When discrepancies occur in the Holy Scriptures and we cannot harmonize them, let it pass, it does not endanger the articles of the Christian faith."[114] Luther did not have to have a perfect form of words in order to have a fully adequate transmission of the Gospel message. It was the central articles of the Christian faith, not technical scientific and historical details, about which Luther was concerned. As an

Augustinian, Luther was able to have faith in God and be guided in His life of faith by God's Word without having first to solve scientific questions. Critical questions were the province of the scholarly study Luther engaged in and recommended as part of the Christian's growth in understanding.

Luther's faith, therefore, was in the subject matter of Scripture, not its form, which was the object of scholarly investigation. An excellent example of the blending of these two facets of Luther's approach may be found in a well-known and oft-quoted statement of Luther's regarding Scripture: "There is no falsehood." When we read that statement in its context, it is evident that Luther was not talking about factual errors or the lack of them.[115] Luther was affirming the reliability of God's Word in accomplishing righteousness in the believer. The passage reads:

> For we are perfect in Him and free from unrighteousness, because we teach the Word of God in its purity, preach about His mercy, and accept the Word in faith. This does away with unrighteousness which does not harm us. In this doctrine there is no falsehood; here we are pure through and through. This doctrine is genuine, for it is a gift of God.[116]

As we observed earlier with Augustine, the emphasis in Luther is on the Bible's absolute trustworthiness in communicating its religious message. The writers never deceive us in transmitting God's promises of judgment and salvation. Neither Augustine nor Luther predicated the trustworthiness of Scripture in communicating its saving message on the technical accuracy of its human accommodated form. Since the purpose of Scripture was to bring people to salvation, it would have been a reversal of priorities to make matters of form the criterion for the Bible's reliability in accomplishing this. Aristotelian Scholastics put questions of the knowledge of the world and a commitment to certain philosophical assumptions prior to acceptance of the Word in faith. But it was at this point that Luther rejected scholasticism and returned the Platonic-Augustinian approach to Scripture. For Luther, faith accepted Scripture because of its divine function. Reason examined Scripture in its human form. Those two attitudes formed a harmonious hermeneutical approach in Luther. For him, the Word of God was a gift to us. He exulted that within this "simple basket of reeds, patched with clay, pitch, and such things . . . there lies . . . a beautiful living boy, like Moses."[117] It was the content, Christ, who made the Bible unique, not its human form of communication: "Christ lies in the crib, wrapped in swaddling clothes."[118]

c. The Swiss Reformation: John Calvin

John Calvin (1509–1564) was raised a Roman Catholic and directed by his father to the priesthood. He received excellent training in Latin and the liberal arts. Calvin switched from theology to law for his graduate study in a university world where Luther's teaching was causing ferment. He evidently experienced a personal conversion on the way to his academic doctorate—and became a Protestant.

Christian Humanism

Calvin's training placed him solidly in the ranks of the Christian humanists.[119] Study of the ancient classics under the guidance of Renaissance humanists decisively affected Calvin's thought.[120] Among the most prominent areas in which Calvin evidenced his humanist training were: his method of exegesis; the importance he attached to the study of the church fathers; his acceptance of a certain kind of "Christian philosophy"; his respect for certain thinkers of pagan antiquity; and his concern for the moral character of Christian experience.[121] The result of Calvin's conversion to the evangelical faith was not a repudiation of classical learning, but a transformation of it, under the guidance of God's Word.[122] Calvin's *Institutes of the Christian Religion* clearly echoed his earlier concentration on the sources of classical antiquity.[123]

Renaissance humanism in itself was, at its core, neither religious nor antireligious. It was a literary and scholarly approach that was pursued by Christians and non-Christians alike.[124] Humanism was not a particular philosophical system but rather a cultural and educational approach to that area of studies known as the "humanities."[125] Among the *studia humanitatis* were: grammar, rhetoric, history, poetry, and moral philosophy. These subjects were studied by reading and interpreting classical writers from Latin and, to some extent, from Greek.[126] This accorded with the purpose of the Renaissance to rediscover and renew interest in the works of classical antiquity.

Christian humanists were a substream within the broader flow of Renaissance humanism. They encompassed those scholars with classical and rhetorical training who treated religious or theological issues in their writings.[127] Christian humanists were unified in their historical approach to the classical texts of the Christian faith. They wanted to answer the questions of what Christ and the apostles really taught and what Christianity was originally intended to be like.[128] The most important elements in the humanist approach to theology were its attack upon the scholastic method and its emphasis on a return to study of the classical

sources, especially the Bible and the church fathers.[129] Among the leading Christian humanists taking this stance were Erasmus, Colet, Johannes Reuchlin (1455–1522), Lefèvre d'Etaples (1455?–1536), Guliel-
mus Budaeus (Budé—1467–1540), and Juan Vives (1492–1540).

A distinctive mark of the Christian humanists was their emphasis on
the rhetorical tradition, which taught the art of speaking and writing
persuasively.[130] They were particularly indebted to Cicero and Plato in
their emphasis on the relative importance of rhetoric over dialectics
(logic). They did not deem logic valueless, but they were more impressed
by the persuasive clarity of truth than they were by the irrefutability of
logic.[131] In *On Christian Doctrine* (Book IV), Augustine had urged the
combining of rhetoric and dialectics. Augustine's primary training was
as a rhetorician, although he acknowledged that dialectics could be quite
useful for the study of Scripture.[132] Augustine took his cue from Cicero
who sought to combine wisdom with rhetoric. Augustine wished his
followers especially to study the biblical writers who fused wisdom and
eloquence.[133] By this study, he hoped that people would learn both *what*
to communicate and *how* to do so.

Christian humanists shared a concern for clarity in the service of
truth. Scholasticism was, for them, associated with sophistry and a pride
in dialectics that sought to find God at the end of a string of logical
distinctions. The Christian humanists preferred an attempt to make the
truth evident in its simplicity and through it to persuade people.[134] The
rhetorically trained humanists thus rejected the medieval concept of
theology as a science and returned to the commitment of the early church
to theology as a practical discipline concerned with salvation and the life
of faith. Theology for the Christian humanists was not *scientia* (science),
but *sapientia* (wisdom). They were concerned not for a systematically
ordered body of certain knowledge, even if supposedly derived from
undemonstrable principles of revelation, but for sacred doctrine derived
directly from the pages of sacred Scripture. They hoped for a holy rhetoric in the humble service of the biblical text that would not be restricted
to the rubrics of Aristotelian logic.[135]

Two aspects of Calvin's rootage in the rhetorical and humanist tradition are particularly important. First, despite the fact that Calvin has long
been regarded as the master logician of Protestantism, it is clear that he
intended to subjugate logic to the Scriptures. Calvin knew the value of
logic as one of the human sciences. Logic along with medicine, law,
astronomy, mathematics, and so on were not to be disparaged since they
were given of God as proper arenas for the study of this world by Christian believers.[136] But the law of noncontradiction, which dialectics taught,
did not, for Calvin, have precedence over the teachings of Scripture. The
power of truth to persuade us through faith was a greater value for Calvin

with his humanist background. He commented, for example, on Matthew 27:43, "He trusts in God; let God deliver him now. . . ." He condemned as "Satan's logic" any interpretation that applied logic to God's providence and then concluded that God does not love us because we suffer.[137] Calvin accepted that God had given logic along with physics, mathematics, and other worldly disciplines "that we may be helped . . . by the work and ministry of the ungodly."[138] But if logic was used to drive persons away from faith in the truths of Scripture, then it was to be categorically rejected.

A second important aspect of Calvin's rootage in humanism was his participation in the rhetorical tradition. Here, Calvin's affinities with Augustine and Cicero (whom he called "the first pillar of Roman philosophy and literature") were apparent.[139] Calvin followed the principle of Cicero's "reform," namely, that wisdom had to go hand in hand with eloquence.[140] Logic and philosophy still retained their value, but added to them was the firm conviction that the truth in its simplicity was convincing. Calvin did not advocate a "frivolous rhetoric" that was only a matter of persuasion whether the case were true or not. Instead he wanted to concentrate, not on rendering the speaker effective, but on rendering the truth effective.[141] Calvin wanted the truth of the Gospel to shine through since he knew that "the cross of Christ is made void, not only by the wisdom of the world, but also by the brilliance of words."[142]

The best example of the right rhetorical approach was found in Scripture itself. Calvin declared that the "rude, uneducated men" who wrote the Gospels and who had "learned nothing in the school of men that they could pass on to others" were the spokesmen for God's truth. He affirmed:

> The truth cries out openly that these men who, previously contemptible among common folk, suddenly began to discourse so gloriously of the heavenly mysteries must have been instructed by the Spirit."[143]

Calvin thus opposed both rhetoric in its negative aspect of embellishment, and dialectics insofar as it placed an excessive confidence in the power of reason. But Calvin was very much committed to the rhetorical tradition in its most positive aspects: the study of classical and patristic texts, and the conviction of the innate persuasiveness of God's truth.[144]

Christian Philosophy

Calvin's purpose in writing his *Institutes* was to provide "a key to open a way for all children of God into a good and right understanding of Holy Scripture."[145] Although "Holy Scripture contains a perfect doctrine," this guide was intended to be helpful for simple people who were seeking their way to salvation.[146] Calvin termed his work, "Christian philosophy"[147] to distinguish it from exegetical commentary on the text of Scripture. Calvin was primarily a biblical theologian, and he intended the *Institutes* to provide expositions of the broader themes of the Bible which he perceived under the illumination of the Spirit to be true and which he had experienced in his own life.[148]

Calvin distinguished his work from that of the "secular philosophers." He had no patience with their presumptions and their confidence in their own wisdom about divine things.[149] Philosophers often had an interest in religion (IV. xx. 9) but they went astray because their only standard of truth was their own human reason. Calvin asserted:

> The Christian philosophy bids reason give way to, submit and subject itself to, the Holy Spirit so that the man himself may no longer live but hear Christ living and reigning within him (Gal. 2:20).[150]

Any truth the pagan philosophers happened to speak came from God's providence, but essentially "the truth of God has been corrupted by them all" (1. x. 3). Christian philosophy, by contrast, depended on the Scriptures and also on the work of the Holy Spirit (I. vii. 4). It was concerned with the truth of God revealed in his "beloved Son" in whom believers hoped and rested. Christian philosophy was, for Calvin, a 'secret and hidden philosophy which cannot be wrested from syllogisms" (III. xx. 1). To mix human philosophy with the teaching of Christ was impious.[151]

At the same time, Calvin was not blind to the achievements of pagan philosophers. He said that the "admirable light of truth shining in them" taught us that "the mind of man, though fallen and perverted from its wholeness, is nevertheless clothed and ornamented with God's excellent gifts."[152] So, Calvin, the believer, studied these philosophers just as he had in the days when he was only a humanist scholar. He accepted some of their teachings and rejected others.

Calvin's approach to philosophy was in harmony with that of his fellow Christian humanists. They did not attempt a synthesis of revealed and reasoned theology in the Thomistic manner. Instead, they used the insights of classical philosophy as an aid in the exposition of Christian theology, and as an admirable example of the fact that God had not left himself entirely without a witness even among the pagans. Thus Calvin did not study the philosophers in order to achieve a unity between the knowledge of the unaided and the enlightened human mind. Rather he used philosophy to point out the approximations to Christian truth that might be seen by the light of nature and to point out also the darkness of error into which pagan philosophy could lead.[153]

Calvin did not wish to substitute theology for philosophy. Each had its own appropriate realm—theology for matters of salvation and the life of faith, and philosophy for matters of worldly wisdom and practice.

Neither did Calvin wish to deny the philosophical influences that had borne on theology in the past. He knew his sources. And he was willing to use philosophical insights that were compatible with the Christian faith. He was, therefore, quite forthright in using philosophical concepts, not as determinative, but as subordinate aids in expounding the truth of Scripture.[154]

Humanistic Education

Calvin's formation as a theologian and biblical exegete was fostered by his humanistic education. In particular, three universities and six teachers played decisive roles.[155]

At fourteen years of age, Calvin journeyed more than sixty miles from his home at Noyon in Picardy to enroll at the University of Paris. He was set on fulfilling his father's wish that he study for the priesthood.[156] Supported by a benefice from the diocese of Noyon, Calvin spent about three months at the Collège de la Marche of the university. In this short period his chief teacher was Mathurin Cordier, an outstanding Latinist.

At the end of 1523, Calvin transferred to the Collège de Montaigu of the university where for the next four years he pursued the licentiate in arts. This degree was basic preparation for further work in the university faculties of law and theology. The ancient Collège de Montaigu had dwindled in numbers and influence under the leadership of Noel Béda (to 1513) and Pierre de la Tempête (to 1528). Calvin frequently deplored their theological conservatism in his later writings, calling them "Sorbonnist" or "Sophist." Under them, Calvin was exposed to "philosophy" or rather "logic." By the end of 1527 (or early 1528) Calvin had completed his arts degree in preparation for theological training. But his father Gerard autocratically decreed that his son should seek the more lucrative life of a lawyer.

The best place in France to study law was at Orléans. Since the ninth century, this university had been eminent, and in Calvin's day it consisted of only one faculty, the faculty of law, divided into two divisions: civil (five professors) and canon (three professors).[157]

For centuries an intimate connection had existed between law and theology, and Calvin's study of methods of legal research became as formative for his theology as any aspect of his education.[158]

By the time Calvin was reading law, the "modern" school of legal study, led by Valla, Politien, and Budé, had developed an impressive body of textual, linguistic, and historical studies of the ancient *Corpus* of civil law.[159] Budé had one of the most substantial humanist influences on Calvin.[160] Calvin's method in his *Commentary on Seneca's De Clementia* owed much to Budé's *Annotationes in Pandectas*.[161] In particular, Calvin turned to

Budé for instruction in legal terms, Roman institutions, political philosophy, philosophy, and literature.[162] Through analyzing literature, Budé taught Calvin the relevance of various disciplines, including those of the historians, jurists, philosophers, poets, and rhetoricians, in understanding life.[163] Calvin's Seneca commentary exhibited a very utilitarian application of poetry to exegesis that was derived from Budé's legal commentaries. This practice of careful word study was learned early by Calvin and served him well later as he applied it to the exegesis of Scripture.[164]

Calvin next attended the University of Bourges where the famous Italian jurist Andreas Alciati had begun to lecture. He remained for two years, then returned to the University of Paris for a year, and then went back to Orléans for a final year of formal study.[165] Calvin's educational pilgrimage was as follows:

Paris	(1523–1527)	Arts
Orléans	(1528–1529; 1532–1533)	Law
Bourges	(1529–1531)	Law
Paris again	(1531–1532)	Literature

Calvin's intellectual development was shaped to a large degree by these educational institutions and especially by the teachers he encountered in them. Although he was undoubtedly influenced and formed by his own reading as well, six teachers left a lasting imprint on young Calvin.

Mathurin Cordier (mid-1523 to end of year)—Calvin acknowledged his debt to Cordier in his *Commentary on First Thessalonians* (1550):

> When my father sent me as a boy to Paris, I had done only the rudiments of Latin. For a short time, however, you were an instructor sent to me by God to teach me the true method of learning, so that I might afterwards be a little more proficient.[166]

Cordier was the greatest Latin teacher of his day. His *Grammatica Latina* was reprinted for over one hundred years. Although Calvin's exposure to this master was short (only four months), it seems to have been decisive in laying the groundwork for Calvin's consummate style of writing in Latin.[167]

Calvin's grounding in philosophy at the Collège de Montaigu does not seem to have had any appreciable effect on his later work. His exposure to scholasticism was more limited than Luther's. But his humanistic training made Calvin's hostility to scholasticism equally great. In the first edition of the *Institutes*, written in 1535, there are sixty-nine references to scholastic theology. Sixty-six of them serve to illustrate Roman error, while the other three are exhibited to show that even the Roman sophists recognized some obvious points.[168]

Pierre de l'Estoile (1528–29; 1532–33?)—Calvin encountered this man, who was regarded as the best French jurist of the time, at Orléans.[169] Conservative both juridically and religiously, de l'Estoile had no sympathy for the Lutheran "heresy" then spreading. He impressed Calvin by his devotion to both the law and religion. He appeared to be a man upheld by his confidence in the truth who was unwilling to waste time on insignificant matters.[170] Both de l'Estoile and his colleagues were traditional in their approach, but they were open to the efforts of the humanists and appropriated their results in the study of juridical science.[171] De l'Estoile probably helped to shape the conservative side of Calvin's views on law and institutions.

Andrea Alciati (autumn 1529–end of 1530)—Along with some friends, Calvin migrated to Bourges in the fall of 1529 to hear Alciati lecture. Alciati's reputation was that he had destroyed the traditional approach of the glossators. He had brought a new humanistic method to the study of the *Corpus* by viewing Roman law within the larger context of Latin language, literature, and history,[172] and applying textual criticism to the study of the law. At the same time, he was a practical lawyer and used the *Corpus* to solve contemporary problems. He was therefore a mediator between the old and the new methods.[173]

Calvin was put off by Alciati's bombastic style, but he respected his scholarship.[174] He imbibed Alciati's critical approach and emulated his search for principles in the historical context of the ancient classical world.[175]

Melchior Wolmar (end of 1530–end of February 1531)—In 1532 when his *Commentary on Seneca's De Clementia* was published, Calvin had a rather limited knowledge of Greek. He had started learning the language, however, only the year before, in 1531 at Bourges under the tutelage of Melchior Wolmar. Wolmar's teaching not only laid the foundation for Calvin's knowledge of Greek, but his inspiration provided the impetus for continuing study. This was especially significant at a time when Greek was still linked with heresy.[176] Calvin paid Wolmar tribute in the dedication of his *Commentary on Second Corinthians* (1546).[177]

Guillaume Budé (1531–1532 ?)—Budé provided Calvin with an extensive literary background on which to draw. He was quantitatively the most influential of Calvin's teachers.[178] Budé's significance, however, also lay in the fact that he persuaded King Francis I to appoint five royal lecturers at the University of Paris who were to provide a progressive counterforce to the dominant reactionary group at the university—the faculty of theology. (The Collège de France eventually sprang from the new appointees, as the Sorbonne represented the older, entrenched group.) These five lecturers under the king's personal protection were champions of humanistic and biblical learning.[179] They embodied the spirit of independent research, unfettered by the decrees of the theological faculty. The whole spirit of the enterprise was one of freedom. The subjects they chose to teach, such as Greek and Hebrew, were regarded as revolutionary and dangerous by the Paris theologians, who cried Lutheranism. But, with the support of the king, the new professors continued to teach and attracted a growing student body.[180]

Pierre Danès (late fall, 1531 ?)—one of those lecturers appointed by Francis I was Pierre Danès, a leading Hellenist. Calvin had hoped to attend his Greek lectures, but evidently due to a summer holiday and an outbreak of the plague in the fall of 1531 was prevented from doing so.[181] Yet, Calvin's contact with him and the other royal lecturers was such that it bore fruit later in Calvin's own educational plans for Geneva.[182]

In summary, Calvin's exposure to these three universities and six teachers contributed significantly to his intellectual formation. He studied under most of them for a short but critical time in his own life development. Almost all of Calvin's teachers were educational innovators whose ideas contributed to his career as a Reformer and to his educational philosophy. Both the humanists and the jurists contributed to making law a lasting influence on the shape of Calvin's thought and upon the institutions he helped found.[183]

Contextualism Versus Literalism

Calvin did not jettison his humanist training upon his conversion. As a Christian he still approached the Scriptures as a classical scholar who had served his apprenticeship commenting on classical texts. After his conversion to the evangelical faith, Calvin's classical learning was transformed. As he says in the *Institutes* (I. viii. 1f), he felt that he had exchanged human rhetoric for a divine rhetoric. He saw the task of the theologian no longer as speculative and primarily philosophical but rather as pastoral and pedagogical (*Inst.* 1. xiv. 4.). As a Christian, Calvin continued to make large, if guarded, use of the rhetorical discipline.[184]

With this background, Calvin approached Scripture with a deep desire to understand the biblical culture in which the texts were set. His humanist approach was quite different from the scholastic style. Scholastic theology was a "stepchild" of canon law. The canonists collected their texts and authorities and set them out dialectically. Abelard's *Yes and No* and Lombard's *Sentences* used this method and were the theological texts of the day. The medieval exegetical tradition added glosses to the text, which then became combined with it to form the data from which further interpretations were drawn. This approach was "stolen" from the juridical pattern. Luther had been trained in this medieval tradition.[185] But Calvin's humanist tutors were part of the forces of change that challenged this method of learning law. The humanists sought direct access to the *Corpus* of Roman law. It became for them a literary and historical sourcebook. The history and social customs of ancient Rome were studied and allowed to inform the understanding of the laws.

As a humanist scholar, Calvin adopted this contextual approach in the exegesis of Scripture. Calvin was always occupied with the circumstances and culture in which the biblical message was set. He knew that this colored the text's meaning. He declared: "There are many statements in Scripture the meaning of which depends upon their context."[186] Calvin wanted to be a student of the whole fabric of biblical culture. His legal education gave him more of a grasp of the context of the ancient world than his contemporary theological curriculum would have given.[187] Calvin followed Erasmus who is his "Introduction to the Edition of the Greek New Testament" (1516) urged a careful study of historical and geographical settings, customs, and institutions. When this was done, Erasmus exclaimed: "Then a marvelous light, and, I might say, life, is given to what is being read, which however, would be boring and dead if this knowledge, and as is so often the case, even a knowledge of the language itself is lacking."[188] Lutheranism had defined "two kingdoms" or two spheres that were sharply separated: church/state; sacred/secular. But Calvin, following the humanists, had developed a more integrative approach. The "secular" could help interpret the "sacred." Indeed, it was crucial for a full understanding of the biblical text that its context be taken into account.

Calvin's humanistic training oriented him, not only to discovering the human context, but also to discerning the divine intention in the Scriptures. Calvin had learned from his legal exegesis that it was not primarily the etymology of the words that was important, but rather an insight into the intent of the author. Calvin categorically rejected a narrow literalism that he called "syllable-snatching" (*syllabarum aucupiis*). In his treatment of the Lord's Supper he spoke of the impossibility of a purely literal interpretation (IV. xvii. 23). Calvin did not reject terms such as "trinity" and "person" just because they did not occur literally in the Bible (I. xiii. 3–4). For Calvin, such legalism resulting from literalism was a sign of ignorance. He believed that the form of the biblical message should never be allowed to obscure the message itself. For Calvin, to hear the divine message, one had at times to go beyond the literal words of the text. He came to the Sermon on the Mount contextually, for example. The Anabaptists said that Christ's prohibition, "Do not swear at all" (Matthew 5:34), must be taken literally and was a prohibition against all oath-taking. Calvin looking beyond such literalistic logic. He pointed to the purpose or intention that Christ had in giving this commandment, and proceeded with his exegesis, commenting: "Here, however, we shall never attain the truth unless we fix our eyes upon Christ's intention and give heed to what he is driving at in that passage" (II. viii. 26).

Calvin also followed the principle of seeking the divine intention when explaining the moral law found in the Ten Commandments. He wrote: "The commandments and prohibitions always contain more than is expressed in words" (II. viii. 8). But he inveighed against those who would use this principle with "wild, precipitate license" by which they would "degrade the authority of the law." He proposed rather that the responsible exegete "inquire how far interpretation ought to overstep the limits of the words themselves so that it may be seen to be, not an appendix added to the divine law from men's glosses, but the Lawgiver's pure and authentic meaning faithfully rendered" (II. viii. 8). Calvin directed attention toward "the reason of the commandment; that is, in each commandment to ponder why it was given to us." He believed that the truth of each commandment would become evident "if we look into the reason or purpose" for which it was given. Calvin looked for the intention of God in giving each law: "Thus in each commandment we must investigate what it is concerned with; then we must seek out its purpose, until we find what the Lawgiver testifies there to be pleasing or displeasing to himself." From his study of rhetoric, Calvin knew that bare literalism was not enough. One had to examine the figures of speech used in presenting a message. He stated: "Obviously, in almost all the commandments there are such manifest synecdoches that he who would confine his understanding of the law within the narrowness of the words deserves to be laughed at" (II. viii. 8).[189]

Accommodation

The concept of "accommodation" (Latin: *accommodare*) Calvin learned from the Latin rhetoricians and jurists.[190] In their usage it meant the process of fitting, adapting, and adjusting language to the capacity of the hearers.[191] It was a matter of building a language bridge between the content of the presentation and the capacity of the audience.[192] Jurisconsults used the term to refer to legal actions adapted to certain specific cases. For these ancients, "accommodation" always had to do with the adaptation of the verbal message to the makeup of the persons being addressed, taking account of their situation, character, intelligence, and emotional state.[193]

As we have observed, most of the early church fathers used the concept of accommodation when dealing with difficulties in the Bible. Calvin expanded on and used the accommodation principle as a consistent basis for not only handling difficulties in Scripture, but also explaining every relationship between God and humankind.[194] Calvin knew there was a great gulf between the highly educated and the comparatively unlearned, between the believer and the unconvinced. It was the task of rhetoric to bridge that gap through the use of simple, appropriate language so that the views of the speaker were persuasively presented. Analogously, the divine rhetoric bridged the infinitely greater gulf between God and humanity through the divine condescension to speak and act in human forms. The divinely appointed human authors of the Bible expressed the divine message under the Spirit's guidance in human forms of thought and speech so that all could benefit.[195] For Calvin, accommodation was the clue to the interpretation of Scripture and thus to the understanding of God's relationship to all of reality.[196]

Certain considerations followed from Calvin's commitment to the accommodation principle[197] as a fundamental component of his under-standing of the nature of God's revelation and of the theologian's task in communicating it.[198] One consideration was that language (form) was always subordinate to content (function). Augustine had made this same discovery after at first being offended by the "rude and barbarous lan-guage" of the biblical writers.[199] Calvin declared that his heart had become "captivated with admiration for Scripture more by grandeur of subjects than by grace of language" (I. viii. 1). For him, "the force of the truth of Sacred Scripture is manifestly too powerful to need the art of words." The Bible's truth "is cleared of all doubt when, not sustained by external props, it serves as its own support" (I. viii. 1).

For Calvin, it was not the style but the content of the Bible that was decisive for us.[200] The variety of forms of writing in Scripture, "crude" and "unrefined" as they were, paled into insignificance for Calvin in light of the biblical message itself. The form of human language did nothing to inhibit the communication of the divine message. Human, imperfect language was the divinely chosen vehicle by which God had revealed the knowledge of himself.[201] God chose to use human forms of thought and speech out of love for his children. In Jesus Christ's taking on human form, we see God's divine condescension "par excellence."[202] When our concentration becomes misplaced and we focus more on the form than on the function of Scripture, then, according to Calvin, we miss the insight that accommodated language is meant to point beyond itself to God, who is spoken of humanly as our Father, Teacher, and Physician.[203]

The insights Calvin derived from his humanist training in both the legal and rhetorical traditions helped form his view of the authority of the Bible and how it was to be interpreted. Calvin had derived from his classical education insights that enabled him to accept the accommodat-ed character of biblical language, a concentration on the intent of the author rather than the form of words, and a concern for the cultural context in which the Divine message was encased. A further determinative aspect of Calvin's humanist education was the influence of a Platonic-Augustinianism on his theological method.

Faith, Reason, and Scripture

Renaissance Platonism was a potent intellectual force in Calvin's day.[204] The Christian humanist tradition of Erasmus made a clear distinction between Plato and Aristotle and sought to emphasize the close relationship between Plato and Christianity. Plato was the humanists' champion in the struggle against Aristotelian scholasticism.[205]

Of the ancient philosophers, Calvin viewed Plato as one of the "sounder class." He described Plato as "the most religious of all and the most circumspect."[206] Although he shunned Plato as a source for his theology, he did confess that Plato knew something about holiness.[207] On the other hand, Calvin quoted Aristotle less than twenty times in the *Institutes.* He apparently knew Aristotle's work well but did not find in Aristotle the spiritual aspiration that was such an appealing dimension of Plato's thought.[208] Plato was the philosopher most cited by Calvin, just as Augustine was the theologian Calvin most preferred.[209] One should not exaggerate Plato's influence on Calvin, however, since Calvin accepted no philosopher or theologian uncritically.[210] Nevertheless, Calvin's theological method was indebted at significant points to Platonism.[211]

Among the church fathers, it was certainly to Augustine that Calvin owed the most. Yet, while constantly acknowledging his debt to Augustine, Calvin did not in the least exempt Augustine's opinions from the test of Scripture. In a creative and critical way, Calvin represented the culmination of the later Augustinian influence.[212] Methodologically he adopted Augustine's basic view of the relationship between faith and reason, following the Augustinian "faith leads to understanding" pattern.

For Calvin, all persons had an inborn knowledge of God. He said: "There is within the human mind, and indeed by natural instinct, an awareness of divinity" (I. iii. 1).[213] It was, he believed, "beyond controversy," that there lay "a sense of deity inscribed in the hearts of all" (I. iii. 1). Calvin called this "a sense of divinity which can never be effaced ... engraved upon men's minds" (I. iii. 3), and "a seed of religion" sown by God in "all men" (I. vi 1).

Calvin did not draw only on Plato's concept of innate ideas, however. He also held to Augustine's notion of original sin. Thus, innate knowledge of God, for Calvin, was suppressed by humans, leaving them responsible for their sinful condition. Calvin wrote:

59423

To prevent anyone from taking refuge in the pretense of ignorance, God himself has implanted in all men a certain understanding of his divine majesty. Ever renewing its memory, he repeatedly sheds fresh drops. Since, therefore, men one and all perceive that there is a God and that he is their Maker, they are condemned by their own testimony because they have failed to honor him and to consecrate their lives to his will (I. iii. 1).

Unlike the scholastics, Calvin was not interested in "idle speculations" that asked: "What is God?" Instead, he felt that "it is more important for us to know of what sort he is and what is consistent with his nature" (I. ii. 2). The knowledge Calvin was concerned with was the kind of knowledge that led to worshipping God rightly and living obediently before him. He was primarily interested in knowledge of our relationship to God, and asked rhetorically: "What help is it, in short, to know a God with whom we have nothing to do?" (I. ii. 2). Calvin's thrust was toward a personal and practical notion of knowledge. He wrote:

Now, the knowledge of God, as I understand it, is that by which we not only conceive that there is a God but also grasp what befits us and is proper to his glory, in fine, what is to our advantage to know of him. Indeed, we shall not say that, properly speaking, God is known where there is no religion or piety.[214]

By "piety" Calvin meant "that reverence joined with love of God which the knowledge of his benefits induces."[215] The nature of pure and true religion for Calvin was "faith so joined with an earnest fear of God that this fear also embraces willing reverence, and carries with it such legitimate worship as is prescribed in the law" (I. ii. 2).

Calvin followed in the Augustinian tradition in believing that sin corrupted the whole person—mind as well as heart. Thus, the distorted knowledge of God that sinners had in their minds would not lead to a valid natural theology. The seed of religion was corrupted or smothered in all humans (I. iv. 1), partly by ignorance and partly by malice.

The innate knowledge of God in human beings was also inscribed by God on "all of His works" according to Calvin. God's whole "workmanship of the universe" and other "innumerable evidences both in heaven and on earth" declare "his wonderful wisdom" so that in reality, "men cannot open their eyes without being compelled to see him" (I. v. 1,2). But this external evidence was also to no avail. Of both internal and external knowledge of God, Calvin said that humans concealed the "signs of divinity" within themselves (I. v. 4). The evidence of God in creation did not achieve its purpose, for very few, in contemplating heaven and earth, think of their maker. Most "sit idly" by, choked by human superstitions and the errors of the philosophers (I. v. 11,12). All humans have shared in this defection from the one true God. Any sparks of divine knowledge kindled in people were smothered before their full light could shine.[216]

Calvin concluded that human beings were responsible for their sorry state. He affirmed: "But although we lack the natural ability to mount up unto the pure and clear knowledge of God, all excuse is cut off because the fault of dullness is within us" (I. v. 15). Because humans sinfully suppressed this innate knowledge of their Creator, Calvin noted that God gave "another and better help" properly to direct us to God our Creator. The purpose of this further revelation was that God might "become known unto salvation" (I. vi. 1). The means of this revelation was Holy Scripture, which functioned as "spectacles":

> Just as old or bleary-eyed men and those with weak vision, if you thrust before them a most beautiful volume, even if they recognize it to be some sort of writing, yet can scarcely construe two words, but with the aid of spectacles will begin to read distinctly; so Scripture, gathering up the otherwise confused knowledge of God in our minds, having dispersed our dullness, clearly shows us the true God.[217]

Human sin made it necessary that God's "general revelation" in creation be made effective through his "special revelation" in Scripture. Therefore, in order to instruct his church, God "not merely uses mute teachers but also opens his own most hallowed lips" (I. vi. 1). Scripture, for Calvin, was the means by which persons came to the knowledge of God and of their salvation. Scripture, was the "Word of God" and was absolutely indispensable for knowledge of salvation and of how to live the Christian life. He declared that "no one can get even the slightest taste of right and sound doctrine unless he be a pupil of Scripture" (I. vi. 2).

In the earliest edition of Calvin's *Institutes* (1536) there was no formal statement of a doctrine of Scripture. In the 1536 edition Calvin's understanding of Scripture was subsumed under the heading of "Faith" in his second chapter. Calvin defined faith in terms of "hope and trust" in "God's good will toward us" which we could know by the promises in Scripture. He stated: "And this is indeed the head and almost the sum of all those things which the Lord by his sacred Word offers and promises us. This is the goal set for us in his Scriptures; this the target he sets."[218] For Calvin, the Bible was this "sacred Word" that persuaded people that God's truth would accomplish its purpose in bringing them to salvation. Calvin declared:

> The Word of God, therefore, is the object and target of faith at which one ought to aim; and the base to prop and support it, without which it could not even stand. And thus this true faith—which can at last be called "Christian"— is nothing else than a firm conviction of mind whereby we determine with

ourselves that God's truth is so certain that it is incapable of not accomplishing what it has pledged to do by his holy Word (Rom. 10:11).[219]

In the final Latin version of the *Institutes* (1559), Calvin dealt with the doctrine of Scripture in three separate sections. A balanced view of Calvin's theory about the Bible must cross-reference his statements from these three places in the 1559 edition: Book I, chapters vi–ix, on Scripture and the knowledge of God; Book III, chapter ii, on Scripture in the context of the redemptive work of the Holy Spirit; and Book V, chapter viii, on the inspiration and authority of Scripture. In addition, these theoretical statements in the *Institutes* must be correlated with the way in which Calvin used Scripture when doing exegesis as shown in his commentaries. Calvin's use of the Bible and his theory about it illumine one another because for him the doctrine of Scripture was tightly tied to the use of the Bible in the Christian community, in preaching and pastoral work in the church.

Calvin's original 1536 *Institutes* were written "to prepare and instruct candidates in sacred theology for the reading of the divine Word, in order that they may be able both to have easy access to it and to advance in it without stumbling."[220] By 1539, Calvin wrote that, given the "means and opportunity" he wished to publish some "interpretations of Scripture."[221] In January of 1551, his *Commentary on the Catholic Epistles* appeared. In his dedicatory letter to King Edward VI of England, Calvin attacked the Council of Trent for elevating tradition to a position of authority alongside Scripture and thus of losing a sure foundation for theology. Protestants, Calvin felt, had to restore a biblical foundation to theology.[222] The exposition of Scripture was a life and death matter. The very existence of the Christian church itself was at stake.

Calvin went about his work as a biblical theologian. His use of Scripture in preaching, and his published exegetical commentaries on Scripture, must be used in interpreting his dogmatic utterances about the Bible in the *Institutes*.

Inner Testimony of the Holy Spirit

"Who can convince us that these writings came from God?" Calvin felt that even to ask such a question was to "mock the Holy Spirit" (I. vii. 1). To ask for proof of the authority of Scripture was like asking: "Whence will we learn to distinguish light from darkness, white from black, sweet from bitter?" (I. vii. 2). The answer, for Calvin, was self-evident: "Indeed, Scripture exhibits fully as clear evidence of its own truth as white and black things do of their color, or sweet and bitter things do of their taste" (I. vii. 2). Calvin thus followed Plato in accepting the notion of innate ideas, and Augustine in assuming that God had already planted a knowledge of himself in human hearts.

According to Calvin, the persuasion that God was the author of Scripture was established in people by the internal testimony of the Holy Spirit (*testimonium Spiritus Sancti internum*). Calvin declared: "We ought to seek our conviction in a higher place than human reasons, judgments, or conjectures, that is, in the secret testimony of the Spirit."[223] Calvin's antischolastic attitude was explicit when he criticized men who "both wish and demand rational proof that Moses and the prophets spoke divinely" (I. vii. 4).[224] Calvin placed himself firmly in the Platonic-Augustinian tradition when he said: "But I reply: the testimony of the Spirit is more excellent than all reason" (I. vii. 4). Calvin repeated that theme in a variety of ways. He proclaimed:

> The Word will not find acceptance in men's hearts before it is sealed by the inward testimony of the Spirit. The same Spirit, therefore, who has spoken through the mouths of the prophets must penetrate into our hearts to persuade us that they faithfully proclaimed what had been divinely commanded.[225]

Scripture, for Calvin, was "self-authenticated" (Gr. *autopiston*), and "hence, it was not right to subject it to proof and reasoning" (I. vii. 5). It was the Holy Spirit who "seals" Scripture in our hearts and

> therefore, illumined by his power, we believe neither by our own nor by anyone else's judgment that Scripture is from God; but above human judgment we affirm with utter certainty (just as if we were gazing upon the majesty of God himself) that it has flowed to us from the very mouth of God by the ministry of men. We seek no proofs, no marks of genuineness upon which our judgment may lean; but we subject our judgment and wit to it as to a thing far beyond any guesswork! (I. vii. 5).

Through the witness of the biblical writers, the Spirit works "a conviction that requires no reasons" and yet produces a certainty that makes persons feel that "the undoubted power of his divine majesty lives and breathes there" in the Bible. This, for Calvin, was what "each believer experiences within himself" (I. vii. 5).

According to Calvin, "Scripture will ultimately suffice for a saving knowledge of God only when its certainty is founded upon the inward persuasion of the Holy Spirit" (I. viii. 13). "Human testimonies," which are meant to confirm Scripture's authority, "will not be vain if, as secondary aids to our feebleness, they follow that chief and highest testimony."[226] Among such "human arguments" that Calvin considered useful for believers were: the unique majesty and impressiveness, and high antiquity of Scripture (I. viii. 1–4); miracles and prophecy (sec. 5–10); simplicity and heavenly character and authority of the New Testament (sec. 11); and the universal consent of the church and fidelity of the martyrs (secs. 12–13). For Calvin these "arguments" for the credibility of Scripture were "human judgments" that were "vain" arguments *in themselves.* Our faith in Scripture, according to Calvin, could be assisted by these arguments, but only *after* we believed in Christ and accepted the authority of the biblical witness to him under the leading of the Holy Spirit. After speaking of Scripture as a book bearing its own authentication, Calvin wrote:

> Unless this certainty, higher and stronger than human judgment, be present, it will be vain to fortify the authority of Scripture by arguments, to establish it by common agreement of the church, or to confirm it with other helps. For unless this foundation is laid, its authority will always remain in doubt. Conversely, once we have embraced it devoutly as its dignity deserves, and have recognized it to be above the common sort of things, those arguments—not strong enough before to engraft and fix the certainty of Scripture in our minds—become very useful aids.[227]

Calvin completely rejected the notion that rational proofs of the divinity of Scripture were necessary before one could have faith in it. He accepted, however, the encouragement such arguments could give to believers after their faith in Scripture had been established by contact with the Word itself and by consent to the inner witness of the Holy Spirit.[228]

Scripture could not be known as authoritative outside of faith in it, according to Calvin. Such a position clearly placed Calvin in the Augustinian stance of faith seeking understanding. It was the very antithesis of a blind faith alone. For Calvin faith was not a leap in the dark; it was not a passive acceptance of what the church taught as true. For Calvin, faith was a kind of knowledge—the personal knowledge of God's benevolence toward us. It was a personal trust in a personal God who had come to us in the person of Jesus Christ.[229]

Calvin wrote of faith: "We hold faith to be a knowledge of God's will toward us, perceived from his Word."[230] Yet for Calvin, "when we call faith 'knowledge' we do not mean comprehension of the sort that is commonly concerned with those things which fall under human sense perception" (III. ii. 14). Faith was concerned rather with that realm "above man's mind." It was *suprarational.* This kind of faith laid the groundwork for further understanding. Calvin stated:

> Even where the mind has attained, it does not comprehend what it feels. But while it is persuaded of what it does not grasp, by the very certainty of its persuasion it understands more than if it perceived anything human by its own capacity (III. ii. 14).

Faith was more than just an intellectual capacity or a feeling capacity for Calvin. It was a consent, a commitment of the whole person to a relationship of trust with a God who had proved Himself gracious in the person of Jesus Christ.[231] Calvin explicitly denied the scholastic notion that one had to have rational proofs before a personal response could be made. Calvin affirmed that believers "are more strengthened by the persuasion of divine truth than instructed by rational proof" and "the knowledge of faith consists in assurance rather than in comprehension" (III. ii. 14).

Calvin very consciously asserted a Platonic-Augustinian theological method that put faith before understanding over against the Aristotelian-Thomistic approach that put reasons before faith. Calvin stated bluntly: "But those who wish to prove to unbelievers that Scripture is the Word of God are acting foolishly, for only by faith can this be known."[232]

Calvin sought the Augustinian middle way in theological method. He fought against two extremes. He rejected the rationalistic scholasticism on the one side which demanded proofs prior to faith in Scripture. And he rejected with equal firmness the spiritualistic sectarians on the other side who claimed leadings of the Spirit apart from Scripture.

For Calvin, the Word and the Spirit belonged inseparably together. He explained:

> The Word itself is not quite certain for us unless it be confirmed by the testimony of the Spirit. . . . For by a kind of mutual bond the Lord has joined together the certainty of his Word and of his Spirit so that the perfect religion of the Word may abide in our minds when the Spirit, who causes us to contemplate God's face, shines; and that we in turn may embrace the Spirit with no fear of being deceived when we recognize him in his own image, namely, in the Word.[233]

The Holy Spirit, according to Calvin, "has not the task of inventing new and unheard-of revelations, or of forging a new kind of doctrine, to lead us away from the received doctrine of the gospel, but of sealing our minds with that very doctrine which is commended by the gospel" (I. ix. 1). For Calvin, the Spirit was the "Author of the Scriptures." Thus, the Spirit "cannot vary and differ from himself. . . . He must ever remain just as he once revealed himself there" (I. ix. 2). And the children of God, "know no other Spirit than him who dwelt and spoke in the apostles, and by whose oracles they are continually recalled to the hearing of the Word" (I. ix. 3).

Incarnational Interpretation of Scripture

For Calvin, all of Scripture was to be interpreted in relation to its purpose, which was to set forth Jesus Christ and His salvation. The central theme of the Bible was Jesus Christ. He was the object of the Christian's faith. Calvin taught: "The Son of God, then who is Jesus

Christ, holds out himself as the object (*scopum*) to which our faith ought to be directed, and by means of which it will easily find that on which it can rest."[234] Or again: "It is Christ alone on whom, strictly speaking, faith ought to look. . . . This . . . is the proper look of faith, to be fixed on ·Christ."[235] For Calvin, it was God's promise of grace in Christ (which was known through the Scriptures) that formed the "foundation of faith because upon it faith properly rests" (III. ii. 29). Calvin wrote: "when we say that faith must rest upon a freely given promise, we do not deny that believers embrace and grasp the Word of God in every respect: but we point out the promise of mercy as the proper goal of faith" (III. ii. 29).

Christ and Scripture were intimately interrelated for Calvin. He contended: "This, then, is the true knowledge of Christ, if we receive him as he is offered by the Father: namely, clothed with his gospel."[236] Since the promise of saving mercy was "the proper goal of faith," Calvin cautioned that we must not interpret Scripture as having any other purpose than of revealing Christ for our salvation. Calvin was clear that:

> we ought to believe that Christ cannot be properly known in any way than from the Scriptures; and if it be so, it follows that we ought to read the Scriptures with the express design of finding Christ in them. Whoever shall turn aside from this object, though he may weary himself throughout his whole life in learning, will never attain the knowledge of the truth; for what wisdom can we have without the wisdom of God?[237]

Calvin did not consider the Bible to have any other purpose, nor concede that the Bible could be interpreted by any other principle, than as the communication that God had come in Jesus Christ.[238]

God's revelation of himself in Christ was a model of God's method of communicating with us, according to Calvin. God accommodated himself to human beings' limited ability to understand him. In language borrowed from Chrysostom, Calvin announced:

> There are two reasons why there can be no faith in God, unless Christ put himself as it were in the middle (*quasi medius interveniat*), for we must first ponder the vastness of the divine glory and at the same time the slenderness of our understanding.[239]

And in language much like that of Origen, Calvin declared:

> All thinking about God, apart from Christ, is a bottomless abyss which utterly swallows up all our senses. . . . Hence it is clear that we cannot trust in God (*Deo credere*) save through Christ. In Christ God so to speak makes himself little (*quodammodo parvum facit*), in order to lower himself to our capacity (*ut se ad captum nostrum submittat*).[240]

God's incarnational style of communication was evident not only in the person of Christ, but in the language of the Bible according to Calvin.

While God's nature is infinite and spiritual, the Bible often represented God as having a mouth, ears, eyes, hands, and feet. Why did the Bible speak in this way? To Calvin, it was because God was communicating with people in accommodated language, adjusting Himself to human capacity. Calvin explained:

> For who even of slight intelligence does not understand that, as nurses commonly do with infants, God is wont in a measure to "lisp" in speaking to us? Thus such forms of speaking do not so much express clearly what God is like as accommodate the knowledge of him to our slight capacity. To do this he must descend far beneath his loftiness.[241]

In both the concept of accommodation, and the parental imagery, Calvin was following the early church fathers. He quoted Augustine approvingly:

> For Augustine also skillfully expressed this idea: we can safely follow Scripture, which proceeds at the pace of a mother stooping to her child, so to speak, so as not to leave us behind in our weakness.[242]

God's method, for Calvin, was "to represent himself to us not as he is in himself, but as he seems to us."[243]

It was not necessary for us to know God as he is in himself, but only to know him as he relates to us, according to Calvin. So also, it was not necessary for God to use precise forms of words. God's saving message was adequately communicated in all the varieties of normal human speech. Calvin asserted:

> It is a very common fault that men want to be taught subtly and scholastically. . . . But how wicked it is for us to yield less reverence to God's speaking because he lowers Himself to our ignorance! Let us know that it is for our sakes that the Lord prattles with us in Scripture in an awkward and common style.[244]

For Calvin, God, as revealed in Scripture, was like a Father, Teacher, and Physician, always taking into account the conditions of his children, pupils, and patients; always nourishing, tutoring, and prescribing according to human needs.[245] For Calvin:

> God, it is true, fills both heaven and earth; but as we cannot attain to that infinite height to which He is exalted, in descending among us by the exercise of His power and grace, He approaches as near to us as is needful, and as our limited capacity will bear.[246]

Calvin knew that what human beings needed was a saving relationship to God and guidance in living the life of faith.

For Calvin, accommodation was a pastoral approach for the building up of believers.[247] The early church fathers had used the notion of accommodation as a means of explaining anthropomorphisms and resolving inconsistencies in the biblical record. Calvin used accommodation to deal with issues such as God's nature (I. xiii. 1); the creation of angels (I. xiv. 3); the function of angels (I. xiv. 11); fate (I. xvi. 9); and God's ways with humans, including questions such as Does God repent? (I. xvii. 12f.). He sometimes began his discussion as an apologist for Scripture. But then he would shift the mode by using the instrument of accommodation to instruct people for their edification.[248] Calvin's pastoral concern was evidenced in these instances. His rhetorical training made Calvin concerned to adapt to the needs of his readers and to show them how God had also condescended to human ways in order to lead people to salvation.

The Concept of Error

Given Calvin's understanding of the accommodated nature of God's communication in Scripture, it is not surprising that Calvin was unconcerned with normal, human inaccuracies in minor matters. For example, Calvin noted that Paul misquoted Psalm 51:4 in Romans 3:4. Calvin generalized about such inaccuracies:

> We know that, in quoting Scripture the apostles often used freer language than the original, since they were content if what they quoted applied to their subject, and therefore they were not over-careful in their use of words.[249]

Similarly in Calvin's commentary on Hebrews 10:6, he affirmed that the saving purpose of the biblical message was adequately communicated through an imperfect form of words:

> They (the apostles) were not overscrupulous in quoting words provided that they did not misuse Scripture for their convenience. We must always look at the purpose for which quotations are made . . . but as far as the words are concerned, as in other things which are not relevant to the present purpose, they allow themselves some indulgence.[250]

Calvin's training as a humanist rhetorician helped him to understand that the Bible's purpose was to persuade persons to be saved. It was not necessary that the Scripture display an exact, technical accuracy. Rather, God had chosen, as a human orator would, to use normal human means of communication, with all of their human weaknesses, to meet human beings at their point of need for God's grace.

Calvin did not think that an exact correspondence was necessary between the literal meaning of an Old Testament passage and its use in the New Testament. In his commentary on Hebrews 2:7, Calvin acknowledged that some felt that the phrase "a little lower than the angels" was not used by the author of Hebrews in the same sense as David had meant it in Psalm 8. Calvin responded:

> I answer that it was not the purpose of the apostle to give an accurate exposition of the words. There is nothing improper if he looks for allusions in the words to embellish the case he is presenting.[251]

Calvin manifested the same attitude in his treatment of Romans 10:6 regarding the phrase: "Say not in thy heart, Who shall ascend?" Against those who questioned the propriety of Paul's application of these words from Deuteronomy 30:12 to the death and resurrection of Christ, Calvin countered:

> If it is alleged that this interpretation is too forced and subtle, we should understand that the object of the Apostle was not to explain this passage exactly, but only to apply it to his treatment of the subject at hand. He does not, therefore, repeat what Moses has said syllable by syllable, but employs a gloss, by which he adapts the testimony of Moses more closely to his own purpose.[252]

Calvin understood Paul to be a preacher of the Good News of Christ, not an historian or linguist concerned with transmitting a past document with minute accuracy. Indeed, Calvin viewed the whole Bible as Good News from a gracious God, communicated in the normal and limited manner of human communication.

The divine character of the biblical message was absolutely unaffected for Calvin the believer when Calvin the scholar discerned technical inaccuracies in the humanly written text. In his commentary on Acts 7:16, Calvin declared that Luke had "made a manifest error" as comparison with the text of Genesis 23:9 showed.[253] As a devout and scholarly student of Scripture, Calvin wrestled with many problems in the biblical text. He did not shrink from facing problems such as the Davidic authorship of the Psalms and the authorship of 2 Peter and Hebrews. He saw and dealt openly with many textual problems in his *Harmony of the first four Books of Moses*, and his *Harmony of the Synoptic Gospels*. For example, in the latter he commented on Matthew 27:9 that "Zechariah" should be read there instead of "Jeremiah" and concluded:

> How the name of Jeremiah crept in, I confess that I do not know, nor do I give myself much trouble to inquire. The passage itself plainly shows that the name of Jeremiah has been put down by mistake, instead of Zechariah (xi.13) for in *Jeremiah* we find nothing of this sort, not any thing that even approaches to it.[254]

For Calvin, technical errors in the Bible that were the result of human slips of memory, limited knowledge, or the use of texts for different purposes than the original were all part of the normal human means of communication. They did not call into question the divine character of Scripture's message. Nor did they hinder the completely adequate communication of God's Word. In fact, they enhanced the telling of the Good News because they were part of God's gracious accommodation of himself to human means and thus made the message more persuasive to human beings. Scholars could and should deal openly and honestly with technical problems according to Calvin's theory and his own practice.

Calvin would not allow, however, that a biblical writer had ever deliberately lied, or knowingly told an untruth. Error in the moral and ethical realm was far removed from the biblical writers. An evidence of Calvin's extreme sensitivity in this matter is provided in his encounter with Michael Servetus. Servetus had produced an edition of Ptolemy's *Geography*. Servetus included in it a statement taken over from another author's work on the subject that it was "sheer misrepresentation" to say that Palestine was a land flowing with milk and honey. Calvin understood Servetus to be alleging that Moses had deliberately lied, that is, that Moses knew that Palestine was actually barren and sterile, but wrote that it was a fertile land. Calvin charged that Servetus had attributed the phrase "vain preacher of Judaea" to Moses. Although Servetus stated that he had not written the original statement, Calvin was not satisfied. And when Servetus responded that there was really nothing wrong with the passage, Calvin was furious.[255] The fact that Calvin apparently misunderstood some of the facts of the case is not at issue here. We are interested in noting his rejection of any attribution of ethical deceit to the biblical writers. Calvin's attitude toward error was equivalent to Augustine's approach, as discussed earlier. Both theologians rejected the notion that the biblical writers had ever intentionally told untruths in communicating the saving message entrusted to them. That was a completely different matter, for both Augustine and Calvin, than the fact that the biblical writers were limited and conditioned by their historical context and that they made technical mistakes in writing as all normal human beings do. Augustine and Calvin were both rhetoricians who concentrated on the saving function of Scripture as the locus of its authority. They dealt with the forms of words in the Bible according to the best scholarship available to them. The Divine purpose for which the Bible was authoritative was not dependent on having a divine form of words. The words were part of the human, accommodated style of God's gracious disclosure of himself to humankind.

Just as Calvin did not expect the Bible to be a repository of technically accurate information on language or history, neither did he expect that the biblical data should be used to question the findings of science. Calvin did not feel that the Bible's teaching had to be harmonized with science. The purpose of Scripture was to bring persons into a right relationship with God and their fellow creatures. Science was in another sphere and was to be judged by its own criteria. In his commentary on Genesis 1:14–16, Calvin faced the issue of the relationship of the Bible to the science of his day. The problem to some people was that the moon was spoken of in the Bible as being one of the two great lights, with the stars being mentioned only incidentally. Astronomers of Calvin's day had proved that Saturn, because of its great distance from earth appeared to be a lesser light than the moon, but was really a greater light. Calvin observed:

> It must be remembered, that Moses does not speak with philosophical acuteness on occult mysteries, but relates those things which are everywhere observed, even by the uncultivated, and which are in common use.... For Moses here addresses himself to our senses, that the knowledge of the gifts of God which we enjoy may not glide away.... By this method (as I have before observed) the dishonesty of those men is sufficiently rebuked, who censure Moses for not speaking with greater exactness. For as it became a theologian, he had respect to us rather than to the stars.[256]

Moses' comments on the natural world were, of course, an example of accommodated communication from God. There was no reason to suppose that Moses knew any more or thought any differently about the natural order than other people of his time and culture. Moses' purpose was not to teach something about natural science. His intent was to benefit his hearers in their life of faith, not to expound scientific matters with technical accuracy. Thus, Calvin noted that Moses "had respect to us rather than to the stars." Calvin continued:

> Moses wrote in a popular style things which, without instruction, all ordinary persons, endued with common sense are able to understand; but astronomers investigate with great labor whatever the sagacity of the human mind can comprehend. Nevertheless, this study is not to be reprobated, nor this science to be condemned.... For astronomy is not only pleasant, but also very useful to be known.... Nor did Moses truly wish to withdraw us from this pursuit.... Had he spoken of things generally unknown, the uneducated might have pleaded in excuse that such subjects were beyond their capacity.[257]

Matters of science, language, and history were all understood by Calvin from the perspective of God's incarnational, accommodated style of communication. The main message of salvation and the Christian life was adequately, indeed admirably, made clear in the biblical writings. The various kinds of scholarly problems that were raised by a serious study of the text could be dealt with by scholarly means. The human form of the biblical record could and should be studied by human means in order to come to a fuller understanding of the human context of the Divine message.

Questions of creation, science, anthropomorphic language, the relationship of the Old and New Testaments, even questions of doctrine, were handled by Calvin under the rubric of accommodation. A notable example is found in Calvin's recognition of problems in harmonizing the various accounts in the Synoptic Gospels.[258] Calvin simply investigated the matter as a humanist scholar would, and, as a believer, assumed that the Holy Spirit had submitted to us an admirable consensus regarding the central message of Scripture through these diverse forms of writing.[259]

The limitations, not only of biblical words but of a preacher's words, were no hindrance to adequate communication of the Divine message, for Calvin. Preaching of the Word of God *was* the Word of God for him.[260] When the preacher proclaimed the Word, it was as if the congregation "heard the very words pronounced by God himself."[261] A person "preaches so that God may speak to us by the mouth of a man" according to Calvin.[262] Calvin asked rhetorically, "What is the mouth of God?" He answered: "It is a declaration that he makes to us of his will, when he speaks to us by his ministers."[263] Calvin asserted that when humans were preaching God's Word, "Christ acts by them in such a manner that he wishes their *mouth* to be reckoned as His *mouth,* and their *lips* as His *lips,*" that is, when they faithfully declare God's Word (Luke x.16).[264] For Calvin, preaching was another form of God's accommodation, His condescension to communicate with humans in a human way. Calvin said of God that "He also provides for our weakness in that he prefers to address us in human fashion through interpreters in order to draw us to himself."[265]

Calvin stressed the very human means by which God's Word came to His people. God had chosen human beings to write His Scripture and to preach His Word. God used humans "that through their mouths he may do his own work—just as a workman uses a tool to do his work" (IV. iii. 1). Neither human preachers nor human writers were always technically accurate. They made human mistakes. But for Calvin, God had chosen to use human agency as the means to accomplish His purposes (IV. iii. 14). Calvin's understanding of the divine intention to use human agency is the necessary background for understanding passages where Calvin spoke of the prophets writing "under the Holy Spirit's dictation" (IV. viii. 6), and of the apostles as "sure and genuine scribes of the Holy Spirit" (IV. viii. 9).[266] Calvin was referring to the divine content of the message transmitted by the prophets and the apostles rather than asserting that the means of transmission were lifted above the possibility of human error. Any assumption that the author's full human personality was overwhelmed, or that the products of human writing were somehow exempted from human error in their form was totally foreign to Calvin's thought. Like Chrysostom, his tutor in exegetical matters, Calvin understood the need for a response on the human writer's part to God's guidance. God used the biblical writers precisely so that His Word might come to us in truly *human* language and forms of thought.[267]

Biblical Exegesis

Calvin examined the human form of Scripture with the best scholarly tools available to him. Having an internal confidence in the Bible's authority, because of the testimony of the Holy Spirit, he did not hesitate to seek understanding of the text through study. Calvin was not a leading but a competent linguist and historian. He used the most reliable work of other scholars at his disposal: Budé on Greek and Erasmus's *Annotations on the New Testament.*[268]

Among the church fathers, Calvin declared Augustine to be without peer as a teacher of doctrine, but acknowledged Chrysostom to be superior as a biblical expositor. Consequently, Calvin turned to Augustine for theology and Chrysostom for biblical exegesis. Calvin felt Augustine was too wordy as an exegete and ranged too far from the text. Calvin wrote:

> Augustine is beyond question the greatest of all in dogmas of faith; he is also outstanding as a devotional interpreter of Scripture; but he is oversubtle, with the result that he is less solid and dependable.[269]

Of Augustine Calvin often said: "What Augustine says is true, but it is not relevant to this passage" or "This is a godly observation, but it has nothing to do with Paul's meaning." On the whole, Augustine was "over subtle," or "too verbose in his method."[270]

In contrast, Calvin did not always agree with Chrysostom's theological conclusions, but he did appreciate Chrysostom's exegetical method. Calvin wrote a Latin preface to a projected French translation of Chrysostom's homilies. In it Calvin stated:

> The outstanding merit of our author, Chrysostom, is that it was his supreme concern always not to turn aside even to the slightest degree from the genuine, simple sense of Scripture and to allow himself no liberties by twisting the plain meaning of the words.[271]

Calvin greatly valued the fact that Chrysostom refused to engage in flights of fanciful, allegorical exegesis. Chrysostom kept to the straightforward meaning of the text in its immediate context, and in this Calvin followed him.[272] Chrysostom had attained two goals to which Calvin dedicated himself. One was that Chrysostom never strayed from a clear elaboration and explanation of the biblical text. The second was that Chrysostom spoke with the common people in mind.[273]

Chrysostom's example lay behind Calvin's two principal requirements for excellence in exegesis: *brevitas* and *facilitas*.[274] *Brevitas* meant that Calvin wished to avoid lengthy commentary that would only exhaust the reader. *Facilitas* meant that he wanted to avoid the discussions of other commentators and come as quickly as possible to the primary meaning of the text.[275] Calvin thus sought the natural and obvious meaning of the text in its context rather than employing allegorical speculation.[276] He branded allegory as a "most disastrous error" and "the source of many evils."[277] Allegorical exegesis was to Calvin a violation of the real sense of Scripture. It evidenced a desire for mysteries deeper than those present in the text itself.[278] Calvin's view was that the plain, genuine, literal, or native sense of Scripture was the record and interpretation of God's revelation and that it was unnecessary to seek another, allegorical meaning.[279] For Calvin, the commentator's primary duty was to reveal the mind of the writer as expressed in the text as clearly and succinctly as possible.[280]

Brevitas and *facilitas* also led Calvin to oppose the Aristotelian rationalistic exegesis that was developing among some of the Reformers, (for example, Melanchthon, Bullinger, Bucer). After examining the commentaries of Melanchthon and Bucer on Romans, Calvin rejected their methodology and set out to develop his own middle way, between what he considered were their excesses in opposite directions.

Melanchthon's method was unacceptable to Calvin because the Lutheran chose to comment only on certain texts that seemed to him to be of worth. Consequently, "he therefore dwells at length on these, and deliberately passes over many matters which can cause great trouble to those of average understanding."[281] Melanchthon's *Loci* ("Topics") while shedding light in necessary places, nevertheless neglected many other issues that needed attention. Calvin feared that the Aristotelian method of Melanchthon could lead to an arbitrary choice of *loci*—one not based on the text, but imposed on it. He also felt that the Aristotelian approach tended to universalize the historical circumstances and cover over delicate nuances of meaning. A danger existed, according to Calvin, that the authors intentions would be treated only as stepping-stones to concepts that were assumed to lie beyond them.[282]

Bucer's excesses went in the opposite direction from those of Melanchthon, but were just as unacceptable to Calvin. Whereas Melanchthon was too arbitarily selective, Bucer was "too verbose to be read quickly by those who have other matters to deal with, and too profound to be easily understood by less intelligent and attentive readers." The length and difficulty of Bucer's comments erected a barrier between the reader and the text in Calvin's view. Calvin responded by comparing Melanchthon and Bucer and explaining his dissatisfaction with their methods. He wrote: "The one did not explain everything; the other explained everything too fully for anyone to be able to read him through quickly."[283]

Calvin's own solution to the problem of achieving comprehensiveness and succinctness was to prepare two different kinds of expositions of biblical truth. He dealt with the "sum of religion" in his *Institutes*. It was there that he undertook "long doctrinal discussion."[284] His expositions of the text of Scripture were given in the form of commentaries written according to the principles of *brevitas* and *facilitas*. The commentaries omitted extensive treatment of the views of other authors.[285] Calvin regarded his *Institutes* and *Commentaries* as complementary works. In both he sought the knowledge of God and he sought to exercise his "gift of interpretation (1 Cor. 12:10) which sheds light upon the word" (IV. xvii. 25).

In summary, then, for Calvin, the Bible was God's Word. But he knew that God did not address human beings directly with divine words. God used human means to communicate his Divine message. The incarnation of Christ was the model of God's method of indirect communication through creaturely means. Thus, the biblical material needed to be studied and understood by the same scholarly means through which all human documents were studied and understood. The humanness of the biblical literature was no hindrance, but the appropriate and adequate vehicle through which God's Divine message could best be communicated to limited and sinful human beings. Calvin did not think it inconsistent to affirm that the apostles were secretaries of the Holy Spirit and at the same time to note grammatical weaknesses or historical inaccuracies in their writings. God, like a good parent, had willingly condescended, adapted, and accommodated himself to the language and thought forms of his children. And God was perfectly able to use these imperfect human forms to communicate his Divine message to people. In Calvin, the humanist scholar had become the Christian theologian.[286]

d. The Reformed Confessions: Swiss, French, Scots, and Belgic

During the sixteenth century, as the Reformation became indigenous in various parts of Europe, local communities, from cities to nations, drew up their own confessions of faith. These statements, sometimes called "symbols," revealed a deep interest in the Bible and its foundational authority for Christian faith. The Reformed Confessions sometimes expressed this concern by devoting a separate article to the doctrine of Scripture. At other times the concern implicitly permeated the whole confession as the Scriptures were assumed to be *the* supreme authority for salvation and the life of the Church.[287]

The sixteenth-century Reformed Confessions, stemming from Calvin's influence, exhibited three differences from Lutheran Confessions of the same period.[288] In the Reformed Confessions, a list of canonical books delineating the documents of Scripture was frequently presented at the beginning. Often this was accompanied by a phrase maintaining that these books were the "Word of God," given by "the inspiration of the Holy Spirit." In the Lutheran Confessions, no such listing was given. The other differences are that in Lutheran Confessions there was no stated doctrine of the inspiration of Scripture. And, in Lutheran Confessions there was also no mention of the special activity of the Holy Spirit in the process of the canonization of the specific biblical books.[289]

Despite these disparities, Reformed and Lutheran Confessions agreed that the authority of Scripture stood supreme over against the authority of any human confession or tradition. The Reformers did not exempt themselves from the possibility of error and asked to be judged by Scripture.

The Reformed Confessions repudiated the Roman Catholic insistence on tradition as a second source of revelation parallel with Scripture.[290] Article I of the Geneva Confession of 1536 put it clearly: "We affirm and desire to follow Scripture alone as rule of faith and religion, without mixing with it any other thing which might be devised by the opinion of men apart from the Word of God" (compare Art. 5 of the French Confession and the preface to the Scots Confession).

Zwingli's Sixty-Seven Articles (1523)

An explicit statement on Scripture was introduced in Zwingli's "Sixty-Seven Articles" of 1523. In his preface, Zwingli proclaimed that the doctrines he preached were formulated "on the basis of the Scripture which is called *theopneustos* (inspired by God)." He expressed his willingness to debate the matters and to be "instructed and corrected, but only from the aforesaid Scripture."

Zwingli's first article: "All who say that the Gospel is nothing without the approbation of the Church err and slander God" rejected the Roman Catholic position. This statement was put at the beginning of his Articles so that opponents of the Gospel would be compelled to argue with him from the Bible without the aid of human teaching.[291] Previous to these articles, Zwingli had written:

> The Word of God ought to be held by us in the highest honor—and by 'Word of God' understand only that which comes from the Spirit of God—and such faith given to no word as to it. For the Word of God is certain and cannot fail; it is bright and does not let man err in darkness; it teaches of itself, it makes itself plain, and illumines the human soul with all salvation and grace.[292]

Zwingli regarded the Scriptures as clearly authoritative, and a textual citation in an argument was decisive for him. The Scripture was "inspired," but Zwingli gave no theory as to how inspiration took place or of its extent. He cared only for the result: a "certain" Word of God which "does not let man err in darkness." In his Articles, Zwingli's emphasis was on the saving message of the Gospel, which was transmitted through the Scriptures, and which called men and women to faith in Jesus Christ (Art. XV).

The Ten Theses of Berne (1528)

In the Ten Theses of Berne, 1528, articles I and II mentioned the "Word of God" through whom the voice of the Head of the Church Jesus Christ was communicated. His Word was the basis for all laws and commandments in the church. Here Scripture was seen as the way through which the will of Christ was made known. In Article IV the basis of teaching about the Eucharist was declared to be in "the biblical writings." Article V spoke against the mass as being "contrary to Scripture" and in Article VI the same argument was used against any other mediator than Jesus Christ. The seventh article rejected purgatory since "Scripture knows nothing of a purgatory." In Article IX the opposite method was employed, stating that marriage was not forbidden since it was "not forbidden in Scripture." And in Article X, Scripture was put forth as the authority for thinking that adultery and fornication were worse for the clergy than for "any other class of men." The Theses were concluded with a resounding: "May all things be to the honor of God and His holy Word!"

The Tetrapolitan Confession (1530)

In the Tetrapolitan Confession of 1530, the first chapter dealt with the "Subject-Matter of Sermons." Preachers were enjoined to preach and teach from the pulpit "nothing else than is either contained in the Holy

Scriptures or hath sure ground therein." It announced that in time of crisis the church had resorted back to the "authority of Holy Scriptures" wishing to regain the preaching of "the doctrine of Christ." Sound doctrine and Christian truth came only from those who "ask counsel of Scripture." It is noteworthy that this confession joined the theological issue of Scripture and its inspiration (quoting 2 Tim. 3:16) with the very practical issue of preaching sermons.

The First Confession of Basel (1534)

The First Confession of Basel, 1534, offered no article on Holy Scripture but ended with the expressed desire

> to submit this our confession to the judgment of the divine Biblical Scriptures. And should we be informed from the same Holy Scriptures of a better one, we have thereby expressed our readiness to be willing at any time to obey God and His holy Word with great thanksgiving.

The presupposition of the whole confession was thus stated in the last article.

The First Helvetic Confession (1536)

In the First Helvetic Confession, 1536, "holy, divine Biblical Scripture inspired by the Holy Spirit and delivered to the world by the prophets and apostles" was named the "Word of God." This symbol affirmed that Scripture guided persons to the true knowledge, love and honor of God, dealing as it does with everything reaching toward that end as well as of "true piety, and the making of a godly, honest and blessed life." (Art. I) In support of these statements, the authors attached "proof texts." The way to interpret Scripture was not by means of rigid logic, but rather "by the rule of faith and love." Early Christian teachers followed this course, the confession noted, and as such were "elect instruments" through whom God operated. All other human doctrines were declared "vile and ineffectual." The purpose (*scopus*) of Holy Scripture was the salvation of persons. The confession urged "that man understand that God is kind and gracious to him and that he publicly demonstrated and exhibited His kindness to the whole human race through Christ His Son." This understanding came from faith alone and showed itself in love for the neighbor. This "purpose" of Scripture was very much the same as in the statement of Article XII on the "Purpose of Evangelical Doctrine": "That we are preserved and saved solely by the one mercy of God and by the merit of Christ."

The Lausanne Articles (1536)

In the Lausanne Articles, 1536, articles I–III began with words about "Scripture" while articles IV–X spoke first of the church. Scripture was affirmed as the source "which teaches only one way of justification, which is by faith in Jesus Christ." Article V maintained that the only valid ministry the church recognized was one that "preaches the Word of God and administers the sacraments," thus continuing in the tradition of Calvin.[293] The emphasis in Article VII was on the practical effects of the Word of God in the ministry of the church, which consisted in the love of God and love of neighbor. This was opposed to any merely "religious" ceremony as a means of serving God.

The Geneva Confession (1536)

The Geneva Confession of 1536 began with an article on the Word of God saying that it alone was "the rule of faith and religion." The one God whom humankind was to "worship and serve" and "place our confidence and trust in" was made known in the Holy Scriptures (Art. II). Faithful pastors were those who preached the Word of God "without mixing the pure doctrine of the Scriptures with their dreams or their foolish imaginings" (Art. XX).

The Confession of Faith of the English Congregation at Geneva (1556)

The Confession of Faith used in the English Congregation at Geneva, 1556, dealt with the question of the Scriptures in the midst of its Article IV on the church. The sufficiency of the Scriptures (Old and New Testaments) for salvation was proclaimed, and this Word of God was indicated as one of the three marks or tokens whereby the visible church could be known (along with the Sacraments and Church Discipline). The Scripture's authority was in its ability to instruct on matters of salvation. In this realm, the Bible's authority stood over and above the authority of any church. Without this Word, no Church, council or decree can establish any point concerning salvation."

The French Confession of Faith (1559)

In the French Confession of 1559, a new element entered. The revelation of God "in his works, in their creation, as well as in their preservation and control" was affirmed as a source of the knowledge of God. The declaration was qualified, however, by the statement that the revelation of God was exhibited "more clearly in His Word," now committed to writing in the Holy Scriptures. The canonical Scriptures were listed book by book (excluding any mention of the Apocrypha). Their canonical status was not validated by church councils but "by the testimony and inward illumination of the Holy Spirit." Thus the Spirit served a double function, in this confession, of enlightening persons to faith in the Gospel (XXI) and of guiding their acceptance of the books of the Bible as God's Word (IV). The Bible was asserted to be the judge of all other authorities. The three articles (III, IV, V) on the Scriptures were placed between two articles on the doctrine of God. The confession did not mention Scripture's inspiration. It confessed the three ecumenical creeds: Apostles', Nicene, and Athanasian "because they are in accordance with the Word of God."

The Scots Confession (1560)

The Scots Confession of 1560 in its preface announced that "if any man will note in our Confession any chapter or sentence contrary to God's Holy Word," he should inform the Confession writers so they might "give him satisfaction from the mouth of God, that is from Holy Scripture, or else we shall alter whatever he can prove to be wrong." The formal treatment of Scripture, however, was not presented until Articles XVIII, XIX, and XX. In Article XVIII the "true preaching of the Word of God" was declared as a mark of the true church. The canonical Scriptures were described as the "written Word of God," in the Old and New Testaments. The Scots Confession held that the Spirit of God and not any individual person or council was the proper interpreter of Scripture. Thus, in controversies over interpretation, the appeal that was to carry the day was not to the authority of what people in other days had said but rather to what the Spirit was currently saying to the churches and "what Christ Jesus Himself did and commanded." God's Spirit could not contradict himself and so if any church of council's interpretation was "contrary to the plain Word of God written in any other passage of Scripture, it is most certain that this is not the true understanding and meaning of the Holy Ghost." The basis on which biblical interpretation was done was the "plain text." The interpretative principle was the "rule of love" (as in Augustine).

Article XIX spoke of the "authority of the Scriptures" and grounded their authority in their authorship by God for the purposes of instructing and making perfect God's people. This stood over against all attempts to make Scripture's authority depend upon the church. The true church "always hears and obeys the voice of her own Spouse and Pastor." Article XX dealt with councils, their power and authority, and maintained that no council gave any authority to the Word of God but rather that they existed to "refute heresies" and to confess the faith publicly. This authority they had gotten from God's "written Word." In this confession, the Scriptures were tied very directly into the life and work of the church.

The Belgic Confession of Faith (1561)

The Belgic Confession of 1561 followed the pattern of the French Confession, but was more elaborate and precise than that earlier one. Like the French, the Belgic knew two sources of revelation: (1) the "creation, preservation, and government of the universe" and (2) the more clear and fully knowable source of the knowledge of God, "his holy and divine Word." The third article dealt specifically with "The Written Word of God" and stressed Scripture's inspiration by the Holy Ghost through the prophets and apostles' writings. A unique feature of this confession was its expression that the two tablets of the law were written by God "with his own finger." The fourth article listed the canonical books, while Article VI stressed the difference between the canonical and apocryphal books. Christians may "read and take instruction from the Apocrypha" but these books do not have "power and efficacy" and cannot "confirm any point of faith or of the Christian religion." The locus and authority of the Scriptures was said to be in the Christian's heart as the Holy Ghost "witnesseth in our hearts that they are from God." The Scriptures thus "carry the evidence in themselves" (Gr. *autopiston*). Here the self-evidence of the Scriptures was recognized as it had been by Calvin.[294]

The seventh article dealt with "The Sufficiency of Holy Scriptures to be the Only Rule of Faith" for salvation. God told people in Scripture how to worship Him and if any one tried to teach otherwise, he must not be listened to. Scriptural doctrine was complete, needing no elaborations by men or tradition. Scripture was declared to be an "infallible" rule (citing Gal. 6:16; 1 Cor. 3:11; 2 Thess. 2:2). All Spirits were to be tested to see if they were from God; if they were not, they were to be rejected.

The Second Helvetic Confession (1566)

The Second Helvetic Confession was originally written by Heinrich Bullinger (1504–1575) as his personal confession. It was published to support the Elector Frederick III of the Palatinate in that ruler's defense of the Reformed faith. This 1566 document dealt very fully with the doctrine of Scripture.

The first two of the confession's thirty chapters dealt with Scripture. Article I combined the topics of Articles I and V of the First Helvetic

Confession, while Article II dealt with subjects included in the First Helvetic's Articles II through IV. The first chapter was entitled: "Of the Holy Scripture being the True Word of God." No list of canonical books was given, but the books of "both Testaments" were said to be the "true Word of God." They did not derive their authority from any source other than themselves (Gr. *autopiston*). In times past God spoke to the "fathers, prophets, apostles, and still speaks to us through Holy Scriptures." The next paragraph presented Scripture's double focus of sufficiency—for saving faith and for the "framing of a life acceptable to God." Here and throughout the confession, the emphasis was both theological and ethical. Nothing was to be added or taken away from Scripture. The canon was closed.

Under the heading "Scripture Teaches Fully All Godliness," the "confirmation of doctrines and the rejection of all errors" were said to be available from the Bible. Its exhortations were to be followed since inspired Scripture was profitable "for teaching, reproof" and so on (2 Tim. 3:16–17). Paul's instructions to Timothy were on "how to behave" (2 Tim. 3:14–15). That Scripture was the "Word of God" was supported by 1 Thessalonians 2:13 and Matthew 10:20; Luke 10:16 and John 13:20. The confession produced no theory of inspiration but, as in other symbols, there was a strong emphasis on the Preaching of the Word of God as the Word of God. When "lawfully called" ministers preached, they proclaimed the very Word of God.

The fact that the Holy Spirit was the One who inwardly illumined believers before they could accept the preaching and come to faith did not eliminate the need for human preaching. Against all manner of sectaries who searched for "inner light" apart from the proclamation of the Gospel, the confession cited Scripture (Jer. 31:34; 1 Cor. 3:7; John 6:44), which maintained that God willed that human preaching be done.[295] The confession affirmed both the centrality of the Preached Word and the complete "sufficiency" of Holy Scripture for "no other Word of God is to be invented nor is to be expected from heaven."

At the same time, it was recognized that "God can illuminate whom and when he will, even without the external ministry, for that is in his power." The freedom of the Spirit was thus upheld and the confession continued in the tradition of Calvin who, when speaking of the workings of Providence, wrote that God's Providence "guides all things, that it works sometimes by the interposition of means, somethings without means, and sometimes against all means."[296] Yet, as the confession pointed out, God's "usual way of instructing men was through the means of his Preached Word."

The confession then listed a number of heresies that were to be rejected. These heresies were to be spurned since they all "denied the

Scriptures proceeded from the Holy Spirit; or did not accept some parts of them, or interpolated and corrupted them."

The concluding section in Chapter 1 was on the Apocrypha, called such by some, and by others "Ecclesiastical." These books, for Bullinger, could be "read in the churches, but not advanced as an authority from which the faith is to be established." Support for this position was given from St. Augustine who wrote concerning the Old and New Testaments, "these books which we have suffice unto godliness" (*De Civitate Dei*, i.e., *The City of God*, XVIII, 38).

Chapter 2 was headed "Of Interpreting the Holy Scriptures; and of Fathers, Councils and Traditions." Citing 2 Peter 1:20, which said that the Holy Scriptures were "not of private interpretations," the Symbol disallowed "all possible interpretations." Nor did it agree with the Roman Catholic view that what the church taught "should be thrust upon all for acceptance." The real problem was *how* to interpret the Scriptures. The confession held that to be "orthodox and genuine," an interpretation must be "gleaned from the Scriptures themselves." To this end, a few rules for hermeneutics were given. Attention was to be paid to "the nature of the language in which they were written," and they must be "expounded in the light of like and unlike passages and of many and clearer passages." Interpretation gleaned thusly should also "agree with the rule of faith and love," so contributing, then, "much to the glory of God and man's salvation."

The "Interpretations of the Holy Fathers" were not despised by Bullinger nor rejected insofar as their works "agree with the Scriptures." Yet where these venerable men taught things different from or contrary to Scripture, "we modestly dissent from them." The same principle was affirmed with regard to decrees and canons of councils. Thus, the confession's "case" was "urged not by these lesser authorities, but only by the supreme judge, God himself, "who proclaims by the Holy Scripture what is true, what is false, what is to be followed, or what to be avoided."

Compared with other Reformed Confessions and particularly with the First Helvetic Confession, the Second Helvetic gave illumination in the believer a larger role alongside the doctrine of an original inspiration. Nearly all the weight was placed on revelation in the living church via preaching and sound exegesis. It was not the work of the Spirit in ancient writers that was emphasized, but the present inward illumination of the living believer. The formal authority was explicitly stated, but the *scopus*, goal, or function of Scripture was the presentation of the redeeming gospel.[297]

The Reformed Confessions of the sixteenth century were built firmly on the foundation of Holy Scripture. They stood on the one hand over against Roman Catholic insistence on church and tradition as independent sources of authority, and on the other against the solely subjective illumination views of sectarian groups. In the Reformed Confessions, Scripture was the Word of God, a certain authority. None of the confessions, however, delved into the intricacies of inspiration or spelled out any elaborate theory as to how the inspired Scriptures came to be such. For these confessions it was enough to confess this belief, for, with Calvin, they affirmed that the Scriptures "carry the evidence in themselves" (Gr. *autopiston*) of their divine origin. Strong emphasis was given to the work of the Holy Spirit as the In-spirer of Scripture *and* the continuing interpreter of Scripture. The Spirit was cited as the author of the believer's trust in Scripture's sufficiency.

The purpose of Scripture in the Reformed Confessions was always tied to bringing persons to salvation and guiding them in living the Christian life. The confessions affirmed that Scripture was "infallible" in achieving its saving purpose. No suggestion was anywhere given that Scripture addressed matters of science, or that it provided technically inerrant information on worldly matters. The authority of Scripture in these confessions resided in its saving function, not in the form of words used. This was emphasized by the equation of the Word of God, not only with the written, but also with the preached Word. Similarly, Scripture was to be interpreted using normal human, hermeneutical rules, but the interpreter was also to be guided by the Holy Spirit and the rule of "faith and love." The message of Scripture was divine while its form was fully human. Heinrich Bullinger summarized the spirit of the Reformed Symbols regarding Scripture:

> We know very well that the Scripture is not called the Word of God because of the human voice, the ink and paper, or the printed letters (which all can be comprehended by the flesh), but because the meaning, which speaks through the human voice or is written with pen and ink on paper, is not originally from men, but is God's word, will, and meaning.[298]

e. Summary

In the early fifteenth century Thomas Bradwardine at Oxford returned to the Platonic-Augustinian methodology as an antidote both to Aristotelian Thomism and to skeptical nominalism. His methodological lead was followed by several pre-Reformers. Wycliffe in England and Huss in Bohemia declared that the Bible alone was the final authority in matters of salvation and living the Christian life. They affirmed that the

Holy Spirit who had inspired the biblical writers would illumine the minds of contemporary interpreters. They combined the use of their regenerate minds with the best available scholarly tools to find the natural, historical meaning of the biblical authors. Their views influenced the sixteenth-century Protestant Reformers.

Luther and Calvin both adopted the Augustinian theological method that faith leads to understanding. They were trained in and used the tools of scholarly study developed by the Christian humanism of the Renaissance. Luther's training in Occamist philosophy and Calvin's study of rhetoric and law strengthened their opposition to scholastic logical systems. The primary source on which they relied for truth about themselves and their relationship to God was the Bible. They followed Augustine theologically: All persons innately possessed a knowledge of God the Creator in their hearts; but human beings sinfully suppressed that awareness. Scripture served, in Calvin's imagery, as spectacles in order to bring that original knowledge into clear focus. In interpretation, they rejected the excesses of allegory and embraced Chrysostom's grammatical-historical method for finding the natural meaning of the biblical authors.

In common with the church fathers, Luther and Calvin held that the authority of Scripture resided in its function of bringing persons into a saving relationship with God in Jesus Christ. Christ was the center of Scripture for both Luther and Calvin. We should look for no other knowledge in the Bible than of Christ and his benefits towards us, according to them. Scripture was not meant to teach us about science. Theology was viewed as a practical discipline, teaching about the life of faith. Theology was not meant to be the Queen of the Sciences, laying the foundation for systems of speculation.

For Luther and Calvin a functional understanding of Scripture was enhanced by the concept of accommodation. The Incarnation exemplified God's style of communication. As did Origen, Chrysostom, and Augustine before them, Luther and Calvin affirmed that God had condescended to use imperfect human forms of communication to accomplish God's perfect, divine function of bringing salvation. The gospel message, not the cultural context or the linguistic forms, was understood to be normative for later readers of the Bible. The Bible was infallible in achieving its saving purpose. Normal human forms of language and thought were used by the biblical writers. These were subject to scholarly investigation, which could help people understand their full meaning.

The Reformers' persuasion that Scripture was the Word of God came from the inner testimony of the Holy Spirit. The Spirit witnessed to the divine, Christological content of Scripture, not its human, linguistic form. Scripture was self-authenticating. It was foolish to try to prove to unbelievers what could only be known by faith. External arguments for the Bible's validity were helpful only after persons had accepted Scripture in faith. The Holy Spirit also illumined the minds of interpreters of Scripture. Luther and Calvin refuted rational scholasticism, which demanded proofs before faith. They rejected with equal firmness the spiritualistic sectarians who claimed leadings of the Holy Spirit apart from the Word. The Word and the Spirit together served as a hallmark of the Reformation.

Luther and Calvin trusted the Bible as an infallible authority in matters of salvation and the life of faith. They vehemently rejected the notion that any biblical writer would deliberately deceive in the religious realm. However, that did not imply, for the Reformers, that the biblical writers were lifted above the human patterns of thought and speech common to others in that writer's cultural context. Normal human flaws and failings could be sorted out by scholarly study. But the Bible never erred by leading the believer into unrighteousness.

The Lutheran Confessions assumed the authority of Scripture but did not give a separate article to discussing it. The Reformed Confessions of the sixteenth century stressed the Augustinian approach to the authority and interpretation of the Bible and affirmed that the Word of God was proclaimed in preaching based on the biblical message.

f. Notes

1. Otto W. Heick, *A History of Christian Thought*, 2 vols. (Philadelphia: Fortress Press, 1976), 1:306. On the Occamist movement, see *HP*, III/1, chap. 9.

2. On Wycliffe, see H. B. Workman, *John Wyclif: A Study of the English Medieval Church*, 2 vols. (Oxford: Clarendon Press, 1926) and J. H. Dahmus, *The Prosecution of John Wyclif* (New Haven: Yale University Press, 1952). See also J. A. Robson, *Wyclif and the Oxford Schools: The Relation of the 'Summa de ente' to Scholastic Debates at Oxford in the Later Forteenth Century* (Cambridge: Cambridge University Press, 1961).

3. See S. H. Thomson, "The Philosophical Basis of Wyclif's Theology," *Journal of Religion* 11 (1931): 86–116, for an appraisal of the relation of Wycliffe's philosophical and theological views.

4. Along with Bradwardine, Gregory of Rimini (d. 1358), General of the Augustinian Hermits, also contributed to the revival of Augustinian thought. He taught at Bologna, Padua, and Perugia. On the other philosophers, Adam Wodham (d. 1358) and Robert Holkot (d. 1349), who were influential Occamists at Merton College, Oxford, see *HP*, III/1, 134–137; *EP*, I, 374.

5. See G. Leff, "Thomas Bradwardine's 'De causa Dei,'" *Journal of Ecclesiastical History* 7 (1956): 21–29.

6. *ODC*, 1502.

7. See J. A. F. Thomson, *The Later Lollards, 1414–1520* (Oxford: Oxford University Press, 1965), pp. 220–238.

8. Heiko A. Oberman, The *Harvest of Medieval Theology*, rev. ed. (Grand Rapids, Mich.: Wm. B. Eerdmans, 1967), p. 372. (Hereafter cited as Oberman, *Harvest.*) See his chap. 11, "Nominalism and Extrascriptural Tradition." See also M. Hurley, *Scriptua sola: Wyclif and His Critics* (Bronx, New York: Fordham University Press, 1960).

9. Oberman, *Harvest*, p. 373. Oberman

contrasts the position of Bradwardine, Wyclif, and Ambrosius of Speier ("Tradition I") with that of Occam, d'Ailly, and Gerson ("Tradition II").

10. *HCT,* 2:327.

11. William Mallard, "John Wyclif and the Tradition of Biblical Authority," *Church History* (hereafter cited as *CH*) 30, no. 1 (March 1961):50.

12. In Mallard, p. 51, citing *De Veritate Sacrae Scripturae,* ed. R. Buddensieg (London: Truebner and Company, 1905–1907), I, c. 1, p. 1.

13. Mallard, p. 51, citing *De Veritate* I, c. 1, p. 2. The center and interpretative principle of Scripture was Christ, see Dahmus, p. 141, citing Bodleian MS, Mus 86.

14. *De Veritate,* i, c. 3, pp. 62; I, c. 2, p. 22.

15. *De Veritate,* I, c. 9, pp. 194–205. Mallard adds: "Wyclif acknowledges the helpfulness of interpretations by the Fathers, but this is very different in his thinking from accepting the interpretation of the hierarchy," p. 58.

16. Mallard, p. 52, citing Thomas Netter, *Doctrinale Antiquitatum Fidei Ecclesiae Catholicae,* ed. F. B. Blanciotti (Venice, 1757), I, c. 34, p. 186. See also Workman, p. 119.

17. Mallard, p. 54.

18. C. A. Briggs, *Study of Holy Scripture,* rev. ed., rep. 1900 (Grand Rapids, Mich.: Baker Book House, 1970), p. 455, citing G. V. Lechler, *Johann von Wyclif* (Leipzig, 1873), I, 483ff.

19. *HI,* p. 279, gives no reference for this remark. Farrar also cites Wycliffe as saying that "the whole error in the knowledge of Scripture, and the source of its debasement and falsification by incompetent persons, was the ignorance of grammar and logic" *Trialog.* i. 8), pp. 278–279.

20. See *De Veritate,* I, c. 1, p. 15. He believed the same essential message was contained in every part of Scripture.

21. Mallard, p. 56. "He was certain that the truth of Christ resided in the statements of Holy Scripture and that the task of the effective preacher was to set forth those statements." See *Sermones,* I, Praefatio.

22. Mallard, p. 58. See *De Veritate,* I, c. 6, pp. 119–124 and I, c. 2, p. 36, Cf. Introduction to *De Veritate,* XXXV. The Bible stood at the center of the church's life for Wycliffe. It was the "law of Christ" and the instrument through which God continued to speak. And we may add one more step, as Mallard does: "To preserve the unity of the Bible

itself he necessarily retained the heritage of the orthodox pastor, the heritage of instruction by allegory," p. 58.

23. *ODC,* 1503. See, however, Matthew Spinka, *John Hus and the Czech Reform* (Chicago: University of Chicago Press, 1941), pp. 12–20, who opposes J. Loserth, *Huss und Wiclif: Zur Genesis der hussitischen Lehre* (Munich: R. Oldenbourg, 1925). See also M. Spinka, *John Hus: A Biography* (Princeton: Princeton University Press, 1968).

24. Oberman, *Harvest,* p. 376.

25. *HI,* p. 279. Farrar further cites Luther as saying in 1520: "I have hitherto unknowingly held and taught all John Hus's doctrines; in a like unknowingness has John Staupitz taught them; briefly we are all unconscious Hussites. Paul and Augustine are Hussites to the letter," p. 312, citing *Martin Luthers Briefe,* ed. Wilhelm Martin Leberecht de Wette, 5 vols. (Berlin: Reimer, 1825–1838), p. 425; Charles Beard, *The Reformation of the Sixteenth Century in its Relation to Modern Thought and Knowledge,* 2d ed., Hibbert Lectures, 1883 (London: Williams & Norgate, 1885), p. 30. (Hereafter cited as Beard, *Reformation.*)

26. Oberman, *Harvest,* p. 88. Luther entered the Augustinian monastery at Erfurt on July 15, 1505, after making a vow to become a monk when his life was spared in a violent thunderstorm. See Roland H. Bainton, *Here I Stand* (Nashville: Abingdon Press, 1950), p. 34. (Hereafter cited as Bainton, *Here I Stand.*) His contact with humanism was limited, a strong contrast with Zwingli, whose education was decisively formed by this movement (see below on Calvin). See Gerhard Ebeling, *Luther: An Introduction to His Thought,* trans. R. A. Wilson (Philadelphia: Fortress Press, 1972), p. 37. (Hereafter "cited" as Ebeling, *Luther.*) On Luther's relationship to Scholasticism and Nominalism, see Brian Gerrish, *Grace and Reason: A Study in the Theology of Luther* (Oxford: Clarendon Press, 1962), chap. 3. (Hereafter cited as Gerrish, *Grace.*)

27. Raymond Larry Shelton, "Martin Luther's Concept of Biblical Interpretation in Historical Perspective" (Ph.D. dissertation, Fuller Theological Seminary, Pasadena, Calif., 1974), p. 146.

28. Translated in Bainton, *Here I Stand,* p. 116. For a study of Luther's attacks on the role of tradition, the authority of Church

councils, etc., see Jaroslav Pelikan, *Obedient Rebels* (New York: Harper & Row, 1964).

29. See Brian A. Gerrish, "Biblical Authority and the Continental Reformation," *Scottish Journal of Theology* (hereafter cited as *SJT*) 10 (1957): 342. (Hereafter cited as Gerrish, "Biblical Authority.")

30. WA 3. 454; 3. 259, as given in A. Skevington Wood, *Captive to the Word* (Exeter: Paternoster Press, 1969), p. 123.

31. Robert Clyde Johnson, *Authority in Protestant Theology* (Philadelphia: Westminster Press, 1959), p. 23, citing *WA* XLVI, 780; VII, 640; XXXIII, 276, 304, and Wood, p. 122, citing *Luther's Works*, ed. Jaroslav Pelikan and Helmut T. Lehmann, 56 vols. St. Louis: Concordia Publishing House and Philadelphia: Muhlenberg Press, 1953–), 23, 174. (Hereafter cited as *LW*.) See Wood's discussion.

32. Wood, pp. 124–125.

33. *LW* 26. 67; *LW* 32. 189, from Wood, p. 125. Again, "we must read the fathers 'with discretion,' he insists, accepting their teaching only when 'they quote clear texts and explain Scripture with clearer Scripture' (WA VII. 639). For 'we must remain with the Scriptures alone' (WA VII. 641)," Johnson, p. 27.

34. WA 40^{II}, 47, cited in Willem Jan Kooiman, *Luther and the Bible*, trans. John Schmidt (Philadelphia: Muhlenberg Press, 1961), p. 208.

35. WA 18, 606, in Kooiman, p. 208.

36. *D. Martin Luthers Werke Tischreden*, ed. Karl Drescher (Leipzig: Big, Teubner, 1912–21), 439 no. 2383, cited in Wood, p. 171. (Hereafter cited as *WATR*.)

37. *Introduction to the OT*, as cited in Gerrish, "Biblical Authority," p. 343. The subject matter of Scripture was Christ's person and His saving work. See WA 16, 113, 22, in Geoffrey W. Bromiley, "The Church Doctrine of Inspiration," in *Revelation and the Bible*, ed. Carl F. H. Henry (Grand Rapids, Mich.: Baker Book House, 1958), p. 211 (hereafter cited as Bromiley, "Doctrine of Inspiration"). See *CD*, I/2, citing *Pred. üb Rom.* 15:4f. (1522): "It holdeth God's word" (WA 10$^{1.2}$ 75,6), p. 492.

38. Hans W. Frei, *The Eclipse of Biblical Narrative* (New Havan: Yale University Press, 1974), p. 19.

39. "Preface to the New Testament," *Works of Martin Luther*, ed. Henry E. Jacobs (Philadelphia, 1915–32), VI, 442, cited in Hugh T. Kerr, ed. *A Compend of Luther's Theology* (Philadelphia: Westminster Press, 1966), p. 9.

40. Bromiley, "Doctrine of Inspiration," p. 211.

41. WA 48, 31, cited in Kooiman, p. 237.

42. Ibid., p. 238.

43. Wood, p. 175, citing WA 3. 515 and 3. 403–04. See also Erich Roth, "On Luther and the Continental Reformation," *Church Quarterly Review* 153 (1952): 173.

44. See also *D. Martin Luthers sämtlicha Schriften*, ed. Johann Georg Walch, 24 vols. revised (St. Louis: Concordia Publishing House, 1880–1910), 3. 21, cited by Wood, p. 176. Hereafter cited as *SL*.)

45. Roland H. Bainton, Warren A. Quanbeck, and E. Gordon Rupp, *Luther Today* (Decorah: Luther College Press, 1957), p. 84, cited by Wood, p. 176.

46. WA 48, 31, in Kooiman, p. 237.

47. Wood, p. 176.

48. SL 3. 21, cited in Wood, p. 140. Heick has identified the several senses that "Word of God" had for Luther: Christ, Creation, God's redemptive acts, as Law or Gospel, Preaching, Bible—all are referred to by Luther as "Word of God," 1: 346–47. Jaroslav Pelikan writes in *Luther the Expositor*, companion volume to *Luther's Works* (St. Louis Concordia Publishing House, 1959) (hereafter cited as Pelikan, *Luther*) that "the Scriptures were the 'Word of God' in a derivative sense for Luther—derivative from the historical sense of Word as deed and from the basic sense of Word as proclamation." This "Word of God" in the Bible "was the same 'Word of God' which God had spoken in the Exodus and in Christ, and the same 'Word of God' which the church was always obliged to proclaim. Ultimately, then, there was only one 'Word of God,' which came in various forms. In its written form it was the Bible," pp. 67, 70. Cf. Heinrich Bornkamm, *Das Wort Gottes bei Luther* (Munich: 1933).

49. WA 4. 535, cited in Wood, p. 140.

50. SL 9, 1775; SL 3, 1890, 1895, cited in Wood, p. 141.

51. WA 18, 653.28–35. See also WA 18, 606.1–609.14; 652.23–653.35, and Luther's the *Bondage of the Will*, trans. J. I. Packer and O. R. Johnston (Westwood, N.J.: Fleming H. Revell, 1957), p. 125. See Gerhard Ebeling, "Word of God and Hermeneutic," trans. James W. Leitch (hereafter cited as Ebeling, "Hermeneutic."), in *The New Hermeneutic*, ed. James M. Robinson and John B.

Cobb, Jr. (New York: Harper & Row, 1964), p. 80 and Wood, p. 135 on the "perspicuity" of Scripture. Cf. Friedrich Geissler, *Claritas Scripturae bei Martin Luther* (Göttingen: Vandenhoeck & Ruprecht, 1966).

52. WA 33, 144, cited in Kooiman, p. 235.

53. Kooiman, pp. 236–237.

54. See WA 3. 250, 255–256, 261–262, 347–348.

55. From Reinhold Seeberg, *Text-Book of the History of Doctrines*, trans. Charles E. Hay, 2 vols. (Grand Rapids, Mich.: Baker Book House, 1966), 2:281, citing *D. Martin Luthers sämtliche Werke*, ed. J. G. Plachmann and J. K. Irmischer, 67 vols. (Erlangen, 1826–1857), 9. 232, 274; 13. 184, 286; 8. 308; 11. 206; 28. 298; 47. 353f. (Hereafter cited as *EA.*) As R. M. Grant says of Luther's view: "We are to understand the words of scripture 'in their kernel and feel them in the heart,'" *SH*, p. 132. See K. Fullerton, "Luther's Doctrine and Criticism of Scripture," *Bibliotheca Sacra* 63 (1906):12.

56. Seeberg, 2. 281 (EA 14. 188). On the "inner" and "outer" Word in Luther, see Seeberg, 2:280–281 and Ebeling, *Luther*, p. 108.

57. Cited in Bromiley, "Doctrine of Inspiration," pp. 211–212, from *Briefwechsel*, ed. Enders and Kawerau, I, 141.

58. *Gospel Sermon, Eighth Sunday After Trinity* (Lenker edition, XIII, 8, in H. T. Kerr, p. 11).

59. Shelton, pp. 120–121, citing *LW*, XXXI, p. 75.

60. "The Papacy at Rome," *Works of Martin Luther*, I, 346f. in H. T. Kerr, p. 4.

61. Gerrish, *Grace*, p. 54.

62. *Epistle Sermon, Twelfth Sunday After Trinity* (Lenker edition, IX, 12–13, in H. T. Kerr, p. 3).

63. See *EP*, V, 112.

64. See Gerrish, *Grace*, p. 1, citing WA 40[1]. 362. 15,22; 365. 18; 275. 17; 344.23 (CDE).

65. Gerrish, *Grace*, p. 2. See his chapter 2, "Luther's Attitude towards Philosophy." Aquinas spoke of Aristotle as "the philosopher."

66. Gerrish, *Grace*, p. 29, citing WA 37. 538. 22 (perhaps an allusion to 1 Corinthians 1:-28) and WA 10[1,2]. 10.14.

67. Gerrish, *Grace*, p. 29, citing *WATR*. 5, no. 5245.

68. Gerrish, *Grace*, p. 30, citing *WATR*. 1, no. 427 and *WATR*. 1, no. 4: *Philosophia est quasi theologia gentium et rationis*. In "Table-Talk" XLVIII Luther says: "Philosophy understands naught of divine matters. I don't say that men may not teach and learn philosophy; I approve thereof, so that it be within reason and moderation. Let philosophy remain within her bounds, as God has appointed, and let us make use of her as of a character in a comedy; but to mix her up with divinity may not be endured." Quoted in H. T. Kerr, p. 4. See also Bernhard Lohse, "Reason and Revelation in Luther," *SJT*, 13 (1960), pp. 337–365.

69. See Gerrish, *Grace*, p. 29.

70. Gerrish, *Grace*, p. 12, citing WA 10[1,1]. 527. 14, 529. 4, 529. 7, 530. 13ff., 531. 5, 531. 6ff.

71. See Gerrish, *Grace*, pp. 15ff. for further discussion.

72. Quoted in Gerrish, *Grace*, p. 22. Reason was not the same *after* the Christian had faith as it was before. See "Table-Talk" CCXCIV, in H. T. Kerr, pp. 4–5.

73. *Nisi convictus fero testimoniis Scripturarum aut ratione evidente* . . . In B. J. Kidd, *Documents Illustrative of the Continental Reformation* (Oxford: Clarendon Press, 1967), p. 85. See *Werke* (1569), IX, 108b.; *LW* 32, 108ff.

74. Gerrish, *Grace*, pp. 24–25. Gerrish rejects Charles Beard's interpretation which claims: "It is impossible to doubt that he here assigns to reason an independent position by the side of Scripture: the words will bear no other interpretation," Beard, *Reformation*, p. 153.

75. From Gerrish, *Grace*, p. 26. In Luther's thought these correspond to: (1) the Earthly Kingdom; (2) the Heavenly Kingdom; (3) serving humbly in the household of faith and always subject to the Word of God. As Gerrish writes: "Within the first context, reason is an excellent gift of God; within the second, it is Frau Hulda, the Devil's Whore; within the third, it is the handmaiden of faith."

76. For Luther, natural reason suffered from the consequences of original sin. Ultimate supernatural truths such as the way to salvation could never be reached by reason. A natural theology was not to be trusted. See Gerrish, *Grace*, p. 102. This revelation on which reason seeks to build is general revelation (p. 102, note 3). When reason led to the conclusion that God could be approached by certain "ceremonies" or "good works," it was no better than a tower of Babel. In this context Luther denounced the Scholastics and their "ladders" to heaven. See Gerrish, *Grace*, p. 103 for a fuller discussion. The greatest thing humans can do, says Luther, is to give God glory, but "it is not reason that does this, but faith." (WA 40¹. 360.24). Cf. "Disputation against Scholastic Theology," (LCC XVI, 266–273), where he says, for example, 44: "The truth is that a man cannot become a theologian unless he becomes one without Aristotle"; 41: "The whole Aristotelian ethic is grace's worst enemy" (p. 269).

77. See Gerrish, *Grace*, pp. 55–56.

78. Shelton, p. 159. See also James Mac-Kinnon, *Luther and the Reformation*, 4 vols. (New York: Russell and Russell, 1962), 1:-249.

79. Paul Oskar Kristeller, *Renaissance Thought: The Classic, Scholastic, and Humanist Strains* (New York: Harper & Row, 1961), p. 87.

80. Kristeller, p. 78.

81. Ibid.

82. Cited in Heiko Oberman, *Forerunners of the Reformation* (New York: Holt, Rhinehart & Winston, 1966), p. 312.

83. Charles Trinkaus, "Erasmus, Augustine, and the Nominalists," *Archive for Reformation History* 67 (1976):31.

84. See Kristeller, p. 82, and his citations (p. 150). Colet's 1497 lectures on Paul's Epistles at Oxford are significant here. For "contrary to medieval scholastic tradition, Colet followed the text of Paul and sought to make clear Paul's meaning in his historical context." See P. A. Duhamel, "The Oxford Lectures of John Colet," *Journal of the History of Ideas* 14 (1953): 493–500. See also Albert Rabil, *Erasmus and the New Testament* (San Antonio: Trinity University Press, 1972), p. 43. Erasmus followed and developed this method that indeed "was the method which was to mark off Renaissance from Scholastic theology.... According to Erasmus, Colet's achievement was the restoration of the old theology, that is, the patristic textual criticism over against the hopeless subtleties of scholasticism" (See *Opus Epistolarum Des. Erasmi Roterodami*, ed. P. S. and H. M. Allen, and H. W. Garrod (Oxford, 1906–47), I, 246–248, lines 19–73. These quotes are from Donald B. Conroy, "Erasmus of Rotterdam: His Formation and Development as Exegete and Theologian," (Pittsburgh Theological Seminary, 1973), p. 23.

85. "To the Councilmen of All Cities in Germany That They Establish and Maintain Christian Schools," *Works of Martin Luther*, IV, 114f. in H. T. Kerr, p. 17. While Luther took advantage of the lexicographical and grammatical assistance, as well as the editions of the biblical text that the Humanists offered, he "could not believe that philosophical studies would reveal the truth of God." Luther stressed the need for the enlightenment of the Holy Spirit (*illuminatio*) if one was truly to understand the Bible. Of the Humanists, he said: "They translate Paul very well, but they do not understand him." In other words, "Luther sought to be more than a philologist of the *sacrae litterae;* he wanted essentially to be a theologian ... Luther is glad to take advantage of the foundation laid by the Humanists, but his concern is not with 'the words,' since his real concern from the beginning to the end is with 'the Word.' The theological view is therefore, for him, primary and dominant," Kooiman, pp. 54, 74–75.

86. Cited in Kooiman, p. 59 (WA 56.371.17).

87. Shelton, pp. 142–143; see also *SB*, chaps. 3 and 4; and Ford Lewis Battles, "Hugo of St. Victor as a Moral Allegorist," *CH* 18, no. 4 (December 1949):220–240.

88. Cited in Wilhelm Pauck, ed., *Luther: Lectures on Romans*, LCC, XV (Philadelphia: Westminster Press, 1961), p. xxx. Found in Shelton, p. 144.

89. See WA, XLII, 71, in Shelton, p. 145.

90. SL 5:335, cited in Wood, p. 162.

91. See *LW* 37, 177 and Ebeling, "Hermeneutic," pp. 78–80. Wood writes: "This comparative technique had been recommended by some of the fathers, including Origen, Jerome and Augustine (Origen, *De Principiis*, 4; Jerome, *Epistolae*, 53. 6.7; Augustine, *De Doctrina*, 2. ix. 14). Luther acknowledged his indebtedness to the past when he wrote: 'The holy fathers explained Scripture by taking the clear, lucid passages and with them shed light on obscure and doubtful passages' (SL. 20. 856). 'In this manner,' he declared, 'Scripture is its own light. It is a fine thing when Scripture explains itself' (SL. 11. 2335)," p. 162.

92. *LW* 9. 21, cited in Wood, pp. 161–162. Luther also writes: "That is the true method of interpretation which puts Scripture alongside Scripture in a right and proper way," from *Works of Martin Luther*, Philadelphia ed. (Philadelphia, 1915–1943), 3.334 (hereafter cited as *PE*), cited in Wood, p. 162.

93. See Paul L. Lehmann, "The Reformers' Use of the Bible," *Theology Today* 3, no. 3 (October 1946): 328 and 340.

94. See *WATR* 1. 136, cited in *SH*, p. 131. He characterized allegories as "mere jugglery," "a merry chase," "monkey tricks," and "looney talk," PE 3. 334; *LW* 9. 7. See also *HI*, p. 338.

95. For a detailed study see James S. Preus, *From Shadow to Promise: Old Testament Interpretation from Augustine to the Young Luther* (Cambridge, Mass.: Harvard University Press, 1969), chap. 11. He writes: "In the course of his lectures on the Psalms, Luther discovered that the Old Testament faith and religion were so much like his own that they could become exemplary for his own faith, and for the Church's self-understanding," p. 166. Preus sees Luther's exegetical understanding emerging into "a future oriented hermeneutic structure, based on God's promise and three advents of Christ," p. 267. This "began to threaten the traditional fourfold structure." See also Gerhard Ebeling, "New Hermeneutics and the Early Luther," trans. Mrs. James Carse, *Theology Today* 21, no. 1 (April 1964): 34–46, esp. p. 40.

96. *LW* 1. 283, cited in Wood p. 165.

97. Heinrich Bornkamm, *Luther and the Old Testament*, trans. Eric W. and Ruth C. Gritsch, ed. Victor I. Gruhn (Philadelphia: Fortress Press, 1969), p. 91, citing WA 31[II]. 242:24. (Hereafter cited as Bornkamm, *Luther*.)

98. Bornkamm, *Luther*, p. 89, citing this insight from Karl Holl. See Karl Holl, "Luthers Bedeutung für den Fortschritt der Auslegekunst," in *Gesammelte Aufsätze zur Kirchengeschichte*, 3 vols. (Tübingen: J. C. B. Mohr, 1948), 1: 558. See also Gerhard Ebeling, "Die Anfänge von Luthers Hermeneutik," (hereafter cited as Ebeling "Luthers Hermeneutik"), *Zeitschrift für Theologie und Kirche* 48 (1951): 172–230, and his *Evangelische Evangelienauslegung* (Munich: Kaiser, 1942) (hereafter cited as Ebeling, *Evangelische*).

99. Bornkamm, *Luther*, p. 89. Preus, chap. 12, details how this linkage between "prophetic," and "literal" occurs in Luther's lectures on the Psalms. The significance of this "new understanding of the *sensus propheticus* is that it makes the qualitative hermeneutical leap necessary for an eventual reuniting of the 'theological' and 'grammatical' senses of the Old Testament. Luther the interpreter has finally thought himself into the pre-advent situation, where he has

found a rich theological reward," pp. 182–183.

To Luther the ancient allegorists had killed the true spiritual meaning of the Old Testament. See *Preface to Old Testament*, 1523 (*Vorrede auf das Alte Testament*), EA 63, 7; *LW* 35, 235, cited in Bornkamm, *Luther*, p. 90. They missed examples of Faith and divine promises in the Old Testament.

For Luther the historical message had a power of its own. See WA 31[II]. 97:26ff., cited in Bornkamm, *Luther*, p. 91. Since all of history is God's work, the present-day believer is united with people of faith in the past and can thus draw help and comfort for their own spiritual lives from the recorded experiences those who have gone before had with God.

100. Bornkamm, *Luther*, p. 91, citing *That These Words of Christ, 'This is My Body,' etc., Still Stand Firm against the Fanatics* (1527) (WA 23. 66:5ff.; *LW* 37, 14).

101. Bornkamm, *Luther*, p. 91, citing *The Deuteronomy of Moses, with Notes* (1525), WA 14. 560:14; *LW* 9, 24. Luther often contrasted false allegory with "history": "One should think much, and magnificently, about history, but little about allegory. You should use allegory like a flower, for it illustrates the sermon rather than strengthens it.... In history you have complete as well as incomplete promises. Allegory does not establish doctrine, but, like color, can only add to it. The painter's colors do not build the house. The human body does not consist of a wreath of flowers, or a beautiful garment, etc. This proves that faith is not grounded in allegories," *Lectures on Isaiah*, 1527–1530. Cited in Bornkamm, *Luther*, p. 90, from WA 31[II], 97:15ff.

102. *LW* 3. 27, cited in Wood, p. 164; see also *LW* 8. 209. Luther says, "It is with the true and actual meaning" that the commentators should be concerned," Wood, p. 164, citing again *LW* 8. 209.

103. One such warning is in his *Lectures on Isaiah*, 1527–1530, as cited above in note 101, but also at WA 31[II], 243:20.

104. *LW* 3. 192; see also 9. 24–5. In lecturing on a different chapter in Genesis he says: "But now that the foundation has been laid on the basis of other sure and clear passages of Scripture, what is there to prevent the additional use of an allegory, not only for the sake of adorning but also for the sake of teaching, in order that the subject may become clearer?" *LW* 8. 269; cf.

9.8, where he speaks of "a proper allegory." In Wood, p. 165.

105. Bornkamm, *Luther*, p. 92.

106. Bornkamm, *Luther*, p. 93, citing: WA 14. 579:34ff; 14. 638:9; 14. 650:20; 14. 693:24ff; and LW 9, 42–43; 9, 108; 9, 136; 9, 205.

107. Bornkamm, *Luther*, agrees with Ebeling who posits the 1529 break. After that date, Luther's use of allegory receded even further. Bornkamm comments of Ebeling: "He is certainly right when he relates both turning points to the experiences which Luther gained in his struggle with the biblical interpretations of the enthusiasts (*Schwärmer*) and of Erasmus and those of the northern Germans" (p. 94, note 57). See Ebeling, *Evangelische*, p. 87; and Ebeling's, "Luthers Hermeneutik."

108. Pelikan, *Luther*, p. 126. He cites three of Luther's "reasons" for not taking a text literally: "the statement of the text itself that it was not to be taken literally; the powerful indication by another passage to this same effect; the clash between a literal interpretation and 'a clear article of the faith,'" pp. 126–127. See Luther's *Confession on the Lord's Supper* (1528), WA 26, 279, 403 and also *Against the Heavenly Prophets* (1525), WA 18, 147.

109. Bornkamm, *Luther*, pp. 96, 95, citing *The Deuteronomy of Moses, with Notes* (1525), WA 14, 561:26; LW 9, 26; *Lectures on Galatians* (1519), WA 2. 549:27ff.; LW 27, 310ff. Heick presents Karl Holl's summary of Luther's contribution to scriptural interpretation: "(1) Scripture has only one meaning. (2) The literal, grammatical interpretation is prior to any other understanding of the text. (3) Every single passage must be seen in the light of the whole Bible. (4) In interpreting the Bible, we are concerned not with its letter, but with its subject matter. (5) The subject matter of the Bible is always clear and intelligible. (6) Because the Scriptures are clear, they are their own interpreters. (7) If the fundamental clarity of Scripture is recognized, its undeniable obscurities and difficulties in details may be freely admitted," 1: 348, citing Holl, 1:544ff. See also Gerrish, "Biblical Authority," pp. 346–347.

110. See Hans-Joachim Kraus, *Geschichte der historisch-kritischen Erforschung des Alten Testaments* (Neukirchen: Neukirchener Verlag, 1969).

111. *HS*, p. 130.

112. See Seeberg, 2:300.

113. Cited in Shelton, pp. 190–191, from LW, XXIII, 96. That Luther calls men and women to faith in Jesus Christ and not in an "inspired Book" is clear, as when he writes: "Christians receive Christ, the Spirit of God, as the central content of Holy Scripture. Having learned to know him, the remainder becomes meaningful to them and all scripture becomes transparent," WA 44. 510, cited in Kooiman, pp. 235–236. Thus people come to the Bible's authority *through* Christ and not the other way around.

114. Cited in Shelton, p. 181 from WA, XLVI, 727. Seeberg, whose *History of Doctrines* J. Theodore Mueller says "represents a most scholarly and reliable treatise on Luther's views of Scripture" "Luther and the Bible," in *Inspiration and Interpretation*, ed. John F. Walvoord [Grand Rapids, Mich.: Wm. B. Eerdmans, 1957], p. 94, says: "In consistency with this view of the Scriptures, historical oversights and errors in the sacred writings disturbed Luther but little (e.g. EA 14. 319; 46. 174; 50. 308f.; 62. 132). They did not affect the real grounds of his confidence" (2:301).

115. Thus it is misleading to characterize Luther as one who can teach us "Lessons . . . on the Inerrancy of Holy Writ." See John Warwick Montgomery "Lessons from Luther on the Inerrancy of Holy Writ," in *God's Inerrant Word*, ed. John Warwick Montgomery (Minneapolis: Bethany Fellowship, 1974), chap. 3. See also Mueller, pp. 102–103, and M. Reu, *Luther and the Scriptures* (Columbus, Ohio: Wartburg Press, 1944), chaps. 5–7. Of Reu's work, Heick comments in a footnote following these words: "Formally Luther followed the terminology of the later Middle Ages in speaking of the Holy Spirit as the author and writer of the Bible. Luther did not draw the same conclusions from these statements as did the orthodox Lutheran teachers of the seventeenth century" (1:347) that "For this reason M. Reu, *Luther and the Scriptures* . . . is unreliable. It gives a distorted view of Luther." Heick concludes about Luther: "In his eyes, the Scriptures were not 'errorless,'" 1:347. See also F. A. D. Tholuck, "The Doctrine of Inspiration," *Journal of Sacred Literature* (July 1854): 342–343. Similarly, Wood's statement: "Luther's recognition of biblical inerrancy was confined to the original autographs, and was not tied to the transmitted text" (p. 145)

comes with no support whatsoever of Luther's ever explicitly mentioning the "original autographs."

116. In Shelton, p. 179, from *LW*, XXIII, 235.

117. WA 16. 82, cited in Wood, p. 178.

118. WA 10. 15, cited in Wood, p. 178.

119. Charles Partee, *Calvin and Classical Philosophy* (Leiden: E. J. Brill, 1977), p. 13. He cites A. M. Hunter, "The Erudition of John Calvin," *Evangelical Quarterly* 18 (1946):200. See also John Leith, "John Calvin-Theologian of the Bible," *Itpn.* (July 1971):336. (Hereafter cited as Leith, "John Calvin.")

120. See Quirinus Breen, *John Calvin: A Study in French Humanism*, 2d ed. (Hamden, Conn.: Archon Books, 1968); Josef Bohatec, *Budé und Calvin: Studien zur Gedankenwelt des französischen Frühhumanismus.* (Graz: Hermann Bohlaus, 1950); André Malan Hugo, *Calvin en Seneca* (Groningen: J. B. Wolters, 1957), and others listed in Partee, p. 13. Note also Francois Wendel, *Calvin et l'humanisme* (Paris: Presses Universitaires de France, 1976). (Hereafter cited as Wendel, *l'humanisme.*)

121. Alexandre Ganoczy, *Le Jeune Calvin: Genèse et Evolution de sa Vocation Réformatrice* (Wiesbaden: Franz Steiner Verlag, 1966), p. 195, quoted in Partee, p. 13. Cf. Robert W. Richgels, "Scholasticism Meets Humanism in the Counter-Reformation: The Clash of Cultures in Robert Bellarmine's Use of Calvin in the *Controversies,*" *Sixteenth-Century Journal* 6 (April 1975):58.

122. Ford Lewis Battles, "The Sources of Calvin's Seneca Commentary" (hereafter cited as Battles, "Sources"), in *John Calvin,* Courtenay Studies in Reformation Theology, I, ed. G. E. Duffield (Appleford: Sutton Courtenay Press, 1966), p. 57. See also *Calvin's Commentary on Seneca's De Clementia,* ed. and trans. Ford Lewis Battles and André Malan Hugo (Leiden: E. J. Brill, 1969). (Hereafter cited as Battles/Hugo.)

123. See index 2, "Author and Source Index" of John Calvin, *Institutes of the Christian Religion,* ed. John T. McNeill, trans. Ford Lewis Battles, 2 vols., LCC (Philadelphia: Westminster Press, 1960). All quotations from the *Institutes* (cited as *Inst.*), many of which are cited in the text by book, chapter, and section, are from this translation unless otherwise indicated. See also indices 3 and 5 in Calvin's *Institutions of the Christian Religion,* trans. Ford Lewis Battles (Atlanta: John Knox Press, 1975). This is cited as the

1536 *Institutes.* On the evolution of the *Institutes,* see Jean-Daniel Benoit, "The History and Development of the *Institutio:* How Calvin Worked," in *John Calvin,* ed. Duffield, pp. 102–117.

124. Kristeller, pp. 74–75.

125. Ibid., p. 10. See Chap. 1, "The Humanist Movement."

126. Ibid., p. 10.

127. Ibid., p. 86.

128. See Robert D. Linder, "Calvinism and Humanism: The First Generation," *CH* 44, no. 2 (July 1975):168ff.

129. Kristeller, p. 75.

130. On this see Quirinus Breen, "John Calvin and the Rhetorical Tradition," in *Christianity and Humanism* (Grand Rapids, Mich.: Wm. B. Eerdmans, 1968). (Hereafter cited as Breen, *Christianity and Humanism.*)

131. Partee, p. 5.

132. Augustine, *On Christian Doctrine,* trans. D. W. Robertson, Jr. (New York: Liberal Arts Press, 1958), II, 31 (*PL* 34, 57).

133. See Cicero, *De Oratore,* III. 35. 141–3; III. 19. 73; and III. 31. 122. Cf. Jerrold E. Seigel, *Rhetoric and Philosophy in Renaissance Humanism* (Princeton: Princeton University Press, 1968), p. 7ff.

134. Partee, p. 6.

135. Eugene F. Rice, Jr., "The Humanist Idea of Christianity: Lefèvre d'Etaples and His Circle," *Studies in the Renaissance* 9 (1962):132.

136. He writes that not only agriculture but "likewise all the arts which contribute to the advantage of mankind, are the gifts of God, and that all that belongs to skillful invention has been imparted by him to the minds of men." He concludes, "Shall we not in them also behold and acknowledge his goodness, that his praise and glory may be celebrated both in the smallest and in the greatest affairs?" *Commentary on Isaiah 28:29 Ioannis Calvini opera quae supersunt omnia,* ed. G. Baum, E. Cunitz, and E. Reuss, 59 vols, from *Corpus Reformatorum* (hereafter cited as CR) (Brunsvigae: C. A. Schwetschke, 1863–1900), 36, 483. (Hereafter cited as *CO.*) See also Partee, p. 5.

137. See *Commentary on Matthew 27:43,* CTS, (*CO* 45, 771). English translations of Calvin's *Commentaries* are indicated as those of the Calvin Translation Society [cited as CTS] or Calvin's New Testament Commentaries [cited as CNTC].

138. *Inst.* II. ii. 16.

139. *Commentary on Seneca's De Clementia,*

Pref. iii. n. 5; cited in Battles, "Sources," p. 49. See the Battles/Hugo edition for the roots of Calvin's rhetoric in the classical rhetoricians of Greece and Rome, pp. 81*–84*.

140. Breen, *Christianity and Humanism*, pp. 112–113.

141. See E. David Willis, "Rhetoric and Responsibility in Calvin's Theology," in *The Context of Contemporary Theology: Essays in Honor of Paul Lehmann*, ed. Alexander J. McKelway and E. David Willis (Atlanta: John Knox Press, 1974), p. 46.

142. *Commentary on 1 Cor. 1:17 (CNTC*, IX, 32; CO 49, 319f.).

143. *Inst.* I. viii. 11. Not everyone sees this because "Three Evangelists recount their history in a humble and lowly style" and "for many proud folk this simplicity arouses contempt," *Inst.* I. viii, 11.

144. Partee, p. 8; see also Willis, p. 47ff., and Linder, pp. 167–181.

145. "Subject Matter of the Present Work" (From the French edition of 1560), p. 7.

146. "Subject Matter," p. 6.

147. On this phrase see the note in the LCC edition of the *Institutes*, and other references *passim.*

148. Wilhelm Niesel, *Die Theologie Calvins*, 2d ed. (Munich: Chr. Kaiser Verlag, 1957), p. 25, as cited in Partee, p. 14. The English translation is *The Theology of Calvin*, trans. Harold Knight (Philadelphia: Westminster Press, 1956), p. 25. (Hereafter cited as Niesel, *Theology.*)

149. See his *Commentary on Romans 1:22 (CO* 49, 25).

150. *Inst.* III. vii. 1. See also III. viii. 9 (note 7), where Calvin criticizes the Stoics to whom he owed much. See Battles/Hugo, pp. 49*–53*; Partee, chap. 8; and Francois Wendel, *Calvin: The Origins and Development of His Religious Thought*, trans. Philip Mairet (London: William Collins, Sons & Co. Ltd., 1965), pp. 28–30; 31–34. (Hereafter cited as Wendel, *Calvin: Origins.*)

151. See *Inst.* I. xiv. 1; I. xiii. 1; and *Commentary on Colossians 2:8* (CO 52, 103).

152. *Inst.* II. ii. 15; see also II. ii. 13. It is pointed out, however, that "in his welcome to truth found in nonscriptural sources and in the natural man, we have no thought of the concept (best represented by Duns Scotus) of two kinds of truth that are not mutually harmonious. Rather, his view is of one God-given truth manifested on two levels, one of which is of value for temporal and mundane concerns only," note 58 to II. ii. 15.

153. Partee, p. 4.

154. Partee, p. 22. He cites A. Mitchell Hunter, *The Teaching of Calvin*, 2d ed. (London: James Clarke and Co., Ltd., 1950), p. 38, who thinks Calvin would have completely denied any influence from philosophy, though philosophical elements are clearly present. Cf. Emile Doumergue, *Jean Calvin, Les hommes et les choses de son temps*, 7 vols. (Lausanne: G. Bridel et Cie, 1897–1927), 4:-21.

155. This section depends on an unpublished paper by Ford Lewis Battles, "Calvin's Humanistic Education, Three Universities: Six Teachers" (Pittsburgh Theological Seminary, 1975). (Hereafter cited as Battles, "Education.")

156. Calvin's early life and career are sketched in the standard biographies. See Williston Walker, *John Calvin: The Organiser of Reformed Protestantism*, rep. 1906 (New York: Schocken Books, 1969); and the recent work by T. H. L. Parker, *John Calvin: A Biography* (Philadelphia: Westminster Press, 1975). Parker pays particular attention to Calvin's educational pilgrimage. (Hereafter cited as Parker, *Biography.*)

157. Parker, *Biography*, p. 13.

158. Battles, "Education," p. 10. For these important developments in the study of law see Battles, "Education," p. 11 ff.; cf. Parker, *Biography*, pp. 14ff and Hastings Rashdall, *The Universities of Europe in the Middle Ages*, ed. F. M. Powicke and E. B. Emden, 3 vols. (Oxford: Oxford University Press, 1936), 1:256–258.

159. Parker, *Biography*, p. 15. Humanists treated Justinian's *Corpus Juris Civilis*, the historical commentary on ancient Roman laws, as a literary and historical sourcebook. They bypassed all medieval accretions to it and read it to learn of ancient language and customs.

160. See Battles, "Sources," pp. 42ff. Along with Erasmus, Budé was one of the "two modern pillars" on which Calvin's *De Clementia* commentary was built. Cf. Battles/Hugo, *passim* and 1536 *Institutes*, pp. 314–315.

161. Parker, *Biography*, p. 27. Bohatec argues that Calvin's famous first sentence in the 1539 *Institutes* and later: "Nearly all the wisdom we possess, that is to say, true and sound wisdom, consists of two parts: the knowledge of God and of ourselves,"

has undoubtedly come from Budé. See *Budé und Calvin*, p. 31, n. 47). He discusses it at length (pp. 241ff.) See 1536 *Institutes*, p. 327f.

162. Battles, "Sources," pp. 42–46.

163. Battles, "Sources," pp. 44–45.

164. Battles, "Sources," p. 45. See T. H. L. Parker, *Calvin's New Testament Commentaries* (Grand Rapids, Mich.: Wm B. Eerdmans, 1971), pp. 147–150 (hereafter cited as Parker, *Commentaries*), for Budé's help to Calvin on the Latin text of the Bible. On Calvin and Valla on the Latin text, see pp. 150ff.

165. After Calvin's father died on May 26, 1531, Calvin returned to the study of theology by way of literary studies in Paris. In a famous passage from the preface to his *Commentary on the Psalms*, he describes how he had been providentially led by God in preparation for his conversion. In this he saw himself as following a spiritual pattern similar to that of David in the Old Testament in being called and used in God's service. See John R. Walchenbach, "The Influence of David and the Psalms on the Life and Thought of John Calvin" (Th.M. thesis, Pittsburgh Theological Seminary, 1969). This "prose-poetic" translation by Ford Lewis Battles gives a taste of Calvin's own style:

> From my early childhood
> My father had destined me
> For theology:
> But after a time,
> Having considered that the knowledge
>   of the law
> Commonly enriches those who follow
>   it,
> This hope suddenly made him change
>   his mind.
> That was the reason
> I was withdrawn
> From the study of philosophy
> And put into the study of law,
> To which, although, in obedience to my
>   father,
> I tried to apply myself faithfully,
> God nevertheless by his secret pro-
>   vidence
> Finally made me turn
> In another direction.

See 1536 *Institutes*, p. xx. See xvi.–xxvii. for a panoramic view of Calvin's "conversion."

On the dating of Calvin's movements, see Parker appendices 1 and 2. The dates followed above come from Battles/Hugo and are presented in an expanded form in "An Analysis of the Institutes of the Christian Religion of John Calvin" by Ford Lewis Battles, 2d rev. ed. (Pittsburgh Theological Semifary, 1972), p. 22*.

166. Battles, "Education," p. 8.

167. Battles, "Education," p. 9. Cordier also influenced Calvin's plans for pedagogy in the Genevan schools. See p. 23.

168. Battles, "Education," p. 10. Speculation has been made that Calvin studied theology under John Major, a Scottish theologian who taught at the Collège of Montaigu from 1525 to 1531. He helped revive the spirit of fourteenth-century Nominalism (See *EP*, V, 138–139). Parker doubts that he studied theology, but says "it is not impossible that Calvin went to Major's philosophy lectures," *Biography*, p. 11. See John Patrick Donnelly, *Calvinism and Scholasticism in Vermigli's Doctrine of Man and Grace*, Studies in Medieval and Reformation Thought, ed. Heiko A. Oberman et al. (Leiden: E. J. Brill, 1976), p. 7–8.

169. Wendel, *Calvin: Origins*, p. 22.

170. In Battles, "Education," p. 12. Cf. Wendel, *Calvin: Origins*, p. 22.

171. Wendel, *Calvin: Origins*, p. 22.

172. Battles, "Education," p. 14.

173. Parker, *Biography*, p. 20.

174. This judgment, along with Calvin's estimate of de l'Estoile, were printed in Calvin's first published piece, *A Preface to the Antapologia of Nicholas du Chemin*, (1531). de l'Estoile had caught Alciati plagiarizing from Budé. See Battles/Hugo.

175. Battles, "Education," p. 15. Battles also thinks that Calvin's idea for doing a commentary and annotating it with classical sources came from Alciati.

176. Parker, *Biography*, p. 21.

177. Translated in Battles, "Education," p. 16 and in *CNTC*, vol. 10. Calvin probably did not master Greek until he was twenty-five. See p. 24.

178. Battles, "Education," p. 19; Cf. Wendel, *l'humanisme*, pp. 66ff.

179. Battles, "Education," p. 18.

180. Battles/Hugo, pp. 3*–4*. Budé's family subsequently embraced the Reformed faith after his death in 1540 and settled in Calvin's Geneva. One of the sons translated Calvin's *Commentary on Daniel* (1552) into French.

181. See Battles/Hugo, p. 5*. Cf. Parker, *Biography*, who says we do not know if Calvin attended the lectures, p. 25.

182. Calvin's Genevan Academy began at Saint-Pierre on June 5, 1559, and served as "the most potent educational force for the Reformed faith, destined to produce leaders and pastors not only for Geneva but for Protestant France and for the other countries which accepted Calvinism," Battles, "Education," pp. 22–23.

183. Battles, "Education," p. 21.

184. See Ford Lewis Battles, "God Was Accommodating Himself to Human Capacity," *Itpn.* 31, no. 1 (January 1977): 19–20. (Hereafter cited as Battles, "Accommodating.") Calvin used tools from classical rhetoric as hermeneutical guides for interpreting Scripture. "Metonymy" helped him interpret the words of institution in the Lord's Supper (*Inst.* IV. xvii. 21) and other Old and New Testament "mysteries." (See his discussion in *Inst.* IV. xvii. 21.) "Synecdoche" was useful for understanding the Ten Commandments (*Inst.* II. viii. 10; cf. I. xv. 4); the phrase "the heavens recount the glory of God" (*Com.* 19:1; *CO* 31.194); as well as the divergent accounts of the number of women at the tomb of the risen Christ (*Com.* Matt. 28:8; *CO* 45.798). "*Hysteron proteron*" (a Greek term meaning that the first is put last) was used by Calvin to understand how Jacob was excused of fraud toward his father-in-law (*Com.* Gen. 30:37; *CO* 23.417) and how the death of Isaac could be put in its "proper order" (*Com.* Gen. 35:28; *CO* 23.475). See H. J. Forstman, *Word and Spirit: Calvin's Doctrine of Biblical Authority* (Stanford: Stanford University Press, 1962), pp. 107–109.

185. See J. Preus, chap. 10, "A Medieval Luther," and Kooiman, p. 9.

186. *Inst.* IV. xvi. 23; see also IV. xv. 18. Hans-Joachim Kraus notes that Calvin's Old Testament commentaries are filled with investigations into the backgrounds of passages, particularly with regard to the settings of the Psalms. See "Calvin's Exegetical Principles," (hereafter cited as Kraus, "Principles"), trans. Keith Crim, *Itpn.* 31, no. 1 (January 1977):14. This article was published originally as "Calvins exegetische Prinzipien," *Zeitschrift für Kirchengeschichte* 79 (1968):329–341.

187. Battles, "Education," p. 25.

188. Cited in Walther Köhler, *Erasmus* (1917), pp. 158, 160. This reference is found in Kraus, "Principles," p. 14.

189. Kraus, "Principles," p. 16.

190. Calvin followed Cicero who sought the integration of "wisdom" (philosophy) and "eloquence" (rhetoric). See Breen, *Christianity and Humanism*, pp. 112–113. Cf. Kristeller, p. 19.

191. The Jurists were fundamentally concerned with a person's relationship with others. See Parker, *Biography*, p. 15.

192. Battles, "Accommodating," p. 22. Cicero wrote that "the oration is to be accommodated to the ears of the multitude," *De Oratore*, II, 159. See p. 22 for other classical references.

193. Battles, "Accommodating," p. 22.

194. Ibid., p. 20.

195. Ibid.

196. Ibid. p. 21.

197. Ibid., p. 19. Calvin never used the noun *accommodatio*, but always either the verb *accommodare* or *attemperare*. See also 1536 *Institutes*, p. 351, and endnote on p. 79. On Calvin's earliest use of these verbs see *Comm. Sen. De. Clem.*, 12.22f. (note), 70.10, 97.31, 139.5.

198. Battles writes that we may see this as Calvin's "fundamental way of explaining how the secret, hidden God reveals himself to us. Everything of which our sense brings knowledge to us, from our puny bodies to the stars, microcosm and macrocosm, is the work of a beneficient Creator who for our sakes thus shows himself in these ways, varied, faceted, yet altogether a unity." He continues: "That, however, we may not give the impression of Calvin as a natural theologian, we must quickly assert that this picture of creation as accommodated revelation of God to us takes its scriptural starting point not in Genesis 1 so much as in Romans 1. The *Institutes* is constructed backward from the incarnation through the law, the fall to the creation, from the second Adam to the first Adam. The theater is built, the stage set, wherein the audience, inexcusable in its blindness, may at last view its true destiny in Christ. Step by step, calculated to our capacity, God moves the drama forward to its heavenly dénouement." In "Accommodating," p. 33.

199. See Augustine, *Confessions*, III, 5.

200. This is the notation over I. viii. 2 in which Calvin discusses the different styles of biblical authors and maintains that all the prophets "far exceed human measure" in the wisdom of their teachings.

201. Battles cites three specific Scriptural uses of accommodation for Calvin: law, Lord's Prayer, and sacraments.

202. See Battles, "Accommodating," pp. 36–38 for "The Incarnation as Accommodation."

203. These are three scriptural portraits of God on which the accommodation principle is grounded. See Battles, "Accommodating," pp. 27ff.

204. See Kristeller, pp. 24, 43, and chap. 3, "Renaissance Platonism." Cf. Partee, pp. 105ff.

205. Partee, p. 110. Erasmus disliked the authority given to the "pagan Aristotle" and saw little connection between him and Christ. See *Opus Epistolarum Des. Erasmi Roterodami*, ed. P. S. Allen (Oxford: Clarendon Press, 1910), II, 110, 101. In his *Enchiridion* he wrote: "Of the philosophers, I should wish you to follow the Platonists, because both in very many sentences and their manner of speaking they came very near to the image of the prophets and the Gospel." See *The Enchiridion of Erasmus*, ed. and trans. Raymond Himelick (Bloomington, Ind.: Indiana University Press, 1963), p. 51. On Luther and Aristotle, see above, pp. 80–81.

206. See *Commentary on Genesis 2:18* (*CO*, 23, 46), afd *Inst.* I. v. 11.

207. See *Commentary on Luke 1:75* (*CO* 45, 50) and Plato's *Protagoras*, 331 d. For a discussion of Calvin's sources of knowledge of Plato, see Partee, p. 111, n. 28, and Battles, "Sources," pp. 63–64.

208. Partee, p. 98. Chapter 7 of his work is "Calvin on Aristotle and the Epicureans."

209. Jean Boisset, *Sagesse et Sainteté dans la Pensée de Jean Calvin* (Paris: Université de France, 1959), pp. 284, 221. Cited in Partee, p. 111.

210. Partee, p. 111.

211. See Roy W. Battenhouse, "The Doctrine of Man in Calvin and in Renaissance Platonism," *Journal of the History of Ideas* 9 (1948): 447–471. See also Joseph C. McLelland, "Calvin and Philosophy," *Canadian Journal of Theology* 11 (January 1965): 47.

212. "Introduction" to *Inst.*, lviii. Calvin's debt to Augustine is shown by Luchesius Smits, *Saint Augustin dans l'oeuvre de Calvin*, 2 vols. (Aussen: Van Gorcum, 1957).

213. *Divinitatis sensum* and "seed of religion" (I. iv. 1) "refer generally to a numinous awareness of God, and are closely related to conscience, which is a moral response to God. Cf. I. i. 3 and *Comm. on John* 11:5, 9" (*Inst.* I. iii. 1 n. 2). See also Edward A. Dowey, *The Knowledge of God in Calvin's Theology* (New York: Columbia University Press, 1965), pp. 50ff. (Hereafter cited as Dowey, *Knowledge of God.*) See Calvin's 1538 *Catechism* which begins with the words: "No human being can be found, however barbarous or completely savage, untouched by some awareness of religion." *John Calvin: Catechism 1538*, trans. and annotated by Ford Lewis Battles (Pittsburgh Theological Seminary, 1972), question 1.

214. I. ii. 1. Dowey writes: "One needs scarcely to prove that Calvin's concept of religious knowledge belongs to those that can be classified as existential. There is scarcely to be found a more passionate thinker than Calvin or one more completely controlled by his knowledge of God. For him the religious or existential response is not something that may or may not come in addition to knowledge of God, but is part of its very definition," *Knowledge of God*, p. 26.

215. Calvin wrote in 1537: "The gist of true piety does not consist in a fear which would gladly flee the judgment of God, but ... rather in a pure and true zeal which loves God altogether as Father, and reveres him truly as Lord, embraces his justice and dreads to offend him more than to die." See *Inst.* I. ii. 1, note 1. The original title of the 1536 *Institutes* was: "The whole sum of piety and whatever it is necessary to know in the doctrine of salvation." Calvin's concept of *pietas* (piety) underlies his *Institutes*. " 'For Calvin,' says Emile Doumergue, 'religion and piety are one and the same thing.' " Cited in "Introduction" to the *Institutes* from *Jean Calvin*, IV, 29. See also Ronald S. Wallace, *Calvin's Doctrine of the Christian Life* (Grand Rapids, Mich.: Wm. B. Eerdmans, 1961) and the discussion, "True Piety According to Calvin" in Ford Lewis Battles, trans. and ed., *The Piety of John Calvin An Anthology Illustrative of the Spirituality of the Reformer* (Grand Rapids, Mich.: Baker Book House, 1978), pp. 13–26.

This sense of the awareness of God that Calvin's writings reflect was, for him, "neither a product of speculative thinking nor an incentive to it. He rejects the intellectual indulgence of detached speculation. If he had any talent for this, it was deliberately checked. He never adopts the attitude of the impersonal inquirer. It is not what God is in Himself—a theme in his view beyond human capacity—that concerns his mind, but what God is in relation to His world and to us ("*Non quis sit apud se, sed qualis erga nos.*" I. x. 2; see also I. ii. 2 and III.

ii. 6). God is not known by those who propose to search him out by their proud but feeble reason; rather, he makes himself known to those who in worship, love and obedience consent to learn his will from his Holy Word." From "Introduction" to *Institutes*, li.

216. On the question of "natural theology" in Calvin there was the explosive Barth/Brunner controversy of the 1930s. See *Natural Theology*, trans. P. Fraenkel (London: Geoffrey Bles, Ltd., 1946), composed of Emil Brunner's *Nature and Grace* and Karl Barth's reply *No!* On this see Dowey, Appendix 3, *Knowledge of God*, and G. C. Berkouwer, *General Revelation* (Grand Rapids, Mich.: Wm. B. Eerdmans, 1968), Chapters 2 and 3. See also *CA*, pp. 33ff., and Kenneth S. Kantzer, "Calvin and the Holy Scriptures," in *Inspiration and Interpretation*, ed. Walvoord, pp. 117ff., who cites his own "The Knowledge of God and the Word of God in John Calvin" (Ph.D. dissertation, Harvard University, 1950) for examples of Protestants who ascribe natural theology to Calvin. Another treatment is John Newton Thomas, "The Place of Natural Theology in the Thought of John Calvin," *The Journal of Religious Thought* (1958): 107–136.

217. *Inst.* I. vi. 1. in the "Argument" to his *Commentary on Genesis* Calvin wrote: "Now, in describing the world as a mirror in which we ought to behold God, I would not be understood to assert, either that our eyes are sufficiently clear-sighted to discern what the fabric of heaven and earth represents, or that the knowledge to be hence attained is sufficient for salvation. And whereas the Lord invites us to himself by the means of created things, with no other effect than that of thereby rendering us inexcusable, he has added (as was necessary) a new remedy, or at least by a new aid, he has assisted the ignorance of our mind. For by the Scripture as our guide and teacher, he not only makes those things plain which would otherwise escape our notice, but almost compels us to behold them; as if he had assisted our dull sight with spectacles" (CTS). The metaphor of the "spectacles" has given rise to a variety of interpretations, related as it is to the question of "natural theology."

218. 1536 *Institutes* II. 2 (p. 58).

219. 1536 *Institutes* II. 3 (p. 58).

220. "John Calvin to the Reader," p. 4.

221. This comes from Calvin's French translation of the "Epistle to the Reader" in the 1539 *Institutes:* "If hereafter our Lord shall give me *le moyen et opportunité.*" The LCC English rendering is: "If, after this road has, as it were, been paved, I shall publish any interpretations of Scripture.... " See Parker, p. 5, who supplied the French. In England at the close of the sixteenth century, Richard Hooker wrote of Calvin: "Two things there are of principal moment which have deservedly procured him honour throughout the world: the one his exceeding pains in composing the Institutions of Christian religion; the other his no less industrious travails for the exposition of holy scripture according unto the same Institutions." See his *Treatise on the Laws of Ecclesiastical Polity*, Pref. ii. 8 in *The Works of Richard Hooker*, arranged by John Keble, 2 vols. (New York: D. Appleton, 1844), 1:127.

222. See Parker, *Commentaries*, p. 4 (CO XIV, 317).

223. *Inst.* I. vii. 4. On this doctrine see *Inst.* III. i. 1; III. i. 3f.; III. ii. 15, 33–36; Dowey, *Knowledge of God*, pp. 106ff.; Niesel, *Theology*, pp. 30–39; Doumergue, 4:54–69; *CA*, pp. 70 –116, and note 12 at I. vii. 4. See too W. H. Neuser, "Theologie des Wortes—Schrift, Verheissung und Evangelium bei Calvin," in *Calvinus Theologus*, ed. W. H. Neuser (Neukirchen-Vluyn: Neukirchener Verlag, 1976), pp. 27ff.

224. He also writes: "We ought to remember what I said a bit ago (I. vii. 1): credibility of doctrine is not established until we are persuaded beyond doubt that God is its Author. Thus, the highest proof of Scripture derives in general from the fact that God in person speaks in it. The prophets and apostles do not boast either of their keenness or of anything that obtains credit for them as they speak; nor do they dwell upon rational proofs. Rather, they bring forward God's holy name, that by it the whole world may be brought into obedience to him" (I. vii. 4). Richard C. Prust sees the concept of "doctrine" as "a bridge between the Holy Spirit, as an agent of the authorship, and the written account, which results through the human agent." See "Was Calvin a Biblical Literalist?" *SJT* 20 (Spring 1967): 317.

225. *Inst.* I. vii. 4. Wendel writes: "For Calvin, the interior witness of the Holy Spirit is the supreme criterion upon which the authority of the Scriptures is founded" and "this formal principle of the witness of the Holy Spirit is affirmed by Calvin with growing conviction in the successive editions of his work," *Calvin: Origins,* pp. 157, 158. As R. C. Johnson puts it: "While the authority of the Bible was, functionally speaking, virtually absolute for Calvin, its authority was completely qualified by the necessity of the presence of the Spirit. Just as Scripture could become an instrument of redemption only by the action of the Spirit, so it could become theologically authoritative only under a personal relationship to the sovereign God through the personal presence of his Holy Spirit," p. 54; see also p. 49 and *Inst.* I. vii. 5. On the question of the relation of faith in Christ to faith in Scripture, G. C. Berkouwer writes: "Calvin mentions the testimony of the Spirit in connection with his discussion of Holy Scripture, but later, in his chapter on faith, he does not mention it (*Inst.* II. ii. 41). This may give the impression that he teaches that faith in Scripture precedes saving faith. However, according to the *Institutes* (I. vi. 2), faith in Scripture and saving faith coincide . . . Krusche is justified in his conclusion that 'Calvin has not torn asunder certainty of Scripture and certainty of faith' (*Das Wirken,* p. 217). Calvin does speak emphatically of the *testimonium* and Holy Scripture, but the manner in which he does so does not warrant the charge of formalizing. Rather, Calvin sees Scripture as the clothes in which Christ comes to us (*Inst.* III. ii. 6); cf. his commentary on 1 Peter 2:8; whereas faith is the knowledge of God's will for us, which is learned from his Word (*Inst.* III. ii. 6). For this reason there is no isolated objectification in Calvin, nor a mere interest in showing that there is a God, but a concern that we learn to know what his will concerning us is," *HS,* pp. 46–47.

226. See the discussions of the "external proofs of Scripture" in Calvin interpreters such as Kantzer, pp. 123ff.; *CA,* pp. 84ff.; and their opponent Dowey, *Knowledge of God,* pp. 114ff. See also Seeberg, 2:395– 396. J. I. Packer, who acknowledges Kantzer's and Warfield's work to have been of "special help," (p. 112), in effect joins hands with Dowey by noting that it is on this question of the "firm proofs" where "Warfield's interpretation of the chapter goes astray." See Packer, "Calvin's View of Scripture," in *God's Inerrant Word,* ed. Montgomery, p. 114. The better perspective is that of Bromiley, that these are "secondary aids but they cannot bring people to the faith whose certainty is founded only on the

persuasion of the Spirit." See *Historical Theology: An Introduction* (Grand Rapids, Mich.: Wm. B. Eerdmans, 1978), p. 225.

227. See Dowey, *Knowledge of God,* pp. 114ff. and Gerrish, "Biblical Authority," p. 356, who, while agreeing with Warfield on some points (p. 355, n. 2), criticizes him for seeing Calvin as teaching that rational arguments work inseparably along with the Holy Spirit to authenticate Scripture as God's Word to the reader—p. 356 n. 2.

228. See Dowey, *Knowledge of God,* p. 137.

229. G. C. Berkouwer, *A Half Century of Theology: Movements and Motives,* ed. and trans. Lewis B. Smedes (Grand Rapids, Mich.: Wm. B. Eerdmans, 1977), p. 157. (Hereafter cited as Berkouwer, *Half Century,*) See *Inst.* III. ii. 1–2.

230. *Inst.* III. ii. 6; cf. Dowey, *Knowledge of God,* pp. 153ff. and Seeberg, 2:401ff.

231. Berkouwer, *Half Century,* writes: The Reformers "thought about the nature of faith and they . . . used various words to get at it: words like *notitia, assensus,* and *fiducia.* Interestingly, they never thought it necessary to set these off into different time periods of Christian experience. Calvin used the word *cognitio,* but did not reduce faith to intellectual knowledge with it because he insisted that this *cognitio* was directed to 'the benevolence of God toward us' and was more an affair of the heart than of the head. They were not offended either by words like *notitia* and *assensus.* Intuitively, they refused to isolate aspects of faith from one another. 'How could it be *fiducia* without at the same time, and because it is *fiducia,* being *notitia* and *assensus* too?' (Barth, *CD* I/1, 269). The reformers never talked as if one first accepted and agreed to something and thereafter believed and trusted," p. 175.

232. *Inst.* I. viii. 13. He concludes, citing Augustine, *The Usefulness of Belief,* xviii. 36 (*PL* 42, 92; LCC VI, 322): "Augustine therefore justly warns that godliness and peace of mind ought to come first if a man is to understand anything of such great matters."

233. *Inst.* I. ix. 3. See also Dowey, *Knowledge of God,* pp. 117ff.; Forstman; J. K. S. Reid, *The Authority of Scripture: A Study of Reformation and Post-Reformation Understanding of the Bible* (London: Methuen, 1962), pp. 45ff.

234. *Commentary on John 14:1* (CTS; *CO* XLVII, 321d, 322a); see also *Inst.* III. ii. 1.; Dowey, *Knowledge of God,* p. 158.

235. *Commentary on John 3:16* (CTS; *CO* XLVII, 64d.). Calvin makes this point repeatedly: "For faith ought to look to him (the Son of God) alone; on him it relies, in him it rests and terminates," *Commentary on Ephesians 4:13* (CO LI, 200c; in Dowey, *Knowledge of God*, p. 158).

236. *Inst.* III. ii. 6. The "permanent relationship between faith and the Word" is emphasized by Calvin when he writes that if faith turns away from its proper goal it becomes "uncertain credulity and vague error of mind. The same Word is the basis whereby faith is supported and sustained; if it turns away from the Word, it falls. Therefore, take away the Word and no faith will then remain."

237. *Commentary on John 5:39* (CTS; CR XLVII, 125); cf. CR XLV, 817 and L, 45.

238. CR LIII, 560, in Niesel, *Theology*, p. 27.

239. From *Commentary on 1 Peter 1:20*, translated in Battles, "Accommodating," p. 38.

240. From *Commentary on 1 Peter 1:20*, in Battles, "Accommodating," p. 38.

241. *Inst.* I. xiii. 1. Berkouwer points to the tendencies toward "accommodation" in the Scriptures at John 16:12; 16:4 and the " 'adjustment' in a pedagogical situation or a certain purpose in approaching someone with the Word of God (Heb. 5:13–14; 1 Cor. 9:20)," *HS*, p. 176.

242. *Inst.* III. xxi. 4, from Augustine, "On Genesis in the Literal Sense," V, 3,6 (*PL* 34, 323). The context is the question of whether or not it is perilous to preach the doctrine of predestifation.

243. *Inst.* I. xvii. 13. The context here is a passage of Scripture where God is said to repent. Forstman sees Calvin protecting "the immutability and wholly otherness of God" by his use of accommodation (p. 115). He cites passages where the concept is either stated explicitly or implied:

God
remembering —Com. Ps. 98:3 (*CO* 32.48) Ex. 6:5 (*CO* 24.79) Ex. 2:23 (*CO* 24.34) Gen. 8:1 (*CO* 23.135)
resting —Com. Gen. 2:2 (*CO* 23.32)
repenting —Com. Jer. 26:17–19 (*CO* 38.533) Gen. 6:6 (*CO* 23.118)
returning —Com. Hosea 5:15 (*CO* 42.316–317)

sleeping —Com. Ps. 44:23 (*CO* 31.447–448)
yearning —Com. Dt. 5:29 (*CO* 24.207–208)
smelling —Com. Gen. 8:21 (*CO* 23.139)
seeing —Com. Dt. 32:19 (*CO* 25.367)
wondering —Com. Matt. 8:9 (*CO* 45.236–237)
laughing —Com. Ps. 2:4–6 (*CO* 31.44)
speaking —Com. Ps. 2:4–6 (*CO* 31.44)
and using spears and bucklers —Com. Ps. 35:2 (*CO* 31.346)

244. *Commentary on John 3:12* (*CNTC*, p. 70). God's purpose in revealing Himself to humans was not to give them a perfect human philosophy. His purpose was to bring people into a relationship to Himself and to strengthen their faith. See Calvin's comments on Peter's escape from prison in *Commentary on Acts 12:10* (*CNTC*, p. 341). The concept of accommodation for Calvin was a key to the manner in which God acted in every area. God's accommodated activity in human affairs was recorded in God's accommodated style of revelation in Scripture. In the 1536 *Institutes* he applied the concept in a discussion of election. See chap. 2 on "Faith," p. 79.

245. These are three scriptural portraits of God identified by Battles as being, for Calvin, the grounds of accommodation ("Accommodating," pp. 27–31). Recall Calvin's rhetorical training and classical rhetoric's concern with accommodation and "intention."

246. *Commentary on Psalm 78:60* (CTS; III, 270).

247. Battles, "Accommodating," p. 26.

248. Ibid., p. 27.

249. *Commentary on Romans 3:4* (*CNTC*, p. 61). Calvin says: "Paul followed the Greek version, which also suited his purpose here better."

250. *Commentary on Hebrews 10:6* (*CNTC*, p. 136). See also Hebrews 11:21 and Ronald S. Wallace, *Calvin's Doctrine of the Word and Sacrament* (Edinburgh: Oliver and Boyd, 1953), pp. 110ff. (Hereafter cited as Wallace, *Word and Sacrament*.)

251. *Commentary on Hebrews 2:7* (*CNTC*, p. 22).

252. *Commentary on Romans 10:6 (CNTC*, p. 225). Cf. 1 Corinthians 10:8 where Paul mentions 23,000 being killed instead of 24,-000 (Numbers 25:9). Calvin says: "It is not a new thing where it is not intended to present a minute enumeration of individuals, to give a number which substantially approximates the actual truth." See Tholuck, p. 345. His attitude is summed up when in commenting on Isaiah 64 and noting that in verse 1 the expression: "That thou wouldest come down" is an example of God "accommodating" himself, Calvin cites Paul's use of the passage in 1 Corinthians 2:9 following the Greek version and "in different words." He says: "In this respect the Apostles were not squeamish; for they paid more attention to the matter than to the words ... " (CTS).

253. *Commentary on Acts 7:16.* See too his comments at Ephesians 4:8 (on Psalm 68: 18), where Paul interprets in such a way as "to serve the purpose of his argument." By so doing he has "departed not a little from the true meaning." Cf. Leith, who notes other instances of Calvin's "textual criticism," "John Calvin," p. 337.

254. *Commentary on a Harmony of the Evangelists* (CTS, 272). Calvin's curiosity is not piqued here to probe behind the biblical text in front of him. The implications of this for speculation about what Calvin might have thought about any "original autograph" of Scripture are assessed differently by Doumergue, 4:76–78 and Dowey, *Knowledge of God*, p. 104. See also John T. McNeill, "The Significance of the Word of God for Calvin," *CH* 28, no. 2 (June 1959): 131–146, who reminds us that Calvin is critical of the "defects in the discourse" of the *original text* as for example at Acts 4:6 and Romans 5:15 where he speaks with reference to the actual biblical writers themselves—Luke and Paul —not just of the "errors" in the text's transmission by careless copyists (pp. 144–145).

255. For a discussion of both the interchange between Calvin and Servetus and the surrounding circumstances see Roland Bainton, *Hunted Heretic: The Life and Death of Michael Servetus, 1511–1553* (Boston: Beacon Press, 1960; rep. 1953), pp. 94–97 and 184–185. Cf. Robert Willis, *Servetus and Calvin* (London: Henry S. King, 1877), pp. 325 –326. Kenneth S. Kantzer has apparently misunderstood the facts of the situation and Calvin's motivation when he asserts that Servetus was indicted because he "taught

that the Bible was not true in a minor geographical detail in the Old Testament." See Kantzer's article, "Evangelicals and the Inerrancy Question," in *Evangelical Roots*, ed. Kenneth S. Kantzer (New York: Thomas Nelson, 1978), pp. 93–94. Cf. Kantzer's article of the same title in *Christianity Today* (April 21, 1978), p. 19. To infer from this incident that Calvin held to the technical inerrancy of the Bible in the sense that Kantzer himself does is entirely unwarranted both by the evidence of the Servetus situation and in view of Calvin's understanding of the accommodated character of biblical language as documented above.

256. *Commentary on Genesis 1:14–15.*

257. *Commentary on Genesis 1:16.*

258. See *HS*, pp. 227–228.

259. *HS*, p. 246.

260. See Wallace, *Word and Sacrament*, chap. 7, "The Preached Word as the Word of God," and T. H. L. Parker, *The Oracles of God: An Introduction to the Preaching of John Calvin* (London: Lutterworth Press, 1947).

261. Parker, *Biography*, p. 90, quoting *Inst.* I. vii. 1.

262. CO LIII, 266, cited in Parker, *Biography*, p. 90. *Commentary on Isaiah 50:10* (CR XXXVII, 224): "God does not wish to be heard but by the voice of His ministers" (CTS).

263. CO XXV, 666f., cited in Parker, *Biography*, p. 90. The Second Helvetic Confession (1566) picks up this understanding also. The title of chapter 1 is "Of the Holy Scripture being the true Word of God." A subheading in that chapter is "The Preaching of the Word of God is the Word of God." See Appendix for text.

264. *Commentary on Isaiah 11:4* (CTS; CR XXXVI. 240).

265. *Inst.* IV. i. 5. See also Sermon on Ephesians 4:11–14 (CR LI. 565).

266. *certi et authentici spiritus sancti amanuenses.* See also *Inst.* IV. viii. 8, where Calvin speaks of Christ's Spirit "dictating the words" (*verba quodammodo dictante Christi Spiritu*).

267. Parker writes: "It is these primary truths of revelation that Calvin seeks to express in the image of dictation to a secretary, an occupation which, as we have seen, was part of his own daily life. The 'speaker' in the Scriptures is God: God the Father reveals himself in the Son by the Holy Spirit: so that man may understand him, God uses completely human speech," *Com-*

mentaries, pp. 58–59. McNeill writes that Calvin's view of the "origin and inspiration of Scripture" is one "in which the writers are not automatons," p. 140.

268. Parker, *Biography*, p. 76. See also Battles, "Sources," pp. 40ff. and Leith, "John Calvin," p. 336.

269. *Praef. in Chry. Hom.* (*CR* IX. 835). For Calvin's opinions of the Greek and Latin Fathers as scriptural commentators see *CR* IX, 834. Origen, Calvin says, "succeeds notably in obscuring the straight-forward sense of Scripture by endless allegories." Cyril is "an outstanding interpreter, . . . second to Chrysostom" among the Greeks. Theophylact received all his "praiseworthy qualities from Chrysostom." Among the Latins, Hilary's commentaries on the Psalter "have little value for understanding the mind of the prophet." Jerome is "almost completely sunk in allegories in which he twists Scripture in far too free a manner." "Better and richer" than Jerome is Ambrose, "despite his extreme brevity." See John Robert Walchenbach, "John Calvin as Biblical Commentator: An Investigation into Calvin's Use of John Chrysostom as an Exegetical Tutor" (Ph.D. dissertation, University of Pittsburgh, 1974) pp. 28, 30. Hereafter cited as Walchenbach, "Calvin as Commentator" See also John H. McIndoe, "John Calvin: Preface to the Homilies of Chrysostom," trans. John H. McIndoe, *The Hartford Quarterly* 5, no. 2 (Winter 1965):19–26.

270. See *Commentary on 1 Corinthians* (*CR* XLIX, 159 and *CR* XLIX, 92). In Walchenbach, "Calvin as Commentator," p. 166. See also Parker, *Commentaries*, pp. 79–80, and *Praef. Chry. Hom.* (*CR* IX, 835).

271. *in simplici verborum sensu contorquendo*, *Praef. in Chry. Hom.* (*CR* IX, 835), in Walchenbach, "Calvin as Commentator," p. 30.

272. See Walchenbach, "Calvin as Commentator," pp. 54, 30. According to Parker, for Calvin, "the context is all-important. Individual words or clauses are not allowed any eccentricity; they are controlled by the context. Conversely, the meaning of the context is understood by the interrelationship of the meanings of the individual parts. Hence these parts are to be interpreted only in relationship to the other parts. This is illustrated clearly by Calvin's practice in the sermons, where he will not single out for special treatment some sublime verse, far less a clause, but builds up the meaning of

the passage from a patient explanation of the members," *Commentaries*, p. 80. See also Frei, pp. 25–27.

273. Walchenbach, "Calvin as Commentator," p. 199.

274. See *Calvinus Grynaeo, Epistula* 191 (*CR* X, 402). In Walchenbach, "Calvin as Commentator," p. 157. See also the translation in *Commentary on Romans* (*CNTC*, p. 1). On the rhetorical roots of these terms, see Parker, *Commentaries*, pp. 50–51.

275. Walchenbach, "Calvin as Commentator," p. 158.

276. See his *Commentary on Galatians 4:22–24*, the *locus classicus* of his severe judgments on allegory and defense of the "genuine," "simple," and "literal" sense of Scripture: "Because he says, 'this is an allegory,' Origen—and many others with him—seized the occasion to corrupt the Scripture in diverse ways, with inferences far removed from its true and natural sense. For they falsely concluded that the literal sense was too inferior and contemptible, and that it was therefore necessary for them to seek the loftier secrets hidden under the bark of the letter, which can only be extracted by forging allegories. This they did readily; for the world has always preferred, and always will prefer, subtle speculations to firm, solid doctrine. In time the most acute forging was accepted and approved, so that not only was the person who simply amused himself interpreting Scripture not restrained, but the greatest praise was conferred upon him. . . . Undoubtedly this [subtle transfiguration of the inviolable Word of God] was an invention of Satan, to diminish the authority of the Scriptures. . . . And the Lord God avenged this profanation with just judgment when he permitted the pure meaning to be buried under corrupt and false glosses" (CTS; CO L, 236f.). See Parker, *Commentaries*, pp. 63–64.

277. *Commentary on II Corinthians 3:6.* See also *Commentary on Daniel 8:25*: "It seems to me far too frivolous to search for allegories."

278. *HS*, p. 129. Calvin does permit a very limited use of allegory but the usage "ought not to go beyond the limits set by the rule of Scripture, let alone suffice as the foundation for any doctrines," *Inst.* II. v. 19 (cf. note 39). His occasions for admitting allegory (see Isa. 33:17–18) in referring to one of the traditional spiritual senses of Scripture are confined to the Old Testament. Because he saw the whole Bible as a record of God's dealings with His people, as salvational-historical, he could deal with even the historical books according to the literal sense and their own context. Calvin is interested in David, for example, "as the object of God's goodness, and he will expound the psalms historically in reference to their writer and his life" (Parker, *Commentaries*, p. 65). But since God is at work in history in Jesus Christ, there is also more to history "than meets the eye," so to speak. Yet for Calvin this "spiritual sense" cannot "be opposed to the historical, for this history is the account of God's activity within history, the account of the earthly life of the incarnate Son of God and of his continued activity through the Church, not needing to be spiritualized" (p. 67). See also Frei, pp. 24–25.

279. Parker, *Biography*, p. 77.

280. Parker, *Commentaries*, p. 68. The "lucid brevity" (*perspicua brevitas*) that Calvin enjoins is defined by his saying that for the commentator "it is almost his only task to unfold the mind of the writer whom he has undertaken to expound." He "misses his mark, or at least strays outside his limits, by the extent to which he leads his readers away from the meaning of his author" ("Dedication" to *Commentary on Romans—CNTC*, p. 1). Thus, this "lucid brevity" "should not be understood as a style of writing that will make the book easier and more pleasant to read, but as the rhetorical method by which the expositor achieves his task of revealing the mind of the writer. *Perspicua* therefore bears now the sense of 'illuminating' and *brevitas* of 'pertinence' or 'relevance,' " Parker, *Commentaries*, p. 54.

281. "Dedication" to *Commentary on Romans* (*CNTC*, p. 2).

282. Parker, *Commentaries*, p. 52.

283. Ibid., p. 3, quoting "Dedication."

284. "John Calvin to the Reader," pp. 4–5.

285. Walchenbach, "Calvin as Commentator," p. 162.

286. See Parker, *Biography*, p. 77. Parker makes five points about Calvin's doctrine of Scripture: "(1) Scripture is the record of God's self-revelation to men; (2) it is also the interpretation of that self-revelation; (3) the record itself is made at the instigation of God; (4) the interpretation is God's own interpretation of the recorded events; (5) the language of the record is given to the writer by God. In this sense the Bible is God's

Word to men, in which he reveals the relationship with them which he has determined and established in Jesus Christ, the relationship of Creator-creature, of Redeemer-redeemed," p. 76.

287. See Edward A. Dowey, "Revelation and Faith in the Protestant Confessions," *Pittsburgh Perspective* (March 1961):9. (Hereafter cited as Dowey, "Revelation and Faith.") Karl Barth notes the same thing in *CD* I/2, 547. Calvin's Catechisms, however do not treat the "Scripture principle" either.

288. The Reformed Confessions are: Zwingli's Sixty-Seven Articles (1523); The Ten Theses of Berne (1528); The Tetrapolitan Confession (1530); The First Confession of Basel (1534); The First Helvetic Confession (1536; also known as The Second Confession of Basel); The Lausanne Articles (1536): The Geneva Confession (1536); The French Confession of Faith (1559); The Scots Confession (1560); The Belgic Confession of Faith (1561); and The Second Helvetic Confession (1566). These are translated and collected in Arthur C. Cochrane, ed., *Reformed Confessions of the 16th Century* (Philadelphia: Westminster Press, 1966). See also Calvin's Geneva Catechism (1541) in T. F. Torrance, ed., *The School of Faith, The Catechisms of the Reformed Church* (Greenwood, S.C.: Attic Press, 1959). Cf. the discussions and selections in *The Faith of Christendom*, ed., Brian A. Gerrish (Cleveland: World Publishing, 1963); *Creeds of the Churches*, ed. John H. Leith (New York: Doubleday & Co., 1963), and Philip Schaff, *Creeds of Christendom*, 3 vols. (New York: Harper & Brothers, 1877), who cite other collections. *A Commentary on the Confession of 1967 and an Introduction to "The Book of Confessions"* (hereafter cited as Dowey, *Commentary*) (Philadelphia: Westminster Press, 1968) was written by Edward A. Dowey. The Book of Confessions is the confessional standard of The United Presbyterian Church in the United States of America and contains some of the sixteenth-century Reformed Confessions.

Lutheran Confessions from this period, found in Theodore G. Tappert, ed., *The Book of Concord* (Philadelphia: Muhlenberg Press, 1959), are The Augsburg Confession (1530); Apology of the Augsburg Confession (1531); The Smalcald Articles (1537); Treatise on the Power and Primacy of the Pope (1537); The Small Catechism of Dr.

Martin Luther (1529); The Large Catechism of Dr. Martin Luther (1529); and The Formula of Concord (1577). Cf. Edmund Schlink, *Theology of the Lutheran Confessions* (Philadelphia: Muhlenberg Press, 1961) and the sections cited in Schaff, Gerrish, and Leith.

289. See Schlink, p. 24. Barth believed that Reformed documents were more explicit since they represent "the common substance of the Evangelical teaching at a later stage, at the stage at which it was already achieving, provisionally, a final form, and therefore with a clarity which had everywhere existed in practice right from the outset, but which was hardly ripe for theoretical expression in the third decade of the century—the great period of the Lutheran reformation," *CD* I/2, p. 547.

290. For a very valuable discussion of the issue of authority in relation to the doctrine of the Church, see Robert S. Paul, *The Church in Search of Its Self* (Grand Rapids, Mich.: Wm. B. Eerdmans, 1972), Chap. 2 (hereafter cited as Paul, *Church*) and his earlier work, *Ministry* (Grand Rapids, Mich. Wm. B. Eerdmans, 1965), chap. 6. Paul shows how three channels of authority—the church, the Bible, and individual revelation—all seen through the eye of human reason, took root historically and expressed themselves in varying ecclesiologies: the church-type; the sect-type; and the "third-type" (modeled after Ernst Troeltsch). Each of these stressed in turn the historical continuity of the church; the restoration of the

Bible; and an appeal to "the Spirit" as its primary basis of spiritual authority. See Paul, *Church*, chaps. 3–5.

291. Rupert E. Davies, *The Problem of Authority in the Continental Reformers: A Study in Luther, Zwingli and Calvin* (London: Epworth, 1946), p. 69. Davies notes that "in Zwingli's writings the word 'Gospel' is as interchangeable with 'Word of God' and 'Scripture' as they are with each other," p. 74.

292. Cited in Davies, p. 69, from *von der Klarheit und Gewissheit usw*, (1522), I, 382 (from Zwingli's *Werke*).

293. See *Inst.* IV. i. 9.

294. *Inst.* I. vii. 2; cf. I. vii. 5. See Robert D. Preus, *The Theology of Post-Reformation Lutheranism*, 2 vols. (St. Louis: Concordia Publishing House, 1970), 1:296–299 for Lutheran equivalents.

295. This caution on the need for preaching was not heeded by later "hyper-Calvinists" such as Joseph Hussey (b. 1660) and John Skepp who, because of their rigid view of predestination and the work of the Holy Spirit, believed it was not proper to hold out the offer of grace to those who might not be elect. See Peter Toon, *Hyper-Calvinism* (London: The Olive Tree, 1967), pp. 70 ff.

296. *Inst.* I. xvii. 1, as translated in Wendel, *Calvin: Origins*, p. 181.

297. Dowey, "Revelation and Faith," p. 14.

298. Dowey, *Commentary*, pp. 204–205, quoting from Bullinger's *Summa Christenlicher Religion* (Zurich: Christoffel Froschouwer, 1576).

g. Selected Bibliography

Battles, Ford Lewis. "God Was Accommodating Himself to Human Capacity." *Interpretation* 31, no. 1 (January 1977): 19–38.

Bornkamm, Heinrich. *Luther and the Old Testament*. Translated by Eric W. and Ruth C. Gritsch. Fortress Press, 1969.

Forstman, H. J. *Word and Spirit: Calvin's Doctrine of Biblical Authority*. Stanford University Press, 1962.

Gerrish, Brian. "Biblical Authority and the Continental Reformation." *Scottish Journal of Theology*, 10 (1957): 337–360.

Gerrish, Brian. *Grace and Reason: A Study in the Theology of Luther*. Clarendon Press, 1962.

Johnson, Robert Clyde. *Authority in Protestant Theology*. Westminster Press, 1959.

Kooiman, Willem Jan. *Luther and the Bi-*

ble. Translated by John Schmidt. Muhlenberg Press, 1961.

Kraus, Hans Joachim. "Calvin's Exegetical Principles." Translated by Keith Crim. *Interpretation* 31, no. 1 (January 1977): 8–18.

Lehmann, Paul L. "The Reformers' Use of the Bible." *Theology Today* 3, no. 3 (October 1946): 328–344.

McNeill, John T. "The Significance of the Word of God for Calvin." *Church History* 28, no. 2 (June 1959): 131–146.

Mallard, William. "John Wyclif and the Tradition of Biblical Authority," *Church History* 30, no. 1 (March 1961): 50–60.

Parker, T. H. L. *Calvin's New Testament Commentaries.* Wm. B. Eerdmans, 1971.

Parker, T. H. L. *John Calvin: A Biography.* Westminster Press, 1975.

Partee, Charles B. *Calvin and Classical Philosophy.* E. J. Brill, 1977.

Pelikan, Jaroslav. *Luther the Expositor.* Concordia Publishing House, 1959.

Shelton, Raymond Larry. "Martin Luther's Concept of Biblical Interpretation in Historical Perspective." Ph.D. dissertation, Fuller Theological Seminary, 1974.

Wallace, Ronald S. *Calvin's Doctrine of the Word and Sacrament.* Oliver and Boyd, 1953.

Wendel, Francois. *Calvin: The Origins and Development of His Religious Thought.* Translated by Philip Mairet. William Collins, Sons & Co. Ltd., 1965.

CHAPTER 3

Concern for Literary Form in the Post-Reformation Period

a. From Reformation to Orthodoxy: Melanchthon, Martyr, Zanchi, Beza

Calvin died in 1564. By that time the Roman Catholic Counter-Reformation had consolidated its strength. The Jesuits were founded in 1540. In 1542, Pope Paul III established the "Congregation of the Inquisition" as the court of final appeal in heresy trials. Protestant doctrines had been repudiated at the Council of Trent (1545–1563). In response, the second generation of Reformers tried to battle Roman Catholicism by using the Roman Catholics' own weapons against them. For example, Protestants tried eventually to prove the authority of the Bible, using the same Aristotelian arguments Roman Catholics had used to prove the authority of the church.

The second generation of Reformers by then were also fighting the extreme rationalism of Faustus Socinus (1539–1604) and the unitarians. Socinus laid great stress on reason, but nonetheless claimed that without revelation, human beings could not know God. "Natural theology," thus rejected by heretics, became an important element in post-Reformation Protestant orthodoxy. When Socinus asserted that reason did not lead to traditional Trinitarian doctrines, orthodox Protestants attempted to defend their stance by reason as well as Scripture.[1]

Intra-Protestant disputes also had arisen that could not be settled by appeal to the biblical text, since both sides claimed scriptural support. Some Protestants, therefore, returned to the resources of medieval scholasticism for philosophical arguments to augment their positions. An upsurge of interest in metaphysical speculation began in the late sixteenth and took root in the seventeenth century.[2] For example, in the Reformed camp, orthodox theologians became so committed to scholasticism that they virtually ceased to refer to Calvin, whose thought no longer had normative value for them.[3] The French national synod of Alais in 1620 passed a rule that every Reformed academy should have a professor of theology whose task would be to expound theological topics "as succinctly as possible, in a scholastic manner, in order that the students may be profited as much as possible and that they may be enabled to apply themselves most forcefully to disputes and metaphysical distinctions."[4]

The followers of Luther and Calvin in the seventeenth century in Europe endeavored to systematize the work of their masters by casting it into an Aristotelian mold. Thus a period of Protestant scholasticism was launched in the immediate post-Reformation period.[5] This Protestant scholasticism rejected the Augustinian approach of faith leading to understanding and reverted to a one-sided Thomistic approach that gave reason priority over faith. There was a significant shift among orthodox Protestants from the Neoplatonic presuppositions of the Reformers to the Aristotelian assumptions of the Reformers' medieval opponents. Two aspects of the central Christian tradition were also progressively abandoned. Theology was no longer viewed as a practical, moral discipline exclusively directed toward the salvation of people and their guidance in the life of faith. Instead it now became an abstract, speculative, technical science that attempted to lay foundations for philosophical mastery of all areas of thought and life. Further, and equally far-reaching in its consequences, the concept of accommodation was discarded. Theologians now unashamedly contended that they thought God's thoughts because the human mind was fitted to think in God's ways. God was no longer the parent who had condescended to speak children's language for their benefit. God was now the supplier, through revelation, of up-to-date scientific information. While scholastic theologians did not claim to know all that God knew extensively, they claimed a one-to-one correspondence between the theological knowledge they had and the way in which God Himself knew it. Precision replaced piety as the goal of theology.

Systematizing Luther: Philipp Melanchthon (1497–1560)

Philipp Melanchthon was born at Bretten, Baden in Germany and died at Wittenberg. His great uncle was the noted humanist scholar Reuchlin, who had a significant influence on his career. Melanchthon studied at Heidelberg and Tübingen. Through Reuchlin's recommendation, Melanchthon became Professor of Greek at the University of Wittenberg.

At Wittenberg, Melanchthon worked closely with Luther, assisting him in translating the Bible into German. Melanchthon saw his chief task, however, as that of giving an exact form to Luther's theology and of setting it forth as an integrated, scientific system. In 1521 Melanchthon published his *Loci Communes Rerum Theologicarum*. This work went through many editions and greatly influenced the transition from Luther's own theology of the cross, to the more philosophical, systematized theology of post-Reformation Lutheranism.[6]

We have already noted Calvin's dissatisfaction with Luther's Aristotelian method of biblical interpretation according to preconceived *loci*. Melanchthon also shifted emphasis away from Luther's concentration on Christ as the central interpretative principle in the Bible. But Melanchthon, in contrast, quoted and used all parts of Scripture as of equal importance, allowing his system, rather than the *kerygma* to be the organizing principle.[7] Melanchthon did not elucidate a doctrine of Scripture in the *Loci*. In succeeding editions of the work, he moved further and further from Luther's own theological method and manner of using biblical texts. The categories of Aristotle's philosophy gained increasing prominence. Despite his early humanistic training, Melanchthon came to utilize as central, Aristotelian terms including final cause, proximate and instrumental causes, undistributed middles, and unproved minors. Melanchthon was an important transitional figure in moving away from the biblical theology of Luther toward a more scholastic, philosophical system of theology.[8]

On the Lutheran side, the movement Melanchthon had begun was carried on and crystallized in the *Loci Theologici* of John Gerhard (1582–1637). Gerhard contended that the Scriptures met Aristotle's qualifications for providing the principles of a science. The doctrine of Scripture, therefore, ceased to be an article of faith for Gerhard. It became, rather, the *principium* (foundation) of other articles of faith.[9]

Scholasticism had not ceased to exist as a theological method during the sixteenth century despite the hostility of Luther and Calvin. Many of those who followed Luther and Calvin as proponents of reformation nevertheless continued to use elements of scholastic methodology mixed with a more Augustinian approach. Pressures of the post-Reformation period encouraged some of the secondary reformers to fall back on methods that promised philosophical certainty. The movement from Melanchthon through Gerhard to a full-blown post-Reformation Lutheranism has been traced elsewhere.[10] Less attention has been given until recently to the sources of scholastic influence among Reformed theologians. Evidence now points strongly in the direction of Italian Aristotelians who became part of the Reformed movement. Peter Martyr Vermigli and Girolamo Zanchi were both Italians who retained strong Aristotelian, scholastic tendencies. Both of them influenced Theodore Beza who assumed Calvin's mantle in Geneva.[11] We need to examine the gradual development from a reformational to a scholastic method in the theology of these three—Martyr, Zanchi, and Beza—in order to understand the final, radical departure from Calvin's theology in the late seventeenth century in the person of Francis Turretin, professor of theology in Geneva from 1653 to 1687.

Aristotle and Accommodation: Peter Martyr Vermigli (1499 or 1500–1562)

A key figure in the rise of Protestant scholasticism was Peter Martyr Vermigli. Martyr was born in Florence and educated by the Augustinians. He studied at the University of Padua, the leading center of Renaissance Aristotelianism, and received his doctorate in theology in 1526. There he became thoroughly grounded in Thomism and acquainted with all the current strands of Aristotelian philosophy. Martyr distrusted Latin translations of Aristotle, and learned Greek on his own in order to master the Greek text of Aristotle at first hand. When he was forced to leave Italy, one of the books he managed to salvage was the Greek *Omnia Opera* of Aristotle.[12]

Martyr spent some fifteen years as a preacher, professor, and superior of the Augustinian order. In 1537 he was promoted to the important post of prior at the monastery of Saint Peter ad Aram in Naples. There for the first time he read the works of the Protestant reformers, particularly Melanchthon, Bucer, and Zwingli. Also, he met and was influenced by the Spanish humanist and religious writer Juan de Valdés (c. 1500–1541). Valdés, while he remained a Catholic, taught ideas similar to themes prominent in Protestant thought. Martyr was stimulated by Valdés's lectures on 1 Corinthians and began to lecture on that Epistle at his monastery.

Martyr began to take on a new theological orientation. In his exegesis of 1 Corinthians 3:11–13, for instance, he suggested that the image of salvation through fire did not mean purgatory in St. Paul's mind. After that, only the support of powerful friends in Rome enabled him to continue preaching. In 1540 Martyr gained an important post as prior of Saint Frediano in Lucca. His zeal for reform made him popular with the monks, but soon it became evident that his doctrinal sympathies were with Calvin, Bucer, Melanchthon, and Zwingli. With the establishment of the Roman Inquisition, Martyr was forced to flee Italy for Zurich.

By December 1542, Martyr had become successor to Wolfgang Capi-
to (1478–1541) as professor of theology in the city of Strassburg. There
he lectured on the minor prophets and the Pentateuch. His care for
method and a precise use of language made him popular as a teacher.
His wide learning was apparent in the use of Patristic quotations to
amplify his exegetical comments. The Interim of Augsburg of 1548
sought a religious settlement between Protestant and Catholic, but under
its threat Martyr was glad to accept Thomas Cranmer's (1489–1556)
invitation to come to England. There he was appointed Regius Professor
of Divinity at Oxford and made a canon of Christ Church. At Oxford in
1549 he participated vigorously in controversies over the Lord's Supper.[13] Along with Bucer, who was Regius Professor at Cambridge, Martyr
helped shape the course of Reformation in England.[14] With the accession
of Mary in 1553, however, he resigned and returned to Strassburg.[15] In
1556 he accepted Heinrich Bullinger's (1504–1575) invitation to become
professor of Hebrew at Zurich. There he taught till he died on December
12, 1562.

Peter Martyr represents a transitional stage between the Augustinian
orientation to Scripture fostered by Calvin and the full-blown Protestant
scholasticism that developed in the century after Calvin. Although Martyr's theology had a humanist-biblical orientation similar to Calvin's,
there were also strong scholastic undercurrents.[16]

In contrast to Luther and Calvin, Martyr, like Aquinas, saw theology
as a *scientia* (science) with its principles borrowed from revelation. When
he discussed the nature of theology he borrowed his content, terminology, and examples from the opening question of Aquinas's *Summa Theologiae* (although Martyr did not acknowledge his source). Martyr affirmed
that theology was an argumentative and a deductive science.[17]

Also like Aquinas, Martyr tried to use as much of Aristotle as was
consistent with Scripture. In his commentary on the *Nicomachean Ethics* he
usually concluded each chapter by showing how Aristotle's teaching
agreed with that of the Bible. In his theological works Martyr referred to
Aristotle ninety-eight times (more than five times the number of references Calvin made to Aristotle in the *Institutes*).[18] Thirteen other Aristotelian philosophers were cited a total of eighty-five times. And twenty
medieval scholastic authors were treated as authorities, particularly Peter
Lombard and Thomas Aquinas. Martyr never cited a nominalist work
with approval. While he agreed with Aquinas more often than he acknowledged, some of his references to Thomas were hostile.[19] Augustine
was quoted more often than any other nonscriptural source. Among the
Fathers, Martyr's favorite exegete was Chrysostom, and, in general, Martyr preferred the Antiochene school of biblical interpretation to the
Alexandrian.[20]

Some passages in Martyr's writings praise reason and its contributions to theology and others warn against oversubtlety and philosophy's invasion of theology. Martyr sought a middle course here. On the one hand, he attacked an antiintellectualism and biblical positivism that posed as Christian piety by accepting nothing not explicitly taught in Scripture. On the other hand, he rejected an excessive rationalism that would reduce Scripture to an equal or subordinate level with the discoveries of reason. He singled out Anabaptists as the antiintellectuals, while Origen and the scholastics generally were charged with excessive rationalism.[21]

Despite the scholastic forms and overtones of much of Martyr's theology, the principle of accommodation was present in his thought. He wrote: "Since God in His own nature is not perceived by sense, He yet condescends to human capacity, and by sensible words shows Himself to be known by men, in corporeal forms and in Sacraments."[22] The fact that humans have any knowledge of God at all was an outstanding testimony to the divine love. Martyr wrote: "God so humbled Himself as to enter into a covenant with man: that comes from His own mere mercy and goodness."[23]

Martyr again distinguished the knowledge and language philosophers used about God from the actual being of God Himself:

> The effects which Philosophers use to know God by their understanding are not equal to His dignity, power and faculties. Wherefore they only declared certain things common and light. But we give to Him attributes or properties, that is, good, just, fair, wise and so on; because we have nothing more excellent, nor names more noble, which can be better applied or agree with Him. Nor yet are these things so in Him as we speak: for, since He is most simple, He is far otherwise good, just and wise than men either are or are called.[24]

The qualities of human thought could not be transferred over into the knowledge of God "since God, who is most simple, is not subject to these."[25]

Since humans could not speak of God properly as He is in Himself, they had to speak of Him in human terms. Martyr commented:

> So is it said that God contracted His soul and was in a way sorry for the miseries of His people. This kind of speech is not proper to God, but improper. For God is not sorry, nor touched with affections. Wherefore it is a speech after the condition of men.[26]

Martyr recognized the accommodated language of Scripture when he realized that God was "said to" operate in the heavens and "said to" descend to designate His presence on earth.[27] The Scripture used this kind of language for a very practical purpose according to Martyr:

But the Holy Scriptures, if they sometimes attribute members to God, doubtless this is the only reason, to help our infirmity: although we cannot comprehend the essence of God in itself, yet by this is provided that by certain symbols and shadows we may somewhat understand. Wherefore members are by a most profitable metaphor attributed to God, that diligently remembering His properties, we may piously and faithfully exercise our minds.[28]

The anthropomorphites of the early church, who attributed a body to God were justly condemned, said Martyr, because "they contended that the nature of God was so in very deed: wherefore they are condemned rightly and worthily."[29] They did not make the distinction between God Himself and language *about* God.

For Martyr the principle of accommodation functioned most strongly in his doctrine of the sacraments.[30] Both Scripture and sacrament were forms of the Word of God.[31] The fact that humans are bodily creatures meant they needed help in the form of accommodated language to understand God.[32] The nontechnical and imprecise language of Scripture was not a stumbling block to the true knowledge of God but rather a great help. The full variety of language forms all moved toward giving true knowledge. Martyr observed:

> The Scriptures do not use exquisite and subtle arguments: and rarely do they bring those most perfect demonstrations, since in respect of God, vision must be accommodated to the doctrinal capacity of the weak. For this reason a good part of its doctrine is composed of parables, narratives, and similes.[33]

Ultimately Scripture must be in accommodated language because of human sinfulness. As humans we cannot have the knowledge of God "engraved on our minds" by the Spirit apart from the "outward writings and the aid of books" because sin has broken human communion with God.[34] It was "our sin that removed us from the sight of God; from this came to us the darkness, blindness and ignorance in heavenly things."[35] Christ the Redeemer, by speaking as he did, was the One who has most fully taken our infirmities to heart. Speaking of Christ, Martyr wrote:

> He ought chiefly to be called *figurator,* who while we live here; takes heed of our infirmity through His kindness, in figures ... there are enough of God's images extant: for Christ is His lively image—let us behold Him and His acts, and in Him we shall know God abundantly.[36]

The ultimate purpose of the accommodated language of Scripture was to bring salvation and union with Christ. Martyr stated:

> And therefore the Holy Spirit, to remedy our weakness, having granted us light and understanding that should excel our own nature, has also humbled

Himself to these metaphors, namely of abiding, dwelling, eating and drinking: so that this divine and heavenly union that we have with Christ may in some way be known to us.[37]

Most of Martyr's published writings were lectures on Holy Scripture. At Oxford he lectured on Romans and 1 Corinthians. In Strassburg and Zurich his chair was in Old Testament and his attention was directed primarily to Old Testament historical books. In interpreting Scripture, Martyr revealed his threefold purpose in the preface to his Corinthian commentary addressed to Edward VI. He outlined three goals of his interpretation: (1) to see that the apostle's meaning was clearly understood and expressed; (2) to see that there was no statement containing superstition; (3) to see that nothing conformable to the Word of God was censured out because of a love for scholarly debate.[38] Martyr always tried to interpret the Scripture according to its natural, historical sense, and sought the meaning of obscure passages on the basis of clearer ones. He buttressed his teachings through citations from the church fathers, and his occasional allegorical interpretations were always brief and most often borrowed from the fathers.[39]

Martyr's usual line-by-line exegesis was occasionally broken up by *loci*, or *scholia*. These were digressions that treated a particular theological subject systematically. The *loci* formed a substantial part of his text. Occasionally editions of his commentaries had special indices for these *scholia* alone. His *Loci Communes*, published posthumously in 1583, was hardly more than a connected series of these *scholia*.[40]

The structure of these *scholia* was varied but two forms were quite prominent. Shorter *scholia* often began with an etymological discussion of the subject, giving Hebrew, Greek, and Latin roots with special focus on biblical usage and examples. This was followed by a philosophical definition using Aristotle's four causes. The definition was then broken down and each of the four causes discussed.[41] Martyr's attention to clear distinctions and definitions endeared him to his students at Strassburg, who preferred him to Bucer.[42]

Longer *scholia* were frequently developed along the lines of the scholastic *quaestio disputata*.[43] Here the *scholia* were posed in the form of questions. Reasons *pro* and *con* were given as answers. Martyr would give a short discussion of the whole problem and then conclude by answering the arguments against the view he supported.[44]

While Martyr praised Aristotle's development of the laws of logic and the syllogism, his writings seldom contained fully developed formal syllogisms.[45] In his *loci*, however, systematic expositions were interjected into his exegesis. These (especially in his Old Testament commentaries) were often only loosely connected with the text itself. He seemed to have introduced them to provide more theological depth and relevance than mere exposition would have allowed.[46] In his Romans lectures, his discourses on predestination and justification were related to his exegesis, and in Martyr's mind were two topics at the very heart of the Protestant attack on Roman theology.

The use of these *scholia* implied that to Martyr the theological process had to go beyond the pure exposition of a text. In this task philosophy was a great help and, in Martyr's eyes, Aristotle in particular was a powerful ally of Calvinism.[47] Yet Martyr did not go beyond this and present any extended part of his theology in the form of a chain of syllogistic deductions derived from given premises.[48] Nor did Martyr collect these *scholia* or *loci* into a single, systematic handbook. This was, however, done by his friends after his death.

Peter Martyr Vermigli was a transitional figure, a neoscholastic. Certain aspects of his thought were closely related to the Protestant scholasticism developed most fully by Zanchi and Turretin. He made extensive use of Aristotle and Aquinas, rather than Augustine, for theological method.[49] Yet his writings quoted Cicero and Virgil more often than Peter Lombard and Thomas Aquinas.[50] He never allowed reason to equal faith or be its superior, thereby jettisoning revelation. Yet, compared to medieval mystics such as Bonaventure and nominalists like Occam, reason played a larger role in his theology.[51] He was quite willing to relate metaphysics to his theology, and explained predestination and reprobation under his doctrine of God and by using the four Aristotelian causes. Yet he did not try to develop a rational theology. His writings did not contain an extended speculative tract into the nature of God such as Aquinas had at the beginning of his *Summa Theologiae* (1, 3–26) and to which Zanchi later devoted 586 folio columns.[52]

Aquinas and Analogy: Girolami Zanchi (1516–1590)

The career of Girolami Zanchi (or Hieronymus Zanchius) was similar to that of Peter Martyr.[53] He was born on February 2, 1516, and raised near Bergamo, Italy. There he entered the monastery of the Augustinian Order of Regular Canons after his parents died when he was fifteen years old. Zanchi received solid theological training in the writings of Thomas Aquinas, the classical languages, and in Aristotle. In 1541 he joined the community led by Martyr at Lucca. Through Martyr he was introduced to the works of the Reformers. For ten years Zanchi remained a secret Protestant believer. In 1552, however, the pressure of conscience and the Inquisition forced him to flee Italy. He spent ten months in Geneva where he studied under Calvin. Zanchi was prepared to join Martyr in England in 1553 but King Edward VI died. So Zanchi went instead to Strassburg.

There he taught philosophy and theology alongside Martyr and the two were closely associated.

Zanchi's lectures on predestination soon drew fire from the Lutheran Johann Marbach.[54] Martyr left for Zurich in 1556 and Zanchi was forced to carry on alone. He gave up the struggle in 1563, apparently on the edge of nervous exhaustion and took a pastorate among Italian Protestants. Five years brought him no peace, however, as his attempts to initiate Calvinistic discipline alienated many of his congregation. They in turn allied themselves with the local anti-Trinitarian party.

In 1568 Zanchi gladly accepted a call to Heidelberg, which Elector Palatine Frederick III had already made a major center of Calvinist theology. There he filled a vacancy left by Zacharias Ursinus (1534–1583). An outbreak of anti-Trinitarianism occurred at Heidelberg in 1570 and, at the request of the Elector, Zanchi wrote and published his first theological work, a defense of the Trinity against Servetus and the Italian radicals in 1572. When Louis VI, a Lutheran, succeeded his father as the Elector in 1576, the Calvinists were driven from the university. Zanchi was offered a chair at Neustadt and taught there with Ursinus until the latter's death in 1583. Zanchi continued his career at Neustadt until he died on November 9, 1590.

Zanchi produced a vast "Summa" of philosophical theology. It was one of the most ambitious undertakings in all sixteenth-century Calvinism.[55] The first four volumes of his *Opera theologica* covered the same material as Aquinas had in the *Pars prima* and *Prima secundae* of his *Summa Theologica* but was twice as long. The text of these four volumes of Zanchi's filled 2886 folio columns.[56]

Unquestionably Zanchi's model was Aquinas's *Summa.* His arrangement of materials very often paralleled that of Aquinas.[57] A prime example of this, and also of how Zanchi differed from Calvin, was Zanchi's treatment of the divine attributes. Calvin was not specifically interested in what God is in himself but rather in how he acts toward his creatures.[58] Aquinas, on the other hand, devoted twenty-three questions in the *Summa* to the divine attributes. Zanchi in his *De natura Dei, seu de divinis attributis* (in five books) had twenty-four chapters on the divine attributes. Nineteen of Aquinas's questions were paralleled by Zanchi. Three of the others (5, 15, 17) did not deal specifically with the topic and so Zanchi did not treat them. Nor did Zanchi deal with the divine unity (probably since he had written extensively on the Trinity and the divine simplicity previously). Four chapters in Zanchi had no parallel in Aquinas. They were on God's graciousness, the divine wrath, hatred, and domination. In these the Calvinistic stress was strong and they prepared the way for Zanchi's treatments of predestination and reprobation.[59]

Zanchi's debt to scholastic method became apparent in his use of the formal deductive syllogism. Throughout his works Zanchi usually stated a thesis, supplied a syllogism to prove the thesis, and then added an additional pair of syllogisms to prove the major and minor premises of the first syllogism.[60] The conclusion of his scriptural exegesis was often marked by a series of deductive syllogisms summarizing what had gone before. In his work on the Trinity, after he gave a long explanation of the Prologue of John, Zanchi gave a series of syllogisms to prove that Christ was the Son of God. He saw the syllogism as a powerful tool to combat the anti-Trinitarians. He believed that most of the struggle was to identify the source of their errors in their faulty logic. As he wrote: "For this Aristotle—or rather God through Aristotle—presents us with a most useful work—his book *Sophistical Refutations.*"[61] Then Zanchi provided an elaborate discussion of the syllogism's proper and improper formulation. This he used to cast his opponents' arguments into syllogisms. The final step was to show, in light of Aristotle, the exact point at which they had misformulated their argument.[62]

Reason played a major role in Zanchi's theology. Although he adhered firmly to the Reformation principle of *sola Scriptura,* for him, much about the divine attributes could not be understood without philosophy. While one could be a Christian without philosophy, one could not be a theologian without it.[63] According to Zanchi, logic and dialectic were indispensable tools for the theologian just as metaphysics was crucially necessary for theology. When Zanchi explained and defended his intended use of Aristotle's *Physics* in the introduction to the second part of his doctrine of creation, he asserted that although physics stood as a part of philosophy, theology must also include physics as the science of creation and the creature since theology included everything relating to our knowledge of God. The theologian and the Christian found physics worthy of the highest praise and study.[64] In this Zanchi differed markedly from Calvin who also found science worthy of praise and study, but who limited science's scope to matters of the world and excluded science from theology.

What role did reason play in providing knowledge of God's revelation? Zanchi wrote:

> Holy Scripture teaches clearly that God is a living God . . . that we should know what is sufficient for our salvation. But what this life of God is, and in what manner it is to be understood (*intelligendum*) that God lives, that is not clearly explained in [Scripture] . . . That we learn, however, from philosophy.[65]

Zanchi saw Scripture as the means God used to reveal Himself and to teach what was sufficient for salvation. But even though Scripture made clear statements about the nature of God, it did not explain *what* God is—his attributes (the "life of God") or "in what manner it is to be understood that God lives." For this the intellect must function. Thus theological knowledge must be a synthesis of two things: God's revelation and human rational understanding (*intellegere*) of this revelation.[66]

For Zanchi, intellectual knowledge was to be carefully distinguished from the knowledge gained by faith in revelation. He wrote:

> Faith is a certain but not evident knowledge. For neither do we believe through faith what is the object of our senses, nor the things that are perceived in the light of the natural intellect. Therefore faith is not evident knowledge. Nevertheless [faith] is a certain knowledge (*certa notitia*) because we know for certain that He, who reveals, is perfectly true. . . .[67]

From this it would appear that for Zanchi no direct knowledge of God was possible apart from faith. If intellectual knowledge must be derived from sensory perceptions, human knowledge of the divine would be impossible without revelation from God. Yet Zanchi, like Thomas, did ascribe to the natural intellect some abilities to come to general knowledge about God. This general knowledge was obtained in two ways: by negation and by analogy.

Since God's essence must be totally beyond the grasp of human intellect it would not be possible to state positively what it is. But what it is *not*, could be stated. God's *simplicity* as the absence of any kind of composition or component parts could be understood. Thus, Zanchi (closely paralleling Aquinas) described the simplicity of God's nature by demonstrating how compositions found in creatures—form and matter, substance and accidents, act and potency, and "the most subtle of all compositions," essence and existence—are absent in God.[68]

Following Aquinas, Zanchi claimed that a natural knowledge of God could be acquired through analogy.[69] Sensible, created things were the "effects" of God the Creator. He was their efficient cause. Via the relationship between cause and effect, one might make positive statements about God by examining His "effects," His creation. God possessed in an eminent degree, all the perfections found in his creatures. This was the doctrine of analogy. Like Aquinas, Zanchi defined it when he wrote that "things having the same name are called analogical, not in that they are altogether the same, nor in that they are of different *ratio* or definition, but in that they have a proportion to one primary thing."[70] The analogy between God and creatures was never one in which they were alike because of something common to them both. That would have put God and creation on the same level. Rather, the analogy was always one in which the creature imitated God. Since every effect resembled its cause, the creature (from which human concepts came), did resemble the Creator.[71]

Zanchi's expansion on Aquinas was built on his use of Aristotelian philosophy. Until his fifty-sixth year, Zanchi's only publication was a preface to a Greek edition of Aristotle's *De Naturali Auscultatione*, published in 1552 in Strassburg. It was written shortly after he left Italy and went to Geneva.[72] This work was perhaps the most sustained defense of Aristotle done by a sixteenth-century Calvinist.[73]

Zanchi granted that many learned and pious men had attacked the study of Aristotelian philosophy. Some felt it was unworthy of a Christian and some claimed it was dangerous to Christianity. Others preferred Plato. Still others saw value in Aristotle but urged that compendia be used in the schools since Aristotle was so obscure. Zanchi refuted each of these views. He wrote: "Mortals owe much to (Aristotle), the best of all authors after God and the sacred scriptures . . . he was the outstanding, best and most perfect philosopher."[74]

Zanchi thus read Scripture through Aristotelian eyes. When he treated the material creation (after devoting fifty-six chapters to the nature and activities of good and bad angels), Zanchi posited two theses: (1) that this was a topic a theologian must discuss; and (2) that Aristotle's method in explaining natural philosophy was identical to that which Moses used under divine inspiration when he recounted the creation story in Genesis. The rest of Genesis was then read through the Aristotelian spectacles.[75]

Zanchi was a Calvinist in dogmatics. His doctrine of absolute predestination was widely circulated and like Martyr and Aquinas he dealt with this doctrine under the doctrine of God rather than linking it with soteriology as Calvin did.[76] This doctrine was central in his theology (he devoted over 600 folio columns to the divine attributes) and is a prime example of the heavy emphasis on metaphysics and causality that were the hallmarks of Protestant scholasticism.

Zanchi was a Thomist in his philosophy and theological methodology. He followed Aquinas's ordering of material closely and referred to him and other thirteenth-century scholastics far more than to the later nominalists.[77] It was the Aristotelian-Thomistic tradition in which he was trained that provided Zanchi with the philosophical categories that so largely influenced his thinking.[78] He did not always agree with Aquinas, however. His arguments, while reaching the same conclusions as Thomas's, did not always follow the same patterns. But where he did not repeat Aquinas, Zanchi's arguments were still distinctly scholastic in form and proceeded from the same basic philosophical and theological points of view.[79] While his chapter on the divine knowledge clearly corresponded with the *Summa Theologiae*, for example, Zanchi never referred to Aquinas in that section.[80]

The combination in Zanchi of material taken from Calvin and form given by scholasticism is well illustrated by his treatment of faith.[81] In outlining the object of faith, Zanchi began scholastically. The act of faith was understood first as assent to the propositions of the entire body of Scripture.[82] In delineating the nature of faith as a virtue or power by which we receive the Word of God with undoubted assent, Zanchi utilized the scholastic terminology of infused habit and act. This was distinctly different from Calvin, who spoke of trust as the essence of faith.[83] Zanchi was departing significantly from Calvin.[84] He believed, however, that the scholastic forms he used enabled him to make distinctions required by Scripture, even though the Bible did not explicitly offer such categories.[85]

In Zanchi we see the effort to remain in continuity with Calvin and others of the early Reformed theologians. We observe with equal clarity Zanchi's self-conscious commitment to a scholastic methodology that diverges significantly from the Augustinian methodology used by Calvin.[86] As a defensive Reformed orthodoxy continued to develop, the scholastic form more and more controlled and changed the Reformation content. Zanchi was a transitional figure who contributed much to the shift from the biblical faith of the Reformers to the philosophical orthodoxy of their followers.

Scholasticizing Calvin: Theodore Beza (1519–1605)

Beza took on the mantle of Calvin in Geneva. One week after Calvin's death Beza was elected Moderator of the Venerable Pastors of Geneva. He succeeded Calvin as professor of theology, while continuing in his own post as rector of the Geneva Academy.[87] Beza was viewed as the outstanding Calvinist theologian, and thus became the most important transitional figure between Calvin and later Reformed orthodoxy.[88] Beza was born into a family of the lesser French nobility. He received an excellent education and used his aristocratic background and training later in life as a diplomat for the Reformed cause. His background probably also accounts for the fact that in Geneva he often sided with those who had been Calvin's opponents (for example the Small Council) over against his fellow pastors. The very training that made him an excellent political envoy to court and to the Huguenot military leaders made him less tolerant of the religious stance of people from the lower social classes.[89]

Beza's education began in Paris, but at the age of nine he was taken to Orléans to live in the house of Melchior Wolmar. Wolmar was a leading Christian humanist with Lutheran sympathies. Wolmar had studied under Lefèvre d'Etaples and Guillaume Budé and was a recognized master of Greek and Latin. Beza credited Wolmar with having initiated him into both the linguistic skills of humanism and the Christian faith.[90] He read Bullinger's work while studying with Wolmar. After his conversion in 1548, Beza wrote to thank Wolmar. He referred to both Wolmar and Bullinger as spiritual fathers. Later in his career, Beza corresponded with Peter Martyr Vermigli and acknowledged Martyr's theological influence on him. Beza called Martyr "my father" and "my other parent." In letters to Bullinger, he cited Martyr's commentaries and other works and stated that he had three times devoured Martyr's *Dialogus*. Beza declared that his own views on the Eucharist did not vary a hair's width from those of Martyr.[91] Evidence within his work suggests strong affinities also with the theology of Giorlami Zanchi.[92] Zanchi too, of course, was associated very closely with Martyr, having received reformation teaching from Martyr at the monastery in Lucca and later having taught with him at Strassburg.

Beza did not immediately commit himself to the Christian faith or the study of theology. His father was displeased with the influence the heretic Wolmar was having on his son and ordered the young Theodore to study law. He did and eventually practiced it in Paris while supported in addition by the income from two ecclesiastical benefices. His real interest, however, was literature and especially poetry. In 1548 Beza published his first volume of Latin poetry. Later that year, an evangelical crisis occurred in Beza's life, precipitated by a severe illness and by his decision to marry Claudine Desnoz. Beza left France and came to Geneva in October 1548. There his secret marriage to Claudine was blessed in the church. During the next two years Beza was declared a heretic and condemned to be burned at stake. He fled from Paris after being officially banished by the Parliament, and his possessions were confiscated. All of his family, friends, literary fame, and fortune were left behind in France.[93]

Beza had apparently hoped to found a printing firm, but in November 1549 he accepted the post of professor of Greek at the new Academy of Lausanne. Beza served there for nine years, teaching theology as well as producing a large number of literary and theological works. By 1558 political events caused him to resign rather than be deposed in Lausanne, and in that same year he accepted a call to Geneva as pastor and professor of Greek. The city was securely in the hands of Calvin and his friends. Within a year, Beza was also appointed rector of the new academy Calvin had designed.[94]

Beza became the guiding spirit of the academy and was responsible for its fame. He chose the professors and guided the curriculum. Calvin had listed Aristotle as one of the authorities whose work might be studied in dialectics and rhetoric, and Beza required the study of Aristotle in both logic and moral philosophy.[95] Beza refused to hire the French Reformed logician Petrus Ramus (1515–1572) because of Ramus's hostility to Aristotle.[96] In some ways, Beza liberalized and secularized the academy, co-operating in this with the secular magistrates. In other ways, his innovations led to a scholasticizing of the curriculum. For example, Calvin had taught theology primarily through exegesis of biblical passages. Beza felt obliged to clarify and systematize the passages cited. The course content then became so unwieldly that two courses had to be taught. In the process, scripture and doctrine were separated. At first, Beza opposed this division, but finally agreed to it in 1595.[97]

There was a strange dualism in Beza's character. He was committed to carrying on the work of Calvin and of assuring doctrinal purity in Geneva. At the same time, he worked against many of the political, social, and ecclesiastical goals Calvin had set, probably because of differences in background and personality.[98] Theologically, Beza contributed to the shift toward a scholastic and away from a Reformation style of doing theology. One important factor in this was Beza's dependence on Aristotle and Aquinas. Calvin had deprecated the value of Aristotelianism and Thomism in the theological enterprise, but there was no trace in Beza's work of the antipathy toward Aristotle that both Calvin and Luther had expressed.[99] Over fifty Aristotelian works were listed in the library catalogue of the academy in 1572. Eight works of Thomas Aquinas were listed and Cardinal Cajetan, a contemporary neo-Thomist, was represented by twelve works.[100] In addition to the Aristotelian influence that came to Beza indirectly through Martyr, Zanchi, and other semischolastic reformers, he studied Aristotelian philosophy for himself. Beza also requested a work by the Italian Aristotelian Pietro Pomponazzi, which heavily emphasized the priority of reason over faith in theology.[101]

One important evidence of Beza's use of scholastic methodology was his treatment of the doctrine of predestination.[102] Following Beza, predestination became the keystone of Protestant scholasticism. Beza referred to predestination as "the principal ground and foundation of our salvation."[103] For him, it was more basic than justification by faith. The Aristotelian notion that real knowledge was based on the discovery of the ultimate cause of events, which was also their logical foundation, played a significant role in Beza's treatment of predestination. This search for ultimate causes and their logical relations took Beza far beyond the position of Calvin.

Beza's work entitled *Tabula* (1555) expounded a scientific system in the Aristotelian sense. God was viewed as the *causa summa* from whose qualities the logical necessity of all events could be deduced. Beza's work was rife with Aristotelian-scholastic terminology and concepts. One result was that the centrality of Christ, which was found in the theology of Calvin, was replaced by a scientific system that had final causation as its key principle.[104] Two important elements of the theological tradition of the early church and the original Reformers were lost in this process. Theology was now viewed by Beza as a scholastic science instead of a practical discipline. And the concept of accommodation was discarded. Theology no longer acknowledged that the revelation of God in Scripture came in human language and thought patterns which God graciously condescended to use. Rather, theology dealt with causes and effects determined by God's nature and thus claimed to view reality from God's perspective.[105]

Beza recognized, with Calvin and Augustine, that sin damaged the whole person, including the reason.[106] Accordingly, Beza often cautioned against the speculative use of reason. Yet he made scholastic distinctions that moved the discussion of predestination away from the stance of Calvin. Beza contended that reason could tell people nothing about the decree of election itself, but reason could be employed by pious people to analyze the secondary means by which God executed the decree. The element of mystery became smaller and smaller as Beza revised his *Tabula.* He felt increasingly able to justify the activities of God through logical argument.

In Beza's work, the concept of God the Father was replaced with the logical principle of God as the highest cause.[107] For Calvin, the omnipotence of God had been tied to God's loving concern for His creatures. In Beza's work, omnipotence was transmuted into the principle of all-causality, which became a philosophical starting point for theology. Beza depersonalized the Holy Spirit by ascribing to the Spirit a logical function. This depersonalization was not to be found in the thought of Calvin.[108] Beza became preoccupied with questions concerning the will of God. These led him deeper and deeper into the arena of speculation.[109]

Like Martyr and Zanchi, Beza was not totally scholastic in his thinking. He demonstrated a dualism that marked such transitional figures. On the one hand he intended to continue the tradition of Calvin, and on the other he responded with scholastic weapons to the pressures of Roman Catholic and other counter movements. He endeavored to expound biblical material, but he loved to use logic as a method for bringing clarity. And often the method distorted the content.[110] Beza was no doubt sometimes torn between the openness to new discovery inculcated by his early humanist training and his desire to organize everything into a stable system, which scholasticism enabled him to do. Beza did move beyond Calvin and furthered the tendencies to scholasticism that were already present in persons like Martyr and Zanchi.

The impact of these tendencies on other Calvinists was exemplified in the writing of, for example, Pierre du Moulin, whose *Elementa logicae* (Leyden, 1596) not only utilized the categories of Aristotle, but repeated the same illustrations Aristotle himself had used.[111] When du Moulin's theology was attacked by the Calvinist theologian Amyraut, du Moulin responded by criticizing Amyraut for making Calvin the "leading theologian."[112] The shifting spirit of the times was evident in du Moulin's response that if Amyraut was permitted to quote Calvin from the pulpit, "why not also Martyr, Zanchius, or Beza, who have not been inferior to Calvin in their teachings?"[113]

Historical circumstances played a role in fostering the growth of a post-Reformation Reformed scholasticism. Beza was active in attempting to consolidate the French Reformed Church along scholastic lines, but he was opposed by Ramus and others of the French Huguenots who held to a more Augustinian position, following Calvin. Nevertheless, Beza was a major influence at the Synod of La Rochelle in 1571. The Synod produced a new confession of faith that contained scholastic terminology appearing to contradict the Second Helvetic Confession on the subject of communion. Ramus was infuriated by the confession and wrote to Bullinger denouncing its innovations. The debate over these matters was suddenly cut short by the Massacre of St. Bartholomew's Day on August 24, 1572, in which Ramus and many other French Protestant leaders were killed. The opposition to Beza's scholasticizing was decimated, as even those who survived were forced to flee. Beza was shocked by this savagery and even his deep sense of the Providence of God seemed shaken as he wrote to Bullinger about the atrocity.[114]

Another historical circumstance that greatly solidified the scholastic approach to Reformed thought was the convening and resultant confession of the Synod of Dort. Beza played an indirect role in that situation. Beza was the first supralapsarian among the Reformers who rooted all theological affirmations in God's eternal decrees.[115] Two Dutch Calvinists who studied with Beza in Geneva had later reacted sharply against his theology. Jacob Arminius (1560–1609; who later departed from Calvin's thought) had been influenced by Ramus and challenged Beza in public lectures. His friend, Uytenbogaert, also took issue with Beza. Uytenbogaert later became the leader of a Remonstrant party that challenged the scholastic decretal theology. The resulting dispute ultimately occasioned the Synod of Dort in 1618–1619.

Beza had died in 1605 at the age of 86. His hyper-Calvinist position was represented in the Netherlands by the Dutch theologian Francis Gomarus (1563–1641). Arminius also had died and his Remonstrant forces were led by Simon Episcopius (1583–1643). The Synod invited representatives from the Reformed churches in most countries and attracted international attention.[116] The Canons of Dort embodied a list of doctrinal statements that purported to define the essential elements of Calvinism. However, the hyper-Calvinist majority at Dort skewed Reformed theology in a scholastic direction by their dependence on Aristotelian notions of causality, by making predestination the central doctrine to be defended in Reformed Christendom and by teaching notions, such as eternal reprobation, not specifically found in Calvin.[117] Even these canons did not go all the way with hyper-Calvinism, however, taking an infra—rather than a supralapsarian—position.[118]

The declarations of Dort, nevertheless, tended to fix Reformed theology on the European continent into a scholastic mold at the beginning of the seventeenth century.

b. The Impact of Changes in Science and Philosophy: Copernicus and Descartes; Voetius and Wittich

The Scientific Revolution: Voetius Versus Copernicus

The adoption of Aristotelian methodology by the Protestant scholastics was occasioned in part by the tremendous revolutions occurring in science and philosophy. The medieval world picture based on the cosmological system developed by Ptolemy of Alexandria (90–168) taught that the earth was the center of the universe and that the apparent motion of the sun, moon, and planets was due to their revolving around the earth (geocentricity). In this Ptolemy was following the teachings of Aristotle, who had once considered the hypothesis set forth by the Pythagoreans that the earth is not the center of the universe, but had rejected it.[119]

Actually the Polish churchman Nicholas Copernicus (1473–1543) began the scientific revolution by upsetting the Ptolemaic geocentric cosmology and postulating that the earth is but one of the planets revolving around the sun, and that it turns on its own axis to create day and night.[120] This he set forth in his treatise *De Revolutionibus Orbium Coelestium* (*On the Revolutions of the Heavenly Spheres*), written in 1530 but not published until 1543. But for some time after the Middle Ages, questions of fact were settled not by experiment but by authority. Broadly speaking, authority in spiritual matters was represented by the Bible, while authority in what we would call scientific questions was represented by Aristotle.[121] This meant that Copernicus's theory did not win immediate acceptance among either "scientists" or theologians, who feared it would destroy the authority of the Bible, which they interpreted as teaching the old Aristotelian-Ptolemaic cosmological view.[122]

Luther did not deal with this "new science" in his authorized works. He made only one comment: "I believe Holy Scripture, for Joshua told the sun to stand still, not the earth." This was recorded in one of his

"Table Talks" when someone told him that according to a certain astronomer, it was impossible for the sun to stand still. But this was likely just
a common sense remark, made when only rumors about Copernicus's
work (not even his name is mentioned in the reminiscence of the report-
er) were circulating (1539). It was only printed (from the memory of one
of his guests) twenty-seven years afterwards (1566).[123] Calvin never mentioned Copernicus, and in developing his theory of accommodation,
while recognizing the discrepancy between the scientific world system of
his day and the biblical text, he did not repudiate the results of scientific
research on that account.[124] As seen above, the influence of Calvin's
humanism led him to be quite open about natural science. Melanchthon,
on the other hand, stood firmly on the Aristotelian/Ptolemaic schema
although in the second edition of his *Initia Doctrinae Physicae,* the passage
advising magistrates to punish those who taught the motion of the earth
was omitted.[125]

Chief among Protestant scholastic objections to the "new thought"
on the "new science" was that these revolutions damaged faith in the
Bible as God's authoritative Word. Scholastic theologians were developing their doctrine of Scripture in such a way that biblical texts became
important as philosophical and factual information. Biblical texts, theological interpretations, and items of scientific knowledge were all treated
as metaphysical data.[126] Among Protestant scholastics, the doctrine of
inspiration was refined and the locus of scriptural authority shifted away
from the Reformation emphasis on the Holy Spirit's witness to Christ
towards rational argumentation to *prove* Scripture's inspiration. In a real
sense, the conception of inspiration was now completely separated from
the idea of revelation.[127]

When the Bible was viewed as a book of knowledge, a decided shift
took place in the way people read and interpreted Scripture. Luther and
Calvin accepted Scripture as normative through faith instilled by the
Holy Spirit. But when the Bible was thought of as a book of metaphysical
knowledge, the technical accuracy of the text became important. The
efficacy of Scripture no longer depended upon the work of the Spirit, but
upon a conception of the Bible as verbally inspired and inerrant. Scholastic theologians forgot the early church and Reformation concept of accommodation. They now identified the biblical message with divine
information given in a book, the very words of which were the Words of
God. The Bible became a book of delivered truths. Theology was the
systematic ordering of these truths. Truths were said to be given in
propositional statements and the Bible was treated as a collection of
propositions.[128]

Both Lutheran and Reformed theologians of the seventeenth century
rejected the new science on theological grounds. The Lutheran Abraham

Calovius (1612–1686) believed Scripture gave answers to the nature of the universe; and reading the Bible literally, he found that the moon could not in itself be dark and getting its light from the sun, since Moses had called it a "light." Calovius also dealt with questions such as the distances of the stars from the earth, the mountains and valleys of the moon, the possibility of life on other planets, and so on. He discussed the views of Kepler, Aristotle, Brahe, Ptolemy, and others, and criticized them on the basis of Scripture.[129] Calovius's rejection of the astronomy of his day, he believed, was based purely on exegetical grounds.[130]

The Calvinist Gisbert Voetius (1589–1676) argued from Scripture in the same way as Calov, citing scriptural verses that said the earth was stationary (Eccles. 1:4; Job 26:7) and that the sun moved (Ps. 19:5–6; Eccles. 1:5,6; Josh. 10:12–14). Voetius went on, however, to cite the opinions of other astronomers and mathematicians as authorities against the new science.[131] Voetius opposed any notion that God accommodated Himself to limited human perspectives. For example, Voetius taught that Psalm 19 was not poetry, but historical and scientific fact. Therefore the Copernican system was in flat contradiction to the text. Voetius declared that if the Holy Ghost had accommodated Himself to the common people of the biblical writer's day that the Holy Ghost would have been telling a lie.[132] For Voetius and other Protestant scholastics the issue was clear. When the findings of science contradicted the apparent literal text of the Bible—the findings of science had to be rejected.

The Method of Doubt: Voetius Versus Descartes

Coupled with the new science in seeking to destroy biblical authority, in the eyes of the "Orthodox," was the new philosophy of Descartes. In 1637 the French philosopher René Descartes (1596–1650) published his *Discours de la Methode de bien Conduire la Raison at Chercher la Vérité dans les Sciences (Discourse on Method)*.[133] In it, he advocated the use of deduction as a method. He rejected all appeals to authority and came to the point where the only thing not to be doubted was the self as a thinking being. His key phrase was *Cogito ergo sum*, "I think therefore I am." From this and his doctrine of innate ideas he revived the ontological proof for God's existence. For him thoughts, rather than external objects, were the prime empirical realities.[134] Space or extension became the fundamental reality in the world, and motion became the source of all change. Mathematics demonstrated relationships between reality and change.[135] Cartesianism, with its exaltation of human reason and its natural skepticism, provided an alternative to the reigning Aristotelianism. Descartes was determined to break with the past. He did not trust the authority of any previous philosopher, and he resolved to rely on his own reason alone.[136] Since the only thing certain was "thought," there was no room in Descartes's philosophy for experience. In effect, Descartes drove a wedge between the mind and its thought on the one hand and the world and experience on the other.[137]

In a very interesting series of events, Descartes ran into stringent opposition to his views from the Calvinist scholastics at the University of Utrecht in Holland led by Voetius.[138] Their reaction to Cartesianism demonstrated the intimate union of scholastic theology with Aristotelian philosophy.

Descartes had resided in the Netherlands since 1638. His "Meditations" were composed there and published on August 28, 1641. Voetius, Utrecht's leading theologian, had, in 1639, used a funeral oration as an occasion to raise the charge of atheism against this new philosophical movement.

What motivations led Reformed orthodoxy to such an attitude regarding Cartesianism? According to Voetius's own *Disputations concerning Atheism* (printed as part of his collected disputations in 1648), they had to do with the perceived consequences (drawn by logical inference!) of Cartesian philosophy.

In his long disputation, Voetius accused the Cartesians of being "contrary atheists." By this he meant a variety of actual atheism in which someone (outwardly) disputed the proposition 'God is' or (inwardly) persisted in his reflection on it, or even came to a negative conclusion.[139] The Cartesians were judged to be such since "they persist in a state of doubt, and while they do not become negative in their deliberations, neither do they wish to reach a conclusion."[140] The scholastics taught that "theory" and "practice" conditioned each other just as the intellect and the will affected each other, so there was no speculative atheism that did not also corrupt morals.[141] Thus Voetius maintained that the charge of atheism included necessarily the charge of libertinism.[142]

Voetius further denounced the Cartesians along with Arminians and Socinians for holding that Scripture alone was the real and sufficient proof of the knowledge of God. If this was so, Voetius acknowledged, the traditional proofs for the existence of God would be impossible. This would mean flying in the face of the theological tradition, according to Voetius, and would leave one bankrupt when having to deal with pagans and Jews. Voetius defended the Aristotelian-Thomistic proofs against Cartesianism. He affirmed

the method of proving the existence of God hitherto common to the whole of Christianity, to all schools and all men of wisdom among theologians and philosophers. The wish to overthrow this method means not only to benefit the atheists, but is a sin, moreover, against sound reason, which is the gift of God, and against the Holy Spirit, who himself applied and used this method.[143]

Here the new philosophy, according to Voetius, deviated from Scripture. The traditional proof for God's existence relied on inferring a cause from an effect, a Creator from a creation. Voetius cited Scripture to substantiate this procedure: Rom. 1:19f.; Acts 14:15,17; Pss. 8:2,4 and 19:1ff; Job 38 and 39; Isa. 40:21,22,26; Jer. 10:10f.[144] He further argued that the Bible draws upon sense experience (Isa. 40:21,26; Acts 17:27; Ps. 19:1ff; Ps. 8:4; Rom. 1:19f.) and this the new philosophy did not do. Thus Cartesianism betrayed its skeptical character. To Voetius this meant that it accused the Holy Spirit of deception.[145]

Voetius linked biblical interpretation that allowed for accommodation to the new philosophy. He charged that people employing such interpretation, "are suspicious of the authority of Holy Scripture because they find in it many things which do not suit their carnal mind, and who so little esteem the Mosaic and Scriptural physics, which after all is dictated by the Holy Spirit [*a Spiritu Sancto dictatam*], that they prefer their own theories of the world and of the nature of things." These people "dispute the divinity of Scripture, accuse *implicite* [implicitly] the Holy Spirit of stupidity, and thereby further atheism."[146]

Voetius defended as scriptural a theological method by which he deduced conclusions from the methods and consequences of his opponent's views. He knew that on the basis of his words, Descartes could not be accused of being an atheist. But, by describing Descartes's method of radical doubt as being a violation of the first commandment; by seeing Descartes's rejection of the cosmological argument denying Scripture's divinity, Voetius could pronounce Descartes an "indirect atheist" or "contrary atheist." Voetius used and developed the analytical and deductive method based on Aristotelian logic that became characteristic of scholastic Reformed orthodoxy.[147]

The Concept of Accommodation: Wittich Responds to Copernicus and Descartes

Not all seventeenth-century Reformed theologians adopted a scholastic approach to Scripture. One who retained the early church and Reformation notion of accommodation was a Dutch Calvinist, Christoph Wittich (1625–1687).[148] Since he believed that the purpose of Scripture was to instruct people about salvation and not about science, he did not feel obliged to reject Copernicanism or Cartesianism. His significant work *Consensus veritatis in Scriptura divina et infallibili revelatae cum veritate philosophica a Renato Des Cartes detecta* (Leiden, 1682) was important for its contribution to the developing interpretation of Scripture. It illustrated how one could deal with the new Copernican conception of the universe as a *theological* problem.

Wittich was teaching in Herborn when, in the early 1650s, Cyriacus Lentulus began to attack him and the Cartesian philosopher Clauberg as "atheists" and "innovators."[149] The two doctrines giving most offence were (1) that the origin of day and night was to be explained by the rotation of the earth and (2) that the earth revolved around the sun. These were considered to be in blatant contradiction to the Bible.[150] In 1659 Wittich dealt with the earth's movement in two works "after the manner of Copernicus" and showed that there was no contradiction of the Scripture involved in the Copernican theory.[151] The theologians at Utrecht, Jacobus du Bois, Peter van Mastricht, and Johannes Herbinius joined them in charging Wittich with denying and destroying the authority of Holy Scripture.

Wittich pointed out that Scripture spoke in the usual expressions of the language of its time. He had no doubt that God had accommodated His message to the limits of human language. For Wittich, Scripture had also taken over the *praeiudicia* (preconceptions) of human language. Expressions such as the rising and setting of the sun were not simply false. They contained, on the contrary, truths which, independently of the preconceptions contained in the words, were directed toward human beings. The question then was not whether Scripture was to be believed or whether it taught something false, but whether one could distinguish between the language and the message. Language was in general taken to be an expression of the world view of the speaker. Scripture simply used the language at hand, even though this language did not correspond exactly to things spoken about. The truth intended in the biblical message could be explained independently of the language in which it was clothed.[152] Wittich claimed the agreement of Scripture and the Reformed Confessions for his position. He appealed also to a letter of Descartes and to a cloud of Reformed witnesses from Calvin to Cappellus.[153] He believed questions concerning science should not disturb true faith and that his opponents should admit this.[154]

As a guide to exegesis, Wittich urged the question: What does the Holy Spirit wish to teach us in a given passage? Since Scripture did not distinguish between the form a truth came in (the language about the truth) and the truth itself, Wittich claimed that the question, where Scripture spoke prescientifically and from a particular world view, was whether one could distinguish between the intended truth and the form in which this truth was expressed. If one could make that distinction between the content and its form, then 'philosophical' things in Scripture could be transformed into philosophical assertions without doing harm to their content. The '*praeiudicium*' with which the biblical writers operated always remained 'in medio' [in the middle]. It did not concern faith, however, but only knowledge, which was of no consequence to faith.[155]

Wittich stated:

> When exegetes have found the universal truth which satisfies the text . . . they are to see whether a prejudice is perhaps implicit in these expressions, which does not have its origin in the Holy Spirit, but rather in common usage, and whether, therefore, the language is 'vulgar,' or is precise and brings pure truth to expression.[156]

Wittich defended the practice of departing from the biblical words in forming a doctrine by appealing to the Reformed doctrine of the Lord's Supper, particularly the eucharistic words of institution. The Lutherans took them literally—"This is my body"; the Reformed pointed out the inner contradiction and subscribed to a "metonymous" interpretation.[157]

Wittich's book was dedicated to presenting and defending the Cartesian conception of the universe. Wittich wanted to show that this view was based on reason and that he would therefore be justified in departing from biblical wordings.[158] His method was clear. He sought to fix the intent of the text in relation to human beings, and he showed that no harm was done to this intent when one accepted the modern conception of the universe. He concluded his book, therefore, with the claim that the views of Descartes did not contradict the Bible.[159]

In 1660 Wittich had to give account of his views to the Synod of Gelderland,[160] but was pronounced orthodox in August 1661. In 1671 he went to teach at Leiden where he remained until his death on May 19, 1687. By introducing the rediscovered concept of "intent" or *scopus* into the debate about Scripture, Wittich affirmed that Scripture was given for salvation and faith, not science and philosophy. By using the notion of accommodation as the early church fathers and Reformers had done, Wittich was able to distinguish between a theory of the universe and theology, and thereby to show a way out of the conflict between science and Scripture into which scholastic theology had fallen.[161] Wittich's commitment to the Augustinian-Calvinist notion of accommodation was reintroduced in nineteenth-century Dutch Calvinism by Herman Bavinck in a manner that enabled Bavinck's followers to avoid the kind of scholasticism engaged in by their contemporaries at Princeton.

c. The Full Development of Reformed Scholasticism: Francis Turretin

A century after Calvin's death, the chair of theology in Geneva was occupied by Francis Turretin (1632–1687). In that interval of one hundred years Reformed Protestants had reacted to Catholic criticism and the new science, and the reigning theological method was closer to that of a Counter-Reformation interpretation of Thomas Aquinas than to that of Calvin.[162] A doctrine of Scripture that made the Bible a formal principle rather than a living witness had been gradually developed. Turretin further solidified this shift of emphasis from the content to the form of Scripture as the source of its authority. He treated the forms of words of Scripture as supernatural and increasingly divorced the text of the Bible from the attention of scholarship and an application to life.[163]

In the generation immediately following Francis Turretin in Geneva, his son, Jean-Alphonse Turretin (1648–1737) led a revolt against scholastic theology that opened the doors to liberalism.[164] Francis Turretin's theology was to be revived, however, and have its greatest influence in America during the era of the old Princeton theology in the nineteenth and early twentieth centuries.[165] At Princeton, further refinements were made in the scholastic doctrine of Scripture, but the foundation had been solidly laid by Turretin.

Francis Turretin was born on October 23, 1623. His father, Benedict Turretin, a pastor and professor of theology, died when Francis was eight years old. After his initial academic training, Francis Turretin decided to specialize in theology. Turretin's instructors in theology at Geneva included two men who had been Geneva's official delegates to the Synod of Dort, John Diodati and Theodore Tronchin. Diodati, an Italian Protestant, at that time occupied the chair of Calvin and Beza. Tronchin was married to Beza's adopted daughter. A third source of Turretin's theological training in Geneva was the equally orthodox scholastic Frederick Spanheim.[166]

After finishing the theological curriculum in Geneva, Turretin traveled to study, as was the custom. He went first to Leyden where he heard the lectures of, among others, the hyper-Calvinists Polyander and Voetius. He proceeded then to Paris where, in addition to theology, he studied physical and astronomical science under Gassendi. Then he visited Saumur and heard Placaeus, Amyrault, and Cappellus, men whose version of Reformed theology he would later vehemently oppose.

In 1648 Turretin became a pastor of the church of Geneva and preacher to the Italian congregation. (Turretin was said to preach with equal ease in Latin, French, and Italian.) In 1650 he declined the chair of philosophy at Geneva. Later, for one year he acted as an interim supply pastor in Leyden. In 1653 Turretin was called to the chair of theology in Geneva. He retained that post and his position as one of the city pastors in Geneva until his death in 1687.[167]

In the century following Calvin's death, Genevan Reformed theology had been challenged by many opposing forces: Counter-Reformation Roman Catholicism; Socinianism; Anabaptist spiritualism; revolutions in natural science; new philosophies from Descartes, Hobbes, and Grotius; and competing interpretations of the Reformed faith in Dutch Arminianism and French Amyrauldianism.[168] The response of the Genevan Reformed had been to rigidify into a defensive posture. Falling back on the philosophy of Aristotle and the theological categories of Thomas Aquinas, Turretin produced a scholastic theology that placed great emphasis on precise definition and systematic, scientific statement.[169] The scholastic method of this theology was exemplified by the treatment of the doctrine of Scripture in Turretin's greatest work, *Institutio Theologiae Elencticae,* published in 1674.

Scholastic Method

The scholastic method of treating theology was widely in use by Reformed theologians in the seventeenth century. Turretin followed the common pattern by distinguishing between formal and material topics in theology. In the first two *loci* (or topics) of Turretin's work, he treated theology and Holy Scripture as the "formal" principles of dogmatics. In the subsequent eighteen *loci* he treated the "material" issues.[170]

The pattern of treating topics in the *Institutio* followed a procedure that had been established by Thomas Aquinas in his *Summa.*[171] The pattern was clear and invariable. A question was asked. Turretin's answer was given. An opponent was named. The relevance of the question was discussed. The question was carefully and accurately defined through an examination of *the state of the question.* At this juncture, the question was first of all approached negatively. Clear distinctions were made in order to eliminate all irrelevant matters. Then, the question was stated positively. The positive statement was always, in essence, Turretin's own position. The positive statement was then followed by further definitions and distinctions if they were needed. When Turretin was satisfied that all doubt about the state of the question had been removed, he proceeded to present the proof for his position. The proof was followed by *the sources of explanation* in which all known or conjectured objections to his position were discussed and refuted. This method was predicated on the dictum that whoever makes distinctions well, teaches well.[172]

Turretin's *Institutio,* following Thomas's method, had a strongly polemical and apologetic character. The author was engaged in a battle with many opponents. Accordingly he cited many authorities both opposed to and supportive of his position.[173] Turretin's chief opponents were the Counter-Reformation Roman Catholics. Thirteen of the twenty-one questions in his treatment of Scripture were directed against the Roman Catholics. Other opponents were also named. Turretin attacked the Anabaptists for discrediting the authority of the Old Testament and for relying upon immediate revelations from the Holy Spirit. Enthusiasts and Libertines were opposed for denying the inerrancy of the Bible. And both the unitarian Socinians and Reformed theologians such as Capellus were severely castigated for critically examining the text of the Bible. Turretin was not trying to develop a Reformed perspective, as Calvin had been. Instead, he had dug in to defend what he considered a finished Reformed orthodoxy. Turretin's personal motto was "Garde le bon depot!" (Guard the good deposit).[174]

Turretin laid great emphasis on the use of proof texts from the Bible. For example, in dealing with just one question, that concerning the perfection of Scripture, Turretin used twenty-nine proof texts. A similar number of citations were used to support each of the other twenty-one questions regarding the Bible. Turretin often appeared to be making the text serve his proof rather than allowing the proof to develop from the text. For example, he cited the words of the Great Commission (Matt. 28:18–20) to prove that the Word of God had to be committed to writing. Also, Turretin often used texts that referred to one specific part of the Bible as if they applied to the whole Bible. For example, the statement in the Psalms that the law of the Lord is perfect was used as a proof text for the perfection of the entire canon.[175] Turretin's use of Scripture evidenced the difficulties we have observed from Origen onward when a theologian has used biblical texts atomistically as items to be fitted into his system, rather than following the theme of the biblical *kerygma*.

Turretin also quoted copiously from nonbiblical sources. In his discussion of Scripture, he cited no less than 175 different authorities including most of the Church Fathers, many of his Roman Catholic opponents, and numerous contemporary Reformed scholastics. The mix of theologians cited exemplified the synthesis of Reformed and scholastic influences. Jerome was cited twenty-six times and Augustine twenty times. On the other hand, Cardinal Bellarmine was used twenty-six times. Eight other contemporary Roman Catholics were used five or more times although Thomas Aquinas was referred to explicitly only once. Turretin's favorite Reformed orthodox authorities were Musculus, Whitaker, Vossius, Rivet, and Daillé. Although Turretin claimed to be expounding a Reformed doctrine of Scripture, he never quoted Calvin.[176] Turretin apparently realized that Calvin's approach to Scripture was antithetical to his own. In Turretin's theology, post-Reformation scholasticism had matured to the point that it could dispense with any attempt to reconcile its teaching with that of the original Genevan reformer.[177]

The Necessity and Authority of Scripture

Turretin's analysis of the doctrine of Scripture occupied 355 pages in his *Institutio*. He asked twenty-one questions, but grouped them under four main headings: the necessity for Scripture, the authority of Scripture, the perfection of Scripture, and the perspicuity of Scripture.[178] These headings corresponded roughly to four marks of Scripture that had been discussed thoroughly at the Reformation. It is significant to note, however, that for the Reformation concept of the "reliability" of Scripture in achieving its function of salvation, Turretin substituted a discussion of the formal "necessity" of Scripture.[179]

Scripture was necessary for Turretin as a formal principle on which to construct a scientific theology. He asserted that the Word was "the sole principle of theology."[180] Turretin recognized the pervasive influence of human sin. He inveighed against those "who believe that there is sufficient assistance in human reason to enable us to live well and happily."[181] He did not believe, however, that fallen humanity was deprived of all light and strength. Humans had sufficient light to direct them in worldly things. But they were not able to come to a true religion that led to worship of God and communion with God.[182] In this, Turretin followed Calvin.

Following Aquinas, however, Turretin concluded that mankind could reason from the natural light to some knowledge of God. In typical Thomistic fashion, Turretin stated that a knowledge of "the existence" and "the power" of God could be learned by reasoning from the knowledge of this world. God's "saving grace and mercy," however, had to be discovered in Scripture.[183]

Turretin's polemical relationship to Roman Catholicism conditioned his approach to the necessity of Scripture. He was concerned to demonstrate that "God has seen fit for weighty reasons to commit His Word to writing."[184] This was directed against the "papists" who discounted the necessity for a written Word. Turretin contended that Christ and the Holy Spirit contacted persons only through Scripture.[185] He announced that the Holy Spirit had not been given "to introduce new revelations, but to impress the Written Word on our hearts."[186] In his concern to reject a Roman Catholic insistence on the Holy Spirit working through oral tradition, Turretin narrowly confined the work of the Holy Spirit in relationship to Scripture. A successive narrowing of the role of the Holy Spirit was evidenced as Reformed scholasticism continued to develop.

By the nineteenth century, the Princeton theologians would allow the work of the Holy Spirit only in inspiring the original authors of Scripture, and not at all in enabling modern readers to understand their Bibles.[187]

Turretin considered the authority of Scripture to be more important than any other subject in theology. He proclaimed: "The authority of the sacred text is the primary foundation of faith."[188] Turretin's formalization of the question of authority was exemplified by the twofold question he posed at the outset of his treatment: "Is the Bible truly credible of itself and divine?"; and "How do we know that it is such?"[189] Calvin had felt that even to ask such a question was to "mock the Holy Spirit."[190] But Turretin did not rely on the internal witness of the Holy Spirit to persuade people of the authority of the Bible's content as Calvin had. Turretin turned rather to an assertion of the inerrant form of Scripture. He declared that the Bible was truly "authentic and divine" because the human writers "were so acted upon and inspired by the Holy Spirit, both as to the things themselves, and as to the words, as to be kept free from all error."[191]

The Concept of Error

Turretin predicated the authority of the Bible on the claim that it was verbally inerrant. He was willing to rest the whole weight of Scripture on the point of one particular. He stated: "The prophets did not make mistakes in even the smallest particulars. To say that they did would render doubtful the whole of Scripture."[192] For Turretin, the function of the Spirit was to provide for the inerrant transmission of information. He said: "The Spirit led the Apostles into all truth so that they might not err."[193] Turretin further based the Scripture's function of communicating salvation and guidance in the Christian life on its form of verbal accuracy. He claimed: "Unless unimpaired integrity characterize the Scriptures, they could not be regarded as the sole rule of faith and practice."[194] Turretin frequently predicated his entire case for the authority of Scripture on the technical perfection of a single passage, not just in the original manuscript, but in the extant copies. He insisted:

> For if once the authenticity of the Scriptures is taken away, which would result even from the incurable corruption of one passage, how could our faith rest on what remains? ... Nor can we readily believe that God, who dictated and inspired each and every word of these inspired men, would not take care of their entire preservation.[195]

Turretin radically departed from the approach of Calvin by resting belief in the authority of Scripture on rational proofs of its inspiration and inerrancy. Turretin followed the Aristotelian-Thomistic method of placing reason before faith. He claimed: "Before faith can believe, it must have the divinity of the witness, to whom faith is to be given, clearly established, from certain marks which are apprehended in it, otherwise it cannot believe."[196] Turretin placed proofs first, whereas for Calvin they were never anything more than "secondary aids to our feebleness" to give comfort to those who had already believed through the witness of the Spirit.[197] Thus, for Turretin, contrary to Calvin, "the Bible with its own marks is the argument on account of which I believe."[198]

The arguments Turretin used in his attempt to demonstrate the authority of the Bible were the same type as those used by Thomas Aquinas and the scholastic tradition. A number of "external marks" were offered. Included were the Bible's "antiquity," its "duration," the "candour and sincerity in the writers," the "blood of the martyrs," the "testimony of the adversaries," and the "consent of all people."[199] Added to these external marks were certain "internal marks" cited as "the most powerful evidences" of the Bible's divinity. Scripture's "matter," its "style," its "form," its "end," and its "effects" were said to testify strongly that Scripture was inspired and inerrant.[200]

Other assertions about the inerrant form of Scripture were added to the external and internal marks to strengthen the statement of Scripture's authority. Turretin asserted that the testimony of the prophets and apostles was authentic.[201] He claimed that antiquity proved that the books were written by those whose names they bore.[202] He further affirmed that the books of Moses were authentic.[203] And finally, he proclaimed that the success of the gospel and the conversion of the world proved the divinity of the Bible.[204] The continual stress on formal questions such as those of authorship stood in marked contrast to Calvin's secondary interest in such matters.

The importance Turretin placed on inerrancy in the form of Scripture was manifested by his efforts to harmonize apparent inconsistencies and contradictions in the biblical text. One of the longest chapters in his *Institutio* (thirty-five paragraphs) was given to this project. Twenty-three apparently inconsistent passages were examined in detail and made to harmonize. Turretin refused to admit that the biblical authors could have had slips of memory or that they could have erred in even the smallest matters.[205] The concept of accommodation utilized by the early church fathers and by Calvin was entirely absent from Turretin. Calvin viewed the language and thought forms of the biblical writers as human products that God had graciously condescended to use. Turretin, in contrast, treated the language and thought forms of the Bible as supernatural entities dictated directly by God.

Some Roman Catholic theologians contended that mistakes in the original manuscripts of the Bible had been corrected in the Vulgate. In response to that extreme position, Turretin took the stance that inconsistencies in the original were not real but only apparent. He acknowledged that some passages were hard to understand, but asserted that they were explainable.[206] He also affirmed, with the Reformers, that the differences between the copies and the original text were so minor that they did not hinder persons from receiving Scripture as the rule of faith and practice.[207] Nonetheless, Turretin continued to be excessively concerned with the purity of the text. He admitted that errors had "crept into the books of particular editions through the negligence of copyists or printers." On the other hand, though, he contended that through textual research the true original could be known. He believed that "corruptions and errors" could be "restored and corrected by any collation of various copies, or of Scripture itself and of parallel passages."[208] This concern for the form of the text dominated Turretin's approach because he believed it was not possible to deny the formal perfection and purity of Scripture and still affirm its objective authority for faith and life.[209]

Canonicity

Another evidence of Turretin's concern for the formal perfection of the biblical text was the approach he took to the question of canonicity. He admitted that even orthodox believers disagreed on some points, for example, as to whether any canonical books had been lost.[210] Turretin himself denied that any books worthy of canonical status had perished. His manner of argument on this point exemplified some of the worst of the scholastic style. He employed a very questionable proof text to support the integrity of the canon. He cited the words of Christ "till heaven and earth pass, one jot or one tittle shall in no wise pass from the law, till all be fulfilled" (Matt. 5:18 KJV), and defended the use of this text by saying it was "permissible to apply these words, which Christ spoke directly of the doctrine of the law, to the books analogically."[211]

After using other proof texts, Turretin resorted to rational proofs to establish the validity of the canon. To prove that the canon was authoritative he cited "the providence of God," the "duty of the Church," and "end of Scripture," and the "practice of the Jews."[212] The burden of these arguments was that the books of the canon had been preserved by the providence of God.

Turretin did not rest his defense of the canon with proof texts and rational arguments, however. He invoked the internal witness of the Holy Spirit in support of canonicity. Calvin had affirmed that the internal witness of the Holy Spirit persuaded believers that Scripture was the Word of God. Turretin had relied rather on rational proofs of the inerrancy of the words of Scripture to persuade people of the authority of the Bible. Having omitted the witness of the Spirit to the content of Scripture, Turretin now invoked the Spirit to testify to the form of the Bible. He claimed: "We know that the books are canonical, not so much from the common consent of the church, as from the internal testimony and persuasion of the Holy Spirit."[213]

A further mark of Turretin's preoccupation with formal matters was the great emphasis he gave to the discussion of editions and versions of the Bible. Five out of the twenty-one chapters in his doctrine of Scripture were devoted to questions about these.[214] For Turretin, an authentic edition and a technically correct translation were essential to an authoritative Bible. Because of his concentration on the form of Scripture, he could not be as open to textual questions as Calvin, for whom authority resided in Scripture's saving function. Calvin was able to leave critical, textual questions for scholarly study to settle. For Turretin, one had to have faith in the form of the text since one's faith was based on the inerrant form of words. He complained: "If every one is allowed to wield a censorious pen and play the critic over it [the Biblical text]" then the basis of the Protestant defense against the Roman Catholics would be destroyed.[215]

Certainly one source of Turretin's concern with versions was a decree of the Council of Trent. According to this Counter-Reformation council, "the Latin Vulgate should be held as authentic in the public reading, disputations, preaching, and expositions, so that no one should dare to reject it under any pretext."[216] Over against the Trent assertion, Turretin held to the position of the Reformers that in controversial matters the original Hebrew and Greek texts should be consulted. He wrote: "The Hebrew of the Old and the Greek of the New Testament have always been and still are the only authentic editions, by which all controversies of faith and religion, and all versions ought to be approved and tested."[217] These were the only editions "in which all things are abundantly sufficient to inspire confidence, and to which the fullest credit is due in its own kind."[218] Copies and translations should be compared with and corrected by the original editions.

This requirement that all editions and versions should be standardized with reference to the oldest authentic sources was a position to which both humanists and Reformers had adhered. But Turretin went further. He asserted that the Holy Spirit had dictated the words as well as the matter of the original Hebrew and Greek manuscripts.[219] And Turretin believed that God had providentially preserved that original integrity in the best available copies. This was not for him just an issue of holding to an infallible saving message as had the church throughout its history. He insisted on an inerrant and technically perfect form.

Inspired Vowel Points

The most notable implication of Turretin's concentration on the form of Scripture was manifested in his insistence on the divine character of the vowel points (small markings or accents to guide in proper pronunciation) in the Hebrew Old Testament. He took sharp issue with the work of Louis Cappel, a Reformed biblical scholar at Saumur. Cappel had written *Arcanum punctationis revelatum,* published anonymously in 1624, and followed it with his *Critica sacra* of 1650. In these works, Cappel demonstrated that the Hebrew vowel points did not date from biblical times, but were additions of Jewish grammarians sometime after the completion of the Babylonian Talmud. Cappel's later work denied the complete accuracy of the received Masoretic text, indicating that the true text of the Old Testament could only be known by a careful collation of all of the Hebrew variants and ancient versions. Cappel was careful to make clear, however, that the variations in the text did not change the essential message of Scripture. It was still an adequate authority for faith and morals.[220]

Reformed scholastics were not open to Cappel's suggestions. The Buxtorfs of Basel (father and son), who were reputed to be great students of rabbinic literature, bitterly denounced Cappel and asserted that the vowel points were original in the text. Francis Turretin took up the cause in Geneva. He wrote:

> We have always thought the truer and safer way to keep the authenticity of the original text safe and sound against the cavils of all profane persons and heretics whatever, and to put the principle of faith upon a sure and immovable basis, is that which holds the points to be of divine origin, whether they are referred to Moses, or to Ezra, the head of the great Synagogue; and therefore, that the adversaries err who wish to impugn the authority of the Hebrew manuscript from the newness of the points.[221]

Turretin argued for the absolute authenticity of the Hebrew Codex. He acknowledged that scribes were human and liable to error. But he claimed nonetheless that the text was inerrant. He asserted that it was

> enough that providence has so watched over the integrity of the authoritative Codex, that although they (the Scribes) might have brought into the sacred text many errors, yet they have not done so, or not in all the copies, nor in such a way as that they cannot be corrected and restored by a collation of the various manuscripts and of Scripture itself.[222]

Turretin predicated faith in Scripture on belief in a particular scholarly theory. In the generation after him, faith in Scripture eroded when people came to see clearly that the scholastics had been wrong about their facts.

Turretin had to define the purpose of translations and versions of Scripture very carefully. They were useful "for the instruction of believers," but they were always to be subordinate to the original text. He explained: "No version either can, or ought to be put on an equality with the original, much less be preferred to it."[223] Then Turretin made a distinction that was necessary in practice, but that undercut his theory. He declared that translations and versions were authentic as to doctrine but not as to words.[224] The words of translations could be corrected because they were not authentic.[225] But the words of the originals were inspired and inerrant. Thus Turretin continued, in theory, to make the technical inerrancy of the words of the original manuscripts prerequisite to their authority. In practice, however, he acknowledged that authentic doctrine was adequately available in imperfect copies and translations.

The Perfection and Perspicuity of Scripture

For Turretin, the perfection of Scripture was intimately related to its authority. It is significant that he substituted the formal notion of "perfection" for the more functional rubric of the "sufficiency" of Scripture which the Reformers had used in contrasting Scripture with ecclesiastical traditions. In content, Turretin followed the Reformers. He felt that the Roman Catholics were denigrating the Bible by giving such a prominent place to unwritten traditions.[226] He said that "the Scripture is a complete and adequate rule of faith and practice."[227] This did not mean for him that everything, even everything religious, was "immediately and expressly" taught in the Bible. Turretin allowed that "many things are to be deduced by legitimate inference" from Scripture.[228] Turretin even allowed that some "historical traditions" and "ritual traditions" had valid uses.[229] His argument was that though traditions were useful, they were not necessary. Scripture was perfect without them. He wrote that the Bible was "so complete as to be an adequate rule of faith and practice without the help of any traditions."[230]

In method, Turretin used the same array of scholastic arguments for the perfection of Scripture that he had for its other attributes of necessity and authority. He again used dubious proof texts. He said: "The Law of God is said [in the Psalms] to be perfect." God, he declared, had forbidden anyone to add to His Word. Turretin contended that "all doctrinal traditions besides the Scriptures are rejected [by the Scriptures]." He argued from external evidences, asserting that no satisfactory reason for tradition could be given. He claimed that the church fathers had testified

that Scripture was perfect. And finally, Turretin stated that the design of
Scripture demanded its perfection.[231] To these formal considerations he
added the functional argument that Scripture's usefulness implied its
sufficiency.[232]

The perspicuity, or clarity, of Scripture was closely related to its
sufficiency. Turretin was with Calvin in affirming that the purpose for
which Scripture was given was the salvation of people. It was not until the
nineteenth-century Princeton theologians that the Bible was expressly
asserted to teach about matters of science and history. Seventeenth-
century scholastics had treated the Bible as a source of information about
science in their practice, but it remained for the nineteenth-century
Princeton theologians to incorporate this scholastic stance explicitly into
their theory about Scripture.

In question 17 of Turretin's *Institutio* he wrote: "The Scriptures are
so perspicuous in things pertaining to salvation, that they can be understood by believers without the external help of oral tradition or ecclesiastical authority." Scripture was "obscure to unbelievers" according to
Turretin. He declared: "The Spirit of illumination is necessary to make
them [the Scriptures] intelligible to believers."[233] This was the closest
approach in Turretin's work to Calvin's concept of the internal testimony
of the Holy Spirit. Yet, even here, Turretin's concern was quite different
from Calvin's. When Calvin spoke of the internal witness of the Spirit,
he meant that the Spirit implanted in people's hearts a trust in Christ and
at the same time a confidence in the Word through which they had
encountered their Savior. The Spirit moved believers to worship and
serve God in their daily lives. Turretin's interest was more formal. He
saw the Spirit's work as enabling people to come to intellectual clarity
about what the Bible said.

All of Turretin's concerns for clarity related to clarification of ideas.
He announced that the perspicuity of Scripture did not mean that there
were no "mysteries" left in the Bible. He opined that "God had a purpose
in making some parts hard to understand." Even matters pertaining to
salvation were not perfectly perspicuous. They were clear "only so far as
they are necessary to be known." For example, the fact of the Trinity was
clear, according to Turretin. But *how* there could be a Trinity was not
clear. Further, some parts of Scripture were more perspicuous than
others.[234] The doctrine of clarity, therefore, did not preclude for Turretin
the use of human means of interpretation. He stated that "the internal
light of the Spirit, attention of mind, the voice and ministry of the
Church, sermons and commentaries, prayer and watching" were all
necessary to render the Bible intelligible.[235]

While the content of Turretin's doctrine of perspicuity was similar to that of the Reformers, the arguments on which he based the doctrine were typically scholastic. He adduced many proof texts which, according to him, proclaimed perspicuity. Then he added rational arguments that sounded familiarly Aristotelian. The "efficient," the "design," the "matter," and the "form" of Scripture all were invoked to prove its perspicuity. The church fathers were called to testify to the Scripture's clarity.[236] And, Turretin claimed, the Bible's perspicuity was borne out by the fact that Scripture had "only one true and genuine sense."[237]

A practical problem toward which Turretin's doctrine of perspicuity was directed was the decree of the Council of Trent forbidding laypersons to read the Bible. Pius IV had modified the decree by leaving its implementation up to individual pastors and bishops.[238] Turretin affirmed that Scripture was sufficiently clear that all Christians should be able to read it. He was, like the Reformers, offended that anyone should be forbidden to read the Bible.[239]

The Helvetic Consensus Formula (1675)

Turretin's approach to Scripture achieved confessional status briefly in the late seventeenth century.[240] The Reformed community already had a rich variety of confessional statements from the sixteenth century. But some Swiss Reformed scholastics felt that yet another was needed, especially to refute what they perceived as the weaknesses of the School of Saumur in France.

Turretin wrote several times to J. H. Heidegger in Zurich and to many other pastors, urging them to support a new confessional statement. On November 6, 1669, he wrote to Heidegger proposing that, just as Calvin and Bullinger had written the *Consensus Tigurinus* in 1549, so now Geneva and Zurich should work together to produce a new *Consensus*.[241] Later in 1669 a group of theologians from the Swiss cantons of Zurich, Basel, Bern, and Schaffhausen met and agreed to prepare a new creed. Much correspondence ensued with many theologians expressing their views. Casper Waser and John Müller of Zurich wrote to Turretin and asked his opinion. In a letter dated July 4, 1674 Turretin replied: "I am convinced of the necessity of a special formula refuting all the points which deviate from the Bible and from our confession."[242] Finally, in 1674, The Evangelical Diet officially ordered the new creed drawn up. J. H. Heidegger of Zurich, the "mother-church of the Reform" was named to draft the document. While the teachings of Descartes, Cocceius, and Piscator were all under attack, only the Salmurian doctrines were to be rejected, and even then, no persons were to be specifically condemned.[243]

The result, published in 1675, was the Helvetic Consensus Formula. Its section on the Bible was directed against textual criticism of the Old Testament. It declared the inspiration of the "Hebrew Original of the Old Testament." This inspiration was found "not only in its consonants, but in its vowels—either the vowel points themselves, or at least the power of the points." The Bible was pronounced inspired "not only in its matter, but in its words." In its third article the confession announced that textual criticism of the Old Testament would "bring the foundation of our faith and its inviolable authority into perilous hazard."

There was resistance to this Swiss creed both from those who thought it did not say enough and from those who felt that it said too much. The principal author, J. H. Heidegger, was denounced in his own city of Zurich because, compared to what he could have said, some felt that he had been too mild.

In other parts of Switzerland, the new confession was resisted for going too far. At Geneva, Tronchin and Mestrezat, both well-established members of the theological faculty, criticized it. The teaching about the inspiration of the vowel points came under heavy fire. Heidegger was accused of misusing proof texts, and of making a confessional statement regarding a matter on which the "best" theologians—Calvin, Pellican, Zwingli, and Luther—had allowed other opinions than those now required. Heidegger explained that the articles on the Bible were meant only to safeguard the authority and authenticity of Scripture and not to decide questions of grammar and criticism. Only with this assurance did the Venerable Company of Pastors in 1678 and the Council in 1679 adopt the confession. This was five years after its adoption by Basel and Zurich.[244]

Turretin, Heidegger, and others utilized all the pressure that they could muster, including civil power, to get the *Consensus* adopted by all the Swiss cantons. Only after considerable struggle was the principle of unity on the basis of a common theological statement maintained. It remained in effect less than a generation. In 1706 the Venerable Company set aside the requirement of subscription to the *Consensus.* It was very soon disregarded in the other cantons and was disapproved from the first by the northern European churches.[245]

The Reformed scholasticism that Turretin and others had brought to full flower, withered and died in a generation. The medieval methodology by which they defended Scripture against Counter-Reformation Catholicism and other threats in the late seventeenth century proved to have little attraction for those who followed them. The scholastic approach to Scripture was, however, to be resurrected in succeeding centuries when orthodox theologians felt similarly threatened by new understandings of the Bible.

d. A Summary of the Shifts That Produced Reformed Scholasticism

We have traced discernible shifts away from the theological method of Calvin in the century following his death. These changes in method often involved distortions of the Reformer's doctrine. That was especially true in regard to the doctrine of Scripture that became the formal principle of a scientific system.

It remains difficult to give a clear and comprehensive definition of Reformed scholasticism. The post-Reformation Reformed theologians, for the most part, intended to reproduce the theology of Calvin. But under many pressures they became devoted to defending what they took to be a finished theological deposit. The defensive weapons they chose were taken from an armory of medieval scholastic argumentation of the type that Calvin himself had rejected as unsuitable for doing theology. The implementation of an alien methodology eventually produced critical changes in Reformed thought concerning the doctrine of Scripture.

Scholasticism represented a spirit, a mood, a mind-set quite different than that of Calvin, the Augustinian-humanist Reformer.[246] We need to speak of shifts of emphasis rather than drastically different doctrines when we contrast Calvin with his scholastic followers. What they had in common, over against Roman Catholicism and Socinianism, for example, was important. But the shifts of emphasis were highly significant, especially in their later historical consequences.[247] Reformed scholastics adopted methods of describing and defending the Bible that they had borrowed from Roman Catholicism and Socinianism. In later centuries, theologians expounded the Reformed doctrine of Scripture in scholastic categories, with no sense of the significant shifts away from Calvin's own approach. By the time of the nineteenth-century Princeton theology, students were given Turretin to study on the erroneous assumption that his doctrine of Scripture was the same as that of Calvin. At the present time, some theologians expound a doctrine of Scripture using the theological method of Thomas Aquinas, and yet do not hestitate to present their work as Reformed theology.[248]

Many scholars in recent years have attempted to outline the main elements of Protestant scholasticism.[249] The following list is a summary of factors that have been identified as representing the post-Reformation Protestant position. They are not intended to be definitive, but are meant to be helpful in stimulating reflection on the material we have presented regarding the development of a scholastic doctrine of Scripture by Reformed orthodoxy.

1. Scholasticism structured theology as a logical system of belief in

reliance on Aristotelian syllogistic reasoning. The emphasis was on a rational defense of a settled deposit of doctrines.

2. Scholasticism revived interest in metaphysical philosophy rooted in a renewed admiration for Thomas Aquinas. There was intense interest in the will of God, in line with the medieval notion that ultimate reality could be known by tracing effects back to their causes.

3. Scholasticism assumed that reason had at least equal standing with faith in religious matters, with the consequence that revelation was often relegated to a secondary position. The Reformation concept of accommodation was dropped and Western logic was assumed to reflect the working of the mind of God.

4. Scholasticism substituted philosophical speculation for growth in the Christian life as the goal of theological work. Theology attempted to return to the medieval ideal of being the queen of the Sciences. A total unified system of knowledge was desired rather than just a deepened insight into the Christian faith.

5. Scholasticism defined faith first as an act of assent by the mind to the deposit of truths in Scripture and only secondarily as a relationship of personal trust in Christ wrought by the Holy Spirit.

6. Scholasticism interpreted Scripture as a nonhistorical body of propositions that offered a base of inerrant information on which to construct a universal philosophy. The emphasis was on texts of Scripture as atomistic units that could be rearranged and fitted into a logical system without reference to the biblical *kerygma*. [250]

Several tendencies that applied particularly to Scripture as a whole should be noted here:[251]

a. The tendency to subject scriptural materal to inappropriate Aristotelian or Cartesian modes of presentation.

b. The tendency to subordinate the inner witness of the Holy Spirit to arguments for the authority and authenticity of Scripture based on external and internal evidences.

c. The tendency to press the notion of verbal inspiration to an unnecessary extreme. A notable example was the insistence that the Hebrew vowel points (which did not exist in the original manuscripts) were inspired.

d. The tendency to treat the human authors of Scripture as mere scribes recording divine words. Even where it was explicitly denied, there were often implications of a dictation theory.

e. The tendency to give false importance to a doctrine of inerrancy. Inspiration was made dependent on the theologian's assertion that the Bible was correct in every detail.[252]

Despite the undoubted intention of the Reformed scholastics to present Reformed theology, it cannot be denied that they departed significantly from the stance of Calvin.[253] In theological method and especially in their view of the authority and interpretation of Scripture, post-Reformation scholastics were more like Thomas Aquinas and his medieval approach than they were like Calvin and his Reformation position. The consequences of these shifts became evident in the pendulum swings of reaction in the centuries that followed.[254]

e. Summary

The followers of Luther and Calvin in the seventeenth century in Europe endeavored to systematize the work of their masters by casting it into an Aristotelian mold. Thus, a period of Protestant scholasticism was launched in the immediate post-Reformation period. This Protestant scholasticism rejected the Augustinian approach of faith leading to understanding and reverted to the Thomistic approach, which gave reason priority over faith. There was a significant shift among orthodox Protestants from the Neoplatonic presuppositions of the Reformers to the Aristotelian assumptions of the Reformers' medieval opponents. Two aspects of the central Christian tradition were also progressively abandoned. Theology was no longer viewed as a practical, moral discipline exclusively directed toward the salvation of people and their guidance in the life of faith. Theology now became an abstract, speculative, technical science that attempted to lay foundations for philosophical mastery of all areas of thought and life. Further, and equally far-reaching in its consequences, the concept of accommodation was discarded. Theologians now unashamedly contended that they thought God's thoughts because the human mind was fitted to think in God's ways. God was no longer the parent who had condescended to speak children's language for their benefit. God was now the supplier, through revelation, of up-to-date scientific information. While scholastic theologians did not claim to know all that God knew extensively, they claimed a one-to-one correspondence between the theological knowledge they had and the way in which God himself knew it. Precision replaced piety as the goal of theology.

Philipp Melanchthon moved Lutheranism away from the Christological concentration of Luther to a more scholastic, philosophical system of theology. Key transitional figures in the movement from reformation theology to a Reformed orthodoxy were Peter Martyr Vermigli, Girolamo Zanchi, and Theodore Beza. Each of these theologians was committed to Aristotelian logic as the means of clarifying and systematizing theology. They intended to reproduce the doctrines of Calvin, but they utilized a theological methodology developed by the scholastic followers of Thomas Aquinas. Sometimes the scholastic method distorted the Reformation content of Calvin's doctrine of Scripture.

At the beginning of the seventeenth century, the Synod of Dort in the Netherlands gave confessional expression to the developing Reformed scholasticism.

The impact of revolutions in science and philosophy in the seventeenth century caused some Reformed theologians to go further in scholastic rigidification. Gisbert Voetius, for example, responded to Copernicus and Descartes by defending Aristotle's view of the universe and Aquinas's arguments for the existence of God. In both instances he claimed to be defending the Bible.

Some theologians, such as Christoph Wittich, remained in the Augustinian-Calvinist tradition and accepted the accommodated character of the Bible's language. Wittich thus avoided unnecessary conflicts with the "new" science and philosophy.

Reformed scholasticism reached its full flowering in the theology of Francis Turretin who held the chair of theology in Geneva one hundred years after Calvin's death. Turretin chose the theological method of Thomas Aquinas's *Summa* as the pattern for his own theology. In developing his doctrine of Scripture, Turretin quoted 175 authorities but did not mention Calvin. Scripture was the formal principle on which he founded a scientific, systematic theology. The authority of Scripture was predicated on the claim that the Bible contained inerrant words. Turretin adduced external and internal arguments to prove that the biblical writers had not erred in the slightest particular. No trace of Calvin's concept of accommodation was to be found in Turretin's work. Not just the content, but the form of the Bible was asserted to be supernatural. Accordingly, Turretin was intensely concerned over the present state of the biblical text. He omitted reference to the internal witness of the Holy Spirit in developing the authority of Scripture, but invoked the Holy Spirit to guarantee an authentic canon and a reliable edition of Scripture. This led Turretin to the extreme of claiming inspiration for the (nonexistent) vowel points in the original Hebrew manuscripts. Turretin's style of Reformed scholasticism was embodied in the Helvetic Consensus Formula in 1675. It declared that textual criticism of the Old Testament would subject faith in Scripture to "perilous hazard."

Reformed scholasticism was a mind-set that, in a period of defensive reaction, made significant changes in the doctrine of Scripture utilized by Calvin. Reason was given priority over faith, and Scripture came to be treated as a compendium of propositions from which logical deductions could be drawn.

f. Notes

1. John Walter Beardslee, III, "Theological Development at Geneva under Francis and Jean-Alphonse Turretin, 1648–1737" (Ph.D. dissertation, Yale University, 1956), p. 18. (Hereafter cited as Beardslee, "Theological Development.")

2. For the influence of scholasticism on post-Reformation Lutherans see Robert P. Scharlemann, *Thomas Aquinas and John Gerhard* (New Haven: Yale University Press, 1964), pp. 3 and 22. For the influence of scholasticism on Reformed theologians in the post-Reformation period see Brian G. Armstrong, *Calvinism and the Amyraut Heresy: Protestant Scholasticism and Humanism in Seventeenth Century France* (Madison: University of Wisconsin Press, 1969), pp. 129–132.

3. John S. Bray, *Theodore Beza's Doctrine of Predestination*, Bibliotheca Humanistica and Reformatorica, Vol. 12 (Neiuwkoop, The Netherlands: B. DeGraff, 1975), p. 12.

4. Jean Aymon, *Tous les synodes nationaux, des églises réformées de France* (The Hague, 1710), II, p. 210, cited in Armstrong, p. 135.

5. See, among others, John H. Leith, *An Introduction to the Reformed Tradition* (Atlanta: John Knox Press, 1977), pp. 114–116 (hereafter cited as Leith, *Reformed Tradition*); and John W. Beardslee, III, ed. and trans., *Reformed Dogmatics* (New York: Oxford University Press, 1965), "Introduction," pp. 3–25. (Hereafter cited as Beardslee, *Reformed Dogmatics*.)

6. *EP*, s.v. "Melanchthon, Philipp."

7. David C. Steinmetz, *Reformers in the Wings* (Philadelphia: Fortress Press, 1971), p. 74.

8. Steinmetz, p. 74.

9. Scharlemann, p. 4.

10. Robert D. Preus, *The Theology of Post-Reformation Lutheranism*, 2 vols. (St. Louis: Concordia Publishing House, 1970). Preus evaluates this development more positively than we do.

11. See Bray, pp. 131–136. See also Armstrong, pp. 38, n. 111; 87 and 158. Jill Raitt, in *The Eucharistic Theology of Theodore Beza*, AAR Studies in Religion, No. 4 (Chambersburg, Pa.: American Academy of Religion, 1972), urges caution in overstressing the Italian Aristotelian influence on Beza until more extensive research is done. However, she does acknowledge that Beza's theological method "became increasingly scholastic" (p. 71). She regards him, as we do, as

a traditional "link between Calvin and Reformed orthodoxy" (p. 73).

12. For an account of Martyr's life see Steinmetz, chap. 14; Marvin W. Anderson, *Peter Martyr A Reformer in Exile (1542–1562)* (Nieuwkoop: DeGraaf, 1975). On his life in Italy see Philip McNair, *Peter Martyr in Italy: An Anatomy of Apostasy* (Oxford: Clarendon Press, 1967).

13. On Martyr's doctrine of the sacraments see Joseph C. McLelland, *The Visible Words of God: An Exposition of the Sacramental Theology of Peter Martyr Vermigli* (Grand Rapids, Mich.: Wm. B. Eerdmans, 1957). (Hereafter cited as McLelland, *Visible Words*.)

14. Martyr's contributions to the English Reformation is assessed in Gordon Huelin, *Peter Martyr and the English Reformation* (Ph.D. dissertation, University of London, 1955). See also John Patrick Donnelly, *Calvinism and Scholasticism in Vermigli's Doctrine of Man and Grace*, Studies in Medieval and Reformation Thought, ed. Heiko A. Oberman et al. (Leiden: E. J. Brill, 1976), chap. 7. (Hereafter cited as Donnelly, *Calvinism*.)

15. Martyr housed and corresponded with numerous English refugees who fled Mary's reign of terror. A close friend was the future Bishop of Salisbury, John Jewel. See W. M. Southgate, *John Jewel and the Problem of Doctrinal Authority* (Cambridge, Mass.: Harvard University Press, 1962), pp. 20, 63, 178. On his correspondence with other Reformers see Charles H. Smyth, *Cranmer and the Reformation under Edward VI* (Cambridge: Cambridge University Press, 1926), pp. 107–138 and Marvin W. Anderson, "Peter Martyr, Reformed Theologian (1542–1562), His Letters to Heinrich Bullinger and John Calvin," *Sixteenth Century Journal* 4, no. 1 (April 1973): 41–64.

16. See John Patrick Donnelly, "Italian Influences on the Development of Calvinist Scholasticism," *Sixteenth Century Journal* 7, no. 1 (April 1976): p. 86. (Hereafter cited as Donnelly, "Italian.") See also Donnelly, *Calvinism*, chap. 8.

17. See *Melachim Id Est, Regum Libri Duo Posteriores cum Commentariis* (Zurich: Froschoverus, 1571), p. 217. Cf. John Patrick Donnelly, "Calvinist Thomism," *Viator* 7 (1976): 443 (hereafter cited as Donnelly, "Calvinist Thomism") and "Italian," p. 89. For Aquinas, *ST*, I, 1, 3, 8.

18. Donnelly, "Calvinist Thomism," p. 443. See also Donnelly, *Calvinism*, chap. 2.

19. See Donnelly, *Calvinism*, p. 28. Martyr's friend Zanchi was nearly always friendly in his references to Aquinas.

20. See Donnelly, *Calvinism*, p. 34. Cf. Marvin W. Anderson, "Word and Spirit in Exile (1542–1561): the Biblical Writings of Peter Martyr Vermigli," *Journal of Ecclesiastical History* 21, no. 3 (July 1970):194f.

21. See Donnelly, *Calvinism*, pp. 43–44.

22. *Proposit, ex Exod. 3, nec. 4*, as cited in McLelland, *Visible Words*, p. 74. In the "benefits of Jesus Christ crucified," Martyr found both the purpose and clarity of Scripture. See Marvin W. Anderson, "Pietro Matire Vermigli on the Scope and Clarity of Scripture," *Theologische Zeitschrift* 30, no. 1 (January–February 1974):94.

23. *In Librum Ludicum ... Commentarii ...* (Zurich: Froschoverus, 1565), 2.23, as cited in McLelland, *Visible Words*, p. 74.

24. Martyr gives an analysis of the knowledge of God in a treatise, *De Visionibus*, appearing *in Iud*, following 6.22., from which the quote is given in McLelland, *Visible Words*, p. 75.

25. In McLelland, *Visible Words*, p. 75.

26. *In Iud. 10.15* as given by McLelland, *Visible Words*, p. 75. See also *In Samuelis* (I Sam. 1.19) as given in McLelland, p. 75.

27. See *In Lamentationes Sanctissimi Ieremiae Prophetae ... Commentarium* (Zurich: J. J. Bodmer, 1629), 1.13 and *In Gen. 11.5*, as cited in McLelland, *Visible Words*, p. 75.

28. Cited in McLelland, *Visible Words*, p. 75, from *De Visionibus*. See also *In Iud. 8.24*, as given in McLelland, p. 76.

29. From McLelland, *Visible Words*, p. 76. The Anthropomorphites were a sect of ancient heretics who understood everything in Scripture in a literal sense, particularly Genesis 1:27: "So God created man in his own image." Thus they maintained that God Himself had a human shape. They were also called "Audiani" after Audius, a Syrian who originated their sect. Origen wrote against certain monks in Egypt who were Anthromorphites. Anthropomorphites reappeared in the tenth century and the seventeenth under Paul Felgenhauer, a Bohemian theosophist and mystic (b. 1620). See John M'Clintock and James Strong, *Cyclopaedia of Biblical, Theological, and Ecclesiastical Literature*, 12 vols. (New York: Harper & Brothers, 1895), s.v. "Anthropomorphites" (hereafter cited as *M&S*). See also *ODC*, s.v. "Audiani."

30. See (In Rom. 4.11, as given in McLelland, *Visible Words*, p. 76.

31. McLelland's title captures Martyr's thought: the sacraments are "the Visible Words of God."

32. See *In Lament. 2.1*, as given in McLelland, *Visible Words*, p. 77. See also *In 1 Cor. 13.12*, p. 77.

33. *In Arist. Eth. pp.* 49f., as given in McLelland, *Visible Words*, p. 77. Only in the life everlasting, said Martyr, would the blessed know "the essence of God ... by soul or mind," *De Visionibus* (McLelland, p. 78).

34. *Enc. Verbi Dei*, as given in McLelland, *Visible Words*, p. 78.

35. *In Iud. 6.22*, as given in McLelland, *Visible Words*, p. 78.

36. *Def. 14* and *in Iud. 8.24*, as given in McLelland, *Visible Words*, p. 78.

37. Preface to the *Tractatio*, as given in McLelland, *Visible Words*, p. 78. Martyr continued by warning against two extremes in interpreting these metaphors—attributing too much or too little to them. The spiritual interpretation demanded a "mean" between these "according to the analogy and convenience of the Holy Scripture," which is—"the hypostatic or essential unity of Christ."

38. See *Corinthios*, f. 3r., as cited in Donnelly, *Calvinism*, p. 59.

39. See Donnelly, *Calvinism*, p. 60, where he cites some instances of Martyr's allegorical interpretation: *Genesis*, ff. 15 v, 33r, 70v, 78r, 103r; *Melachim*, 214v, 233v; *Iudicium*, f. 90rv. These allegories seem to have been used because Martyr had in mind the future preaching needs of his listeners.

40. See Donnelly, *Calvinism*, p. 60.

41. Ibid., p. 61. Examples of this method are in Martyr's treatment of: temptation (*Genesis*, f. 85r); heresy (*Iudicium*, ff. 38v–39r); and fortitude (*Samuelis*, f. 231v). The four causes are heavily used in Martyr's sacramental writings: Material cause is the material object used, water, bread, wine. The formal cause is the words of the rite. The final cause is to stir human hearts to claim God's promise by faith. The efficient cause is God. See *Romanos*, pp. 106–107.

42. Martyr, however, lacked the gift of wit and sense of humor. See Donnelly, *Calvinism*, p. 62. Donnelly finds no trace of Ramism in Martyr's writings as he attributes his emphasis on logical distinctions to Aristotle, the foe of Ramus.

43. See M. D. Chenu, O. P., *Toward Understanding Saint Thomas*, trans. A. M Henry and

D. Hughes (Chicago: Regnery, 1964), for a further discussion of the scholastic *quaestio* and how an article was built up.

44. Examples of this method are Martyr's discussion of works of supererogation (*Corinthios*, ff. 225r–229v) and the legitimacy of administering communion under one species (*Corinthios*, ff. 263r–271v). See Donnelly, *Calvinism*, pp. 62–63.

45. Martyr did use syllogisms for example in his *Defensio* (pp. 355, 359) and his ethics. Donnelly writes: "The formal syllogism actually plays far less a role in Martyr than in many Protestant scholastics. In most of Jerome Zanchi's writings each subsection starts with a formal syllogism which the whole subsection then explains and defends," *Calvinism*, p. 63.

46. See Donnelly, *Calvinism*, p. 63.

47. See *Ethicorum*, p. 265. Martyr gave three reasons for using Aristotle: "First he believes the Aristotelian world view is fundamentally correct, although it must be supplemented and corrected from biblical revelation on such points as the eternity of the world. Secondly, Aristotle provides Martyr with much that reinforces and gives systematic coherence to his theology. Finally, Aristotle provides weapons for attack. For Martyr, Aristotle is not a neutral in the doctrinal controversies of the sixteenth century; he is Calvinism's ally." See Donnelly, "Italian," p. 93.

48. See Donnelly, *Calvinism*, p. 200.

49. Ibid., p. 35.

50. Ibid., p. 202.

51. Ibid., p. 200.

52 Ibid., p. 201. When Martyr did attempt to explore the Godhead, he concentrated on the divine will and the sovereign freedom of the act of predestination. Cf. Joseph McLelland, "The Reformed Doctrine of Predestination according to Peter Martyr," *SJT* 8 (1955): 255–271.

53. For a detailed biography of Zanchi see C. Schmidt, "Girolamo Zanchi," *Theologische Studien und Kritiken*, 32 (1859): 625–708. (Hereafter cited as Schmidt, "Girolamo Zanchi.") An extensive bibliography is given by C. Schmidt and Joh. Ficker, s.v. "Zanchi," *Realencyklopädie für protestantisch Theologie und Kirche*, ed. J. J. Herzog, 3 Aufl. (1908), Bd. XXI. See also the summary in Otto Gründler, "The Influence of Thomas Aquinas upon the Theology of Girolamo Zanchi (1516–1590)," in *Studies in Medieval Culture*, ed. John R. Sommerfeldt (Western Michigan University, 1964), pp. 106–107

(hereafter cited as Gründler, "Influence") and Donnelly, "Italian," pp. 87–88.

54. Zanchi's controversy in Strassburg is treated in Jürgen Moltmann, *Prädestination und Perseveranz* (Neukirchen: Neukirchener Verlag, 1961), pp. 72–109. Cf. Joseph N. Tylenda, "Girolamo Zanchi and John Calvin: A Study in Discipleship as Seen through Their Correspondence," *Calvin Theological Journal* 10, no. 2 (November, 1975): 107ff.

55. At least three editions of Zanchi's *Opera theologica* (hereafter cited as Zanchi's *Opera*) were published—all after his death: 1605, 1613, 1619. Zanchi's thought is dealt with in Otto Gründler, "Thomism and Calvinism in the Theology of Girolamo Zanchi (1516–1590)," (Ph.D. dissertation, Princeton Theological Seminary, 1961), published as *Die Gotteslehre Girolami Zanchis und ihre Bedeutung für sein Lehre von der Prädestination* (Neukirchen: Neukirchener Verlag, 1965). (Hereafter cited as Gründler, *Gotteslehre*.)

56. The first volume dealt with the Trinity, the second with the divine attributes, the third with creation, and the fourth with Adam's fall, sin, and the law of God. Zanchi stated that he planned to do further tomes on the person and office of the Redeemer and on the Church in time and eternity. After he left Heidelberg and assumed other duties, time did not permit him to do the final volumes. See Donnelly, "Calvinist Thomism," p. 444.

57. See Gründler, *Gotteslehre*, pp. 64–75.

58. See *Inst.* (1559), I. x.2; I. v. 9; I. xiv. 1; II. ii. 6,7; and I. ii. 2. Cf. Gilbert Rist, "Modernité de la méthode theologique de Calvin," *Revue de théologie et philosophie* 1 (1968): 23–29.

59. See Donnelly, "Calvinist Thomism," p. 447 for a comparative table.

60. See Donnelly, "Italian," p. 90.

61. From Zanchi, *Opera* (1605), I, 381, as cited in Donnelly, "Italian," p. 91.

62. See Zanchi, *Opera* I, 381ff. and especially p. 388, as cited in Donnelly, "Italian," p. 91.

63. See Schmidt, "Girolamo Zanchi," p. 694, as cited in Gründler, "Influence," p. 109.

64. Schmidt, "Girolamo Zanchi," p. 698, as cited in Gründler, "Influence," p. 109.

65. *De natura Dei*, in Zanchi, *Opera* (1613), II col. 83, as cited in Gründler, "Influence," p. 109.

66. Gründler, "Influence," p. 109. Zanchi used Aristotle and Aquinas to expound on the nature of human knowledge. See *De natura Dei* in *Opera*, II, 83, as cited in Gründler, "Influence," p. 110. Like Aristotle and Aquinas, Zanchi presupposed that all natural knowledge was derived from the sensible world and came to us through our senses. See *De natura Dei* in *Opera*, II, 196f; see also in *Opera*, II, 84, 65, 196.

67. *De natura Dei* in Zanchi, *Opera*, II, 196, as cited in Gründler, "Influence," p. 111.

68. See *De natura Dei* in Zanchi, *Opera*, II, 33; see also *ST* I, q. 13, a.2. Like Aquinas, Zanchi began his discussion of the nature of God by dealing with the concept of God's *simplicity.*

69. See chap. 1 in this work on Aquinas and chap. 1, notes 220ff.

70. *De natura Dei*, in Zanchi, *Opera*, 23; see also *ST* I, q. 13, a.5, as cited in Gründler, "Influence," p. 113.

71. See Gründler, "Influence," pp. 113–116 for more detail.

72. The full title was *Aristotelis de naturali auscultatione, seu de principiis, cum praefatione Doctoris Zanchi* (Strasbourg: V. Rihelius, 1554). It was not reprinted in the *Opera.* See Donnelly, "Italian," p. 94.

73. This is the opinion of Donnelly, in "Italian," p. 94.

74. *Aristotelis de naturali auscultatione,* f. d6, as cited by Donnelly, "Italian," p. 94.

75. See Zanchi, *Opera*, III, 217–219. Zanchi also developed a physico-theology in which he attempted to integrate a large treatise on physical reality with theology. Lambert Danäus, a French Protestant divine (b. 1530), was the first Calvinist to develop physico-theology. These theologies were popular in the seventeenth century but in the eighteenth sometimes merged into various strands of Deism. Danäus wrote to attack Aristotelian physics and its tendency to divorce nature from its Creator and thus lead to atheism. Danäus wanted to examine all the multiplicity and beauty of nature so as to inspire his readers toward praise and admiration for God. Zanchi too had this pious purpose in mind. But he sought expressly to build upon Aristotelian physics. See Donnelly, "Italian," pp. 94–95 and Ernst Bizer, *Frühorthodoxie und Rationalismus* (Zurich: Evz-Verlag, 1963), p. 50. When Zanchi defended the immortality of the soul, he did so on the basis of twenty-five articles developed from fourteen passages from Aristotle. Calvin had defended the

doctrine primarily on scriptural grounds. See *Inst.* (1559), I. v. 5; I. xv. 2; III. xxv. 3; xxv. 6. (On Zanchi's correspondence with Calvin, see Tylenda, pp. 113ff.) Martyr had denied there were rational arguments for the immortality of the soul. See *Melachim Id Est, Regum Libri Duo Posteriores cum Commentariis* (Zurich: Froschoverus, 1571), pp. 217, 232, cited in Donnelly, "Italian," p. 95. Cf. Donnelly, *Calvinism*, pp. 96–100. For Zanchi's arguments see *Opera*, III, 638–678, as cited in Donnelly, "Italian," p. 95. Zanchi concluded that Aristotle accepted or at least did not deny the immortality of the soul. While there were some Platonic elements in his thought, Zanchi's basic substructure was Aristotelian. See Donnelly, "Italian," pp. 95–96 and "Calvinist Thomism," p. 449.

76. Zanchi's views on predestination were spread in England partially through William Perkins's *A Golden Chaine* (1590), which examined the causes of predestination. In the eighteenth century, the Calvinist Augustus Toplady (1740–1778) sought to oppose John Wesley's Arminian tendencies by translating not Calvin but Zanchi's treatise on predestination. He titled it *The Doctrine of Absolute Predestination.*

77. See Donnelly, "Calvinist Thomism," p. 448.

78. Gründler, "Influence," p. 117.

79. Donnelly, "Calvinist Thomism," p. 448. Zanchi used Aquinas for an ally on many theological fronts. In one work he claimed he would refute the Thomist, Domingo de Soto (1494–1560) and the Council of Trent on man's total corruption, based on the writings of Thomas Aquinas. When Zanchi had summarized his own teaching against de Soto he added: "Just as your Aquinas also teaches." See Zanchi, *Opera*, IV, 59, as cited in Donnelly, "Calvinist Thomism," p. 451.

80. Donnelly, "Calvinist Thomism," p. 448.

81. See the discussion of this matter in Bray, pp. 15 and 130, and in Armstrong, pp. 138–139. Both of them rely on Gründler's dissertation at Princeton Theological Seminary, which was later published in German. Bray cites the German edition. Gründler's interpretation is disputed by Norman Shepherd, "Zanchius on Saving Faith," *The Westminster Theological Journal* 36 (1973): 31–47. We have tried to take account of Shepherd's valid objections. At depth, the most important difference between the two is that

Gründler evaluates post-Reformation Reformed scholasticism negatively while Shepherd evaluates it as a positive development.

82. Gründler, (English ed.), p. 57, (German ed.), p. 49, as cited in Bray, p. 15. See also Shepherd, pp. 32–33. See Zanchi, *Opera*, Tom. 7, Part I, Col. 352, as translated by and cited in Shepherd, pp. 33–34.

83. Shepherd, p. 40, states: "It must be readily acknowledged that there are obvious differences in the ways in which Zanchi and Calvin describe the nature of faith. Zanchi consciously and deliberately employs the scholastic terminology of infused habit and act. Calvin does not characteristically speak in this way. Even more striking is the fact, noted by Gründler, that Zanchi expressly differs from those who, like Calvin, speak of trust (*fiducia*) as the essence of faith."

84. Shepherd, p. 43, notes that Zanchi "is unwilling to define faith as trust." This departure from Calvin is, according to Shepherd, "only in a formal sense."

85. Shepherd, p. 41.

86. Shepherd, pp. 43–44, comments: "The difference between Zanchi and Calvin is not unimportant and is laden with significant practical consequences; but Zanchi is not conscious of introducing a novelty. He finds the distinction already within the generation of the Reformers."

87. Bray, pp. 9 and 29.

88. Many scholars depict Beza as a transformer as well as transmitter of Calvin's theology. Among those previously cited are Armstrong, Bray, Beardslee, Dowey, and Raitt. See in addition the important study of Ernst Bizer, "Reformed Orthodoxy and Cartesianism," trans. Chalmers MacCormick, *Journal for Theology and the Church* 2 (1965): 20–82. This is translated from Bizer's "Die reformierte Orthodoxie und der Cartesianismus," *Zeitschrift für Theologie und Kirche* 55 (1958): 306–372. Note also two helpful articles by Basil Hall, "The Calvin Legend" (pp. 1–18), and "Calvin against the Calvinists" (pp. 19–37) in *John Calvin: A Collection of Distinguished Essays*, ed. Gervase E. Duffield (Grand Rapids, Mich.: Wm. B. Eerdmans, 1966).

89. Bray, pp. 22, 30–33.

90. Ibid., p. 22.

91. Ibid., pp. 22–24 and 135.

92. Armstrong, pp. 38–40. Cf. *HCT*, 3:246.

93. Bray, pp. 23–24.

94. Ibid., pp. 25–27.

95. Ibid., pp. 28, 121. This introduction of Aristotle into the curriculum was parallel to Melanchthon's initiatives in Wittenberg.

96. Bray, p. 28, n. 47. See also Walter J. Ong, *Ramus: Method and the Decay of Dialogue: From the Art of Discourse to the Art of Reason* (Cambridge, Mass.: Harvard University Press, 1958), p. 28, and Ralph Bronkema, *The Essence of Puritanism* (Goes, The Netherlands: Oosterbaan & LeCointre, 1929), p. 113. For an overview of Ramus's influence on Reformed theology and especially on that of the Westminster Divines see Jack Bartlett Rogers, *Scripture in the Westminster Confession* (Grand Rapids, Mich.: Wm. B. Eerdmans, 1967), pp. 87–95 and 236–239. (Hereafter cited as *SWC.*)

97. Bray, pp. 32–33.

98. Ibid., pp. 30–33.

99. Ibid., pp. 121–122.

100. Ibid., p. 132.

101. Ibid., pp. 132–136. See also Armstrong, pp. 38–39. Raitt correctly cautions lest too much weight be given one piece of evidence such as Beza's request for a book by Pomponozzi. Her own work, however, corroborates, on other grounds, the scholasticizing tendencies in Beza's theology.

102. See Bray, chapter 6, "Rationalism and Scholasticism in Beza's Treatment of Predestination," pp. 119–136.

103. *Tractationes*, I, 199, cited in Bray, p. 120.

104. Walter Kickel, *Vernunft und Offenbarung bei Theodor Beza* (Neukirchen: Neukirchen Verlag, 1967), pp. 167–168, cited in Bray, pp. 122–123.

105. Armstrong, p. 136.

106. *Quastiones*, pp. 38–42, 47–48, 74–75; *Theses*, pp. 18, 34, cited in Bray, p. 124.

107. *Tractationes*, III, 417, cited in Bray, p. 127.

108. Bray, p. 127.

109. Bray, p. 129, offers as an example, *Quastiones*, pp. 93–115.

110. See Bray, who cites *Tractationes*, III, 415–416 on Romans 9:8–9 (p. 129) and *Tractationes*, III, 412–413 (p. 130) on Romans 11, where Beza "logically" deduced that God was glorified through the punishment of the reprobate.

111. Bray, p. 121. On du Moulin see Armstrong, pp. 83–88.

112. Armstrong, p. 158.

113. *Examen de la doctrine de MM Amyrault and Testard*, p. 99, cited in Armstrong, p. 87.

114. Bray, p. 35.

115. Philip C. Holtrop, "Predestination in Calvin, Beza, and the Later Reformed Orthodoxy," (Grand Rapids, Calvin Seminary lecture, February 10, 1977), p. 6. Holtrop is preparing a two-volume study of Beza's theology.

116. For background see "The Synod of Dort and the Arminian Controversy (A.D. 1619)" in Jack Rogers, *et al.*, *Case Studies in Christ and Salvation* (Philadelphia: Westminster Press, 1977), pp. 83–96.

117. Holtrop, pp. 6–7.

118. Armstrong, pp. 59–60. See also Holtrop, p. 7.

119. On the Ptolemaic/Aristotelian cosmology, see John Dillenberger, *Protestant Thought and Natural Science* (Nashville: Abingdon Press, 1960), pp. 21–28, (hereafter cited as Dillenberger, *Protestant Thought*) and A. R. Hall, *The Scientific Revolution 1500–1800* (Boston: Beacon Press, 1960), chap. 1.

120. On Copernicus see: William Cecil Dampier, *A History of Science*, 4th ed. (Cambridge: Cambridge University Press, 1966), pp. 109–113; Herbert Butterfield, *The Origins of Modern Science*, rev. (New York: Macmillan, 1961), pp. 17–36; and other works on the history of science. See also Dillenberger, *Protestant Thought*, pp. 21–49 and E. A. Burtt, *The Metaphysical Foundations of Modern Science*, rev. ed. (New York: Doubleday, 1954), pp. 36–41.

121. Alan Richardson, *The Bible in the Age of Science* (Philadelphia: Westminster Press, 1961), pp. 9–10.

122. See Dillenberger, *Protestant Thought*, pp. 29–49 and Paul A. Kocher, *Science and Religion in Elizabethan England* (San Marino, Calif.: Huntington Library, 1953), chap. 9. The religious resistance on the continent is also treated in Dorothy Stimson, *The Gradual Acceptance of the Copernican Theory of the Universe* (Gloucester, Mass.: Peter Smith, 1972 [rep. 1917]), pp. 95–106.

123. R. Hooykaas, *Religion and the Rise of Modern Science* (Grand Rapids, Mich.: Wm. B. Eerdmans, 1972), pp. 121ff. See also Dillenberger, *Protestant Thought*, pp. 37–38; Kocher, p. 8; and Heinrich Bornkamm, "Kopernikus im Urteil der Reformatoren," *Archiv für Reformations-Geschichte* 40 (1943):171–183.

124. Hooykaas, p. 120. Cf. Dillenberger, *Protestant Thought*, pp. 38–39 and Kocher, p. 9.

125. Hooykaas, p. 122. Cf. Dillenberger, *Protestant Thought*, pp. 39–41.

126. Dillenberger, *Protestant Thought*, p. 59.

127. Heinrich Heppe, *Reformed Dogmatics*, edited by E. Bizer. Translated by G. T. Thomson (London: Allen & Unwin, 1950), p. 17.

128. Dillenberger, *Protestant Thought*, p. 59. Cf. pp. 96–97.

129. R. Preus 2:228. Preus points out that Lutheran resistance did not arise until the middle of the seventeenth century and that "this is understandable, for it was only then that the new world picture had established itself as being generally acceptable to any except a few savant astronomers," 2:227.

130. R. Preus. 2:228–229. On this last point, "all the Lutherans, even those who did not enter into the present discussion, were at one" with Calovius. Preus cites Calovius, *Systema*, I, 608; Mentzer, *Opera Latina*, I, 776; Gerhard, *Loci Theologici*, II, 36; Dannhauer, *Hodosophia Christiana*, p. 39; Dorsch, *Synopsis Theologiae Zacharianae*, I, II, ll. It was Calovius's opinion that Scripture's authority extended also to those places where Scripture happened to mention the things of nature, and this was the position of his contemporaries. Calovius, *Systema*, I, 552. See also *Socinismus Profligatus*, p. 62; Quenstedt, *Systema, P.I, C.4, S.2, Q.5, fons sol. (I, 116)*.

131. See R. Preus, 2:228, note 8, citing Voetius, *Selectarum Disputationum Theologicarum Pars Prima* (Utrecht, 1648), pp. 638, 700; *and Matthias Martini, Quaestiones Theologicae & Philologicae in Librum Josuae* (Bremen, 1624), p. 20. Johann Heinrich Alsted (1588–1638) was also a leading Calvinist who resisted the new science. Dillenberger writes: "At the very time that Galileo was making his discoveries, Alsted developed a conception of theology and its relation to metaphysics in which Aristotle was enshrined in the very citadel of theology. The new result was that the Aristotelian-Ptolemaic world-picture, buttressed by a profusion of Biblical passages, could not be denied without challenging the Christian position itself" (*Protestant Thought*, p. 58). In short, "in the Protestant orthodox development of the seventeenth century, philosophical and Biblical motifs were intertwined" (p. 95).

132. Hooykaas, p. 131, citing Voetius, *Thersites heautontimoroumenos Ultratecti* (1635), pp. 266, 281, 283. Hooykaas comments: "Cal-

vin's accommodation theory was precisely the sort of reasoning that Voetius opposed as much as possible." See Calvin's accommodating exegesis, *Commentary on Psalm 19* (CTS, 312–316).

133. On Descartes see the standard texts, Emile Brehier, *The Seventeenth Century*, trans. Wade Baskin, The History of Philosophy (Chicago: University of Chicago Press, 1966), chap. 3; *HP*, s.v. *Descartes to Leibniz*, IV; *EP*, II, 344–354; Hugh Kearney, *Science and Change 1500–1700* (New York: McGraw-Hill, 1974), pp. 151–162; and Burtt, chap. 4.

134. Bertrand Russell, *A History of Western Philosophy* (New York: Simon & Schuster, 1945), p. 567.

135. John Herman Randall, *The Making of the Modern Mind* (Boston: Houghton Mifflin, 1926), p. 241.

136. *HP* IV, 78.

137. Colin Brown, *Philosophy and the Christian Faith* (Chicago: Inter-Varsity Press, 1969), p. 53.

138. The account is in Bizer.

139. Bizer, p. 31. Voetius's theses about atheism may be found in his *Disputationes Selectae*, I, 114–226.

140. Bizer, p. 32, citing *Disputationes*, I, 151

141. Bizer, p. 32.

142. Ibid.

143. Ibid., citing *Disputationes*, I, 172.

144. See Bizer, p. 33.

145. See Bizer, p. 34, citing *Disputationes*, I, 176.

146. From *Disputationes*, I, 177, as given by Bizer, p. 34.

147. Bizer, p. 38. A much more detailed study of scholasticism and its relationship to Cartesianism is found in Josef Bohatec, *Die cartesianische Scholastik in der Philosophie und reformierten Dogmatik des 17. Jahrhunderts* (Hildesheim: Georg Olms Verlagsbuchhandlung, 1966) and Paul Althaus, *Die Prinzipien der deutschen reformierten Dogmatik im Zeitalter der aristotelischen Scholastik* (Darmstadt: Wissenschaftliche Buchgesellschaft, 1967).

148. See Donald G. Dawe, *No Orthodoxy but the Truth* (Philadelphia: Westminster Press, 1969), pp. 70–71, who writes of Wittich's concept of God vis-à-vis Spinoza. On Wittich see also *M&S*, XII, 960; *HCT*, 3:297; and Althaus, chap. 6.

149. Bizer, p. 52.

150. Bizer, p. 52, points out that Jacobus Revius had attacked the Copernican theory before, in 1648 and 1650.

151. Bizer, pp. 52–53. Cf. Dillenberger, *Protestant Thought*, p. 101.

152. Bizer, p. 54, citing *Consensus*, pp. 6–7. Helmut Thielicke writes: "Only in Christopher Wittig's *Consensus* ... does one get slight hints that the importance of the new awareness of the ego was suspected. For if Wittig does not discuss the subjectivity of present-day believers, he does reflect on the ego of the authors of Scripture as this was conditioned by time, situation, and knowledge. These men were entangled in *praejudicium* (preconception), e.g., cosmological and scientific concepts," in *The Evangelical Faith*, trans. and ed. Geoffrey W. Bromiley, 2 vols. (Grand Rapids, Mich.: Wm. B. Eerdmanns, 1974), 1:35. Dillenberger calls this the concept of accommodation, *Protestant Thought*, p. 101.

153. Bizer, pp. 54–55, citing *Consensus*, p. 6; Epist. 100 (Theologia pacifica defensa, p. 27; and *Consensus*, 31.

154. Bizer, p. 55. See *Consensus*, "Praef.," pp. 6 and 8.

155. Bizer, p. 55. Wittich poses the question in *Consensus*, p. 8.

156. *Consensus*, p. 209. In Bizer, p. 55.

157. Bizer, pp. 55–56.

158. See Bizer, p. 56ff. for a discussion of the contents of Wittich's book.

159. Bizer, p. 58, citing *Consensus*, cap. L, 938.

160. Bizer, p. 58. See *HS*, p. 137. Berkouwer sees a continuity between the views of Wittich and, for example, Bavinck, who in the nineteenth century also returned to the notion of Scripture's purpose of salvation and accomodated style of communication.

161. Bizer, p. 58; see also pp. 58ff. for his account of "The Dispute about the Conception of the Universe" (Wittich and Maresius).

162. Beardslee, "Theological Development" p. i. Beardslee states: "Preliminary conclusions include: the theology of F. Turretin took its strength from two great men, Aquinas and Calvin, and its Calvinism is often lost in scholasticism."

163. Beardslee, "Theological Development," p. 1. "General conclusions begin with the fact that F. Turretin failed in his purpose, the consolidation of the Reformation. Factors in his theology that contributed to this result are his excessive 'supernaturalism' and 'rationalism'.... A particular manifestation is the doctrine of

Scripture, which is so supernatural as to be divorced from scholarship and life."

164. Beardslee, *Reformed Dogmatics*, Introduction, pp. 14–15: "It was an orthodoxy that was virtually to evaporate in the next generation, as Geneva became the city of Jean-Alphonse Turretin, Jacob Vernet, and Jean-Jacques Rousseau."

165. Beardslee, *Reformed Dogmatics*, p. 15. "But this eclipse of Reformed theology is in part only an interlude. Turretin's work, reprinted in 1847, exercised a real influence on the theology of the nineteenth century, especially of American Presbyterianism, through its place in the background of the Princeton movement that culminated with the *Systematic Theology* of Charles Hodge." See also Leith, *Reformed Tradition*, p. 125.

166. "Turretin," *The Biblical Repertory and Princeton Review* 20 (1848): 455. No author is given for this article, which was occasioned by the republication in 1847 of Turretin's Latin *Institutio Theologiae Elencticae* in 4 volumes (hereafter cited as *In.*). The author is presumably Charles Hodge. See also Beardslee, "Theological Development," p. 2.

167. "Turretin," p. 456. See Beardslee, "Theological Development," pp. 2–3.

168. Beardslee, *Reformed Dogmatics*, p. 10. See also Beardslee, "Theological Development," pp. 17–18.

169. Beardslee, *Reformed Dogmatics*, p. 10. See Leith, *Reformed Tradition* pp. 115–116. Leith comments: "It represents a high, technical level of theology. These virtues gave scholastic theology great power. The theologies of this period are today still impressive and indispensable for their intellectual thoroughness. The danger of scholastic theology is that in seeking careful and precise definitions, theology becomes very remote and abstract from life. It forgets that life is more than reason."

170. Leon McDill Allison, "The Doctrine of Scripture in the Theology of John Calvin and Francis Turretin" (Th.M. thesis, Princeton Theological Seminary, 1958), p. 83. All citations from Turretin's *Institutio* are taken from this most helpful study.

171. Gerrit Keizer, *François Turrettini, Sa Vie Et Ses Oeuvres Et Le Consensus* (Lausanne: Georges Bridel, 1900), p. 235, cited in Allison, p. 83.

172. Allison, pp. 83–84. See also "Turretin," pp. 461–462, where [Hodge] comments regarding Turretin: "His distinguishing excellence is perspecuity

and discrimination. His intellect was admirably fitted and trained for perceiving and stating the real principles involved in theological questions. He furnishes the best illustration within our knowledge of the maxim *qui bene distinguit bene docet.*"

173. Allison, p. 89.

174. Allison, p. 90.

175. The American publishers of another of Turretin's works felt it necessary to disclaim responsibility for his every interpretation of Scripture. See Francis Turretin, *Turretin on the Atonement of Christ*, trans. James R. Willson (New York: Board of Publication of the Reformed Protestant Dutch Church, 1859), p. iv, in Allison, p. 91. The citation by the publishers reads: "The work as now published is believed to present in simple and perspicuous English the exact line of thought and argument presented by the great Genevan professor. It only remains to be added, that while the Board of Publication approves of the work as a whole, it is not to be considered responsible for every shade of opinion on minute points, or every interpretation of quoted Scripture."

176. Allison, p. 92. "John Calvin was not mentioned at all in Turretin's doctrine of Scripture," John H. Gerstner, "The Church's Doctrine of Biblical Inspiration," in *The Foundation of Biblical Authority*, ed. James Montgomery Boice (Grand Rapids, Mich.: Zondervan, 1978), p. 41; and p. 56, note 14 misconstrues Allison. Whereas Allison is referring only to the sources of Turretin's doctrine of Scripture, Gerstner ignores this and refers to Turretin's citing of Calvin in other *loci*.

177. Allison, pp. 92–93.

178. Allison, p. 57.

179. See *HS*, Chapter 9. Berkouwer comments: "The reliability of Scripture is correlated with trust as surrender, relying on Scripture to banish all doubt and uncertainty," p. 241.

180. *In.* II, 1, 1, cited in Allison, p. 57.

181. Ibid.

182. *In.* II, 1, 3 and II, 1, 4, cited in Allison, p. 58.

183. *In.* II, 1, 5, cited in Allison, p. 58.

184. *In.* II, 2, 2, cited in Allison, p. 58.

185. *In.* II, 2, 12, cited in Allison, p. 59.

186. *In.* II, 29, cited in Allison, p. 59.

187. B. B. Warfield, for example, was also very conditioned by an anti-Roman Catholic polemic. Section X, Chapter I of the Westminster Confession of Faith, "Of the Holy Scripture," states: "The Supreme judge, by which all controversies of religion are to be determined ... can be no other but the Holy Spirit speaking in the Scripture." Warfield responds by saying that "it is wholly as in the Word that He [the Spirit] is here spoken of, and not as also in the heart," p. 255 in *The Westminster Assembly And Its Work* (New York: Oxford University Press, 1931). Warfield's scholastic view is at variance with statements by the Westminster Divines themselves on this subject. See *SWC*, pp. 426–429.

188. *In.* II, 12, 1, cited in Allison, p. 59.
189. *In.* II, 4, 1, cited in Allison, p. 59.
190. *Inst.* I, vii. 1.
191. *In.* II, 4, 5, cited in Allison, pp. 59–60.
192. *In.* II, 4, 22, cited in Allison, p. 60.
193. *In.* II, 4, 24, cited in Allison, p. 60.
194. *In.* II, 5, 7, cited in Allison, p. 60.
195. *In.* II, 5, 7, cited in Allison, p. 60.
196. *In.* II, 4, 13, cited in Allison, p. 61.
197. *Inst.* I. viii. 13.
198. *In.* II, 6, 5, cited in Allison, p. 61.
199. *In.* II, 4, 8, cited in Allison, p. 62.
200. *In.* II, 4, 9, cited in Allison, p. 62.
201. *In.* II, 4, 14, cited in Allison, p. 62.
202. *In.* II, 4, 17, cited in Allison, p. 62.
203. *In.* II, 4, 18, cited in Allison, p. 62.
204. *In.* II, 4, 21, cited in Allison, p. 62.
205. *In.* II, 5, 3, cited in Allison, p. 62.
206. *In.* II, 5, 3, cited in Allison, p. 63.
207. *In.* II, 5, 4, cited in Allison, p. 63.
208. *In.* II, 5, 5, cited in Allison, p. 63.
209. *In.* II, 6, 3, cited in Allison, p. 64.
210. *In.* II, 6, 17 and *In.* II, 7, 3, cited in Allison, p. 72.
211. *In.* II, 7, 4, cited in Allison, p. 72.
212. *In.* II, 7, 5, cited in Allison, p. 72.
213. *In.* II, 6, 14, cited in Allison, p. 73.
214. Allison, p. 74.
215. *In.* II, 12, 11–12, cited in Allison, p. 75.
216. *In.* II, 11, 2, cited in Allison, p. 75.
217. *In.* II, 11, 2, cited in Allison, p. 75.
218. *In.* II, 11, 3, cited in Allison, p. 75.
219. *In.* II, 11, 6, cited in Allison, p. 75.
220. Armstrong, p. 125. See also Beardslee, "Theological Development," pp. 24–25.
221. *In.* II, 11, 13, cited in Allison, p. 76.
222. *In.* II, 12, 14, cited in Allison, p. 76.
223. *In.* II, 13, 13, cited in Allison, p. 77.
224. *In.* II, 13, 14–15, cited in Allison, p. 77.
225. *In.* II, 13, 20, cited in Allison, p. 77.
226. *In.* II, 16, 1, cited in Allison, p. 78.
227. *In.* II, 16, 9, cited in Allison, p. 78.
228. *In.* II, 16, 2–3, cited in Allison, pp. 78–79.
229. *In.* II, 16, 7, cited in Allison, p. 79.
230. *In.* II, 16, 5, cited in Allison, p. 79.
231. *In.* II, 16, 15–20, cited in Allison, p. 79.
232. *In.* II, 16, 13–14, cited in Allison, p. 79.
233. *In.* II, 17, 2, cited in Allison, p. 80.
234. *In.* II, 17, 3–4, cited in Allison, p. 81.
235. *In.* II, 17, 6, cited in Allison, p. 81.
236. *In.* II, 17, 11–12, cited in Allison, p. 81.
237. *In.* II, 19, 2, cited in Allison, p. 81.
238. Allison, p. 82.
239. *In.* II, 18, 3, cited in Allison, p. 81.
240. The English translation of *The Helvetic Consensus Formula* (1675) is found in Archibald Alexander Hodge, in *Outlines of Theology*, (New York: A. C. Armstrong and Son, 1879), pp. 656–663. It is reprinted in John H. Leith, ed., *Creeds of the Churches: A Reader in Christian Doctrine from the Bible to the Present*, rev. ed. (Richmond: John Knox Press, 1973), pp. 308–323.
241. Donald G. Grohman, *The Genevan Reactions to the Samur Doctrine of Hypothetical Universalism: 1635–1685* (Th.D. dissertation, Knox College, Toronto, Canada, 1971), p. 381. See pp. 379–384 for further background.
242. Turretin to Waser, cited in Grohman, p. 382.
243. Beardslee, "Theological Development," pp. 56–57.
244. Beardslee, "Theological Development," pp. 58–59.
245. Beardslee, "Theological Development," pp. 60–65.
246. Armstrong, p. 32.
247. Geoffrey W. Bromiley, "The Church Doctrine of Inspiration," in *Revelation and the Bible* ed. Carl F. H. Henry (Grand Rapids, Mich.: Baker Book House, 1958), p. 213. David Sabean notes the significances of Moise Amyraut's (1596–1664) departure from Calvin on matters of faith and reason. For Amyraut, "belief in Scriptural truths must be founded on reason and be consistent with proper logic." See "The Theological Rationalism of Moïse Amyraut," *Archiv für Reformationgeschichte* 55 (1964):204–215. The quote is from p. 208.
248. For example, R. C. Sproul, following John Gerstner. In an address entitled "The Philosophical Roots of the Hermeneutical Problem" at the Philadelphia Conference on Reformed Theology in Pasadena, California on February 10, 1978, Sproul contended that first among the philosophical roots of the contemporary crisis in modern hermeneutics was "the loss of the medieval synthesis of Christian theology and philos-

ophy achieved by St. Thomas Aquinas," Sproul emphasized: "That's right. You heard it. You can quote it. I said it. A Reformed, Calvinistic, evangelical Protestant said it."

249. Armstrong, pp. 31–32; Bray (who generally follows Armstrong), pp. 12–17; Beardslee, *Reformed Dogmatics,* pp. 3–24; Leith, *Reformed Tradition,* pp. 114–116 and 124–126; and, Bromiley (who concentrates on consequences for the doctrine of the inspiration of Scripture), pp. 212–214; Holtrop, pp. 2–4. The six points that follow are based on a collation and adaptation of the summaries presented by Armstrong and Bray.

250. See Holtrop's comparison of Calvin and later Reformed orthodoxy on this point, p. 4.

251. This listing of tendencies utilizes the material presented by Bromiley, pp. 213–214, but arranges the elements in a different order.

252. Bromiley, p. 213, himself prefers to retain the term *inerrancy* and comments: "To be sure, inspiration is itself the basis of

inerrancy, and there is no obligation to prove the latter."

253. Armstrong comments: "This new outlook represents a profound divergence from the humanistically oriented religion of John Calvin and most of the early Reformers. The strongly biblical and experientially based theology of Calvin and Luther had, it is fair to say, been overcome by the metaphysics and deductive logic of a restored Aristotelianism," p. 32.

254. Bromiley summarizes his view of Protestant scholasticism stating: "It is also to be recalled that in the matters referred to we are dealing for the most part only with tendencies within a general loyalty, or intention of loyalty, to the Reformation position. Yet the fact can hardly be disputed that a new and non-Biblical rationalism of presupposition, method and approach threatens the Protestant doctrine with these dogmaticians, that they clearly repeat in some degree the same kind of Judaizing movement as that of the early and medieval Church, and that in so doing they incur a measure of both positive and negative responsibility for the disasters which follow," p. 214.

g. Selected Bibliography

Allison, Leon McDill. "The Doctrine of Scripture in the Theology of John Calvin and Francis Turretin." Th.M. thesis, Princeton Theological Seminary, 1958.

Armstrong, Brian G. *Calvinism and the Amyraut Heresy: Protestant Scholasticism and Humanism in Seventeenth Century France.* University of Wisconsin Press, 1969.

Beardslee, John W., ed. and trans. *Reformed Dogmatics.* Oxford University Press, 1965.

Beardslee, John W. "Theological Developments at Geneva under Francis and Jean-Alphonse Turretin (1648–1737)." Ph.D. dissertation, Yale University, 1956.

Bizer, Ernst. "Reformed Orthodoxy and Cartesianism." Translated by Chalmers MacCormick. *Journal for Theology and the Church* 2 (1965): 20–82.

Bray, John S. *Theodore Beza's Doctrine of Predestination.* B. DeGraff, 1975.

Bromiley, Geoffrey W. "The Church Doctrine of Inspiration." In *Revelation and the Bible,* edited by Carl F. H. Henry. Baker Book House, 1958, pp. 205–217.

Dillenberger, John. *Protestant Thought and Natural Science.* Abingdon Press, 1960.

Donnelly, John Patrick. *Calvinism and Scholasticism in Vermigli's Doctrine of Man and Grace.* E. J. Brill, 1976.

Donnelly, John Patrick. "Calvinist Thomism." *Viator* 7 (1976): 441–451.

Donnelly, John Patrick. "Italian Influences on the Development of Calvinist Scholasticism." *Sixteenth Century Journal* 7, no. 1 (April 1976): 81–101.

González, Justo L. *A History of Christian Thought* Vol. 3. Abingdon Press, 1975.

Gründler, Otto. "The Influence of Thomas Aquinas upon the Theology of Girolamo Zanchi (1516–1590)." In *Studies in Medieval Culture*, edited by John R. Sommerfeldt, Western Michigan University, 1964.

Gründler, Otto. "Thomism and Calvinism in the Theology of Girolamo Zanchi (1516–1590)." Ph.D. dissertation, Princeton Theological Seminary, 1961.

Hall, Basil. "Calvin against the Calvinists." In *John Calvin: A Collection of Distinguished Essays*, edited by Gervase E. Duffield. Wm. B. Eerdmans, 1966, pp. 19–37.

Heppe, Heinrich. *Reformed Dogmatics*. Revised and edited by E. Bizer. Translated by G. T. Thomson. Allen and Unwin, 1950.

Hooykaas, R. *Religion and the Rise of Modern Science*. Wm. B. Eerdmans, 1972.

Leith, John H. *An Introduction to the Reformed Tradition*. John Knox Press, 1977.

CHAPTER 4

Shifts from Concentration on Function to Concern for Form in Great Britain

a. Staying in Touch with the Reformation Tradition Regarding Scripture: The Westminster Confession of Faith

The English Reformation underwent a separate and distinctive development from that on the continent.[1] The Church of England stood between Roman Catholic and Protestant. Within that church was a Puritan party, which pressed for reform in a Calvinistic direction theologically and a Presbyterian direction governmentally. Usually in control and opposed to the Puritans were the High Church Anglicans, who maintained an Aristotelian-Thomistic theology and an hierarchical episcopal form of church government. By the seventeenth century these two church parties were identified with political forces—the Puritans with parliamentarians and the High Church party with the king. The political gap widened until it finally split, issuing in a civil war.

The Westminster Assembly of Divines was called by the Puritan Parliament in 1643 to advise them on religious reform. As the Westminster Divines began to meet (1643–1649), the military fortunes of the parliamentary army worsened. The English Parliament then turned to Scotland for aid in their struggle against Charles I. One condition for that aid was a solemn league and covenant binding England and Scotland to secure a uniformity of confession of faith, form of church government, and a directory for worship and catechizing. Scottish representatives were sent as envoys to the English Parliament and to participate in the Assembly.

The Assembly of Divines was composed of some 150 delegates, who met at Westminster Abbey from 1643 until the confession was finished in December of 1646 and then with less regularity until 1649. Eleven people comprised the committee to draft the confession of faith, seven Englishmen (Cornelius Burges, Thomas Gataker, Robert Harris, Charles Herle, Joshua Hoyle, Edward Reynolds, and Thomas Temple) and four Scots (Robert Baillie, George Gillespie, Alexander Henderson, and Samuel Rutherford). The most important outside resources on which the Divines drew were the Irish Articles of 1615 prepared by Dublin professor James Usher, and a work of Usher's entitled *A Body of Divinity*, which was a compendium of Reformed theology in use at that time.

The Westminster Assembly became progressively estranged from the English Parliament as that body changed from being dominantly Presbyterian to predominantly Independent (Congregational). For example, Scripture proofs were annexed to the confession of faith at the insistence of Parliament. The Divines were reluctant, fearing misuse of the method of citing proof texts. A primarily Independent Parliament finally accepted the Westminster Confession in 1648, with modifications in church government and discipline. However, conformity to the confession was never implemented in England. Meanwhile, the general assembly of the Church of Scotland adopted the confession in 1647. Thus the Westminster Confession became the official creed of Scottish Presbyterianism while England soon reverted to Anglicanism. An erroneous impression that the Westminster Confession was primarily a Scots product was thereby conveyed to later generations.

By 1649 Cromwell's militarily victorious Independents cut off Charles I's head, and the Westminster Assembly dissolved. The Presbyterians who had been trying to maintain loyalty both to the authority of the Bible and to the king were undone as a political force. In later years they even conspired with the High Church party to restore the king's son, Charles II, to the throne, in hopes of some sort of ecclesiastical compromise. Instead, at the Restoration, the vengeful Bishops demanded complete conformity to episcopacy from every minister or face expulsion from their parishes. Later Protestant histories naturally looked upon those who were banished as heroes and read their attitudes and theology back into the Westminster Confession. The work of those who actually wrote the Westminster Confession was often neglected. A prime example is of this was Edward Reynolds, the most important individual in the writing of the confession, who later conformed and became an Anglican Bishop. Subsequent generations of nonconformists shunned his work. Later attitudes, conditioned by the bitterness of civil war and ecclesiastical strife, ceased to treat the Westminster Confession in its own historical context.[2]

Faith and Reason

Britain was distinctive not only politically, but philosophically. A British anti-Aristotelian Augustinianism was a deep-rooted tradition carried on in the Puritan party. One especially important influence on the Westminster Divines was the Augustinian concept of "right reason." For Augustine, only the righteous could rise to an understanding of truth.[3] Truth was considered valuable only if it led to godliness. Edward Reynolds declared: "For the Rules of Living and Doing well are the Statutes (as it were) and Dictates of right Reason."[4] Right reason was reason that acknowledged the authority of God and which functioned for moral, not speculative ends.

The Westminster Divines opposed Anglican and Roman Catholic scholastics regarding the purpose of theology. The Divines affirmed that theology was a practical discipline that aimed at the reform of life rather than a scientific discipline that fostered contemplation.[5]

Another antischolastic philosophical influence was that of Peter Ramus (1515–1572), a Protestant martyr in the St. Bartholomew's Day massacre in Paris. Ramus continued the Ciceronian rhetorical tradition as Augustine had applied it to theology. He attacked Aristotelian logic as artificial and contrived and the university curriculum based on Aristotle as confused and disorganized. (Beza had refused Ramus a teaching position in Geneva because of his anti-Aristotelianism.) Ramus developed a simplified logic based not on syllogisms, but on self-evident propositions. He worked in a Platonic way from universals to particulars, and from these axioms he laid ideas out in pairs in a neat outline organization.

Ramism was introduced in England as a counterforce to the Aristotelian domination at the Royalist-controlled universities.[6] The best known English expositor of Ramist logic was William Temple, whose son Thomas chaired the committee that drafted the Westminster Confession. Thomas Temple's preaching showed that he had mastered the Ramist logic, which was considered just the outlining preparatory to expository preaching. Temple contended that by Ramist outlining, the one natural sense of a biblical passage could be set forth. Ramist analysis was a help to Puritan divines in achieving their ideal of a plain style of preaching the Word of God.[7]

Philosophically, the Westminster Divines remained in the Augustinian tradition of faith leading to understanding. Samuel Rutherford stated the position: "The believer is the most reasonable man in the world, he who doth all by faith, doth all by the light of sound reason."[8] Faith not only took precedence over reason, but for the Divines, faith was the only way to know spiritual matters. Edward Reynolds declared that those who know God's judgments only by sense, "are said, in Scripture ... not to know any of this, or to lay it to heart:—and the reason is, because they knew it not by faith, nor in a spiritual manner in order unto God."[9] Rutherford contended that the more persons relied on Scripture and the less on reason, the greater would be their Christian growth. Rutherford claimed: "The more that the word of promise hath influence in believing, and the lesse of convincing reason and appearances, the greater Faith."[10]

Authority of Scripture and the Testimony of the Spirit

Chapter 1 of the Westminster Confession was entitled, "Of the Holy Scripture."[11] The first five of the ten sections of this chapter represented a development of the theme of the Holy Spirit's relationship to Scripture.

Section i: The Light of Nature

Section i spoke in Platonic-Augustinian fashion of the "light of nature" that was understood as a direct revelation of God in every person's heart. As with Augustine and Calvin, the Divines held that humans suppressed but could never wholly eradicate that sense of the divine within them. The "works of creation and providence" reinforced in persons that knowledge which had been suppressed and because of which persons were inexcusable for their sins. The Divines expounded no "natural theology" in the Thomistic fashion, asserting that people could know God by reason based on sense experience prior to God's revelation. When they spoke of "natural theology," the Divines meant the knowledge God had implanted in their inner nature. Samuel Rutherford spoke of man's

> reasonable soul, which to me is a rare and curious book, on which essentially is written by the immediate finger of God, that natural Theology, that we had in our first creation.[12]

For the Westminster Divines there were not two sources of revelation, nature and Scripture, but only one, God's Word. God had implanted a knowledge of himself in the human heart, and humans with that internal knowledge also recognized God as the Creator in nature. But humans sinfully suppressed that original knowledge of God's Word. So God revealed himself in a person, Jesus Christ, and that personal revelation was clearly recorded in the pages of Scripture. There was no two-source theory of revelation, as in scholastic theology. Rather, there was a recognition of the one Word of God repeatedly and persistently confronting sinful humankind.[13]

For the Westminster Divines, both Christ and Scripture bore the designation the Word of God. Edward Reynolds noted: "We may observe how Christ is frequently pleased to honour his gospel with his own titles and attributes. And therefore the apostle speaks of him and his word, as of one of the same thing." Reynolds exclaimed: "The which is the 'Word' in one verse, is 'Christ himself' in another."[14]

Puritans applied the title, the Word of God, not only to Christ and Scripture, but to preaching that set Christ forth as presented in Scripture. This threefold designation of the Word of God was actually a means of concentration on the saving act of God in Jesus Christ. Edward Reynolds declared:

> Preaching of the Word, is called preaching of Christ,—and ministers of the Word, ministers of Christ,—and learning of the Word, learning of Christ; because our faith, our works, and our worship . . . have all their foundation, growth, end and virtue, only in and from Christ crucified.[15]

The necessity of Scripture that the Westminster Divines maintained was not the theoretical necessity of a formal principle of theology, but rather the necessity of all persons to trust in Christ for their salvation. Scripture and preaching set forth the Savior, Jesus Christ.[16]

Section ii: The Canon

The question of how the canon was formed was apparently not discussed by the Westminster Assembly. The Divines deliberately omitted mention of any test or mark of canonicity. They simply asserted that all canonical Scripture was given by inspiration of God and thereby denied that the authority of Scripture was based on the authority of the church.[17]

The Westminster Confession was Reformed, as distinct from Lutheran, in giving a list of canonical books. It was also unique among Reformed confessions in omitting disputed designations of authorship. In this, the Westminster Divines and their confession took exactly the opposite stance of Turretin and the Helvetic Consensus Formula. Protestant scholastics made the defense of traditional authorship of the biblical books a necessary concomitant of the Bible's inspiration. The Westminster Confession took care, with Calvin, to leave such questions open to scholarly debate. Also, the confession differed from its closest source, the Irish Articles of 1615, for example, by not listing the Epistle to the Hebrews as one of Paul's letters.[18]

The Westminster Divines gave no definition or theory of inspiration in the confession. They were primarily concerned that inspiration from God not be sought apart from the text of Scripture as they believed was done by the scholastic Roman Catholics and the spiritualistic Sectarians.[19]

Section iii: Inspiration

The Westminster Confession excluded the Apocryphal books from the canon because the Divines did not consider them divinely inspired. Unlike the Anglican Thirty-nine Articles and the Irish Articles, the Westminster Confession did not grant the Apocrypha any special use in the church.[20] The Westminster Confession reflected the open attitude of Calvin, which affirmed the inspiration of Scripture's divine message but left theologians free to deal with critical questions through scholarship.[21]

Section iv: The Authority of Scripture

The authority of Scripture in section iv was not made dependent on the testimony of any person or church, but on God, the author of Scripture. There was no recourse, as in Aristotelian scholasticism, to rationally demonstrable external evidences of the Bible's authority. Edward Reynolds declared that faith is an assent "grounded upon the *authority or authenticalness of a Narrator,* upon whose report ... we relye *without* any evidence of the thing itself."[22]

The Westminster Divines strongly affirmed that God was the author of the saving and life-directing message of Scripture. The High Church Anglicans, especially Richard Hooker, acknowledged only the general doctrinal principles of Scriptures as authoritative. Hooker felt that theologians should be left free to accept or reject the details. Samuel Rutherford opposed Hooker's views. Rutherford's concern was that his High Church opponents claimed the right to introduce ceremonies, policies, and forms of government into the church that were not found in Scripture, on the thesis that Scripture did not regulate these areas. Rutherford found the High Church procedures and practices objectionable and contended that they were illegitimate unless they were commended in Scripture. In the controversy, Rutherford appealed to God as the author of every detail of Scripture. He declared:

> But as the Authority of God hath imprinted a necessity on them, so are they obligatory to us: I am obliged to receive this as scripture, that *Paul left his cloak at Troas;* no lesse then this, *Christ came into the world to save sinners,* in regard of Canonicall authority stamped upon both.[23]

Rutherford opposed any dissection of Scripture that made some parts the Word of God and other parts not God's Word. All of Scripture was from God.

At the same time, the Westminster Divines, including Rutherford, were clear that the purpose of Scripture was to bring people into relationship to God, not to communicate interesting information in all branches of learning. Scripture was not to be used, for example, as a source of information in the sciences to refute what the scholars were discovering. The Westminster Divines aligned themselves with the Parliament and supported the idea of a new university in London to teach natural science because the ancient Royalist-dominated universities were not doing so.[24] Samuel Rutherford was very explicit that Scripture's purpose was to mediate salvation, not communicate information on science. He listed areas in which Scripture is *not* our rule, for example, "not in things of Art and Science, as to speak Latine, to demonstrate conclusions of Astronomie." But Scripture was our rule, Rutherford affirmed "1. in fundamentalls of salvation. 2. In all morals of both first and second table."[25]

The Westminster Divines received Scripture as the Word of God because in so doing they were receiving the Word of God, Jesus Christ. Edward Reynolds stated that "Christ and his gospel have the same attributes of glory frequently given unto them."[26]

The authority of Holy Scripture was not merely to be "believed," but "obeyed," according to the Westminster Divines. Therefore people were exhorted to receive the Word and to walk, or live, according to it. Puritans were not opposed to experimental science because they knew that Christians grew by experiencing God's will as they sought to put God's Word into practice.[27]

Section v: Internal Witness of the Holy Spirit

Section v climaxed the development of the first half of the Westminster Confession's chapter on Scripture with the statement that while many arguments for the truth and authority of Holy Scripture could be adduced, only the witness of the Holy Spirit in a person's heart could persuade that person that Scripture is the Word of God. The wording of this section very closely paralleled a work of George Gillespie, one of the Scots commissioners. However, while Gillespie twice said evidences "prove" Scripture to be God's Word, the confession was more restrained. It said instead that external evidences "are arguments" by which Scripture does "abundantly evidence" itself to be God's Word. This was in the same vein as Calvin's "secondary aids to our feebleness." Gillespie's work was an argument for the union of Word and Spirit against the Antinomians who claimed the Lord speaking to them apart from Scripture. Even in that context Gillespie asserted: "I heartily yeeld that the Spirit of the Lord is a Spirit of Revelation, and it is by the Spirit of God, that we know the things which are freely given us of God."[28]

The Westminster Divines stood steadfastly with Calvin in stating that "our full persuasion and assurance" of the authority of Scripture came from the internal testimony of the Holy Spirit.[29]

Despite the pressure from sectarian appeals to private interpretations of the Spirit, and scholastic citations of external evidences, the Westminster Divines would not give up their firm conviction that it was the Spirit who brought them to the authority of the Word. Samuel Rutherford in a tract against the Roman Catholics asked: "How do we know that Scripture is the Word of God?" If ever there was a place where one might expect a Divine to use the Roman Catholic's own style of rational arguments as later scholastic Protestants did, it was here. Rutherford instead appealed to the Spirit of Christ speaking through Scripture to the human subject:

> Sheep are docile creatures, Ioh. 10.27. *My sheep heare my voyce, I know them and they follow me* . . . so the instinct of Grace knoweth the voyce of the Beloved amongst many voyces, *Cant.* 2.8. and this discerning power is *in the Subject.*[30]

For Rutherford, as for Calvin, Scripture was self-authenticating. Rutherford averred that the believer experienced a personal relationship to Christ and Scripture that needed no external confirmation. He said:

> To the new Creature, there is in *Christ's* Word some character, some sound of Heaven, that is in no voyce in the world, but in his only, in *Christ* represented to a beleevers eye of Faith; there is a shape and a stampe of Divine Majesty, no man knoweth it, but the beleever.[31]

Later, scholastic Protestants no longer felt secure in appealing to a personal relationship to Christ in Scripture as the foundation of the Bible's authority and tried instead to find objective certainty in arguments based on external evidences.[32]

Interpretation of Scripture by the Spirit and Scholarship

The last five sections of the confession dealt especially with how Scripture could be interpreted by a regenerate mind in light of its purpose of bringing us to salvation in Christ.

Section vi: Sufficiency of Scripture

In section vi the saving content of Scripture was clearly delineated: "The whole counsel of God concerning all things necessary for His own glory, man's salvation, faith and life." Scripture was not an encyclopedia of answers to every sort of question for the Divines. They asserted that some things were to be ordered by our natural reason and Christian prudence. Those things even included some circumstances of worship and church government. In these matters the English Divines were somewhat more flexible than their Scottish counterparts.[33] Yet even the conservative Scot, Samuel Rutherford, was explicit that not all human activities, but only the moral dimensions of human acts, were regulated by Scripture.[34]

In emphasizing salvation and guidance in the life of faith as the purpose for which Scripture was given, the Westminster Confession followed the Reformation confessions and the immediately antecedent British Symbols, the Irish Articles, and the Anglican Thirty-nine Articles. These confessions and the Westminster Divines' other primary reference point, Usher's *A Body of Divinitie,* define "the whole counsel of God" in relationship to salvation and the Christian life, and not more broadly, as did scholastic thought. Usher wrote:

> Again, seeing the Minister is bound to disclose the whole counsell of God to his people, (*Acts* 20:27) he being thereunto fully furnished out of the Scriptures they may also be abundantly taught to salvation.[35]

It was in accomplishing salvation and instructing believers in the Christian life that the Westminster Divines affirmed Scripture to be sufficient.

The related phrase, "or by good and necessary consequence may be deduced from Scripture" has been subject to much misunderstanding. The Westminster Divines insisted that valid Christian truth could be deduced from Scripture. This was a median position between those of opponents on either side. The High Church Arminians on the one side insisted that reason alone, without reference to Scripture, gave normative guidance in the religious realm. Against this position, the Divines insisted that religious deductions were valid only if made with reference to the norm of Scripture. On the other side, the Sectarian Antinomians and Anabaptists claimed direct personal revelations from the Holy Spirit. Again, the Westminster Divines refused a separate source of guidance apart from the written Word of God. The prime concern of the authors of the Westminster Confession was to hold Scripture, regenerate reason, and the Spirit together. Their contention was that none of these was intended by God to operate independently of the others. Together, they were used by God to communicate saving truth to humankind.

The Westminster Divines rejected a biblicism that demanded a proof text from Scripture to prove each theological point. They equally opposed rational speculation or sectarian spiritualism that claimed truth apart from the written Word. The way in which the Westminster Confession expressed the balanced view of the Divines was to state that the "whole counsel of God" was either "expressly set down in Scripture," or "by good and necessary consequence may be deduced from Scripture."[36]

It is essential to note in this section that the Westminster Divines refused to separate the Word and the Spirit in the interpretation of Scripture. Despite sectarian appeals to the Spirit, the Divines did not overreact as did the later Protestant scholastics who banished all illumination of the Spirit from the interpretation of Scripture. The Westminster Divines affirmed: "Nevertheless, we acknowledge the inward illumination of the Spirit of God to be necessary for the saving understanding of such things as are revealed in the Word."

The Socinians (Unitarians) contended that the Bible could be *understood* by unregenerate persons. For the Westminster Divines, however, any knowledge that was not saving did not merit the name "knowledge" at all. Edward Reynolds announced:

> Absurd is the doctrine of the Socinians, and some others, *That unregenerate men by a meer natural perception, without any divine superinfused light* (they are the words of Episcopius, and they are wicked words) *may understand the whole Law,* even all things requisite unto faith and godliness. Foolishly confounding, and impiously deriding the spiritual and divine sense of holy Scriptures, with the Grammatical construction.[37]

Reynolds compared the knowledge a nonbeliever had of Scripture with the ability of a person to draw up a mathematical formulation without understanding its meaning.

Section vi of the Confession of Faith, as understood through the writings of its authors, was a very careful delineation of the intimate interrelation of Scripture, the Spirit, and regenerate reason. The Spirit working through the Scripture brought people to saving faith in Jesus Christ. Saved persons glorified God in faith and life by the use of their renewed reason. They followed the explicit commands and the general principles of Scripture. Scripture was a book with implications for all of life. But for the Westminster Divines, the central purpose of Scripture was to bring the message of new life in Jesus Christ. The "whole counsel of God" discernible in Scripture was not a general compend of information about life, but a guide to the new life of faith in Jesus Christ. That guidance was only available to those illumined by the Holy Spirit.

Section vii: Clarity of Scripture

The Westminster Divines acknowledged that there were two levels in the Bible. One level was the central saving message available by God's grace to everyone who desired to know it. The other level was less plain because to penetrate it required scholarly understanding of the cultural context in which the prime message was given. The proximate sources of the Westminster statement, Usher's *A Body of Divinitie* and the Irish Articles, both made the same distinction.[38]

Edward Reynolds, in a passage full of appealing imagery, made the same distinction between helpful material to be mined from Scripture by scholars, and essentials of salvation that were plainly available to the simplest people. He wrote:

> It is true, there are [*dusnoēta*], hard things, to exercise the study and diligence, the faith and prayers of the profoundest scholars; waters wherein an elephant may swim.—But yet as nature hath made things of greatest necessity to be most obvious and common, as air, water, bread, and the like; whereas things of greater rarity, as gems and jewels, are matters of honour and ornaments, not of daily use;—so the wisdom of God hath so tempered the Scriptures, as that from thence the wisest Solomon may fetch jewels for ornament, and the poorest Lazarus, bread for life: but these things which are of common necessity as matters of faith, love, worship, obedience, which are universally requisite unto the common salvation, (as the apostle expresseth it,) are so perspicuously set down in the Holy Scriptures, that every one who hath the Spirit of Christ, hath therewithal a judgement to discern so much of Gods will, as shall suffice to make him believe in Christ for righteousness, and, by worship and obedience, to serve him unto salvation. The way of holiness is so plain, that simple men are made wise enough to find it out; and wayfaring men, though fools, do not err therein.[39]

Many of the Westminster Divines were extraordinarily learned for their time in the languages and cultural backgrounds of the biblical milieu, and were well aware of the impact of cultural context on the biblical writers. They could evaluate the quality of the human literary style of the biblical writers without in any sense derogating from the divine character of their message. Scripture was not all on one flat plain for the Divines. The Bible was like a relief map with peaks and valleys. All parts belonged rightfully to Scripture, but they had places nearer to or farther from the central Christian content of the Bible. Thomas Gataker expressed this difference:

> All Scripture, saith the Apostle, *is divinely inspired,* and *is profitable to instruct.* And *Every word of God,* saith Agur, *is pure:* even as *pure* as gold or *silver* that hath past *seven times* through the fire *in the furnace.* But yet, as some gold and silver is finer than other; and some golden vessels are more usefull than others are: so betweene Scripture and Scripture (though all pure, pretious, and profitable) there is great difference: some is of greater excellency, and of more ordinarie use.[40]

Gataker's attitude is characteristic of the Westminster Divines in affirming the divine content of all the biblical writing while analyzing the human literary form.[41]

The Westminster Divines were in harmony with the Reformation notion that God had condescended to speak through human language and cultural forms. The Bible's message was genuinely divine and its form fully human. To understand that was essential to understanding the clarity of Scripture.

All Scripture was not alike to the Westminster Divines. There was a central message that could be known by anyone. It included "those things necessary to be known, believed, and observed for salvation." They were clear "in some place of Scripture or other." Anyone could understand this basic saving message of Scripture, "not only the learned, but the unlearned." The "due use of ordinary means" recommended generally meant a willingness to go to church and hear the Bible expounded by a preacher—often for four hours at a stretch! That made preaching a grave responsibility for Puritan divines. They dug deeply into the Bible, not to gain esoteric knowledge, but to know Jesus Christ more fully and to present him to people more persuasively.[42]

Section viii: The Authenticity of the Text and Translations

What about the parts of the Bible that were not plain? For the Divines, those parts related not to the central message of Christ, but to the surrounding context. These were the matters that caused "controversies in religion." Matters of controversy were to be dealt with by scholarship. The Divines then urged recourse to the biblical text in the original Hebrew and Greek. Section viii exemplified the constant dual concern of the Divines: to meet the demands of careful scholarship and to meet the spiritual needs of ordinary people. After urging scholarly study in the original Hebrew and Greek, they also urged that the Bible "be translated into the vulgar language of every nation." Thus all persons, without having to depend on the scholars could worship God in an acceptable manner, and, "through patience and comfort of the Scriptures, have hope." This was a reiteration of the Westminster Divines attitude that theology was a practical and not a theoretical activity. For the Divines, right interpretation of the Bible was rooted in faith, and was encouraged to develop in understanding through scholarly study.

The Divines were biblical scholars accustomed to referring to the Old and New Testaments in the Hebrew and Greek texts. Their sermons illustrate careful linguistic study, comparison of translations, and utilization of insights from cognate languages and ancient thought forms. They were well aware that people in ancient cultures not only used different languages but employed different forms of thought than seventeenth-century Britishers.[43] Robert Baillie, one of the Scots Divines, was reputed to have mastered thirteen languages including Hebrew, Chaldee, Syriac, Arabic, and Ethiopic.[44] In a sermon preached to the House of Lords, Baillie illustrated both his commitment to Scripture and the carefulness of his scholarship. He publicly adhered to what he believed was the correct translation of the original text even when it raised theological problems for him. Baillie said:

> But the great difficulty is in the third, How the Lord causes us to erre from his way: This would seem to make God the cause and author of sin, which is a horrid blasphemy against many Scriptures, and all reason. To exchew this huge, great and intolerable inconvenience, sundry famous interpreters do translate the originall otherwayes then we read it; Not, *Why hast thou made or caused us to erre?* but, *Why hast thou suffered or permitted us* to erre? So *Junius* an excellent translator: And many hundred yeers before him, the *Chaldee* Paraphrast did render it, *Why hast thou cast us away to erre from thy wayes?* This interpretation is approved by very Learned and Orthodox Divines, who bring this reason for it, That the *Hebrew* word here, is not simply in the active form, not in *Kal*, but, as they speak, in *Hiphil*, whose signification oftentimes is not to make or cause, but to permit. Indeed, this translation does eschew fully the difficulty; yet we dare not venture upon it; for as it seems it were to make too bold with the Scripture.[45]

Such seriousness on the part of the Divines about what the biblical text actually said sets their work in sharp contrast with that of later Protestant scholastic theologians who strove to harmonize every text.[46]

The authors of the Westminster Confession apparently meant by the word *authentical* that the text of Scripture in the original language was to be considered the final source of reference for understanding. This was a defense of responsible scholarship in opposition to the claims of the Roman Catholic Council of Trent that only the Latin Vulgate was an authentic text from which to derive Christian teaching. The Divines also opposed the High Church Anglican exaltation of the Septuagint above the Hebrew text of the Old Testament. Both Roman Catholics and Sectaries used the fact of variant readings in the extant Hebrew and Greek manuscripts to deprecate the use of texts in the original language. The Divines dealt with all of these issues on scholarly grounds. They did not react defensively as the Reformed scholastics in Switzerland did a few years later and claim a pure text down to the vowel points. Even one of the Westminster Divines chief proximate sources, Archbishop Usher, contended that the original Hebrew text had vowel points; the Divines themselves maintained a cautious and critical judgment, refraining from any pronouncement about the points.[47]

For the Westminster Divines the saving Word of God was adequately communicated through copies and translations. Their concern was not apologetics, but preaching. The Divines wanted Scripture available in the common language of all persons so that everyone could study the word and compare it with the exposition of preachers trained to use the original languages. The Divines condemned the High Church practice of holding services of prayer at which there was no exposition of Scripture. Edward Reynolds expressed positively the passionate desire of the Westminster Confession's authors:

> O! therefore that every parish had an endowment fit for a learned, laborious, and worthy pastor,—and pastors worthy of such endowments,—that provision were made, that every family might have a Bible in it, and (if by law it might possibly be procured) the exercises of religion therewithal: this would be the surest magazine to secure the happiness of a kingdom.[48]

The Divines' deepest concern was that all persons should come to know Christ in Scripture. The saving power of the Word of God, for them, lay not in the original Hebrew and Greek letters of the Bible, but in the available English sense of the words. It was in that message, translated into their own contemporary idiom that all persons could find challenge and hope.[49]

Section ix: The Interpretation of Scripture

In section ix, the Westminster Divines contended that Scripture was a unity, that particular texts had a single, not multiple meaning, and that the analogy of faith was the basic interpretative principle. Joshua Hoyle, an Irishman, disallowed allegorizing and challenged his Roman Catholic opponent:

> Wherein consists the Scripture or written word of God? in Words and letters onely, or sense and meaning too? body onely, or soul and life withall? ... And what do we else than joyne *words* with *meaning*.[50]

Edward Reynolds preferred the grammatical sense of Scripture, but as with Augustine, he also allowed his own Christian experience of what was doctrinally and morally proper to guide him. He wrote:

> The most immediate and grammatical sense whereof is ever soundest, where there doth not some apparent and unavoidable error in doctrine, or mischief in manners, follow thereupon.[51]

That Scripture should be compared with Scripture and interpreted according to the analogy of faith was a basic Reformation principle. The wording of section ix of the Westminster Confession bears strong similarities to Chapter II of the Second Helvetic Confession and Chapter

XVII of the Scots Confession of 1560. Parts of the Thirty-nine Articles, the Irish Articles, and Usher's *A Body of Divinitie* also parallel this section of the confession.[52]

The "analogy of faith" meant that the meaning of any particular passage of Scripture had to be sought in the light of the general meaning of Scripture as a whole. The Westminster Divines were quite clear that the Bible was a collection of writings unified by a common theme, *kerygma,* or story. Thomas Gataker opposed the interpretation given a passage by his Antinomian opponents stating: "First, that this can not be the meaning of the place, because it evidently crosseth the main tenor of the *story,* and the *truth of God's Word.* "[53] Edward Reynolds dealt with the principle of the analogy of faith in a sermon preached to his colleagues in the Westminster Assembly. After alluding to the danger of allegorizing, Reynolds proceeded to outline a two-point program for the interpretation of Scripture. He urged humility and adherence to the analogy of faith. He declared:

> Whensoever, therefore, we judge it needful to interpose any opinion or sense of our own, let us, first, do it with humility and submission, with reservation of honour and reverence unto others from whom we differ; not magisterially or tribunitially, with a *eurēka* as if we spake rather oracles than opinions. Secondly, let us in this case take heed of departing, 'vel latum unguem,' from the analogy of faith, and that knowledge which is according to godliness, into diverticles of fancy, or critical curiosity; but let us resolve ever to judge those expositions best and soundest, which are most orthodox, practical, heavenly, and most tending unto the furtherance of duty and godliness.[54]

For Reynolds, Gataker, and the other Westminster Divines, the analogy of faith was a continual pointer to the story, the central saving message of Scripture by which all of the diverse parts were to be interpreted.

The true sense of Scripture was "not manifold, but one," according to the Westminister Confession of Faith. That unity of the Bible was provided by the story of God's salvation in Jesus Christ, which was the central theme of both Old and New Testaments. For example, Thomas Temple utilized the typological interpretation characteristic of the early church fathers and declared:

> This second psalme is an exact description of the Kingdome of Christ, as it was prophesied of by David, who was himself a type and figure of Christ in his Kingdome, and the Father of him according to the flesh: which, as it appeares out of the frame of the whole psalme, so we finde this Psalme clearly expounded of Christ and his Kingdome by the Apostles in the new Testament.[55]

Samuel Rutherford, in the same vein spoke of: "Ceremonies of *Moses* his law which did shadow out *Christ* to us."[56]

For these seventeenth-century Reformed theologians the doctrine of the covenant was a further rubric that bound the two Testaments together in unity. The details of their covenant theology are beyond the scope of this study. We are concerned only with how it functioned as a principle of biblical interpretation for them. The covenant gave an overall unity, centered in Christ, to their view of Scripture. That sense of the unified message of the whole Bible freed the authors of the Westminster Confession from dependence on literal word-for-word evidence for every aspect of their theology. They were concerned with the overarching themes of God's relationship to his people. Cornelius Burges used the covenant theme polemically against the Anabaptists, arguing:

> If in the judgment of all the Churches of Christ, it be sufficient (as indeed it is) to confute all the Anabaptists in the world, that infants are within the covenant, & therefore ought not to be debarred of the seale of it, . . . therefore in all these respects they may be baptized, notwithstanding that no Text of scripture enioyne it in so many words.[57]

However, for most Westminster Divines most of the time, the theme of covenant was simply a synonym for the message of God's salvation in Jesus Christ, revealed in Scripture and applied personally to them. Robert Harris proclaimed sermonically to his hearers that if they were in covenant, all contained in the covenant was theirs, which was the same as saying all in the Bible, all in Christ was theirs; indeed God was theirs.[58] Joshua Hoyle linked being in covenant with God to obedient listening to God's Word in Scripture. Hoyle wrote:

> He that would raise his heart to such a degree of walking in covenant with God shall do well to meditate *Davids* example, Psal. 119.105 to the 112. He sets up Gods Word for his lamp at home, and lanthorn abroad; he is resolved to walk by no light but Gods.[59]

Edward Reynolds identified the word of the gospel with Christ and referred to the gospel as a covenant of mercy. For Reynolds, the covenant theme was a summary of the gospel message. He concluded:

> I said before, that I approve not the mincing and crumbling of holy Scriptures. Yet in these parts of them, which are written for models and summaries of Christian doctrine, I suppose there may be weight in every word, as, in a rich jewel, there is worth in every sparkle. Here then, first, we may take notice of Christ's propriety to his people; *thy people;* all the elect and believers do belong unto Christ. They are his people.[60]

For the Westminster Divines, the Bible was a book that told one unified story—the saving grace of God in Jesus Christ. They referred to that theme sometimes as the gospel and sometimes as the covenant. The proper interpretation of Scripture did not take verses individually and plug them in as proof texts of a systematic theology. The right interpretation of Scripture allowed the analogy of faith to operate. It interpreted the individual verses as parts of the overall message. This was the interpretative model that informed the statement: "The infallible rule of interpretation of Scripture is the Scripture itself." The Scripture could be "searched and known" by understanding all the verses as parts of a whole unified biblical story.[61]

Section x: Holy Spirit Speaking in Scripture

In the final section of their chapter on Scripture, the Westminster Divines ended where they began with an affirmation of the union of the Spirit and the Word. They concluded: "The Supreme judge, by which all controversies of religion are to be determined . . . can be no other but the Holy Spirit speaking in the Scripture." Thomas Gataker used the phrase "the Spirit of God in the Word" in speaking of how people might find happiness and contentment.[62] Robert Harris spoke of the Spirit and the Word as one rule: "If you would have your heart made one, you must go all by one rule, inward, the Spirit; outward, the Word."[63]

For Edward Reynolds, the Spirit was the Spirit of Christ who worked in the Word to persuade persons:

> Which should teach us, what to look for in the *Ministry of the Word*, namely that which will convince us, that which puts an edge upon the Word, and opens the heart and makes it burn, the Spirit *of Christ; for by that only we can be brought unto the righteousness of Christ.*[64]

For the Westminster Divines, the final judge in controversies of religion was not just the bare word of Scripture interpreted by human logic, nor a Spirit speaking apart from the Word, but the Spirit of Christ leading persons in Scripture to its central saving witness to Him.

There is a striking parallel between this final section of the Westminster Confession on Scripture and a sentence in the Scots Confession of 1560 (Chapter XVIII). The Scots Confession reads: "When controversy arises about the right understanding of any passage or sentence of Scripture, or for the reformation of any abuse within the Kirk of God, we ought not so much to ask what men have said or done before us, as what the Holy Ghost uniformly speaks within the body of the Scriptures and what Jesus Christ himself did and commanded."[65]

The authors of the Westminster Confession separated the statement about the "infallible rule of interpretation of Scripture" in section ix from the statement on the "Supreme judge by which all controversies of religion are to be determined" in section x. Their intention perhaps was more clearly to answer opponents who separated these same questions. The Roman Catholics acknowledged Scripture to be a rule, but contended that the church was the judge who applied the rule. To the Protestants' assertion that Scripture was both the rule and judge, the Roman Catholics replied that the judge needed to be a present living person.[66]

Protestant scholastics from Turretin, through the Helvetic Consensus formula, and down to the nineteenth-century Princeton theologians overreacted to the Roman Catholic position. They insisted that the letter of Scripture alone was rule and judge. They relied on their own logic and rejected any illumination of the Holy Spirit in interpreting Scripture.[67]

The Westminster Divines retained the Reformation balance, however, holding to a dynamic, present interaction of both Word and Spirit. They insisted that the Holy Spirit did not simply inspire the Scripture and then, like a deist God, go away and leave humans to interpret the Bible on their own. The Divines relied on the Spirit of God to guide them in understanding God's Word. Edward Reynolds, for example, illustrated this attitude in expounding a passage when he said:

> This union of the faithful to Christ, being one *of those deep things of God,* which are not discernible without the Spirit, is yet set forth unto us in the Scriptures under sundry vulgar and obvious similitudes, which I will but touch upon.[68]

The authors of the Westminster Confession maintained a confidence that the Spirit of God not only had inspired the Bible, but that the Spirit led people into ever new and better understandings of it. Alexander Henderson, for example, argued with King Charles I that an evidence of the Spirit's leading was the better exegesis of Scripture done by the Protestant Reformers than by their medieval predecessors.[69]

The balance of Word and Spirit displayed by the Westminster Divines is the more remarkable because of pressures exerted on them from opponents on both sides. On the one side stood the Roman Catholics and the High Church Anglicans, who attributed authority to "decrees of councils" and "opinions of ancient writers" independent of or as interpreters of the Scripture. These "doctrines of men" generally attributed an authority to human reason independent of Scripture. On the other side stood the Sectarians. The Sectarians also preached what, to the authors of the Confession of Faith, were "doctrines of men" but which the Sectarians themselves claimed to be the revelations of the Spirit. According to those who claimed to receive them, the revelations of "private spirits" transcended the Scripture's authority. The Westminster Divines tried to return a balanced answer to their opponents on both sides. They did not deny the use of human reason, nor did they wholly discount the opinions of theologians, either individually or in council. But they claimed that all opinions of men were valid only insofar as they agreed with the Scripture. Furthermore, the Scripture was only rightly understood by those whose minds were enlightened by the Holy Spirit. But neither the reason apart from Scripture, nor the Spirit apart from Scripture, was authoritative in religious matters. Only the Spirit speaking in the Scripture was the "supreme judge" in controverted points.[70]

The Westminster Divines were deeply committed to the unity of the church. They were often caustic with their opponents on either side, whom they felt had broken the balance of Word and Spirit on which the church was founded. Robert Harris sarcastically defined the position of the Roman Catholics as those who "leaving the old rule (the written Word) put themselves wholly into the hands of a weak man, who (confessedly) is apt to reele, unlesse his Chaire hold him up."[71] Edward Reynolds stated that one of the troubles with the spiritualistic Sects was their "usurped authority" over the Word by which

> all controversies of religion are turned, not into means to discover doctrine, that they may be rested in, which doth appear to have in it most intrinsecal majesty, spiritualness, and evidence; but into factions and emulations of men, that that sect may be rested in, who can, with most impudence and ostentation, arrogate a usurped authority to themselves.[72]

The Westminster Divines recognized that God's Spirit continually worked through his Word. That meant that all councils, including the Westminster Assembly, stood in need of correction. Despite their rejection of "new Light" not rooted in Scripture, the Divines acknowledged the need for a continuing Reformation guided by the Spirit and based on the Bible. George Gillespie eloquently affirmed their stance, saying:

> It is the duty, not only of particular Christians, but of reforming, yea reformed, yea the best reformed Churches, whensoever any error in their doctrine, or any evill in their Government or forme of worship, shall be demonstrated to them from the word of God, . . . to take in and not to shut out further light: to imbrace the will of Christ held foorth unto them, and to amend what is amisse, being discovered unto them.[73]

For the authors of the Confession of Faith, the final judge in all controversies of religion was the living Word of God—the Spirit of Christ speaking in Scripture.

b. A Transition Toward Protestant Scholasticism: John Owen

John Owen (1616–1683), a younger contemporary of the Westminster Divines, gave leadership to the developing Independent or Congregational movement. After the completion of the Westminster Confession in 1646, the membership of Parliament shifted from dominantly Presbyterian to largely Independent. Oliver Cromwell, an Independent, dissolved the Parliament in 1653 and declared a Commonwealth.

During Cromwell's reign as Lord Protector, Owen served as dean of Christ's Church, Oxford, and was vice-chancellor of the University.[74] During the Civil War, Owen had accompanied Cromwell to Ireland and Scotland as a chaplain and retained his close relationship with the Lord Protector, becoming Cromwell's chief adviser in churchly matters.[75]

During the period from 1652 to 1657, when Cromwell was chancellor and Owen vice-chancellor of Oxford, even Owen's opponents acknowledged that he ruled the university fairly and efficiently.[76] Owen lectured in divinity, preached, and governed the university. He also served on a commission for licensing translations of the Bible and for approving public preachers (the "Triers") and served as chairman of a committee of referees appointed to devise a plan for the Christian reconciliation of differences in the church of Scotland.[77] Owen later was unseated as an elected Member of Parliament from Oxford University because he was a clergyman. But he continued to take major responsibility for framing the "Fifteen Fundamentals of Christianity." Cromwell and Parliament promised religious toleration to those who subscribed to this document.[78] In addition to all of this, Owen also served on a commission appointed by Cromwell to study the petition of Menasseh ben Israel for the readmission and toleration of Jews in England.[79]

Owen's relationship with Cromwell cooled, however, when Owen vigorously opposed Parliament's efforts to make Cromwell king. In fact, Owen drafted a petition on behalf of the military against the monarchy.[80] A month after Cromwell's death in September 1658, Owen lost his post of vice-chancellor, and his deepening involvement in the political interests of Independency led to the loss of his deanery in March 1660.

In 1658 Owen was active in the Savoy Synod, which produced the Savoy Declaration, the first and most basic English Congregational confession of faith and statement on church polity. Owen wrote the preface to this work, which essentially reproduced the Westminster Confession except in church polity. Owen always represented his work as being in harmony with that of the Westminster Divines whose younger contemporary he was. From 1660 until his death in 1683, Owen produced over half his writings, never ceasing to confront Arminians, Socinians, Roman Catholics, Quakers, and others whom he deemed unorthodox. His major piece of biblical interpretation was a massive four-volume work on the Epistle to the Hebrews.

John Owen's views on the authority and interpretation of Scripture mark him as a transitional figure between the Reformation stance of the

Westminster Divines and the Protestant scholasticism of his continental contemporaries. Owen's thought on Scripture is particularly clear in three of his treatises.[81] The most significant works are: "Of the Divine Original of the Scriptures"; "A Vindication of the Purity and Integrity of the Hebrew and Greek Texts of the Old and New Testament"; and a Latin work directed against the Quakers "*Pro Sacris Scripturis Exercitationes Adversus Fanaticos*" (1659).[82] In addition, Owen's "The Reason of Faith," and "Causes, Ways, and Means of Understanding the Mind of God," parts 1 and 2, Book VI, of his large *Discourse on the Holy Spirit* (1677–1678) also contribute to an understanding of his concerns and emphases regarding the Bible.

Reformation Emphases on Inspiration and the Spirit

When Owen's thought is compared to the several scholastic tendencies regarding Scripture (see page 186, number 6, a-e) his approach can be seen to be like that of the Westminster Divines in some regards, while it moved his English Reformed constituency toward scholasticism in others.[83]

First, seventeenth-century scholastic theologians made the inspiration of the Bible dependent in every detail on its inerrancy (6.e). For Calvin and the Reformers the authority of Holy Scripture had rested on the fact that it reported the real acts of God in revelation. The authority of Holy Scripture did not rest on the form of its recording, but on its content, that is, on the reality of the revelation committed to writing. For the continental Reformed orthodox, Scripture was affirmed to be inspired because of its alleged errorless form.[84]

John Owen was not a scholastic in this regard. For him, Scripture was true "and every part of it was given by divine inspiration."[85] Biblical writers "witness that *what* they wrote was received by *inspiration from God.*"[86] But the authority of Scripture stemmed not from the *form* in which it was given, but rather from its function—that *God* spoke through it. Owen wrote: "By its spiritual light, which it derives from its author alone, it infallibly shows itself to be the Word of God."[87] For Owen it was the divine origin of Scripture which was the "sole foundation of its authority."[88] When he defended the "Perfection of Holy Scripture" against the Quakers he saw this "perfection" as "their completeness as regards their proper purpose" which is "to instruct us in knowledge of God and our duty to this end, that we may pursue eternal life to the glory of God."[89] By focusing on this purpose of Scripture—to lead to salvation—Owen stood with Calvin, Westminster, and the sixteenth-century Reformed confessions.

Second, Protestant scholasticism tended to subordinate the inner witness of the Holy Spirit to arguments for the authority and authenticity of Scripture based on external and internal evidences (6.b.).[90] Calvin's emphasis on Scripture's self-authenticating and self-evidencing power was maintained in the sixteenth-century confessions and Westminster. Continental dogmatics in the seventeenth century, however, tended to stress the validity of external rational arguments to give credence to biblical authority.[91]

Owen opposed turning the work of "faith" into a work of "reason." He recognized that "external" arguments which claimed to prove that Scripture was from God were "all human and fallible."[92] And he discounted the notion that assent to the Scriptures was a work of the natural faculties of the mind. He stated:

> On this supposition, the whole *work of believing* would be a work of *reason.* 'Be it so,' say some: 'nor is it meet it should be otherwise conceived.' But if so, then the object of it must be things so evident in themselves and their own nature as that the mind is, as it were, compelled by that evidence unto an assent, and cannot do otherwise. If there be such a light and evidence in things themselves, with respect unto our reason, in the right use and exercise of it, then is the mind thereby necessitated unto its assent: which both overthrows the nature of faith, substituting an assent upon natural evidence in the room thereof, and is absolutely exclusive of the necessity or use of any work of the Holy Ghost in our believing, which sober Christians will scarcely comply withal.[93]

To avoid losing sight of the vital importance of the Spirit, Owen stressed the role of the Spirit in authenticating the Word of God.[94]

Owen, therefore, upheld Reformation emphases with regard to inspiration of Scripture and the internal witness of the Holy Spirit. He moved toward scholasticism, however, with three other emphases. In these areas he appears to have assisted in the process of rigidifying the doctrine of Scripture on the English scene.

A Scholastic Stress on Inspired Vowel Points

A third mark of Protestant Scholasticism was the tendency to subject scriptural material to inappropriate Aristotelian or Cartesian modes of presentation (6.a.).[94] This tendency was exhibited in Owen's treatise on "The Divine Original of the Scripture." In it he wished to show "that the whole authority of the Scripture in itself depends solely on its divine original."[96] To do this he adduced arguments to persuade people of Scripture's divine origin and thus divine authority.[97] For Owen, God's works had "that expression of God upon them" and "by being *what* they are, they declare *whose* they are."[98] Owen stressed the innate knowledge of God that should lead to the acceptance of Scripture as God's Word when one saw that Scripture confirmed what humans already knew within themselves—that all things had their origins from God.

Here Owen clearly demonstrated the influence of his training in Aristotelian logic.[99] He also exhibited a Cartesian emphasis on human ability to know eternal truth through the "innate principles of reason."[100] His arguments proceeded from human reason and natural knowledge to the eventual perception of the Scriptures as the Word of God. Methodologically he was willing to reverse the Augustinian order of "faith seeking understanding." In this he exemplified a Protestant scholasticism.

Fourthly, Protestant scholastics rigidified the Reformed doctrine of Scripture through the tendency to treat the human authors of Scripture as mere scribes recording divine words (6.d.).[101] In writing about the prophets, Owen clearly exhibited this tendency. He wrote:

> God was so with them, and by the Holy Ghost to spake in them—as to their receiving of the Word from him, and their delivering of it unto others by speaking or writing—as that they were not themselves enabled, by any habitual light, knowledge or conviction of truth, to declare his mind and will, but only acted as they were immediately moved by him. Their tongue in what they said, or their hand in what they wrote, was *'et sofer,* no more at their own disposal than the pen is in the hand of an expert writer.[102]

Thus, in Owen's view, the biblical writers were passive instruments for recording God's Word.

The fifth scholastic trend was the tendency to press the notion of verbal inspiration to an unnecessary extreme by insisting that the Hebrew vowel points were inspired (6.c.).[103] Here too Owen joined hands with later continental scholastic theologians. For him *God's* words were recorded in the Bible and even the smallest grammatical details of Scripture were products of God's direct inspiration. He referred to the "infallible and divinely inspired" original copies of Scripture in which "every iota and tittle of it [was] the word of the great God."[104] The biblical writers themselves produced "no change or alteration to the least iota or syllable."[105] For Owen it was not "enough to satisfy us, that the doctrines mentioned are preserved entire; every tittle and iota in the Word of God must come under our care and consideration, as being, as such, from God."[106]

Owen exhibited affinities with both the Augustine/Calvin/Westminster tradition and that of later Protestant scholasticism. In matters of methodology, human authorship, and the extent of inspiration, Owen stood with the Reformed scholastics. Yet he did not make inerrancy the basis of inspiration or sever the connection of Word and Spirit by advancing thoroughgoing rationalistic arguments as the ultimate criterion for the Bible's authority. Thus, John Owen was a transitional figure between Reformation Calvinism and post-Reformation scholastic orthodoxy.

Since Owen tried to maintain the dynamic tension between Word and Spirit, why did he at the same time, take such a rigid position regarding the biblical text itself? What made him take recourse to the nonexistent divine *autographa* (original text)? His writings from 1659, when he writes about "jots and tittles", seem more in line with the Helvetic Consensus Formula of 1675 than with the Westminster Confession of 1646.[107]

The answer lies perhaps in a theological controversy in which Owen became involved. In 1659 a man named Brian Walton published a Polyglott Bible in England. It introduced variant readings of the Old Testament text and questioned the antiquity of the Hebrew punctuation. Owen responded with a polemical treatise entitled, "Of the Integrity and Purity of the Hebrew and Greek Text of the Scripture." Just as Turretin did fifteen years later, Owen reacted to textual criticism by trying to prove that the Bible had been providentially preserved in its original state. On punctuation, Owen held that the Hebrew vowel points were an ancient, sacred, and inspired part of the original Hebrew text.

Walton responded by attacking Owen in "The Considerator considered and the Biblia Polyglotta Vindicated." Walton successfully defended his own position and was able to hold Owen up to the ridicule of the learned world.[108] Lacking much knowledge of biblical manuscripts, Owen was pushed farther than he had previously gone when he sensed an apparent threat to the Bible's foundational authority. He tried to meet the onslaught on rational grounds and with rational weapons. In doing so, he shifted the grounds of faith to the grounds of reason. And in doing so he lost the battle.[109]

A similar scholasticizing of the spirit of the Westminster Confession was taking place in Scotland. There, an unofficial and anonymous commentary on the Westminster Confession entitled *The Sum of Saving Knowledge* appeared in 1650. It manifested a much more rigid and scholastic spirit than the Westminster Confession itself. It was, however, often published in the same volume as the confession. Many thought, therefore, that it was a product of the Westminster Assembly and interpreted the confession through this later, more scholastic commentary.[110]

The Westminster Divines still belonged to the Reformation era in Great Britain. Until the middle of the seventeenth century the "Age of Faith" prevailed. The "Age of Reason" came quickly but unexpectedly thereafter.

c. Changes in Science and Philosophy in Seventeenth-Century England: Newton and Locke

The impact of new currents in natural science and philosophy did not significantly affect England until after the restoration to the throne of Charles II in 1660. Sir Francis Bacon (1561–1626) had rejected the Aristotelian scholastic tradition and provided a new inductive approach to science as early as 1620. *Novum Organum* had offered a new method for all scientific work. Bacon maintained that Truth was twofold: there was a truth in religion and a truth in science. These two, he felt, should be kept in separate spheres because the truths of religion could not be confirmed by the principles of science.[111] While Bacon's work eventually had far-reaching effects, the writings from the period immediately following his death showed little trace of his influence. His genius was recognized, and he was quoted now and again on special points, but the philosophical and theological implications of his method were generally ignored. No new logic appeared along the lines suggested in his *Novum Organum*.[112]

Puritans were open to new and experimental approaches to science, but had little opportunity to exercise their interests until stability was returned to the country after the civil war and Cromwell's *Interregnum*. The Aristotelianism that reigned in the English universities prior to the mid-seventeenth century was not the inductive philosophy of Aristotle based on sense perception, but the syllogistic Aristotle that had become traditionalism taught from commentaries on commentaries and that stifled new thought. It was this kind of scholasticism that was supplanted by the new science and philosophy after the mid-seventeenth century.[113]

The English response to new developments in science, even among theologians, stood in sharp contrast to the reactions of the Protestant scholastics on the Continent. In general, the theological tone in England had been set by Calvin and transmitted there by those who shared his opinion that science did more good than harm to religion.[114] While the Copernican system was having difficulty on the Continent, in England, the theological censure was mild. There was never the outright repression that occurred abroad. This more lenient attitude may be attributed to many distinctive English elements: the relatively greater religious freedom in England; the native moderation and practicality of the English temperament; the existence of a strong Neoplatonic tradition in English thought; and, the relatively lesser dominance of Aristotelianism in the English unversities.[115]

Scientists Who Affirmed Theology: The Virtuosi

Most of the new group of professional scientists coming to prominence in England had been thoroughly schooled in religion and had
university training similar to the theologians. Eventually this group
became known as the *virtuosi*, a term used to designate those specifically
interested in the natural sciences and experimental philosophy. It was
these scientists who formed the Royal Society in 1660. On the whole they
represented a viewpoint that was interested in harmonizing science and
religion.

These *virtuosi* followed Bacon's lead in making science and religion
separate spheres with distinct tasks. That left each sphere open for free
development. As long as scientists and theologians followed the Augustinian method of "faith seeking understanding" all went well. They accepted the Bible in faith and recognized the accommodated character of
its human language and thought. The Bible's purpose was to guide
persons to salvation and the life of faith. The purpose of science was to
teach about the material world. When scientists and theologians shifted
to an Aristotelian-Thomistic method, things changed. When reason was
given precedence over faith in the religious realm, scientists and theologians tried to prove the validity of the Bible by evidence from science.
In this, religion and science were at first treated as separate, but as
complementary and harmonious.

An early member of the *virtuosi* group who exemplified an Augustinian approach to harmonizing science and religion was John Wilkins (1614
–1672). Wilkins was an avid natural scientist and later Bishop of Chester
(he was also Oliver Cromwell's brother-in-law). Debating with the
learned Alexander Ross, an avowed opponent of the new science, Wilkins
declared in *A Discourse Concerning a New Planet* that the Bible did not speak
about scientific matters. For him, "while it is supreme and unquestioned
as a spiritual authority, the Bible makes no pretense of delivering scientific truths. If it speaks of the sun and the moon rising, it does not intend
to comment on astronomy, for the Bible is merely accommodating its
language to the vulgar conceptions of its time."[116] Wilkins wrote:

> There is not any particular by which philosophy has been more endan-
> gered, than the ignorant superstition of some men, who in stating the con-
> troversies of it, do so closely adhere unto the mere words of Scripture. . . .
> It were happy for us, if we could exempt Scripture from philosophical con-
> troversies: If we could be content to let it be perfect for that end unto which
> it was intended, for a Rule of our Faith and Obedience, and not stretch it also
> to be a Judge of such Natural Truths, as are to be found out by our own
> Industry and Experience. [The Holy Spirit could have easily given us infor-

mation on the latter yet] He has left this travel to the sons of men to be exercised with.[117]

Thus religion and science were kept in their own spheres and could proceed without conflict. The potential for a shift in method was also present, however. For Wilkins and many of his contemporaries, for example, astronomy was a positive intellectual aid to religion. He wrote:

> It proves a God and a providence, and incites our hearts to a greater admiration and fear of His omnipotency. . . . A deeper study of astronomy only reveals the Creator's excellency the better. Astronomy likewise serves the moral teachings of religion by helping to correct man's estimation of himself and of his actions.[118]

Other transitional people who followed Wilkins's lead and deeply believed in the harmony of scientific studies with religion were Sir Kenelm Digby (*Two Treatises*, 1644); John Ray (*Physico-theological Discourses*, 1692); Thomas Sprat, Joseph Glanvill, and the foremost example of all—Robert Boyle (1627–1691), the "father of chemistry." These men believed their studies in natural science confirmed and strengthened belief in the providential hand of God active in Creation. They viewed their whole scientific enterprise as a religious experience. Asserting that the revelation in nature could not contradict the written word, they defended science and praised it as a religious act. All truth is one, they continually said. Natural philosophy did not and could not contradict Christianity, according to them.[119]

On the theological side, it is important to examine the attitude of English churchmen toward the Bible and science. In the early seventeenth century there was nothing in any of the creeds of Catholicism, Anglicanism, or Puritanism that made any one of them more or less favorable to science in general. There was, however, a diversity of receptiveness to science within each group. Considerations such as ecclesiastical organization, lay intervention, and economic alliances entered in to make Puritans more hospitable than Anglicans, and Anglicans perhaps more hospitable than Catholics to the input of the new science.[120] Among Puritans who were totally committed to the Copernican system, for example, were Mark Ridley (1560–1624), Dr. John Bainbridge (1582–1643), Henry Briggs (1561–1630), Henry Gellibrand (1597–1636), the mathematician John Wallis (1616–1703), and John Wilkins. These men combined their scientific interests with an equally strong commitment to Reformed theology.[121]

In particular Gresham College became known as a hotbed of Puritanism, as well as a kind of central clearinghouse for new ideas.[122] The Puritan attitude toward science was influenced greatly by Francis Bacon.[123] Using the inductive approach and keeping the spheres of religion and science separate, Bacon believed that religious knowledge was, nonetheless, primary. He wrote: "All knowledge is to be limited by religion, and is to be referred to use and action.[124] In effect, God revealed himself to humankind by means of two scriptures: first, through the written word, but also, second, through his handiwork, the created universe. To study nature was considered part of the duty humans owed to the Creator of the world.[125] Religion, according to these Puritans, should protect and promote all increase of natural knowledge. They viewed the superstitious and the enthusiasts—Roman Catholics and Anabaptists—as the obstacles to scientific enquiry.[126] Bacon's thought provided a powerful tool for those Puritans seeking to maintain their faith while also being open to the advances in scientific thinking, particularly in the 1640s and 1650s.[127] His principle of making science subordinate to religion seemed to harmonize well with their Augustinian "faith seeking understanding" stance.

In 1660 the Royal Society was formed at Gresham College. Four of the founding twelve members were Gresham College professors.[128] In defense of those Christian *virtuosi* involved in the Society's work as it progressed, Joseph Glanvill (1636–1680), a clergyman and scientist, warned that it was "a sin and a folly either in the one or the other [that is, in layman or cleric] to censure or discourage those worthy undertakings" since "the study of nature is useful in most of the affairs wherein religion is concerned." Glanvill believed that science cultivated an outlook fatal to all the principal enemies of belief. It overthrew atheism, sadducism, superstition, enthusiasm, and the humor of disputing.[129] In this Glanvill continued in the *virtuosi* tradition by seeing science as a positive aid to religion. The authority of Scripture was not undermined, according to him, since the study of nature produced a knowledge of God in His works and thus caused people to love Him and His world. So, one could be a member of the Royal Society and a religious person without any sense of conflict.[130]

Yet it was this very "complementary" spirit and the desire to harmonize science and religion that eventually proved to undermine the very biblical authority the *virtuosi* tried to uphold. Despite the reverent attitude with which the *virtuosi* approached their studies, they accepted and elaborated a conception of nature that eventually challenged some traditional doctrines of Christianity.[131] The most acute problem was the relationship of divine Providence and natural law. The *virtuosi* held to an atomic or mechanistic philosophy. They rejected the Aristotelian scheme in which natural phenomena were explained by the actions of substantial forms. The new science (via Galileo and Kepler) insisted that nature was a mechanically determined order. Bodies obeyed laws—not laws whereby each body sought its highest end as Aristotle taught, but ascertainable laws that could be discovered by the human mind. Nature was viewed as a machine made up of unconscious material parts controlled by external mechanical forces.[132] If this was so, what part could a doctrine of particular Providence play, a doctrine that taught God's personal control and intervention in His universe?[133] The only consistent route for the *virtuosi* to follow was to interpret God's Providence as His general benevolence in creation and His further continued sustenance of the created order. "Particular providence" was lost.[134]

The discarding of this doctrine proved to be less damaging to biblical authority than was the underlying means whereby the *virtuosi* sought to defend the Christian faith. Their basic belief was that natural philosophy was an aid to religion. To counter the general "secularization" of the culture and the supposedly rising tide of atheism, the *virtuosi* believed a clear demonstration of God's existence with unanswerable proofs would carry the day for Christianity. "Natural religion" was supposed to be the sure defender of the Faith. In theory natural religion was intended to supplement Christianity, by providing it with a rational foundation. In practice, though, natural religion began to displace the biblical faith.[135]

A large number of scientists joined the fight against atheism: Walter Charleton, John Wilkins, John Ray, Nehemiah Grew, Joseph Glanvill and Robert Boyle. Each, from his own discipline, sought to solidify the rational basis for belief in God apart from the Bible. In addition to combating the atheistic threat, these scientists wanted to provide rational certainty for the Christian faith to combat the excesses of religious zeal manifested by certain sects. After the civil war with its religious strife, many devout Christians sought for fundamentals on which to agree, and in reaction to the "enthusiasm" of the sects, looked for a rational basis for faith. Accordingly, the *virtuosi* elaborated on natural religion as an apologetic for the Christian faith. Because sectarians questioned the possibility of finding absolute authority in the Bible, and enthusiasts challenged the faith of reasonable men, natural revelation seemed to promise the means of restoring certainty.[136] But in the arguments of Wilkins, Boyle, and Ray, the loving God of redemption, the Father of the Lord Jesus Christ, gave way to an omnipotent Creator. In the works of Boyle, for example, few references were made to Christ. The Bible was seen less as a record of God's relationship to people than as a further and higher revelation of His power. The nature of God progressively was adjusted to fit the nature of the universe as science viewed it.[137] By accommodating their view of the nature and function of Scripture to the prevailing canons of scientific enquiry, these well-meaning men of science and faith lost hold of the very Bible they really wished to uphold.

With William Petty (1623–1687), founder of modern statistics and economics, the relationship of reason to faith took a new turn. It popularized a little rhyme:

Religion's natural and good
For king or state, if understood;
If not, 'tis but a mere illusion,
Begetting bloodshed and confusion.

The words "Religion's natural and good for king and state, if *understood"* made reason a tool for the criticism of religion. In the work of the other *virtuosi,* reason supported religion. In the work of Petty, the power of reason to determine matters of faith was asserted. When this step was taken, natural religion actually ceased to support Christianity and gradually began to replace it.[138]

All in all, by concentrating on the rational features of faith, the *virtuosi* tended to forget in practice what they admitted in principle—that the Christian faith finally transcended proof. Christianity as they interpreted it was a reasonable religion for reasonable people with the spiritual profundity of traditional Christianity pushed aside.[139]

Theologians Who Affirmed Reason: The Cambridge Platonists and the Latitudinarians

In theology, the drift away from faith toward reason as the locus of certain authority was seen in the works of the Cambridge Platonists and the Latitudinarians.

At the height of their influence when Charles II was restored to the throne, the Cambridge Platonists comprised a small group of brilliant thinkers who sought a "middle way" between the Anglicans and Puritanism. Against the Anglicans they stressed that morality was more important than church polity. Against the Puritans they maintained that reason must have priority over faith. Their seat of authority was the individual conscience governed by reason. Leading figures of the group were: Benjamin Whichcote (1609–1683); John Smith (1616–1652); Ralph Cudworth (1617–1685); and Henry More (1614–1687). Being Puritan in background, these men did not want to destroy religious tradition but sought rather to restore to it what they felt was vital. They were vigorously anticreedal in approach, and found many agreeable elements in Platonic philosophy. Since the Platonic tradition was strong in England, with an authority second only to that of Scripture, they used its language in their religious exhortations. They implied without aggressively proclaiming, that there were other means of expressing the Christian faith than those currently being practiced.[140] The Cambridge Platonists sought a unity between all parties on what they saw as the real essentials of religion, permitting disagreement on minor points. As Benjamin Whichcote said: "The maintenance of truth is rather God's charge, and the continuation of charity ours." For Whichcote: "The essentials of belief are contained in the Scriptures, and are so clearly set forth that any one using his reason can scarcely miss them."[141]

It was this emphasis on reason that was most characteristic of the Cambridge school. For them there was no split between reason and faith. Whichcote wrote: "The reason of men is the candle of the Lord; lighted by God and lighting unto God. *Res illuminata illuminans*" (see Proverbs 20:27).[142]

The significance of the Cambridge Platonists in the development of the doctrine of Scripture was the role they played in preparing the theological climate of the end of the seventeenth century. They were instrumental in placing reason in the foreground as the unquestioned authority for theological decision making.

The Latitudinarians also contributed to the shift in religious thought. The name and the numbers of this group are rather ill defined. Their approach was seen in the sermons of some of the most influential pre-Revolutionary London preachers: Patrick, Lloyd, Tillotson, Burnet, and Stillingfleet. After the Restoration many of these became bishops in the Church of England. They were seen as the propagators of a progressive liberalism and were closely allied with the Cambridge Platonists in attempting to strike a middle ground between the fanatic excesses of "enthusiastic" sects and the purely rationalistic arguments of the atheists. The avowed purpose of the Latitudinarians was to eliminate the irrational from religion. They claimed that the use of human mental powers could only advance the cause of faith. They advocated a restoration of reason to its rightful place. For them to grasp the truth "is the most natural perfection of the rational soul."[143] The Latitudinarians also believed in a law of nature that could communicate what was morally right. Perhaps their most characteristic emphasis was on the human obligation to fulfill moral laws. By emphasizing philanthropic good works, they stressed practical religion more than creeds. Yet these concerns gradually degenerated into mere complacency. Nevertheless, the Latitudinarians do represent an important transitional stage between the reliance on authority that characterized the early seventeenth century and the rationalism of the early eighteenth century.[144]

God Inferred from Nature: Isaac Newton

The two most influential figures of the late seventeenth century in England were Isaac Newton (1642–1727) and John Locke (1632–1704). Newton brought to fulfillment the scientific revolution begun by Copernicus, Kepler, and Galileo. Through his discovery of the law of universal gravitation, Newton synthesized his predecessors' work into a coherent picture and solved many of the day's scientific confusions. His solution was orderly and relatively simple, bursting upon the world with the publication of his *Principia* in 1687. All bodies reacted to each other according to their natural properties:

> We are to admit no more causes of natural things than such as are both true and sufficient to explain their appearances ... therefore to the same natural effects we must, as far as possible, assign the same causes.... We must ... universally allow, that all bodies whatsoever are endowed with a principle of mutual gravitation.[145]

Stated innocently enough, this discovery unlocked doors of explanation for the movement of planets and made possible the projection of planetary movements as yet unknown. Speed and direction could be determined within a single conception of motion. No longer was motion to be explained by the authority of Aristotle or an antiquarian philosopher. No more could the occult be reckoned as cause for movement. For with Newton's theory, there were no hidden purposes to discover. His basic purpose was "to subject the phenomena of nature to the laws of mathematics ... from the phenomena of motions to investigate the forces of nature, and then from these forces to demonstrate the other phenomena."[146] Everything was put on an experimental, mechanical, mathematical basis.

Newton stood as the culmination of the Christian *virtuosi*. He did not want his momentous discovery to exclude God from the universe, and he wrote to Richard Bentley (1662–1742), the English scientist and classical scholar:

> When I wrote my treatise about our system, I had an eye upon such principles as might work with considering men for the belief of a Deity; and nothing can rejoice me more than to find it useful for that purpose.[147]

At the end of the second edition of the *Principia*, Newton appended a note in which he said that he did not profess to know the nature of the cause of gravity that made bodies tend to approach one another. As a religious man, his mechanistic system still left room for God. Newton proclaimed:

> This most beautiful system of the sun, planets and comets, could only proceed from the counsel and dominion of an intelligent and powerful Being.... He endures forever, and is everywhere present; and by existing always and everywhere, he constitutes duration and space.[148]

Like the other *virtuosi*, the harmony of science and religion was Newton's basic presupposition.

But despite his piety, Newton's work had an adverse effect on traditional Christianity. Besides reducing the size of the body of phenomena explained as "mystery," Newton perpetuated the *virtuosi's* picture of

God. God's personality was lost and ultimately His Being was made to fit into the scientific theory of the universe. In his statement on God as "duration and space," Newton nearly identified the Almighty with the eternity and infinity of the world, and made God a metaphysical projection of the creation. In explaining how the Genesis account might plausibly be explained when it presented God as having created everything in six ordinary days, Newton developed a picture of God starting the earth's acceleration from rest and then speeding it up to its present velocity. He concluded then that earlier "days" were longer since the earth was then rotating more slowly. This approach portrayed God as a mechanical force bound even in Creation to the *Principia*'s universal laws. Newton believed that this universe required a Creator. He did not anticipate that a God deduced from nature would become no more than a projection of nature.[149]

Beyond this, Newton wrote on other theological matters. His writings indicate a basic theological sympathy with Arianism. In this he reflected a trend noticeable among certain of his contemporaries. Many felt that if they could eliminate the doctrine of the Trinity from Christianity it would be easier for them to reconcile theology with science.[150] In a treatise, "A Short Scheme of the True Religion," Newton revealed his contention that the Golden Rule taught by Jesus was dictated by the light of reason. When Newton equated Christ with reason, he eliminated all supernatural elements from Christianity.[151]

God Deduced from Reason: John Locke

While Newton was shaping the physical world, John Locke was fashioning the mental world. His two influential treatises *An Essay Concerning Human Understanding* (1690) and *The Reasonableness of Christianity* (1695) sought to bring reason to the defense of traditional Christian doctrine but also to prune the faith of all doctrines that were not reasonable. His *Essay* moved steadily toward the certainty of God's existence. He contended that we intuitively know we ourselves exist. He then asserted that by demonstration humans could come to the assurance that there was a God. Indeed this knowledge of the existence of "a God" is "the most obvious truth that reason discovers," its evidence being "equal to mathematical certainty." Yet persons must apply themselves "to a regular deduction of it from some part of our intuitive knowledge, or else we shall be as uncertain and ignorant of this and other propositions which are in themselves capable of clear demonstration."[152] Locke rejected *innate ideas* as the source of human knowledge of God. Yet he declared:

Though God has given us no innate *ideas* of himself, though he has stamped no original characters on our minds wherein we may read his being: yet, having furnished us with those faculties our minds are endowed with, he hath not left himself without witness, since we have sense, perception, and reason and cannot want a clear proof of him, as long as we carry ourselves about us. Nor can we justly complain of our ignorance in this great point, since he has so plentifully provided us with the means to discover and know him, so far as is necessary to the end of our being and the great concernment of our happiness.[153]

Locke's approach well matched the spirit of the times for its emphasis on reason, but even more because he seemed to offer an eminently "reasonable" (and "simple") account of what many felt was the true origin of the idea of God. While Newton was disclosing the secrets of the heavens, Locke was disclosing the secrets of the mind. The principle that changed chaos into order was the same in both realms. The evidence of reason permeated all things. Locke reaffirmed the role of reason in religion. He also promoted reason's authority to a new plane.[154] Reason became the judge of revelation. Locke wrote:

> *Reason* is natural *revelation,* whereby the eternal Father of light, and Fountain of all knowledge, communicates to mankind that portion of truth which he has laid within the reach of their natural faculties. *Revelation* is natural *reason* enlarged by a new set of discoveries communicated by God immediately, which reason vouches the truth of, by the testimony it gives that it comes from God.[155]

Where reason was not sufficient, human beings needed revelation. But, the revelation people received was judged by reason, since "revelation cannot be admitted against the clear evidence or reason, and therefore no proposition can be received for divine revelation if it be contradictory to our clear intuitive knowledge."[156]

Locke's influence in theology was monumental during the next hundred years. Only a few of the *virtuosi* such as the orthodox Calvinist John Wallis, Sir Thomas Browne (1605–1682), Isaac Barrow (1630–1677) and John Mapletoft (1631–1721) resisted the shift toward natural religion.[157] Locke provided the groundwork on which deism was soon to rise.

Deism

When the Glorious Revolution of 1688 saw the abdication of the English throne by the Catholic James II and the establishment of the Protestants William of Orange and Mary as rulers, various conditions made it possible to open a new phase of religious discussion. Calvinism had been on the decline since the 1660s but Protestantism in general had triumphed. Freed from the struggle with the Roman Catholics, and from the question of toleration for Independents, the time was ripe for an exploration of the basic content and foundation of Protestant theology.[158]

The movement that gained strength was deism, the final extension of "natural religion." Its primal roots were in the writings of Lord Herbert of Cherbury (1583–1648) who in 1639 set out five fundamental truths he believed to be sufficient for salvation. These five fundamentals were proposed as the basis of a universal religion.[159] The fundamentals were amplified by Charles Blount (1654–1693), who attacked the Christian doctrine of revelation as superstition and Jesus Christ as little better than the pagan miracle-worker Apollonius of Tyann.[160] But it was with John Toland's (1670–1722) book *Christianity Not Mysterious* published in 1696, one year after Locke's *Reasonableness of Christianity*, that deism began its period of greatest activity.[161] In the preface, Toland indicated his aims:

> I prove first, that the true religion must necessarily be reasonable and intelligible. Next I show that these requisite conditions are found in Christianity ... thirdly I demonstrate that the Christian religion was not formed after such a manner, but was divinely revealed from heaven.[162]

For the deists, the supreme reality was reason. Revelation only gave supplementary information. Reason must govern revelation. There was no room left for mystery in the Christian faith. Toland's dependence on, yet development of, Locke was evident. Where Locke wished to prove Christianity to be reasonable, Toland taught that nothing contrary to reason or above it could be part of Christian doctrine.[163] No deference was granted any authority past or present. For the deists, Scripture recorded God's appeal to the reason of humankind.

England's seventeenth century was of tremendous significance, both as an end and as a beginning. It marked, on the one hand, the end of the time when the Bible was accepted uncritically as a sure and certain authority for salvation and for leading a moral life. Intellectual events had brought men and women into a strange new world. No longer did they feel completely at the mercy of divine Providence. Instead, they could now *understand* the world about them because of Sir Isaac Newton. They could understand their relation to that world because of John Locke. As far as Scripture was concerned it was not that people rejected it as false. It was rather that "natural religion" came more and more to seem all-sufficient. Revelation increasingly appeared to be secondary, and slightly inconvenient.[164]

England's seventeenth century marked, on the other hand, the beginning of the steady acceptance of the claims of reason (now approximated to the standards of common sense), which led to its virtual enthronement as *the* supreme authority. An earlier age, which had believed that Scripture presented an absolute divine message in weak and fallible human language, gave way to a new age where the Bible was valid only insofar as its form could be verified by the researches of human reason. While most of the shapers of this thought maintained faith in God and allegiance to the Christian church, their efforts set in motion attempts to adjust Christian beliefs into accord with the conclusions of science and philosophy. The old certainty of the biblical message had eroded away. "New thought" now offered rational certainty in its place. The "Age of Faith" had ended. The "Age of Reason" had begun.

The Concept of Error

It is appropriate to the developments we have just sketched and relevant to events that followed that the first recorded use in English of the word *inerrant* occurred in 1652. The context was "Astronomy. Of a star: Fixed; not 'wandering' as a planet." Gaule, *Magastrom*, xxvi, was quoted as saying "The sunne . . . after which the moon and, beneath these, the rest errant and inerrant."[165] The attention of ordinary people had turned from God's personal interaction with his children to humans' ability to describe the working of the world with mechanical precision. This attitude also affected theologians who uncritically adopted a mechanistic, mathematical model by which the Bible was judged. Scripture's message had to accord with Lockean reason and Scripture's language had to conform to Newtonian notions of perfection. Because Scripture failed to measure up to the mechanical standards of the new science, increasing numbers of theologians and church people felt drawn to the rational religion of deism in the late seventeenth century. By the beginning of the eighteenth century Reformed Protestants fought back against the inroads of deism. They did so, just as post-Reformation Protestants on the continent had done earlier, by using the enemy's weapons to do battle. Scots Presbyterians defended the Bible by claiming that it conformed to Locke's empirical philosophy and Bacon's scientific methodology. Scripture as well as the stars began to be discussed in terms of errancy and inerrancy.

d. Eighteenth-Century Scottish "Common Sense" Philosophy: Thomas Reid

Philosophically, the seventeenth century is known as the age of rationalism. Descartes, followed by Spinoza (1632–1716) and Leibniz (1646–

1716), had overemphasized one dimension of classical realism, the Platonic notion of innate ideas and deductive reasoning. They had sought to prove everything deductively using the syllogistic logic developed by Aristotle. Reason was made independent of and prior to faith. This mode of thought made heavy inroads into post-Reformation scholasticism on the European continent. However, as we have seen, the peculiar circumstances in England held back the influences of deductive rationalism there.

British philosophy dominated the eighteenth century, often called the "Age of Enlightenment."[166] John Locke had turned to another aspect of Aristotelianism, and proposed to found certain knowledge on sense experience and inductive reasoning alone. Again, reason was made prior to faith but using a different method. An Irish Anglican bishop, George Berkeley (1685–1753), followed Locke's lead but tried to save Christianity by claiming that God, not matter, was the source of the sense perceptions we receive. The result was an idealism which posited that only minds and ideas really existed. The Scot, David Hume (1711–1776), worked out the logic of Locke's position. Hume's conclusion was skepticism. The only thing we know by sense experience alone is that we have sensations. He attacked the notion of cause and effect and substituted habit or custom as the link between events in our minds. Hume argued that miracles were improbable. This argument was especially challenging to the rising Protestant scholasticism, which made miracles one of the chief evidences of the truth of the Bible.

English Presbyterians followed the drift toward deism, which accompanied the increasing commitment to scientific categories, as conclusive even in religion. Much of Presbyterianism in England eventually turned into Unitarianism.[167] In Scotland, the inroads of the Enlightenment produced a different result. Thomas Reid (1710–1796) opposed both Hume's skepticism and Berkeley's idealism while remaining philosophically in the reigning empiricist tradition. Reid believed that Hume had brought the entire fabric of natural philosophy into great intellectual danger. Reid responded by assuming an Aristotelian realism, which based all knowledge on sense experience. He was also self-consciously committed to the correctness of the scientific method of "chaste induction" spelled out a century earlier by Sir Francis Bacon. By an "inductive analysis" of the faculties and powers of the mind, Reid, and the realist school that followed him, hoped to lay a firm philosophical foundation. Reid's goal was to give philosophical validation to the practice of inductive science, the rationality of the received Christian tradition, and the common sense beliefs of ordinary people.

Thomas Reid was the son of a Scots Presbyterian minister. He studied divinity at Aberdeen and was licensed to preach. His parishioners proved very hostile toward him perhaps because he was more bookish than pastoral.[168] In 1751 Reid was appointed to a professorship at King's College Aberdeen. There he taught mathematics, physics, and "mental philosophy." Reid helped to found the Aberdeen Philosophical Society. Papers he read to its meetings were collected and published in 1764 as his *Inquiry into the Human Mind*. He was chosen that same year as Adam Smith's successor at Glasgow in the chair of moral philosophy. Reid retired in 1780, but continued to publish. His *Essays on the Intellectual Powers of Man* appeared in 1785 and were followed in 1788 by the *Essays on the Active Powers of Man*.[169]

Reid's philosophy came to be known as Scottish realism, or Scottish common sense philosophy. It was the first real "school" of British philosophy after the Cambridge Platonists.[170] It has generally been considered the only competent attempt to refute Hume's philosophy as a whole.[171] The leading Scottish realist of the next generation, and the one who exerted the most influence in America, was Dugald Stewart (1753–1828). Stewart was the son of a mathematics professor at Edinburgh. He studied under Adam Ferguson (1723–1819), professor of moral philosophy at Edinburgh, who presented Reid as the chief authority in philosophy. In 1771 Stewart attended Reid's lectures in Glasgow. He returned to Edinburgh, first to take over his father's mathematics classes, and later to assume Ferguson's chair upon his retirement in 1785. For twenty-five years thereafter, Stewart was professor of moral philosophy at Edinburgh.[172] He devoted his career to the development and dissemination of Reid's philosophy although he avoided the use of the term "common sense" and spoke instead of "the fundamental laws of human belief" or "the primary elements of human reason." Stewart's classes inspired a generation of Scottish literary figures, and drew listeners from the Continent and America. He wrote prolifically, his first work being *Elements of the Philosophy of the Human Mind* in 1792 and his last being his *Philosophy of the Active and Moral Powers of Man* in 1828.[173]

Aristotle and Bacon Versus David Hume

Reid began from a commitment to Aristotelian realism. He wrote a brief but accurate *Account of Aristotle's Logic*.[174] Reid's closest friends on the faculties of Aberdeen and Glasgow were mathematicians and scientists. He was personally competent in Newtonian mathematics and in chemistry, in which he conducted experiments. His lectures in philosophy included discussions of statics, dynamics, astronomy, magnetism, electricity, hydrostatics, pneumatics, and optics. For twelve years at Glasgow he lectured on Newton's *Mathematical Principles of Natural Philosophy*. Stewart was only slightly less involved in science than Reid. Stewart lectured not only in mathematics but also in astronomy and may have dealt with algebraic methods in physics.[175]

Reid and Stewart believed that their whole philosophical program was the carrying out of the inductive plan of research proposed in Sir Francis Bacon's *Novum Organum*.[176] The question of methodology was central for them. Their embrace of Newton was based on the notion that Newton was a disciple of Bacon. Lord Bacon had performed little actual inductive research himself, and Newton had developed the Baconian method by giving what Reid called "the first and noblest examples of that chaste induction, which Lord Bacon could only delineate in theory."[177] Reid approved the new inductive Aristotelianism rather than the syllogistic, Aristotelian deductionism of scholasticism. Bacon, he believed, had disclosed an infallible procedure for exposing the structure and laws of the universe by "the slow and patient method of induction."[178]

In a manner characteristic of the Enlightenment, Reid and Stewart easily moved from natural philosophy to a "science of man." They were performing what they considered to be an inductive analysis of the faculties and powers by which the mind knows, feels, and wills. While their concentration was on what we would call "psychology," their underlying concern was for the foundation of the inductive method itself. The Scottish realists were involved in a certain circularity by attempting to validate the inductive method by means of induction. They genuinely attempted to do just that and claimed as a result that they had discovered that the human mind was a structure "designed" exactly and only for the inductive method of knowing.[179]

When Reid studied Hume's *Treatise on Human Nature,* he realized that the accepted assumptions about how the mind knew were unacceptable. Reid acknowledged that the mind-body problem bequeathed to the Enlightenment by Descartes had not been solved. Scottish philosophy (Baconianism) accepted the fact that reality was divided into "two great kingdoms"—bodies and minds. The problem for empiricists was how to bridge that gap between matter and mind.[180] Locke had asserted that the middle term, the object of perception, was an "idea." Berkeley carried that logic a step further and claimed that all that existed were minds and ideas. And ideas existed as they were perceived by minds. Reid, in his youth had accepted Berkeley's system, "till, finding other consequences to follow from it, which gave me more uneasiness than the loss of a material world, it came into my mind ... to put the question, What evidence have I for this doctrine, that all the objects of my knowledge are ideas in my own mind?"[181] Reading Hume, and reflecting on what all people affirmed by their common sense, Reid departed from Berkeley's views.

But Reid was reluctant to accept Hume's skeptical conclusion. He declared:

> For I am persuaded, that absolute scepticism is not more destructive of the faith of a Christian than of the science of a philosopher, and of the prudence of a man of common understanding.[182]

Hume had exposed the fallacy of Locke's fundamentally subjective premise. If human beings only know ideas, then Hume was right that there was no way of knowing that things existed objectively beyond those ideas.

Reid responded by rejecting the modern problem and retreating to the ancient Aristotelian epistemology. He discarded ideas and retained only minds and matter.[183] Reid asserted that what the mind perceived was not an idea but the real thing itself. Reid announced: "Perception . . . hath always an object distinct from the act by which it is perceived."[184] Stewart was wholly in accord, asserting that it was "the external objects themselves, and not any . . . images of these objects, that the mind perceives."[185]

The skeptical response to Reid's assertion was to ask how one could know that the mind was actually encountering the external object. Reid's confident assertion, in which he was followed by all Scottish realists, was that the act of perceiving an object was accompanied by an intuitive belief or "judgment" that the object really existed. This judgment was not something transmitted to the mind by the senses. It existed a priori (before the experience). Judgment was both logically and psychologically prior to the awareness of sensations. It validated the objective existence both of the external object and of its field of causal relationships. This judgment evidenced itself by "a strong and irresistible conviction and belief."[186] Reid compared this "belief" to religious "faith."[187] Judgment was the basic unit of knowledge in Reid's inductive scheme. But the judgment itself was not known inductively, but intuitively. It was not the product of scientific inquiry, but of personal faith.

For Reid, every perception as it arrived at our senses was already interpreted by these "natural judgments." This intuitive realism was thus declared the secure base on which the veracity of sense perceptions and the validity of scientific induction could rest. Reid declared:

> If there are certain principles, as I think there are, which the constitution of our nature leads us to believe, and which we are under a necessity to take for granted in the common concerns of life, without being able to give a reason for them—these are what we call 'the principles of common sense'; and what is manifestly contrary to them, is what we call absurd.[188]

Despite their investment in intuition, the Scottish realists continually appealed to "trust in the senses" and decried any confidence in "pure reason." The focus was on "facts" known directly by the senses. Realists tended to characterize opposing viewpoints as "rational speculation."[189]

As people, the Scottish realists manifested great confidence in the certainty of their knowledge. As philosophers, they were forced to concede some of the major elements of Hume's skepticism.[190] Reid's concept of "judgment" had bridged the chasm between matter and mind for practical purposes. But he admitted that he had no knowledge of the actual operations of the process of knowing. Reid declared his mystification quite openly:

> We know, that when certain impressions are made upon our organs, nerves, and brain, certain corresponding sensations are felt, and certain objects are both conceived and believed to exist. But in this train of operations nature works in the dark. We can neither discover the cause of any one of them, nor any necessary connection of one with another.[191]

Both Reid and Stewart were forced to admit candidly the correctness of Hume's doctrine that "causation is not an object of sense."[192] Judgment affirmed the existence of causal agency for the Scottish realists, but they had no empirical information about causation. Hume had denied human ability to know cause and effect through the senses. The Scottish realists restored cause and effect, but as a *presupposition*, not as the conclusion of empirical investigation.[193] "First principles," were supplied by intuition, and as Stewart admitted, "abstracted from other *data*, they are perfectly barren in themselves."[194] Reid, in his role as a careful philosopher, severely restricted the scope of scientific inquiry. He announced:

> We are very much in the dark with regard to the real agents or causes which produce the phenomena of nature.... [For example] A Newtonian philosopher inquires what proof can be offered for the existence of magnetic effluvia, and can find none.... He confesses his ignorance of the real [efficient] cause of [magnetically induced] motion, and thinks, that his business, as a philosopher, is only to find from experiment the laws by which it is regulated.... What has been said of this, may be applied to every phenomenon that falls within the compass of natural philosophy. We deceive ourselves, if we conceive, that we can point out the real efficient cause of any one of them.[195]

The scientific method, in its strictest Baconian interpretation, was limited to observable facts. Reid affirmed: "What can fairly be deduced from facts, duly observed, or sufficiently attested, is genuine and pure."[196] Stewart attested that the main thrust of Reid's philosophy was "to remind us of the limited powers of the human understanding." He insisted that the fundamental purpose of all Baconian science was not to "flatter the pride of man" but to "lead to a confession of human ignorance."[197]

Common Sense and Religious Authority

The philosophic caution that the Scottish realists evinced was matched by the personal confidence they manifested. After admitting the severe limits of certain knowledge, they appealed to the probable knowledge accepted by all people of common sense. Their appeal was both democratic and pragmatic. It suited the spirit of the Enlightenment. And, it was especially adapted to the attitudes of nineteenth-century Americans, on whom it would exert such a special influence. Reid argued that even philosophers, in the end, should accept what the common sense of mankind dictated:

> It is a bold philosophy that rejects, without ceremony, principles which irresistibly govern the belief and conduct of all mankind in the common concerns of life; and to which the philosopher himself must yield, after he imagines he hath confuted them.[198]

This popular appeal was the more powerful because it was rooted in religious authority. Reid grounded his argument for the validity of sense experience (as had philosophers before him like Locke and Descartes) in the assertion that a benevolent God would not allow us to be deceived. Reid urged:

> Indeed, if we believe that there is a wise and good Author of nature, we may see a good reason, why he should continue the same laws of nature, and the same connections of things, for a long time; because, if he did otherwise, we could learn nothing from what is past, and all our experience would be of no use to us.[199]

Reid produced no formal treatise on natural theology, but he assumed that something like it was part of the equipment of all people's common sense. He declared, for example: "that the most perfect moral rectitude is to be ascribed to the Deity," and that "man is a moral and accountable being, capable of acting right and wrong, and answerable for his conduct to Him that made him," are "principles prescribed by every man's conscience."[200]

Thus Reid provided what Enlightenment conservatives most wanted, an absolute moral sense built in to humankind. Reid had no awareness of historical or cultural relativism, or of concepts of moral development. For him duty was a presupposition, a power that belonged to the "moral sense," the "moral faculty," or "conscience." He contended:

> By an original power of the mind, when we come to years of understanding and reflection, we not only have the notions of right and wrong in conduct, but perceive certain things to be right and others wrong.... There must, therefore, be in morals, as in all other sciences, first or self-evident prin-

ciples, on which all moral reasoning is grounded, and on which it ultimately rests.[201]

For Reid, both the design of the universe and the dictates of conscience were indelibly inscribed by God in the nature of reality. Common sense and inductive investigation were adequate instruments for knowing them.[202]

Along with Thomas Reid and Dugald Stewart a number of other names were prominently associated with Scottish realism. Two less able popularizers of Reid's position, James Beattie (1753–1803) and James Oswald (1715–1769), received much public acclaim but brought Reid's thought into disrepute by oversimplifying it. A third generation of Scottish realists took common sense philosophy into new areas. Thomas Brown (1778–1820) developed a mechanistic psychology that enjoyed immense popularity in Great Britain and the United States for twenty years. Sir William Hamilton (1788–1856) was the last of the major figures of the school. He put Reid together with Kant and provided a synthesis that was very acceptable in his time.[203]

e. Scottish Realism Moves to America: John Witherspoon

John Locke was America's philosopher from about 1714 (when a number of his books were given to Yale University) through the period of the Revolutionary War.[204] In the early 1800s Scottish common sense philosophy began to replace Locke as the dominant influence in American thought.[205]

Scottish Realism and the Framers of the Constitution

American intellectual historians have recently discovered that Scottish realism exerted a significant influence on some of the prominent political leaders in the early years of the American Republic. Thomas Jefferson was indebted for both his religious views and his working philosophy not only to Locke, but also to Dugald Stewart. Jefferson met Stewart in Paris in 1789 and thereafter contended that Stewart was one of the greatest of thinkers. Jefferson's concept of the moral sense was very much like that of Reid and Stewart. Jefferson affirmed with the Scottish realists that religious belief had to be based on reason and evidence. His definition of belief was "the assent of the mind to an intelligible proposition."[206] John Adams agreed with Jefferson in his estimation of Stewart, whom Adams called a genius. James Madison learned the principles of Scottish realism at Princeton from John Wither-spoon to whom we will shortly return.[207]

Scottish realism remained the most powerful force in American intellectual and academic life until after the Civil War. Most American colleges were church-sponsored at this time. Scottish common sense provided an antidote to the philosophical heresies of Hume and Berkeley and a bulwark against the infidelity fostered by the French Revolution (1789–1799).[208] This Scottish realism, which seemed to fit the American situation so well, was the reigning school of thought at the time when philosophy was introduced into the academic curriculum of many American colleges. It was adapted to liberal uses at Harvard and served to strengthen the status quo at Princeton.[209] Generally, Scottish realism was identified as the view of a moderate Enlightenment and moderate Calvinist position. Scottish common sense arguments were used not only against skeptics and deists, but also against mystics and emotionalists in religion.[210]

Baconianism in American Culture

Another name for Scottish realism in American was "Baconianism." In 1823, Edward Everett, a spokesperson for popular culture, declared: "At the present day, as is well known, the *Baconian* philosophy has become synonymous with the true philosophy."[211] American intellectuals were reading Thomas Reid and even more Dugald Stewart (because of his more elegant style).[212] By 1860, Bacon's name had been attached to every area of life to add authority to it. People attributed the beneficient state of poetry, science, philosophy, religion, psychology, medicine, law, and agriculture in America to the guidance given them by the scientific method of Bacon as transmitted by the Scottish realists. A contributor to a religious magazine published in Baltimore in 1841 proclaimed "the noble spirit of the Baconean philosophy" responsible for "the sacredness of the marriage tie, the purity of private life, the sincerity of friendship, charity towards the poor, and general love of mankind" as it was exercised in Anglo-Saxon countries.[213]

In this climate of opinion, Bacon was viewed as an exemplar of Protestant piety.[214] True science and true religion were seen as ultimately harmonious. In the period between 1800 and 1860, probably the majority of scientists and their popularizers were Christians who were eager to demonstrate that science supported religious belief.[215] James Dwight Dana, a leading scientist of the 1850s and editor of the *American Journal of Science* wrote confidently in 1856 that "almost all works on science in our language, endeavor to uphold the Sacred Word."[216] The combination of Newtonian science and Protestant religion formed a distinctively

American ethos during the first half of the nineteenth century.[217] Scientists and churchmen functioned much as the *virtuosi* in England during the seventeenth and eighteenth centuries by applying their philosophy to every area of life.[218]

Scottish realism, which seemed always to confirm the harmony of science and religion in this period, proved incapable of handling the changes in science that occurred after the middle of the century. The publication of Darwin's *On the Origin of Species* in 1859 signaled a new era of conflict rather than harmony between science and religion. Baconian philosophy was so wedded to the concept of static design in nature and to an overly objective view of science that it inhibited its followers from adapting to the turn science was taking. In the religious realm, the doctrine of the scientific inerrancy of the Bible, which had seemed so promising in the seventeenth century, now demanded that people chose between Genesis and geology.[219]

Princeton and John Witherspoon's Moral Philosophy

Books by Scottish common sense philosophers had been available in America early in its history. America gained its own living exponent of Scottish realism when John Witherspoon came to take the presidency of the College of New Jersey (later Princeton College) in 1768. Princeton was located geographically halfway between New York and Philadelphia. During the Revolutionary War the College's Nassau Hall was a place of refuge for the American military forces. Under Witherspoon's presidency, Princeton College became a defender of the orthodox Calvinist faith, buttressed by the philosophy of Scottish common sense philosophy.[220]

John Witherspoon (1723–1794) was a Covenanter by ancestry and a Lowland Scotsman by birth. He studied at the University of Edinburgh and became a minister in the Church of Scotland. Witherspoon became a champion of the Popular (Calvinistic) party in the Scottish Kirk, which opposed the aristocratic Moderate party. In the process he made many enemies. When President Samuel Finley of the College of New Jersey died in 1766, the trustees turned to Scotland for someone who had not been involved in disputes between revivalists and conservatives in America. A young American who was studying medicine in Edinburgh, Benjamin Rush, urged Witherspoon to accept the invitation. He argued that Witherspoon's staunch Calvinism, which had made advancement impossible for him in Scotland, was just what had commended him to the Americans.[221]

Witherspoon came, and is known to most Americans now as the only clergyman to sign the Declaration of Independence. As president at Princeton, he was far from being a revolutionary. Before Witherspoon, the theology of Jonathan Edwards and the idealist philosophy of Berkeley had been powerful at Princeton. Within a year, Witherspoon had gotten rid of all tutors who favored the "new divinity" and had installed Scottish realism as the official philosophy of the college.[222] Witherspoon denounced idealism:

> The truth is, the immaterial System, is an evil and ridiculous attempt to unsettle the principles of common sense, by metaphysical reasonings, which can hardly produce any thing but contempt in the generality of persons who hear it, and which I verily believe never produced conviction even in those who pretend to espouse it.[223]

He offered a solution in the form of Scottish common sense philosophy, contending:

> In opposition to these, some late writers have asserted with great apparent reason, that their [*sic*] are certain first principles or dictates of common sense, which are either simple perceptions, or seen with intuitive evidence. These are the foundation of all reasoning, and without some such principles, to talk of reason, is to use words without any meaning. They can no more be proved than an axiom in mathematical science.
> Authors of Scotland have lately produced and supported this opinion, to resolve at once all the refinements and metaphysical objections of some infidel writers.[224]

Witherspoon coupled these philosophical certainties with simple maxims of the Whig political tradition and began a conservative tradition that proved to have great power in America. Princeton was especially influential in training the leadership of the church and state in the American South. James Madison, the architect of the Constitution, typified many Virginians who felt that the College of William and Mary was too liberal and went instead to Princeton to study under Witherspoon.[225] Princeton graduates founded seminaries in Virginia, Kentucky, and Tennessee, and colleges throughout the South and West.[226] Southern regional conservatism was given a philosophical base in Scottish realism.[227]

Year after year, in unchanged form, Witherspoon delivered a series of lectures on moral philosophy to the seniors in Nassau Hall. (They were published after his death.) For Witherspoon, the great enemy was rationalistic deism. His response was to commend Scottish common sense philosophy as rationally more acceptable.[228] Witherspoon faithfully reflected the Scottish realist approach to religion and passed it on to those who would later found Princeton Seminary. Witherspoon had unbounded confidence in human reason. He said:

> We must distinguish between the *light* of nature and the *law* of nature; by

the first is to be understood what we can do or discover by our own powers, without revelation or tradition: by the second, that which, where discovered, can be made to appear to be agreeable to reason and nature.[229]

The process of discovery in the natural world was always by induction from sense data. Witherspoon sounded the constant note of realist empiricism by appealing first of all to the senses. He stated: "That our senses are to be trusted in the information they give us seems to me to be a first principle because they are the foundation of all our reasonings."[230] Witherspoon continued to commend induction: "It is always safer in our reasonings to trace facts upwards, than to reason downwards upon metaphysical principles."[231] Yet, when it came to Christian doctrines, Witherspoon felt comfortable drawing deductions. He proclaimed: "From reason, sentiment and tradition, the Being and infinite perfection and excellence of God may be deduced."[232] Despite all the appeal to induction to lay an evidential foundation for faith, the followers of Scottish realism blithely switched to deduction for developing doctrine.

Reason and Scripture were always asserted to be harmonious in accord with the principles of Scottish realism. Witherspoon affirmed:

> There are few things more delightful, than to observe that the latest discoveries in philosophy, have never shewn us anything but what is perfectly consistent with Scripture doctrine and history.[233]

Witherspoon laid down the strategy that had become standard in Protestant scholasticism. He urged that the enemy be met on their own grounds with their own weapons, and asserted:

> If the Scripture is true, the discoveries of reason cannot be contrary to it.... It is true that infidels do commonly proceed upon pretended principles of reason.... But as it is impossible to hinder them from reasoning on this subject, the best way is to meet them upon their own ground and show from reason itself the fallacy of their principles.[234]

Thus Witherspoon brought from Scotland to America the apologetic approach to Scripture that had led to conflicts between Scripture and emerging science in Switzerland and England. He prepared the groundwork on which the nineteenth-century Princeton theology would be built. The later fundamentalist-modernist controversy over the inerrancy of Scripture in the twentieth century was, in principle, already set in motion. At the same time, Witherspoon himself did not press Scripture for information in every area as some of his successors would do. He taught: "I am of the opinion that the whole of Scripture is perfectly agreeable to sound philosophy; yet certainly it was never intended to teach us everything."[235] Witherspoon was not as scholastic as Turretin and the Helvetic

Consensus Formula. He said that he found the then-current dispute over the age of the Hebrew vowel points "attended with great uncertainty."[236] Yet he bequeathed a philosphical heritage to American Calvinism that, when later combined with the theology of Turretin, would produce the Princeton scholasticism. That Princeton theology would develop a doctrine of the scientific and historical inerrancy of Scripture that would engender continuing strife on the American religious scene.

f. Summary

The English Reformation underwent a development quite distinct from that on the Continent. The civil war retarded the incursion of the new science and philosophy and thus also slowed the scholastic reaction to them until after the mid-seventeenth century. Puritanism in England drew on native resources of Augustinian anti-Aristotelianism. This Neo-platonic philosophical orientation was supported in the seventeenth century by the simplified logic of French Protestant philosopher Peter Ramus.

The Westminster Divines, meeting from 1642–1649, carried on the Augustinian middle way in theological method, holding that faith leads to understanding. For them the authority of Scripture resided in its central saving message and was affirmed to them by the inner witness of the Holy Spirit. The purpose of the Bible was to join people to Jesus Christ, not to judge matters of science. This central saving message could be known by anyone who read the Bible or heard the gospel preached. Matters of controversy in religion were to be dealt with by scholarship. The historical setting and cultural context of the biblical message were important in understanding the difficult passages, and the grammatical-historical method of exegesis was preferred. The Westminster Divines fought the excesses of High Church rationalists on the one side, and spiritualistic Sectarians on the other. They maintained the Reformation stance that the Word and the Spirit always work together.

John Owen was a transitional figure who illustrated the move toward scholasticism soon after the Westminster Assembly. In reaction to biblical criticism, he contended that the Hebrew original of the Old Testament had been verbally inspired down to the (nonexistent) vowel points. A similar scholasticizing occurred in Scotland through an anonymous commentary on the Westminster Confession of Faith.

After the Restoration of Charles II in 1660, the Royal Society was founded. It became a means of introducing the new science and philosophy in England. Its members were clergymen and scientists who divided religion and science into separate spheres. Gradually reason was given priority over faith even in religious matters. Isaac Newton stood as the final flowering of this trend, introducing mechanical laws governing the universe, but holding to his belief in God. John Locke applied empirical methods to philosophy, hoping to find certain knowledge based on sense experience alone. For him as well reason became the judge of what was appropriate in religion. Theologians adopted a mechanistic, mechanical model by which the Bible was to be judged. Scripture's message had to conform to Newtonian notions of perfection. Many followed the lure of the new science into deism. By the end of the eighteenth century David Hume had followed Locke's lead to the conclusion of skepticism.

Thomas Reid founded a school of Scottish common sense philosophy that sought to answer Hume while remaining solely empirical in method. Reid assumed a simple Aristotelian realism and accepted as normative Bacon's naive method of scientific induction. Reid claimed that the mind directly encountered objects in nature. His assurance that this was so was provided by an intuitive judgment of the mind.

Scottish realism dominated the academic philosophy taught in American colleges during their first half-century. It was brought to Princeton by John Witherspoon in 1768 when he became president of the College of New Jersey. Witherspoon's Scottish realism laid the foundation for the theories of biblical interpretation developed in the late nineteenth and early twentieth centuries at Princeton Seminary.

g. Notes

1. John W. Beardslee, III, ed. and trans., *Reformed Dogmatics* (New York: Oxford University Press, 1965), p. 5.
2. *SWC*, chap. 3, pp. 117–220. For other, very brief treatments of this material, see Jack Rogers, *Confessions of a Conservative Evangelical* (Philadelphia: Westminster Press, 1974), pp. 93–105 and Jack Rogers, ed., *Biblical Authority* (Waco, Tx.: Word Books, 1977), pp. 31–35.
3. *SWC* pp. 82–83. Cf. Robert Hoopes, *Right Reason in the English Renaissance* (Cambridge, Mass.: Harvard University Press, 1962), p. 64.
4. Edward Reynolds, *A Treatise of the Passions and Faculties of the Soule of Man, with the severall Dignities and Corruptions thereunto Belonging* (London, 1640), p. 518, cited in SWC, p.

231. (Hereafter cited as Reynolds, *Treatise.*)
5. *SWC* pp. 234–236. Cornelius Burges, in "The Second Sermon: Preached to the Honourable House of Commons, April 30, 1645. Discovering the Vanity and Mischief of the Thoughts of a Heart Unwashed," caustically characterized a scholastic, charging: "Hee now was the onely man that could chop *Divinitie* into smallest shreds, and drive it nearest together: placing Religion rather in Contemplation rather than action," p. 6, cited in *SWC* p. 235. See also the comments of Edward Reynolds in *Treatise,* p. 397, cited in *SWC,* p. 243.
6. *SWC*, pp. 87–89. Cf. Donald K. McKim, "Ramist Influence on Amesian Methodology," (Pittsburgh Theological Seminary, 1975).

7. *SWC*, pp. 90–94 and 237–238.

8. Samuel Rutherford, "A Sermon Preached to the Honourable House of Commons: At Their Late Solemne Fast, Wednesday, Janu. 31, 1643" (London, 1644), cited in *SWC*, p. 247.

9. Edward Reynolds, "Israel's Prayer in Time of Trouble, With God's Gracious Answer Thereunto; or an Explication of the Fourteenth Chapter of the Prophet Hosea, in Seven Sermons, Preached upon So Many Days of Solemn Humiliation" (1645), *Works* (1826), p. 408, cited in *SWC*, p. 248. (Hereafter cited as Reynolds, "Israel's Prayer.")

10. Samuel Rutherford, *The Tryall and Triumph of Faith* (London, 1645), p. 259 cited in *SWC*, p. 248. (Hereafter cited as Rutherford, *Tryall.*)

11. See the text of the Westminster Confession used here (taken from *The Confession of Faith of the Assembly of Divines at Westminster: From the Original Manuscript Written by Cornelius Burges in 1646*, ed. S. W. Carruthers [London: Presbyterian Church of England, 1946]) in the appendix.

12. Samuel Rutherford, *The Divine Right of Church-Government and Excommunication . . . To Which Is Added, a Brief Tractate of Scandal* (London, 1646), cited in *SWC*, p. 267. (Hereafter cited as Rutherford, *Divine Right.*) A helpful and historically reliable treatment of the Westminster Divines' views on the Bible is contained in John H. Leith, *Assembly at Westminster* (Richmond, Va.: John Knox Press, 1973).

13. *SWC*, pp. 283–285.

14. Edward Reynolds, "An Explication of the Hundred and Tenth Psalm, Wherein the Several Heads of the Christian Religion Therein Contained, Touching the Exaltation of Christ, the Sceptre of His Kingdom, the Character of His Subjects, His Priesthood, Victories, Sufferings, and Resurrection, Are Largely Explained and Applied" (1632), in *Works* (1826), p. 124, cited in SWC, p. 288. (Hereafter cited as Reynolds, "Psalm 110.")

15. Reynolds, "Psalm 110," pp. 5–6, cited in *SWC*, p. 290.

16. Nineteenth-century interpreters often read back into the Westminster Confession a natural theology of the kind that gained a firm place in British Protestant theology only in the eighteenth century. See John Dillenberger, *Protestant Thought, and Natural Science: A Historical Interpretation* (Nashville:

Abingdon Press, 1960, pp. 137–138 (hereafter cited as Dillenberger, *Protestant Thought*), and *SWC*, pp. 291–294.

17. *SWC*, p. 295.

18. *SWC*, pp. 296–297.

19. *SWC*, pp. 298–301.

20. *SWC*, pp. 302–303.

21. Later scholastic theologians such as A. A. Hodge required external evidences to validate the Canon, and asserted an inerrant form of Scripture as an evidence of its inspiration. See *SWC*, pp. 303–305 and A. A. Hodge, *The Confession of Faith: A Handbook of Christian Doctrine Expounding The Westminster Confession* [1867] (London: The Banner of Truth Trust, rep. 1961), pp. 33–34. (Hereafter cited as A. A. Hodge, *Confession of Faith.*) This unhistorical approach on the Westminster Confession has been continued in the twentieth century, for example, by Gordon H. Clark, *What Do Presbyterians Believe? The Westminster Confession: Yesterday and Today*, rev. ed. (Philadelphia: Presbyterian and Reformed Publishing, 1965), p. 15. Clark says: "Against the fundamentalists, who insisted on the inerrancy of the Bible, the modernists asserted that the Confession does not say the Bible is inerrant." Clark sides with the fundamentalists and claims inerrancy as the position of the confession. He perpetuates the false dichotomy between errancy and inerrancy by ignoring the historical middle ground of accommodation. Positions that claim either errancy or inerrancy for the Bible are concentrating on Scripture's form of words. The early church and Reformation position by contrast found the Bible to be inspired and authoritative because of its function of bringing a saving content or message to people.

22. Edward Reynolds, "The Life of Christ" (1631), in *Works* (1658), pp. 269–270, cited in *SWC*, p. 312. (Hereafter cited as Reynolds, "Life of Christ.") One of the nineteenth-century Reformed orthodox writers, E. D. Morris, *Theology of the Westminster Symbols* (Columbus, Ohio: n.p., 1900), pp. 105–106, was forced to admit: "The general fact is that none of the Protestant Confessions attempted any description of that strong external evidence on which primarily the whole question of authoritativeness now rests: they simply appealed even from the judgment of the Church and the historic Councils to this interior proof, and were content with the responsive approval of the

soul that for itself has tasted and seen that the Word is precious." A. A. Hodge had difficulty reconciling the clear teaching of the Confession with his own position at this point. See A. A. Hodge, *Confession of Faith*, pp. 35–36.

23. Rutherford, *Divine Right*, p. 64. To counteract Hooker's view that minor matters of church order were left to human invention, Rutherford was, on occasion, driven to a theory of dictation. He contended, in controversy, that the biblical writers, "in writing every jot, tittle or word of Scripture, they were immediately inspired, as touching the matter, words, phrases, expression, order method, majesty, stile and all: So I think they were but Organs, the mouth, pen and *Amanuenses;* God as it were immediately dyting, and leading their hand at the pen," p. 66. Rutherford was much more circumspect in other writings; and others of the divines, especially the English members, were careful to reject such a scholastic reaction. See *SWC*, pp. 299–302.

24. *SWC*, pp. 103–106 and 244–245.

25. Rutherford, *Divine Right*, p. 99, cited in *SWC*, pp. 366–367.

26. For examples see Reynolds, "Psalm 110," p. 150, cited in *SWC*, p. 313.

27. Christopher Hill, *Intellectual Origins of the English Revolution* (Oxford: 1965), p. 295. (Hereafter cited as Hill, *Intellectual Origins.*)

28. George Gillespie, "A Treatise of Miscellany Questions: Wherein Many Usefull Questions and Cases of Conscience are Discussed and Resolved: For the Satisfaction of Those, Who Desire Nothing More, Then to Search for and Finde out Precious Truths, in the Controversies of These Times," (1649) in *Works* (Edinburgh, 1846), pp. 259–260, cited in *SWC*, p. 321. Gillespie was concerned about persons appealing to a voice of the Spirit they claimed condoned their sins. Gillespie replied: "Tis granted to us that if the voice which speaks peace in a man be not according to the written word of God, it is not the Spirit of the Lord."

29. *Inst.* I, viii, 13: "Therefore Scripture will ultimately suffice for a saving knowledge of God only when its certainty is founded upon the inward persuasion of the Holy Spirit."

30. Rutherford, *Tryall*, p. 98, cited in *SWC*, p. 324.

31. Rutherford, *Tryall*, p. 98, cited in *SWC*, p. 324.

32. Contemporary Reformed scholastics continue to assert that their view is that of the Westminster Confession, without offering evidence from the writers of the Confession. John H. Gerstner published *A Biblical Inerrancy Primer* (Grand Rapids, Mich.: Baker Book House, 1965) in which he attempted to prove that the Bible was inspired and inerrant by arguing from external evidences. He asserts, "That the approach of this *Primer* was abundantly used by the Westminster divines and seventeenth century Orthodoxy, in general, could be extensively illustrated were there any necessity to prove what no one questions," p. 17. Gerstner's thesis was questioned in 1967 by Rogers in *Scripture in the Westminster Confession*, but Gerstner has offered no evidence from the sources to support his claim.

33. See A. F. Mitchell, *Lecture on the Westminster Confession of Faith: Being a Contribution to the Study of Its Historical Relations, and to the Defense of its Teaching*, 2d ed. (Edinburgh: T. Paton, 1866), p. 12, Cf. *SWC*, p. 367.

34. See many citations from Rutherford in *SWC*, pp. 360–367. The nineteenth-century Princeton theologians were not as careful to make that distinction as Rutherford was. A. A. Hodge treats the Bible as a compendium of information on every subject. He says, "The inspired Scriptures of the Old and New Testaments are a *complete* [emphasis his] rule of faith and practice: they embrace the whole of whatever supernatural revelation God now makes to men, and are abundantly sufficient for all the practical necessities of men or communities," *Confession of Faith*, p. 37.

35. James Usher, *A Body of Divinitie, or the Summe and Substance of Christian Religion, Catechistically Propounded, and Explained, by Way of Question and Answer: Methodically and Familiarly Handled* (London, 1645), p. 19, cited in *SWC*, p. 328.

36. *SWC*, pp. 339–347. B. B. Warfield takes the Westminster Divines' statement out of its historical context and uses it to justify a rationally developed system of doctrine. See Warfield, *The Westminster Assembly And Its Work* (New York: Oxford University Press, 1931), pp. 226–227.

37. Reynolds, "The Sinfulness of Sin," (1631) (hereafter cited as Reynolds, "Sinfulness of Sin"), in *Works* (1658), p. 61, cited in *SWC*, pp. 354–355. Warfield, in the interest of promoting rational objectivity, makes just the kind of distinction between knowledge and saving knowledge that Reynolds rejects. See Warfield, pp. 227–228.

38. Usher, p. 21, cited in *SWC*, pp. 369–370 and Article V of the Irish Articles found in E. F. K. Muller, *Die Bekenntnisschriften der reformierten Kirche* (Leipzig: A. Diechert, 1903), pp. 526–527, cited in *SWC*, p. 370.

39. Reynolds, "Israel's Prayer," pp. 412–413, cited in *SWC*, pp. 370–371.

40. Thomas Gataker, "David's Instructer. A Sermon Preached at the Visitation of the Free-Schoole at Tunbridge in Kent by the Wardens of the Worshipfull Company of Skinners," in *Certaine Sermons* (London, 1637), p. 1, cited in SWC, pp. 299–300. (Hereafter cited as Gataker, "David's Instructor.")

41. See Gataker, "David's Instructer," p. 1, cited in *SWC*, p. 300.

42. *SWC*, pp. 375 and 387. Recent interpreters, both scholastic and antischolastic, have generally ignored the Westminster Divines' emphasis on preaching as "means." Interpreters as unlike as Warfield and George Hendry have emphasized the ability of any intelligent person to understand Scripture without taking account of the Westminster Divines' qualifying phrases.

43. See *SWC*, pp. 388–390 for examples. Robert Harris, "A Treatise of the New Covenant: Delivered Sermon-Wise Upon Ezech. 11. ver. 19,20" (1634) (hereafter cited as Harris, "New Covenant") in *Works* (1654), p. 74, states "In that *Rom.* 13 there is an Hebraisme, the soule for the whole man: In this we now urge there is a Grecisme, as we would show if it were needful and with us it is ordinary to use body for the whole man; as when we say, he is a very good body, or a naughty body, that the Greeks often put [*sōmata*] for persons."

44. *Dictionary of National Biography*, ed. Sidney Lee (London: Smith, Elder, 1898), s.v. "Baillie, Robert, D.D." "As a scholar, Baillie was remarkable."

45. Robert Baillie, *Errours and Induration, Are the Great Sins and the Great Judgments of the Time. Preached in a Sermon before the Right Honourable House of Peers, in the Abbey-Church at Westminster, July 30, 1645, the Day of the Monethly Fast.* (London, 1645), pp. 6–7, cited in *SWC*, p. 390.

46. The approach of the Westminster Divines is compatible with the stance of the contemporary "Confession of 1967." See *The Constitution of the United Presbyterian Church in the United States of America, Part I:*

Book of Confessions (Philadelphia: Office of the General Assembly of the UPCUSA, 1967), "The Confession of 1967" 9.29. The whole paragraph, with which the Westminster Divines could well have concurred, reads:

"The Bible is to be interpreted in the light of its witness to God's work of reconciliation in Christ. The Scriptures, given under the guidance of the Holy Spirit, are nevertheless the words of men, conditioned by the language, thought forms, and literary fashions of the places and times at which they were written. They reflect views of life, history, and the cosmos which were then current. The church, therefore, has an obligation to approach the Scriptures with literary and historical understanding. As God has spoken his word in diverse cultural situations, the church is confident that he will continue to speak through the Scriptures in a changing world and in every form of human culture."

47. *SWC*, pp. 391–394. See also "Recent discussion of authenticity," in *SWC*, pp. 394–398.

48. Reynolds, "Israel's Prayer," p. 201, cited in *SWC*, p. 401.

49. The artificial character of the inerrancy position is illustrated by the fact that even Warfield had to admit that Scripture in translation is actually the Word of God. The Word clearly resides in the meaning, therefore, not in some one, pristine set of words. Warfield says, "The sharp distinction that is drawn between the inspired originals and the uninspired translations is, therefore, not permitted to blind men to the possibility and reality of the conveyance in translations, adequately for all the ordinary purposes of the Christian life and hope, of that Word of God which lies in the sense of Scripture, and not in the letter save as in a vessel for its safe conduct," pp. 240–241.

50. Joshua Hoyle, *A Reioynder to Master Malone's Reply* ["to Mr. James Usher"] *Concerning Reall Presence* (Dublin, 1641), p. 220, cited in SWC, p. 415.

51. Reynolds, "Psalm 110," p. 136, cited in *SWC*, p. 415.

52. For the texts see *SWC*, pp. 403–406.

53. Thomas Gataker, *God's Eye on His Israel, or a Passage of Baalam, out of Numb. 23.21. Containing Matter Very Seasonable and Suitable to the Times; Expounded and Cleared from Antinomian Abuse; with Application to the Present Estates of Things with Us* (London, 1645) in

Certaine Sermons, p. 3, cited in *SWC,* p. 407. See also p. 30, cited in *SWC,* p. 407.

54. Edward   Reynolds,.   "Self-Denial. Opened in a Sermon before the Reverend Assembly of Divines on a Day of Their Private Humiliation" (1648), in *Works* (1826), p. 343, cited in *SWC,* p. 411.

55. Thomas Temple, *Christ's Government In and Over His People. Delivered in a Sermon before the Honourable House of Commons, at Their Late Publick and Solemne Fast, Octob. 26, 1642.* (London, 1642), p. 1, cited in *SWC,* p. 419.

56. Rutherford, *Divine Right,* p. 37, cited in *SWC,* p. 419.

57. Cornelius Burges, *Baptismall Regeneration of Elect Infants, Professed by the Church of England, according to the Scriptures, the Primitive Church, the Present Reformed Churches, and Many Particular Divines Apart* (Oxford, 1629), p. 113, cited in *SWC,* p. 420. On pp. 113–114 Burges concludes: "Then this also ought to satisfie all ingenious and moderate men, that by like sound and necessary consequences I have from the scriptures made good this point in hand."

58. Harris, "New Covenant," p. 90, cited in *SWC,* p. 421.

59. Joshua Hoyle, *Jehojadah's Iustice against Mattan, Baals Priest: or the Covenanters Justice Against Idolaters* (London, 1645), p. 2, cited in *SWC,* p. 421.

60. Reynolds, "Psalm 110," p. 124, cited in *SWC,* p. 421.

61. Nineteenth-century Reformed scholastics such as Morris shifted ground from the *kerygmatic* meaning of "searched and known" in the Westminster Confession to a discussion of the need for rational evidences in support of Scripture's authority. Such an endeavor is completely out of harmony with the approach of the Westminster Divines. See Morris, pp. 117–118, cited in *SWC,* p. 417.

62. Gataker, "True Contentment in the Gaine of Godliness, with its Self-Sufficiencie. A Meditation on I Timoth. 6.6," in *Certaine Sermons* (1637), p. 125 cited in *SWC,* p. 426.

63. Harris, "New Covenant," p. 24, cited in *SWC,* p. 427.

64. Reynolds, "Sinfulness of Sin," p. 135, cited in *SWC,* p. 323. Reynolds continues: "Yet it is the Word alone which the Spirit worketh by.... We should therefore pray for the Spirit to come along with his Word."

65. See *SWC,* p. 424 for further discussion of the proximate sources of this section.

66. *SWC,* pp. 425–426.

67. B. B. Warfield, p. 255, for example, wished to restrict this reference in the Westminster Confession to the letter of Scripture rather than including its interpretation by the Spirit. Warfield asserted: "This passage deals with the objective right of Scripture to rule not with the subjective recognition of that right on our part. Nor, even yet can it be read as Dr. Candlish appears to read it, as if the phrase were intended to express the two-fold fact that Scripture is given by the Holy Spirit and our eyes opened to its meaning by the same Spirit, so that it is He, the combined inspirer and illuminator, who is the Judge in all controversies," cited in *SWC,* p. 428. In the twentieth century some theologians reacted too far in the opposite direction in their aversion to the extreme objectification of Scripture by the scholastic Princeton theologians. George Hendry, *The Holy Spirit in Christian Theology,* rev. ed. (Philadelphia: Westminster Press, 1965) notes that phenomenon, commenting: "It is significant, as a reaction against this doctrinal proposition, that a large and vigorous body in contemporary Christendom has turned to seek the authentic demonstration of the Spirit in the unsystematic and the inarticulate," p. 153, cited in *SWC,* p. 429.

68. Reynolds, "Life of Christ," p. 240, cited in *SWC,* p. 426.

69. Alexander Henderson, *The Papers Which Passed at New Castle betwixt His Sacred Majestic and Mr. Al: Henderson: Concerning the Change of Church Government. Anno Com. 1646* (London, 1649) p. 30, cited in *SWC,* pp. 426–427.

70. *SWC,* p. 430. Cf. George Hendry, *The Westminster Confession for Today: A Contemporary Interpretation,* Library of History and Doctrine (London: SCM Press, 1960), pp. 38–39.

71. Robert Harris, "Saint Pauls Confidence" (1628) in *Works* (1654), "To the Printer," p. 27. A marginal reference to the words "leaving the old rule (the written Word)" reads "which was done at Trent." See *SWC,* p. 431.

72. Reynolds, "Psalm 110," p. 248, cited in *SWC,* p. 433.

73. Gillespie, pp. 124–125, cited in *SWC,* p. 436. Cf. Robert McAfee Brown, "Tradition as a Protestant Problem," *Theology Today,* 18 (January 1961): 439.

74. On the life and labors of Owen see the works of Peter Toon: *God's Statesman* (Exet-

er: Paternoster Press, 1971) and his edited works, *The Correspondence of John Owen* (Cambridge, England: James Clarke & Co., 1970) (hereafter cited as Toon, *Correspondence*); and *Oxford Orations*, trans. supervised by John Glucker (Cornwall: Gospel Communications, 1971). See also the older works of William Orme, *Memoirs of the Life, Writings, and Religious Connexions of John Owen D.D.* (London: Printed for T. Hamilton, 1820) and Andrew Thomson, "Life of Dr. Owen," in *The Works of John Owen*, ed. William Goold, 16 vols. (London: Banner of Truth Trust, rep. 1968), 1. (Hereafter cited as Owen, *Works*.) Other information comes from David Masson, *The Life of John Milton: Narrated in Connexion with The Political, Ecclesiastical, and Literary History of His Time*, 7 vols. (London: MacMillan and Co., 1859–94), *passim*.
75. Robert S. Paul, *The Lord Protector, Religion and Politics in the Life of Oliver Cromwell* (Grand Rapids, Mich.: Wm. B. Eerdmans, 1964), p. 204. (hereafter cited as Paul, *Lord Protector*.) It was Cromwell who named him dean of Christ's Church in 1651, and the following year as vice-chancellor of Oxford.
76. Toon, *Correspondence*, p. 47.
77. *Dictionary of National Biography* (Oxford University Press, 1968), XIV, 1319 (hereafter cited as *DNB*.) This article notes of Owen: "When the royalist rising was anticipated in the spring of 1654–55, he made himself responsible for the security of the town and county of Oxford, and was frequently to be seen riding at the head of a troop of horse, well mounted, and armed with sword and pistol."
78. Masson, 5:12. See also Paul, *Lord Protector*, pp. 256–257.
79. See Paul, *Lord Protector*, p. 255, and Masson, 5:71–76.
80. See Paul, *Lord Protector*, pp. 367 and 371. See also Thomson, lxvi–lxvii. and Toon, *Correspondence*, p. 48.
81. For a somewhat more detailed study, see Donald K. McKim, "John Owen's Doctrine of Scripture in Historical Perspective," *The Evangelical Quarterly* 45, no. 4 (October–December 1973): 195–207. (Hereafter cited as McKim, "Owen's Doctrine.")
82. This last work was translated in 1970 by Mrs. Ann F. Castro (M.A. Classics, U. of Indiana) of New Wilmington, Pennsylvania.
83. See also Geoffrey W. Bromiley, "The Church Doctrine of Inspiration," in *Revela-*

tion and the Bible, ed. Carl F. H. Henry (Grand Rapids, Mich.: Baker Book House, 1958), pp. 213–214.
84. Heinrich Heppe, *Reformed Dogmatics*, revised and edited by E. Bizer. Translated by G. T. Thomson (London: Allen & Unwin, 1950), pp. 16–17. See also Robert D. Preus, *The Inspiration of Scripture* (Edinburgh: Oliver and Boyd, 1955) and *The Theology of Post-Reformation Lutheranism*, 2 vols. (St. Louis Concordia Publishing House, 1970), vol. 1, for the Lutheran scholastics.
85. Owen, *Works*, 4:35.
86. Owen, *Works*, 4:32. Italics are Owen's.
87. Owen, "Pro Sacris," Ex. I, sect. 1.
88. Owen, *Works*, 16:297.
89. Owen, "Pro Sacris," Ex. III, sects. 1, 28.
90. Cf. Bromiley, p. 213.
91. See Heppe, p. 26 who speaks of the Holy Spirit's subordinate role "in favour of a false autonomy of Holy Scripture."
92. See Owen, *Works*, 4:20, 50.
93. Owen, *Works*, 4:54. Cf. 4:148. Italics are Owen's.
94. See Owen, *Works*, 4:47, where Owen writes that to say our faith is "the effect and product" of these rational arguments "is both contrary to the Scripture, destructive of the nature of divine faith, and exclusive of the work of the Holy Ghost in this whole matter."
95. Cf. Bromiley, p. 214.
96. Owen, *Works*, 16:309.
97. These are arguments from works of creation and providence; from the innate light of nature implanted by God in men's minds; from "arguments expressing the ways and means of revelation itself." See Owen, *Works*, 16:337, 310.
98. Owen, *Works*, 16:311. Italics are Owen's.
99. See Toon, *Correspondence*, pp. 5–6. Owen's tutor at Queen's College, Oxford (B.A. – 1632) was Thomas Barlow, a distinguished Aristotelian scholar who was regarded as "a master of casuistry, logic, and philosophy." See *DNB*, I, 1144–1145. As Mark Curtis has demonstrated, "the work of college tutors was definitely in the seventeenth century the most important influence on a scholar's education." See *Oxford and Cambridge in Transition* (Oxford: Clarendon Press, 1959), p. 107. Indeed, "from the letters of the time we learn that many a student continued throughout his days to show in his life and conduct the spiritual influence of his college tutor" as well. See Wal-

lace Notestein, *The English People on the Eve of Colonization, 1603–1630* (New York: Harper & Row, 1954), p. 138.

Toon points out that "unlike Puritan contemporaries at Cambridge, he [Owen] never seems to have been introduced to the Ramist critique of Aristotelianism," *Correspondence*, p. 6. Hugh Kearney in *Scholars and Gentlemen: Universities and Society in Pre-Industrial Britain 1500–1700* (Ithaca, N.Y.: Cornell University Press, 1970), writes of Barlow: "He did not recommend Ramus or any of his followers." Kearney attributes the continuation of the old-style scholastic curriculum at Oxford to the influence of Barlow, librarian of the Bodleian Library there from 1642 to 1646. He composed a guide: "A Library for Younger Scholars" which, "in its intellectual tone, pushes us back at once to the Oxford of the 1630s," p. 124.

100. To maintain consistency with the second point listed above, Owen still would have to insist that the Holy Spirit is the agent who causes even these "arguments" to have a persuasive effect.

101. Cf. Bromiley, p. 213.

102. Owen, *Works*, 16:298. See also p. 299.

103. Cf. Bromiley, p. 213.

104. Owen, *Works*, 16:355.

105. Owen, *Works*, 16:350.

106. Owen, *Works*, 16:303. Cf. 16:305. For Owen, "translations contain the word of God, and are the word of God, perfectly or imperfectly, according as they express the words, sense, and meaning of these originals," 16:356.

107. Owen's position is expanded further with a consideration of his *"Pro Sacris"* treatise and how it accords with his other views. For this, see McKim, "Owen's Doctrine," pp. 204–205.

108. See "Prefatory Note" by editor in Owen, *Works*, 16:282. See also discussion in F. F. Bruce, *Tradition: Old and New* (Grand Rapids, Mich.: Zondervan, 1970), pp. 156ff. Bruce gives an historical survey of "tradition and the text of Scripture" and points out that neither Calvin nor his disciples who produced the Geneva Bible in 1560 were disturbed by textual variants. The Geneva Bible in fact drew its readers' attention to such variants by noting them in the margin and did not imagine that "they were confusing their minds or disturbing their faith," p. 155. See also Bruce Metzger, "The Geneva Bible of 1560," *Theology Today*, 17 (1960): 339ff. and Bruce's further discussion, "The

Battle for the Vowel Points," pp. 159–162.

109. "Prefatory Note" by editor in Owen, *Works*, 16:346. See also Orme, p. 269. A. F. Mitchell assigns Owen the role of bringing a more restrictive interpretation to the Westminster Confession because Owen was not satisfied with the degree of its dogmatic strictness. See Alexander F. Mitchell and J. Struthers, eds. *Minutes of the Sessions of the Westminster Assembly of Divines (November 1644 to March 1649) from Transcripts of the Originals Procured by a Committee of the General Assembly of the Church of Scotland* (London, 1874), p. xx. Robert S. Paul has seen a parallel development in terms of Owen's doctrine of the Atonement. Hatred and fear of Socinianism and Arminianism led Owen and other seventeenth-century Calvinist theologians "to render more precise, and therefore more rigid, the penal interpretation of the Atonement." They felt that an attack on their theory of the atonement was an indirect attack on the doctrine of the Trinity. See Robert S. Paul, *The Atonement and the Sacraments* (Nashville: Abingdon Press, 1960), p. 126. See his whole discussion, pp. 117–131.

110. G. D. Henderson, *Religious Life in Seventeenth-Century Scotland* (Cambridge: The University Press, 1937), p. 97. John Macleod, *Scottish Theology in Relation to Church History Since the Reformation* (Edinburgh: Publication Committee of the Free Church of Scotland, 1943), p. 85, attributes the commentary to David Dickson and James Durham. See *SWC*, p. 449.

111. On Bacon see W. R. Sorley, *A History of British Philosophy to 1900* (Cambridge: Cambridge University Press, 1965; rep. 1920), chap. 2 (hereafter cited as Sorley, *British Philosophy*); Basil Willey, *The Seventeenth Century Background* (London: Chatto and Windus, 1967; rep. 1934), chap. 2; and Hill, *Intellectual Origins*, chap. 3. Willey maintains Bacon's chief wish was "to keep science pure from religion," p. 29 while Hill thinks that his separation of science and religion "was in the best Protestant tradition," pp. 92–93. G. R. Cragg, *Freedom and Authority: A Study of English Thought in the Early Seventeenth Century* (Philadelphia: Westminster Press, 1975), chap. 2, maintains that "the effect of Bacon's thought was to encourage the doctrine of twofold truth. He wished to safeguard science against interference by theology," p. 55. (Hereafter cited as Cragg, *Freedom and Authority*.)

112. Sorley, *British Philosophy*, p. 34. See also Hill, *Intellectual Origins:* "Only after 1640 did he acquire the great reputation and influence which he was so long to retain," pp. 14–15. Bacon wrote: "There are two ways, and can only be two, of seeking and finding truth. The one, from sense and reason, takes a flight to the most general axioms, and from these principles and their truth, settled once for all, invents and judges of all intermediate axioms. The other method collects axioms from sense and particulars, ascending continuously and by degrees so that in the end it arrives at the most general axioms. This latter is the only true one, but never hitherto tried," *Novum Organum*, Book I, XIX. In A. R. Hall, *The Scientific Revolution 1500–1800*, 2d ed. (Boston: Beacon Press, 1972; rep. 1962), p. 161.
113. See *SWC* pp. 110–114 and 244–245.
114. Kocher, pp. 10–11. A detailed account of the Reformed attitude to science cannot be given here but Hooykaas points out the influence of Calvin's notion of accommodation; see Hooykaas, pp. 117–124. See also Christopher Hill, *The Century of Revolution 1603–1714* (New York: W. W. Norton, 1966), pp. 92–93. The flow of Calvinism into England is detailed in Charles D. Cremeans, *The Reception of Calvinistic Thought in England, Illinois Studies in Social Sciences*, 31 (Urbana; University of Illinois Press, 1949).
115. Kocher, p. 191. Dillenberger cites "the absence of the intense Catholic problem of the Continent" as another reason why "the relation between science and theology developed differently than on the continent," *Protestant Thought*, p. 104. Hill points out that "over ten per-cent of the books listed in the Short Title Catalogue between 1475–1640 deal with natural science. Nine out of ten of these books were in English. With the doubtful exception of Italy, no country has like so high a proportion of vernacular scientific books at this date," *Intellectual Origins*, p. 16.
116. Richard S. Westfall, *Science and Religion in Seventeenth-Century England* (Ann Arbor: University of Michigan Press, 1973; rep. 1958), p. 34. Dillenberger, *Protestant Thought*, pp. 105–110, details the struggle with Ross.
117. John Wilkins, *A Discourse Concerning a New Planet* (London, 1640), p. 48, as cited by Westfall, p. 34 and Wilkins's comments on Ecclesiastes 3:10 (Prop. II), as cited in Hooykaas, p. 116. Wilkins's attitude resem-

bles that of the Reformed minister Philip van Lansbergen (1561–1632) who was a strict Calvinist and famous astronomer, being "the most zealous propagator of Copernicanism in the Netherlands. He took the view (1619; 1629) that Scripture does not speak about astronomical matters 'according to the real situation but according to appearances.' The testimony of Scripture, so he said, is truth itself, but its authority was wrongly adduced to demonstrate the motions of the heavens; 'Scripture is given by inspiration of God, and is profitable for doctrine, for reproof, for correction, for instruction in righteousness, but it is not meet for instruction in geometry and astronomy,'" cited in Hooykaas, p. 123.
118. Wilkins, pp. 237–239, cited in Westfall, pp. 34–35.
119. Westfall, p. 48. On the *virtuosi* see Dillenberger, *Protestant Thought*, pp. 112–117 and Hooykaas, pp. 126–130; 170–194.
120 This is Kocher's conclusion after discussing the question of whether or not early Puritans were intrinsically attracted to science, p. 4.
121. See Hooykaas, p. 133, and Hill, *Intellectual Origins*, chap. 2, where he expands the list (p. 24).
122. Hill, *Intellectual Origins*, p. 37. See his discussion of the Gresham College circle, pp. 34–63. The question of the relationship between Puritanism and science is a highly controversial one. See Hugh Kearney, *Science and Change 1500–1700*, (New York, McGraw-Hill, 1974), pp. 209–215 (hereafter cited as Kearney, *Science and Change*) and the debates between Kearney and Christopher Hill along with other essays on this theme collected in *The Intellectual Revolution of the Seventeenth-Century*, ed. Charles Webster (London: Routledge & Kegan Paul, 1974). (Hereafter cited as Webster, ed., *Intellectual Revolution*).
123. See *SWC*, pp. 104–106.
124. Bacon, *Works*, III, 218, as cited by Hill, *Intellectual Origins*, p. 91, who calls Bacon "the decisive figure," p. 11. Cf. Kearney, *Science and Change*, pp. 88–95; Hall, pp. 164ff. and Cragg, *Freedom and Authority*, chap. 11.
125. Willey, p. 35. This was a crucial first step toward the rise of scientific deism.
126. Hill, *Intellectual Origins*, p. 93, from F. H. Anderson, *The Philosophy of Francis Bacon* (Chicago: University of Chicago Press, 1948), p. 95.
127. See Hill, *Intellectual Origins*, p. 117,

who claims John Wilkins was "the man who did most to popularize Bacon (and Galileo too)." Hill cites approximately twenty prominent names on which Bacon's influence is traceable; many of these are Puritans. Cf. Hooykaas, pp. 139–141. But see also the opinion of Kearney in "Puritanism and the Scientific Revolution," in Webster, ed., *Intellectual Revolution*, pp. 222ff.

128. Hill, *Intellectual Origins*, p. 125f. See Hall, chap. 7. Histories of the Royal Society are: Thomas Sprat, *History of the Royal Society* (London, 1667) and Dorothy Stimson, *Scientists and Amateurs: A History of the Royal Society* (New York: Greenwood Press, 1968; rep. 1948). Margery Purver and E. J. Bowen, *The Royal Society: Concept and Creation* (Oxford: Clarendon Press, 1960) stresses the role of Baconianism.

129. Joseph Glanvill, *Essays Upon Several Important Subjects in Philosophy and Religion* (London, 1676), IV, 31, as cited in G. R. Cragg, *From Puritanism to the Age of Reason* (Cambridge: Cambridge University Press, 1966), p. 95. (Hereafter cited as Cragg, *Puritanism*.) Glanvill, in an address to the Royal Society exclaimed: "How providentially are you met together in days when people of weak heads on the one hand, and vile affections on the other, have made an unnatural divorce between being wise and good," *Scepsis Scientifica* (1665), cited in Cragg, *Puritanism*, p. 72.

130. Dillenberger, *Protestant Thought* p. 130. He further notes that "statistical evidence points to a predominant Puritan membership in the Royal Society. This does not mean that the Royal Society was unopposed by Puritans; but it does mean that the Puritans more than any other group contributed to the work of the society." The Society and church were seen as complementary agents for reformation in science and religion, p. 129.

131. Westfall, p. 70.

132. Westfall, p. 72. On Aristotle's "Physics," see among other discussions, Bertrand Russell, *A History of Western Philosophy* (New York: Simon & Schuster, 1945), chap. 23.

133. Westfall, pp. 76–77. The problem is further heightened of course, with respect to mechanism and miracles.

134. See Westfall's account of Robert Boyle's and John Ray's dealings with this issue, pp. 83–101.

135. Westfall, p. 106.

136. Westfall, p. 117.

137. Westfall, pp. 125 and 199. Boyle's works are *The Works of the Honourable Robert Boyle*, ed. Thomas Birch, 6 vols. (London, 1772). For a recent and thorough study of Boyle's theology of creation see Eugene M. Klaaren, *Religious Origins of Modern Science* (Grand Rapids, Mich.: Wm. B. Eerdmans, 1977).

138. In Westfall, pp. 133–134, from *The Petty Papers. Some Unpublished Writings of Sir William Petty*, ed. Marquis of Lansdowne. 2 vols. (London: Constable, 1927), 2:251–252.

139. Westfall, pp. 117–118. He states: "In abandoning the true ground of Christianity and arguing religion as though it were natural philosophy, the *virtuosi* did more to challenge traditional Christianity than all of the 'atheists' with whom they did battle."

140. Willey, p. 134.

141. Cragg, *Puritanism*, p. 42 citing, Benjamin Whichcote, *Letters to Tuckney* (London, 1753), p. 118. On the Cambridge Platonists see selections from their writings in C. A. Patrides, ed., *The Cambridge Platonists* (Cambridge, Mass.: Harvard University Press, 1970) (hereafter cited as Patrides, ed., *Cambridge Platonists*); G. R. Cragg, ed., *The Cambridge Platonists*, Library of Protestant Thought (New York: Oxford University Press, 1968). Other studies are by F. J. Powicke, *The Cambridge Platonists* (New York: G. Olms, 1970; rep. 1926); William Cecil de Pauley, *The Candle of the Lord* (Freeport, N.Y. Books for Libraries Press, 1970) and James Deotis Roberts, Sr., *From Puritanism to Platonism in Seventeenth-Century England* (The Hague: Martinus Nijhoff, 1968). The older standard work was John Tulloch's *Rational Theology in England in the Seventeenth-Century*, 2 vols. (Edinburgh: William Blackwood and Sons, 1874), volume 2 dealing with the Cambridge Platonists.

142. Benjamin Whichcote, *Aphorisms*, No. 916. In Patrides, ed., *Cambridge Platonists*, p. 334. On Whichcote see Paul Miles Davenport, *Moral Divinity with a Tincture of Christ: An Interpretation of the Theology of Benjamin Whichcote, founder of Cambridge Platonism* (Nijmegen: n.p., 1972.) See also Whichcote, *Aphorisms*, Nos. 644, 76; and his sermon on Romans 1:18—"The Use of Reason in Matters of Religion" in Patrides, ed., *Cambridge Platonists*, p. 42. John Smith put it positively: "To follow Reason is to follow God," in Willey, p. 72.

The Bible confirmed natural truth for the

Cambridge Platonists. Natural truth was to be known both from Creation and Scripture. As Whichcote put it: "God hath set up two Lights; to enlighten us in our way: the Light of *Reason*, which is the Light of his Creation; and the light of *Scripture* which is the after-Revelation from him. Let us make use of these two Lights; and suffer neither to be put out," *Aphorisms*, No. 109, in Patrides, ed., *Cambridge Platonists*, p. 327. See also Joseph Addison's famous hymn: "The Spacious Firmament on High." On Addison (1672–1719) see *DNB* I, 122–131 and *NIDCC*, p. 12. The hymn is found in many hymnbooks. See for example *The Worshipbook* of The United Presbyterian Church in the United States of America (Philadelphia: Westminster Press, 1970), pp. 595–596.

143. Cragg, *Puritanism*, p. 65, quoting Bishop Edward Stillingfleet (1635–1699), *Origines Sacrae*, 3d ed. (London, 1666), pp. 1–2. This work was apologetic in nature and dealt with the divine authority of Scripture. See *ODC*, 1311.

144. G. R. Cragg, *The Church and the Age of Reason 1648–1789*, Pelican History of the Church, 4 (Middlesex, England: Penguin Books, 1966), p. 72. Cf. Cragg's *Reason and Authority in the Eighteenth-Century* (Cambridge: Cambridge University Press, 1964) (hereafter cited as Cragg, *Reason and Authority*), pp. 43–61, for the story of the Latitudinarians in the eighteenth century.

145. Isaac Newton, *Mathematical Principles of Natural Philosophy*, Great Books of the Western World (Chicago: Encyclopaedia Brittanica, 1952), 34:270–271. Cf. Hall, chap. 9.

146. Dillenberger, *Protestant Thought*, p. 119, citing Newton's *Mathematical Principles*, p. 1.

147. On December 10, 1692. *In Four Letters from Isaac Newton to Doctor Bentley. Containing Some Arguments in Proof of a Deity* (London, 1756), p. 1.

148. *General Scholium* concluding the *Principia*, cited in Hall, p. 273.

149. Westfall, p. 200.

150. Cragg, *Puritanism*, p. 101.

151. Westfall, p. 208.

152. John Locke, *An Essay Concerning Human Understanding* (London: J. M. Dent & Sons, 1974), IV, 10. 1. (Hereafter cited as Locke, *Essay*.) Willey writes: "Locke's Deity, in a word, is that of the contemporary reconcilers of science and religion, such as Glanvill or Boyle, and that of the eighteenth-century as a whole—a Deity to be approached by demonstration, and whose existence, proclaimed by the spacious firmament on high, is as well attested as any proof in Euclid. . . . Newton's Great Machine needed a mechanic, and religion was prepared ahead with that which could serve this purpose," p. 279.

153. Locke, *Essay*, IV. 10. 1. For Locke's thought see R. I. Aaron, *John Locke*, 2d ed. (Oxford: Clarendon Press, 1963); John W. Yolton, *John Locke and the Way of Ideas* (Oxford: Clarendon Press, 1968); James Gibson, *Locke's Theory of Knowledge and its Historical Relations* (Cambridge: Cambridge University Press, 1960; rep. 1917); John W. Yolton, "Locke and the Seventeenth-Century Logic of Ideas," *Journal of the History of Ideas* 16, no. 4 (October 1955): 431–452; and Douglas Greenlee, "Locke and the Controversy over Innate Ideas," *Journal of the History of Ideas* 33, no. 2 (April–June 1972): 251–264.

154. Cragg, *Puritanism*, p. 117. See his chap. 6.

155. Locke, *Essay*, IV. 19. 4.

156. Locke, *Essay*, IV. 18. 5. On Locke's and Newton's religious beliefs see Herbert McLachlan, *The Religious Opinions of Milton, Locke, and Newton* (Manchester: Manchester University Press, 1941).

157. On these men see Westfall, chap. 9.

158. Sorley, *British Philosophy*, p. 145. For a study of the growth of toleration and the later period see Harry Grant Plum, *Restoration Puritanism* (Chapel Hill: University of North Carolina Press, 1943). Cf. A. A. Seaton, *The Theory of Toleration under the Later Stuarts* (New York: Octagon Books, 1972; rep. 1911). The theological struggles of the Socinians are detailed in Herbert J. McLachlan, *Socinianism in Seventeenth-Century England* (London: Oxford University Press, 1951).

159. In John Orr, *English Deism: Its Roots and its Fruits* (Grand Rapids, Mich.: Wm. B. Eerdmans, 1934), p. 62. These were: (1) That there is one Supreme God. (2) That he ought to be worshipped. (3) That virtue and piety are the chief parts of divine worship. (4) That we ought to be sorry for our sins and repent of them. (5) That divine goodness doth dispense rewards and punishments both in this life and the next. See also Willey, chap. 7.

160. See Orr, pp. 109–113, and *ODC*, 181.

161. On Toland, see Cragg, *Puritanism*, pp. 136–155 and F. H. Heinemann, "John Toland and the Age of Enlightenment," *Review of English Studies* 20 (1944), pp. 125–146 and the supplementary note, 25 (1949), pp. 346–349. See also *ODC*, 1383.

162. John Toland, *Christianity Not Mysterious* (London, 1695), cited in Cragg, *Puritanism*, p. 142. See also Orr, pp. 116–121. Cragg, *Reason and Authority*, chap. 3, deals with eighteenth-century deism.

163. See the comparison of Locke and Toland in Sir Leslie Stephen, *History of English Thought in the Eighteenth-Century*, 2 vols. (New York: Harcourt, Brace and World, 1962), 1:78–100.

164. Willey, p. 75.

165. See James A. H. Murray, ed. *A New English Dictionary on Historical Principles*, 11 vols. (Oxford: The Clarendon Press, 1901), 5 (Letter I): 242–243.

166. See, for example, Peter Gay, *Age of Enlightenment*, Great Ages of Man: A History of the World's Cultures (New York: TIME, 1966) Also valuable are his two volumes: *The Enlightenment, An Interpretation: The Rise of Modern Paganism* (New York: Alfred A. Knopf, 1975; rep. 1966) and *The Enlightenment, An Interpretation: The Science of Freedom* (London: Wildwood House, 1973; rep. 1969). See also Franklin L. Baumer, *Modern European Thought* (New York: Macmillan, 1977), pp. 141ff. We are concerned in this work only with the manifestations of the Enlightenment spirit in Great Britain and the United States. In a new and insightful study Henry F. May, *The Enlightenment in America* (New York: Oxford University Press, 1976), p. xiv, defines the word *Enlightenment* in its simplest terms. He states: "Let us say that the Enlightenment consists of all those who believe two propositions: first, that the present age is more enlightened than the past; and second, that we understand nature and man best through the use of our natural faculties." May divides the Enlightenment into four stages: moderate, skeptical, revolutionary and didactic. We are primarily concerned with his fourth category, the didactic enlightenment, "a variety of thought which was opposed to both skepticism and revolution, but tried to save from what it was as the debacle of the Enlightenment the intelligible universe, clear and certain moral judgments, and progress. Its chief center was Scotland. It began before the middle of the eighteenth century, but its principal triumphs in America took place in the first quarter of the nineteenth."

167. May, p. 18. The Dr. Williams Library in London, one of the finest collections of materials on English Presbyterianism, is now a Unitarian foundation. Cf. Lefferts A. Loetscher, *A Brief History of the Presbyterians*, 3d ed. (Philadelphia: Westminster Press, 1978), p. 52.

168. John Herman Randall, Jr., *The Career of Philosophy*, vol. 2, *From the German Enlightenment to the Age of Darwin* (New York: Columbia University Press, 1965), pp. 510–511. Randall states that Reid's uncle "had to defend him at the foot of the pulpit stairs with a drawn sword. Only gradually did they become reconciled to his lack of critical originality in his sermons."

169. Randall, p. 511.

170. Rudolf Metz, *A Hundred Years of British Philosophy* (New York: Macmillan, 1938), p. 30, cited in Theodore Dwight Bozeman, *Protestants in an Age of Science: The Baconian Ideal and Antebellum American Religious Thought* (Chapel Hill: University of North Carolina Press, 1977), p. 5. (Hereafter cited as *PAS*.)

171. Sorley, *British Philosophy*, p. 203. Hume conceded the power of Reid's criticism and wrote a gracious, though noncommital, letter to Reid. See Randall, p. 516.

172. Randall, p. 511.

173. Sorley, *British Philosophy*, pp. 207–208.

174. Randall, p. 513. Reid declared the "inutility" of the syllogism for scientific research. See *PAS*, p. 180, n. 16. Reid's *Aristotle* is found in *The Works of Thomas Reid*, ed. Sir William Hamilton, 2 vols. (Edinburgh, 1846), 2:681–714. (Hereafter cited as Reid, *Works*.) Recently there has been a renewed appreciation of Reid. This follows the reintroduction of realism in Great Britain by, for example, G. E. Moore and Bertrand Russell. A recent collection of critical studies of Reid's work has appeared, including a complete bibliography of works by and about him. See Stephen F. Barker and Tom L. Beauchamp, eds. *Thomas Reid: Critical Interpretations*, Philosophical Monographs, First Annual Series (Philadelphia: Temple University Press, 1976).

175. *PAS*, p. 6 and p. 180, n. 10.

176. *PAS*, pp. 5–7. Stewart observed that the influence of "Lord Bacon" upon Reid "may be traced in almost every page." See Stewart, *Account of the Life and Writings of Thomas Reid* in Reid, *Works*, p. 9. Reid once said of Bacon, "I am very apt to measure a man's understanding by the opinion he en-

tertains of that author," *Works*, p. 11. Robert Blakely, an intellectual historian, remarked that Stewart's enthusiasm for Bacon was "intense and indiscriminate." See Robert Blakely, *A History of the Philosophy of Mind*, vol. 4 (London: Longmans, Brown, Green, & Longman, 1850), p. 8, cited in *PAS*, p. 180, n. 8.

177. Thomas Reid, *Essays on the Intellectual Powers of Man* (Cambridge, Mass.: M.I.T. Press, 1969), Essay 2, chap. 8, p. 145 (hereafter cited as *IP*), cited in *PAS*, p. 7. Stewart claimed that "Newton ... had the rules of the *Novum Organum* constantly in his eye." See Reid, *Works*, 2:712, cited in *PAS* p. 180, n. 14.

178. *IP*, Essay 6, chap. 8, p. 701, cited in *PAS*, p. 8.

179. *PAS*, p. 8.

180. *PAS*, pp. 8–9.

181. Cited in Randall, pp. 513–514.

182. Cited in Randall, p. 514.

183. Randall, p. 514.

184. Thomas Reid, *An Inquiry into the Human Mind*, ed. Timothy Duggan (Chicago: University of Chicago Press, 1970), chap. 6, sec. 20, p. 206, cited in *PAS*, p. 10. Bozeman comments: "Scholars are not agreed upon whether Reid assumed a direct or mediate knowledge of objects 'perceived,' " p. 181, n. 23.

185. Stewart in *The Collected Works of Dugald Stewart*, ed. Sir Thomas Hamilton, 11 vols. (Edinburgh: Thomas Constable, 1854), vol. 2: *Elements*, ch. 1, sec. 3, p. 112 (hereafter cited as *CWDS*), cited in *PAS*, p. 10.

186. *IP*, Essay 2, chap. 5, pp. 111–113, cited in *PAS*, p. 10.

187. *IP*, Essay 2, chap. 20, p. 290, cited in *PAS*, p. 181, n. 24.

188. Cited in Randall, p. 517.

189. *PAS*, p. 11. For a comparison of Reid with Kant see Randall, pp. 516–520.

190. Meyrick H. Carré, *Phases of Thought in England* (Oxford: At the Clarendon Press, 1949), p. 285.

191. *IP*, Essay 2, chap. 20, p. 288, cited in *PAS*, p. 11. Reid, *Inquiry*, chap. 6, sec. 21, p. 216 admits: "[We have] no means of knowing how the body acts upon the mind, or the mind upon the body ... There is a deep and dark gulf between them, which our understanding cannot pass," cited in PAS, p. 181, n. 27.

192. *IP*, Essay 6, chap. 6, p. 655, cited in *PAS*, p. 12.

193. *PAS*, pp. 12–13.

194. *CWDS*, vol. 3: *Elements*, pt. 2, chap. 1, sec. 2, p. 45, cited in *PAS*, p. 13.

195. Thomas Reid, *Essays on the Active Powers of the Human Mind* (Cambridge, Mass.: M.I.T. Press, 1969), Essay I, chap. 6, pp. 43, 45–46, cited in B, p. 13.

196. *IP*, Essay I, chap. 3, p. 46, cited in *PAS*, p. 14.

197. *CWDS*, 2: *Elements*, pt. I, chap. 1, sec. 3, p. 109, cited in *PAS*, p. 14.

198. Cited in May, p. 345.

199. Cited in May, p. 345.

200. Cited in Randall, p. 521.

201. Cited in Randall, p. 520.

202. *PAS*, p. 18. *PAS*, p. 21, lists the principal elements of "Baconianism" that were transferred from Scotland to America: (1) a spirited enthusiasm for natural science; (2) a scrupulous empiricism, grounded upon the confident "trust in the senses" and in the reality of the outer world supplied by the realist doctrine of "judgment"; (3) a sharp accent upon the limits of scientific method and knowledge, directed to the inductive control of generalizations by continuous reference to "facts." Abstract concepts not immediately forged from observed data have no place in scientific explanation; and (4) a celebratory focus upon "Lord Bacon" as the progenitor of inductive science; a flat identification of Newtonian methods with Bacon's "induction."

203. See Randall, pp. 511–512 and Sorley, *British Philosophy*, pp. 209–210.

204. May, p. 33.

205. *PAS*, pp. 21–24. See also I. Woodbridge Riley, *American Philosophy: The Early Schools* (N.Y.: Dodd, Mead, 1907), pp. 475–479.

206. May, pp. 294–295.

207. May, p. 346. Cf. Garry Wills, *Inventing America: Jefferson's Declaration of Independence* (Garden City, N.Y.: Doubleday, 1978), who also recognizes the influence of the Scottish realists on Jefferson. See Part 3, "A Moral Paper."

208. *PAS*, p. 22; see also May, p. 207.

209. Randall, p. 530, notes that John Dewey learned Scottish realism at the University of Vermont.

210. May, pp. 346–347.

211. *PAS*, p. 3.

212. *PAS*, pp. 22–23.

213. *PAS*, pp. 24–26. *PAS*, p. 28, notes that the Disciples of Christ founded Bacon College in 1836 "in honor of Lord Francis Ba-

con, father of the inductive method of reasoning and the new science."

214. *PAS*, pp. 72–76.

215. *PAS*, p. 77.

216. Cited in *PAS*, p. 79.

217. *PAS*, pp. 165–166.

218. *PAS*, p. xiii.

219. *PAS*, pp. 167–168 and xiv. See also May, pp. 358–359. May speaks of an American culture based on a fear of many things that Scottish realism was designed to combat. He contends, p. 359: "What is clear is that whatever its utility, the Scottish Philosophy was not adequate to its task."

220. Riley, p. 481.

221. Riley, p. 485; May, p. 62.

222. May, pp. 62–63. Cf. Sydney E. Ahlstrom, "The Scottish Philosophy and American Theology," *CH* 24 (September 1955): 262.

223. Cited in May, p. 64.

224. Cited in May, p. 64.

225. May, pp. 71 and 96. May says that Madison "arrived at a consistent, lifelong defense of Christianity on the basis of reason and intuition, shifting gradually like many contemporaries from the first to the second."

226. May, pp. 320–321.

227. *BC*, p. 6. Bozeman points out that Baconian philosophy was used to support pro-slavery thought during the 1840s (*PAS*, pp. 25–26).

228. Ahlstrom, p. 262, comments: "Believing as his whole generation seemed to,

moreover, that the then regnant views of Locke and Berkeley led inexorably to the 'skepticism' of Hume or, worse yet, to the materialism of Condildac and the French *ideologues*, they saw no other recourse but to defend orthodox theology with weapons forged in the Scottish universities for quite another kind of battle."

229. John Witherspoon, "Lectures on Moral Philosophy," in *The Works of John Witherspoon, D.D.*, 9 vols. (Edinburgh: Printed for J. Ogle, 1851), 3:368 (hereafter cited as Witherspoon, *Works*), cited in John Oliver Nelson, "The Rise of the Princeton Theology," (Ph.D. dissertation, Yale University, 1935), p. 188.

230. Witherspoon, *Works*, 6:22, 9f., cited in Donald K. McKim, "Archibald Alexander and the Doctrine of Scripture" (hereafter cited as McKim, "Alexander"), *Journal of Presbyterian History* (hereafter cited as *JPH*) 54, no. 3 (Fall 1976):359.

231. Witherspoon, *Works*, 3:390, cited in Nelson, p. 185.

232. Witherspoon, *Works*, 3:388, cited in Nelson, p. 190.

233. Witherspoon, *Works*, 4:53, cited in Nelson, p. 188.

234. Witherspoon, *Works*, 6:22, 9f., cited in McKim, "Alexander," pp. 359–360.

235. Witherspoon, *Works*, 3:369, cited in Nelson, p. 188.

236. Witherspoon, *Works*, 4:501, cited in Nelson, p. 189.

h. Selected Bibliography

Ahlstrom, Sydney E. "The Scottish Philosophy and American Theology," *Church History* 24 (September 1955); 257–272.

Bozeman, Theodore Dwight. *Protestants in an Age of Science.* University of North Carolina Press, 1977.

Carré, Meyrick H. *Phases of Thought in England.* Clarendon Press, 1949.

Cragg, G. R. *Freedom and Authority: A Study of English Thought in the Early Seventeenth Century.* Westminster Press, 1975.

Cragg, G. R. *From Puritanism to the Age of Reason.* Cambridge University Press, 1966.

Cragg, G. R. *Reason and Authority in the Eighteenth-Century.* Cambridge University Press, 1964.

Dillenberger, John. *Protestant Thought and Natural Science.* Abingdon Press, 1960.

Hill, Christopher. *Intellectual Origins of the English Revolution.* Oxford University Press, 1965.

Leith, John H. *Assembly at Westminster.*

John Knox Press, 1973.

McKim, Donald K. "John Owen's Doctrine of Scripture in Historical Perspective." *The Evangelical Quarterly* 45, no. 4 (October–December 1973): 195–207.

May, Henry F. *The Enlightenment in America.* Oxford University Press, 1976.

Powicke, F. J. *The Cambridge Platonists.* G. Olms, 1970 (rep. 1926).

Randall, John Herman, Jr. *The Career of Philosophy.* Vol. II. Columbia University Press, 1965.

Rogers, Jack B. *Scripture in the Westminster Confession.* Wm. B. Eerdmans, 1967.

Sorley, W. R. *A History of British Philosophy to 1900.* Cambridge University Press, 1965.

Tulloch, John. *Rational Theology in England in the Seventeenth Century.* 2 vols. William Blackwood and Sons, 1874.

Westfall, Richard S. *Science and Religion in Seventeenth-Century England.* University of Michigan Press, 1973 (rep. 1958).

Willey, Basil. *The Seventeenth Century Background.* Chatto and Windus, 1967 (rep. 1934).

PART II

Contemporary Response:

Reformed Scholasticism in America and the Recovery of Alternatives in the Reformation Tradition

CHAPTER 5

The Development of Reformed Scholasticism in America

a. Religious Experience and Common Sense Philosophy: Archibald Alexander (1772–1851)

Reformed theology moved from Britain to the New World in several streams. New England was largely settled by the Congregationalists, or Independents as they were known in England. Puritans with Presbyterian sympathies who remained within the Church of England entered the South. Scotch-Irish immigration brought another stream of Calvinism, also modified since the Westminster Assembly, into the middle colonies. People nurtured by these divergent traditions merged to form the Presbyterian Church in its first presbytery in 1706. The significant differences between the traditions have been responsible for the splits and reunions that have marked Presbyterian history since that time.[1]

Alexander's Training

The Presbyterian Church had no center of theological training until the founding of Princeton Seminary in 1812. Until that time it was customary for young men to study with tutors in preparation for ordination examination by the presbytery. One such young man was Archibald Alexander, born on April 17, 1772, in a log cabin seven miles east of Lexington, Virginia, to William and Ann Alexander, Scotch-Irish Presbyterians. In his boyhood young Archibald showed a love for nature as well as a love for learning, being able to read in the New Testament and recite the Westminster Shorter Catechism by the time he was seven years old.[2]

At seven he was sent to school at Timber Ridge; later he went to a series of other schools where he progressed in his study of Latin and Greek. Determined to provide his son with a good education, William Alexander enrolled Archibald in Liberty Hall school (now Washington and Lee College) for which he himself had donated the land. The boy's tutor at this institution was William Graham, a graduate of Princeton College who had studied there under John Witherspoon. Many of the old patriot's Princeton lecture notes were handed on verbatim to Alexander and other students by Graham.[3] Graham was an amateur scientist who impressed on young Alexander an ardor for "the Newtonian system."[4] Later Alexander paid high tribute to Graham, who was also a thoroughly grounded classicist with particular interest in the "philosophy of the mind," acknowledging him to be the prime director of his thoughts and molder of his character.[5]

After seven years studying with Graham, Alexander became a private tutor for the family of General John Posey. Using the household library, he read a great deal and spent hours in solitary meditation. Though he had learned the Shorter Catechism and most of the Larger, "but without reflection," he was utterly averse to spiritual things and committed to his own religion only because he had been brought up in it.[6] He also disliked the common revivalism which was growing in that area for he had "never heard of any conversion among Presbyterians."[7] While earnestly seeking a religious experience, the young man candidly confessed that his moments of spiritual uplift were brief and seldom.[8]

About this time Alexander found a tract entitled "Internal Evidences of the Christian Religion by Soame Jenyns, Esq." in an old trunk of books. Alexander described his reading of this work by saying, "At every step conviction flashed across my mind, with such bright and overwhelming evidence, that when I ceased to read, the room had the appearance of being illuminated."[9] A theological interest was thus awakened. He began to do more theological reading and to have deeper concerns about his own salvation.

In this period Alexander took a trip with Graham to visit the scenes of the various revivals in the Blue Ridge region. Though he heard many revival sermons and had long theological discussions, he felt himself full of inner conflicts, doubts, and fears about his own "hardness of heart" and hopes for salvation.[10] At times he "rolled on the ground in anguish of spirit."[11] He spent long periods in the woods in prayer and Bible reading but still emerged tasting the "bitterness of despair."[12] After this time of spiritual struggling, he had several experiences in which "the whole plan of grace appeared as clear as day."[13] He knew that "Christ as an Advocate was able to save me."[14] Thus Alexander came to make a profession of his Christian faith in 1789. He felt that the "Sun of Righteousness began to rise on me, though under a cloud." Yet in later years he concluded that his regeneration took place the year before at General Posey's. This demonstrated to him "how seldom believers can designate with exactness the time of their revival."[15] Nonetheless, in his own personal experience Alexander knew the potency of the revival spirit.

After returning home and being dangerously ill for a time, he recovered to face the question of his profession. He was inclined toward the gospel ministry but had doubts about his fitness for such a work. Nevertheless he went to his old teacher Mr. Graham and asked him to direct his reading. Graham smiled and told him, "If you mean ever to be a theologian, you must come at it not by reading but by thinking."[16] This piece of advice he remembered for the rest of his life. Nevertheless, in preparation for ordination, he read theological works including Edwards's *Freedom of the Will, Original Sin,* and *Religious Affections* as well as works by John Owen and Thomas Boston (1676–1732). At this point, Witherspoon's *Lectures on Moral Philosophy* did not interest Alexander much. But he did become familiar with Francis Turretin's theology by reading it in a Latin compendium.[17]

Alexander intended to go home for study after being ordained, but the opportunity for a preaching tour of the "circuit rider" type became available. Alexander accepted it. Later he was called to a co-pastorate that involved six churches in an area sixty miles long and thirty miles wide. So, during the closing years of the eighteenth century, the new minister did the work of a rural pastor and itinerant missionary on the colonial frontier of Virginia and Ohio, where he enjoyed success and a high reputation for his abilities.[18]

In 1797 Alexander accepted the presidency of Hampden-Sydney College where he also taught science for a time.[19] He resigned in 1801 to take a tour of New England where he was exposed to the "New Theology" of the post-Edwardian era. After he returned, his views, which had been somewhat modified by eastern suggestions, began to fix themselves more definitely in the direction of the theology received from his tutor Mr. Graham.[20] Socially and politically, Alexander was confirmed in his stance as a Virginian and Southerner.[21]

Alexander married Janetta Waddel in 1802 and resumed his college presidency. In 1807 he accepted the call to the Third (Pine Street) Presbyterian Church in Philadelphia. He quickly became a well-known preacher and pastor, while beginning a number of new projects including Sunday evening services, an Evangelical Society using street preaching and two-by-two visitations, the Philadelphia Tract Society, and a Foreign Missions Society.[22] In 1810 he received the Doctor of Divinity degree from the College of New Jersey.

Another project that claimed Alexander's attention was the creation of a theological seminary. As the Presbyterian Church then had no such institution, it became Alexander's increasing conviction that this situation should be remedied. So, in 1808 he preached a sermon to this effect to the General Assembly of which he had been moderator the previous year. The challenge was picked up and in 1809 a seminary was proposed. By 1810 it was clear that interest was great. In 1811, Alexander chaired a committee that drew up plans for the establishment of Princeton Theological Seminary the following year. In 1812, "amid the tears and prayers of the church" Alexander was elected Princeton's first professor.[23] Most felt that no one in the Church, except Alexander himself, had any doubt that he was the man best suited for the job.[24] On August 12, 1812, Archibald Alexander was inaugurated and set out on the great work of planning and instituting the courses of instruction at Princeton Seminary, which were to have such a strong influence in the years to come.

The Influence of Turretin and Scottish Realism

Alexander centered seminary studies in the works of Turretin and the Scottish common sense philosophy popularized in America by Witherspoon. Alexander's biographer wrote:

> Dr. Alexander . . . conceived that theology was best taught by a wise union of the text book with the free lecture. Finding no work in English which entirely met his demands he placed in the hands of his pupils the *Institutions* of Francis Turretin.

Despite the fact that the works of Calvin and the Westminster Divines were available, it was Turretin in Latin that became the standard text at Princeton. It remained so for sixty years until in 1872 Charles Hodge's *Systematic Theology* replaced it as an updated English version of the same theology. Alexander's practice was to assign twenty to forty pages of Turretin in Latin and at the next class to ask the students for an exact repetition of what they had read. He acknowledged that Turretin's work was "ponderous, scholastic and in a dead language." Nonetheless, he felt that if seminarians studied "this athletic, sinewy reasoner of the faith," they "were apt to be strong and logical divines."[25]

Alexander's course in "mental science" at Princeton Seminary was almost a transcript of the thought of Thomas Reid and Dugald Stewart adapted to theological concerns.[26] Alexander declared that when theologians confronted the topics of "speculative philosophy" they would "seldom err," if they were "governed by the plain principles of common sense." Scottish common sense philosophy was identified with correct thinking by Alexander. He asked his theology class in 1837: "What is reasoning?" The students recorded his answer in their notebooks: "The exercise of comparing facts with each other and impressions with external things."[27] Alexander inculcated in his students a single standard of knowing—that of Baconian empiricism. He stated that "knowledge is the apprehension of truth," for example, that birds *do* sing and that honey *is* sweet.[28] The effect of this commitment to Scottish empiricism for Alexander was to make reason prior to faith. Alexander concluded that "unless the Christian religion is attended with sufficient evidence, we cannot believe in it, even if we would."[29] He believed that the Bible itself supported the empiricist approach. He read Christ in the New Testament as urging his disciples rationally to weigh the empirical evidence of His divinity. Unquestionably his miracles were credible, they were "capable of satisfactory proof from testimony." And this proof was decisive for Alexander. For by the "constitution of his nature" one was "under the necessity of believing what he saw with his eyes, heard with his ears, and handled with his hands."[30]

Antideist Apologetics

The original "Plan" of Princeton Seminary was organized around the effort to combat deism. The deists held that the only revelation needed was the moral law evident in nature and discovered by reason.[31] The Princeton theologians wanted to show "the right use of reason in religion" and also the need for biblical revelation.[32] Witherspoon earlier had laid down the strategy of meeting the enemy on his own ground with his own weapons. Princeton theologians were to "show from reason itself the fallacy of their [deists'] principles."[33] To this end Alexander asserted:

> Without reason we can form no conception of a truth of any kind; and when we receive any thing as true, whatever may be the evidence on which it is founded, we must view the reception of it to be reasonable. Truth and reason are so intimately connected that they can never with propriety be separated.[34]

Thus the "Plan of the Seminary" provided that "every student ... must have read and digested the principal arguments and writings relative to what has been called the deistical controversy—Thus he will be qualified to become a defender of the Christian faith."[35] For Alexander, reason was a beneficial tool through which Scripture was to be interpreted since "it is reasonable to believe whatever God declares to be true." In fact, it was just as "reasonable" to believe this as it was "to believe what by our senses we perceive to exist."[36] Alexander thus began to treat verbal statements in Scripture as equivalent to objects in nature, an approach Charles Hodge would develop more self-consciously.[37]

There was a double thrust, an epistemological dualism, in Alexander's thought. True knowledge could come both through reason *and* religious experience. This was graphically portrayed in the preface to his volume *Religious Experience:*

> Thus it is found, that nothing tends more to confirm and elucidate the truths contained in the word, than an inward experience of their efficacy on the heart. . . . Genuine religious experience is nothing but the impression of divine truth on the mind, by the energy of the Holy Spirit.[38]

To bring the battle to the deists, Alexander upheld the potency of human reason. But from his firsthand knowledge of the vitalities of Christian experience, Alexander held both reason and religious experience to be valid ways of knowing truth.[39] In the academic realm, reason was accented, although, in the personal realm, experience was approved.[40]

Princeton's antideistical orientation gave rise to an apologetic defense of Christianity based on "evidences." To help prove that Princeton had an unshakably "reasonable" religion and a "certain" basis for authority in the Bible, Alexander contributed his *Evidences of Christianity* in 1825 and enlarged it in 1836. Besides dealing with "evidences" for Scripture's authenticity, inspiration, and canonical authority, Alexander devoted considerable space to two subjects supremely essential for the Christian apologetic: miracles and prophecy.[41] The attacks of David Hume on biblical miracles did much to provoke these concerns, so it is not surprising that Alexander continually pointed to fallacies in Hume's work. In his *A Brief Compend of Bible Truth* Alexander crystallized the Princeton position when he wrote: "The truth of Christianity then, rests on this single point, Is the testimony of these miracles true, or a mere fable?"[42] Prophecy was an even more powerful persuader, according to Alexander, since "no one but God himself can foretell distant events which depend entirely on the purpose of Him 'who worketh all things after the counsel of his own will.' "[43]

Eleven chapters of Alexander's *Evidences* provided his doctrine of Scripture. One of these was on the Bible's internal evidence of its divine origin (that is, from the intrinsic sublimity of the gospel message itself); two were on inspiration; and eight were on the canonical authority of scriptural books. The primacy given to internal evidences reflected Alexander's own religious experience through reading the Bible. The extensive treatment given to external evidences for canonicity evidenced the influence of Turretin's scholastic concerns.

Alexander believed that "more instances have occurred of skeptical men being convinced of the truth of Christianity by the internal than by the external evidences."[44] They were thus to him one of Christianity's "firmest props."[45] In particular they were a bulwark against the deists who wanted to use unbridled reason as the judge of revelation. But this method was most "unreasonable" Alexander argued.[46] Instead, Alexander felt that one could become convinced of the Bible's divine origin by studying the Book itself, and letting its own "evidence" speak to the heart. Saving faith belonged to this "internal evidence," not as "perceived by the unaided intellect of man, but as it is exhibited to the mind by the illumination of the Holy Spirit."[47] This evidence could come only through Bible study and

> cannot easily be put into the form of logical argument, for it consists in moral fitness and beauty; in the adaptation of truth to the human mind; in its astonishing power of penetrating and searching the heart and affecting the conscience. There is a sublime sanctity in the doctrines and precepts of the gospel; a devotional and heavenly spirit pervading the Scriptures; a purity and holy tendency which cannot but be felt by the serious reader of the word of God; and a power to sooth and comfort the sorrowful mind; all which qualities may be perceived, and will have their effect, but cannot be embodied and presented, with their full force, in the form of argument.[48]

Alexander's own experience with Scripture had brought him to a posture close to that of Calvin.

However, in order to present his readers with a "salutary impression" Alexander developed three of these internal evidences in a more scholastic manner: (1) "That the Scriptures speak of God and His attributes in a way which accords with what right reason would lead us to expect in a divine revelation." (2) "The account which the Bible gives of the origin and character of man accords very exactly with reason and experience." (3) "That the Scriptures contain explicit information on those points on which man stands most in need of instruction." (These are: the doctrine of the future state or retribution, pardon of sin, and restoration from the depraved nature.)[49] These three evidences summarized Alexander's complete apologetical concerns: (1) that Scripture provided a correct theology that could be reasonably defended; (2) that the biblical accounts were affirmed by the reality of human experience; and (3) that humans could not go "all the way with Reason" as the deists wished, since revelation was still needed. Alexander thus incorporated his concern for the internal work of the Spirit into the framework of a philosophical apologetic. In doing so he moved away from the convictions of the Reformers and toward the style of scholasticism.[50]

Degrees of Inspiration

On the question of inspiration, Alexander made concessions that his later followers rejected.[51] Inspiration was confined to those men who wrote the biblical books whereas "illuminating," an enabling of the soul to receive revealed truths, was available to all. Inspiration consisted, for Alexander, of three kinds: (1) superintendence, (2) suggestion, and (3) elevation.[52] "Superintendence" indicated guidance but no new revelation of facts to the writer. The second type of inspiration, "suggestion," had the function of communicating new information. Here the Spirit inspired ideas, "suggesting" them to the writers. The third type of inspiration, "elevation," took place when a writer spoke or wrote in ways or words "far more sublime and excellent than they could have attained by the exercise of their own faculties."[53]

Alexander's distinctions regarding inspiration enabled him to take a mediating position on the question of whether the words as well as the ideas of Scripture were given by inspiration. He wrote: "It is probable, that in this controversy as in many others, both parties are right; or rather that the truth will be fully possessed by adopting the views entertained on both sides, and endeavoring to reconcile them." [54] With the revealing of new truths, "it is necessary to suppose that the words as well as ideas, were immediately suggested by the Holy Spirit."[55] "But," continued Alexander,

> as in the narration of well-known facts, the writer did not need a continual suggestion of every idea, but only to be so superintended, as to be preserved from error; so in the use of language in recording such familiar things, there existed no necessity that every word should be inspired; but there was the same need of a directing and superintending influence as in regard to the things themselves.[56]

By arguing in this way, Alexander preserved each writer's characteristic style. He used the imagery of "a father conducting a child along a narrow path. The child walks by its own activity and takes steps according to its ability; but the father preserves it from falling and keeps it in the straight path."[57] Biblical writers thus retained their own peculiar style of writing and expression "as fully, as if they were writing or speaking without inspiration."[58] Alexander's use of the imagery of God as parent relating to the biblical writers as children functioned quite differently than that same imagery when used by Origen, Chrysostom, Augustine, and Calvin. For the earlier theologians, the parent entered the world of the child's experience and accepted the child's limitations. For Alexander, the parent hovered over the child and guided the child in the parent's path. The distinction is subtle but important.

Alexander rejected as groundless objections from those who "object to this theory of superintendence, under the impression that it is less perfect, than if everything were inspired by direct suggestion of the Holy Spirit."[59] He regarded the "clear intuitive knowledge which we possess of truths" as a "sort of permanent inspiration."[60]

The Concept of Error and Canonicity

Because of his roots in Turretin, however, Alexander held fast to the postulate of the Bible's inerrancy in all things. He wrote: "And could it be shown that the evangelists had fallen into palpable mistakes in facts of minor importance, it would be impossible to demonstrate that they wrote anything by inspiration."[61] For Alexander, plenary inspiration was "such a divine influence upon the minds of the sacred writers as rendered them exempt from error, both in regard to the ideas and the words."[62]

Originally Alexander had predicated the divine origin of the Bible primarily in internal evidence—the power of the gospel message. As time passed he sought more objective external criteria to prove that the canonical Scriptures were authoritative. Alexander sought to certify the list of inspired biblical books by appealing to the authority of Christ with the sanctions of Christ and his apostles: He wrote: "The unqualified testimony in favor of the Old Testament by Christ and his apostles already referred to, ought to be decisive on this point, if all other evidence was wanting."[63] He rejected the Apocrypha as canonical Scripture on the basis of both external and internal evidence. For the New Testament Scriptures, the testimony of the church could not establish authority, nor could the internal evidence of the book. If canonical status was gained solely by internal evidence, he felt "this principle would have a tendency to unsettle the canon, and there would be no certainty as to the rule of our faith."[64] Therefore, Alexander wished to shift from "faith" to "sight" by having the criterion for canonicity be a matter of fact:

> It is whether the books which compose the New Testament, were written by inspired men; that is, by the men whose names are affixed to them, the apostles and disciples of our Lord, who were eyewitnesses of the facts which they have recorded.[65]

The rudiments of the Princeton theology as set forth by Archibald Alexander remained unchanged for over one hundred years. But the emphases did change as the Princeton theologians rigidified in the face of mounting opposition to their scholastic style.[66] For Alexander, Christian experience was foundational. Reason and evidence were utilized to confirm experience. Alexander approximated the Reformation balance of the Word and the Spirit, and acknowledged that the practical purpose of theology was to bring persons into a relationship with God which would lead to worship and right living. One of Alexander's arguments against deism was that the deists had not been "most zealous and consistent worshippers of God."[67] He felt that no miracle could give stronger evidence of the divine origin of the gospel than that it was used of God to reform wicked men.[68] This emphasis on religious experience and the inner working of the Holy Spirit was gradually subordinated and finally suppressed in the Princeton theology.[69]

b. Piety and Turretin's Systematic Theology: Charles Hodge (1797–1878)

Charles Hodge, the son of a surgeon, was born in Philadelphia.[70] His father died when he was six months old due to overwork during the yellow-fever epidemic of 1797. Hodge recorded that his mother saw to his religious training: "She took us regularly to church, and carefully drilled us in the Westminster Catechism, which we recited on stated occasions to Dr. Ashbel Green, our pastor."[71] His mother enabled Charles and his older brother Hugh to get college educations in part by moving to Princeton and boarding college students. The move to Princeton came in 1812, the year that Princeton Seminary was founded and Archibald Alexander was installed as its first professor. Hodge stated many years later: "I can well remember, then a boy of fourteen, lying at length on the rail of the gallery [of the Presbyterian Church] listening to the doctor's inaugural address and watching the ceremony of investiture."[72] During that same summer, Alexander sought out the young Hodge and established a friendship with him that remained unbroken. Hodge entered the sophomore class at Princeton College in the fall of 1812. With the founding of the seminary, an agreement had been reached to suspend the teaching of theology at the college. Princeton College had only four faculty members, and Hodge studied the Bible, belles-lettres, moral philosophy, and logic with the president, Dr. Ashbel Green, who had been the Hodge family's pastor in Philadelphia. The students were required to memorize the Westminster Shorter Catechism in Latin. In philosophy they studied former President Witherspoon's lectures in moral philosophy.[73] It was during a revival at the college in 1815 that the young Hodge felt himself to be converted.[74]

Hodge attended Princeton Seminary from 1815 to 1819. His study of theology under Archibald Alexander fixed his thought and determined his vocation. After graduation from seminary, Hodge followed a plan proposed by Alexander, and spent the next school year at home in Philadelphia studying the system of punctuating and accenting Hebrew with points (a system with which Alexander was not familiar). Hodge studied Hebrew with a Dr. Joseph Banks of the Associate Presbyterian Seminary in Philadelphia and also broadened his education by attending lectures in anatomy and physiology at the medical department of the University in Philadelphia.[75] During this year, Hodge was licensed to preach and did so, often several times each Sunday.[76] In May 1820, the General Assembly of the Presbyterian Church approved the hiring of "an assistant teacher of the original languages of Scripture" and the professors of the Seminary appointed Charles Hodge to the position.[77] He returned to Princeton Seminary in June 1820 and boarded in Alexander's home until Hodge married in 1822.[78] Charles Hodge remained on the faculty at Princeton for fifty-eight years. He was made professor of oriental and biblical literature in 1822 and in 1840 was transferred to the chair of didactic theology. He continued to teach New Testament exegesis, however, until his death.[79]

After teaching four years, Hodge asked for and was granted a leave for two years study in Europe. He felt very inadequately trained in languages and also wanted the broadened knowledge of contemporary theology which that experience would afford him. Alexander was reluctant to have Hodge exposed to German thought but consented.[80] Hodge provided as his substitute for the two-year period a member of the newly graduated class, John W. Nevin (1803–1886). (Later, Nevin helped develop the "Mercersburg Theology," which provided an alternative to the Princeton theology among the German Reformed Churches in America.)[81] Hodge left his wife and two children in the care of his mother and his brother Hugh, who was a medical doctor. First he went to Paris where he studied French, and Arabic and Syriac with De Sacy.[82] In Germany he sought out the more conservative theologians, those whose thought was substantially the same as Alexander's. From August Tholuck at Halle, Hodge learned arguments to counter the prevailing German rationalist thought. At Berlin Hodge learned from Hengstenberg how to reply to the technical arguments of the higher critics. Hodge heard Schliermacher and the critic Gesenius as well, but their thought and that of other more liberal theologians seemed only to have the effect of strengthening him against them.[83]

Hodge's Influence

In 1825, just prior to leaving for Europe, Charles Hodge began the publication of a quarterly journal known first as *Biblical Repertory: A Collection of Tracts in Biblical Literature*. For the first four years it was filled almost exclusively with reprints and translations of essays by European scholars. The name was changed in 1829 to *Biblical Repertory and Theological Review* and after 1836 it was known as the *Biblical Repertory and Princeton Review.* [84] Hodge edited this journal for forty-six years. He was also the principal contributor to its pages. His 142 articles and innumerable reviews would have filled about ten volumes. They covered the range of every controversial subject of his day, including theology and biblical criticism, metaphysics and psychology, personal, ecclesiastical, and political ethics, and all phases of ecclesiastical theory and practice.[85] Hodge's views were thus presented piecemeal and in relation to particular issues. From the beginning to the end of his tenure, however, his views never changed.[86] His *Systematic Theology*, published in three volumes near the end of his career in 1872–1873, was largely composed of the material developed earlier in the pages of this journal. Hodge was proud of his unbending consistency. He held to the same views, for example, of slavery, both before and after the Civil War. He wrote in 1865: "With regard to slavery, both in its moral and political aspect, we stand now just where we always have stood. The doctrine advocated in his journal in 1836 is still our doctrine."[87] (He contended that slaveholding was not necessarily a sin and opposed abolitionism, while at the same time abhoring the evils of slavery and the defense of it by the South.)[88] In a retrospective of the History of the *Princeton Review* in 1868 Hodge asserted his lack of originality:

> It is with unfeigned and humble gratitude to God that the conductors of the *Biblical Repertory and Princeton Review* can look over the comparatively long period of its existence with the conviction that from first to last it has been devoted to the vindication of that system of doctrine contained in our standards, and which, as all Presbyterians believe, is taught in the word of God. No article opposed to that system has ever appeared in its pages . . . Whether it be a ground of reproach or of approbation, it is believed to be true that an original idea in theology is not to be found in the pages of the *Biblical Repertory and Princeton Review* from the beginning until now. The phrase 'Princeton Theology,' therefore, is without distinctive meaning.[89]

This same attitude of unchanged commitment to a particular system of theology was manifested by Hodge in his remarks at the celebration of his fiftieth year as professor at Princeton. He declared:

> Again, Drs. Alexander and Miller were not speculative men. They were not given to new methods or new theories. They were content with the faith once delivered to the saints. I am not afraid to say that a new idea never originated in this Seminary. Their theological method was very simple. The Bible is the word of God. That is to be assumed or proved. If granted; then it follows, that what the Bible says, God says. That ends the matter.[90]

Hodge rearranged, but never consciously altered, any article in the system of doctrine he received from his mentors.[91]

Through his writing and training of students, Charles Hodge exerted a powerful conservative force in the Presbyterian Church and in other denominations. Preachers, teachers, and college presidents went forth from Princeton carrying Hodge's thought to others in all parts of the country.[92] Hodge taught over 3,000 seminary students, more than any other American in the nineteenth century. Thousands more agreed with Princeton Seminary President Francis L. Patton's evaluation of Hodge's 2,000 page *Systematic Theology* as "the greatest system of dogmatics in our language."[93] Each year, with one exception, from 1835 to 1867 Hodge wrote a critical review of the annual meeting of the General Assembly of the Presbyterian Church, which exerted great influence in his denomination.[94] In the controversies in the Presbyterian Church between the New School, which favored revivalism and more liberal measures, and the more conservative Old School, Hodge sided consistently with the Old School in both doctrine and polity. The New School men tended to follow the New England theology of Jonathan Edwards, which stressed personal experience. They inclined toward philosophical idealism. And many were abolitionists. The Old School adherents favored the more objective theology of Turretin's scholastic Calvinism. Philosophically, they held to Scottish common sense realism. And the Old School partisans deemphasized the slavery issue out of deference to their southern adherents. When the Old School party gained control of the General Assembly in 1837, the more liberal presbyteries were ejected. Hodge defended the division in the church and served as moderator of the (Old School) Presbyterian Church in 1846. He resisted the proposed reunion of the two bodies in 1867 as not sufficiently guaranteeing what he considered the distinctive doctrines of Calvinism. He nonetheless acquiesced to the union when consummated in 1869.[95]

Hodge wrote a *Constitutional History of the Presbyterian Church in the United States* in 1840 in which he set forth a logical argument for the Old School position as essential Presbyterianism. In addition to that and his *Systematic Theology*, Hodge produced other influential works. His first, in 1835, was *A Commentary of the Epistle to the Romans*, which went through nineteen editions by 1880. He published other commentaries: on Ephesians (1856), First Corinthians (1857), and Second Corinthians (1859).

One of his most widely read works was a popular presentation of systematic theology, *The Way of Life*, published by the American Sunday School Union in 1841 and bearing the recommendation of all evangelical denominations. It was reprinted by the London Religious Tract Society and translated into other languages.[96] *The Way of Life* exhibited the balance of objective and subjective elements, of doctrine, and of application more than any of Hodge's other works. In it, for example, he stressed the power of the internal evidence of Scripture itself in producing faith, whereas external evidences were more prominent in his more scientific theological writings.[97] The genuine piety and personal warmth evidenced in this work were embodied by Hodge in the Sabbath Conferences with Princeton Seminary students and faculty. These weekly sessions were held for the discussion of questions of experiential religion and the duties of the Christian life. Hodge and the other faculty appeared as friends and pastors rather than instructors. The cold logic of controversy was replaced by the warmth of living concern.[98] The last book Hodge wrote was *What Is Darwinism?* in 1874.[99] It symbolized the change in circumstances that had overtaken Hodge and the Princeton theology. When Princeton Seminary began, the faculty had confidence that the leading authorities in natural science supported their position. By the time of Hodge's death, the scene had changed drastically. From then on, the Princeton theology was increasingly on the defensive as its static system no longer cohered with the directions that developmental science was taking.[100]

Biblical Criticism

The developmental approach of the natural sciences was also being adapted to the study of historical documents in the nineteenth century. Textual Criticism (also called "Lower Criticism") was the attempt to determine the original state of the biblical text and its content by a comparison of all the available manuscript evidence. This had been known, and resisted, by Turretin and the Reformed scholastics of the seventeenth century.[101] By the time of the Princeton theology, this science was considered acceptable, and one of Hodge's purposes in going to Europe was to learn more of it. Gradually, during the nineteenth century, a new threat appeared on the horizon. It was Higher Criticism.[102] The term came into common use only after the appearance in 1881 of W. Robertson Smith's book, *The Old Testament in the Jewish Church.* Smith's articles in the 1875 and 1880 editions of the *Encyclopaedia Britannica* brought this critical scholarly approach to the attention of the general public.

Higher Criticism recommended the application to the Bible of the same methods of literary and historical analysis as those applied to other books. Questions were asked concerning authorship, location, and date of writing, the intent of the writers, and the influences of the historical and cultural environment on the writings. Much of the impulse toward such literary criticism had come from the skeptical attitude towards authority of the eighteenth-century Enlightenment. Although the full development of Higher Criticism in Germany came after Hodge's sojourn in 1826–28, he was appalled by what he termed the "rationalist" and "pantheist" approach to the Bible that he found there. He followed it closely all of his life and determinedly opposed all attempts to subject the Bible to the same analysis as other books. In an article entitled, "The Latest Form of Infidelity," published in 1840, Hodge attacked German Higher Criticism and its acceptance in America. He used as an example, David Friedrich Strauss (1808–1874), whose *Leben Jesu* had appeared in 1835–36.[103]

Between the years 1829 and 1850 some seventy articles opposing the emerging Higher Criticism appeared in the *Princeton Review,* and the flow increased after 1850.[104] Hodge was a student of ancient languages. He proposed that the problem with Higher Criticism lay not in its philological study, but in its philosophical presuppositions.[105] During the middle part of Hodge's career, beginning in the 1840s, the Princeton theologians proclaimed confidently that continental European scholarship was swinging back in a more orthodox direction.[106] By the end of his life, that confidence was gone, but the real conflicts between the Princeton theologians and the Higher Critics did not come until the era of Hodge's son, A. A. Hodge, and his colleague B. B. Warfield. Charles Hodge further prepared the foundation, already laid by Archibald Alexander, from which the later Princeton theologians would wage their battle.

The Influence of Turretin

Hodge and the Princeton theologians always assumed that the foundation on which they built their theology was first, Scripture and second, the Westminster Confession of Faith and Catechisms. Hodge had been brought up on the Westminster standards and he instinctively used their phraseology in articulating his theology.[107] Furthermore, the Professors at Princeton Seminary took a vow of subscription to the Westminster standards.[108] The notion that there was a system of doctrine taught in Scripture and that this system was set forth in the Westminster Confession was taken for granted by the Princeton professors. To vow never to teach anything other than that implied in the Westminster standards surely provided powerful psychological reinforcement to believe that what they taught was indeed consonant with Westminster, and Scripture. But, in fact, the Princeton professors, and thus their students, did not study the Westminster Confession in its historical setting. They studied the theology of Francis Turretin, which breathed a very different spirit. They assumed and asserted that the theology of Turretin was the same as that of Westminster and Calvin. The terms used in the Westminster

Confession's chapter on Scripture were defined by concepts taken from Turretin. The concentration was on Turretin, and the Princeton theologians did not differentiate between Turretin and other, more authentic, Reformation sources.

In 1840, due to Archibald Alexander's advancing age, Charles Hodge replaced Alexander as professor of didactic theology. For eight or nine years, Alexander and Hodge shared the teaching of systematic theology. Alexander would continue to lecture on a topic until Hodge had prepared his lectures in that area, then Hodge would take over. Their method of teaching was the same and it relied heavily on Turretin. Both Alexander and Hodge had written commentaries on Turretin for classroom use.[109]

Hodge met both the middle and senior classes twice a week. His biographer described the routine:

> Before the first meeting of either class for the week, the Professor assigned a topic and a corresponding section of Turretin's Institutes of Theology in Latin for previous study. When they met the hour was occupied by a thorough discussion of this subject in the form of question and answer.[110]

Hodge encouraged the students to develop their own system of theology, but the assumption was strong that it would conform to Turretin, and the assignments encouraged that assumption. A. A. Hodge recorded his father's methodology:

> At the same time the Professor gave them a list of questions on the topic, numbering from twenty-five to forty, answers to which, written out in full, were to be read to him at the meeting of the class nine days afterwards. These answers were elaborated out of materials drawn from Turretin, and the notes taken in the classroom, and from any other source rendered accessible by the Seminary library.[111]

This method of instruction and the constant reiteration of praise for Turretin certainly had the effect of fixing in the students' minds that Turretin's theology was normative.

Hodge was unremitting in his acclaim of Turretin. In an 1845 article in the *Princeton Review,* Hodge wrote that Turretin was "on the whole, the best systematic theological writer with whom we are acquainted, and notwithstanding the tincture of scholasticism which pervades his work, it is remarkable adapted to the present state of theology in this country."[112] In 1848 Hodge hailed the publication in New York of a new Latin edition of Turretin's *Institutio Theologiae Elenticae.* In his review of the work Hodge declared: "It has long been admitted that Francis Turretin was the best expounder of the doctrine of the Reformed Church, as matured into completeness of form in the period following the Synod of Dort." Hodge classified Turretin among the "giants of Protestant theology," and categorized his work among the "monuments of reformation theology" while obliquely acknowledging that some referred to it as "Scholastic rubbish."[113] For Hodge, however, there were no ambiguities in his feelings for Turretin. Hodge announced of Turretin that: "His adherence to the received doctrine of the Reformed church is so uniform and strict, that there is no writer who has higher claims as an authority as to what that doctrine was."[114] After urging students of theology to purchase the newly available Latin work and exhorting laymen to present copies to their ministers, Hodge concluded:

> We were once told by Chief Justice Ewing, . . . that it was the uniform practice of Mr. Justice Washington, to read through the whole of Blackstone's Commentaries once a year; and that he did so to give consistency, method and unity, to all the otherwise scattered and heterogeneous acquisitions of the year. We entertain no doubt, that a similar practice with regard to the equally logical and more commanding system of Turretin, would do more for a masculine theology and an energetic pulpit, than cart loads of religious journals, epitomes from the German, and occasional sermons.[115]

It was Turretin's logical system that impressed and delighted Hodge. In his biography he is quoted as saying, in an aside: "So, as has often been said, the best way to make a logician is to set him to study Euclid, or, as any old student of Princeton Seminary would say, set him to study Turretin."[116] Near the end of his life Hodge preached an historical sermon on the occasion of reopening a refurbished chapel at Princeton Seminary. In it he referred to Turretin's institutes of theology as "one of the most perspicuous books ever written."[117] Hodge's own three-volume *Systematic Theology* was not intended to implement any change from Turretin's theology. It was rather meant to make Turretin's style of theology available in English and adapted to the issues of Hodge's time. The admiration for Turretin at Princeton continued unabated until the seminary was reorganized in 1929. Francis Landley Patton, president of Princeton Seminary in Warfield's day approvingly called Turretin, "the Thomas Aquinas of Protestantism."[118]

Verbal Inspiration

The Princeton theologians found a normative authority for theology in the writings of Francis Turretin. But they assumed that Turretin was only putting into systematic form a system of doctrine already implicit in Scripture. For them, authority rested finally on the Bible. The authority of the Bible resulted from the fact that it was inspired by God. All the Princeton theologians believed that. But the subject of inspiration was not given systematic treatment until Hodge presented an exposition entitled "Inspiration" in the *Princeton Review* in 1857.[119] Hodge's views on inspiration were again presented, somewhat more concisely, in his *Systematic Theology* fifteen years later.[120] Apparently because of increasing attack on his position, Hodge wrote another brief summary of his stance on inspiration just seven months before his death.[121]

Hodge was not an historian of doctrine. He often erroneously asserted that the whole church held to a position that was actually peculiar to Protestant scholasticism.[122] This was true of his concept of inspiration Hodge seemed totally unaware of the concept of accommodation, which had been central to the principal theologians of the early church and the Reformation. For them, Scripture contained a divine message from God communicated in the language and thought forms of human beings. The saving function was divine, but the words, while adequate to bear the meaning, were fallible in the very humanness of their form. Not so for Hodge. The whole purpose of inspiration for him was to produce a carbon copy of God's language. He wrote in his *Systematic Theology:*

> The common doctrine of the Church is, and ever has been, that inspiration was an influence of the Holy Spirit on the minds of certain select men, which rendered them the organs of God for the infallible communication of his mind and will. They were in such a sense the organs of God, that what they said God said.[123]

He had asserted earlier in his article, "Inspiration": "The whole end and office of inspiration is to preserve the sacred writers from error in teaching."[124]

Inspiration, for Hodge, was different from both revelation and illumination. The object of revelation was to communicate knowledge to a person and make that person wiser. The intent of illumination was to enable persons to understand revelation and thus become holy. But the purpose of inspiration was purely mechanical. It applied only to the biblical writer and "was to preserve him from error in teaching."[125] The passive character of the recipients of inspiration was pointed out repeatedly by Hodge. The Holy Spirit worked on the biblical writers to make them "infallible organs of God, so that what they taught, God taught."[126] The imagery was no longer that of children receiving from God what was good for them, but of grown men uttering thoughts they perhaps did not even understand.[127] Hodge wrote to the Scottish theologian, Marcus Dods:

> An inspired man stood in the same relation to God that Aaron stood to Moses in his intercourse with Pharoah. What Aaron said, God said: "I will put my words in your mouth"; "holy men of old spake as they were moved by the Holy Ghost." Therefore, what David said, the Holy Ghost said. What Jeremiah said, the Holy Ghost said.[128]

Hodge drove his point home, again by an incorrect assessment of history. He asserted that "the accepted formula to express the doctrine of the Church in all ages on this subject is, that the Scriptures were written *dictante Spiritu Dei* (dictation by the Spirit of God)."[129]

When the mechanical character of his view of inspiration was pointed out, Hodge simply denied it. He declared that the inspired penmen were "men not machines; not unconscious instruments, but living, thinking, willing minds, whom the Spirit used as his organs."[130] Inspiration did not take away the writers' human characteristics. Nor did it elevate a biblical author "in the secular knowledge above the age in which he lived," but it did prevent him from teaching, for example, "that the earth is the centre of our system." When that person wrote Scripture, he spoke errorlessly according to Hodge's view of scientific fact even if the opposite "may have been his own conviction" when not writing Scripture.[131] This was the genius of verbal inspiration according to Hodge. He wrote: "Verbal inspiration, therefore, or that influence of the Spirit which controlled the sacred writers in the selection of their words, allowed them perfect freedom within the limits of truth."[132] With respect to the mode of the Spirit's operation Hodge professed to be "entirely ignorant."[133]

Hodge's modesty was not quite as thoroughgoing as he claimed. He did assert as essential to his view of inspiration that God selected the words to be used. At the conclusion of his denial that verbal inspiration involved dictation, Hodge asserted: "Nevertheless, and none the less, they spoke as they were moved by the Holy Ghost, and their words were his words."[134]

Hodge's model for interpreting this seeming inconsistency was the relationship between providence and free will. Hodge held it to be a "fundamental principle of scriptural theology that a man may be infallibly guided in his free acts."[135] Hodge did not know how this could be. He simply believed that it was so. More importantly, he interpreted the meaning of that dictum very narrowly and with a Newtonian notion of the way that the world worked.

Just as the world worked according to rigid, mechanical laws for Hodge, so thought could only be communicated through precise words. This was a presupposition Hodge had picked up from Scottish realism. He uncritically affirmed:

> No man can have a wordless thought, any more than there can be a formless flower. By the law of our present constitution, we think in words, and as far as our consciousness goes, it is as impossible to fuse thoughts into the mind without words, as it is to bring men into the world without bodies.[136]

The notion that Semites such as the Old Testament Hebrews, for example, could think in pictures rather than employing syllogistic logic was incomprehensible to Hodge. He had no understanding of the enormous varieties of world views held in various cultures. The differences in the manner of thinking between ancient and modern and between Eastern and Western peoples was something he had to deny.[137] Conflict between the Princeton theologians and the Higher Critics, who studied comparative religion, was inevitable at this point.

Hodge appealed for his views of how the mind worked to the Scottish principle of the common sense of mankind. This philosophical premise had important ramifications for Hodge's theory of biblical interpretation. It also impinged on his view of verbal inspiration. He told his classes early in his teaching career that "all mankind have certain feelings and agree in certain obvious truths. There is something fitly called the common sense of all mankind."[138] In 1859 Hodge authored an article entitled "The Unity of Mankind."[139] Hodge's article was a review of a book that supported his notion that all people came from a common set of parents. In it he repeated the constant claim of Princetonians that all true science supported their side of the argument. Confident of that support, Hodge exclaimed: "The church, as we have said, bows to the facts of nature, because they are the voice of God. Theories are the stammering utterances of men before which she holds her head erect."[140] The conclusion of this was a passionate, if somewhat patronizing, plea to recognize that all persons are the same. Hodge wrote:

> The Bible says that all men are children of a common Father. Accordingly, wherever we meet a man, no matter of what name or nation, we find he has the same nature as ourselves. He has the same organs, the same senses, the same instincts, the same faculties, the same understanding, will and conscience, the same capacity for religious culture. He may be ignorant and degraded; he may be little above the idiot brother who sits with us at our father's table, but we cannot but recognize him as a fellow man.[141]

Because Hodge thought in absolute categories, his defense of human unity forced him to overlook the importance of the cultural diversity within that unity. Similarly, with regard to inspiration, Hodge affirmed with the Reformers that God infallibly communicated a divine saving message to humankind. But, for Hodge, that could only occur if God chose the exact words the biblical authors were to write. For Hodge, to deny his understanding of how inspiration took place was tantamount to denying that it did take place. His scholastic concentration on the form of Scripture separated him from the Reformers who found authority in Scripture's saving function. But Hodge was unable to make that distinction. He asserted: "The denial of verbal inspiration is in our view the denial of all inspiration, in the scriptural sense of the doctrine."[142]

The Concept of Error

In all the areas in which the doctrine of Scripture was coming into debate Charles Hodge was a transitional person. He belonged emotionally to the settled world of Archibald Alexander when all learning supported a static view of reality, which was elaborated by Scottish common sense philosophy and Turretin's theology. As the Higher Critics increasingly raised questions about the validity of that world view, Hodge was drawn into polemical and apologetic stances for which he was hardly prepared. He empathized with the language and the intent of the Westminster Confession of Faith, that Scripture was given to lead people to salvation and guide them in the life of faith. But when new science raised questions about the old science that Hodge had trusted, he felt obliged to claim that Scripture gave valid information about science as well as salvation. He treated the English translation of the Bible as the infallible Word of God but, under pressure from critics who pointed to discrepancies, he began to retreat toward the original autographs of the Bible as alone being error free. Hodge was even willing to admit that there could be some errors in minor matters in Scripture, which did not affect its saving message. But when confronted with inconsistencies in his doctrine of inspiration, he fell back on the scholastic theory that the Scripture was an inerrant communication of information in all areas that it touched. Hodge's views often seem inconsistent because he lived and worked in a transitional period. His followers, A. A. Hodge and B. B. Warfield, knew that the Princeton theology no longer reigned supreme, and rigidified it into a rationalistic, apologetic stance. They authored another article entitled "Inspiration," in 1881 to plug the gaps Hodge's view of inspiration had left open.

Hodge admitted that "there are difficulties connected with this theory" that God controlled the language as well as guided the thought of the biblical writers. With that admission, the ambiguity in Hodge's approach was manifested. He declared that no great doctrine was free of difficulty. Then he stated that a person "will soon find that his faith must rest on the proper evidence of the doctrine, and not on his ability to solve all the difficulties connected with it." By the end of the paragraph Hodge had moved farther saying: "The only rational, and indeed the only possible course for men to pursue, is to believe what is proved to be true, and let the difficulties abide their solution."[143] Hodge continually confused the presentation of evidence in support of a position with a proof of that position. Because he was committed to a certain stance it was easy for him to claim that partial evidence constituted proof.

For Hodge, the teacher, the evidence of inconsistency among the biblical writers was no problem. His principal tack was that the difficulties were so few that they were inconsequential. He wrote in "Inspiration" that "the difficulties are so minute as to escape the notice of ordinary intelligence." He contended that they "must be sought as with a microscope, and picked out with the most delicate forceps of criticism." The example he gave was of one writer stating that "on a certain occasion twenty-four thousand persons were slain; another, a thousand years after, says there were twenty-three thousand." He conceded that there were other objections and "some of a more serious kind" but in the end concluded that the objections were "pitiful" and "miraculously small."[144] In his *Systematic Theology* Hodge added to this discussion a now famous illustration. He wrote:

> The errors in matters of fact which skeptics search out bear no proportion to the whole. No sane men would deny that the Parthenon was built of marble, even if here and there a speck of sandstone should be detected in its structure. Not less unreasonable is it to deny the inspiration of such a book as the Bible, because one sacred writer says that on a given occasion twenty-four thousand, and another says that twenty-three thousand, men were slain. Surely a Christian may be allowed to tread such objections under his feet.[145]

Hodge the teacher was able to dismiss such problems as minor. Hodge the theorist, however, was unable to admit that the problem might reside in his understanding of the issue. Rather than foregoing the theory that the Scripture was composed of verbally inspired propositions, Hodge plunged ahead to claim that the Bible harmonized at every point, both internally and when compared with external evidence from science.

As a teacher Hodge was helpful in interpreting changes in world view to his students. He pointed out:

> There is also a distinction to be made between the Bible and our interpretation. The latter may come into competition with settled facts; and then it must yield. Science has in many things taught the Church how to understand the Scriptures. The Bible was for ages understood and explained according to the Ptolemaic system of the universe; it is now explained without doing the least violence to its language, according to the Copernican system. Christians have commonly believed that the earth has existed only a few thousands of years. If geologists finally prove that it has existed for myriads of ages, it will be found that the first chapter of Genesis is in full accord with the facts, and that the last results of science are embodied on the first page of the Bible. It may cost the Church a severe struggle to give up one interpretation and adopt another, as it did in the seventeenth century, but no real evil need be apprehended.[146]

Such a passage was prophetic of the problems the Princeton theology would encounter in subsequent years. If the advice of Hodge, the teacher, had been followed, the fundamentalist-modernist controversy of the 1920s might have been averted for many.

But Hodge's theory about the nature of the Bible and its inspiration experienced the same inability to adapt to new science as had its predecessor scholastic theory in the seventeenth century. Hodge refused to affirm the approach of, for example, Augustine, Calvin, and Rutherford, that the Bible was not meant to teach us about matters of science such as astronomy. Hodge instead held to the notion that it was a purpose of the Bible to convey information on scientific matters—"the last results of science." Hodge stated as his main premise: "If the Bible be the word of God, all the great questions which for ages have agitated the minds of men are settled with infallible certainty."[147] Hodge attempted to hold the theory that the inspiration of Scripture resided in its verbal form while taking account of ancient views of science. He did so by introducing the distinction between what a biblical writer thought and what he taught. Hodge wrote: "For example, it is not the question Whether they thought that the earth is the centre of our system? but, Did they teach that it is?"[148] If Hodge at this point had simply affirmed that the biblical writers taught what all people of the time believed concerning matters of science, but that these matters were not relevant to the Christian's salvation and life of faith, no conflict would have arisen. But Hodge attempted to hold two contradictory positions. On the one hand he declared:

> An inspired man could not, indeed, err in his instruction on any subject. He could not teach by inspiration that the earth is the centre of our system, or that the sun, moon, and stars are mere satellites of our globe, but such may have been his own conviction. Inspiration did not elevate him in secular knowledge above the age in which he lived; it only, so far as secular and scientific truths are concerned, preserved him from teaching error.[149]

On the other hand, Hodge, with his conviction that science and Scripture harmonized at all points could not be content to say that the biblical writer did not deal with science. Instead, he felt compelled to declare that the biblical writer taught something different from what he thought. Hodge asserted confidently:

> It is true, when astronomy first began to unfold the mechanism of the universe there was great triumph among infidels, and great alarm among believers, at the apparent conflict between science and the Scriptures. But how stands the case now? The universe is revealed to its profoundest depths, and the Bible is found to harmonize with all its new discovered wonders. No man now pretends that there is a word in the Bible, from Genesis to Revelation, inconsistent with the highest results of astronomy.[150]

Hodge went on to assert in 1857 that anyone "must be blind indeed not to see that geology will soon be found side by side with astronomy in obsequiously bearing up the queenly train of God's majestic word."[151]

By 1874 Hodge was no longer so confident. In *What Is Darwinism?* he declared: "The conclusion of the whole matter is, that the denial of design in nature is virtually the denial of God. Mr. Darwin's theory does deny all design in nature, therefore his theory is virtually atheistical."[152] For Hodge, the acceptance of development meant the denial of design. And his wrath was directed at geologists as well as biologists who accepted developmental theories that contradicted his notion of static design.[153] Hodge thus helped to set the scene for the drama that would be acted out years later by William Jennings Bryan and Clarence Darrow in a small town in Tennessee.

Hodge's theory about Scripture asserted the errorlessness, by (his) modern standards, of Scripture in all matters about which Scripture spoke. In the *Systematic Theology* he summarized his views saying:

> It means, first, that all the books of Scripture are equally inspired. All alike are infallible in what they teach. And secondly, that inspiration extends to all the contents of these several books. It is not confined to moral and religious truths, but extends to the statements of facts, whether scientific, historical, or geographical. It is not confined to those facts the importance of which is obvious or which are involved in matters of doctrine. It extends to everything which any sacred writer asserts to be true.[154]

He also claimed incorrectly that this was "the Church doctrine on this subject."[155]

When pressed to reconcile his doctrine with the dissimilarities between biblical data and the data of modern science, Hodge, late in life, moved towards a theory of the inerrancy of the original autographs of Scripture. In his letter to Marcus Dods, Hodge insisted that:

> It is of the Bible as it came from the hands of the sacred writers, and of the Bible as properly interpreted, that this infallibility is asserted. There may be discrepancies between one part of the Scripture and another, arising from errors of transcribers. Far more numerous and important difficulties have their origin in erroneous interpretations.[156]

This "autograph" theory had not been put forth explicitly by Hodge in his earlier treatment of the doctrine of inspiration. And he did not elaborate and refine it into an apologetic tool, as his son A. A. Hodge and his student B. B. Warfield were later to do. Charles Hodge was primarily the biblical expositor and theologian. He practiced all his life the position he took at the very beginning of his teaching career. Then he wrote: "The Bible we now have, is essentially the Bible, which proceeded from the sacred writers."[157] That was good enough for Hodge in practice. It was not good enough for his successors in polemics. Hodge, in response to criticism, moved in directions that allowed for the narrowing of the doctrine of inspiration that took place in the next generation.

The Influence of Scottish Realism

There is no carefully developed theory of biblical interpretation (hermeneutic) to be found in the writings of the Princeton theologians.[158] Interpretation was apparently no problem to them. They had the framework of a system of theology given in the Thomistic categories of Francis Turretin's theology. Furthermore, they uncritically accepted the principles of Scottish common sense philosophy as determinative of how all knowledge was acquired. With these two systems assumed as valid the Princeton theologians proceeded with confidence in the certainty of their knowledge.[159]

Charles Hodge wrote: "Every theology is in one sense a form of philosophy. To understand any theological system, we must understand the philosophy that underlies it and gives it form."[160] That axiom was certainly true of the Princeton theology in its reliance on Scottish realism. Between 1830 and 1860 at least fourteen articles in the *Princeton Review* endorsed and interpreted the views of the Scottish philosophers of common sense. We need to examine a number of those principles as they were applied by Hodge to his method of doing theology as a science.

Hodge began, as all Baconian scientists did, with a commitment to the validity of sense perceptions and our rational deductions from them. Hodge began his *Systematic Theology* with these words: "In every science there are two factors, facts and ideas; or, facts and the mind." Knowledge in theology was acquired just as knowledge in the natural sciences, according to Hodge. His definition of epistemology was: "Knowledge is the persuasion of what is true on adequate evidence."[161] After outlining and rejecting two other methods of doing theology, the speculative and the mystical, Hodge proceeded to his own preference, "the inductive method." For Hodge, "it is so called because it agrees in everything essential with the inductive method as applied to the natural sciences."[162]

Hodge noted that the scientist "comes to the study of nature with certain assumptions." The first of these assumptions for the scientist was the validity of sense experience. Hodge wrote:

> He assumes the trustworthiness of his sense perceptions. Unless he can rely upon the well-authenticated testimony of his senses, he is deprived of all means of prosecuting his investigations. The facts of nature reveal themselves to our faculties of sense, and can be known in no other way.[163]

Hodge adopted wholeheartedly the naive inductive method of Bacon as mediated through the Scottish realists. He evidenced no awareness of any elements within the observer that were brought to that observer's encounter with the data of nature.

Hodge's second assumption was a trust in his own powers of reason. Hodge wrote concerning the man of science:

> He must also assume the trustworthiness of his mental operations. He must take for granted that he can perceive, compare, combine, remember, and infer; and that he can safely rely upon these mental faculties in their legitimate exercise.[164]

The overriding influence of Scottish realism and its coherence with the Thomism of Francis Turretin was evidenced here. Despite the constant profession of faithfulness to Calvin and the Augustinian tradition, the Princeton theologians seemed never to fear that their minds had been affected by sin. Their later followers worked out the full implications of this faculty psychology.[165] The Princeton men were sure that sin had made the emotions unreliable. But they held an almost Pelagian confidence that the mind was essentially undisturbed by sin's influence.

The factors necessary for certain knowledge that were not attributable to sense experience or reason were confidently derived by Hodge from intuition. He concluded his opening paragraph on the inductive method of the scientist by saying:

> He must also rely on the certainty of those truths which are not learned from experience, but which are given in the constitution of our nature. That every effect must have a cause; that the same cause under like circumstances, will produce like effects; that a cause is not a mere uniform antecedent, but that which contains within itself the reason why the effect occurs.[166]

Thus Hodge followed the Scottish realists again. Where they could not refute David Hume, they merely ignored him. Hume had proved that principles such as cause and effect could not be demonstrated on empirical grounds. The Scottish realists, and Hodge, simply appealed to intuition to provide the principles lacking in empiricism. But, they continued nonetheless to maintain that their method was strictly empirical.

Hodge followed Scottish common sense philosophy, not only regarding sense experience, reason, and intuition, but also with reference to the nature and function of language. We have already shown an effect of this influence on Hodge's view of verbal inspiration. The Scottish realists and Hodge treated words like things that were directly knowable. Reid had written: "Language is the express image and picture of human thoughts."[167] At another place he contended: "The meaning of the word is the thing conceived."[168] Reid and Stewart asserted, and Hodge agreed, that persons could not think without words.

Hodge regarded words in much the same way as he regarded objects in nature. As early as 1823 he told his students that "Words excite ideas

... or sensations."[169] Hodge's notion, already discussed, that all persons in all cultures and periods of history basically thought alike enabled him to assume that his understanding of the meaning of words corresponded to that of the biblical writers. He taught:

> All men are affected very much in the same way by external objects ... there is a considerable similarity in all languages ... [There exists] a general [linguistic] construction which is the foundation of universal grammar.[170]

Hodge later wrote with firm confidence in a univocal meaning of words: "Such language when interpreted according to established usage, and made to mean what it was intended to express, is not only definite in its import, but it never expresses what is false to the intellect."[171] He could assume that nineteenth-century philologists had a firm grasp on the "established usage" of words. One implication of this rather rigid and mechanical view of language was that for Hodge, even "figurative language" is "just as definite in its meaning and just as intelligible as the most literal."[172]

The implications of this view of language for biblical interpretation were immense. The biblical writers perfectly portrayed what they saw and experienced. Once the modern interpreter understood the established usage of the words in the biblical account, the interpreter was brought into direct contact with the event itself. To read the biblical words was to encounter the biblical thought or deed just as if the interpreter had had direct experience of it.

A further assumption of Scottish realism that Hodge shared was that memory brought one into direct contact with past occurrences. And further, that through the testimony of others we could have direct access to what they experienced. Thomas Reid had contended that "memory is an original faculty given us by the author of our being" and was designed to bring us into actual contact with past occurrences.[173] Reid was confident that memory was clear and accurate. He wrote: "It is by memory that we have an immediate knowledge of things past ... Every man who remembers must remember something.... Every man can distinguish the thing remembered from the remembrance of it."[174] Thus one remembered, for example, not the idea of Rome, but Rome itself. Reid claimed: "The object remembered must be something which did exist in time past."[175] Historical events were thus mediated as the "remembered testimonies" of others. Reid concluded:

> This belief, which we have from distinct memory, we account real knowledge, no less certain if it was grounded on demonstration; no man in his wits calls it into question.... The testimony of witnesses in causes of life and death depends upon it, and all the knowledge of mankind of past events is built upon this foundation.[176]

Reid's view was generally accepted in the America of Hodge's time. Levi Hedge, a philosopher at Harvard averred that events recorded in the past were facts that could be accepted "on the testimony of others, vouching their observation and experience."[177]

Hodge applied these common sense notions to the interpretation of the Bible. He submitted some five rules by which a "testimony" should be tested in order to be accepted as trustworthy. These rules were almost identical to those of the Harvard logician, Hedge.[178] Hodge then affirmed: "Some things we believe on the testimony of our senses; other things we believe on the testimony of men."[179] Hodge maintained that to deny the certainty of our knowledge of past events led to skepticism and nihilism. Hodge wrote in *Systematic Theology* concerning belief in miracles that it "must rest on historical testimony."[180] He declared: "It is . . . a false assumption that human testimony is inadequate to produce absolute certainty." Hodge affirmed: "We cannot help confiding in good men."[181] His conclusion lent great confidence to biblical interpreters of the Princeton persuasion. He wrote: "The testimony of other men, under these conditions, may be as coercive as that of our own minds."[182]

These Scottish common sense assumptions account for the (by modern standards) strange way in which the Princeton theologians treated history. In 1840, Charles Hodge produced *The Constitutional History of the Presbyterian Church in the United States of America.* His method was to identify "official" sources, quote the "testimonies," explain the natural meanings of the words, and produce a history that claimed an identity of the Presbyterian past with the views of the Princeton theology.[183] His son, A. A. Hodge, wrote a commentary on the Westminster Confession of Faith. In it, A. A. Hodge showed no concern to investigate the thought world or the sources of the Westminster Divines. He simply developed what for him were the logical meanings of their statements and presented it as an historical commentary. When such methods were used by the Princeton theologians in interpreting the Bible, they were bound to collide with the findings of critical scholars who were investigating the thought world of the ancient Near East.

Biblical Interpretation as Baconian Induction

The manner in which Hodge interpreted the Bible arose from his Scottish common sense assumptions. Words in the Bible were treated like facts in nature. It was assumed that the nineteenth-century reader of the Bible came into direct contact with the biblical realities through the historical testimony of the biblical writers. And just as the natural scientist could never be wrong in his conclusions if he followed the Baconian method of induction rigorously, so the theologian could never be doctrinally wrong if he carefully organized all the biblical propositions on a given topic. Hodge wrote in the first chapter of his *Systematic Theology:*

> The Bible is to the theologian what nature is to the man of science. It is his store-house of facts; and his method of ascertaining what the Bible teaches, is the same as that which the natural philosopher adopts to ascertain what nature teaches.[184]

The theologian's job, like that of the natural scientist, was to collect and organize the available facts and then to deduce "laws" from them. Hodge declared on the opening pages of his *Systematic Theology:*

> The Bible is no more a system of theology, than nature is a system of chemistry or of mechanics. We find in nature the facts which the chemist or the mechanical philosopher has to examine, and from them to ascertain the laws by which they are determined. So the Bible contains the truths which the theologian has to collect, authenticate, arrange, and exhibit in their internal relation to each other. This constitutes the difference between biblical and systematic theology. The office of the former is to ascertain and state the facts of Scripture. The office of the latter is to take those facts, determine their relation to each other and to other cognate truths, as well as to vindicate them and show their harmony and consistency. This is not an easy task, or one of slight importance.[185]

According to Hodge, it was the will of God that people use the inductive method to discover biblical truths. Hodge declared of God:

> He does not teach men astronomy or chemistry, but He gives them the facts out of which those sciences are constructed. Neither does He teach us systematic theology, but He gives us in the Bible the truths which, properly understood and arranged, constitute the science of theology. As the facts of nature are all related and determined by physical laws, so the facts of the Bible are all related and determined by the nature of God and his creatures. And as He wills that men should study His works and discover their wonderful organic relation and harmonious combination, so it is His will that we should study His Word, and learn that, like the stars, its truths are not isolated points, but systems, cycles, and epicycles, in unending harmony and grandeur.[186]

Induction from the facts of Scripture was, therefore, not inconsistent with holding to a system like that of Turretin. Hodge assumed that a systematic theology was to the biblical data as the laws of nature, reflecting God's order and design, were to the objects in nature.[187]

Hodge proceeded to outline the inductive method of forming a scientific systematic theology. First one had to make the assumptions of Scottish realism.[188] Second, "the duty of the Christian theologian is to ascertain, collect, and combine all the facts which God has revealed concerning himself and our relation to Him." Here Hodge made an enormous claim. Essentially, he asserted that the integration of all knowledge could be accomplished on the basis of the data in the Bible.[189] Hodge asserted:

> Lest we should err in our inferences from the works of God, we have a clearer revelation of all that nature reveals, in his word; and lest we should misinterpret our own consciousness and the laws of our nature, everything that can be legitimately learned from that source will be found recognized and authenticated in the Scriptures.[190]

Hodge and the Princeton theologians worked hard toward the integration of all knowledge into a monumental, integrated system, as articles over the years in the *Princeton Review* indicate.

Hodge next repeated the Baconian caution that all induction must be done with the greatest care. Hodge contended that a complete induction from all the available facts was necessary. He wrote: "Illustrations without end might be given of the necessity of a comprehensive induction of facts to justify our doctrinal conclusions."[191] Other followers of Reid's brand of Baconian induction came to realize that a complete induction of all the pertinent facts was an impossible goal. Samuel Tyler was the most admired American philosopher of science from the 1840s to 1860s. He was a close friend of Charles Hodge, and virtually became the "house" philosopher for the Old School Presbyterian Church during that period. Most of Tyler's writings on philosophical induction appeared first as articles in the *Princeton Review*. Tyler was careful to rehabilitate deduction as a fully approved Baconian device whereby the generalizations gained from induction were extended in their consequences. According to Tyler, both induction and deduction were necessary for a complete conception of science.[192] He wrote: "The two together constitute one complete system of processes by which knowledge is acquired and perfected."[193]

Hodge felt no actual conflict between the "facts" of Scripture and many other sources of input, including those truths he considered intuitively true, and the inward teaching of the Holy Spirit, or religious experience. Hodge reconciled all of those potentially devisive sources of truth by the assertion of two premises:

> First, All truth must be consistent. God cannot contradict himself. He cannot force us by the constitution of the nature which He has given us to believe one thing, and in His Word command us to believe the opposite. And, second, All the truths taught by the constitution of our nature or by religious experience, are recognized and authenticated in the Scriptures. This is a safeguard and a limit.[194]

For Hodge, the inward teaching of the Spirit produced a theology of the heart that found expression in prayers and hymns. Hodge allowed that "the facts of religious experience should be accepted as facts, and when duly authenticated by Scripture, be allowed to interpret the doctrinal statements of the Word of God." Hodge went so far as to assert that: "It would be safe for a man to resolve to admit into his theology nothing which is not sustained by the devotional writings of true Christians of every denomination."[195] Princeton theologians of the next generation were not so generous. Hodge had removed the inner testimony of the Spirit from the place Calvin had given it as the authenticator of the authority of Scripture.[196] But for Hodge the work of the Holy Spirit still warmed the heart and provided a complementary theology that should be compared with the more rational scientific kind. By Warfield's time, the fear of "mysticism" and the necessities of apologetics allowed the Holy Spirit only to make persons love that which the reason had accepted as true.

Faith as Assent

Hodge's notion of theology as scientific induction influenced his view of faith. In volume 3 of the *Systematic Theology* Hodge devoted a chapter to it. Although he used terms in ambiguous ways, he was quite clear that faith was understood in the scholastic sense as assent to truth. He began a discussion of the psychological nature of faith by saying: "Faith in the widest sense of the word, is assent to the truth, or the persuasion of the mind that a thing is true."[197] The ambiguity appeared when he used the word *trust* to describe this rationalistic definition of faith. Hodge wrote: "From all of this it appears that the primary idea of faith is trust." But immediately he put his use of the word *trust* in an intellectual setting: "The primary idea of truth is that which is trustworthy; that which sustains our expectations, which does not disappoint, because it really is what it is assumed or declared to be."[198]

Later in his discussion, Hodge defined faith as "a conviction of truth founded on testimony." He attempted to demonstrate that this had support throughout church history. He first quoted Augustine and next the Scottish realist philosopher William Hamilton. After appealing to the Alexandrian school and the medieval scholastics, Hodge asserted: "Such also was the doctrine of the Reformers, and of the theologians of the subsequent age, both Lutheran and Reformed." Hodge then proceeded to quote Thomas Aquinas and Francis Turretin in support of his stance, quoting no sixteenth-century Reformer at all.[199] Hodge's basic appeal was, as always, to "common sense." He claimed: "This view of the nature of faith is all but universally received, not by theologians only, but by philosophers, and the mass of Christian people." No consideration was given to the Reformation sense of faith as a trustful commitment of the whole person to God as a person. Rather faith was reduced to an often repeated rationalistic formula: "The Scriptures teach that faith is the reception of truth on the ground of testimony or on the authority of God."[200]

Hodge allowed one exception. Saving faith was different from faith in the authenticated facts of Scripture. Saving faith rested on a separate and later work of the Holy Spirit. Hodge wrote:

> That faith which secures eternal life; which unites us to Christ as living members of his body; which makes us the sons of God; which interests us in all the benefits of redemption; which works by love, and is fruitful in good works; is founded, not on the external or the moral evidence of the truth, but on the testimony of the Spirit with and by the truth to the renewed soul.[201]

For the Reformers, faith in Christ and faith in Scripture had been indistinguishable aspects in one movement of personal trust. In Hodge they became separate and sequential moments. One first knew that Scripture was the Word of God by rational evidences. Then one came to trust in Christ as one who was demonstrably the Son of God. And then the Holy Spirit worked with this evidence to renew the soul. The Augustinian approach of faith seeking understanding as a theological method had been reversed. Hodge self-consciously and carefully followed the Thomistic order that reason had to precede faith.

Biblical Facts Equal Scientific Facts

Hodge's Thomist theological method worked well as long as the "common sense" of most people in his generation accepted the evidence he offered. At the beginning of Hodge's career, he confidently appealed for support to the leading natural scientists of his day and found his views confirmed. When a Darwinian, developmental world view began to challenge the neat, Newtonian model of reality, however, things changed. Hodge had committed the *Princeton Review* to a policy of openness toward science. He had written that "scientific men" should be allowed to pursue "their investigations, according to their own methods." That was, of course, at a time when the methods of science were roughly the same as the Baconian induction Hodge recommended for theology. Even more importantly, it was at a time when the presuppositions of the scientists and the theologians both were derived from Scottish common sense philosophy. But a time came when the conclusions to which the biologists and geologists were coming differed from those to which Hodge was committed. Such conclusions were characterized as "crude and hasty generalizations" that conflicted with the fundamental facts of Scripture.

At this point, Hodge urged that "the friends of religion may wisely rebuke" the intrustion of scientific views.[202]

The key to the coming conflict was a subtle shift that had taken place in the concept of fact through Hodge's reliance on Scottish realism. Verbal propositions extracted by the theologians from Scripture were equated with objects observed by the scientist in nature. Hodge had no sensitivity to the significant difference between a verbal statement and a material thing. His Scottish common sense view of language allowed him to identify words with things. He had so objectified biblical statements, that they functioned for him like static objects. Thus, when conflicts arose between the "facts" of nature and the "facts" of the Bible, Hodge declared that the biblical facts were correct and the scientific evidence was false, or at least misunderstood. Hodge contended in good conscience that it was "unphilosophical" for the scientist to ignore scriptural "facts" when making his investigations.[203] No genuine Baconian induction was complete until both the data of the Bible and the results of field or laboratory investigation were correlated.[204] It was but a short step from there to the position that the biblical data were to be given a priori (before experience) acceptance. Hodge was aghast that Louis Agassiz, a leading natural scientist, long in favor with the Princeton theologians, had lent his name to the polygenist theory that mankind had arisen from several sources of origin. Hodge firmly declared that Agassiz would not have become mired in that error "if he had appreciated the immense *a priori* probability against that theory arising from the teachings of the Bible."[205] Hodge's view that the Bible contained all the data on all matters of human knowledge had originally appealed to scientific findings as a support. Now the Bible was used to refute the findings of science.

This position laid the foundation for the antiintellectual fundamentalism that was to come. During Hodge's era most clergymen were relatively well versed in the principles of science, which was still in the embryonic stage of development. Hodge urged them to exercise their right of review over the findings of science.[206] He held that the Bible contained all the facts also discoverable in nature. And he was confident that the biblical data could be used to correct the findings of the scientists. It was only a small step from there to the stance that any believer with his Bible could wage war effectively on untrue theories of atheistic scientists. The stage was set for the twentieth-century conflict between science and religion. Hodge did not live to see it. But his followers in the next generation simply polished the weapons he had provided and rushed into the fray.

Hodge lived during the "golden age" of the Princeton theology. The principles of Scottish common sense philosophy were generally ac-

cepted. Turretin's system seemed universally adequate as a framework
for theology. And Hodge and his Princeton colleagues proceeded with
absolute confidence in the certainty and permanence of their views. They
lived in a setting and with a style that few people in the future would ever
know. Charles Hodge lived in the same house most of his adult life. His
children were born there and he died there. Because of his lameness he
sat exclusively in one particular chair in one particular place in his study
during thirty-eight years. And he patronized the same tailor shop in
Princeton for sixty years. The people he met and with whom he worked
all shared the same comfortable and enclosed world of experience. His
personal habits and his habits of thought remained the same and functioned usefully in that relatively unchanging environment.[207] One of his
sons, Caspar Wistar Hodge, became his colleague in New Testament
studies. Another son, Archibald Alexander Hodge, was briefly his colleague and became his successor in the chair of systematic theology. The
age of doubt and development was looming on the horizon, but for
Charles Hodge its sun had not yet risen.

In this context of conservatism and moderation, Hodge declared that
with the few rules of biblical interpretation he had provided, all people
could agree on the meaning of biblical statements. Having described his
theological method in detail, Hodge concluded the introduction to his
Systematic Theology with these words:

> The fact that all the true people of God in every age and in every part of
> the Church, in the exercise of their private judgment, in accordance with the
> simple rules above stated, agree as to the meaning of Scripture in all things
> necessary either in faith or in practice, is a decisive proof of the perspicuity
> of the Bible, and of the safety of allowing the people the enjoyment of the
> divine right of private judgment.[208]

This assumption that the "true people of God" all agreed set the Princeton theologians against the German Higher Critics and all who followed
new interpretations. When Hodge could not fault German scholarship,
he complained that the Bible was being "irreverently treated."[209] With
Charles Hodge, the period of reverent agreement with the conclusions
of the Princeton Theology came to an end.

c. Retreat to the Original Autographs: Archibald Alexander Hodge (1823–1886)

A. A. Hodge was a man whose life was molded by devotion to the
person and the ideals of his father.[210] He was born one year after Charles

Hodge began his long professional career at Princeton, and was nurtured as a child and youth in that environment. He attended Princeton College and graduated in 1841. He studied especially under the natural scientist Joseph Henry, a close friend of his father and later the founding director of the Smithsonian Institution.[211] A. A. Hodge studied at Princeton Seminary under his father and was one of a group of students who could reproduce Charles Hodge's lectures in systematic theology nearly verbatim. He graduated in 1847. That same year he married and went with his bride to serve as a missionary in Allahabad, India. Three years and two children later, their health was impaired and they returned to the U.S.[212] A. A. Hodge then served three pastorates in succession. They were at Lower West Nottingham, Maryland (1851–55), Fredericksburg, Virginia (1855–61), and Wilkes-Barre, Pennsylvania (1861–64). He was reputed to be a warm and good-humored pastor and inspiring preacher. In 1864 he was called to the chair of systematic theology at Western Seminary in Allegheny, Pennsylvania. During most of his time there he served the North Presbyterian Church. In 1877 A. A. Hodge went to Princeton Seminary as an associate of his aged father. The next year, Charles Hodge died. Archibald Alexander Hodge, named for the first professor of theology at Princeton, became its third professor of theology, succeeding his father, as the one best suited "to perpetuate the traditional character of Princeton Seminary."[213]

Tightening the Princeton Tradition

A. A. Hodge and his colleagues at Princeton believed and proclaimed that they were simply carrying on an unbroken tradition. In actuality the intellectual world around them was changing and they were forced to change. Part of that change was a matter of attitude and style. Instead of being able to count on general public acceptance, they had to develop an apologetic for their position. In 1869 Hodge published, *The Confession of Faith: A Handbook of Christian Doctrine Expounding the Westminster Confession*. At that time he correctly anticipated the reunion of the New School and Old School Presbyterian Churches later in the year. The doctrinal basis of that union was the Westminster standards "pure and simple." Hodge provided a guide to those standards that gave a consistent Old School interpretation. In good Scottish common sense fashion he, of course, insisted that he was only bringing "into full relief the natural, obvious, and generally admitted sense of the text."[214] His interpretation of the confession's chapter on Scripture bore little resemblance to the thinking of Westminster's British authors. When Hodge "set forth these standards in their plain, native sense" they read like a transcript of his father's lectures in systematic theology. All the familiar themes were there in his definition of "inspiration":

> The books of Scripture were written by the instrumentality of men, and the national and personal peculiarities of their authors have been evidently as freely expressed in their writing, and their natural faculties, intellectual and moral, as freely exercised in their production, as those of the authors of any other writings. Nevertheless these books are, one and all, in thought and verbal expression, in substance and form, wholly the Word of God, conveying with absolute accuracy and divine authority all that God meant them to convey, without any human additions or admixtures. This was accomplished by a supernatural influence of the Spirit of God acting upon the spirits of the sacred writers, called "inspiration;" which accompanied them uniformly in what they wrote; and which, without violating the free operation of their faculties, yet directed them in all they wrote, and secured the infallible expression of it in words. The nature of this divine influence we, of course, can no more understand than we can in the case of any other miracle. But the effects are plain and certain—viz., that all written under it is the very Word of God, of infallible truth, and of divine authority; and this infallibility and authority attach as well to the verbal expression in which the revelation is conveyed as to the matter of the revelation itself.[215]

The theology was the same as that of Charles Hodge. But the reasons given were more apologetic in attitude, as well as terse in style. A more combative and cautionary note had crept in. A. A. Hodge asserted: "The fact that the Scriptures are thus inspired is proved because they assert it of themselves." But to this he immediately added: "And because they must either be credited as true in this respect, or rejected as false in all respects." To this Hodge added the apologetic appeal that "God authenticated the claims of their [the Scriptures] writers by accompanying their teaching with 'signs and wonders and divers miracles.' Heb. ii.4." Hodge could not accept the authority of Scripture as the Westminster Divines had because of the internal testimony of the Holy Spirit. He felt compelled even more than his father to shift the accent to external evidences of authenticity. He concluded his definition of inspiration by saying that it was impossible that God would "unconditionally command belief except to truth infallibly conveyed."[216]

At least two major factors accounted for A. A. Hodge's more refined and scholasticized doctrine of inspiration. The first was the growing impact of biblical criticism.

In nineteenth-century Germany, the scientific tools of the Enlightenment were being extensively used for the critical study of the Bible. In the first half of the century some scholars at Harvard and Andover seminaries had imported this method of biblical study to America. But such leaders as Moses Stuart (1780–1852), Theodore Parker (1810–1860), and Edward Robinson (1794–1863) died shortly before or during the 1860s and left no prominent successors.[217] Thus it was not until after the Civil War that the full impact of European critical studies began to be felt in America.

When A. A. Hodge came to Princeton Seminary as a systematic theologian in 1877, he devoted his inaugural address to a defense of systematic theology over against the new claims of the "biblical theology" movement. Hodge stressed the doctrinal interpretation of Scripture rather than just its history of salvation as the proper object of Christian faith. He repudiated skepticism that questioned the methods and conclusions of metaphysics when he said: "Whether this policy of preserving the truth by means of its disintegration be urged upon us by subtle enemies or by silly friends, we intend to refuse it utterly."[218] The questioning of biblical "facts" which were clear to the Princeton theologians was now increasingly being done by biblical scholars themselves.

A second influential factor on Hodge's doctrine of inspiration was the changing concept of nature and science. In 1859 Charles Darwin's *On the Origin of Species* had appeared. This monumental work set off a series of intellectual explosions that had far-reaching effects on conservative Calvinism for the rest of the nineteenth century and after.[219] The Princeton theologians' belief that the findings of science led to praise of the Creator was also united to a certain view of nature. It was a doctrine of static design. Each structure in nature was "designed" for a particular function or end. An eye was "intended" for seeing, clouds were intended to nourish the earth with water, and so on.[220]

But Darwin's view of evolution challenged this. It taught a developmental view of nature. Whereas before science had echoed that the firmament proclaimed the glory of God, now it was constructing a universe in which God's benevolent governance was not necessary. A Christian who had seen in nature the evidence of God's marvelous design was now being told that in nature there were countless violent struggles with only the "fittest" surviving.[221] In 1871 Darwin's developmental hypothesis reached out to include humans when his *The Descent of Man* was published.

Due to the upheavals of the Civil War the full impact of Darwinism was not felt on the American scene until after 1869.[222] The increasing acceptance of Darwinism thereafter accelerated the asking of questions that had already arisen from the science of geology as well as from biblical criticism of the Book of Genesis.[223] The new paths science began to take led in directions the Princeton theologians did not approve of. The synthesis of "faith" and "knowledge," which seemed so evident and promising before the Civil War, was now being shattered.[224] Forced to cling to their increasingly outmoded concepts of nature and science for fear of capitulating to atheism, the Princeton defenders drifted farther and farther away from vital contact with ongoing science.[225]

The developments in biblical criticism and the natural sciences were part of a whole "crisis of historical consciousness" in the nineteenth century.[226] Traditional notions of the past were challenged by a dynamic view of history.[227] The feared outcome of this, exemplified in the Princeton attacks on Darwin was the elimination of God from the arena of world history.[228] There was no flexibility in the Princeton thought for a fundamental philosophical change of world view. The Princeton theology was bound to an eighteenth-century Newtonian view of nature and to an eighteenth-century Scottish realist perspective in philosophy. The Princeton theologians were not able to separate their observation of the world or their exegesis of the Bible from the eighteenth-century theories that had determined their interpretation. No view that advocated a dynamic view of historical development could be accepted by them.

Nor did the Princetonians distinguish between science as a method of knowing and science as a content of knowledge.[229] The "holy alliance" between religion and science had held strong in the first half of the century, and Princeton had adopted the tools and methods of its counterparts in the scientific community. The "fact" was sovereign. Christian theology could proceed according to the canons of the "science" of the day. Reason could apply the same rules of investigation to the Bible as to any other book, with the sure confidence that in the end the truth of God would be vindicated.[230] But with the coming of new challenges the Princeton theologians' methodological commitments led to open warfare with scientists. The "philosophy of facts" wedded so closely to static creationism meant that there was no way for Princeton to adapt to new scientific "facts" that seemed to challenge the traditional views. The new body of knowledge could not be accounted for on the basis of the philosophical and methodological commitments previously made.

From Plenary Inspiration to the Original Autographs

Under the pressure of these changed circumstances, A. A. Hodge changed not only the style but the content of the Princeton defense of Scripture. This shift is evident in changes made from the first (1860) to the revised (1879) edition of his *Outlines in Theology*. The first edition was prepared prior to the Civil War; the second edition came after changes in thought had occurred subsequent to that conflict. The first edition had been prepared while Hodge was in the pastorate in Fredricksburg, Virginia. The revised edition was issued after thirteen years of teaching theology at Western Seminary. And more importantly, it came after A.

A. Hodge had assumed the heavy burden of perpetuating and defending a Princeton theological tradition that was increasingly under attack.

The chapters of the 1860 edition of *Outlines of Theology* were originally given as Sabbath evening lectures to Hodge's congregation. He produced the work as "a syllabus of theological study for the use of theological students generally" and for pastors who had neither the time nor resources to pursue the study of theology in depth.[231] The format of the book took a question and answer form. The questions were the ones used by Hodge's father Charles "to his classes of forty-five and six," the years in which young Archibald sat under his father's tutelage. Hodge added two or three chapters and adapted the questions for his purposes, but throughout he had consulted with his father.[232]

In 1879 after succeeding his father at Princeton, Hodge published a revised and enlarged edition of his *Outlines.* The new work contained "nearly fifty per cent more matter than the former one" and represented Hodge's increased knowledge as a teacher with fourteen years experience. The appendix to this work included English translations of Calvin's "Consensus Tigurinus" and of the "Formula Consensus Helvetica" authored by J. H. Heidegger and inspired by Francis Turretin.[233] The significant expansions and shifts in emphasis from Hodge's 1860 edition to his revised edition of 1879 were evidence of the increasing rigidification of the Princeton theology in response to criticism.[234]

In 1860, after discussing the nature of inspiration, how it differed from revelation, spiritual illumination, and the extent of inspiration, Hodge offered his definition of plenary inspiration. He described inspiration as

> a divine influence full and sufficient to secure its end. The end in this case secured is the perfect infallibility of the Scriptures in every part, as a record of fact and doctrine both in thought and verbal expression. So that although they come to us through the instrumentality of the minds, hearts, imaginations, consciences and wills of men, they are nevertheless in the strictest sense the word of God.[235]

Then followed a defense of the sacred writers as inspired historians and of an inspiration that extended to their language as well as thoughts.[236]

The revised edition of 1879 gave the same definition of plenary inspiration (question 3). But it was *preceded* by this question and answer as 2:

> In what sense and to what extent has the Church universally held the Bible to be inspired? That the sacred writers were so influenced by the Holy Spirit that their writings are as a whole and in every part God's word to us—an authoritative revelation to us from God, indorsed by him, and sent to us as a rule of faith and practice, the original autographs of which are absolutely infallible when interpreted in the sense intended, and hence are clothed with absolute divine authority.[237]

Then followed the question on plenary inspiration (3) and a definition of "verbal inspiration" as

> that divine influence, of whatever kind it may have been, which accompanied the sacred writers in what they wrote, extends to their expression of their thoughts in language, as well as to the thoughts themselves. The effect being that in the original autograph copies the language expresses the thought God intended to convey with infallible accuracy, so that the words as well as the thoughts are God's revelation to us.[238]

Four reasons for this were then advanced.[239]

Several things are significant about Hodge's later revision. First, Hodge now taught that it was the "original autographs" of Scripture that were "absolutely infallible when interpreted in the sense intended." In 1860 his definition of plenary inspiration had asserted "the perfect infallibility of the Scriptures in every part, as a record of fact and doctrine both in thought and verbal expression" (question 7). By 1879 he had backed up one step by introducing the notion of the autographs in the question before the definition of plenary inspiration. A reader of the earlier version would doubtlessly have thought that Hodge's belief about the "perfect infallibility of the Scriptures in every part" and their plenary inspiration referred to the present text of Scripture as it was then received. To prevent this opinion from arising in 1879, Hodge qualified his definition of plenary inspiration by introducing the notion of autographs. In 1860 there was no hint of it. By 1879 it was the controlling framework.

Second, Hodge claimed in 1879 that the absolute infallibility (he meant "inerrancy") of the original autographs when properly interpreted had been the sense in which the church universally had held the Bible to be inspired. He produced no evidence for this assertion. In the 1860 discussion, no mention of the church had been made on this point. His argument in 1860 began from the proposition: "The Scriptures of the Old and New Testaments are inspired, and therefore infallible."[240] (Again, no mention was made of the autographs; the present texts were apparently assumed.) In 1879 the first two major divisions of Hodge's discussion were: "Statement of the Church Doctrine of Inspiration" (questions 2–5) and "The Proof of the Church Doctrine of Inspiration" (question 6).[241] At the end of his chapter on inspiration, Hodge added "Authoritative Statements" from the Council of Trent, the First Vatican Council, Formula Concordiae Epitome, the Second Helvetic Confession, the Belgic and Westminster Confessions. These were statements on inspiration to be sure. But they did not necessarily support Hodge's assertion that the "original autographs" were inspired and infallible in the way that Hodge claimed.

Third, when Hodge argued that the words as well as the thoughts of the Bible were inspired, he again appealed to the "original autograph copies."[242] It was in these that the full effects of inspiration were to be felt. These copies expressed "the thought God intended to convey with infallible accuracy." The four points Hodge used to prove this were the same he had used in 1860. But then there had been no hint that the "original autographs" alone were meant.

Discrepancies Denied

The importance of the "original autographs" qualification became clear when Hodge in 1879 discussed "What objection to the doctrine of Plenary Inspiration is drawn from the alleged fact that 'Discrepancies' exist in the Scriptural Text? and how is this objection to be answered?"[243] The similar question in 1860 had been: "Upon what principles are we to answer the objections founded upon the alleged discrepancies between the sacred writers, and upon their alleged inaccuracies in matters of science?"[244]

In the earlier volume Hodge had said that "if either of these objections were founded on facts, it would clearly disprove the doctrine we maintain."[245] He believed that neither were founded on facts and then went on to tell why. But by 1879 Hodge was not willing to concede that inconsistencies in Scripture itself or inconsistencies "with some certainly ascertained facts of history or of science" would damage the case for inspiration. The science that seemed so much in support of the Princeton position prior to 1860 had begun to turn hostile. Hodge wrote:

> It is obvious that such a state of facts, even if it could be proved to exist, would not, in opposition to the abundant positive evidence above adduced, avail to disprove the claim that the Scriptures are to some extent and in some degree the product of divine inspiration. The force of the objection would depend essentially upon the number and character of the instances of discrepancy actually proved to exist, and would bear not upon the fact of inspiration, but upon its nature and degree and extent.[246]

Hodge then listed five "considerations" he felt were "evidently well-grounded, and sufficient to allay all apprehension on the subject." His strategy in these "considerations" was to define precisely what would constitute a "discrepancy."

Here the genius of the appeal to the autographs shone through. Hodge's first point was that "the Church has never held the verbal infallibility of our translations, nor the perfect accuracy of the copies of the original Hebrew and Greek Scriptures now possessed by us. These copies confessedly contain many 'discrepancies' resulting from frequent transcription."[247] While these "variations embarrass the interpretation of many details," Hodge asserted that the "unanimous testimony of Christian scholars" was that no essential fact or doctrine of Christianity was lost or abated by these variations. Further, in 1879, Hodge claimed, the church possessed "a more perfect text of the original Scriptures than she has enjoyed since the apostolic age." Thus "discrepancies" in the present biblical text presented no major problems to Hodge's view.

His second point was that

the Church has asserted absolute infallibility only of the original autograph copies of the Scriptures as they came from the hands of their inspired writers. And even of these she has not asserted infinite knowledge, but only absolute infallibility in stating the matters designed to be asserted. A 'discrepancy,' therefore, in the sense in which the new critics affirm and the Church denies its existence, is a form of statement existing in the original text of the Hebrew and Greek Scriptures evidently designed to assert as true that which is in plain irreconcilable contradiction to other statements existing in some other portions of the same original text of Scripture, or to some other certainly ascertained element of human knowledge. A 'discrepancy' fulfilling in every particular this definition must be proved to exist, or the Church's doctrine of plenary verbal inspiration remains unaffected.[248]

Hodge's statement in 1860 had been simply that "with regard to apparent discrepancies between the sacred writers, that nothing presents any difficulty short of a clear and direct contradiction."[249] Once again Hodge's doctrine was further developed by introduction of the unavailable autographs.

Hodge's third point shifted the responsibility to his critics when he asserted that the existence of "discrepancies" was a "violent improbability." Those who asserted them must find them and have them verified by competent judges to prove that "all the elements of the above definition meet in each alleged instance, not probably merely, but beyond the possibility of doubt." This, Hodge observed would be for them "a very difficult task to perform, one in any instance indeed hardly possible." He set the criteria of judgment in his fourth point:

(1) That the alleged discrepant statement certainly occurred in the veritable autograph copy of the inspired writing containing it. (2) That their interpretation of the statement, which occasions the discrepancy, is the only possible one, the one it was certainly intended to bear.... (3) He must also prove that the facts of science or history, or the Scriptural statements, with which the statement in question is asserted to be inconsistent, are real facts or real parts of the autograph text of canonical Scripture, and that the sense in which they are found to be inconsistent with the statement in question is the only sense they can rationally bear. (4) When the reality of the opposing facts or statements is determined, and their true interpretation is ascertained, then it must, in conclusion, be shown not only that they appear inconsistent, nor merely that their reconciliation is impossible in our

present state of knowledge, but that they are in themselves essentially incapable of being reconciled.[250]

Hodge's fifth point was that "no single case of 'discrepancy,' as above defined, has been so proved to exist as to secure the recognition of the community of believing scholars." This then was Hodge's "unassailable" case to show that no "discrepancy" (which really meant no "scientific error") could be proved to exist in the autographs of Scripture (now lost) using then-current scientific methods. Not only must the text be established as part of the autographs, but it must be interpreted in its "intended sense" and must be shown to be a statement of direct teaching rather than mere assertion. Finally a reconciliation of "discrepant" texts had to be shown to be impossible, not only on the basis of *present* knowledge, but beyond that as "essentially" unharmonious.

Loss of Support from Science

A final point showed another shift in Hodge's attitude from 1860 to 1879. This concerned what he perceived to be the effects of current science on his doctrine of inspiration. The failure of natural science any longer to support the Princeton theology was perhaps why his doctrine was so elaborated in the 1879 *Outlines.*

In 1860, on the question of the Bible's "apparent inaccuracies in matters of science," Hodge had recognized that

> the sacred writers having for their design to teach moral and religious truth, and not physical science, use on all such subjects the common language of their contemporaries [*sic*], always speaking of natural phenomena as they appear, and not as they really are.[251]

But then Hodge went on to add this revealing statement:

> And yet revelation does not present one single positive statement which is not consistent with all the *facts* known to men, in any department of nature. In the progress of science, human ignorance and premature generalization have constantly presented difficulties in the reconciliation of the word of God with man's theory of his works. The advance of perfected knowledge has uniformly removed the difficulty.[252]

Clearly in 1860 Hodge viewed science as a powerful ally. He had adopted its inductive methods for doing theology just as his father had done.[253] And like other earlier Princeton theologians, A. A. Hodge assumed that the scientist could uncover design, benevolence, and order in nature and that they would lead him to the "doxological praise" of nature's Creator.[254] Science in 1860 had been a potent ally of belief.

A. A. Hodge wrote in 1860 that Scripture did not present "one single positive statement which is not consistent with all the *facts* known to men, in any department of nature" (italics are Hodge's). At that time he felt on secure ground. Nine years before the *Southern Presbyterian Review* had claimed with certainty that

> no *fact* in any department of human knowledge has yet been discovered even in appearance contradictory of any of the statements of the Bible. It is the *reasoning* of men on facts which conflicts with it.[255]

The way to meet a scientific claim that seemed to clash with a religious doctrine was to show how the claim *went beyond* the limits of support rendered by the factual evidence.[256] So successful were the Princeton theologians at doing this that from his position as the son of the most eminent Princetonian and as a working pastor, A. A. Hodge could confidently assert in 1860 not only that there were then no biblical contradictions to known scientific facts, but also that the further advance of "perfected knowledge has uniformly removed" any difficulty of reconciling the Bible and the facts of science. So confident was he, in fact, that he was willing to allow that a "clear and direct contradiction" would, indeed, "clearly disprove the doctrine we maintain."[257]

By 1879 A. A. Hodge was not so bold. Then, after painstakingly having described what would constitute a legitimate discrepancy in the autographic text, he concluded with these words:

> Difficulties in interpretation and apparently irreconcilable statements exist, but no 'discrepancy' has been proved. Advancing knowledge removes some difficulties and discovers others. It is in the highest degree probable that perfect knowledge would remove all.[258]

Here Hodge displayed confidence that he had constructed an unassailable apologetic case for the "scientific errorlessness" of the Bible in its original autographs. But gone was the earlier unbridled confidence in the support of contemporary science.

Developments in biblical criticism and the natural sciences were symptomatic of a general revolution in historical thinking that was becoming widespread by the late 1870s. The changes in A. A. Hodge's presentation of the doctrine of Scripture reflected Princeton reaction to the advances of biblical criticism and to changing conceptions of nature and science. The Princeton theologians felt that a firmly secured Scripture was needed. In the face of critical studies and new scientific "facts," the Bible now had to be defended in a new way. Princeton saw it as imperative to defend the Scriptures as scientifically "errorless" documents. The "specks of sandstone" Charles Hodge had admitted could be detected in the "marble of the Parthenon" were becoming more numerous. A. A. Hodge therefore found it necessary to clarify and rigidify the Princeton doctrine. Hence in 1879 he asserted that only the original autographs of the Scriptures were verbally inerrant. Since no "discrepancy" (as he defined it) could ever be proved to reside in the nonexistent autographs, the doctrine of inspiration seemed perfectly secure. And for good measure, he added that this newly developed view had always been the position of the church universal.

This new doctrine of inspiration was the one to be defended by the third generation of Princeton theologians, A. A. Hodge and B. B. Warfield. The three volumes of Charles Hodge's *Systematic Theology* published from 1871 to 1873 represented the culmination of his half-century of teaching. His doctrine of inspiration was the source from which A. A. Hodge had worked in his 1860 *Outlines.* Charles Hodge's views and methods reflected his confidence that a theologian could work in the manner of the natural scientist and that science and the Bible would never ultimately be in conflict.[259] But by the time A. A. Hodge took his father's place, religious and scientific claims were often at variance rather than in harmony with one another. Thus A. A. Hodge produced his expanded 1879 *Outlines,* and began to erect a bulwark to defend Princeton's theory about Scripture against the onslaughts of critical scholars and natural scientists.

d. Summary

Princeton Seminary was founded in 1812 as the first American institution to train Presbyterian clergy. Systematic theology was taught according to the post-Reformation scholastic methodology of Francis Turretin. The theory of hermeneutics (biblical interpretation) was taken from the philosophy of Scottish realism. For over 100 years, the Princeton theologians uniformly predicated the authority of Scripture on its supposed form of inerrant words. The Bible became a sourcebook on every area of knowledge including science and history. Statements in the Bible were treated like objects in nature. It was assumed that the mind knew directly the reality spoken of in the Bible. No trace of the central Christian notion of accommodation affected the Princeton theologians. With supreme confidence in their own correctness, they arranged the facts of Scripture into a systematic whole according to Turretin's framework.

Despite the intended uniformity of thought among the Princeton theologians, significant changes were made in successive generations. Archibald Alexander began with religious experience and used reason and evidence to confirm it. Charles Hodge continued to honor religious experience as a valid basis for personal religion. He preferred the internal evidence the Bible presented to the reader over external evidences of its authority. But in the classroom and in writing Hodge asserted that theology was a science and stressed objective proofs of the Bible's divinity. By the time of his son, A. A. Hodge, the sciences were no longer supporting Princeton theories of biblical inerrancy. A. A. Hodge rested his case on external evidences, but shifted the object of inerrancy to the original (lost) autographs of the biblical text.

e. Notes

1. Lefferts A. Loetscher, *A Brief History of the Presbyterians*, 3d. ed. (Philadelphia: Westminster Press, 1978), pp. 57–62. See also *BC*, chap. 1 and John H. Leith, *An Introduction to the Reformed Tradition* (Atlanta: John Knox Press, 1977), pp. 43–48. (Hereafter cited as Leith, *Reformed Tradition*.)

2. James W. Alexander, *The Life of Archibald Alexander, D.D.* (New York: Charles Scribner's Sons, 1854), pp. 8, 15. (Hereafter cited as *LAA*.)

3. John Oliver Nelson, "Archibald Alexander: Winsome Conservative," *Journal of the Presbyterian Historical Society* 35, no. 1 (1957):17. (Hereafter cited as Nelson, "Archibald Alexander.")

4. *PAS*, p. 40.

5. *LAA*, pp. 17, 18.

6. *LAA*, p. 36.

7. Cited in Nelson, "Archibald Alexander," p. 17. See John B. Boles, *The Great Revival 1787–1805* (Lexington: University of Kentucky Press, 1972), p. 62 for his confirmation of this caution.

8. Elwyn A. Smith, *The Presbyterian Ministry in American Culture: A Study in Changing Concepts, 1700–1900* (Philadelphia: Westminster Press, 1962), pp. 124–125. While serving as a reader for a Baptist woman, Mrs. Taylor, who was nearly blind, Alexander read one of John Flavel's sermons on Revelation 3:20 portraying Christ standing at the door. That Sabbath evening as he read to her he remembers: "As I read along every word I read seemed applicable in my own case." His voice faltered, he was moved to tears and ran from the room pouring out his heart in prayer and then experiencing a flood of joy. "It soon occurred to me that possibly I had experienced the change called the new birth." But within a week he had given in again to temptation and "my

9. *LAA*, p. 43. See Herbert M. Morais, *Deism in Eighteenth-Century America* (New York: Russell and Russell, 1960), pp. 97, 99–100 for other reactions to Jenyns' work.

10. *LAA*, p. 61.

11. *LAA*, p. 61.

12. *LAA*, p. 70.

13. *LAA*, p. 70

14. *LAA*, p. 64.

15. *LAA*, p. 72. His son includes these accounts in the biography to show Alexander's acquaintance with religious awakening, since his later opposition to enthusiastic excesses and false doctrines led his opponents to treat him as a "rigid bookdivine, who had grown up in cold forms without acquaintance with great outpourings of the Holy Spirit," *LAA*, p. 72.

16. *LAA*, p. 83

17. *LAA*, p. 109.

18. John A. Mackay, "Archibald Alexander: Founding Father," in *Sons of the Prophets*, ed. Hugh T. Kerr (Princeton, 1963), p. 7.

19. *PAS*, p. 40–41. Alexander apparently maintained an intense interest in mathematics and natural science throughout his life. See *LAA*, pp. 17, 36, 177, 200, 297, 382, 540, 685.

20. See A. A. Hodge, *The Life of Charles Hodge D.D. L.L.D.* (New York, 1880), p. 48. (Hereafter cited as *LCH*.)

21. Alexander was said, by his friends, to be "decidedly a Southern man." See *Biblical Repertory and Princeton Review*, index volume from 1825 to 1868, s.v. "Archibald Alexander." Archibald Alexander's son and biographer, James W. Alexander, declared his father "a Virginian to the last," who seized "any opportunity for vindicating the honour of 'the old colony and dominion,' " in

LAA, pp. 403–404. Bozeman, *PAS*, pp. 35 and 36, comments that "Alexander's southern proclivities were not uncharacteristic of the Old School [conservative Presbyterians] as a whole, which both before and after 1837 attempted as rigorously as possible to exclude debate on the subject of slavery from its courts and took a conciliatory position in its periodicals and other publications toward this divisive question."

22. An incident showing his preaching abilities occurred when "upon a certain occasion, after preaching a very long sermon, he announced the dismissal of the congregation by a hymn, but not a person moved. The whole congregation was stirred with deepest feeling and he arose and spoke forty-five minutes longer." See Hughes O. Gibbons, *A History of Old Pine Street* (Philadelphia, 1905), p. 140. This volume gives a record of Alexander's pastorate.

23. *LAA*, pp. 328–329.

24. John DeWitt, "Archibald Alexander's Preparation for his Professorship," *Princeton Theological Review* 3, no. 4 (October 1905):591.

25. *LAA*, p. 368.

26. *LAA*, pp. 177, 366.

27. Archibald Alexander, "Sketches of Moral and Mental Philosophy," *Biblical Repertory and Princeton Review* 20 (October 1848):529; and James Green, "Dr. Alexander on Mental Science," MSS notebook, Alexander Papers in Firestone Library of Princeton University, cited in *PAS*, p. 54.

28. Green, p. 5, cited in *PAS*, p. 57.

29. Archibald Alexander, *Evidences of the Authenticity, Inspiration and Canonical Authority of the Holy Scriptures* (Philadelphia: Presbyterian Board of Publication, 1836), p. 89. (hereafter cited as *Evidences.*)

30. *Evidences*, p. 65.

31. See Morais; H. D. MacDonald, *Ideas of Revelation: An Historical Study A.D. 1700 to A.D. 1860* (London: MacMillan, 1959), pp. 75ff. See also Donald G. Dawe, *No Orthodoxy but the Truth* (Philadelphia: Westminster Press, 1969), chap. 5, pp. 89–105. Dawe traces the influence of deism on emerging patterns of Christology. His title "No Orthodoxy but the Truth" was a slogan of the deist John Toland.

32. The phrase "the right use of reason in religion" is the title of chapter 1 of *Evidences*. See *PAS*, p. 141 and 206, n. 37 where he notes that the passage "may be intended as a sarcastic play upon a similar and well-known passage from Hume's *An Enquiry Concerning Human Understanding*."

33. This is John Witherspoon's phrase, as found in *The Works of John Witherspoon, D.D.*, 9 vols. (Edinburgh: Printed for J. Ogle, 1815), 6:10.

34. *Evidences*, p. 10.

35. In *BC*, p. 21, from *The Plan of a Theological Seminary Adopted by the General Assembly . . . A.D. 1811* (Philadelphia, 1811), p. 13. Henry F. May, *The Enlightenment in America* (New York: Oxford University Press, 1976), pp. 22–23, observed that this strategy did not always work: "Benjamin Franklin was not the only person converted to deism by reading antideist arguments. In answering the deists on their own terms the Christians had taken on the job of proving their religion rational and moral in every detail. This was a tactical mistake, and a gigantic failure of religious and historical imagination."

36. *Evidences*, pp. 10, 12, 18.

37. *PAS*, pp. 138–139 observes: "The twentieth-century expositor of eighteenth-and early nineteenth-century thought will quickly observe that the age made no clear distinction between natural, social and psychological phenomena . . . Briefly put, the Evidences of Christianity were an affirmative theological response to the demand for sensible evidence advanced by Newtonian science. The basic premise was that items of biblical revelation, like propositions in science, could and must be verified empirically." See also *PAS*, pp. 140–141: "The whole weight of the *Evidences* thus rested upon an empirical conception of biblical events and doctrines as *facts* directed to the senses."

38. Archibald Alexander, *Thoughts on Religious Experience* (Philadelphia: Presbyterian Board of Publication, 1841), pp. 5, 8. Ernest Sandeen notes that this dualism is "not however, noticeable in the Princeton Theology after the time of Archibald Alexander." See Ernest R. Sandeen, *The Roots of Fundamentalism* (Chicago: University of Chicago Press, 1970), p. 320. (Hereafter cited as Sandeen, *Roots.*) See chapter 5 of this work for his analysis of the alliance of the Princeton theology with dispensationalism to form fundamentalism. His *The Origins of Fundamentalism: Toward a Historical Interpretation*, Facet Books (Philadelphia: Fortress Press, 1968), pp. 12ff., makes the same point.

39. As will be seen, the later Princeton line gradually elevated reason at the expense of religious experience. Theologically this expressed itself in their undervaluing the work of the Holy Spirit. See Sandeen, *Roots,* p. 310. See further Ernest R. Sandeen, "The Princeton Theology: One Source of Biblical Literalism in American Protestantism," *CH* 31, no. 3 (1962):310.

40. W. Andrew Hoffecker, Jr., in "The Relation between the Objective and the Subjective Elements in Christian Religious Experience: A Study in the Systematic and Devotional Writings of Archibald Alexander, Charles Hodge and Benjamin Breckinridge Warfield" (Ph.D. dissertation, Brown University, 1970), p. 109, asserts: "In forging a *via media* between Orthodox Presbyterian confessionalism and revivalist enthusiasm Alexander attempted to draw on the best and put aside the worst aspects of each position. He was not always successful at the latter as traces of scholastic methodology and rationalistic presuppositions often assume a place of prominence in his thinking."

41. On the use of miracles and prophecy in eighteenth- and nineteenth-century apologetics, see Dulles, pp. 138ff. and 169ff., and Alan Richardson, *Christian Apologetics* (New York: Harper & Row, 1947), chaps. 7 and 8.

42. Archibald Alexander, *A Brief Compend of Bible Truth* (Philadelphia: Presbyterian Board of Publication, 1846), p. 15 (Hereafter cited as *Bible Truth.*)

43. *Evidences,* p. 131. See also *Bible Truth* p. 17, and John Dillenberger, *Protestant Thought and Natural Science: A Historical Interpretation* (Nashville: Abingdon Press, 1960), p. 145. (Hereafter cited as Dillenberger, *Protestant Thought.*)

44. *Evidences,* p. 187. An expanded treatment of what has gone before here and of Alexander's views is found in Donald K. McKim, "Archibald Alexander and the Doctrine of Scripture," *JPH* 54, no. 3 (Fall 1976):355–375. (Hereafter cited as McKim, "Archibald Alexander.")

45. *Evidences,* p. 188.

46. Alexander used Thomas Chalmers (1780–1847) as support against the deists and asked how human creatures could possibly know what was proper for the infinite God to do? See *Evidences,* pp. 187–188.

47. *Evidences,* p. 189.

48. *Evidences,* pp. 189f.

49. *Evidences,* pp. 190, 197, 200.

50. Hoffecker, p. 57, comments: "For Calvin the natural knowledge that one has is implanted by God and is not the result of reason's competence. (II. 2. 20) There are hints of this in Alexander's thought, nevertheless, a dependence on reason which would be totally abhorrent in Calvin's thought is present in Alexander."

51. See A. A. Hodge, *Outlines of Theology,* rev. ed. (New York: Robert Carter and Brothers, 1879), pp. 77f. (hereafter cited as *Outlines* [1879]), where he calls "superintendence," "elevation," "direction," and "suggestion"—"defective statements of the doctrine." This edition was reprinted in 1886 in London by Thomas Nelson and Sons. See also Hodge, *Outlines of Theology* (New York: Robert Carter and Brothers, 1860), p. 69. (Hereafter cited as *Outlines* [1860].)

52. *Evidences,* p. 224. Cf. McKim, "Archibald Alexander," p. 364 for further distinctions. Alexander wrote that "Superintendence was operative when an historian was influenced by the Holy Spirit to write, and in writing is so directed as to select those facts and circumstances which will answer the end proposed; and so assisted and strengthened in the narrative of events, so as to be preserved from all error and mistake." *Evidences,* pp. 223ff.

53. *Evidences,* p. 225.

54. *Evidences,* p. 226.

55. *Evidences,* p. 226.

56. *Evidences,* pp. 226ff.

57. *Evidences,* p. 227.

58. *Evidences,* p. 227.

59. *Evidences,* p. 227.

60. *Evidences,* p. 228.

61. *Evidences,* p. 229.

62. *Evidences,* p. 230.

63. *Evidences,* p. 258.

64. *Evidences,* p. 267.

65. *Evidences,* pp. 267–268. See particularly Alexander's work on the canon: *The Canon of the Old and New Testaments Ascertained* (Philadelphia: Presbyterian Board of Publication, 1851), Part II, Section 1, especially pp. 118 and 141.

66. Loetscher in *BC,* p. 23, remarks: "In Dr. Alexander is to be found, in germ, the entire Princeton Theology. Later writers were principally concerned with sharpening definitions—and in doing this they tended progressively to narrow the theology—and with relating its basic principles to the problems of their day."

67. *Evidences,* p. 27.

68. Nelson, "Archibald Alexander," pp. 74
–75.

69. See Smith, pp. 136–137 and 149ff. and
Sandeen, *Roots,* p. 310.

70. For brief biographies of Charles Hodge
see *Dictionary of American Biography,* ed.
Dumas Malone (N.Y.: Charles Scribner's
Sons, 1932), s.v. "Hodge, Charles" (he-
reafter cited as *DAB*) and *The New Schaff-
Herzog Encyclopedia of Religious Knowledge,* ed.
Samuel Macauley Jackson (N.Y.: Funk and
Wagnallis Company, 1909), s.v. "Hodge,
Charles" (hereafter cited as *NSH*).

71. *LCH,* p. 13.

72. *LCH,* p. 18.

73. *LCH,* p. 23.

74. *LCH,* p. 30.

75. *LCH,* p. 68. Cf. *PAS,* pp. 41–44.

76. *LCH,* pp. 69–74.

77. *LCH,* p. 75. The General Assembly's
resolution went on to say: "Provided a suitable person can be obtained at a salary consistent with the funds of the Seminary; and
provided also that such salary does not exceed the sum of four hundred dollars."
Hodge struggled to make ends meet finan-
cially all his life. The seminary salary was
inadequate to support a wife and seven children and was often not even paid on time.
Hodge often had to appeal for money to his
brother Hugh, a successful Philadelphia ob-
stetrician and professor of medicine. Hugh
was frequently the material provider for the
Hodge family. See letters from Charles to
Hugh Hodge in *LCH,* pp. 343–344 and 347.

78. *LCH,* p. 76. Hodge began at this time to
suffer from a pain in his right thigh which
made him lame most of his life. In 1822 just
after being appointed professor, Charles
Hodge married Sarah Bache a great-grand-
daughter of Benjamin Franklin and a family
friend whom he had known nine years.
Hodge was devoted to his family and allowed the children to come and go freely
into his study while he worked. See *LCH,*
pp. 28–29 and 96. His first wife died in 1849
and Hodge married Mrs. Mary (Hunter)
Stockton in 1852 who survived him in
death.

79. *NSH,* s.v. "Hodge, Charles."

80. We are very grateful for insights into
the theological and philosophical background of Charles Hodge to The Rev. John
W. Stewart of Westminster Presbyterian
Church, Grand Rapids, Michigan, for sharing with us his unpublished manuscript on
Charles Hodge's response to biblical criticism (1975), and for his advice in letters and
personal conversations. Subsequent references to J. W. Stewart refer to his unpublished paper, "The Princeton Theologians:
The Tethered Theology" (1975).

81. It is ironic that Nevin later became an
opponent of Hodge. Nevin along with
Philip Schaff (1819–1893) was a founder of
the "Mercersburg Theology," named after
the Pennsylvania town where both taught at
the German Reformed Seminary. In common with Hodge's Old School Presbyterianism, Nevin challenged the prevailing
revivalistic theology of American Protestantism. His solution, however, was quite
different from that of Hodge. Nevin and the
Mercersburg theologians wished to bring
the Reformed Churches back into closer
continuity with the Reformation and early
church understanding of the church and the
sacraments. Nevin believed that rationalism, Puritanism, and revivalism had defect-
ed from the real direction of the Reformers.
He and his colleagues stressed liturgical
renewal and a return to Calvin's objective
and Christ-centered sacramental theology.
These views were set forth in Nevin's works
The Anxious Bench (1843), *The History and
Genius of the Heidelberg Catechism* (1847), and,
The Mystical Presence (1846), as well as in the
pages of the *Mercersburg Review.* The Mercersburg theology apparently drew on the
resources of German theologians such as
Schleiermacher, Neander, and Dorner and
has been compared with British movements
such as the Oxford Movement and the Cambridge Platonists. See *The Westminster Dictionary of Church History,* ed. Jerald C. Brauer
(Philadelphia: The Westminster Press,
1971), (hereafter cited as *WDCH*) s.v. "Mercersburg Theology," and *ODC,* s.v. "Mercersburg Theology." Cf. Jack M. Maxwell,
*Worship and Reformed Theology: The Liturgical
Lessons of Mercersburg.* Pittsburgh Theological Monographs Series no. 10, ed. Dikran Y.
Hadidian (Pittsburgh: Pickwick Press,
1976).

82. *LCH,* pp. 103 and 109.

83. J. W. Stewart, III, C, 15–17. See *LCH,*
pp. 115–159.

84. *LCH,* pp. 247–250. References to this
journal under its various titles will be ab-
breviated *PR.* The objectives of the reorganized journal were stated in 1829 in an
advertisement:

1st, to furnish Christian readers with "facilities for a right understanding of the divine oracles;" 2d, "to bring under strict, impartial review the philosophy and literature of the time, and show their influence, whether for good or evil, on biblical interpretation, systematic theology, and practical religion, in doing which it will be necessary to correct and expose the error of founding religious doctrines on isolated passages, and partial views of Bible truth, or forcing the Scriptures to a meaning which shall accord with philosophical theories;" 3d, "To notice and exhibit the dangers of the particular form of error prevailing in the period;" 4th, "To present the history of religious doctrine and opinion, to notice the revival of old and exploded doctrines, and their effects on vital religion," 5th, "To consider the influence of different principles of ecclesiastical polity on piety, morals, literature and civil institutions;" 6th, "To observe and sustain the various enterprises of Christian benevolence, especially the vast and growing interest of Sabbath-schools;" 7th, "Such attention as the limits of the work will admit, will be bestowed on the important interests of general knowledge, and select literary information will be given in every number;" 8th, "The work is not designed to be controversial in its character, but to state temperately and mildly, yet firmly and fearlessly, Bible truth in its whole extent."

A. A. Hodge commented:

"This commendatory advertisement is signed by the following leading ministers of the day: Ashbel Green, Samuel Miller, Archibald Alexander, John H. Rice, Ezra Fisk, Ezra Styles Ely, Francis Herron, Thomas Cleland, Samuel H. Cox, Thomas H. Skinner, James Hoge, Henry B. Weed, William Nevins, Joseph Sanford, Thomas J. Biggs, Samuel L. Graham, Luther Halsey. Thus some of the strongest and most prominent partizans of each of the two Schools, into which the Presbyterian Church divided in 1831, were in 1829 united in laying the foundations of the *Biblical Repertory*, destined to take so decided a part in the coming conflict."

See *LCH*, pp. 247–248.

85. *LCH*, pp. 250–251.
86. Nelson, "Archibald Alexander," p. 332. Nelson comments regarding the founding of this journal by Hodge: "Here was an impressive textual safeguard of the Biblicist assumptions which Alexander had set up. Princeton Seminary had begun to explicate its tradition for the world to see," p. 289.
87. Charles Hodge, "The Princeton Review on the State of the Country and of the Church," *PR*, 38 (1865): 637, cited in William S. Barker, "The Social Views of Charles Hodge (1797–1878): A Study in 19th Century Calvinism and Conservatism," *Presbyterion: Covenant Seminary Review* 1 (Spring 1975):5.
88. Barker, while generally in sympathy with Hodge's conservative and moderate approach to social issues, comments: "To apply the social norms of Roman society in the New Testament age directly to 19th century American society, as Hodge did with regard to slavery, manifests a blindness to the differences in the forms of slavery in the two societies and to the general development of civilization over the centuries of time between the two eras. With this kind of sensitivity the inherently conservative and moderate aspects of Calvinism can be balanced with the essentially reforming and socially activist aspect of that same Biblical Reformed tradition," p. 22.
89. *LCH*, pp. 256–257. Historically seen, of course, Hodge was wrong. See Sandeen, *Roots*, p. 106 where Sandeen comments:

"Most twentieth-century Fundamentalists and many twentieth-century historians have mistakenly assumed that Protestantism possessed a strong, fully integrated theology of biblical authority which was attacked by advocates of the higher criticism. As we shall see, no such theology existed before 1850. What did exist was a great deal of popular reverence for the Bible, the eighteenth-century literature defending the authenticity of the Scriptures and providing 'evidences' of their supernatural orgin—all of which was beside the point—and an apologetic stance which had conditioned defenders of the faith to respond to any challenge to the Bible with the cry 'heresy.' A systematic theology of biblical authority which defended the common evangelical faith in the infallibility of the Bible had to be created in the midst of the nineteenth-century controversy. The formation of this theology in association with the growth of the millenarian movement determined the character of Fundamentalism."

90. *LCH*, p. 521. A recently (1977) created organization calling itself the International Council on Biblical Inerrancy uses Hodge's exact language as one of its slogans: "What the Bible says, God says," adding the phrase "through human agents and without error." See James Montgomery Boice, "Biblical Inerrancy—The Debate Is Not Over," *Evangelical Newsletter* 5 (July 14, 1978):4. The twentieth-century transmitter of Hodge's theology, B. B. Warfield, perpetuated Hodge's maxim. See his essay, " 'It Says:' 'Scripture Says:' 'God Says' " in *The Presbyterian and Reformed Review.* (1899):472–510 (hereafter cited as *PRR*), reprinted in *The Inspiration and Authority of the Bible,* ed. Samuel G. Craig (Philadelphia: Presbyterian and Reformed Publishing, 1970; rep. 1948), pp. 299–348.

91. Nelson, "Archibald Alexander" p. 332. Nelson comments: "Few men except Charles Hodge would deny that such a phenomenal record of self-avowed changelessness is itself a remarkable distinction," p. 301.

92. George P. Schmidt, *The Old Time College President* (N.Y.: Columbia University Press, 1935), p. 29, refers to the *Princeton Review* as the then "strongest theological journal in the English-speaking world" and affirms "the domination of higher education by the Presbyterians," cited in *PAS*, p. 35. Bozeman comments, p. 132, that "Presbyterians considered themselves missionaries to the American intellect." See Sandeen, *Roots,* pp. 103–131, 168–172, who contends that a coalition of the Princeton theology and the millenarian movement determined the character of fundamentalism.

93. *NSH,* s.v., "Hodge, Charles." Patton is the writer of this article.

94. See the article, "Charles Hodge" in *PR,* index volume for 1825–1868, p. 207, cited in Barker, p. 3.

95. *BC,* pp. 5–8. In addition to the differences cited in the text, the New School Presbyterians were more inclined toward congregationalism and decentralization whereas the Old School partisans insisted on the connectional church and some centralized authority. Loetscher comments (*BC,* p. 8): "Once again in 1869, as in 1758 [New Side-Old Side controversy, *BC,* p. 3], the Presbyterian Church was restoring unity not by resolving its differences, but by ignoring and absorbing them." See also *PAS,* p. 33. Bozeman notes: "To match Hodge, the South had James Henley Thornwell, 'the Calhoun of the [Southern] Church,' probably the most gifted Presbyterian of his day," *PAS,* p. 36. For the background on Southern Presbyterians whose theology parallels that of the Princeton theologians, see Leith, *Reformed Tradition,* pp. 147–149, and especially Morton H. Smith, *Studies in Southern Presbyterian Theology* (Amsterdam: Jacob Van Campen, 1962), who gives a thorough and sympathetic treatment of the principal figures of influence.

96. *LCH,* pp. 324–325.

97. William D. Livingstone, "The Princeton Apologetic as Exemplified by the Work of Benjamin Breckenridge Warfield and J. Gresham Machen: A Study in American Theology, 1880–1930," (Ph.D. dissertation, Yale University, 1948), pp. 226–227. See also Nelson, "Archibald Alexander," p. 336. The opening sentences of Hodge's inaugural address as professor of oriental and biblical literature in 1822 are indicative of his mood and motivation (see *LCH,* p. 94):

> "The moral qualifications of an Interpreter of Scripture may all be included in Piety; which embraces humility, candor, and those views and feelings which can only result from the inward operation of the Holy Spirit.
>
> It is the object of this discourse to illustrate the importance of Piety in the Interpretation of Scripture."

See also *PAS,* p. 171.

98. *LCH,* pp. 457–459.

99. *LCH,* p. 576. Hodge was 77 years old by this time. He had just seen the publication of his *Systematic Theology.*

100. Loetscher, *BC,* p. 10, notes that there was "little explicit discussion of evolution among Presbyterians … until the Bryan flurry of the 1920s threatened to stampede the General Assembly into obscurantist action." He accounts for this by saying that, "the larger truth of course is that theories of development … were conditioning the climate and in part defining the problems of all theological discussion."

101. *BC,* p. 20.

102. For definitions, see *WDCH,* s.v. "Criticism, Biblical Higher (United

States)," and *ODC*, s.v. "Higher Criticism." The broader background is sketched in Alan Richardson's chapter, "The Rise of Modern Biblical Scholarship and Recent Discussion of the Authority of the Bible," in *CHB*, vol. 3, *The West from the Reformation to the Present Day*, ed. S. L. Greenslade (Cambridge: At the University Press, 1963), pp. 294–338. Loetscher brings the issue to bear on the American Presbyterian scene at the time of the Princeton theology in *BC*, chapter 3, pp. 18–29.

103. Charles Hodge, "The Latest Form of Infidelity," *PR*, 12 (January 1840):54. Cf. *ODC*, s.v. "Strauss, David Friedrich." Hodge may well have drawn on the evaluation of his colleague in the biblical department, Joseph Addison Alexander, who wrote of Strauss's work in 1837 that the "'infidel theology' ... appears to have reached its consummation. In this one book are [sic] concentrated all the unbelief of the age," *PR*,9(1837): 198.

104. J. W. Stewart, IV, p. 2.

105. J. W. Stewart, III, C, 8.

106. J. W. Stewart, IV, 17. This was no doubt due to Hodge's heavy dependence on Tholuck and Hengstenberg as evidenced in Hodge's article cited in note 103. Joseph Addison Alexander also studied in Europe and was thoroughly acquainted with the works of the German Higher Critics. He urged readers of the *Princeton Review* to learn from their labors, even to "seize upon their valuable products and convert them to our own use," *PR*, 18 (1846):561f. There was a strong tension in his theology, however, between thoroughly appropriating the work of the Europeans—even of such critics as Hengstenberg, and the rigidities of the fully defined Princeton theology. In his failure to unify these two intellectual forces, J. A. Alexander prefigures the coming struggles between Princeton and the biblical critics. See James H. Moorhead, "Joseph Addison Alexander: Common Sense, Romanticism and Biblical Criticism at Princeton," *JPH*, 53, no. 1 (Spring 1975):54ff.; 58ff; 61ff.

107. J. W. Stewart, IV, 6–7 gives numerous examples from Hodge's writings.

108. See *Plan of the Theological Seminary of the Presbyterian Church in the United States of America Located in Princeton, New Jersey* (Elizabeth, N.J.: Kollock, 1816), p. 11, cited in Nelson, "Archibald Alexander," p. 234.

109. J. W. Stewart, IV, 8, notes that both commentaries are extant in manuscript in the Speer Library at Princeton Theological Seminary. Hodge's commentary is dated 1833, before he began teaching systematic theology. Alexander's has no date on it, but Stewart surmises that it was written as early as 1818.

110. *LCH*, p. 323.

111. *LCH*, p. 324.

112. Hodge, *PR*17 (1845):190, cited in Nelson, "Archibald Alexander," p. 273.

113. Hodge, *PR*, 20 (July 1848):452.

114. Hodge, *PR*, 20 (July 1848):461.

115. Hodge, *PR*, 20 (July 1848):462–463.

116. *LCH*, p. 24.

117. *LCH*, p. 553.

118. Cited in Charles Augustus Briggs, *Theological Symbolics* (N.Y.: Charles Scribner's Sons, 1914), p. 378.

119. Charles Hodge, "Inspiration," *PR* 29 (October 1857):660–698 (Hereafter cited as "Inspiration.")

120. Charles Hodge, *Systematic Theology*, Vol. I (N.Y.: Charles Scribner's Sons, 1871), pp. 153–182. (Hereafter cited as Hodge's *ST*.)

121. Letter to Marcus Dods, Free Presbytery of Glasgow, November 2, 1877. Printed in *The Presbyterian*, 48 (January 12, 1878):9. (Hereafter cited as Letter to Dods.) We are indebted for information on this source of Hodge's doctrine of inspiration to James L. McAllister, Jr., "The Nature of Religious Knowledge in the Theology of Charles Hodge" (Ph.D. dissertation, Duke University, 1957), p. 201f.

122. McAllister, in the conclusion of his dissertation, pp. 369–370, comments: "What he [Hodge] cited as the authoritative testimony of the Church was, in fact, the testimony of only some parts of the whole church, and even some parts of the Protestant churches. The truth is that Hodge was not the scholar of historical theology which he appeared to be, and among his contemporaries George P. Fisher did the best job of making that evident."

123. Hodge's *ST*, I, 154.

124. "Inspiration," p. 685.

125. Hodge's *ST*, I, p. 155.

126. Hodge's *ST*, I, p. 156.

127. "Inspiration," p. 669. Hodge said: "Much contained in the New Testament has a fulness of meaning which the apostles themselves little imagined."

128. Letter to Dods, cited in McAllister, p. 204.

129. Ibid.

130. Hodge's *ST*, I, 157.

131. "Inspiration," p. 669. Hodge continued: "We may therefore hold that the Bible is in the strictest sense the Word of God, and infallible in all its parts, and yet admit the ignorance and errors of the sacred writers as men. It was only as sacred writers they were infallible."

132. "Inspiration," p. 678.

133. "Inspiration," p. 666.

134. Hodge's *ST*, I, 157. In "Inspiration," p. 675, Hodge avers that "unless the language is determined by the Spirit, the communication after all is human, and not divine."

135. "Inspiration," pp. 677–678.

136. "Inspiration," p. 677.

137. Among the many resources indicating different thought patterns in different cultures see *e.g.*, Thorleif Boman, *Hebrew Thought Compared with Greek*, trans. Jules L. Moreau (Philadelphia: Westminster Press, 1960) and the response to it in James Barr, *The Semantics of Biblical Language* (London: Oxford University Press, 1961). See also Ralph Stob, *Christianity and Classical Civilization* (Grand Rapids, Mich.: Wm. B. Eerdmans, 1950), p. 7, and Kenneth E. Bailey, *Poet and Peasant* (Grand Rapids, Mich.: Wm. B. Eerdmans, 1976), pp. 29–37, where he calls for "oriental exegesis of the New Testament." For a recent anthropological study of the relationship between cultural diversity and human commonality see Walter Goldschmidt, *Comparative Functionalism* (Berkeley: University of California Press, 1966) and the application of his work to theology by Charles Kraft, *Christianity in Culture* (Maryknoll, N.Y.: Orbis, 1979).

138. Charles Hodge, "Lectures on Hermeneutics, February, 1824," *MSS*, Speer Library, Princeton Theological Seminary, Alumni Alcove, cited in J. W. Stewart, IV, 26.

139. Charles Hodge, "The Unity of Mankind," *PR*, 31 (January 1859):103–149. (Hereafter cited as "Unity.")

140. "Unity," p. 148.

141. "Unity," pp. 148–149.

142. "Inspiration," p. 677. Hodge said on page 676 that the trustworthiness of the Bible "depends on the fact that the language employed is the word of God, and not the word of man."

143. "Inspiration," p. 682.

144. "Inspiration," pp. 682–683.

145. Hodge's *ST*, I, 170.

146. Hodge's *ST*, I, 171.

147. Hodge's *ST*, I, 171.

148. Hodge's *ST*, I, 169.

149. "Inspiration," p. 669.

150. "Inspiration," p. 683. See also *PAS*, pp. 126–128. Bozeman characterizes the Princeton view by saying: "So flawless had been the operation of God's Spirit in guiding the scriptural authors that the polemical needs of nineteenth-century exegesis already had been taken into account."

151. "Inspiration," p. 683.

152. Hodge, *What is Darwinism?* (N.Y.: Scribner, Armstrong, and Company, 1874), p. 173. (Hereafter cited as *Darwinism*.) See also *PAS*, pp. 168–169. Hodge had quoted Professor Thomas Huxley's assessment that Darwin's *On the Origin of Species* was "the death-blow of teleology, i.e. of the doctrine of design and purpose in nature." (Hodge's *ST*, II, 16) when he devoted a section to Darwin in the second volume of his *Systematic Theology* (1871–73). It was under the heading "Anti-Scriptural Theories" of the origin of man. See Hodge's *ST*, II, 12ff.

153. *Darwinism*, pp. 133–134. See also *PAS*, pp. 81–86. In 1844 a work by Scottish publisher Robert Chambers (1802–1871), *The Vestiges of Creation*, was published. A devout theist, Chambers believed that an evolutionary theory of human origins actually supported the argument from design. Hodge claimed that Chambers's theories had "fallen into utter disrepute among scientific men" by the time he wrote. See Alan Richardson, *The Bible in the Age of Science* (Philadelphia: Westminster Press, 1961), pp. 48–49. (Hereafter cited as Richardson *Age of Science*.) In the same year that Hodge published *What is Darwinism?*, John Fiske (1842–1901) infused the whole evolutionary process with divine purpose by coining the phrase: "Evolution is God's way of doing things." This was later popularized as a slogan by Lyman Abbott (1835–1922). See Fiske's *Outline of Cosmic Philosophy*, as cited in Winthrop S. Hudson, *Religion in America*, 2d ed. (New York: Charles Scribner's Sons, 1973), p. 267. Cf. Sydney E. Ahlstrom, *A Religious History of the American People* (New Haven: Yale University Press, 1973; rep. 1972), p. 770. (Hereafter cited as Ahlstrom, *History*.) Hodge's neighbor, President James McCosh (1811–1894) of Princeton University said, "I am inclined to think that

the theory contains a large body of important truths." He interpreted "natural selection" as being the product of "supernatural design," *Christianity and Positivism* (New York: R. Carter & Brothers, 1871). See Hudson, p. 267 and Ahlstrom, *History*, p. 770. Charles Hodge maintained, however, that "a more absolutely incredible theory was never propounded for acceptance among men." See *Darwinism*, p. 177, as cited in *PAS*, p. 168. Later his son would agree.

154. Hodge's *ST*, I, 163.
155. Hodge's *ST*, I, 163.
156. Letter to Dods, cited in McAllister, p. 210.
157. McAllister, pp. 209–210.
158. John W. Stewart in a letter to Jack Rogers (July 21, 1976) commented: "After thorough searching, I have never been able to track down a systematic, fully developed hermeneutic position. Hodge's class lectures on 'Biblical Criticism' are the closest thing I can find and, on the whole, are not typical of Hodge's usual thoroughness. The few paragraphs in his *Systematic Theology* are equally unsatisfying." Moorhead, p. 56, confirms this judgment in his study of Joseph Addison Alexander.
159. J. W. Stewart, in the letter cited above remarks: "One matter puzzles me greatly: apparently, as informed and careful as Hodge *et al* were, I have never been able to find a shred of evidence that these earlier Princeton theologians ever questioned the ingredients of common sense philosophy."
160. Hodge, "What is Christianity?" *PR*, 32 (January 1860):121.
161. Hodge's *ST*, I, 1.
162. Hodge's *ST*, I, 9.
163. Hodge's *ST*, I, 9.
164. Hodge's *ST*, I, 9.
165. See, for example, John H. Gertsner, "The Origin and Nature of Man: Imago Dei," in Carl F. H. Henry, ed. *Basic Christian Doctrines*, Contemporary Evangelical Thought (New York: Holt, Rinehart and Winston, 1962), p. 92: "The intellectual nature of man is usually designated as the image of God in the broader sense; the moral, or holy, nature is the image of God proper in the narrower sense. The former is inalienable even in hell; the latter was losable even in paradise."
166. Hodge's *ST*, I, 9.
167. *The Works of Thomas Reid, D.D.*, ed. Sir William Hamilton, 7th ed. (Edinburgh: Ma-

clachlan and Stewart, 1872), 1:440. See J. W. Stewart, IV, 29–31.
168. *Works of ... Reid*, 1:364.
169. Charles Hodge, "Biblical Criticism and Hermeneutics," *MSS*, 1823, Speer Library, Princeton Theological Seminary, Alumni Alcove, cited in J. W. Stewart, IV, 32. (Hereafter cited as "Hermeneutics.")
170. "Hermeneutics," cited in J. W. Stewart, IV, 42.
171. Charles Hodge, "Professor Park's Sermon," a review of Edward A. Park's address, "The Theology of the Intellect and that of the Feelings," *PR*, 22 (October 1850):652. (Hereafter cited as "Park's Sermon.")
172. "Park's Sermon," p. 651.
173. *Works of ... Reid*, 1:340. Reid concluded: "It is the inspiration of the Almighty that gives me this understanding," 1:341.
174. *Works of ...Reid*, 1:339.
175. Ibid., 1:298. Reid claimed: "Nor is it to be doubted that, by the faculties which God has given us, we can conceive things that are absent, as well as perceive those that are within the reach of our sense."
176. *Works of ... Reid*, 1:340.
177. Levi Hedge, *Elements of Logic; or a Summary of the General Principles and Different Modes of Reasoning*, 4th ed. (Buffalo: Phinney & Co., 1851), pp. 58–72, cited in J. W. Stewart, IV, 35.
178. *St.*, I, 634. Stewart, IV, 36, suggests that Hodge used Hedge as a textbook at Princeton.
179. Hodge's *ST*, I, 40.
180. Hodge's *ST*, I, 633.
181. Hodge's *ST*, I, 634.
182. Hodge's *ST*, I, 634.
183. *LCH*, pp. 279–284. See J. W. Stewart, IV, 37.
184. Hodge's *ST*, I, 10.
185. Hodge's *ST*, I, 1–2. Hodge's approach was perpetuated in the biblical department at Princeton by Joseph Addison Alexander. See Moorhead, p. 57.
186. Hodge's *ST*, I, 3. Bozeman notes that the word *fact*, or its equivalent, *truth*, occurs twenty-seven times in the first three pages of Hodge's *Systematic Theology* (*PAS*, p. 147). He further notes: "Hodge is at once the most thoroughgoing and revealing statement of the identification of theological method with the inductive understanding of natural science to which the Old School had come to be devoted." (p. 155). Of the Princeton theologians he writes: "Having

collected the 'direct Scripture proof,' blocks of passages ordered under relevant readings, they considered the matter settled by proof 'more firm than the enduring earth and glorious sky,' " p. 147.

187. *PAS*, pp. 157–159. On p. 157 Bozeman comments: "For Hodge and his colleagues, the 'wonderful organic relation and harmonious combination' of things was as real in revelation as in nature."

188. Hodge's *ST*, I, 10.

189. Hodge's *ST*, I, 11. Hodge wrote: "Everything revealed in nature, and in the constitution of man concerning God and our relation to Him, is contained and authenticated in Scripture." This led his later followers to use the Bible as a basis for constructing a unified field of knowledge to compete with other philosophies and sciences. See, for example, Francis A. Schaeffer, *The God Who Is There* (Downers Grove, Ill.: Inter-Varsity Press, 1968), pp. 92–93, "It is plain, therefore, that from the viewpoint of the Scriptures themselves there is a unity over the whole field of knowledge. God has spoken, in a linguistic propositional form, truth concerning Himself and truth concerning man, history and the universe." For background on Schaeffer's relationship to the Princeton Theology see Jack Rogers, "Francis Schaeffer: the Promise and the Problem," *The Reformed Journal* (May and June 1977):12–15 and 15–19.

190. Hodge's *ST*, I, 11.

191. Hodge's *ST*, I, 12.

192. *PAS*, pp. 65–68. *PR* 30 (1858):735, stated that "Mr. Tyler is second to no American metaphysical writer of the present generation," cited in *PAS*, p. 65.

193. Samuel Tyler, *A Discourse of the Baconian Philosophy*, 2d ed. (New York: Baker and Scribner, 1850), p. 168, cited in *PAS*, p. 67. Hodge added as a fourth point that "in theology as in natural science, principles are derived from facts, and not impressed upon them." The theologian's job was to set forth "God's system," not the theologian's own. See Hodge's *ST* I, 13–14. Hodge's conviction that God had implanted one system of theology in Scripture and that this system was known (and best expressed in Turretin) vitiated the practical value of his insistence on induction. See Hodge's *ST*, I, 18. Hodge counted himself an Augustinian.

194. Hodge's *ST*, I, 15.

195. Hodge's *ST*, I, 16–17. See Hodge's own devotional book, *The Way of Life*.

196. Hodge's *ST*, III, 69. Hodge wrote: "This witness of the Spirit is not an affirmation that the Bible is the Word of God." A statement more directly opposite to Calvin's position could hardly be made.

197. Hodge's *ST*, III, 42.

198. Hodge's *ST*, III, 43.

199. Hodge's *ST*, III, 60–61.

200. Hodge's *ST*, III, 62.

201. Hodge's *ST*, III, 68.

202. Cited in *PAS*, p. 99

203. Cited in *PAS*, p. 111. See also pp. 108, 142, 152.

204. Benjamin M. Palmer, a Southern Presbyterian adherent of the Princeton theology, argued that Bacon would never have omitted biblical data from his scientific inductions. Palmer wrote in an article in the *Southern Presbyterian Review* of 1852 entitled, "Baconianism and the Bible," that: "The very genius of inductive philosophy forbids the exclusion of a single pertinent fact from its generalizations.... The philosophy ... which will ignore the Bible ... has apostatized from the fundamental articles of the Baconian creed," cited in *PAS*, p. 110. Bacon had already been beatified as a paragon of Protestant virtue. See *PAS*, pp. 72–74. Some of the more extravagant statements came from Palmer: "There never could have been a Bacon without the Bible.... Francis Bacon was an offspring of the Reformation"; and from his fellow Southern Presbyterian John Holt Rice who stated that Bacon imbibed "the first great truths of philosophy" while poring over his Bible. Cited in *PAS*, pp. 129–130.

205. "Unity," pp. 104–105, cited in *PAS*, p. 111. For more on Agassiz and the controversy, see *PAS*, pp. 79, 83, 93, and 98.

206. See *PAS*, pp. 63, 98, 100, 109.

207. Barker, p. 4. A. A. Hodge, his son and biographer, characterized his father as conservative and moderate. See *LCH*, p. 253.

208. Hodge's *ST*, I, 188.

209. Charles Hodge, *A Dissertation on the Importance of Biblical Literature* (Trenton, N.J.: Printed by G. Sherman, 1822), pp. 45–46, cited in J. W. Stewart, IV, 46.

210. For brief biographies of A. A. Hodge see *DAB*, s.v. "Hodge, Archibald Alexander" and *NSH*, s.v. "Hodge, Archibald Alexander."

211. See *PAS*, p. 41.

212. After the death of his first wife, Elizabeth Holliday Hodge, A. A. Hodge in 1862 married Mrs. Margaret McLaren Woods.

213. Letter from J. C. Backus to A. A. Hodge (April 25, 1877), cited in *BC*, p. 24.
214. "Author's preface," in a reprint edition (London: Banner of Truth Trust, 1961), p. xvi. (Hereafter cited as A. A. Hodge, *Confession of Faith.*)
215. A. A. Hodge, *Confession of Faith*, pp. 33–34.
216. A. A. Hodge, *Confession of Faith*, p. 34.
217. See Jerry W. Brown, *The Rise of Biblical Criticism in America 1800–1870* (Middletown, Conn.: Wesleyan University Press, 1969), p. 180 and *BC*, pp. 20–21. Cf. Charles A. Briggs, *General Introduction to the Study of Holy Scripture* rev. ed., (Grand Rapids, Mich.: Baker Book House, 1970; rep. 1900), chap. 11.
218. A. A. Hodge, *Addresses at the Inauguration of . . .* (Philadelphia, 1887), pp. 25–26, 34–38, as cited in *BC*, p. 25.
219. See *PAS*, p. 167–168.
220. See *PAS*, pp. 82–83. See also Richard Westfall, *Science and Religion in Seventeenth Century England* (Ann Arbor: University of Michigan Press, 1973; rep. 1958), pp. 50, 69 and Dillenberger, *Protestant Thought*, pp. 114, 115.
221. See Ahlstrom, *History*, pp. 768–769.
222. Ahlstrom, *History*, p. 768. Ahlstrom points to the contributions of Herbert Spenser, the greatest popularizer of Darwin in Britain and America (see p. 767). Martin Marty writes that "after about 1860, American Protestants began to undergo an extensive assault on their old world view and an impressive change to a new one," *Righteous Empire* (N.Y.: Dial Press, 1970), p. 189. He mentions Spenser, Hegel, and John Henry Newman as contributing to this new world view. "The Hegelian or Darwinian world views meant that as people looked out at their worlds, they found some principle of development, evolution, or change operative," p. 190.
223. See the account of these developments and the reaction of New School Presbyterians in George M. Marsden, *The Evangelical Mind and the New School Presbyterian Experience* (New Haven: Yale University Press, 1970), chap. 7.
224. *PAS*, p. 169.
225. *PAS*, p. 168.
226. The phrase is Marty's, p. 189. Ahlstrom, *History*, lists five challenges to the traditional views: (1) "uniformitarian" principles applied to the interpretations of past events to the exclusion of miracle and di-

vine providence; (2) the Scriptures themselves were interpreted in the same manner as other important historical documents; (3) historical theology came into its own as a discipline; that is, anxiety about specific doctrines (such as the Atonement or the nature of Christ) came to be resolved by the scientific study of that doctrine in the history of Christianity; (4) comparative religion; and (5) "historicism," pp. 772–773. Richardson writes: "The real challenge of the nineteenth-century revolution in human thinking lay not in the realm of natural science but in the realm of history," *Age of Science*, p. 49.
227. See Richardson, *Age of Science*, pp. 49ff.
228. Charles Hodge wrote that Darwin's theory meant that "hundreds or thousands of millions of years ago God called a living germ, or living germs, into existence, and that since that time God has no more to do with the universe than if He did not exist. This is atheism to all intents and purposes, because it leaves the soul as entirely without God, without a Father, Helper, or Ruler, as the doctrine of Epicurus or of Comte," Hodge's *ST*, II, 16. He was profoundly sure of his own position: "God has revealed his existence and his government of the world so clearly and so authoritatively, that any philosophical or scientific speculations inconsistent with these truths are like cobwebs in the track of a tornado." See Hodge's *ST*, II, 15, 17; and 29 where he writes: "The immutability of species is stamped on the very face of nature."
229. See *PAS*, p. 168.
230. *PAS*, p. 168. Cf. p. 143.
231. *Outlines (1860)*, p. iv.
232. Ibid., iv–v.
233. *Outlines (1879)*.
234. Interestingly, the chapter on the evidences of Christianity was dropped in 1879 and attention turned directly from the "sources of theology" to the Bible's inspiration. Works on the evidences of Christianity are cited in his chapter 3 (1879) to prove that "it is an historical fact that Christianity is such a supernatural revelation," p. 61. But the traditional full arguments of "Evidences" from miracle and prophecy are noticeably absent here though Hodge had developed them in the 1860 edition.
    In the Princeton tradition Archibald Alexander's *Evidences* was the pioneering work. The significance of the approach of this work lies in the underlying assumption

that Christianity (and the Bible) could be approached by the inductive methods of then-current natural science. As one thinker said: "By the induction of facts we prove that the Bible comes from God." See *PAS*, p. 143. James W. Alexander (Archibald Alexander's son) wrote: "A book comes to us purporting to be a revelation from God. Examine the proofs which it brings to substantiate this claim. If they are incontrovertible, believe the book . . . . If they are insufficient, burn the volume," *Forty Years of Familiar Letters of James W. Alexander*, ed. John Hall, 2 vols. (New York: Charles Scribner, 1860), 1:55. See *PAS*, pp. 139–143.

A. A. Hodge's approach in 1879 certainly was still the same as in 1860 and in the Princeton tradition itself. He cites miracles and prophecies in questions 8 and 13 of chap. 3 (1879) as a proof of inspiration. But as will be suggested, his heightened concern to defend the Bible from the onslaught of Higher Critics and Darwinian science led him to tighten his case by arguing an errorless autograph of the Bible rather than by arguing that the present text was the errorless revelation of God.

235. *Outlines* (1860), p. 70. A. A. Hodge tightened the Princeton doctrine of inspiration at this point. The man for whom he was named, Archibald Alexander, had distinguished three "kinds" or "species" of inspiration. Alexander specifically rejected the argument that there could be only one method of inspiration. Now A. A. Hodge claimed that "it is injurious to distinguish between different degrees of inspiration, as if the several portions of the Scriptures were in different degrees God's word, while in truth the whole is equally and absolutely so," *Outlines* (1860), p. 69. See also *Outlines* (1879), pp. 77f. Alexander surely would have rejected Hodge's charge that his (Alexander's) view produced a Bible that was not fully and thoroughly the Word of God! Joseph Addison Alexander also renounced the view of "different degrees of inspiration" as being a "dangerous tendency." See Moorhead, p. 58, citing *The Prophecies of Isaiah* (1870 edition), I, 8.

236. Questions 8 and 9, *Outlines* (1860), pp. 71–72.

237. *Outlines* (1879), p. 66.

238. *Outlines* (1879), pp. 66–67.

239. These four reasons are exactly the same ones he used in the 1860 edition to prove that inspiration extended to words as well as to thoughts (question 9).

240. *Outlines* (1860), p. 67.

241. *Outlines* (1879), pp. 66, 69. This latter proof had two parts: from the statements of the Scriptures themselves; and from the phenomena of Scripture when critically examined.

242. *Outlines* (1879), p. 67.

243. *Outlines* (1879), p. 75 (question 20).

244. *Outlines* (1860), p. 76 (question 24).

245. *Outlines* (1860), pp. 76–77.

246. *Outlines* (1879), p. 75.

247. *Outlines* (1879), p. 75.

248. *Outlines* (1879), pp. 75–76.

249. *Outlines* (1860), p. 77.

250. *Outlines* (1879), pp. 76–77.

251. *Outlines* (1860), p. 77.

252. *Outlines* (1860), p. 77.

253. See *PAS*, pp. 153–155.

254. See *PAS*, pp. 81–86.

255. See A. A. Porter, "The Unity of the Human Race," *Southern Presbyterian Review*, 4 (1851):367, as cited in *PAS*, p. 104. Charles Hodge taught that: "There is of course a vast difference between facts and theories. The former, and not the latter are authoritative." See "Unity," p. 107, as cited in *PAS*, p. 105.

256. This was the method regularly used in the *Princeton Review* when laying to rest some specious scientific claim. See *PAS*, pp. 104–105. Charles Hodge wrote: "There is a great distinction between theories and facts. Theories are of men. Facts are of God. The Bible often contradicts the former, never the latter," Hodge's *ST*, I, 171. Thus the fact, not the theory was to be authoritative for the Hodges.

257. *Outlines* (1860), pp. 76, 77.

258. *Outlines* (1879), p. 77.

259. Charles Hodge proclaimed: "Science has in many things taught the Church how to understand the Scriptures. . . . The Bible has stood, and still stands in the presence of the whole scientific world with its claims unshaken," Hodge's *ST* I, 171.

f. Selected Bibliography

Ahlstrom, Sydney E. "The Scottish Philosophy and American Theology." *Church History*, 24 (September 1955):257–272.

Bozeman, Theodore Dwight. *Protestants in an Age of Science.* University of North Carolina Press, 1977.

Leith, John H. *An Introduction to the Reformed Tradition.* John Knox Press, 1977.

Loetscher, Lefferts A. *The Broadening Church.* University of Pennsylvania Press, 1957; rep. 1954.

Marsden, George M. *The Evangelical Mind and the New School Presbyterian Experience.* Yale University Press, 1970.

May, Henry F. *The Enlightenment in America.* Oxford University Press, 1976.

McKim, Donald K. "Archibald Alexander and the Doctrine of Scripture." *Journal of Presbyterian History*, 54, no. 3 (Fall 1976):355–375.

Moorhead, James H. "Joseph Addison Alexander: Common Sense, Romanticism and Biblical Criticism at Princeton." *Journal of Presbyterian History*, 53, no. 1 (Spring 1975):51–65.

Nelson, John Oliver. "The Rise of the Princeton Theology." Ph.D. dissertation. Yale University, 1935.

Sandeen, Ernest R. "The Princeton Theology." *Church History*, 31 (September 1962):307–321.

Sandeen, Ernest R. *The Roots of Fundamentalism.* University of Chicago Press, 1970.

Smith, Elwyn A. *The Presbyterian Ministry in American Culture.* Westminster Press, 1962.

CHAPTER 6

The Defense of Reformed Scholasticism in America

a. From Inductive Science to Deductive Apologetics: Benjamin Breckinridge Warfield (1851–1921)

A. A. Hodge died, suddenly and unexpectedly, at the age of 63 in 1886. He had taught at Princeton for just nine years. That seminary, which had had only two professors of systematic theology in its first sixty-five years, now had to seek a fourth occupant for its central chair. The Princeton Seminary faculty again reached out to Western Seminary in Pennsylvania and picked its Professor of New Testament Language and Literature, Benjamin Breckinridge Warfield.[1] Warfield had been a student of Charles Hodge and an intimate friend of A. A. Hodge. Warfield had collaborated with the younger Hodge in writing a new article on inspiration in 1881.[2]

Warfield's father's family had been English Puritans who settled in Virginia, and his mother had descended from Scotch-Irish immigrants to Pennsylvania.[3] His maternal grandfather, Robert Jefferson Breckinridge, had been moderator of the General Assembly of the Presbyterian Church (Old School) in 1841 and was the founder and president of the Theological Seminary at Danville, Kentucky. Warfield's father was a wealthy landowner and breeder of horses and cattle.[4] In his family home a child was expected to have completed study of the Westminster Shorter

Catechism by the sixth year. That exercise was followed by study of proofs from Scripture and then the Larger Catechism, with a considerable amount of Scripture memorization done in the course of Sabbath afternoons. Warfield joined the Second Presbyterian Church in Lexington when he was sixteen.[5]

Warfield attended private schools and studied with tutors, two of whom later became college presidents. He entered Princeton College in 1868, the same year that James McCosh (1811–1894) came from Scotland to be its president. Warfield's interests lay in natural science. McCosh combined a commitment to Scottish realist philosophy with an acceptance of Darwinian evolution. Warfield already was a "Darwinian of the purest water," having studied the *On the Origin of Species* before coming to Princeton. Later, however, he rejected Darwin's evolutionism. He insisted that God had created everything distinctively new by a miracle, although he did not deny that God had used evolution to bring created beings to their present level of development.[6] Warfield concentrated his college studies in mathematics and physics. He intended to seek a fellowship to pursue graduate work in experimental science. His father dissuaded him by arguing that he did not need the money and would do better to travel in Europe without being bound to any particular course of study. Warfield graduated with the highest honors in 1871 at the age of nineteen, having won prizes for essay and debate.[7]

Warfield left for Europe the following February. He went first to Edinburgh. In the following summer, he wrote from Heidelberg that he had decided to enter the ministry. The announcement came as a surprise to his family and friends, perhaps because Warfield had always been reticent to speak about personal matters.[8] At home again he edited for a short time the *Farmer's Home Journal,* dealing with livestock. He attended Princeton Seminary from 1873 to 1876 during the last years of Charles Hodge's life. He was licensed to preach by the Presbytery of Ebenezer (Kentucky) in 1875 and supplied churches that summer and the next. He declined a call to the First Presbyterian Church of Dayton, Ohio, on graduation in order to go abroad for further study.[9] Warfield married Annie Pearce Kinkead, daughter of a prominent lawyer, and sailed soon after for Leipzig. The year was marred by tragedy when, during a walk in the Harz Mountains, the Warfields encountered a severe thunderstorm. The experience apparently had a shattering effect on Mrs. Warfield's nervous system and she was practically an invalid the rest of her life.[10]

Returning to America, Warfield spent some time as assistant pastor of the First Presbyterian Church of Baltimore. In the fall of 1878 he accepted the call to become instructor in New Testament Language and Literature at Western Theological Seminary in Allegheny, Pennsylvania.

The following year he was made professor and ordained. He remained at Western for nine years. When the invitation from Princeton came to succeed A. A. Hodge, many sought to persuade Warfield to remain in the field of New Testament. Warfield, however, recalled that Charles Hodge himself had begun as a professor of languages and of New Testament, and he accepted the call.[11]

The Shift to Apologetics

B. B. Warfield was Professor of Didactic and Polemical Theology at Princeton for thirty-three years. He lived very much the life of the scholarly recluse, partly because of his temperament and partly because of his wife's health. He seldom left the environs of Princeton Seminary to which he was passionately loyal. He had little to do with the activities of the church, seldom preached in neighboring cities and did not serve on committees or boards of the denomination. Yet, through his teaching and writing, his influence was immense. He was chief editor of the *Presbyterian and Reformed Review* from 1890 to 1903 and contributed many articles to it and its successor the *Princeton Theological Review.*[12]

Nearly all of Warfield's writing was piecemeal and polemical. When friends asked why he did not write a systematic theology, he replied that the times were not ripe for another effort in that area. Charles Hodge's work provided the constructive base. But Warfield felt that all of the principal doctrines of Christianity were under severe attack, and he saw his job as defending them.[13]

When Archibald Alexander founded Princeton he set forth a mixture of philosophical and pastoral theology. Charles Hodge drew together all the strands of thought he had inherited and compressed them into a systematic theology. Warfield now saw that system under attack. For him then, the task was defense and the technique was apologetics.

Warfield assumed all the traditional commitments of the Princeton theology: the scholastic methodology of Thomas Aquinas and Turretin; the philosophy of Scottish common sense; the interpretation of Scripture based on Baconian induction; the priority of reason over faith; and the necessity for factual evidences of the Bible's authenticity. None of these needed to be developed. But all of them needed to be defended. The sources on which the Princeton theology drew receded more into the background with Warfield than they had with any of his predecessors. He insisted ever more strongly that he was only defending what Scripture plainly taught and what the church had always believed. His emphasis shifted from inducing facts to deducing conclusions. While strengthening the theory that theology was based on induction, Warfield actually worked increasingly by deduction. Charles Hodge had reduced theology to a science. Warfield refined it into a technology. Conclusions were drawn on the basis of technical definitions, minute word studies, and scholastic refinements of language.

Warfield was asked to contribute a memorial essay to A. A. Hodge's biography of his father. In it, both Warfield's commitment to the principles of Charles Hodge and Warfield's own penchant for technical refinements are revealed. Warfield wrote:

> I thought then, and I think now, that Dr. Hodge's sense of the general meaning of a passage was unsurpassed.... He seemed to look through a passage, catch its main drift and all its theological bearings, and state the result in crisp sentences, which would have been worthy of Bacon.... He had, however, no taste for the technicalities of exegesis.... He made no claim, again, to critical acumen; and in questions of textual criticism he constantly went astray.... He was great here, but not at his greatest. Theology was his first love.... I can only say that in that room of Systematic Theology, I think I had daily before me examples of perfect teaching.[14]

Warfield needed no new theology. The Princeton theology, systematized by Charles Hodge was enough. In his inaugural address at Princeton, Warfield announced:

> Though the power of Charles Hodge may not be upon me, the theology of Charles Hodge is within me, and ... this is the theology which, according to my ability, I have it in my heart to teach to the students of the coming years. Oh, that the mantle of my Elijah might fall upon my shoulders; at least the message that was given to him is set within my lips.[15]

What Warfield added to the Princeton theology was a technical expertise, a skill in logic and argumentation, a polemical power that continued to be influential during a time when it was increasingly under attack. Warfield was perhaps the man most capable of perpetuating the Princeton tradition as it moved from the nineteenth into the twentieth century.

Warfield knew where to begin. The Bible was the first line of defense. The enemy was Higher Criticism. His inaugural address in 1880 was entitled "Inspiration and Criticism." That same year he wrote a pamphlet on "The Divine Origin of the Bible."[16] After his death, his writings were collected and published in ten volumes. The first volume, *Revelation and Inspiration,* was devoted to articles in apologetic defense of the authenticity and authority of the Bible.

Revelation and Reason

Like Charles Hodge, Warfield believed in both "natural" revelation and "supernatural" revelation.[17] Natural revelation was God's revelation of Himself "in the course of Nature or of history." Warfield's deep commitment to a natural theology was revealed in his attitude toward the relationship between general and special revelation. He wrote:

> Without special revelation, general revelation would be for sinful man incomplete and ineffective. . . . Without general revelation, special revelation would lack that basis in the fundamental knowledge of God as the mighty and wise, righteous and good, maker and ruler of all things, apart from which the further revelation of this great God's interventions in the world for the salvation of sinners could not be either intelligible, credible or operative.[18]

For Warfield, even God could not operate other than through the Aristotelian epistemology in which all knowledge began in sense experience and was objectified and categorized by the intellect.

At the same time, Warfield attempted to follow Calvin in the belief that the knowledge of God was innate, "naturally engraved on the hearts of men."[19] This was the *sensus divinitatis* or *sensus deitatis* through which "all men know there is a God, who has made them, and to whom they are responsible."[20] But Warfield quickly went beyond Calvin to find fully developed arguments for the existence of God. Warfield assumed that Calvin held that the traditional theistic proofs were "sound," but he did note that in both richness and fullness of presentation on these matters, Calvin was surpassed by Zwingli. Warfield acknowledged, however, that "it is to Melanchthon that we shall have to go to find among the Reformers a formal enumeration of the proofs for the divine existence."[21] Warfield overlooked Calvin's antipathy to Aristotle and Thomas Aquinas. And he omitted mention of the reversal in theological method from the first to the second generation of Reformers. In Warfield's view these Thomistic proofs had been "traditional in the Church from its first age."[22]

Warfield also dealt with Calvin's teaching that this "light which God has kindled in the breasts of men has been smothered and all but extinguished by their iniquity."[23] But here also he was very careful to redefine how Calvin was to be interpreted on this point of the "noetic effects of sin."[24] Calvin taught the "bankruptcy of the natural knowledge of God" for obtaining salvation to be sure, according to Warfield. He also taught that the corruption of the human heart had corrupted the knowledge of God and that this had rendered humans inexcusable before God.[25] Only through the "testimony of the Spirit" or "regeneration" could these noetic effects of sin be removed.[26] But Warfield stressed that Calvin should not be interpreted as teaching the unknowableness of God. For Warfield it was important to read Calvin as saying at this point that:

> The 'testimony of the Holy Spirit in the heart' does not communicate to man any new powers, powers alien to him as man: it is restorative in its

nature and in principle merely recovers his powers from their deadness induced by sin.[27]

Despite his acknowledgement of all of Calvin's stricture's against the natural person's ability to know God, Warfield laid his stress not on the supernatural, but on the natural knowledge of God.[28]

Apologetics as the Foundation of Theology

The significance of Warfield's interpretation of Calvin on these points is that it provided a theoretical and theological basis by which the use of reason in theology could be justified. Warfield's view of natural revelation, the effect of sin on the human mind, and the testimony of the Spirit provided the foundation on which his apologetics were built. For Warfield, apologetics stood "at the head of the departments of theological science."[29]

Warfield described apologetics not only as the first, but the most fundamental activity for the Christian scholar. The task of apologetics was

> not the defense, not even the vindication, but the establishment, not, strictly speaking, of Christianity, but rather of that knowledge of God which Christianity professes to embody and seeks to make efficient in the world and which it is the business of theology scientifically to explicate.[30]

Warfield rejected definitions of theology as "the science of faith" with its subject matter the "subjective experiences of the human heart" and theology as "the science of the Christian religion" which investigated "the purely historical question of what those who are called Christians believe." Properly, theology was "the science of God" which dealt with "a body of objective facts" and had as its subject matter the "knowledge of God." If this was so, argued Warfield, then apologetics "must begin by establishing the reality as objective facts of the data upon which it is based."[31] The business of apologetics was:

> to establish the truth of Christianity as the absolute religion. . . . It has for its object the laying of the foundations on which the temple of theology is built, and by which the whole structure of theology is determined.[32]

For Warfield, therefore, philosophy preceded theology. The requirements of human reason had to be met before God could give faith.

Warfield's greatest enemies from the standpoint of apologetics were the extremes of rationalism and mysticism. He did not even acknowledge the option of an Augustinian "faith leads to understanding" approach. Every theology that did not conform to his Thomistic tendencies, Warfield classed as rationalism or mysticism. Albrecht Ritschl (1822–1889) was the epitome of rationalism for Warfield. Ritschl, according to Warfield, grounded religious knowledge on utility rather than on fact and therefore cut off the possibility of rational proof.[33] The "mystical tendencies" at work in Warfield's time he saw as paralleling rationalism in their "widespread inclination to set aside apologetics in favor of the 'witness of the Spirit.' "[34] Warfield asserted:

> It seems to be forgotten that though faith be a moral act and the gift of God, it is yet formally conviction passing into confidence; and that all forms of convictions must rest on evidence as their ground, and it is not faith but reason which investigates the nature and validity of this ground. 'He who believes,' says Thomas Aquinas, in words which have become current as an axiom, 'would not believe unless he saw that what he believes is worthy of belief.'[35]

In keeping with his avowed commitment to Thomistic scholasticism, Warfield stressed formal issues and did not acknowledge that the church fathers and Reformers had seen theology as a practical task of bringing people to salvation and obedience to Christ.

Warfield's views on apologetics can most clearly be seen in contrast to those of his contemporaries in the Netherlands, the Calvinist theologians Abraham Kuyper (1837–1920) and Herman Bavinck (1854–1921).[36] These men saw apologetics as not the first but the last of the theological disciplines. They used Apologetics only after their theology was completed and then as a means to answer philosophical objections to Christianity.[37] Warfield reacted against this "minifying of apologetics."[38] He argued:

> Faith is, in all its exercises alike, a form of conviction, and is, therefore, necessarily grounded in evidence. And we are arguing that evidence accordingly has its part to play in the conversion of the soul; and that the systematically organized evidence which we call Apologetics similarly has its part to play in the Christianizing of the world.[39]

Warfield believed apologetics was to play a "primary part" and a "conquering part" in the Christianizing of the world. In fact, Christianity was distinct for him in that

> it has come into the world clothed with the mission to *reason* its way to its dominion. Other religions may appeal to the sword, or seek some other way to propagate themselves. Christianity makes its appeal to right reason, and stands out among all religions, therefore, as distinctively 'the Apologetic religion.'[40]

According to Warfield:

> It [apologetics] concerns itself with the solid objective establishment, after a fashion valid for all normally working minds and for all ages of the world in its developing thought, of those great basal facts which constitute the

Christian religion; or better, which embody in the concrete the entire knowledge of God accessible to men, and which, therefore, need only explication by means of the further theological disciplines in order to lay openly before the eyes of men the entirety of the knowledge of God within their reach.[41]

Warfield held, with the medieval scholastics, that theology was the Queen of the Sciences. And apologetics, for him, was the ruling consort of the Queen.

Warfield's differences with his Dutch counterparts came through clearly in his review of Bavinck's *De Zekerheid des Geloofs* (*The Certainty of Faith*).[42] This work revealed the deep methodological differences between those in the Amsterdam and the Princeton traditions.

Faith and Evidence

Warfield quoted Bavinck as saying that "Apologetics is the fruit, not the root of faith."[43] Warfield claimed that Bavinck had confused the certainty of the truth of Christianity with the assurance of salvation. Warfield's uncritical commitment to the epistemology of Scottish realism forced him to separate these two factors, which the Reformers had seen as inseparably joined in Christian experience. Warfield could conceive of "no act of faith of any kind which is not grounded in evidence: faith is a specific form of persuasion or conviction, and all persuasion or conviction is grounded in evidence."[44] Because Bavinck stated that the direct act of personal faith was necessary before an individual could have the certitude of the truth of the Christian religion, Warfield argued that Bavinck had reversed "the natural order." For Warfield, reason always had to precede faith. He declared:

> On the face of it, conviction of the truth of the Christian religion would appear to be the logical prius of self-commitment to the Founder of that religion—who is also its Heart—as the redeemer of my soul.[45]

Faith Without the Holy Spirit

Warfield failed to recognize Bavinck's stance as that of a wholistic Augustinian approach. Warfield operated only within the dichotomy of Thomistic rationalism or irrationality. For Warfield the Holy Spirit worked to produce acceptance of the humanly devised evidential reasons for faith:

> Does God the Holy Spirit work a blind and ungrounded faith in the heart? What is supplied by the Holy Spirit in working faith in the heart surely is not a ready-made faith, rooted in nothing and clinging without reason to its object; nor yet new grounds of belief in the object presented; but just a new

power to the heart to respond to the grounds of faith, sufficient in themselves, already present in the mind.[46]

Because of his Scottish realist assumptions, Warfield decreed that knowledge of persons and God came in the same way as knowledge of inanimate objects, through the senses first. He had no room for the kind of personal knowledge of God, wrought by the Spirit, which Augustine and the Reformers held. Without giving concrete historical examples, Warfield claimed that his position was that of the Reformed tradition.[47]

Warfield then went further to assert that reasons for faith were actually a type of faith in themselves:

> The Holy Spirit does not produce faith without grounds. But the 'grounds' may and do produce a faith without that specific operation of the Holy Spirit by which alone saving faith can be created in the soul.[48]

Bavinck had labeled this merely as "historical faith." But Warfield insisted on formally calling this "faith" since " 'historical faith' is faith—is a conviction of the mind." The Holy Spirit did not produce faith for Warfield. The Spirit only made the "faith" which was already produced in the mind by reason into "saving faith":

> The truth therefore is that rational argumentation does, entirely apart from that specific operation of the Holy Ghost which produces saving faith, ground a genuine exercise of faith. This operation of the Spirit is not necessary then to produce faith, but only to give to a faith which naturally grows out of the proper grounds of faith, that peculiar quality which makes it saving faith.[49]

Warfield's position was in sharp contrast to that of Calvin who had stated flatly: "But those who wish to prove to unbelievers that Scripture is the Word of God are acting foolishly for only by faith can this be known" (*Inst.* I. vii, 13). Warfield's apparent inability to understand Calvin's stance was rooted in Warfield's assumption that Scottish realist philosophy adequately described all human thought processes. Clearly Warfield conceived "faith" to be primarily mental assent to rational propositions that were logically compelling to an individual. The "proper grounds" of faith were "reasons" or "evidences." Warfield believed that while an individual "ordinarily does not require the whole 'body of evidences' to convince him" of the truth of Christianity, "surely he does require that kind and amount of evidence which is requisite to convince him before he can really be convinced: and faith, in all its forms, is a conviction of truth, founded as such, of course, on evidence."[50]

Warfield was still working with an eighteenth-century Baconian notion of the complete objectivity of science, including theological science. As with Charles Hodge, the necessity of having all faith grounded in evidence induced Warfield sometimes to accept very little evidence and call it adequate. Warfield exhibited this tendency in his essay, "Faith in Its Psychological Aspects."[51] To Warfield, "belief" or "faith" was not an "arbitrary act of the subject's; it is that of a mental state or act which is determined by sufficient reasons."[52] He was careful to argue that faith was not a product of the volition or an act of the consent of the will. He wrote: "It would seem to be fairly clear that 'belief' is always the product of evidence and that it cannot be created by volitions, whether singly or in any number of repetitions." Undoubtedly there was an "interacter of belief and volition," but "one cannot be successfully transmuted into the other, nor one be mistaken for the other."[53] Belief was always "forced consent," that is, it was always "determined by evidence, not by volition." Warfield acknowledged that to say "faith" was the product of evidence was not the same as saying that "consent was produced only by compelling evidence, that is, evidence which is objectively adequate."[54] This was because "objective adequacy and subjective effect are not exactly correlated." Yet he held strongly that "there is no 'faith,' 'belief' possible without evidence or what the mind takes for evidence; 'faith,' 'belief' is a state of mind grounded in evidence and impossible without it."[55] It was true for Warfield that

> the mind knows and can know nothing of objectively and subjectively adequate grounds in forming its convictions. All it is conscious of is the adequacy or inadequacy of the grounds on which its convictions are based.[56]

But this was where the decision was made. If the grounds "appeal to it as adequate, the mind is convinced; but if they do not, it remains unconvinced."[57] Curiously, Warfield's concept of faith, as always founded on evidence, had a twofold effect. It maintained the theory of the primacy of the intellect. But in practice it encouraged apologists to use any evidence that was adequate for their audience, even though that evidence did not objectively prove the case.

If reason produced both faith and knowledge, how were these two factors to be distinguished? Warfield asserted that the difference was the ground on which each rested. Knowledge was based on human perception; faith was based on testimony. Warfield wrote: "Those convictions which rest on our rational perceptions are called 'knowledge,' while those which rest on 'authority' or 'testimony' receive the name of 'belief,' 'faith.' "[58] Warfield thus utilized the Scottish realist theory that history (remembered events) was equivalent to sensorily perceived objects as evidence. In other words, "the difference is only that they rest on different kinds of evidence—knowledge on 'sight' and faith on 'testimony.' "[59] In "faith" there was an element of "trust" which had "retired into the background in those other acts of assent which we know as 'knowledge.' "[60] Warfield followed Charles Hodge's scholastic notion of trust as intellectual assent to evidence. Warfield could then reiterate that faith was not unreasonable. He affirmed:

> We are moved to this act of conviction by the evidence of testimony, by the force of authority—rationally determined to be trustworthy—and not by the immediate perception of our own rational understanding.[61]

For Warfield the central movement of faith was assent (*assensus*). But it depended not on the will but the intellect—"the *assensus* issues from the *notitia*" (knowledge).[62] In short, faith depended on reason. There had to be reasons before there could be faith. Warfield thus felt that he had protected theological objectivity. But by admitting that evidence could convince people even when it was not intrinsically compelling, he opened the door for later followers of the Princeton apologetic to claim proof when the evidence was at best only probable and at worst simply psychologically appealing to the audience.[63]

Warfield taught that "the action of the Holy Spirit in giving faith is not apart from evidence, but along with evidence; and in the first instance consists in preparing the soul for the reception of the evidence."[64] The evidence was what Warfield termed the "*indicia* of the divinity of Scripture."[65] These were the "proofs" of the divine origin of Scripture. Warfield dealt with these most fully when he wrote on "Calvin's Doctrine of the Knowledge of God." He argued that while Calvin did not explicitly speak of "their part in forming faith under the operation of the testimony of the Spirit,"[66] yet, "it is a complete misapprehension of Calvin's meaning . . . when it is suggested that he represents the *indicia* of the divinity of Scripture as inconclusive or even as ineffective."[67] While "the *indicia* are wholly insufficient to assure us of the divinity of Scripture apart from the testimony of the Spirit," Calvin, according to Warfield, "thought of the *indicia* as co-working with the testimony of the Spirit to this result."[68] To Warfield, Calvin taught that "when the soul is renewed by the Holy Spirit to a sense for the divinity of Scripture, it is through the *indicia* of that divinity that it is brought into its proper confidence in the divinity of Scripture."

This assertion was made in spite of Calvin's clear priority to the witness of the Spirit and subordination of arguments to "secondary aids to our feebleness" (*Inst.* I, viii, 13). Warfield thus followed the persistent Princeton practice of reinterpreting Calvin in light of Aristotelian assumptions that would have been alien to the Reformer. Warfield claimed: "We must accredit Calvin as thinking of the newly implanted spiritual sense discerning the divinity of Scripture only through the mediation of the *indicia* of divinity manifested in Scripture."[69]

Thus the Bible became authoritative according to Warfield not primarily because of the Holy Spirit's witness to Jesus Christ and his message of salvation but rather because one was convinced rationally of the proofs of Scripture's divinity. This was Warfield's main thrust even though he conceded a few pages later that to Calvin "this testimony is just God Himself in His intimate working in the human heart, opening it to the light of the truth, that by this illumination it may see things as they really are and so recognize God in the Scriptures with the same directness and surety as men recognize sweetness in what is sweet and brightness in what is bright."[70]

On Calvin's Neoplatonlc presuppositions the authority of Scripture was self-evident to the Christian believer. On Warfield's Aristotelian assumptions the authority of Scripture could be deduced from evidence that was claimed to be intellectually compelling to the nonbeliever. Because of sin, however, the Spirit had to confirm the evidences for Scripture's authenticity in order to move persons to affirm in their hearts what their minds had accepted. Evidences for the authenticity of Scripture were exalted to a status above Scripture itself.[71] Faith was grounded solely on the *indicia* of Scripture.[72] And the Holy Spirit was relegated to the secondary role of moving the will to follow the mind.

Authority and Canonicity

For Warfield the Scriptures were authoritative because God had spoken through the biblical authors. Warfield wrote: "It is because the apostles were Christ's representatives, that what they did and said and wrote as such, comes to us with divine authority."[73] It was not the church that had the authority on which the canon of Scripture was founded. Rather, the church existed because the apostles founded it on the authority of Christ. It was apostolicity that determined the authority of Scripture for Warfield. He wrote:

> The authority of the Scriptures thus rests on the simple fact that God's authoritative agents in founding the Church gave them as authoritative to the Church which they founded. All the authority of the apostles stands behind the Scriptures, and all the authority of Christ behind the apostles. The Scriptures are simply the law-code which the law-givers of the Church gave it.[74]

Warfield's concept of authority had the unfortunate practical consequence of introducing the Bible as a law book rather than as a saving good news. In addition, and equally unfortunately, Warfield predicated the authority of the Bible on his ability to prove the traditional apostolic authorship or sanction for each of the books. This set him in constant opposition to the Higher Critics.[75]

Warfield was careful to make the distinction between apostolic authorship and apostolic sanction. He wrote: "The authority of the apostles, as founders of the Church by divine appointment, was embodied in whatever books they imposed on the Church as law, not merely in those which they themselves had written."[76] This led Warfield to extensive historical investigations to prove whether or not certain books or passages had apostolic sanction and imposition. To preserve a book's canonical status and also its inspiration as authoritative, the "evidence" had to be examined so there would be a proper "reason for faith."[77]

Warfield felt that the "court of simple common sense" might rightly be able to judge the validity of judgments made about the possible canonicity of early writings.[78] With this Scottish realist principle he investigated the evidence for canonicity among second-century writings and concluded that "every one of the twenty-seven books which now constitute our New Testament is assuredly genuine and authentic."[79] 2 Peter was the greatest question mark but "sober criticism fails to find adequate grounds for rejecting 2 Peter from the circle of apostolic writings."[80] Thus the authority of "testimony" (the proper grounds for faith) made certain by historical investigation, judged by the canons of common sense, produced for Warfield and his colleagues at Princeton a sure "reason" for faith in the received canon of Scripture.[81] This canon was authoritative because it was God speaking through the biblical authors, and because the apostolic authorship of the books could be proved by evidence Warfield deemed sufficient.

The Proof of Inspiration

With proof of the authenticity, historical credibility, and thus general trustworthiness of the Bible, Warfield was next able to "prove" its inspiration.[82]

For Warfield, God's revelation in Scripture was very closely connected to inspiration. The connection between the two was found in the concept of "progressive revelation." There were three stages or periods in history in which God worked his redemptive acts. Each of these had one characteristic method of revelation.[83] The first was the patriarchal age in which God spoke in "outward manifestations, and symbols, and theophanies." In the prophetic age, God's mode of communication was "inward prophetic inspiration." Then "God spoke to men characteristically by the movements of the Holy Spirit in their hearts." In the New Testament period, "which is preeminently the age of the Spirit," revelation was through "the medium of the written word, what may be called apostolic as distinguished from prophetic inspiration." In sum, these modes of revelation were: "(1) external manifestations, (2) internal suggestion, and (3) concursive operation."[84] The historical development the Scriptures traced or rather embodied in their own growth was "the record of the steady advance of this gracious revelation through definite stages from its first faint beginnings to its glorious completion in Jesus Christ."[85] Warfield said that revelation had as its "proximate end just the production of knowledge, though not, of course, knowledge for its own sake, but for the sake of salvation."[86] Redemptive acts and their explanations (since God has not left the revelation to explain itself) existed side by side. Scripture was, for Warfield, "in one word, itself a redemptive act of God and by no means the least important in the series of His redemptive acts."[87]

Warfield further refined the Princeton doctrine of inspiration. He contended:

> The apostles claim to be attended in their work of giving law to God's Church by prevailing superintending grace from the Holy Spirit. This is what is called inspiration.[88]

In his inaugural address at Allegheny Seminary in 1880, Warfield had defined inspiration more fully as the

> extraordinary, supernatural influence (or, passively, the result of it) exerted by the Holy Ghost on the writers of our Sacred Books, by which their words were rendered also the words of God, and, therefore, perfectly infallible.[89]

Warfield continually stressed that there were both divine and human elements involved in inspiration:

> The Church, then has held from the beginning that the Bible is the Word of God in such a sense that its words, though written by men and bearing indelibly impressed upon them the marks of their human origin, were written, nevertheless, under such an influence of the Holy Ghost as to be also the words of God, the adequate expression of His mind and will.[90]

Warfield was more careful than Hodge in describing the relationship of human and divine factors. Warfield realized that at times in the Church's history there had been "a tendency toward so emphasizing the divine element as to exclude the human." This had led to a dictation theory of inspiration by some seventeenth-century divines in various Protestant communions. At other times the divine factor had been excluded all together, Warfield felt, and the Scriptures seen as "purely human in both origin and character."[91] To do justice to both elements, Warfield wished to use the term *concursus*. For him, this term meant that "every word is at once divine and human. The philosophical basis of this conception is the Christian idea of God as immanent as well as transcendent in the modes of his activity."[92] Both factors "are conceived of as flowing confluently and harmoniously to the production of a common product. And the two elements are conceived of in the Scriptures as the inseparable constituents of one single and uncompounded product."[93]

While more exact than Hodge in developing a concept of inspiration, Warfield essentially followed Hodge in outlining its consequences. Warfield continued the Princeton policy of asserting that implications of inspiration developed in post-Reformation scholasticism had always been held in the Church. He wrote:

> It [the Church] has always recognized that this conception of co-authorship implies that the Spirit's superintendence extends to the choice of the words by the human authors (verbal inspiration), and preserves its product from everything inconsistent with a divine authorship—thus securing, among other things, that entire truthfulness which is everywhere presupposed in and asserted for Scripture by the Biblical writers (inerrancy).[94]

While Warfield insisted that he wished to guard against a mechanical dictation theory of the mode of inspiration, he occasionally seemed to embrace it. In his review of G. Rooke's *Inspiration* he reacted against Rooke's theory that inspiration meant the impartation of "sufficient knowledge" that the writer could then record in his own way. Warfield argued this was inconsistent with biblical texts where the writer went beyond his own knowledge and with those passages where "the authority of Scripture is shown to inhere even in its vocables, its tenses, its numbers, and its forms of speech as God's Words."[95] On the other hand, while he claimed at times that an author's style made no difference as to whether or not a work was inspired, Warfield felt it necessary to defend the style of 2 Peter against E. A. Abbott who had characterized the style as from "a pseudepigrapher of the baser sort."[96]

Warfield also took care to reject the analogy of the divine and human natures of Christ as an explanation of the divine and human in Scripture. He observed that:

> There is no hypostatic union between the Divine and the human in Scripture; we cannot parallel the 'inscripturation' of the Holy Spirit and the incarnation of the Son of God.... In the one they unite to constitute a Divine-human person, in the other they cooperate to perform a Divine-human work.[97]

He preferred analogies to the Spirit's work in conversion and sanctification and to the activities of God in providence and grace.[98]

External Evidence

Warfield's aim in his numerous expositions of inspiration was to assert what he believed the Scriptures taught about themselves. In so doing he emphasized his belief that the divine influence on the biblical writers produced an immediate divine oracle or Word of God. While he held that in the New Testament a real distinction between a writer's inspiration and the product of that inspiration could not be made, he laid heavy stress on the "writtenness" of the biblical message. This can be seen in his treatment of the Greek terms *graphē* (document), *graphō* (to write), and *logion* (oracle).[99] For example:

> This emphasis on the *written* Scriptures as themselves the product of a divine activity, making them as such the divine voice to us, is characteristic of the whole treatment of Scripture by Paul . . . Generally it must be observed that no difference is made between the word spoken and the word written.[100]

Warfield claimed to base his proof of the Bible's inspiration on its own teachings. At the same time, he asserted that, independent of an inspired Bible, biblical authors could be shown to be accredited messengers from God. Miracles demonstrated their credibility.[101] After asserting that premise, Warfield proceeded to logical deductions so characteristic of his apologetic style. He contended that these creditable messengers of God would not lie about their inspiration if they were inspired by God since God himself would not lie. Nor would God permit these spokesmen to do so.[102]

For Warfield inspiration was a mode of revelation although he also distinguished the two. Revelation was the communication of information to the biblical writers while inspiration was God's superintendence of the writers' communication of that information.[103] A consequence of this concept for Warfield was that "we must indeed prove the authenticity, credibility and general trustworthiness of the New Testament writings before we prove their inspiration."[104] Once both these tasks had been accomplished, the next step was "the test of the truth of the claims of the Bible to be inspired of God through comparison with its contents, characteristics and phenomena."[105] For Warfield claimed as did the Princeton professor before him, that the whole case rested on the "facts." In words that echoed Charles Hodge, Warfield declared:

> By all means let the doctrine of the Bible be tested by the facts and let the test be made all the more, not the less, stringent and penetrating because of the great issues that hang upon it. If the facts are inconsistent with the doctrine, let us all know it, and know it so clearly that the matter is put beyond doubt.[106]

Warfield then admitted more forthrightly than Hodge the merely probable character of their "proof." Even though he knew that all the evidence was "not in the strict logical sense 'demonstrative,'" he was not dismayed. Since the case was built on historical and empirical data it could never attain the status of strictest certainty. The evidence for Scripture's inspiration was " 'probable' evidence." Thus, it "leaves open the metaphysical possibility of its being mistaken." Yet Warfield felt on safe ground. He proclaimed:

> It may be contended that it [the evidence] is about as great in amount and weight as 'probable' evidence can be made, and that the strength of conviction which it is adapted to produce may be and should be practically equal to that produced by demonstration itself.[107]

Warfield's Scottish common sense presuppositions apparently made him insensitive to the weight of his own bias. He too easily shifted from the claim that "facts" put the matter "beyond doubt" to the assertion that the "strength of conviction" produced was "practically equal to that produced by demonstration." Satisfied for himself that the external evidence was decisive, Warfield approached "the study of the characteristics, the structure, and the detailed statements of the Bible."[108]

Internal Evidence

The chief passages to which Warfield referred for his doctrine of inspiration were 2 Timothy 3:16; 2 Peter 1:19–21; and John 10:34f. Warfield built his case around the Greek term *theopneustos*. He dealt in detail with this term in three major articles.[109] His translation of *theopneustos* was "God-breathed." In the first article Warfield emphasized the nature of Scripture rather than its origination: God breathed "tells us nothing expressly of how the Scriptures originated, but confines itself to telling us of their essential nature."[110] In his second article Warfield said exactly the opposite. He stated that the term was "primarily expressive of the origination of Scripture, not of its nature and much less of its effects."[111] In the third article Warfield spoke of *theopneustos* as indicating origin and then added the idea of function. The Scriptures originated from "the creative breath of God." As such "they are of Divine origin and therefore of the highest value for all holy purposes."[112] In this piece he spoke of the inspired Scriptures as being of "great advantage" and "of supreme value for all holy purposes." Here Warfield seemed to connect the inspiration of Scripture in some sense with the function which it was able to perform for believers (in the context it was for Timothy—2 Timothy 3:16).[113] In the second piece, however, he had denied that the inspiredness of Scripture referred to both its "nature" and its "effects."

Warfield's differing views were perhaps occasioned by the theological opponents with whom he was debating. Since apologetics was his style, answering every new attack was more important than consistent exposition. In the first article Warfield stressed the character and not the mode of inspiration. The Scripture passage with which he dealt was not answering the question of "how" Scripture was inspired but rather "what" the product of this inspiration was and what its nature was. *Theopneustia* secured a God-breathed product. Warfield asserted that it did not refer to the mode of inspiration. Warfield's second article, however, combatted the "new view" of *theopneustos* propounded by Drs. Hermann Cremer (1834–1903) and Heinrich Georg August Ewald (1803–1875). They held the term meant "God-filled" and accented the active sense of the term "God-breathing."[114] The "new view" defined Scripture, based on 2 Timothy 3:16, "not according to its origin, but according to its effect—not as 'inspired by God,' but as 'inspiring its readers.' "[115] Warfield reacted by zealously guarding the passive sense of the term. He decided that this passage expressed "an epithet or predicate of 'Scripture'—*theopneustos.*"[116] Warfield saw the Holy Spirit as the "responsible author" of Scripture and declared:

> The fact that all Scripture is conceived as a body of Oracles and approached with awe as the utterances of God certainly does not in the least suggest that these utterances may not be described as God-given words or throw a preference for an interpretation of *theopneustos* which would transmute it into an assertion that they are rather God-giving words.[117]

When confronted with what he considered an unacceptable implication of his former position, Warfield shifted his stress to *theopneustos* as indicating the divine origination of the Scriptures.

Apologetic concerns determined the careful distinctions Warfield made as he wrote about inspiration. He guarded against any view that elevated "subjective" elements, that is, the Scriptures were inspired because they are inspiring. First and foremost Warfield had to maintain that the Bible was a source of truth. He was willing to acknowledge that the inspired Scriptures had "supreme value" for the believer (third article). But he came down hardest on the objective character of Scripture. Warfield introduced five technical discriminations. The Greek term was not "*in*spirating" or "*in*spiration," it was "spiring" or "spiration"—God had "breathed out" the Scriptures. They were the products of the creative breath of God.[118] Warfield was careful not to speculate on the method God used in producing them.

Warfield also dealt exegetically with 2 Peter 1:19–21. The Greek phrase *hupo pneumatos hagiou pheromenoi* Warfield preferred to translate: "as borne by the Holy Spirit" (RSV: "men moved by the Holy Spirit spoke from God."—2 Peter 1:21b).[119] The Holy Spirit, said Warfield, operated in a way said to be a "bearing" of the biblical authors. Warfield felt that this was a special technical term, "not to be confounded with guiding, or directing or controlling, or even leading in the full sense of that word."[120] Warfield explained:

> It goes beyond all such terms, in assigning the effect produced specifically to the active agent. What is 'borne' is taken up by the 'bearer,' and conveyed by the 'bearer's' power, not its own. The men who spoke from God are here declared, therefore, to have been taken up by the Holy Spirit and brought by His power to the goal of His choosing. The things which they spoke under this operation of the Spirit were therefore His things, not theirs.[121]

Again, Warfield sought to safeguard the Scripture as an "immediately Divine Word" that was divinely trustworthy. In an apologetic confrontation, Warfield was not as careful to accent the confluence of divine and human factors. He was concerned to emphasize that Scripture was divine.

Warfield defined his understanding of the divine trustworthiness of Scripture more fully when he interpreted John 10:35: "If he called them gods to whom the word of God came (and scripture cannot be broken) . . . " (RSV). Warfield argued that the terms *law, prophecy,* and *Scripture* used in the John 10:34f. passage were "strict synonyms." The phrase "and the scripture cannot be broken" spoke of Scripture (now, for Warfield, the whole Bible) as an "irrefragable authority." The phrase was "the strongest possible assertion of the indefectible authority of Scripture." This meant for Warfield that Scripture had inviolable authority even in its "most casual clauses"; even in "the very form of its expression in one of its most casual clauses." Warfield attributed this technical, apologetic distinction to Jesus. According to Warfield, for Jesus "the indefectible authority of Scripture attaches to the very form of expression of its most casual clauses. It belongs to Scripture through and through, down to its most minute particulars, that it is of indefectible authority." Warfield linked this passage with many more to develop this case. He claimed that Jesus and the other New Testament writers appealed to Scripture as "an indefectible authority whose determination is final." He continued:

> Both He and they make their appeal indifferently to every part of Scripture, to every element in Scripture, to its most incidental clauses as well as to its most fundamental principles, and to the very form of its expression.[122]

Relying on his Scottish realist assumptions, Warfield unquestioningly attributed to Jesus attitudes that had arisen in the nineteenth century in an apologetic context. He thus believed that:

> The writers of the New Testament books looked upon what they called 'Scripture' as divinely safeguarded in even its verbal expression, and as divinely trustworthy in all its parts, in all its elements, and in all its affirmations of whatever kind.[123]

Warfield contrasted his view of inspiration with what he called "accommodation." He wrote:

> Shall we then take refuge in the idea of *accommodation,* and explain that, in so speaking of the Scriptures, Christ and his apostles did not intend to teach the doctrine of inspiration implicated, but merely adopted, as a matter of convenience the current language, as to Scripture, of the time?[124]

Warfield did not take his understanding of accommodation from its use in the early fathers and Calvin. He seemed to be totally unaware of the concept as they used it—to refer to God condescending to human limitations for human benefit. Warfield, rather, was reacting to James Stuart, a Scottish theologian.[125] Warfield claimed that Stuart's doctrine of accommodation was

> a method by which they [New Testament writers] did and do not undeceive but deceive; not a method by which they teach the truth more winningly and to more; but a method by which they may be held to have taught along with the truth also error.

With accommodation as a starting point, Warfield claimed "we must impeach the New Testament writers as lacking either knowledge or veracity."[126] Unfortunately, both Warfield and Stuart were overreacting to the relatively new notion of cultural conditioning. Stuart used it to deny validity to the message given through the biblical writers. Warfield responded by canonizing even the ancient cultural forms in order to protect their saving function.

Interpretation by Inference

Warfield's formal position was that the whole truth of Christianity did not depend on the verbal inspiration of the Bible.[127] However, he did believe that "the Spirit's superintendence extends to the choice of the words (verbal inspiration), and preserves its product from everything inconsistent with a divine authorship (inerrancy)."[128] His operative position was the traditional Princeton one that "the Scriptures are the word of God in such a sense that their words deliver the truth of God without error."[129] In the past, the Princeton theologians had been able simply to assert that their doctrine of Scripture was biblical. By the late nineteenth century, however, Warfield was called upon to defend this doctrine on exegetical grounds. A well-known instance of this defense was Warfield's controversy with his fellow Presbyterian, the Old Testament Professor at Lane Theological Seminary, Henry Preserved Smith (1847–1927).[130] In April 1882 Smith published an article in *The Presbyterian Review* on "The Critical Theories of Julius Wellhausen." This was the fourth in a series of articles that were to debate the pros and cons of biblical criticism. While Smith criticized facets of Wellhausen's work, he also observed that the textual corruption of the Bible implied its noninfallibility.[131] Smith later supported Union Seminary's Old Testament Professor, Charles Augustus Briggs, during a protracted trial for heresy from 1891 to 1893. Smith was himself tried for heresy during this period by the Presbytery of Cincinnati. On December 13, 1892, he was suspended from the Presbyterian ministry for denying the prevalent Princeton doctrine of Scripture.[132] Smith, in 1893, published a full account of his views on Scripture and defended them against Warfield's position, which at that time was dominant in the Presbyterian church.

Smith questioned Warfield's main thesis that the scriptural phrase "it is written" was equivalent to "God says it." Smith wrote:

> Now, turning to the First Epistle to the Corinthians (iii, 19), we read: 'For it is written, He that taketh the wise in their craftiness.' The quotation from the Old Testament is found in Job v, 13, in a speech of Eliphaz the Temanite. But the speeches of Eliphaz are not accepted by the most stringent inerrancist as 'infallible in all their utterances.'[133]

Warfield's Princeton position had earlier taught that, in relation to the Book of Job where various doctrines were taught, "all our doctrine demands, is that the writer of that book was inspired to give a true account, first of what the men said, and then of what God said."[134]

Smith seized on this inconsistency:

> We have the prosecution, then, conceding that the speeches of Eliphaz, as recorded for us by inspiration, are not guaranteed as infallible. Yet one of these speeches is quoted by the very formula which, as the prosecution assert, declares Scripture to be infallible in all its utterances. The inconsistency is apparent. The phrase *it is written* is in one case, at least, not an assertion of infallibility, and of course it cannot be made such an assertion anywhere else.[135]

Smith then scoured the Old Testament for other instances where the Princeton doctrine of inspiration would guarantee no more than an infallible account of error. Discrepancies between the books of Samuel/Kings and Chronicles were found; differing numbers of chariots, cubits, battle casualties, and so on were noted.[136]

When Warfield was confronted with conflicting "facts" in the biblical account he retreated to an assertion of the traditional Princeton theory. He claimed that his doctrine was grounded in the teachings of Christ and asserted that he would not be disturbed by other theories of inspiration that did not accord with this truth. Warfield replied, not exegetically, but dogmatically: "If we accept the full authority of Christ and of his apostles in all things, we must accept the infallible Bible at their hands."[137] For

Warfield the issue was clear: "Whether the basis of our doctrine is to be what the Bible teaches, or what men teach."[138] While Smith attempted to discuss what the Bible *did* teach on the basis of biblical data, Warfield withdrew to higher ground. He declared that Smith's view of inspiration had compromised itself by its emphasis on the inductive difficulties of Scriptural interpretation. Despite all of Princeton's earlier emphasis on interpreting the Bible by induction from the "facts," Warfield now announced that this was a "human" view of inspiration rather than a scriptural view. He charged Smith with forfeiting the principle by which any Christian doctrine could be established. Warfield wrote of Smith:

> It is everywhere apparent that when he denies that the Scriptures are free from error, he means as much as those words can be made to include, not as little as possible: and that his object is not leave the way open enough to be disturbed by 'specks in the marble of the Parthenon' or slight blemishes in accuracy of statement; but to leave it open wide enough to reject the authority of this or the whole section of Bible history or this or the other whole sphere of Bible declarations.[139]

With this norm firmly in mind, Warfield debated Smith not on the level of biblical exegesis but on the level of theological doctrine as defined by the Princeton theology. Warfield then resorted to *ad hominem* argumentation. He charged Smith with making himself the judge over history rather than submitting to the authority of the biblical record. Warfield confidently identified his own position with that of the church and declaimed:

> The difference between him and the church in this matter does not lie where he fancies it does. It lies here: he has more confidence in his own historical judgments than in Scriptural statements, and prefers to harmonize the Scriptural statements with his opinions. The church has more confidence in the Scriptural statements than in his historical opinions, and prefers that he shall harmonize his opinions with the Scriptural statements. Dr. Smith says it cannot be done. Well, then, the issue is sharply drawn. And in the last analysis it is simply this: Infallible Scripture *versus* Infallible Science.[140]

The final shift in the Princeton attitude toward science had been accomplished. Science was no longer viewed as a support. Scripture now was to be contrasted with and used to critique science.

Inerrancy by Deduction

The concept of biblical inerrancy at which Warfield finally arrived was based on deductions from premises peculiar to the Princeton theology rather from the "facts" and phenomena of Scripture. As other Christians increasingly came to question the Princeton stance, Warfield made calm discussion difficult by refusing to reflect on his presuppositions and by continually attributing his position to the New Testament writers. He claimed:

> The New Testament writers in all their use of it treat it as what they declare it to be—a God-breathed document, which, because God-breathed, as through and through trustworthy in all its assertions, authoritative in all its declarations, and down to its last particular, the very Word of God, His 'oracles.'[141]

This meant for Warfield "the complete trustworthiness of Scripture in all elements and in every, even circumstantial statement."[142] The Bible "in all its parts and in all its elements, down to the least minutiae, in form of expression as well as in substance of teaching, is from God."[143] For Warfield this "complete trustworthiness" and "entire truthfulness" of Scripture included its accuracy and correctness in matters of history and science.[144] Thus, the Princeton position as brought to its most refined form by Warfield, allowed no practical manifestation of the human element in Scripture. While acknowledging humanity in theory, in practice even the most minute form of expression was attributed directly to God. What made matters even more difficult as biblical criticism became the center of growing public discussion was that Warfield treated any questioning of the Princeton apologetic position as an attack on the Bible itself. Warfield linked any denial that a purpose of the Bible was to speak with technical accuracy on science and history with a wholesale denial of the Bible's authority and trustworthiness for salvation. He wrote:

> The present controversy concerns something much more vital than the bare 'inerrancy' of the Scriptures, whether in the copies or in the 'autographs.' It concerns the trustworthiness of the Bible in its express declarations, and in the fundamental conceptions of its writers as to the course of the history of God's dealings with his people. It concerns, in a word, the authority of the Biblical representations concerning the nature of revealed religion, and the mode and course of its revelation.[145]

Warfield's doctrine technically stated that it was the original autographs of Scripture that were inspired and without error.[146] Warfield claimed that this was the doctrine of the Westminster Confession of Faith.[147] He knew that scribal slips and printers' errors had crept into the text as it has been transmitted to the church through the years. But as with other books where errors had intruded "and as we do not hold the author responsible for these in an ordinary book, neither ought we to hold God responsible for them in this extraordinary book which we call the Bible."[148] He continued: "It is *the Bible* that we declare to be 'of infallible truth'—the Bible that God gave us, not the corruptions and slips which scribes and printers have given us, some of which are in every copy."

Warfield was not bothered by the fact that the *autographa* of Scripture were now lost. It was the autographic *text*, not the *codex* that was in question. Warfield believed that God had providentially preserved enough texts that a near approximation of the original was within reach of textual criticism. He wrote:

> God has not permitted the Bible to become so hopelessly corrupt that its restoration to its original text is impossible. As a matter of fact, the great body of the Bible is, in its autographic text, in the worst copies of the original texts in circulation; practically the whole of it is in its autographic text in the best texts in circulation; and he who will may today read the autographic text in large stretches of Scripture without legitimate doubt.[149]

In practice, Warfield repeatedly expressed the older Princeton position that the phenomena of Scripture were being investigated and no errors were to be found. He asserted that the "progress of investigation has been a continuous process of removing difficulties, until scarcely a shred of the old list of 'Biblical Errors' remains."[150] Further there was a distinction between "*real* discrepancies" and "*apparent* discrepancies." Warfield contended:

> The Church does indeed affirm that the genuine text of Scripture is free from real discrepancies and errors; but she does not assert that the genuine text of Scripture is free from those apparent discrepancies and other difficulties, on the ground of which, imperfectly investigated, the errancy of the Bible is usually affirmed.[151]

But when pressed to explain facts that did not fit the Princeton theory, Warfield appealed to faith. Warfield urged faith not just in the Bible, but in the Princeton theory about it. He expressed his hope and faith, saying:

> Earnest study of the Word may remove these difficulties yet, as it has removed so many more serious ones in the past. And if they are never removed until the trump of doom sounds, why our doctrine of Scripture does not depend on our understanding them. In the exercise of a due modesty, we may manage to credit the doctrine taught us by the Lord and His Apostles, even though some 'difficulties' stand in the way.[152]

Only once did Warfield admit any uneasiness as to whether or not the remaining difficulties might invalidate the Bible's doctrine of inspiration. Warfield said: "It may be true that they do. But I for one—let me say—I for one do certainly hope and believe that they do not."[153]

Warfield's apologetic asserted the inductively demonstrable inerrancy of Scripture. He was fond of saying that, "no single error has as yet been demonstrated to occur in the Scriptures as given by God to His Church."[154] To make that assertion secure, Warfield simply defined "indisputable errors" in such a way that they were impossible to prove.

Warfield's joint article with A. A. Hodge in 1881 set up the Princeton criteria for proving "errors" in Scripture.

> Let (1) it be proved that each alleged discrepant statement certainly occurred in the original autograph of the sacred book in which it is said to be found. (2). Let it be proved that the interpretation which occasions the apparent discrepancy is the one which the passage was evidently intended to bear. It is not sufficient to show a difficulty, which may spring out of our defective knowledge of the circumstances. The true meaning must be definitely ascertained, and then shown to be irreconcilable with other known truth. (3). Let it be proved that the true sense of some part of the original autograph is directly and necessarily inconsistent with some certainly known act of history, or truth of science, or some other statement of Scripture certainly ascertained and interpreted. We believe that it can be shown that this has never yet been successfully done in the case of one single alleged instance of error in the Word of God.[155]

Warfield, with Hodge, thereby shifted the arena of discussion away from what the actual Bible said and was. They based their entire apologetic case on the inability of anyone to bring forth evidence from the nonexistent autographs. With such an unassailable, though artificial, position Warfield felt secure. Individual facts that arose from critical study could never topple the Princeton theory of inerrancy. Warfield affirmed:

> We cannot set aside the presumption arising from the general trustworthiness of Scripture, that its doctrine of inspiration is true, by any array of contradictory facts, each one of which is fairly disputable.[156]

Warfield claimed that the place to start in interpreting Scripture was with Princeton's apologetically developed doctrine of inspiration rather than "with a collection of the phenomena, classifying and inducing from them alone" since "we may be ignorant and unstable enough to wrest them to our own intellectual destruction, and so approach the Biblical doctrine of inspiration, set upon explaining it away."[157]

The shift in Princeton's method of biblical interpretation was now complete. From the late eighteenth until the mid-nineteenth century, the Princeton theologians claimed to approach the Bible with Baconian induction. And the sciences of the times tended to support their conclusions. When the sciences became critical rather than corroborative of Scottish realist presuppositions, the Princeton theologians argued from their preestablished doctrine, rather than from the data. Warfield completed the shift from inductive investigation to deductive apologetics. The premises from which the Princeton theologians proceeded were no longer available for public perusal. Warfield did not appeal, as Archibald

Alexander did, to the Scottish realists. Nor did he acknowledge Princeton's dependence on Turretin as Charles Hodge had. The Princeton theology had absorbed these sources into its own tradition. The authority of the whole, gradually developed, Princeton theory about the Bible was now identified with the authority of the Bible itself. Warfield's task was apologetics. He defended the Princeton tradition by logical deduction from Scripture. He did it with great passion and technical expertise.

b. Princeton Scholasticism's Resistance to Biblical Criticism: B. B. Warfield Versus C. A. Briggs

In the late nineteenth century, the academic battle between Princeton scholasticism and Higher Criticism developed into an ecclesiastical struggle between B. B. Warfield and Charles Augustus Briggs. This conflict within the Presbyterian Church had much wider consequences. It triggered a chain of events which, in the early twentieth century, caused a major reconfiguration of American theological seminaries and a rethinking of denominational distinctives. The Warfield-Briggs controversy in many ways set the terms for the fundamentalist-modernist controversy that preoccupied the whole country in the 1920s and 1930s. And its effects are with us yet.

Briggs's Introduction of Biblical Theology

It was natural that the prime antagonist of the Princeton theologians should be Charles Augustus Briggs (1841–1913), whose chief mission in life was to introduce the views of German Higher Criticism into the Presbyterian Church. Briggs studied at Union Theological Seminary in New York from 1861 to 1863. Due to the illness of his father, he interrupted his studies and assumed management of the family business for three years. In 1865 he married Julie Valentine of New York City. Briggs had given much thought to study abroad, and after his father's recuperation he and his wife sailed for Germany in the summer of 1866. In Germany Briggs became greatly enamored with and stimulated by German theology and its critical approach to the Bible. At the University of Berlin Briggs studied for three years under I. A. Dorner, E. W. Hengstenberg, Emil Roediger, and H. G. A. Ewald. He was so impressed by them that after only five months there he wrote home to an uncle: "I cannot doubt but what I have been blessed with a new—divine light. I feel a different man from what I was five months ago. The Bible is lit up with a new light."[158] Reflecting on the American scene Briggs felt that "the great fault with American theology is that it is too little critical."[159] Briggs had been raised an Old School Presbyterian and went to Germany with the Old School conservative approach to biblical interpretation. His studies there convinced him that he was "defending a lost cause."[160]

Briggs returned to the United States in 1869 and in 1870 assumed the pastorate of the First Presbyterian Church of Roselle, New Jersey. Shortly after his return home, Briggs published perhaps the first article on biblical theology authored in the United States. He said: "Biblical Theology has for its range . . . the entire Scripture. It seeks to reach and realize the unity of Scripture amidst the manifold forms of its presentation."[161] In 1874 Briggs was called to teach at Union Seminary in New York. In 1876 he was elected Davenport Professor of Hebrew and Cognate Languages. The inaugural address he gave on September 21 was one in which he urged that critical biblical study not be bound by tradition or dogmatic views.[162] Instead of looking upon scientific methods as a danger to the supernatural character of biblical revelation, Briggs welcomed them and urged their wider use. He declared: "So long as the Word of God is honored, and its decisions regarded as final, what matters it if a certain book be detached from the name of one holy man and ascribed to another, or classed among those with unknown authors?"[163] Briggs wanted the new scholarship to be interpreted by evangelical Christians rather than to be monopolized by enemies of historic Christianity.[164]

Seeking a sustained outlet for his views, Briggs provided leadership in the founding of a theological journal, *The Presbyterian Review*. This venture had representation from Northwest, Auburn, Union, Lane, and Princeton seminaries. It was intended to express the interests and hopefully reconcile the views of previous Old and New School partisans.[165] A. A. Hodge of Princeton and Briggs were chosen as the two managing editors. But initial goodwill soon turned toward hostility as the paper ran a series of articles dealing with questions raised by the Higher Criticism.

The Literary Debate over Higher Criticism

The opponents of Higher Criticism proposed that the new journal treat issues raised by the heresy trial of Professor W. Robertson Smith (1846–1894) in Scotland.[166] It was decided that each editor of the *Review* should choose four contributors to express alternately a positive and negative position about biblical criticism. The first response was jointly authored by A. A. Hodge and B. B. Warfield and appeared in April 1881.[167] Its topic was inspiration and as its implications later became apparent, this essay stood as the classic statement of the scholasticized orthodoxy of the Princeton school regarding the Bible. In his portion of the article, A. A. Hodge defined inspiration as:

> the superintendence by God of the writers in the entire process of their writing, which accounts for nothing whatever but the absolute infallibility of the record in which the revelation, once generated, appears in the original autograph.[168]

Hodge after admitting the fallibility of human language and judgment went on to contend:

> Nevertheless the historical faith of the Church has always been, that all the affirmations of Scripture of all kinds, whether of spiritual doctrine or duty, or of physical or historical fact, or of psychological or philosophical principle, are without any error, when the *ipsissima verba* of the original autographs are ascertained and interpreted in their natural and intended sense.[169]

Warfield, in his part of the article, narrowed the burden of proof to one demonstrated error. He insisted: "A proved error in Scripture contradicts not only our doctrine, but the Scripture claims and, therefore, its inspiration in making those claims."[170] He removed any practical possibility of testing his claim, however, by setting up conditions that were impossible to fulfill. He qualified his claim, saying: "We do not assert that the common text, but only that the original autographic text was inspired. No 'error' can be asserted, therefore, which cannot be proved to have been aboriginal in the text."[171] Although in debate the burden of proof is always with the affirmative proposal, Warfield, as part of his apologetic, asserted that all the burden rested with critics of his position. The question the critics were opening for inductive examination was what doctrine of Scripture would actually best accord with the character of the biblical data. But the Princeton theologians begged the question and assumed as proven what their opponents were challenging. Hodge and Warfield reiterated the historically false claim that their position was both primitive and perpetual in the church. Thus by their definition, inspiration *had to* mean scientific and historical inerrancy, and the only way for this to be disproved was for someone to prove that an error existed in the original (lost) *autographa* or original text of Scripture.[172] Hodge and Warfield thus imposed immediate and stringent restrictions on the methods of Higher Criticism. And they exercised *a priori* vetoes on the possible conclusions of scholarly research. Hodge wrote:

> Every supposed conclusion of critical investigation which denies the apostolical origin of a New Testament book, or the truth of any part of Christ's testimony in relation to the Old Testament and its contents, or which is

inconsistent with the absolute truthfulness of any affirmation of any book so authenticated, must be inconsistent with the true doctrine of Inspiration.[173]

Though Hodge had said earlier in the article that inspiration "is not in the first instance a principle fundamental to the truth of the Christian religion," by the end of the article it had emerged as the absolutely crucial center of their apologetic argument.

Briggs responded in the July, 1881, issue under the title: "The Right, Duty, and Limits of Biblical Criticism."[174] He launched a violent attack on Princeton's "scholastic theology" as the real but misguided foe of evangelical biblical criticism. He rejected inerrancy and also the Princeton position that canonicity depended on authorship or tradition. Instead Briggs appealed to the Reformers and interpreted them as teaching that canonicity depended upon the witness of the Holy Spirit. He also made a distinction between "plenary" and "verbal" inspiration. Briggs accepted plenary inspiration, which acknowledged errors and inconsistencies in the Bible but which nonetheless held Scripture to be the infallible rule of faith and practice. But he rejected verbal inspiration. Briggs wrote:

> *Verbal* Inspiration is doubtless a more precise and emphatic definition, than *plenary* Inspiration; but this very emphasis and precision imperil the doctrine of Inspiration itself by bringing it into conflict with a vast array of objections along the whole line of Scripture and History.[175]

This piece put Briggs under suspicion by some in the Presbyterian Church, yet others were sympathetic. As the articles in the *Review* continued to be published public reaction increased. In January, 1882, Hodge wrote to Briggs: "I shall unite with you in doing all I can to prevent controversy in Newspapers and otherwise on the matter of Biblical Criticism until the series in our Review is finished."[176] Further disagreements evolved, however, and in October, 1882, A. A. Hodge resigned as coeditor. He was replaced by Francis Landley Patton who had joined the Princeton faculty from McCormick Seminary the previous year. Also in 1882, the General Assembly noted the "introduction and prevalence of German mysticism and 'higher criticism' and of philosophic speculation and so-called scientific evolution." The General Assembly statement warned

> those who give instruction in our Theological Seminaries, against inculcating any views, or adopting any methods which tend to unsettle faith in the doctrine of the divine origin and plenary inspiration of the Scriptures, held by our Church, or in our Presbyterian systems of doctrine.[177]

The seventh article of the *Review* series was written by Briggs. In it he conceded that the Pentateuch was a compilation of four main documents written soon after Moses.[178] The eighth and last article was by

Patton. In it he warned against an overemphasis on the witness of the Spirit to the extent that the intellectual defenses of Christianity were belittled. He also wrote that "any opinion inconsistent with the inerrancy of Scripture is contra-confessional." Contra-confessional too, according to Patton, was "belief in the non-Mosaic authorship of the Pentateuch."[179]

The 1883 General Assembly, having received overtures from five Presbyteries, reminded its Presbyteries that

> it is incumbent upon them to see to it that the appropriate constitutional action be taken, if at any time it should become manifest, that any member of our Church was promulgating theories of dangerous tendency, or contra-confessional doctrines concerning the Holy Scriptures.[180]

Briggs's Attack on Princeton Scholasticism

During this time Briggs became more daring as a writer. In 1883 he produced *Biblical Study: Its Principles, Methods and History.* In it he denounced Protestant scholasticism contrasting it with the spirit and principles of the Westminster Divines.[181] 1885 marked the publication of his *American Presbyterianism,* in which he contended that in the colonial history of this church, the Old Side-Old School tradition embodied by Princeton was actually a corruption of the true orthodoxy. The foreign elements in Old Side-Old School theology were the tinctures of Protestant scholasticism.[182]

In 1888, Patton resigned his coeditorship of the *Presbyterian Review* to become president of Princeton College. B. B. Warfield was elected by the Princeton Seminary faculty to replace Patton as their editorial representative. Initially Briggs was pleased. But strains soon developed. Warfield had taken the job "to do what little I can to forward the Old School interest in the Review." He began to exert pressure on Briggs in areas the latter had long considered his editorial prerogative.

To the theological and personal tensions an ecclesiastical one was soon added. The General Assembly of 1889 sent overtures to all the presbyteries asking: "Do you desire a revision of the Confession of Faith? If so, in what respects and to what extent?" According to previous agreement it was Briggs's turn to discuss the action of the 1889 General Assembly in the *Review.* Warfield insisted on inserting a statement of his own regarding confessional revision. Eventually Briggs and Union Seminary were identified in the church as leaders of the revision movement. Warfield and Princeton led the antirevision party.

The editorial conflict between Briggs and Warfield continued and on September 22, 1887, Briggs resigned as editor and the Union faculty

then voted to discontinue the *Review*. The last link of cooperation between the New School and Old School parties dissolved in the controversies over Higher Criticism and confessional revision.[183]

Briggs's boldest attack on Princeton came one week before he resigned as editor of the *Review*. He published *Whither? A Theological Question
for the Times* as a defense of the revision movement. In it he sought to
show by actual quotations that leading conservative theologians (chiefly
the whole Princeton school and others such as Dr. Howard Crosby and
Briggs's own Calvinist colleague W. G. T. Shedd [1820–1894]) had led
American Presbyterianism astray from the Westminster Confessional
standards into the direction of Reformed scholasticism.[184] Summarizing
his assault Briggs charged:

> This drift has been gradual and imperceptible under the leadership of able
> divines who did not take trouble to study the Westminster divines, the au-
> thors of the standards, but who relied on their *a priori* logic for the correct
> interpretation of the standards as well as the Scriptures, and accordingly
> they interpreted both the Scriptures and the standards to correspond with
> that system of scholastic Calvinism which had become to them the rule of
> faith. It was an evil day for Presbyterianism when the Puritan and Presbyteri-
> an fathers were laid aside, and the scholastic divines of Switzerland and
> Holland were introduced into our universities and colleges as the text-books
> of theology, and the tests of Orthodoxy. The Westminster symbols were
> buried under a mass of foreign dogma. Francis Turretin became the rule of
> faith, and the Westminster Confession was interpreted to correspond with
> his scholastic elaborations and refinements.[185]

In opposition to Princeton, Briggs outlined his view of the Westminster
Confession's statement on Scripture:

> The Westminster doctrine of the Scriptures is an admirable doctrine. It
> corresponds with the statements of the Scriptures themselves, as well as with
> the faith of the Reformation. The advance in the science of Biblical criticism
> in recent times has brought evangelical critics into entire sympathy with it.
> It corresponds with the facts of the case and the results of a scientific study
> of the Bible. They accept the Confession of Faith, and build upon it, and use
> it to destroy the false doctrines that dogmaticians have taught in its place.
> These false doctrines are partly extra-confessional, sharpening the defini-
> tions of the Westminster symbols by undue refinements and assumed logical
> deductions, such as, (a) the addition of the adjective *verbal* to inspiration, and
> (b) the use of the term *inerrancy* with reference to the entire body of the
> Scriptures. They are chiefly contra-confessional, substituting false doctrines
> for the real faith of the Church in these two particulars, (c) basing the
> authority of the Scriptures upon the *testimony of the ancient Church,* and (d)
> making the inspiration of the Scriptures depend upon their supposed *human
> authors.*[186]

Briggs then began to refute the Princeton theologians individually by citing their own words. On verbal inspiration he took A. A. Hodge to task and held that "no confession of faith or catechism of recognized standing in the Reformed or Lutheran Church, teaches that the Scriptures are inspired in their verbal expressions."[187] In elaborating, Briggs wrote:

> Verbal inspiration makes the original Hebrew, Aramaic, and Greek documents as they came from the hands of their writers, the only inspired Word of God. If the line cannot be drawn between the thoughts and words of Scripture, we cannot separate the inspired thoughts from the inspired words,—we cannot transfer the inspired thoughts into other words. . . . The theory of verbal inspiration cannot admit inspired thoughts in other than inspired words. It therefore results in the denial that there are inspired thoughts in the English Bible. It cuts off the Christian people from the real word of God and gives them a human substitute.[188]

Briggs maintained vigorously that "it is sheer assumption to claim that the original documents were inerrant. No one can be persuaded to believe in the inerrancy of Scripture, except by *a priori* considerations from the elaboration of the doctrine of verbal inspiration."[189] After citing contemporary European theologians who rejected inerrancy, Briggs made three points against Hodge and Warfield who claimed that the inerrancy of the original autographs had always been part of the historic faith of the Church:

> (1). The historic faith of the Church is to be found in the official symbolical books and nowhere else. None of these symbols state that the '*ipsissima verba* of the original autographs are without error.' (2) It is well known that the great Reformers recognized errors in the Scriptures and did not hold to the inerrancy of the original autographs. Are these Princeton divines entitled to pronounce Luther and Calvin heterodox, and to define the faith of the universal Church? (3). The Westminster divines did not teach the inerrancy of the original autographs.[190]

To Briggs all this meant that "the doctrine of the inerrancy of Scripture not only comes into conflict with the historical faith of the Church, but it is also in conflict with Biblical criticism."[191] Briggs openly declared his own position:

> It seems to me that it is vain to deny that there are errors and inconsistencies in the best texts of our Bible. There are chronological, geographical, and other circumstantial inconsistencies and errors which we should not hesitate to acknowledge.[192]

Yet for Briggs these minor errors in detail did not destroy the Bible's credibility and trustworthiness as a witness. He wrote: "The question of credibility is to be distinguished from infallibility. The form is credible, the substance alone is infallible."[193] Warning against Princeton, Briggs continued:

> But whatever interpretation we may give to these errors, however much we may reduce them in number, the awkward fact stares us in the face, that these Princeton divines risk the inspiration and authority of the Bible upon a single proved error. Such a position is a serious and hazardous departure from Protestant orthodoxy. It imperils the faith of all Christians who have been taught this doctrine. They cannot escape the evidence of errors in the Scriptures.[194]

His pastoral concern pushed Briggs onward:

> What an awful doctrine to teach in our days when Biblical criticism has the field! What a peril to precious souls there is in the terse, pointed sentence, 'A proved error in Scripture contradicts not only our doctrine but the Scripture claims, and therefore its inspiration in making those claims'! No more dangerous doctrine has ever come from the pen of men. It has cost the Church the loss of thousands. It will cost us ten thousand and hundreds of thousands unless the true Westminster doctrine is speedily put in its place.[195]

The vehemence of Briggs's attack did not cease until he had examined what he considered the "contra-confessional" positions of Princeton: basing Scripture's authority on the testimony of the ancient church; and making the inspiration of Scripture depend on its supposed human authors.[196]

The whole Princeton line from Archibald Alexander through Charles and A. A. Hodge was indicted by Briggs. Alexander, for example, by appealing to the authority of the church on canonicity, was accused by Briggs of falling in with the Jesuits in fearing mysticism or enthusiasm.[197] And "by mixing inspiration and canonicity with the questions of authenticity," both of the Hodges departed further than Alexander from the Westminster position.[198] A. A. Hodge had written:

> We determine what books have a place in this canon or divine rule by an examination of the evidences which show that each of them, severally, was written by the inspired prophet or apostle whose name it bears, or, as in the case of the gospels of Mark and Luke, written under the superintendence and published by the authority of an apostle.[199]

According to Briggs, this position meant that "the inspiration, the canonicity, and the authority of the Bible depends, therefore, upon the results of the Higher Criticism."[200] Briggs observed that it cannot be proved that all New Testament writings were written by the man whose name the book bears or published by the authority of an apostle. This led Briggs to chide that "if the elder and younger Hodge are correct in their theory of inspiration, that a very large portion of the Bible is in peril from the Higher Criticism, and that the only way to save the Bible is to destroy the 'higher critics.' "[201] Regrettably, B. B. Warfield also was "following in the same path of error."[202] For Briggs, "the Reformers found the essence of the authority of the Scriptures in the Scriptures themselves and not in human theories about them. Hence they were not anxious about human authorship."[203] Appealing to both the Reformers and the Westminster Divines who "did not determine these questions of the Higher Criticism for us," Briggs found that neither they nor any of the Catechisms or Confessions mingled questions of inspiration and canonicity and authenticity. The testimony of the Westminster Confession was explicit for Briggs: "The Westminster Confession excludes human authorship from the inspiration and divine authority of the Scriptures, when it states: 'The authority of the Holy Scripture, for which it ought to be believed and obeyed, dependeth not upon the testimony of any man.' "[204]

How was it that Briggs, an Old Testament scholar, had such a grasp of Reformation history and such a thorough acquaintance with the writings of the Westminster Divines? The answer lay in two areas. Briggs's early studies in Germany had included research into the history of doctrine under Isaac Dorner. Briggs had then undertaken a study of the doctrine of justification by faith and its relationship to sanctification. When he investigated the Westminster Confession on this point he was surprised to find that it accorded with the theology of the sixteenth-century Reformers and was distinctly different from the American Reformed theology he had earlier been taught. He thereafter continued his study of the history of theology and particularly of the Puritan roots of Presbyterianism. The second and decisive factor was that a friend of Union Seminary in New York, David Hunter McAlpin, had underwritten the expense of collecting for the seminary's library all the extant writings of the Westminster Divines. Over a period of fourteen years, prior to the writing of *Whither?*, Briggs had made numerous trips to Britain researching and purchasing materials for this collection. He commented in the preface to *Whither?* that he had "spared no time, labor, or expense in searching the original editions and manuscript sources of all documents relating to this subject; spending many months in the chief libraries of Great Britain and in the lesser Puritan libraries; and diligently searching in old book-stores for every book, tract, and manuscript that could be found and purchased."[205] All of this research was funded by McAlpin to whom Briggs dedicated *Whither?*

Warfield's Defense of the Princeton Theology

Warfield replied to Briggs's charges on the doctrine of Scripture in the Westminster Confession in a number of articles which appeared in the years 1889 to 1894. These were later collected and expanded into a book entitled *The Westminster Assembly and Its Work.* Warfield responded, not as an historian, but as an apologist. The grip of the Princeton tradition was such that Warfield proved unable to enter afresh into a discussion of the sources of Reformed theology. He operated with only two categories: the orthodoxy of the Princeton theology; and "liberalism," to which Briggs's approach was consigned. Warfield began from what he considered "the obvious fact that the Westminster Confession teaches the verbal or plenary inspiration and infallibility or inerrancy of the original Scriptures." Without entering into any analysis of the historical circumstances that produced the Westminster position, Warfield charged that Briggs was seeking to explain away the "obvious meaning of the document."[206]

The basic thrust of Warfield's argument was the assumption that the Westminster Divines were identical in their theology to that of the post-Reformation scholastics such as Turretin. Warfield did not prove that this was the case. He postulated it. The Scottish common sense philosophy, so long before absorbed by the Princeton theology had taught an identity of past historical views with those of the present. Warfield took for granted that there was one Reformed system of theology and that all those whom he considered Reformed, of whatever historical period, held to that system. Warfield found it incomprehensible that "the Reformed theologians of Britain were in violent (though assuredly unconscious) opposition to their brethren on the Continent, in the most fundamental postulate of their system."[207] Warfield attempted to show that Briggs's quotations were taken out of context or in other ways misrepresented the views of the Westminster Divines.[208]

Warfield went on to develop what he considered the real Westminster doctrine of inspiration. He did this by quoting from members of the Assembly who had no direct hand in framing and defining the section on Scripture in the Westminster Confession. Warfield again assumed a uniformity of viewpoint among the members of the Assembly that was historically not valid. He therefore chose to cite those Divines whose writings were most amenable to his own position. Furthermore, Warfield attributed to the words of the Westminster Divines "technical and unmistakable" meanings that had been developed by the Princeton theology but of which the Westminster Divines themselves were wholly innocent.[209]

Warfield did not attempt a direct refutation of Briggs's charges of "contra-confessional" doctrines. He fell back instead on the philosophical assumptions of the Princeton theology and claimed that they were necessary in any Reformed system of thought. With reference to Briggs's assertion that the Princeton theology based its authority of Scripture on the testimony of the early church, Warfield replied that persons need: "A preparation of the spirit, as well as an exhibition of the evidences, in order to be persuaded and enabled to yield faith and obedience."[210] This premise—that all knowledge was based on evidence—was so much a part of Warfield's presuppositions that he stated: "If this be not true the whole Reformed system falls with it."[211] For Warfield, an appeal to the testimony of the Holy Spirit apart from a prior exhibition of evidences would be unthinkable "mysticism."

Warfield, the apologist, never responded to the real issue, which was whether, on historical grounds, the Princeton theology had been faithful to the Westminster Confession and the sixteenth-century Reformation confessions. Warfield, as an apologist, took the normativity of his position for granted and then read it back into those sources of which he approved. The most blatant example of this kind of argument was his use of Charles Hodge's *Systematic Theology* as an example of "all Reformed systems," when the status of Hodge's theology was the question at issue.[212]

Warfield made no direct answer to Briggs's last objection, that the Princeton theology predicated the inspiration of Scripture on its supposed human authors. When Warfield dealt with the Westminster Divines' views of canonicity he noted that what he called the "common distinction" between revelation and inspiration (that is, the distinction made by the Princeton theology) was not drawn. He felt that it was implicit in, for example, John Lightfoot's writings.[213]

Briggs's Trial and Suspension

Despite the fact that Briggs was historically correct, Warfield's views prevailed. The majority of ministers, and through them members, of the Presbyterian Church had been trained in the Old School scholasticism Warfield espoused. They had been taught Scottish realism and Turretin and been told that it was the Westminster Confession and Calvin.

During the 1880s Briggs had become identified as the spokesperson for two controversial issues in the Presbyterian Church: biblical criticism and confessional revision.[214] In 1891 Briggs was transferred to the newly created chair of Biblical Theology at Union Seminary in New York. The intention of the faculty and board was to give Briggs a more effective platform from which to disseminate Higher Criticism. At the insistence of the donor of the chair who was also chairman of Union's board of directors, Briggs devoted his inaugural to the issues of biblical criticism and confessional revision. It was entitled "The Authority of Holy Scripture." Briggs later commented: "The aim of the address was to maintain and assert in the strongest terms the divine authority of Holy Scripture in connection with a full recognition of the results of modern Biblical criticism and modern thought in all departments."[215] Briggs also admitted that he was filled with passion in view of what he considered unjust attacks on himself.[216] Briggs noted three sources of divine authority: the church, the reason, and the Bible. He further gave as examples of those who had found God by these various methods: Newman, the Roman Catholic; Martineau, the Unitarian; and Spurgeon, the Protestant. Briggs then shocked some in his audience by asserting that "no one of these ways has been so obstructed as the Holy Bible."[217] He went on to enumerate six "barriers" that hindered the functioning of the divine authority of Holy Scripture. They were elements of the Princeton theory of the inerrancy of Scripture and efforts to resist biblical criticism.[218] Briggs added fuel to the fire of conservative reaction by raising questions about the traditional doctrine of original sin and espousing the notion of progressive sanctification after death.[219] Briggs later clarified his stand on the sources of authority. He declared that Scripture alone was an infallible rule of faith and practice and that reason and the church were only means of understanding and applying the Bible. He claimed that his other controversial views were not at variance with the Westminster Confession but were in areas to which it did not speak and were thus legitimate items of scholarly discussion.[220] But the damage had already been done. Even some of Briggs's friends and supporters regretted the vehemence and lack of reserve with which he had spoken.

When the General Assembly convened in May 1891 it had overtures from sixty-three presbyteries concerning the Briggs address. These were referred to the Standing Committee on Theological Seminaries chaired by Francis L. Patton, President of Princeton College, and composed completely of anti-Briggs selectees. This committee moved, and the Assembly adopted, a motion to veto Briggs's election to the Union Seminary professorship of Biblical Theology.[221]

Following the Assembly, pressure was exerted on the Presbytery of New York to bring Briggs to trial for heresy.[222] In October 1891 a committee of New York Presbytery presented two formal charges of heresy, one concerning Briggs's views on the authority of the Bible and the other his position on progressive sanctification. Briggs's carefully prepared response persuaded the Presbytery to dismiss the charges by a vote of 94 to 39. The prosecution committee, however, was unwilling to let the matter rest and appealed, not to the next higher court, the Synod of New York, but directly to the General Assembly.[223]

The General Assembly of 1892 met in Portland, Oregon. That body, in an action without precedent, accepted the prosecuting committee's appeal, which had bypassed the Synod. The Assembly then voted 429 to 87 to send the Briggs case back to New York Presbytery for a full trial.[224] On the day of adjournment an overture was introduced and adopted that came to be known as the "Portland Deliverance." Clearly directed at Briggs, it asserted: "Our Church holds that the inspired Word as it came from God is without error." It continued in part:

> The assertion of the contrary cannot but shake the confidence of the people in the sacred books. All who enter office in our Church solemnly profess to receive them as the only infallible rule of faith and practice. If they change their belief on this point, Christian honor demands that they should withdraw from our ministry. They have no right to use the pulpit or the chair of the professor for the dissemination of their errors until they are dealt with by the slow process of discipline.[225]

Briggs complained that this decision prejudiced his case, which was still to be tried. Some felt that the prosecution of Briggs was a determined effort to institute a new and narrower definition of orthodoxy in the Presbyterian Church.[226]

In November 1892, the Presbytery of New York brought Briggs to trial on a list of six charges. Chairman Birch of the prosecuting committee exemplified the attitude toward Scripture of the extreme conservatives who were now pushing the case. In his opening statement he said of the Bible:

> God is the arranger of its clauses, the chooser of its terms, and the speller of its words so that the text in its letters, words, or clauses is just as divine as the thought.[227]

Briggs for his part assured the Presbytery that he believed the Holy Scriptures to be the only infallible rule of faith and practice. Citing the Westminster Confession he noted: "The Scriptures are the final appeal in religious controversies; matters of faith and practice, not for questions of science."[228] Again the presbytery acquitted Briggs of each charge. And again the prosecution appealed directly to the General Assembly.[229]

The intervening months saw a concerted effort by the conservative press to ensure Briggs's conviction by the General Assembly. False letters were published, Briggs's views were misrepresented, and untrue rumors were circulated that Briggs and Henry Preserved Smith were planning to bolt the denomination and form a new church.[230] The prosecution was now in the hands of ultra-conservatives who went even beyond the Princeton theology. But the Princeton men did nothing openly to disavow or moderate the actions being taken.[231]

The General Assembly met in the New York Avenue Presbyterian Church in Washington, D.C., in May 1893. The retiring moderator, W. C. Young, used his keynote address to attack Higher Criticism. Despite some illegalities in procedure, the Assembly entertained the appeal from the Presbytery of New York and proceeded to try the case on the floor. Briggs acted as his own attorney and was said to have represented himself to good advantage. The Rev. Joseph J. Lampe presented the opening argument for the prosecution. He climaxed his presentation with the statement: "It is the Bible and Christ against Dr. Briggs."[232] After three days of arguments, the commissioners voted 383 to 116 to sustain the appeal. On the following day a Committee of Judgment recommended that Briggs be suspended from the Presbyterian ministry. The recommendation was adopted by a voice vote.[233]

Sixty-three commissioners signed a formal protest against the sentence.[234] The Assembly proceeded, however, to strengthen the scholastic position by two further actions. It disavowed any further relationship with Union Seminary in New York because Union had declined to dismiss Briggs.[235] And, it adopted a recommendation which read in part:

> This Assembly reaffirms the doctrine of the deliverance of the Assembly of 1892 touching the inspiration of Holy Scripture, namely, that the original Scriptures of the Old and New Testaments, being immediately inspired of God, were without error, and in so doing declares that the said deliverance enunciates no new doctrine and imposes no new test of orthodoxy, but interprets and gives expression to what has always been the belief of the Church taught in the Westminster Confession of Faith.[236]

Dr. Herrick Johnson, a professor at McCormick Seminary was joined by eighty-six other commissioners in formally protesting this pronouncement. They listed as one of the grounds: "Because it is setting up an imaginary Bible as a test of orthodoxy." They further branded the pronouncement "an interpretation of our standards which they never have borne."[237] In response, the Assembly adopted a supplementary statement saying: "The Bible as we now have it, in its various translations and versions, when freed from all errors and mistakes of translators, copyists, and printers, is the very Word of God, and consequently wholly without error."[238] The General Assembly thus took a final step toward fundamentalism. They removed even the technical, apologetical safeguards with which the Princeton theology had hedged the doctrine of inerrancy. Now, at least in the popular mind, the English Bible in the layperson's hands was declared to be a technically true source of information on science as well as religion. Conflict between those two spheres in American life in the coming decades was assured.

c. The Scholastic Separation from Princeton Seminary: J. Gresham Machen

Religious matters made front page news in the late nineteenth and early twentieth centuries. The inerrancy of the Scriptures along with the evolution of the species formed the core of the famous fundamentalist-modernist controversy that affected most of American Protestantism.[239] The conflict in the Presbyterian Church had importance far beyond that denomination. The Princeton theologians provided scholarly sanction for a theory of the inerrancy of the Bible that was the practical, functioning belief of millions of people in other churches and parachurch movements. Dispensational millenarianism was exerting wide influence through the Scofield Reference Bible, the Bible Conference movement, and Bible schools across the country. Although the Princeton theologians disapproved of the particular interpretation of biblical prophecy used by the dispensationalists, they tended to form a working coalition on the more central issues on which all fundamentalists agreed. And the Princeton theology of Hodge and Warfield was allowed by nearly all fundamentalist groups to provide the theory regarding the inerrancy of the Bible. Without treating the issues independently, people in other denominations and movements tended to take sides with the biblical critics or with the Princeton theologians and to incorporate that controversy into the categories of their own traditions.[240]

Tensions over the question of the inerrancy of Scripture marked the next three decades in the Presbyterian Church. In 1894 the General Assembly suspended from the ministry Professor Henry Preserved Smith of Lane Seminary in Cincinnati for refusing to teach that the Bible was inerrant in the Princeton sense.[241] The first two decades of the twentieth century saw the development of two increasingly self-conscious parties within the denomination. The one group was committed to a larger theological inclusiveness. The other group desired to preserve a homogeneous scholasticism.[242] Until the mid-twenties, it appeared that the scholastics were gaining in strength. In 1910 the General Assembly adopted five points that all ordination candidates had to affirm as "essential and necessary doctrines." The first of these stated:

> It is an essential doctrine of the word of God and our standards, that the Holy Spirit did so inspire, guide and move the writers of the Holy Scriptures as to keep them from error.[243]

These five points were treated by the scholastics as the church's real, working confession. They were increasingly challenged by others who felt that they represented a fundamentalist narrowing of the Presbyterian theological stance.[244]

The clash between liberals and scholastics crystalized in the mid-twenties. A number of notable events served to bring matters to a head. There was a proposed merger of the evangelical churches in the United States which evoked much discussion between 1918 and 1920. A renewed interest in foreign missions began in 1921. And Harry Emerson Fosdick preached a famous sermon, "Shall the Fundamentalists Win?" in the First Presbyterian Church in New York City in 1922.[245] It was countered by a sermon entitled, "Shall Unbelief Win?" by Clarence E. Macartney of the Arch Street Presbyterian Church in Philadelphia. Macartney followed this by initiating charges, which were successful in crowding Fosdick, a Baptist, from the pulpit of the First Presbyterian Church. Macartney's election to the moderatorship of the General Assembly in 1924 was closely related to the Fosdick case. Macartney was the second youngest person ever to serve as moderator.[246] He was nominated by William Jennings Bryan, who said in his speech nominating Macartney:

> It was his vigilance that detected the insidious attack made upon the historic doctrines of the Presbyterian Church; it was his courage that raised the standard of the protest about which the Church rallied; it was his leadership that won a decisive victory for evangelical Christianity and historical Presbyterianism. He was the man of the hour and linked himself with the fundamental tenets of the creed of our church.[247]

Christianity and Liberalism

Perhaps the central figure of controversy in this period was Macartney's close personal friend, Professor J. Gresham Machen of Princeton Seminary. Machen was the last in the line of notable names of the old Princeton theology. Like many of his predecessors he came from a family of wealth and culture with strong Southern ties. Machen graduated Phi Beta Kappa from Johns Hopkins University and went on to study at Princeton Seminary under B. B. Warfield in 1902. At Warfield's death in 1921, Machen called him "the greatest man I have known."[248] Machen spent a year studying in Germany and returned to Princeton in 1906 to begin a twenty-three-year period on the faculty. He was first instructor and then Assistant Professor of New Testament until 1929. Machen followed Warfield in using his New Testament scholarship for apologetic purposes. He declared: "You can hardly have evangelism, unless you have Christian scholarship."[249] Machen's approach to Scripture adhered to the apologetic stance of the Princeton theology. He wrote:

> Christian experience is rightly used when it confirms the documentary evidence. But it can never possibly provide a substitute for the documentary evidence. We know that the gospel story is true partly because of the early

date of the documents in which it appears, the evidence as to their authorship, the internal evidence of their truth, the impossibility of explaining them
as being based upon deception or upon myth. This evidence is gloriously
confirmed by present experience, which adds to the documentary evidence
that wonderful directness and immediacy of conviction which delivers us
from fear.[250]

To this account of how revelation was authenticated, Machen added a
statement on inspiration. He said: "This latter doctrine means that the
Bible not only is an account of important things, but that the account
itself is true, the writers having been so preserved from error, despite
a full maintenance of their habits of thought and expression, that the
resulting Book is the 'infallible rule of faith and practice.' "[251]

In 1923 Machen issued a book entitled *Christianity and Liberalism* in
which he contended that Christianity and liberalism were two distinct and
utterly different religions. He wrote: "We shall be interested in showing
that despite the liberal use of traditional phraseology, modern liberalism
not only is a different religion from Christianity but belongs in a totally
different class of religions."[252] According to Machen two such different
ideologies could not exist together in one church. One or the other had
to go.[253] Machen did not deny the title Christian to all individual liberals.
But the domino theory was very much at work in his thinking. He argued:

> That does not mean that all liberals hold all parts of the system, or that
> Christians who have been affected by liberal teaching at one point have been
> affected at all points. . . . But the true way in which to examine a spiritual
> movement is in its logical relations; logic is the great dynamic, and the
> logical implications of any way of thinking are sooner or later certain to be
> worked out. And taken as a whole, even as it actually exists to-day, naturalis-
> tic liberalism is a fairly unitary phenomenon; it is tending more and more
> to eliminate from itself illogical remnants of Christian belief.[254]

Soon after the first publication of this book, Machen became the stated
supply of the First Presbyterian Church of Princeton. Dr. Henry van
Dyke, a noted professor of English literature at Princeton University and
a Presbyterian minister, gave up his pew in the church to protest what
he called, "the schismatic and unscriptural preaching of Dr. J. Gresham
Machen."[255]

The Auburn Affirmation

In 1923 liberal leadership in the church drew up and published in
1924 a document popularly called the Auburn Affirmation. This state-

ment was signed by 1,274 Presbyterian clergymen, about 13 percent of the ministers in the church. It objected to the five-point doctrinal deliverance of the General Assembly of 1910, which had been reaffirmed by the Assembly in 1916 and again in 1923.[256] In its crucial paragraph, the Affirmation stated:

> Furthermore, this opinion of the General Assembly attempts to commit our church to certain theories concerning the inspiration of the Bible, and the Incarnation, the Atonement, the Resurrection, and the Continuing Life and Supernatural Power of our Lord Jesus Christ. We all hold most earnestly to these great facts and doctrines; we all believe from our hearts that the writers of the Bible were inspired by God; that Jesus Christ was God manifest in the flesh; that God was in Christ, reconciling the world unto Himself, and through Him we have our redemption; that having died for our sins He rose from the dead and is our ever-living Saviour; that in His earthly ministry He wrought many mighty works, and by His vicarious death and unfailing presence He is able to save to the uttermost. Some of us regard the particular theories contained in the deliverance of the General Assembly of 1923 as satisfactory explanations of these facts and doctrines. But we are united in believing that these are not the only theories allowed by the Scriptures and our standards as explanations of these facts and doctrines of our religion, and that all who hold to these facts and doctrines, whatever theories they may employ to explain them, are worthy of all confidence and fellowship.[257]

The lines were clearly drawn. Machen and the conservatives claimed an identity between their doctrines and the biblical facts. The signers of the Auburn Affirmation distinguished between facts and doctrines and desired latitude regarding doctrinal theories. The Auburn Affirmation particularly deplored the theory of inerrancy, which was "intended to enhance the authority of the Scriptures," but in their view "in fact impaired their supreme authority for faith and life."[258] Machen, on the other hand, had inherited an ambivalence from his predecessor Princeton theologians. With them, he acknowledged that only faith in Christ was necessary in order to be a Christian. But the Princeton theologians had so built their apologetic approach on biblical inerrancy that it now had to be treated as essential. Since the 1910 General Assembly pronouncement, scholastics like Machen were committed to defending inerrancy as the first in their list of "essential and necessary" doctrines.[259]

In 1925, the General Assembly appointed a special theological commission of fifteen members to deal with the contrasting positions of Machen and the Auburn Affirmation. It was charged "to study the present spiritual condition of our Church and the causes making for unrest, and to report to the next General Assembly, to the end that the purity, peace, unity and progress of the Church may be assured."[260]

The Reorganization of Princeton Seminary

At this time, events were taking place at Princeton Seminary that would decisively affect matters in the denomination as a whole. A moderate named J. Ross Stevenson had been elected president of Princeton Seminary to succeed Francis L. Patton in 1914. Stevenson openly declared that he wished Princeton Seminary to represent the whole church rather than to perpetuate the particular Old School theology. A majority of the faculty, including Machen, were, therefore, opposed to the president. Stevenson feared that if the homogeneous Princeton theology were allowed to continue, the institution might become "an interdenominational Seminary for Bible School-premillennial-secession fundamentalism."[261] Machen, and others feared that any change would allow Princeton Seminary eventually to become a modernist institution. Two boards governed the institution. The board of directors was responsible for the educational program, and a majority of them sided with the scholastic faculty majority. A board of trustees governed the financial operations, and a majority of the trustees sided with the president, a minority of the faculty, and a minority of the directors in desiring a more inclusive policy at the seminary.[262] The faculty had nominated and both boards had approved the appointment of J. Gresham Machen to be professor of apologetics and ethics. In 1926 President Stevenson recommended to the General Assembly that Machen's appointment be held up until the seminary could be investigated for "conditions subversive of Christian fewllowship."[263]

Report of the Special Theological Commission

In the meantime, the special theological commission of the General Assembly was at work. In addition to researching the constitutional and theological history of the denomination, they heard many witnesses, including Machen. In 1926 the commission made an interim report to the Assembly amidst much excitement. The historical part of the commission's report developed the idea that "the Christian principle of toleration" was deeply embedded in the denomination's constitution. The report added that "toleration does not involve any lowering of the Standards. It does not weaken the testimony of the Church as to its assured convictions.[264] Two central convictions of Machen and the Princeton conservatives were thus denied. The first was their contention that the true history of the church was one of uniform theological conservatism. The report argued that diversity had always been an enriching aspect of the denomination. The second conservative contention to be denied was

Machen's assertion that conservative Christianity and liberalism were mutually exclusive and incompatible elements in the denomination. The report believed that there was a place for both.[265]

The General Assembly of 1927 elected as its moderator, Robert E. Speer, head of the Board of Foreign Missions, and one of the most beloved persons in the church. The special commission presented its final report and applied its principles to the matter of "essential and necessary articles." The right to judge what was necessary for ordination was a right reserved to the ordaining body, the Presbytery. The General Assembly could only exercise those rights specifically granted to it. The report asserted that the only way for an Assembly to declare any article of faith essential and necessary would be for it "to quote the exact language of the article as it appears in the Confession of Faith."[266] The five points adopted in 1910, 1916, and 1923 were thus declared without authority. The principal set forth was that no body, including the General Assembly, had the constitutional power to make binding definitions of the church's essential faith. Conservative control was thus broken by asserting that there was no central control at all over the belief system of the denomination.[267] Machen, among others, realized that the possibility of scholastics again directing the denomination was nil.[268]

Scholastic Protest and Withdrawal

In 1929 the General Assembly approved the reorganization of Princeton Seminary. The two previous boards were merged into a single board of trustees, with one-third of the members coming from each of the previous boards and another third from the church at large. This reorganization was made possible by the votes of a "third party" in the denomination, theological evangelicals who nonetheless wanted an inclusive policy in the church and the seminary. Machen expressed his greatest anger at these people calling them "indifferentists" and "theological pacifists."[269]

Machen felt that he could not be part of an inclusive seminary, and in 1929 he left Princeton to form Westminster Seminary in Philadelphia. Three other faculty members (Robert Dick Wilson, Oswald T. Allis, and Cornelius Van Til) and twenty students made the break with him. A total of fifty students enrolled at Westminster for the first semester. The majority came from evangelical colleges like Wheaton, Asbury, and Taylor University. Carl McIntire and Harold J. Ockenga were members of the original class who became prominent conservative leaders.[270] Westminster Seminary was committed to continue the Hodge-Warfield tradition of old Princeton.

Soon after founding the seminary, Machen acted to counter what he felt was the influence of liberalism in the Presbyterian Church's mission program. He organized the Independent Board for Presbyterian Foreign Missions and became its president. The General Assembly declared this competition with a denominational agency schismatic and ordered all who were Presbyterians to withdraw from it. Machen refused, was tried, and on March 29, 1935, was suspended from the ministry of the Presbyterian Church.[271] The language of the judgment rendered was reminiscent of the suspension of C. A. Briggs in 1893. But now the roles were reversed. Princeton theologians were no longer in control of the denomination. They were everywhere on the defensive.

In October 1935, one faculty member and a majority of the board of Westminster Seminary, including Clarence E. Macartney, resigned rather than endorse the aggressive ecclesiastical separatism of Machen and the faculty majority. The General Assembly of 1936 heard four judicial cases appealing censures of members of the Independent Board. In each of the cases the Assembly upheld the censure imposed by lower judicatories. Within nine days of these judicial decisions, Machen and some of his most vocal followers formed a new denomination named "The Presbyterian Church of America." Machen was elected its first moderator. (The name was changed in 1939 to The Orthodox Presbyterian Church.) The movement was soon fragmented, as in 1937 Carl McIntire and some others broke with Machen over their desire to maintain premillenialism, total abstinence from alcoholic beverages, and a more congregational form of government. They formed the Bible Presbyterian Synod as their denomination and Faith Seminary in Philadelphia as their training school. Machen died a few weeks later while on a trip to North Dakota. He was, to the end, trying to hold together the few churches of his denomination. His funeral was held in the Spruce Street Baptist Church in Philadelphia.[272]

The era of the Princeton theology was ended. But the theological problems were unsolved. Princeton theology's equation of inerrancy with the position of the Westminster Confession was never repudiated. Rather, the Presbyterian Church simply agreed not to make any interpretation of the Westminster Confession binding. The Westminster Confession then practically ceased to function and the church was left without a clear confessional position. Those who left the denomination and those in other groups sympathetic to the Princeton theology's theories about Scripture were thus allowed to believe that they were the inheritors of the true Reformation tradition. The large and amorphous movement known as evangelicalism in America continued the Princeton doctrine of Scripture, often without any longer being aware of its origins.

d. Summary

When B. B. Warfield succeeded A. A. Hodge as Professor of Theology at Princeton, he completed the shift in theological method from induction to deduction. Apologetics was now the primary task in a time when the Princeton theories were under increasing attack from within the church. Warfield no longer acknowledged the philosophical and theological sources of the Princeton theology in Scottish realism and Turretin. He identified the Princeton position with the Bible itself and claimed that the church had always held to the Princeton particularities.

The Princeton theologians' denial of any difference between their own views of language and culture and that of the ancient Near Eastern biblical writers brought them into violent conflict with biblical criticism. The academic battle between scholasticism and criticism developed into an ecclesiastical struggle between C. A. Briggs and B. B. Warfield. Briggs correctly labeled the Princeton theology as post-Reformation scholasticism. However, the majority in the Presbyterian Church in 1893 sided with Warfield; and Briggs was suspended from the ministry.

Between 1893 and 1910 the Presbyterian Church treated the Hodge-Warfield view on inerrancy as confessional and read it back into the history of Reformed theology. Conflict increased between liberal and scholastic factions in the Church until in 1927 the General Assembly declared that no one had the right to interpret the Westminster Confession. In 1929 J. Gresham Machen withdrew from Princeton Seminary and founded Westminster Seminary to perpetuate the Hodge-Warfield tradition. In the ensuing decade, however, it was scholastics who were ejected from or left the leadership of the denomination. The era of the Princeton theology was ended. But the theological problems remained unresolved.

e. Notes:

1. For summary biographies, see *DAB*, s.v. "Warfield, Benjamin Breckinridge," and *NSH*, s.v. "Warfield, Benjamin Breckinridge."
2. Wilber B. Wallis, "Benjamin B. Warfield: Didactic and Polemical Theologian," Part I: "The Testimony of B. B. Warfield," *Presbyterion: Convenant Seminary Review* (April 1977):4.
3. Ethelbert D. Warfield, "Biographical Sketch of Benjamin Breckinridge Warfield," in Benjamin Breckinridge Warfield, *Revelation and Inspiration* (New York: Oxford

University Press, 1927), p. v. (Hereafter cited as E.D.W.) E. D. Warfield was B. B. Warfield's brother.
4. Samuel G. Craig, "Benjamin B. Warfield," in Benjamin Breckinridge Warfield, *Biblical and Theological Studies* (Philadelphia: Presbyterian and Reformed Publishing, 1952), p. xi.
5. E.D.W., p. vi.
6. Craig, pp. xi–xii. See also James McCosh, *The Scottish Philosophy* (N.Y.: R. Carter & Brothers, 1875).
7. E.D.W., p. vi.

370 *The Authority and Interpretation of the Bible*

8. E.D.W., pp. vi–vii.

9. E.D.W., p. vii.

10. Wallis, p. 4. Mrs. Warfield died in 1915.

11. E.D.W., p. vii.

12. Francis Landley Patton, "Benjamin Breckinridge Warfield—A Memorial Address," *The Princeton Theological Review* 19 (July 1921):pp. 369–391, cited in Craig, p. xvi.

13. Craig, p. xliii.

14. *LCH*, pp. 589, 590, from Warfield's essay "Dr. Charles Hodge as a Teacher of Exegesis," in *LCH*, pp. 586–591; also reprinted in *Selected Shorter Works of Benjamin B. Warfield—I*, ed. John E. Meeter (Nutley, N.J.: Presbyterian and Reformed Publishing, 1970), pp. 437–440. (Hereafter cited as *SWW-I.*)

15. "The Idea of Systematic Theology Considered as a Science," inauguration of the Rev. Benjamin B. Warfield, D.D., as Professor of Didactic and Polemic Theology, Princeton Theological Seminary, May 8, 1888. Printed as *The Idea of Systematic Theology Considered as a Science* (New York: Anson Randolph & Co., 1888), pp. 5,6. This was expanded in the *PPR* 7 (April 1896):243–271, and reprinted in Warfield, *Studies in Theology* (New York: Oxford University Press, 1932), pp.49–87. (Hereafter cited as *Studies.*)

When Caspar Wistar Hodge, Jr., grandson of Charles Hodge and nephew of A. A. Hodge, who had assisted Warfield in the Department of Theology for twenty years, succeeded him after Warfield's death he said at his inauguration on October 11, 1921: "Relying on the help of God, I shall teach the same theology they taught, and give myself whole-heartedly to its exposition and defense." "The Significance of Reformed Theology," *Princeton Theological Review* (hereafter cited as *PTR*) 20 (January 1922):2.

16. Wallis, p. 7.

17. Hodge's *ST*, I, chap. II, question 2: "The Facts of Nature Reveal God," p. 22. Warfield also calls these "general" and "special" revelation or "natural" and "soteriological revelation." See "The Biblical Idea of Revelation," in his *The Inspiration and Authority of the Bible* (Philadelphia: Presbyterian and Reformed Publishing, 1970; rep. 1948), p. 74. (Hereafter cited as *IAB.*) This was the article "Revelation" in *The International Standard Bible Encyclopaedia*, ed. James Orr (hereafter cited as *ISBE*; 1915), 4:2573–2582.

18. *IAB*, p. 75.

19. See his essay "Calvin's Doctrine of the Knowledge of God" in *CA*, p. 33.

20. *CA*, p. 34. Warfield says that the knowledge of God as innate was "the common property of the Reformed teachers," note 4.

21. See "Calvin's Doctrine of the Knowledge of God," in *CA*, pp. 148–149.

22. *CA*, p. 147.

23. *CA*, p. 43, citing *Inst.* I. iv. 4.

24. *CA*, p. 150.

25. *CA*, p. 44.

26. *CA*, p. 151. See also pp. 68ff.

27. *CA*, p. 151.

28. *CA*, p. 151. Warfield also stressed this in Augustine. See *CA*, pp. 474ff., the conclusion of his essay "Augustine's Doctrine of Knowledge and Authority." For Warfield, "special revelation is not ... a substitute for general revelation but only a preparation for its proper assimilation." *CA*, p. 474.

29. See "Apologetics," in *Studies* p. 4.

30. *Studies*, p. 3.

31. *Studies*, p. 7.

32. *Studies*, p. 9. Warfield subdivided apologetics into five parts: philosophical, psychological, distinguishing theology from other sciences, historical, and bibliological apologetics, p. 13.

33. *Studies*, p. 15.

34. *Studies*, p. 15. See also Warfield's "Introduction" to Francis R. Beattie's *Apologetics*, in *Selected Shorter Writings of Benjamin B. Warfield—II*, ed. John E. Meeter (Nutley, N.J.: Presbyterian and Reformed Publishing, 1973), p. 94 (Hereafter cited as *SWW—II.*)

35. *Studies*, p. 15.

36. Kuyper's and Bavinck's views on Scripture will be discussed more fully in chapter 7.

37. *SWW—II*, pp. 95–96. See Abraham Kuyper, *Principles of Sacred Theology*, trans. J. Hendrik DeVries (Grand Rapids, Mich.: Wm. B. Eerdmans, 1965; rep. 1954), with an introduction by Warfield. In 1898, Warfield did not mention this fundamental difference between his and the Dutch tradition although he did express it later. See also Cornelius Van Til, "As I Think of Bavinck," *International Reformed Bulletin*, no. 27 (October 1966):20ff., where Van Til imagines Warfield's first reading of Bavinck's *Gereformeerde Dogmatiek.*

38. *SWW—II*, p. 100.

39. *SWW—II*, p. 99.

40. *SWW-II*, pp. 99–100. In opposition to Kuyper and Bavinck, Warfield felt it was possible to meet the non-Christian on the "neutral ground" of "right reason" and "to validate the Christian 'view of the world.' " This is because for Warfield, reason has been left unimpaired by the Fall and its attendant sin. He also followed the Scottish realism tradition in stressing human commonality to the point of denying the significance of cultural diversity. He assumed that his type of Euro-American reasoning was in principle standard and in form superior to all other thought forms. He declared: "All minds are after all of the same essential structure." See *SWW—II*, pp. 100ff., 117–120.

The Princeton position was reechoed in 1910 when C. W. Hodge gave reasons why the "distinction or dualism between the natural religious consciousness and the Christian consciousness is not absolute as it is conceived to be by Kuyper." See "Christian Experience and Dogmatic Theology," *PTR* 8 (January 1910):18. (Hereafter cited as C. W. Hodge, "Christian Experience.")

41. *SWW—II*, p. 105. Further discussion of these issues is found in Jack B. Rogers, "Van Til and Warfield on Scripture in the Westminster Confession," in *Jerusalem and Athens*, ed. E. R. Geehan (Nutley, N.J.: Presbyterian and Reformed Publishing, 1971), chap. 5; and in other essays in the same volume: Robert D. Knudsen, "Progressive and Regressive Tendencies in Christian Apologetics," chap. 14; and Clark H. Pinnock, "The Philosophy of Christian Evidences," chap. 23. On Warfield and Kuyper see also Cornelius Van Til, *The Defense of the Faith*, 3d rev. ed. (Philadelphia: Presbyterian and Reformed Publishing, 1967), chap. 11.

42. *PTR* (January 1903):138–148, reprinted in *SWW—II*, 106–123.

43. *SWW—II*, p. 114.

44. *SWW—II*, p. 112.

45. *SWW—II*, p. 113.

46. *SWW—II*, p. 115. Warfield summed up his view of reason and faith when he wrote:

"Though faith is the gift of God, it does not in the least follow that the faith which God gives is an irrational faith, that is, a faith without cognizable ground in right reason. We believe in Christ because it is rational to believe in Him, not even though it be irrational. Of course mere reasoning cannot make a Christian; but that is not because faith is not the result of evidence, but because a dead soul cannot respond to evidence. The action of the Holy Spirit in giving faith is not apart from evidence, but along with evidence; and in the first instance consists in preparing the soul for the reception of the evidence (*Studies*, p. 15)."

Warfield had just quoted Aquinas: " 'He who believes,' says Thomas Aquinas, in words which have become current as an axiom, 'would not believe unless he saw that what he believes is worthy of belief.' "

47. *SWW—II*, p. 115.

48. *SWW—II*, p. 115.

49. *SWW—II*, p. 115.

50. *SWW—II*, p. 120.

51. *PTR* 9 (1911):537–566, reprinted in *Studies*, pp. 313–342.

52. *Studies*, p. 314.

53. *Studies*, p. 317. For Warfield, in matters of faith especially, the will follows the understanding. See John H. Gerstner, "Warfield's Case for Biblical Inerrancy" (hereafter cited as Gerstner, "Warfield"), in *God's Inerrant Word*, ed. John Warwick Montgomery (Minneapolis: Bethany Fellowship, 1974), pp. 122–124.

54. *Studies*, p. 318.

55. *Studies*, p. 318.

56. *Studies*, p. 320.

57. *Studies*, p. 320. Warfield's colleague and successor Caspar Wistar Hodge later asserted: "Apart from the blinding effects of sin [faith] could not be withheld when the evidence is present." See "The Witness of the Holy Spirit to the Bible," *PTR* 11 (1913):64

58. *Studies*, p. 329. In Warfield's "Augustine's Doctrine of Knowledge and Authority," he "appears to be setting forth his own. For example, he interprets Augustine as a rationalist in the sense that 'the reason acting under laws of its own supplies the forms of thought without which no knowledge can be obtained; whether by sensation or experience.' " In the relation of faith to reason Warfield interpreted Augustine as giving the priority to reason. Gerstner, "Warfield," p. 121. See also *CA*, pp. 422ff. and *Studies*, pp. 325ff. John J. Markarian, "The Calvinistic Concept of the Biblical Revelation in the Theology of B. B. Warfield" (Ph.D. dissertation, Drew University, 1963), p. 57, also deals with this.

59. *SWW—II*, 121. See also *Studies*, pp. 330 and 326: "Knowledge is seeing, faith is crediting."

60. *Studies*, p. 331.

61. *Studies*, p. 326.

62. *Studies*, pp. 341–342. Caspar Wistar Hodge exemplified the Princeton position when he wrote that "*Assensus* is the logical prius of *fiducia*." See "Christian Experience," p. 20. See also William D. Livingstone, "The Princeton Apologetic as Exemplified by the Work of Benjamin B. Warfield and J. Gresham Machen: A Study in American Theology, 1880–1930" (Ph.D. dissertation, Yale University, 1948), pp. 187ff. and Markarian, pp. 88–93.

63. See, for example, Thomas V. Morris, *Francis Schaeffer's Apologetics: A Critique* (Chicago: Moody Press, 1976), p. 81.

64. *Studies*, p. 15.

65. See *CA*, pp. 84ff. Warfield cites the Westminster Confession I. 5.

66. *CA*, p. 88.

67. *CA*, p. 85. Warfield claimed Calvin believed that miracles were "part of the objective evidence of the deity of Scripture" and that he did not place miracles below the testimony of the Spirit in importance, p. 86, note 60. On Warfield and miracles see Gerstner, "Warfield," pp. 128–130.

68. *CA*, p. 89.

69. *CA*, pp. 87, 90. Warfield continued: "To taste and see that the Scriptures are divine is to recognize a divinity actually present in Scripture; and of course recognition implies perception of the *indicia* of divinity manifested in Scripture." Warfield commented, though, that "it must be admitted that Calvin has not at this point developed this side of his subject with the fulness which might be wished, but has left it to the general implications of the argument," p. 90.

70. *CA*, pp. 111–112. See also Markarian, p. 96, and note 2, and Andrew Hoffecker, "The Relation between the Objective and the Subjective Elements in Christian Religious Experience: A Study in the Systematic and Devotional Writings of Archibald Alexander, Charles Hodge, and Benjamin Breckinridge Warfield" (Ph.D. dissertation, Brown University, 1970), pp. 253 and 263.

71. See Edward A. Dowey, *The Knowledge of God in Calvin's Theology* (New York: Columbia University Press, 1965), p. 116.

72. See Daniel P. Fuller, "Benjamin B. Warfield's View of Faith and History: A Critique

in the Light of the New Testament," *Journal of the Evangelical Theological Society* 11, no. 2 (Spring 1968):77, who comments that these *indicia* "are a part of the empirical stuff of the world around us."

73. *SWW—II*, p. 537. The article was originally published in the *Westminster Teacher* 17 (September 1889):324–326, and is reprinted in *SWW—II*, pp. 537–541.

74. *SWW—II*, p. 537. Cf. p. 538.

75. Warfield said of the present canon: "That this collection as a whole is 'the Word of God' is experimentally verifiable." See B. B. Warfield, *Critical Reviews* (New York: Oxford University Press, 1932), p. 121. This is from Warfield's review of Marcus Dods's, *The Bible, Its Origin and Nature*, reprinted from *PTR* 4 (1906):109–115.

76. *Studies*, p. 645, from the essay "The Latest Phase of Historical Rationalism" in *The Presbyterian Quarterly* 9 (1895):36–67 and 185–210, reprinted in *Studies*, pp. 585–645. Again, "the principles of canonicity was not apostolic authorship, but *imposition by the apostles as 'law,'*" p. 645. See also Warfield's *The Canon of the New Testament* (Philadelphia: American Sunday School Union, 1892). He appealed to Augustine on this point. See *CA*, pp. 433ff. Also of importance is "The Canonicity of Second Peter," *Southern Presbyterian Review* 33 (January 1882):45–75, reprinted in *SWW—II*, pp. 48–79.

77. On these grounds he rejected the ending of the Gospel of Mark as the Word of God. See "Inspiration and the Spurious Versus at the End of Mark," *Sunday School Times* 25 (January 20, 1883):36f. See also his earlier article in the same publication "The Genuineness of Mark 16:9–20" 24 (December 2, 1882):755f. and "A Defence of the Article on 'The Genuineness of Mark 16:9–20,'" *The Presbyterian*, 53, no. 3 (January 20, 1883):8f. See also Markarian, p. 164.

78. *IAB*, p. 429, from "Inspiration and Criticism," which was Warfield's inaugural address at his induction to the Chair of New Testament Literature and Exegesis at Western Theological Seminary in 1879.

79. *IAB*, p. 429.

80. *IAB*, p. 431. See *SWW—II*, pp. 48–79; Markarian, pp. 158–165; and Warfield's *Syllabus on the Special Introduction to the Catholic Epistles* (Pittsburgh: W. W. Waters, 1883), as well as his *The Bible Doctrine of Inspiration Not Invalidated* (New York: Ketcham, 1893). (hereafter cited as Warfield, *Bible Doctrine*).

81. Markarian rightly notes: "Warfield uses

the very same tools to establish this external authority of Scripture as his opponents use to evaporate it—historical investigation based upon human reason. The only difference is that the presuppositions governing the search differ. On the one hand there may be an antisupernaturalistic bias or a bias against external authority. But for Warfield there is an opposite bias. The basis is no different. The one says, 'historical investigation,' and so does the other," p. 173. Cf. Dowey, p. 118. For Warfield, "the authority which cannot assure of a hard fact is soon not trusted for a hard doctrine," *IAB*, p. 181.

82. See Otto Piper, "The Authority of the Bible," *Theology Today*, 6 (April 1949–January 1950):160.

83. See the sections of "The Biblical Idea of Revelation"; "The Process of Revelation" and "Modes of Revelation" in *IAB*, pp. 79–96.

84. *IAB*, pp. 82–83. Warfield drew from A. B. Davidson, *OT Prophecy* (1903).

85. *IAB*, p. 79.

86. *IAB*, p. 80.

87. *IAB*, p. 81.

88. *SWW—II*, p. 540.

89. *IAB*, p. 420. See also Warfield's article "Inspiration" from Johnson's *Universal Cyclopaedia*, IV (1909 edition), reprinted in *SWW—II*, pp. 614–636.

90. "The Real Problem of Inspiration," *PRR* 4 (1893):177–221, reprinted in *IAB*, pp. 169–226. The quoted passage is from p. 173.

91. *SWW—II*, p. 543, from "The Divine and Human in the Bible," in the *Presbyterian Journal* 19, no. 18 (May 3, 1894):280, reprinted in *SWW—II*, pp. 542–548. See also p. 628.

92. *SWW—II*, p. 546. Warfield wrote: "The fundamental principle of this conception is that the whole of Scripture is the product of divine activities which enter it, however, not by superseding the activities of the human authors, but confluently with them; so that the Scriptures are the joint product of divine and human activities, both of which penetrate them at every point, working harmoniously together to the production of a writing which is not divine here and human there, but at once divine and human in every part, every word and every particular," p. 547; see also p. 629.

93. *SWW—II*, p. 547; see also p. 629.

94. *IAB*, p. 173. In "The Church Doctrine of Inspiration," published in *Bibliotheca Sac-*

ra 51 (October 1894):614–640 as "The Inspiration of the Bible," reprinted in *IAB*, pp. 105–128, Warfield wrote that "the writers of the New Testament books looked upon what they called 'Scripture' as divinely safeguarded in even its verbal expression, and as divinely trustworthy in all its parts, in all its elements, and in all its affirmations of whatever kind," p. 115.

95. *PRR* 5 (January 1894):177. See Markarian, p. 126. This same tendency is seen in his comment that "what Calvin has in mind is not to insist that the mode of inspiration was dictation, but that the result of inspiration is as if it were by dictation, viz., the production of a pure word of God free from all human admixtures," *CA*, pp. 63–64. Gerstner comments: "One can only remark that while talking about inerrancy, Warfield on this occasion spoke errantly!" in "Warfield," p. 134.

96. See E. A. Abbott *From Letter to Spirit* (London: A. & C. Black, 1903), p. 400. Warfield's comment was made in "Dr. Edwin A. Abbott on the Genuineness of Second Peter," *Southern Presbyterian Review* 34 (April 1883):390–445. Markarian comments: "Warfield takes each word and phrase which Abbott has handled to refute the former's testimony in arraignment of the style of the letter. Also in a notebook of *Mss Materials on the New Testament* Warfield has an unpublished article on II Peter 2:8 attempting to show that the Epistle is not making a crude use of *blemma* for a sense of sight by translating it as a passive 'appearance.' The question here is not with the scholarship of either Abbott or Warfield, but with the fact that Warfield felt the necessity of defending the style of II Peter even though according to his principle of *concursus*, the author's style could not be used as an argument against inspiration," p. 127, note 2.

97. *IAB*, p. 162, from the "The Biblical Idea of Inspiration," published as "Inspiration," from *ISBE*, III, 1473–1483, reprinted in *IAB*, pp. 131–166. For a discussion of "A Christological Analogy for Two Natures" from another perspective see Markus Barth, *Conversation with the Bible* (New York: Holt, Rinehart & Winston, 1964), chap. 5.

98. See "Professor Henry Preserved Smith on Inspiration," *PRR* 5 (October 1894):600–653. Smith argued that there was the analogy of the divine and human in the Bible with sanctification. The Holy Spirit can be present within fallibility. Warfield answered that sanctification in believers was a process working towards completion. The Scriptures, however, were a completed work. Markarian writes: "Warfield's Doctrine of Inspiration is carefully stated. He seeks to guard against confusion of the work of the Spirit in accrediting and assimilating Scripture. This is the interest of preserving its objective character.... " p. 130. See also *SWW—II*, p. 546.

99. See Warfield's "The Terms 'Scripture' and 'Scriptures' as Employed in the New Testament" in *IAB*, pp. 229–241, reprinted from Hastings's *Dictionary of Christ and the Gospels*, II, 583–588; " 'It Says:' 'Scripture Says:' 'God Says,' " in *IAB*, pp. 299–348 from *PRR* 10 (1899):472–510; and " 'The Oracles of God' " in *IAB*, pp. 351–407, from *PRR* 11 (1900):217–260.

100. *IAB*, pp. 318, 320. For Warfield, "revelation is but half revelation unless it be infallibly communicated; it is but half communicated unless it be infallibly recorded," *IAB*, p. 442.

101. See Gerstner, "Warfield," pp. 128–130 and Warfield's *Miracles: Yesterday and Today; True and False* (Grand Rapids, Mich.: Wm. B. Eerdmans, 1953) and "The Question of Miracles," *The Bible Student*, 7 (March, April, May, June 1903):121–126, 193–197, 243–250, 314–320, reprinted in *SWW—II*, pp. 167–204.

102. *SWW—II*, pp. 631ff. See also Gerstner, "Warfield," p. 131.

103. *IAB*, p. 160. He distinguished sharply between them: "The former being used to denote the divine activity in supernaturally communicating to certain chosen instruments the truths which God would make known to the world; while the term 'inspiration' is reserved to denote the continued work of God by which—his providential, gracious, and supernatural contributions being presupposed—he wrought within the sacred writers in their entire work of writing, with the design and effect of rendering the written product the divinely trustworthy Word of God," *SWW—II*, p. 615.

104. *IAB*, p. 212.

105. *IAB*, p. 217.

106. *IAB*, p. 217.

107. See *IAB*, pp. 218–219. See also Fuller, p. 77.

108. *IAB*, p. 219.

109. "Paul's Doctrine of the Old Testament," *Presbyterian Quarterly*, 3 (July

1889):389–406; " 'God-Inspired Scripture,' " *PRR* 11 (January 1900):89–130, reprinted in *IAB*, p. 245; and "The Biblical Idea of Inspiration" in *IAB*, pp. 131–166.

110. "Paul's Doctrine of the Old Testament," p. 396.

111. *IAB*, p. 296.

112. *IAB*, pp. 133, 134.

113. *IAB*, p. 134.

114. See *IAB*, p. 276.

115. *IAB*, p. 247.

116. *IAB*, p. 245.

117. *IAB*, p. 295.

118. *IAB*, p. 133. Scripture is not " 'breathed into by God' " or "the product of the Divine 'inbreathing' into its human authors" but is "breathed out by God."

119. Warfield says there is some possibility the term could be rendered as "brought" but he clearly preferred "borne." See *IAB*, pp. 136, 137, 150, 151.

120. *IAB*, p. 137.

121. *IAB*, p. 137.

122. See *IAB*, pp. 139, 140.

123. *IAB*, p. 115.

124. *IAB*, p. 117.

125. See Warfield's quotes from James Stuart, *The Principles of Christianity* (London: Williams & Norgate, 1888), p. 67 seq. and the discussion in *IAB*, pp. 190ff. Stuart said the apostles adapted their teachings to the people of their time and "were themselves, to a very great extent, men of their own time, sharing many of the common opinions and even the common prejudices." Stuart also said, however, that because the New Testament writers were "so completely dominated by the spirit of the age ... their testimony on the question of Scripture inspiration possesses no independent value." Warfield saw Stuart as rejecting both Biblical inspiration and the doctrine of sacrificial atonement.

126. *IAB*, p. 195.

127. *IAB*, p. 210.

128. "The Present Problem of Inspiration," *Homiletic Review* 21 (May 1891):411. (Hereafter cited as Warfield, "Present Problem.")

129. *IAB*, p. 208.

130. On Smith, see *BC*, pp. 33–35, 63–68.

131. *The Presbyterian Review* 3 (1882): 357–388. See *NIDCC*, s.v. "Henry Preserved Smith."

132. The immediate occasion for Smith's trial was an action directed against Briggs, the "Portland Deliverance" of the 1892

General Assembly, which said in part: "The General Assembly would remind all under its care that it is a fundamental doctrine that the Old and New Testaments are the inspired and infallible Word of God. Our Church holds that the inspired Word, as it came from God, is without error." See *The Presbyterian Enterprise*, ed. Maurice W. Armstrong, Lefferts A. Loetscher, and Charles A. Anderson (Philadelphia: Westminster Press, 1956), p. 249. See also *BC*, pp. 56–57, 61–62.

133. Henry P. Smith, *Inspiration and Inerrancy: A History and a Defense* (New York: Robert Clarke & Co., 1893), p. 270. (Hereafter cited as H. P. Smith, *Inspiration and Inerrancy*.) See also Warfield's statement: "If we are to occupy the attitude toward Scripture which Christ occupied, the simple 'It is written!' must have the same authority to us in matters of doctrinal truth, of practical duty, of historical fact and of verbal form that it had to him; and to us as truly as to him, the Scriptures must be incapable of being broken," in "Reviews of Recent Theological Literature," *PRR*, 4 (1893):499. See the account of these debates in Edward J. Carnell, *The Case for Orthodox Theology* (Philadelphia: Westminster Press, 1959), pp. 102ff.

134. *PR* 29 (1857):685.

135. H. P. Smith, *Inspiration and Inerrancy*, p. 270.

136. Carnell set some of these troublesome passages in parallel columns:

2 Samuel	8:4	1 Chronicles	18:4
	10:6		19:6
	10:18		19:18
	24:9		21:5
	24:24		21:25
1 Kings	4:26	2 Chronicles	9:25
	6:2		3:4
	7:26		4:5

See Carnell, pp. 103–104 and James Barr, *Fundamentalism* (Philadelphia: Westminster Press, 1978; rep. 1977), pp. 224–225; 309–310.

137. *PRR* 4 (1893):499.

138. *IAB*, p. 226.

139. *PRR* 5 (1894):650.

140. *PRR* 5 (1894):646.

141. *IAB*, p. 150.

142. *PRR* 4 (1893):499.

143. *IAB*, p. 150. Markarian writes that Warfield "maintained that the Scripture as a formal norm is an inerrant propositional revelation which is an immediate Word of God," p. 182.

144. See Warfield's joint article with A. A. Hodge, "Inspiration," *The Presbyterian Review* 2 (April 1881):238. Markarian writes: "Scripture has within it marks of its human authorship but Warfield claims that in studying the human element in Scripture we must adjust our theories if they lead to claims of fraud, deceit, mistakes. There may be different views of Jehovah but not false views; underdeveloped morality but not immorality; incomplete and partial but not incorrect and false views. The record was not written to teach true science to all generations, but the cosmology of Genesis is in harmony with that of the nineteenth-century," p. 120. He cites Warfield's "Paul's Doctrine of the Old Testament."

145. *SWW—II*, p. 581, "The Inerrancy of the Original Autographs," *The Independent* 45 (March 23, 1893):382f., reprinted in *SWW—II*, pp. 580–587.

146. See *SWW—II*, p. 581.

147. See "The Westminster Confession and the Original Autographs," *The Presbyterian Messenger* 1, no. 50 (September 13, 1894):1181f., reprinted in *SWW—II*, pp. 588–594; and "The Westminster Doctrine of Inspiration," *The Independent*, 43 (April 23, 1891):595f., reprinted in *SWW—II*, pp. 572–579.

148. *SWW—II*, p. 582.

149. *SWW—II*, p. 584. Warfield also wrote: "The autographic text of the New Testament is distinctly within reach of criticism in so immensely the greater part of the volume, that we cannot despair of restoring to ourselves and the Church of God, His book, word for word, as He gave it by inspiration to men," *An Introduction to Textual Criticism of the New Testament* (Toronto: S. R. Briggs, 1887), p. 15, as cited by Gerstner, "Warfield," p. 137.

150. Warfield, "Present Problem," p. 416. See also *IAB*, p. 225.

151. *SWW—II, p. 585.*

152. Warfield, *Bible Doctrine*, p. 181. See also Livingstone, p. 277.

153. Warfield, *Bible Doctrine*, p. 181.

154. Warfield, "Present Problem," p. 416.

155. *Presbyterian Review* 2 (April 1881):242.

156. Warfield, "Present Problem," p. 416.

157. Warfield, "Present Problem," p. 416. Though Warfield claimed to be an apostle of an inductive approach, he worked more through deduction from his preestablished theory or doctrine. Ernest R. Sandeen, *The Roots of Fundamentalism* (Chicago: University of Chicago Press, 1970) (hereafter cited as Sandeen, *Roots*), p. 130 comments: "The Princeton professors' insistence that they were doing nothing new, while creating a unique apologetic which flew in the face of the standards they were claiming to protect, cannot be judged as a historically honest or laudable program."

158. Max Gray Rogers has written an extensive article entitled "Charles Augustus Briggs: Heresy at Union," in *American Religious Heretics*, ed. George H. Shriver (Nashville: Abingdon Press, 1966), pp. 89–147. He draws on private papers and the correspondence of Briggs. The letter to his uncle is identified as Briggs Transcript (hereafter cited as *B.T.*) I, 34, 317a. January 8, 1867 (?). See M. G. Rogers, p. 90.

159. Cited in Carl E. Hatch, *The Charles A. Briggs Heresy Trial* (New York: Exposition Press, 1969), p. 23 from a letter from Briggs to Dr. Henry Boynton Smith on May 6, 1868 (B.T. III, 461–465).

160. C. A. Briggs, *The Higher Criticism of the Hexateuch* (New York: Charles Scribner's Sons, 1892), p. 62, cited in M. G. Rogers, p. 90.

161. C. A. Briggs, "Biblical Theology with Especial Reference to the New Testament," *The American Presbyterian Review*, New Series, 2 (January 1870):120, cited in M. G. Rogers, p. 91.

162. *BC*, p. 27. See his chap. 3, "Biblical Criticism," for accounts of the contexts and responses made to the rise of biblical criticism.

163. C. A. Briggs, "Exegetical Theology, Especially in the Old Testament," an address on the occasion of his inauguration as Davenport Professor of Hebrew and Cognate Languages in the Union Theological Seminary, New York City, on September 21, 1876 (New York: Rogers and Sherwood, 1876), p. 15, cited in M. G. Rogers, p. 91.

164. Lefferts A. Loetscher, *A Brief History of the Presbyterians*, 3d ed. (Philadelphia: Westminster Press, 1978), p. 129.

165. See *BC*, chap. 4. Loetscher comments, "The first number . . . January, 1880, contained a broad and irenic statement of purpose," *BC*, p. 30.

166. See Warner M. Bailey, "William Robertson Smith and American Biblical Studies," *JPH* 51, no. 3 (Fall 1973):285–308, and his "Theology and Criticism in William Robertson Smith" (Ph.D. dissertation, Yale University, 1970).

167. At this time Warfield was teaching at Western Seminary in Pittsburgh. He joined the faculty of Princeton in 1887. The article appeared in the *Presbyterian Review* 2 (April 1881):225–260. (Hereafter cited as "Inspiration.") Warfield wrote pp. 238–260.

168. "Inspiration," pp. 225–226.

169. "Inspiration," p. 238.

170. "Inspiration," p. 245.

171. "Inspiration," p. 245. See also p. 242 where Warfield challenges: "Let it be proved that each alleged discrepant statement certainly occurred in the original autograph of the sacred book in which it is said to be found." Warfield wrote extensively on the doctrine of Scripture. See his *IAB*, and collected articles in part 5 of *SWW —II*, especially: "The Inerrancy of the Original Autographs," pp. 580–587, and "The Westminster Confession and the Original Autographs," pp. 588–594. Warfield's views are examined in Gerstner, "Warfield," pp. 115–142. A valuable guide to Warfield's work is John E. Meeter and Roger Nicole, *A Bibliography of Benjamin Breckinridge Warfield 1851–1921* (Philadelphia: Presbyterian and Reformed Publishing, 1974).

172. This was the position of A. A. Hodge in the revised edition of his *Outlines of Theology*. (New York: Robert Carter and Brothers, 1879), pp. 66–67, 75–76.

173. "Inspiration," p. 236. See also pp. 244 –245 for Warfield's agreement.

174. *Presbyterian Review* 2 (July 1881):550– 579.

175. C. A. Briggs, "The Right, Duty, and Limits of Biblical Criticism," *Presbyterian Review* (July 1881):551. For amplification of this controversy see *SWC*, pp. 28–43.

176. B.T. VI, 111–113, no. 1719, December 27, 1882, cited in M. G. Rogers, p. 93. Briggs's correspondence and papers are housed in the library of Union Theological Seminary in New York City.

177. *Minutes*, General Assembly of the Presbyterian Church in the U.S.A., 1882, p. 92; see also p. 116. See *BC*, p. 35.

178. Charles A. Briggs, "A Critical Study of the History of the Higher Criticism with Special Reference to the Pentateuch," *Presbyterian Review* 4 (January 1883):69–130.

179. Francis L. Patton, "The Dogmatic Aspect of Pentateuchal Criticism," *Presbyterian Review* 4 (April 1883):341–410. See pp. 363, 371. By Scripture, Patton meant the original autographs.

180. *Minutes*, General Assembly of the Presbyterian Church in the U.S.A., 1883, pp. 631–632. See also General Assembly *Minutes*, 1884, pp. 47–48.
181. C. A. Briggs, *Biblical Study: Its Principles, Methods and History* (New York: Charles Scribner's Sons, 1883).
182. C. A. Briggs, *American Presbyterianism* (New York: Charles Scribner's Sons, 1885).
183. M. G. Rogers, pp. 93–95. See also *BC*, pp. 38–39.
184. C. A. Briggs, *Whither? A Theological Question for the Times* (New York: Charles Scribner's Sons, 1889), p. viii. and *passim*. (Hereafter cited as *Whither?*)
185. *Whither?*, pp. 20–21. In his later work, *Theological Symbolics* (Edinburgh: Charles Scribner's Sons, 1914), p. 378, Briggs continued this theme:

"The Helvetic Consensus unfortunately became the Symbol of the Old School Calvinists of America, which they followed rather than the Westminster Confession. The *Institutions* of Francis Turretin became their textbook, and the Westminster divines were ignored, and became altogether unknown. And so the American Calvinists were plunged into a century of unnecessary and unfruitful conflict, for which the Princeton divines have been chiefly responsible. In a recent publication Francis L. Patton goes so far as to name Francis Turretin the 'Thomas Aquinas of Protestantism.' "

186. *Whither?*, pp. 63–64.
187. *Whither?*, p. 64.
188. *Whither?*, p. 65. Hodge and Warfield taught that "infallible thought must be definite thought, and definite thought implies words.... *The line* (of inspired or not inspired, or infallible or fallible) *can never rationally be drawn between the thoughts and words of Scripture*," in "Inspiration," pp. 234–235 (italics theirs). Briggs cites then "the opinions of a few Presbyterians of the seventeenth century on this subject, in order to show how far modern divines have departed from the Westminster doctrine of the Bible," p. 66. Pp. 66–68 contain the quotations.
189. *Whither?*, pp. 68–69.
190. *Whither?*, p. 69. Briggs then quotes Samuel Rutherford and Richard Baxter.
191. *Whither?*, p. 71.
192. *Whither?*, p. 72.
193. *Whither?*, p. 72.

194. *Whither?*, pp. 72–73.
195. *Whither?*, p. 73.
196. On the former point, Briggs believed Princeton had actually destroyed the Reformed doctrine of the authority of Scripture and had decisively changed the base of Protestantism. See *Whither?* p. 90.
197. *Whither?*, pp. 77–81.
198. *Whither?*, p. 81.
199. *Whither?*, p. 84, quoting A. A. Hodge, *Commentary on the Confession of Faith*, pp. 51–52.
200. *Whither?*, p. 84.
201. *Whither?*, p. 86.
202. See *Whither?*, pp. 86–87, quoting Warfield, *Presbyterian Review*, 10:506.
203. *Whither?*, p. 87.
204. *Whither?*, p. 82. Westminster Confession, I, 4. Briggs concluded his attack with a quote from A. F. Mitchell, the leading authority on the history of the Westminster Confession of Faith. See *Minutes of the Sessions of the Westminster Assembly of Divines (November 1644 to March 1649) From Transcripts of the Originals Procured by a Committee of the General Assembly of the Church of Scotland*, eds. A. F. Mitchell and J. Struthers (London, 1874), "Introduction," p. xlix. See *Whither?*, p. 89.
205. *Whither?*, pp. vii–viii.
206. Benjamin B. Warfield, *The Westminster Assembly and Its Work* (New York: Oxford University Press, 1931), pp. 262–263. (Hereafter cited as Warfield, *Westminster Assembly*.)
207. Ibid.
208. Ibid., pp. 263–271.
209. Ibid., pp. 262–263 and 269–271.
210. Ibid., p. 212.
211. Ibid.
212. Ibid., p. 213.
213. *SWC*, pp. 41–42.
214. M. G. Rogers, p. 97.
215. Cited in M. G. Rogers, p. 97.
216. M. G. Rogers, p. 98.
217. Charles A. Briggs, "The Authority of Holy Scripture," in *Documents of the Briggs Case*, vol. 1 (New York: n.p., 1891), p. 24ff. (Hereafter cited as Briggs, "Inaugural.")
218. Briggs, "Inaugural," pp. 30–39.
219. Ibid., pp. 50–56. See also M. G. Rogers, pp. 97–99; *BC*, pp. 49–51; and Armstrong, et al., pp. 251–253, for excerpts from Briggs's address.
220. M. G. Rogers, pp. 115–118.
221. Ibid., pp. 103–104. See also *BC*, pp. 51–55, for a summary of relationships be-

tween Union Seminary and the General Assembly during this period.

222. Hatch, p. 90.

223. M. G. Rogers, pp. 105–109.

224. Ibid., pp. 109–110.

225. Cited in M. G. Rogers, pp. 110–111.

226. *BC*, p. 56.

227. M. G. Rogers, p. 116.

228. *The Defense of Professor Briggs before the Presbytery of New York, December 13, 14, 15, and 19, 1892* (New York: Charles Scribner's Sons, 1893), p. 97, cited in M. G. Rogers, p. 116. Loetscher in *BC*, p. 58, notes that Briggs cited from the works of Origen, Jerome, Augustine, Luther, Calvin, and others to show that these theologians "testify that there are errors in Holy Scripture."

229. M. G. Rogers, pp. 119–121.

230. Ibid., pp. 121–122. Rogers comments: "One observer later described the situation as one in which every single trick known in the political game was used."

231. M. G. Rogers, pp. 122–123.

232. Ibid., p. 133.

233. Ibid., p. 137. Briggs entered the priesthood of the Protestant Episcopal Church in 1899 and spent his remaining years working for Christian unity (*BC*, p. 62 and M. G. Rogers, p. 139). Briggs consistently maintained the attitude he had expressed in the preface to *Whither?*, p. x: "The author does not want to exclude from the Church those theologians whom he attacks for their errors. He is a broad-churchman and all his sympathies are with a comprehensive Church, in which not only these divines shall be tolerated, but all other true Christian scholars shall be recognized, and wherein all Christians may unite for the glory of God." Looking back in later years, Briggs felt that he had been simply a convenient target for those opposed to biblical criticism and confessional revision. See M. G. Rogers, p. 139.

234. M. G. Rogers, p. 137.

235. Ibid., pp. 137–138.

236. Cited in M. G. Rogers, p. 138.

237. Cited in M. G. Rogers, p. 138 and *BC*, pp. 61–62.

238. M. G. Rogers, p. 138 and *BC*, p. 62.

239. William Hordern, *A Layman's Guide to Protestant Theology*, rev. ed. (New York: Macmillan, 1968), pp. 51–53. The whole of chap. 3 is helpful. See also on fundamentalism, *BC*, p. 91.

240. *PAS*, pp. 172–174; Sandeen, *Roots*, pp. 168–170.

241. *BC*, pp. 67–68.

242. *BC*, p. 95.

243. Cited in *BC*, p. 98. The other four "essential and necessary" doctrines were: the virgin birth of Christ, Christ's death as a sacrifice to satisfy divine justice and reconcile us to God, Christ's bodily resurrection and ascension to heaven and intercession, and Christ's mighty miracles which made changes in the order of nature. For the exact statement of these doctrines see Armstrong, et al., pp.280–281. The ambiguity revealed in Armstrong, et al., pp. 281–282, is that while these articles are declared essential and necessary "others are equally so." But the others are never specified. Loetscher in *BC*, p. 98, remarks: "Though not mentioning premillennialism, the 'five points' noticeably resembled the points of the Niagara Bible Conference in 1895."

244. *BC*, p. 99.

245. *BC*, pp. 103–104.

246. C. Allyn Russell, *Voices of American Fundamentalism: Seven Biographical Studies* (Philadelphia: Westminster Press, 1976), pp. 206–208.

247. Cited in Russell, p. 208. See further chap. 8, "Clarence E. Macartney: Preacher—Fundamentalist"; and chap. 7, "William Jennings Bryan: Statesman—Fundamentalist."

248. Cited in Russell, p. 136. See the whole of chap. 6, "J. Gresham Machen: Scholarly Fundamentalist." Machen, a bachelor, reserved for his mother the title "the best and wisest person" he had ever known. See also Machen's biography by Ned B. Stonehouse, *J. Gresham Machen: A Biographical Memoir* (Grand Rapids, Mich., Wm. B. Eerdmans, 1954) and Paul Wooley, *The Significance of J. Gersham Machen Today* (Nutley, N.J.: Presbyterian and Reformed Publishing, 1977).

249. Cited in Russell, p. 140.

250. J. Gresham Machen, *Christianity and Liberalism* (New York: Macmillan, 1923), p. 72. (Hereafter cited as Machen, *Christianity*.)

251. Machen, *Christianity*, p. 73.

252. Ibid., p. 7.

253. Ibid., pp. 159–160, 166–167. Machen felt the liberals should withdraw. But if they wouldn't, then the "Christians" should.

254. Machen, *Christianity*, pp. 172–173. Machen's stress on "logical implications" was continued by his colleague at Westminster Seminary, Cornelius Van Til.

255. Cited in Russell, pp. 153–154.

256. *BC*, pp. 117–118; Russell, p. 152. See

also Paul Wooley, "American Calvinism in the Twentieth Century," in *American Calvinism*, ed. Jacob T. Hoogstra (Grand Rapids, Mich.: Wm. B. Eerdmans, 1957), p. 46; and Charles E. Quirk, "Origins of the Auburn Affirmation," *JPH* 53, no. 2 (Summer 1975):120–142, and his "A Statistical Analysis of the Signers of the Auburn Affirmation," *JPH* 43, no. 3 (Fall 1965):182–196.

257. Cited in *BC*, p. 118.

258. Armstrong, et al., p. 286.

259. *BC*, pp. 116–117.

260. Cited in *BC*, pp. 127–128; Russell, p. 152.

261. Cited in Russell, p. 153.

262. Russell, p. 153.

263. Ibid., pp. 154–155.

264. Cited in *BC*, p. 131.

265. *BC*, pp. 134–135.

266. Cited in *BC*, p. 134.

267. *BC*, pp. 134–135. Loetscher, p. 135, comments trenchantly: "But in sweeping away by a stroke of interpretation much of the previously exercised power of the General Assembly to define and thus to preserve the Church's doctrine, the commission established a principle which has much broader implications than the Church has yet had occasion to draw from it."

268. *BC*, pp. 132–133.

269. Russell, p. 155.

270. Russell, pp. 155–156. See also *BC*, pp. 148–149. For an account of these events from the perspective of the founders of Westminster Seminary, see Edwin H. Rian, *The Presbyterian Conflict* (Grand Rapids, Mich.: Wm. B. Eerdmans, 1940).

271. Russell, p. 156. *BC*, p. 151, notes that "the Church was moving simultaneously towards administrative centralization and theological decentralization."

272. *BC*, pp. 150–155, and Russell, pp. 156–158 and 209.

f. Selected Bibliography

Carnell, Edward J. *The Case for Orthodox Theology*. Westminster Press, 1959.

Gerstner, John H. "Warfield's Case for Biblical Inerrancy." In *God's Inerrant Word*, edited by John Warwick Montgomery. Bethany Fellowship, 1974.

Hatch, Carl E. *The Charles A. Briggs Heresy Trial*. Exposition Press, 1969.

Livingstone, William D. "The Princeton Apologetic as Exemplified by the Work of Benjamin Breckenridge Warfield and J. Gresham Machen: A Study in American Theology, 1880–1930." Ph.D. dissertation. Yale University, 1948.

Loetscher, Lefferts A. *The Broadening Church*. University of Pennsylvania Press, 1957, rep. 1954.

Markarian, John J. "The Calvinistic Concept of the Biblical Revelation in the Theology of B. B. Warfield." Ph.D. dissertation. Drew University, 1963.

Rogers, Jack B. "Van Til and Warfield on Scripture in the Westminster Confession." In *Jerusalem and Athens*, edited by E. R. Geehan. Presbyterian and Reformed Publishing, 1971, pp. 154–165.

Rogers, Max Gray. "Charles Augustus Briggs: Heresy at Union." In *American Religious Heretics*, edited by George H. Shriver. Abingdon Press, 1966.

Russell, C. Allyn. *Voices of American Fundamentalism: Seven Biographical Studies*. Westminster Press, 1976.

Sandeen, Ernest R. "The Princeton Theology." *Church History* 31 (September 1962):307–321.

Sandeen, Ernest R. *The Roots of Fundamentalism*. University of Chicago Press, 1970.

CHAPTER 7

Evangelical Reactions to Reformed Scholasticism

a. In Scotland: T. M. Lindsay and James Orr

Lindsay's Historical Critique of the Princeton Theology

Criticism of the developed Princeton doctrine of Scripture came from across the Atlantic and the pen of Thomas M. Lindsay (1843–1914). Lindsay was a Scottish church historian educated at Glasgow and Edinburgh who served for many years as professor and later principal of the staunchly evangelical United Free Church College, Glasgow.[1] His major works are *Luther and the German Reformation* (1900) and *A History of the Reformation* (2 vols. 1906, 1907). In the last chapter of volume 1 of his *History,* "The Religious Principles Inspiring the Reformation," Lindsay discussed the Reformation conception of Scripture.[2] He was drawn into this question not only as an historian but also through his defense of W. Robertson Smith in his trial for heresy by the Free Church of Scotland (1877–1881).[3] Lindsay believed Smith's doctrine of Scripture "while it agreed with that of the Reformers it differed from what is commonly called the doctrine of the Princeton School."[4]

At the urgings of "several American correspondents, personally unknown to myself," Lindsay set out to show how Princeton had deviated from the theology of the Reformation.[5] To set the stage, Lindsay first summarized his view of the Reformation doctrine "under two principal and four subordinate statements."[6] In short these were: (1) The Reformers opposed medieval theology in that for them "the *supreme* value of the Bible did not consist in the fact, true though it be, that it is the ultimate source of theology, but in the fact that it contains the whole message of God's redeeming love to every believer—the *personal* message to *me*."[7] (2) Faith for the Reformers "was not mere assent to propositions, but personal trust on the personal God revealing Himself in His redeeming purpose—a trust called forth by the witness of the Spirit testifying in and through the Scripture, that God was speaking therein."[8] Thus Lindsay stressed that

> these two thoughts of Scripture and faith always correspond. In medieval theology they are primarily intellectual and propositional; in Reformation theology they are primarily experimental and personal. Hence the witness of the Spirit, which emphasizes this experimental and personal character of Scripture, forms part of almost every statement of the Doctrine of Scripture in Reformation theology.[9]

Lindsay elaborated four points at which the theology of the Princeton school was more medieval than Reformed in its doctrine of Scripture. These were:

> In the purely intellectual apprehension which they have of Scripture, in their reduction of the real distinction between the Word of God and Scripture to a merely formal difference, in their formal as opposed to a religious reading of the thoughts of the infallibility and authority of Scripture, and in their still more formal relegation of the strict infallibility of Scripture to unknown and unknowable original autographs of the Scripture records.[10]

Lindsay developed four substantial criticisms of the Princeton theology:

1. *The Princeton theologians had a purely intellectual apprehension of Scripture.* Lindsay cited Charles Hodge's *Systematic Theology* (ed. of 1871, p. 155), where Hodge distinguished between revelation that had as its main object the communication of knowledge and inspiration that was to secure infallibility in teaching. Lindsay then charged that the "supreme thought of the witness of the Spirit, which marked the personal as opposed to the merely intellectual idea of Scripture introduced by the Reformers, is not made a distinctive and essential part of the doctrine of Scripture."[11] Hodge had *omitted* in his quotations from Reformed creeds, "those portions which include the thought of the witness of the Spirit as an integral part of the doctrine of Scripture": the fifth paragraph of the Second Helvetic Confession; the fourth paragraph of the French Confession; and the fourth and fifth paragraphs of the Westminster Confession.[12] Hodge brought forth the witness of the Spirit doctrine "when confuting the idea that Scripture is to be received on the authority of the Church, and when he turns from systematic to experimental theol-

ogy, as in a powerful essay on the *Ground of Faith in Scripture.*"[13] But the doctrine was not used "to make clear the supreme contention of the Reformers, that the Bible is above all things a record of God's personal dealing in deeds and by words with the saints of old, and therefore with us."[14] Lindsay freely admitted that the Reformers found a communication of knowledge in the Scriptures as Hodge and Princeton contended. He distinguished the Reformers' emphasis, however, saying:

> Their universal thought is that all such passages describe Scripture not in its primary but in its secondary aspect, and their universal contention is that Scripture is above all things the record of God's words and deeds of love to the saints of old, and of the answer of their inmost heart to God. It is this personal manifestation of God which is the main thing: the knowledge which comes along with that manifestation is important, and makes men wise *unto salvation;* but the doctrine comes from and through the promise, not the promise in and through the doctrine."[15]

To reverse this order as Princeton did was to follow Thomas Aquinas, Lindsay contended. The Princeton "formalist idea" of the Bible led them to thrust the personal element in Scripture into the background and to present Christ "in the form of a doctrine rather than of a personal Saviour, and the transformation of faith into assent to a proposition instead of personal trust in a personal Saviour."[16]

2. Lindsay further criticized the Princeton theology for: *their reduction of the real distinction between the Word of God and Scripture to a really formal difference.* Citing Luther, Calvin, Zwingli and the Scots' Confession, Lindsay argued that "it is because Scripture is the Word of God that it is authoritative and infallible."[17] The Reformers when they said, "Scripture is the Word of God" did not use "is" to "denote logical identity. They made it clear that while they could honestly and earnestly say that Scripture is the Word of God, they could nevertheless make a real distinction between the two."[18] They interpreted "is" by such words as "*contains, presents, conveys, records.*" Noting the Westminster Confession (XIV. 2), Lindsay claimed:

> The Word of God consists of God's commands, threatenings, promises, and, above all, of the Gospel offer of Christ to us, and these are conveyed to us in every part of Scripture. These, and none other, are the things which faith receives as infallibly true and authoritative, and neither the Westminster nor any other Reformed Confession recognizes an infallibility and authority which is apprehended otherwise than by faith.[19]

After studying the Hodge/Warfield article in the *Presbyterian Review* (October 1881), Lindsay concluded that the Princeton theologians "do not believe what the Reformers so definitely taught."[20] He cited A. A. Hodge's *Commentary on the Confession of Faith* (1870 ed., pp. 204–207), where Hodge held that, "we must first settle what books belong to the canon of Scripture before we can accept with faith the whole Word of God." Lindsay then observed:

> He makes faith include: *first,* assent to propositions; and *secondly,* trust in a personal Christ, making in genuine medieval fashion the promise come from the doctrine, and not the doctrine from the promise."[21]

3. Lindsay objected as well to: *their formal as opposed to a religious idea of the infallibility and authority of Scripture.* Summarizing the Princeton position in both Charles Hodge (Hodge's *ST,* I, 153, 155) and A. A. Hodge and Warfield (*Presbyterian Review,* 2:232), Lindsay said Princeton taught that the essence of inspiration is

> a superintendence exercised upon the writers of Scripture by the Holy Spirit, and the result of this superintendence is to secure a book free from all error, whether of fact, or precept, or doctrine. This inerrancy is infallibility, and this infallibility gives Scripture its authority and testifies to its Divine Authorship.[22]

And, "what corresponds to inspiration in the writers is inerrancy in the writings. Thus the inerrancy of Scripture is its characteristic, which is the test both of its infallibility and of its Divine origin."[23]

Lindsay responded by saying that "this whole question of the formal inerrancy of Scripture seems to be to be trivial in the extreme."

> The small verbal discrepancies, errors if you will, in Samuel and Chronicles are nothing to me: formal inerrancy, if proved, would not make these works more a part of Scripture than they are at present. Infallibility does not consist in formal inerrancy at all, but in the power which compels me to know that God is through this Scripture speaking to me now as He spoke not merely *by* the prophets and holy men of old, but *to* them and in them, and giving me through them in word and picture the message of His salvation.[24]

Moreover Lindsay argued:

> Whatever my private opinions may be, the formal idea of infallibility which makes it to consist in verbal inerrancy was not that of the Reformers, nor is it the view of the Westminster Confession. The Reformers did not take Inspiration to mean a Divine superintendence exercised over the writers of Scripture in order to produce an errorless record. When they spoke of Inspiration in a strictly technical sense, they applied it to the writings and not to the writers of Scripture. It was the writing that was *theopneustos,* breathed of God, or inspired. This is the use of the word in all the Reformed Confessions, and is its use in the Westminster Confession of Faith.[25]

To Lindsay, "the universal line of thought is that Scripture is inspired because it conveys the authoritative and infallible Word of God: it is not infallible and authoritative because it is inspired."[26]

Princeton, according to Lindsay, had substituted a full-blown theory of inspiration for what in Reformed statements on the doctrine of Scripture was taken up by a doctrine of the witness of the Holy Spirit. In Reformed statements, "a theory of Inspiration is seldom or never given." But now Lindsay noted, "the Princeton theory of Inspiration is an attempt to bestow on Scripture, primarily and in itself, qualities which it really possesses, but possesses only because it is the record of God's words to men and of his dealings with them."[27] To anchor his point still further, Lindsay referred to Calvin (*Inst.* I. vii. 4) and to "the Scotch Confession," which says that in Scripture, the "true kirk alwaies heares and obeyes the voice of her awin Spouse and Pastor" (Art. 19). For Lindsay, "this is a religious theory of infallibility and authority very different from the merely formal ideas of the Princeton School."[28]

4. Finally, Lindsay castigated: *the Princeton theology's still more formal relegation of the strict infallibility of Scripture to unknown and unknowable original autographs of Scripture.* While agreeing with Princeton on "some simple canons for testing so-called errors or mistakes," Lindsay pointed out that "when all is said they are bound to admit that the attribute of formal inerrancy does not belong to the Scriptures which we now have, but to what they call 'the *ipsissima verba* of the original autographs' of Scripture when these are interpreted in their natural and intended sense."[29] From Princeton's own use of these words, "it follows that the Scriptures as we now have them are neither infallible nor inspired."[30] And this, Lindsay remarked, is "frankly and courageously said by themselves, 'We do not assert that the common text, but only that the original autographic text was inspired.' "[31]

In a series of rhetorical questions, Lindsay hammered away at "the lengths the School are driven to maintain their theory":

> Where are we to get our errorless Scripture? In the *ipsissima verba* of the original autographs. Who are to recover these for us? I suppose the band of experts in textual criticism who are year by year giving us the materials for a more perfect text. Are they to be created by-and-by when their labours are ended into an authority doing for Protestants what the 'Church' does for Roman Catholics? Are they to guarantee for us the inspired and infallible Word of God, or are we to say that the unknown autographs are unknowable, and that we can never get to this Scripture, which is the only Scripture inspired and infallible in the strictly formal sense of those words as used by the Princeton School?[32]

Lindsay declared:

> If I am asked why I receive Scripture as the Word of God and as the perfect rule of faith and life, then certainly I do not answer: Because it is the slightly imperfect copy of original autographs, which, if I could only get at them, I

could show you to be absolutely errorless writings. I answer—Because the Bible is the only record of the redeeming love of God, because in the Bible alone I find God drawing near to man in Christ Jesus, and declaring to us in Him His will for our salvation. And this record I know to be true by the witness of His Spirit in my heart in and with the Word, whereby I am assured that none other than God Himself is able to speak such words to my soul.[33]

It was Lindsay's belief that:

This is the answer of all the Reformers, and it was also the answer of the Puritans—of Luther, and Calvin, and Knox, and John Owen. It is the answer of Dr. Charles Hodge himself when he is not writing formal systematic but experimental theology, when he is dealing not with theological formulae but with living men and women.[34]

As an historian in a Scottish Presbyterian theological college, Lindsay knew that the Princeton theologians had forsaken a Reformation doctrine of Scripture for a scholastic one. As an evangelical theologian in a Scottish Presbyterian Church, Lindsay accepted Scripture not because of formal proofs of its authority but because of its function in bringing persons to a saving relationship with God in Jesus Christ.

Orr's Theological Critique of the Princeton Position

Another nineteenth-century Scottish theologian who rejected the Princeton theory of inerrancy was James Orr (1844–1913).[35] Orr was born in Glasgow and studied at the university there. He was trained further in the Theological Hall of the United Presbyterian Church and served as a pastor in that denomination for seventeen years. From 1874 until 1901 he served as Professor of Church History at the Theological College of the United Presbyterian Church of Scotland. He had long worked for union between the Free and the United Presbyterian Churches in Scotland. After that union occurred, Orr became Professor of Theology and Apologetics at the United Free Church college in Glasgow. There he was a colleague of T. M. Lindsay from 1901 until his death in 1913.

James Orr was recognized worldwide as an evangelical theologian of undisputed orthodoxy. He lectured many times at seminaries in the United States, including Princeton in 1903 during Warfield's tenure. Orr was the general editor of the prestigious *International Standard Bible Encyclopedia*. He invited Warfield to write the article on "Inspiration" for it. And Orr contributed to the series of books known as *The Fundamentals*.[36]

Despite all of this similarity to the Princeton theologians, and the mutual respect that existed between them, Orr decisively rejected their scholastic doctrine of Scripture. Orr was grounded in church history in a way the Princeton theologians were not. Thus he was able to hold on to the Reformers' functional approach to authority rather than yielding to the scholastic formalism the Princeton theologians had adopted.[37]

Because of his grounding in Reformation soil, Orr was an outspoken critic of the scholastic theories of the Princeton theology. He recognized the strong grip the Princeton theology had established in the evangelical world, but he rejected their domino theory that the authority of the Bible would fall if the Princeton scholastic method were questioned.

He acknowledged the medieval usage of the scholastic method and its revival by the Princeton theology, but forthrightly rejected it:

> The older method was to prove first the inspiration (by historical evidence, miracles, claims of writers), then through that establish the revelation. This view still finds an echo in the note sometimes heard—'If the inspiration of the Bible (commonly some *theory* of inspiration) be given up, what have we left to hold by?' It is urged, *e.g.*, that unless we can demonstrate what is called the 'inerrancy' of the Biblical record, down even to it minutest details, the whole edifice of belief in revealed religion falls to the ground. This, on the face of it, is a most suicidal position for any defender of revelation to take up.[38]

Orr flatly denied that "inerrancy"—"*i.e.*, hard and fast literality in minute matters of historical, geographical and scientific detail"—was "a point in the *essence* of the doctrine of inspiration." He went on to observe that

> at best, such 'inerrancy' can never be demonstrated with a cogency which entitles it to rank as the foundation of a belief in inspiration. It must remain to those who hold it a doctrine of faith; a deduction from what they deem to be implied in an inspiration established independently of it; not a ground of belief in the inspiration.[39]

Orr had similar difficulties with the notion of "verbal inspiration." He wrote: "The phrase 'verbal inspiration' is one to which so great ambiguity attaches that it is now very commonly avoided by careful writers.[40] Orr noted of verbal inspiration that:

> It is apt to suggest a *mechanical* theory of inspiration, akin to dictation, which all intelligent upholders of inspiration now agree in repudiating. In the result it may be held to imply a *literality* in narratives, quotations, or reports of discourses, which the facts, as we know them, do not warrant.[41]

As part of the "facts" that Orr derived from Scripture itself he pointed to "the *reports of the Lord's own sayings* in the Gospels." He declared:

> It is well known that in the reports of Christ's words in the Synoptic Gospels there is often a very considerable variation in expression—a difference in phraseology—while yet the *idea* conveyed in all the forms is the

same. . . . Here the advocates of verbal inspiration are themselves compelled to recognize that absolute literality is not of the essence of inspiration—that the end is gained if the *meaning* of the saying is preserved, though the precise form of words varies. There may be compression, combination, change of construction—even (as in John) interpretation; but the truth is purely given.[42]

In common with the Reformers, Orr noted in the biblical account a "freedom in regard to the letter, while the sense is accurately conveyed" in the manner in which the New Testament writers themselves quote the Old Testament.[43]

Orr followed in practice the inductive method of establishing the doctrine of Scripture, which the Princeton theologians held only in theory. By examining the actual data of the Bible and taking seriously the cultural context in which they were expressed, Orr developed a doctrine that affirmed the divine function of Scripture but left freedom for the scholarly examination of its human form. Orr was quite critical of much of biblical criticism as it was practiced in his time. But in principle, he was open to the findings of scholarship in a way that the Princeton theologians were not.[44]

Orr fully took the historical and cultural setting of the biblical writers into account and accepted the normal human consequences of it for their writings. The Reformers had used the concept of accommodation to explain this combination of divine and human factors in Scripture. Orr introduced the notion of "progressive revelation" as a rubric to explain the same phenomenon. Orr wrote:

> Revelation is not complete all at once. If the light with which it starts is dim, it grows clearer as the ages advance. The world into which it comes is one deeply sunk in sin, and in the evils which sin brings with it. Revelation has to take up man as it finds him, with his crude conceptions, his childlike modes of thought and expression, his defective moral ideas and social institutions, and has to make the best of him it can. Imperfect conditions have to be borne with for the time, while germs of truth and principles are implanted which, in their development, gradually throw off the defective forms, and evolve higher.[45]

The Princeton theologians were committed to a logical, deductive approach to Scripture that treated the biblical text as if it had been written directly to the nineteenth-century mentality. Orr viewed the Bible as an historical document and recognized development and change within it, conceding the significant differences between modes of thought in the ancient Near East and the nineteenth-century West.

Orr clearly rejected the Princeton doctrine of Scripture. But he embraced the Bible itself with evangelical fervor as the authority for his life. He concluded his work on *Revelation and Inspiration* with the words:

> The word of God is a 'pure word.' It is a true and 'tried' word; a word never found wanting by those who rest themselves upon it. The Bible that embodies this word will retain its distinction as *the Book of Inspiration* till the end of time![46]

One result of the work done in the nineteenth century by Reformed evangelicals was that there is now a healthy tradition of evangelical biblical scholarship in Britain that is not preoccupied with formalistic questions.

b. In the Netherlands: Abraham Kuyper and Herman Bavinck

During the same period that the Princeton theology was developing in America, a distinctly different Reformed tradition was evolving in the Netherlands. At the height of nineteenth-century liberalism in the Netherlands there were two splits from the national Reformed Church, each endeavoring to recover Calvinistic orthodoxy. One was a spontaneous pietistic movement, whose greatest theologian was Herman Bavinck (1854–1921). Bavinck took his doctorate at Leiden under Scholten, the father of Dutch theological liberalism. Bavinck studied the Reformers, however, and wrote his dissertation on *The Ethics of Ulrich Zwingli.* Bavinck later taught at a small theological seminary of his denomination and produced a four-volume systematic theology, *Gereformeerde Dogmatiek,* between 1895 and 1901. Only a part of volume two was published in English under the title *The Doctrine of God.* [47] His doctrine of Scripture in volume one has never been available to American readers.

The other split from the state church was deliberate and well organized. Its leader, politically and theologically, was Abraham Kuyper (1837–1920). Kuyper also studied at Leiden under liberal teachers and also researched the Reformers. He wrote his doctoral dissertation on the idea of the Church in John Calvin and Johannes a Lasco. Kuyper was brought back to an orthodox Augustinian-Calvinist orientation both through his studies and the piety of the common people in his first pastoral charge. Kuyper wrote voluminously, but only a small part has been translated into English. Kuyper's organizing genius was expressed in the creation of institutions based on Christian principles. He founded the Free University of Amsterdam, edited a daily newspaper, led a political party, and eventually became the prime minister of the Netherlands.

In 1892 these two splinter denominations merged to form the Gerefor-meerde Kerken (the Reformed Churches).

When Kuyper left for government leadership in 1902, Bavinck succeeded him as Professor of Dogmatics at the Free University. Both Kuyper and Bavinck were respected in America as evangelicals and Calvinists. Each gave the celebrated Stone Lectures at Princeton, Kuyper in 1898 on *Calvinism,* and Bavinck in 1908 on *The Philosophy of Revelation.* Warfield contributed enthusiastic introductions to the English translations of a part of Kuyper's *Principles of Sacred Theology* in 1898, and to Kuyper's *The Work of the Holy Spirit* in 1900. Later, in 1903, Warfield expressed concern about Kuyper's view of apologetics.[48]

Together, Kuyper and Bavinck perpetuated a theological method which, particularly with regard to Scripture, followed the line of Augustine and the Reformers rather than that of the post-Reformation scholasticism preferred by the Princeton theology. The Dutch Reformed tradition held to the Augustinian method that faith leads to understanding rather than the medieval scholastic view that reasons were necessary prior to faith. Thus, the primary issue for the Dutch Reformed tradition was the functional one of how God related to humankind rather than the philosophical issue of whether God's existence could be proved. In relation to the Bible, that meant the Holy Spirit moved persons to accept Scripture as authoritative because of the saving message it expressed rather than that human reason compelled persons to believe the Bible because of evidential or logical proofs of its divine character.

Authority and the Testimony of the Spirit

The authority of Scripture, in the Dutch Reformed tradition, was affirmed to persons by the internal testimony of the Holy Spirit. Kuyper said: "The Reformers wisely appealed on principle to the 'witness of the Holy Spirit.' By this they understood a testimony that went out directly from the Holy Spirit, as author of the Scripture, to our personal *ego.* "[49] Kuyper specifically positioned himself with the Reformers in denying the efficacy of external evidences to prove the authority of Scripture.[50]

Bavinck spoke succinctly to the same subject: "Scripture is the word of God because the Holy Spirit witnesses of Christ in it, because it has the incarnate Word as its subject matter and content."[51] Also:

> The real object to which the Holy Spirit gives witness in the hearts of the believers is no other than the *divinitas* of the truth, poured out on us in Christ. Historical, chronological and geographical data are never in themselves, the object of the witness of the Holy Spirit.[52]

For Bavinck, the witness of the Spirit to the authority of Scripture was inseparably related to rebirth and conversion. He said: "The *testimonium Spiritus Sancti* is first an assurance that we are children of God."[53] For Bavinck, "our faith in Scripture increases and decreases according to our trust in Christ."[54]

Salvation Not Science

The purpose or function of Scripture was the central concern for Kuyper and Bavinck. Bavinck declared that biblical criticism became a problem only when the critics lost sight of the purpose of Scripture.[55] Bavinck was unequivocal that the purpose, goal or "destination" of Scripture "is none other than that it should make us wise to salvation."[56] He declared: "Scripture is the book for Christian religion and Christian theology. For that end it is given. For that end it is suited. And therefore it is the word of God, poured out upon us through the Holy Ghost."[57] Scripture was, therefore, not meant to give people technically correct scientific information:

> The writers of Holy Scripture probably knew no more than their contemporaries in all these sciences, geology, zoology, physiology, medicine, etc. And it was not necessary either. For Holy Scripture uses the language of daily experience which is always true and remains so. If the Scripture had in place of it used the language of the school and had spoken with scientific exactness, it would have stood in the way of its own authority.[58]

Because of their clear understanding that the purpose of Scripture was to bring persons to salvation in Christ, the Dutch Reformed tradition responded very differently to science than did the Princeton theology. In the nineteenth century while Hodge and Warfield were rejecting biblical criticism, Kuyper and Bavinck were meeting the issue openly and constructively. Kuyper wrote:

> If in the four Gospels, words are put in the mouth of Jesus on the same occasion which are dissimilar in form of expression, Jesus naturally cannot have used four forms at the same time, but the Holy Spirit only intended to create an impression for the church which perfectly answers to what went out from Jesus.[59]

Accommodation

Bavinck, like Calvin, recognized that God had accommodated himself to our human forms of thought and speech in communicating his divine message. Bavinck noted: "Even in historical reports, there is sometimes distinction between the fact that has taken place and the form in which it is set forth."[60] This did not deflect from the truth of Scripture for Bavinck. He said: "Then finally it appears that Scripture is certainly true in everything, but this truth is absolutely not the same nature in all its component parts."[61]

Kuyper expressed his understanding of the accommodated character of God's revelation by reflecting on the fact that the Savior and the Scripture had appeared "in the form of a servant."[62] He wrote:

> As the Logos has not appeared *in the form of glory,* but in the form of a servant, joining Himself to the reality of our nature, as this had come to be through the results of sin, so also, for the revelation of His Logos, God the Lord accepts *our* consciousness, our human life *as it is.* ... The 'spoken words,' however much aglow with the Holy Ghost, remain bound to the limitation of our language, disturbed as it is by anomalies. As a product of writing, the Holy Scripture also bears on its forehead the mark of the form of a servant.[63]

For the nineteenth-century Dutch Reformed tradition, the Bible was a functional, not a philosophical book. Its function was to present Christ as Savior. Conversion to Christ and commitment to Scripture were caused, not by reason, but by the Holy Spirit. Not a rational grasp of evidences, but one's personal response to God in Christ moved a person to accept Scripture as authoritative. Kuyper and Bavinck's focus, as Christians and as theologians, was on the divine content of Scripture, not on its human form. The Bible's function was to give people encouragement in salvation not information about science. Therefore, the human forms in which Scripture's message came could be examined by scholarship. Scientific findings were not an obstruction to faith, but an occasion to understand more fully the ways in which God had revealed Himself through human needs.

Organic Inspiration

The basic interpretative principle of the Reformation had been stated in several ways: the analogy of faith, or Scripture is its own interpreter. The meaning of these phrases was that each part of the Bible was to be understood in relationship to the overall saving message of Scripture. Bavinck attempted to express this relationship of the parts to the whole through the image of the human body. Bavinck's concept, which he called "organic inspiration," drew attention to the fact that there is a center and a periphery to Scripture. Bavinck said:

> In the human organism nothing is accidental, neither the length, nor the breadth, nor the color, nor the hue; but all does not therefore stand in the same close connection with the life center. Head and heart have a much more important place in the body than hand and foot, and these again stand in worth above nails and hair.[64]

This did not imply differences or grades of inspiration for Bavinck, but just that each part had its own function and some parts were more centrally important than others. In this Bavinck was attempting to do full justice to both the divine and human in Scripture as Augustine and Calvin had with the concept of accommodation and James Orr had with the rubric of progressive revelation.[65] Informed by this perspective, Bavinck denied the post-Reformation emphasis on each word and letter of Scripture.

> In the thoughts are included the words, and in the words, the vowels. But from this it does not follow that the vowel points in our Hebrew manuscripts are from the writers themselves. And it also does not follow that all is full of divine wisdom, that each jot and tittle has an infinite content. All has its meaning and significance very certainly, but there in the place and in the context in which it comes forth.[66]

When each word and letter was viewed as having its own divine content, according to Bavinck, that "leads to the false hermeneutical rules of the Jewish Scribes, and does not honor, but dishonors Scripture."[67]

The Necessity for Scholarly Study

For Kuyper and Bavinck, the Reformation concept that Scripture is its own interpreter did not take away the need for interpretation, but focused on the way in which interpretation must be done. For Bavinck, every kind of scholarly study of Scripture is necessary because the word of God, Scripture, like the incarnate Christ, has "gone into the creaturely ... into humanity, weak and despised and ignoble; the word became writing, and has, as writing, subjected itself to the fate of all writing."[68] This circumstance led Kuyper to call for "freedom of exegesis." This he felt was necessary "if theology is to discharge her duty to the confessional life of the Church."[69] Kuyper set forth the reason in simple imagery:

> For this provides the constant stimulus to turn back from the confession to the Word of God, and so prevents the Church from living on the water in the pitcher, and allowing itself to be cut off from the Fountain whence the water was drawn.[70]

These Reformed theologians did not fear scholarly investigation but considered it an essential aspect of a responsible faith. Kuyper stated that hermeneutics was a "mixed science." On the one hand, it had to deal with the Bible by the same rules of interpretation used with any other book. On the other hand, the interpreter should listen for what God has to say to us and therefore interpretation could not be separated from faith in Scripture.[71]

The clarity of Scripture was, therefore, continually related to its central saving message, not to the particular words and sentences. According to Bavinck, the central truth of salvation was set forth in a form so simple and intelligible "that someone in search of salvation will come to known the truth."[72]

At the same time Bavinck affirmed "that certainly not everything recorded in Scripture should be normative authority for our faith and life."[73] Bavinck was not distinguishing between inspired and uninspired parts of Scripture, nor between revelational and nonrevelation elements in the Bible. None of those formal or quantitative distinctions applied. Rather, Bavinck provided a theory that explained the distinction most Christians make in practice. That is, Scripture has a central message and a lot of surrounding material. For Bavinck, the intrepretation of Scripture was always to be governed by keeping this center, purpose, or "destination" of Scripture in mind. He declared "that destination is none other than that it should make us wise to salvation."[74]

By distinguishing between the center and the periphery in Scripture, Kuyper and Bavinck's tradition freed their followers *from* scholarship and *for* scholarship. The central saving message of Scripture could be received in faith without waiting for scholarly reasons. The supporting material of Scripture, the human forms of culture and language, were open to scholarly investigation. A scholarly interpretation of the human forms of Scripture could ýield dividends of deepened faith. Scripture fulfilled God's intention to reveal saving truth. No human mistakes could frustrate that divine motivation. It was not meaningful, therefore, to equate human inaccuracy with error in the biblical sense of intent to deceive. Human scholarship could deal with the methods by which God accommodated his message of salvation to human means of understanding.

c. In England: P. T. Forsyth

The British Congregationalist Peter Taylor Forsyth (1842–1921) has often been called a "forerunner of Neo-orthodoxy," a "Barthian before Barth," or a "liberal evangelical."[75] In many ways, Forsyth's thought paralleled aspects of other British theologians of his time. He was contemporary with Orr and Lindsay but did not share their evangelical upbringing and training. With them, however, he reacted against the Reformed scholasticism of his American contemporary, B. B. Warfield.

Authority in Christ

Forsyth was schooled in the "sunny liberalism" of the nineteenth century under F. D. Maurice (1805–1872) and Albrecht Ritschl (1822–1889). He gradually found himself more and more drawn, however, toward a rediscovery of the doctrine of grace and of God's holy love expressed supremely in Jesus Christ and His work on the Cross. From this stemmed his major works on the Atonement and Christology.[76] But even behind this stood his preoccupation with the problem of authority, which he repeatedly called "the greatest question of the age"[77] and "the central question of religion."[78] In his theological work, Forsyth reacted against the then-current stream of Protestant theology that, in the nineteenth century, had shifted from the far right to the far left, from post-Reformation scholastic dogmas of biblical authority to the vageries of subjective religious experience.[79] Forsyth believed that the anthropocentric, methodological reorientation from the far right, which had occurred during the nineteenth century, had obscured the primacy of grace in Christianity. Forsyth perceived that the Christian faith began with the movement of God to humankind, not with a movement of people to God.[80]

For Forsyth this meant finding ultimate authority for faith in the cross of Jesus Christ. As he wrote: "The last authority is God in His supreme saving act of grace to mankind in Christ's Cross, which is the power of God addressed to what is at once the power and weakness in us, our will, conscience and total moral self."[81] Authority for Forsyth had to be internalized—"divine authority must be inward."[82] But the experience of Grace had to lead to concrete ethical obedience. To Forsyth the moral authority of the Cross demanded "action, obedience and sacrifice, and not merely echo, appreciation, stirrings and thrills."[83]

Thus revelation was supremely an "action" rather than "words" or "truths." Revelation was God's self-communication, "his actual coming and doing . . . not the mere offer of Himself but the actual bestowal of Himself."[84]

In light of this, Forsyth viewed the Bible as absolutely essential. It was the Word of God through which the Gospel was made known to humans. The Bible was "the medium of the Gospel." Forsyth wrote:

> It [the Bible] was created by faith in the Gospel. And in turn it creates faith among men. It is at once the expression of faith and its source.[85]

While "the book is not the act, true enough; . . . yet it is quite a necessary part of the act and its effect." But, as in the crucifixion of Christ, no one saw its purpose in the plan of God, so man must have "God's version of the act." Forsyth declared: "God must be his own interpreter. He must explain himself and his action. . . . None but himself can reveal his own revelation."[86] God had now given "His version" through "the incarnate fact, then the word or interpretation of it by apostles and thereby, the fact again, but the fact enshrined in the soul of the believing Church."[87] The result was the Bible, God's "last phase of the revelatory act and deed."[88] Indeed the Scriptures as a form were "part of the whole act."[89] Forsyth noted that an action of a legislature passed as law (or a treaty) is then printed and circulated with the government's seal upon it, sharing in its authority and being an integral part of the action passed. Forsyth then declared:

> So also do the Scriptures form part, an indispensable part of the great deed itself. . . . They are part of the whole transaction, integral to the great deed. And we do not get the whole Christ or his work without them.[90]

For "the material revelation and consummation in Christ is not complete without a formal consummation in its *interpretation.*"[91]

Forsyth then, insisted upon the Bible as the "outward sign of the objectivity of our religion."[92] This was its "grand value."[93] But this must never obscure the fact that the Bible was a "medium" through which the supreme authority, the Gospel was transmitted.[94] Forsyth stated: "Christ did not come to bring a Bible but to bring a Gospel."[95] The authority of the Gospel was beyond any other authority. Thus the real authority for the Christian faith was in a message, not a book.[96] Forsyth wrote:

> We have but one great sacrament. It is God's redeeming Word in Christ's cross. In this sacrament the Bible as a book takes the place of the elements. It is not the Bible that contains God's Word so much as God's Word that contains the Bible. . . . The letter of the Scripture is the revered bread and wine, but the consecrating Word and the power they convey is the gospel.[97]

Inspiration and Biblical Criticism

Forsyth devoted two chapters in *The Person and Place of Jesus Christ* to the question of "Apostolic Inspiration"—"in General" and "in Particular." In these sections he was not trying to ground the authority of Scripture on external proofs, but rather to speak from the perspective of faith about what faith knew to be true about Scripture. He believed that inspiration should be seen less in terms of a book and "more in terms of the men that wrote it and of the nation that bred them."[98] Christ spoke through his apostles and their interpretations so that "inspiration has not to do with information but with insight."[99] The apostles' inspiration was "to set forth in word and thought the principle and power of that supreme sacrament of the Word, namely Christ; it was to exhibit formally the truth materially embodied in the manifestation."[100] The New Testament grew as preaching concerning Christ and was accepted by the church as "the inspired part of the revelation of which Christ was the incarnate redeeming agent."[101]

Forsyth, however, did not believe that inspiration guaranteed every statement or view even of an apostle. He wrote:

> The inspiration is not infallible in the sense that every event is certain or every statement final. You may agree with *what* I say without agreeing with *all* I say. The Bible's inspiration, and its infallibility, are such as pertain to redemption and not theology, to salvation and not mere history.[102]

The main question for Forsyth was not one of the "integrity of the Bible, but of its efficacy for grace, its sufficiency for salvation."[103] He believed that:

> To stake the gospel upon the *absolute* accuracy of the traditional view of the Bible, its inerrancy, or its authorship by apostles, is just to commit, in a Protestant form, the Roman error of staking the sacrament on the correctitude of its ritual or the ordination of its priest.[104]

Thus Forsyth did not believe in verbal inspiration. He felt that such a view made the Bible a "closed book."[105] Yet he did remark that while "we can no more believe in the infallibility of the Bible . . . we must believe in its finality."[106] Its truth had value for all times as part of the revelation of God and "the true minister ought to find the words and phrases of the Bible so full of spiritual food and felicity that he has some difficulty in not believing in verbal inspiration."[107]

Forsyth wholeheartedly endorsed the use and findings of biblical criticism. He believed that "modern scholarship has made of the Bible a new book. It has in a certain sense rediscovered it. You might say that the soul of the Reformation was the rediscovery of the Bible; and in a wider sense that is true today also."[108] Again he wrote: "The Higher Criticism is a gift to us of the Spirit" for "the Gospel not only tolerates, it demands science and criticism."[109] Yet the Bible must not be "put on the rack of mere literary criticism, or historical, or even ethical" and only critical findings accepted.[110] For the work of criticism should be more the work of the church than of the schools. For "from the Church must come the final correction and appraisement of the criticism of the schools."[111] The historic Jesus was more than just the historic Jesus, He was the Christ of faith and though "not immune from critical action, [He is] secure" since "our real faith is fixed—on the finished redeeming work of the Saviour on the Cross."[112] Throughout his own spiritual pilgrimage, Forsyth maintained his "faith in critical methods" and his acceptance of many of their new results.[113] He always believed, however, that criticism was the handmaid of the gospel. He asserted:

> The critical study of Scripture is at its best, and the higher criticism is at its highest, when it passes from being analytic and becomes synthetic. And the synthetic principle in the Bible is the gospel. The analysis of the Bible must serve the history of grace.[114]

This meant that hermeneutically Forsyth always read the Bible with the Gospel as his standard.[115] He wrote that "the selective principle is the *gospel of grace* in Christ crucified. Whatever carries that home, whatever is indispensable for that, is of prime value and obligation."[116] Thus, he wrote: "We are free, nay, forced, therefore to deal critically with all parts of the Bible under the ruling principle of redemption."[117] His test for Scripture was "actually Luther's test—does this or that passage 'ply Christ, preach Christ'?"[118] This was where the one purpose of the Bible lay: in reconciliation. And this was where the Bible had its "organic unity of idea and purpose."[119] For Forsyth, this unity was, "organic, total, vital, evangelical; . . . not merely harmonious, balanced, statuesque. It is not the form of symmetry, but the spirit of reconciliation."[120] It was the power of the Bible's message, not its form, that Forsyth valued above all. And it was in this "corporate unity of grace" that the real power of the Bible was to be found. The church must begin taking the Bible as a whole, not atomistically using its texts and sections, Forsyth taught.[121]

Religious Experience and Biblical Authority

P. T. Forsyth always insisted, however, that even the objective authority of the Bible as it bears witness to the act of grace in Christ's cross, could not be understood except in the "evangelical experience of regeneration." This was "the soul's re-creation, surrender, and obedience once and for all in a new creation and direct communion with the God of the moral universe."[122] In other words, Christian experience could not be divorced from the process of one's accepting the Bible's authority. Forsyth stressed that authority "must be inward, it must be in the soul."[123] Indeed, he said: "We shall be sure of an actual, final authority in proportion as we have had the experience of being absolutely mastered by the moral act of redemption which made Christ King of human history."[124] This authority, then, was personal, "it is a relation of person in holy love."[125] Yet, while "a real authority . . . is indeed *within* experience . . . it is not the authority *of* experience, it is an authority *for* experience, it is an authority experienced."[126] Thus Forsyth urged:

> The Christian experience is not something we bring rationally to the Bible to test scriptural truth; it is something miraculously created in us by the Bible to respond to divine power acting as grace ... it is not our independent verification but our appropriation and completion of God's gift and revelation of Himself by faith of the most intimate, and therefore mysterious kind.[127]

This experience received by faith as the "last authority" was "not demonstrable, it is only realisable, as *the* religious experience of the conscience. It is the moral imperative of holy love acting upon our moral experience in historic grace."[128]

Peter Taylor Forsyth, then, was significant in the Reformed tradition for signaling a break from both of the prevailing nineteenth-century types of theology: from liberalism, which emphasized religious experience as the seat of authority; and from scholastic orthodoxy, which stressed the objectivity of the Bible with little concern for the role of Christian experience or the church.[129] Though he developed no theory of the church,[130] Forsyth did recognize it along with the Bible and Christian experience as one of the media of grace through which the Gospel was made known.[131] He focused attention on the Bible's message rather than its form: "The charter of the church is not the Bible but the redemption."[132] He was not threatened but rather welcomed biblical criticism since he believed: "Christianity will not stand or fall by its critical attitude to its documents, but by its faithful attitude to its gospel."[133] The function the Bible performed in witnessing to the Gospel was what made the Bible authoritative. Indeed, through the centuries for Forsyth:

> The Bible has done its great work, not as a document of history, but as a means of grace, as a servant of the gospel, lame, perhaps, and soiled, showing some signs of age, it may be, but perfectly faithful, competent and effectual always.[134]

Forsyth, though trained in liberalism, returned to the functional authority of Scripture in much the same manner as his nineteenth-century evangelical counterparts, Lindsay and Orr in Scotland, Kuyper and Bavinck in The Netherlands, and Briggs and Henry Preserved Smith in America. Some had come to the Reformation position through the study of historical theology, others through exegetical research, and Forsyth perhaps most through a personal religious encounter with the Bible. They all to a degree foreshadowed the response to Scripture of the dominant figure in mid-twentieth century Reformed theology, Karl Barth, who brought together the personal, exegetical, and historical motifs in an impressive synthesis.

d. Summary

The late nineteen and early twentieth centuries saw a severe polarization between liberalism, with its subjective embrace of the new, and conservative scholasticism, with its objectifying grip on the old. Some theologians trained in each camp, however, refused to be part of that false dichotomy.

Some Reformed theologians reared in an evangelical orientation strongly reaffirmed their Reformation roots. For example, Thomas Lindsay and James Orr were noted nineteenth-century Scots evangelicals who rejected the reigning Hodge-Warfield theory of inerrancy as historically false and theologically unfruitful.

In the Netherlands, at the same time, two theologians reforged their links with the Reformed tradition. Kuyper and Bavinck both studied under liberals, but researched the Reformers. They reaffirmed a Reformed tradition that found authority in the saving content, not the supernatural form of Scripture. The Bible's authority was brought home to their hearts by the inner witness of the Holy Spirit. They accented God's accommodated method of communicating with humankind. The Bible was understood to speak in ordinary language about salvation, not technical terminology about science. Bavinck introduced an "organic" model of inspiration. This enabled him to treat all of Scripture as God's Word, but to recognize a center and a periphery to the message, as opposed to the mechanical model of scholasticism, which tended to treat every verse of the Bible as of equal importance.

P. T. Forsyth, a British Congregationalist trained in liberalism, returned to a strong accent on biblical authority. For Forsyth, authority resided in God, who acted in saving grace. The Bible witnessed to God's act and so became a vital part of that action.

e. Notes

1. See *NIDCC*, p. 597, and *ODC*, p. 825.
2. *A History of the Reformation*, 2d ed., 2 vols. (Edinburgh: T. & T. Clark, 1959; rep. 1907), pp. 453–467. (Hereafter cited as Lindsay, *History*.) This selection was reprinted in an issue of *Union Seminary Review*, a publication of Union Theological Seminary, Richmond, Virginia, devoted to "The Reformers and the Bible." It is volume 43, no. 1 (October 1931):11–24. The editor of this journal wrote that "Lindsay's discussion of the Reformation Conception of Scripture has never been surpassed," p. 6.
3. On Smith see John S. Black and George Chrystal, *The Life of William Robertson Smith* (London: Adam and Charles Black, 1912). Principal Lindsay's relationship to Smith is mentioned throughout. See also Warner M. Bailey, "William Robertson Smith and American Biblical Studies," *JPH* 51, no. 3

(Fall 1973) and "Theology and Criticism in William Robertson Smith" (Ph.D. dissertation, Yale University, 1970).

4. T. M. Lindsay, "The Doctrine of Scripture. The Reformers and the Princeton School," *The Expositor*, 5th series, 1 (1895):278. (Hereafter cited as "Doctrine.") See Lindsay's article in *The Expositor* for October 1894: "Professor Robertson Smith's Doctrine of Scripture," 4th series, 10 (1894):241–264. He mentions the Princeton Theology on p. 262.

5. "Doctrine," p. 278. Lindsay characterizes this as a "real departure."

6. His earlier article on Smith's "doctrine of scripture" and later treatment in his *History* provide Lindsay's elaborated documentation.

7. His statements are found in "Doctrine," pp. 279–280. We cite here the corresponding points made in Lindsay, *History*, p. 455: "The Reformers saw in it [the Bible] a new home for a new life within which they could have intimate fellowship with God Himself —not merely knowledge about God, but actual communion with Him."

8. "Doctrine," p. 279. See also Lindsay, *History*, pp. 457–460: "Saving faith was not intellectual assent at all. It was simple trust —the trust of a child—in their Father's promises, which were Yea and Amen in Christ Jesus," p. 458. He further wrote: "To the Reformers the chief function of Scripture was to bring Jesus Christ near us; and as Jesus always fills the full sphere of God to them, the chief end of Scripture is to bring God near *me*. It is the direct message of God's love to *me*,—not doctrine, but promise (for apart from promise, as Luther said unweariedly, faith does not exist); not display of God's thoughts, but of God Himself as *my* God," p. 460.

9. "Doctrine," p. 279. In his footnote, Lindsay lists these: First Helvetic Confession, par. 5; Second Helvetic Confession, pars. 1, 5; French Confession of 1559, pars. 2, 4; Belgic Confession of 1561, pars. 2, 5; Scotch Confession of 1560, pars. 4, 19; Westminster Confession, ch. 1, 4, 5. He notes: "For a fuller discussion see the Preface to Luther's German Bible, Luther's *Freiheit eines Christenmenschen*, [*Freedom of the Christian Man*], and Calvin's *Institutes*, Bk. I. vii., Bk. III. ii. 6. See also "Doctrine," pp. 279–280; and Lindsay, *History* for elaborations of the points: no. 1:pp. 461–463; no.

2:pp. 463–464; no. 3:pp. 464–466; no. 4:pp. 466–467.

10. "Doctrine," pp. 280–281.

11. "Doctrine," p. 281.

12. "Doctrine," p. 281, citing Hodge's *ST*, I, 151–152.

13. "Doctrine," p. 281, citing Hodge's *ST*, I, 129, and *Essays and Reviews*, p. 188ff.; Lindsay mentions too in this connection, Hodge's *Way of Life*, a devotional book.

14. "Doctrine," pp. 281–282.

15. "Doctrine," p. 282.

16. "Doctrine," p. 283.

17. "Doctrine," p. 283.

18. "Doctrine," p. 283.

19. "Doctrine," p. 284.

20. "Doctrine," p. 284.

21. "Doctrine," pp. 284–285.

22. "Doctrine," p. 286.

23. "Doctrine," p. 286.

24. "Doctrine," pp. 287–288. Lindsay cited the Scripture passages 2 Samuel 24:24 and 1 Chronicles 21:35 and used the Latin phrase from Calvin's *Commentary on Matthew* 27:9: *nec anxie laboro*—"I do not care." The discrepancy is over the price David paid for Ornan's (Araunah's) threshing floor and oxen. Lindsay commented "I do not go to Scripture to learn the price of threshing floors and oxen."

25. "Doctrine," p. 288.

26. "Doctrine," p. 288.

27. "Doctrine," pp. 288–289. Earlier Lindsay noted that A. A. Hodge and Warfield had followed Charles Hodge "who devotes a few lines to the doctrine of Scripture, and nearly thirty pages to a doctrine of Inspiration," p. 286.

28. "Doctrine," pp. 289–290. Lindsay held that the Westminster Confession taught that the infallibility of Scripture is recognized by faith. And, "inerrancy, if it exists is merely a matter of fact to be recognized by the ordinary reason." This note is struck also in his *History*, pp. 464–465:

> "With the medieval theologian infallibility was something which guaranteed the perfect correctness of abstract propositions; with some modern Protestants it consists in the conception that the record contains not even the smallest error in word or description of fact— in its inerrancy. But neither inerrancy nor the correctness of abstract propositions is apprehended by faith in the Reformers' sense of that word; they are matters of fact, to be accepted or reject-

ed by the ordinary faculties of man. The infallibility and authority which need faith to perceive them are, and must be, something very different; they produce the conviction that in the manifestation of God in His word there lies infallible power to save. This is given, all the Reformers say, by the Witness of the Spirit."

29. "Doctrine," p. 291, citing *Princeton (sic Presbyterian) Review*, (1881), 2:245–246 and p. 238.

30. "Doctrine," p. 291.

31. "Doctrine," pp. 291–292, citing *Princeton (sic Presbyterian) Review*, (1881), 2:245. To make such a statement Lindsay says, "is a very grave assertion and shows to what lengths the School are driven to maintain their theory, and it is one which cannot fail, if seriously believed and thoroughly acted upon, to lead to sad conclusions both in the theological doctrine of Scripture and in the practical work of the Church," p. 292.

32. "Doctrine," p. 292. Lindsay held "with all the Reformers, and with all the Reformed Creeds, that the Scriptures, *as we now have them*, are the inspired and infallible Word of God, and that all textual criticism, while it is to be welcomed in so far as it brings our present text nearer the *ipsissima verba* of the original autographs, will not make the Scriptures one whit more inspired or more infallible in the true Scriptural and religious meanings of those words than they are now; for infallibility is not formal inerrancy, but what produces the conviction of infallibly saving power," p. 293.

33. "Doctrine," p. 293.

34. "Doctrine," p. 293. Lindsay refers here to Hodge's *Way of Life*. Ernest R. Sandeen in noting this reference comments: "This may seem true, but little of the personal element is allowed to creep into the argument as evidence, and with late Princeton theologians seems entirely absent," "The Princeton Theology: One Source of Biblical Literalism in American Protestantism," *CH* 31, no. 3 (September 1962):320.

35. For brief biographical sketches of James Orr see *NSH*, s.v. "Orr, James" and *NIDCC*, s.v. "Orr, James."

36. Between 1910 and 1915 a series of twelve small books were published in the United States bearing the title *The Fundamentals: A Testimony to the Truth*. (Hereafter cited as *The Fundamentals*.) Funded by several wealthy Christian laymen, the series

brought together contributors from both the dispensationalist and the Old School Calvinist parties. The purpose of the series was to defend traditional doctrines similar to "5 points" set forth by the Presbyterian General Assembly in 1910. See *WDCH*, s.v. "Fundamentalism"; *Baker's Dictionary of Theology*, ed. Everett F. Harrison (Grand Rapids, Mich.: Baker Book House, 1960), s.v. "Fundamentalism"; and James Barr, *Fundamentalism* (Philadelphia: Westminster Press, 1978), p. 2. Edward John Carnell, *The Case for Orthodoxy* (Philadelphia: Westminster Press, 1959), p. 113, offers the terse definition: "Fundamentalism is orthodoxy gone cultic." He urges that "we must distinguish between the movement and the mentality." See especially, chap. 8, in which he discusses J. Gresham Machen, among others.

37. In the conclusion of his book *Revelation and Inspiration*, Orr wrote: "In the last resort, the proof of the inspiration of the Bible ... is to be found in the life-giving effects which that message has produced, wherever its word or truth has gone. This is the truth in the argument for inspiration based on the witness of the Holy Spirit. The Bible has the qualities claimed for it as an inspired book. ... It leads to God and to Christ; it gives light on the deepest problems of life, death, and eternity; it discovers the way of deliverance from sin; it makes men new creatures; it furnishes the man of God completely for every good work," *Revelation and Inspiration* (New York: Charles Scribner's Sons, 1910), pp. 217–218. (Hereafter cited as Orr, *Revelation*.) See also the discussion in Carnell, pp. 99–102, of the differences between the Princeton theology and Orr.

38. Orr, *Revelation*, pp. 197–198. Orr went on to contend positively: "It is certainly a much easier matter to prove the reality of a divine revelation in the history of Israel or Christ, than it is to prove the inerrant inspiration of every part of the record through which that revelation has come to us." For Orr "the doctrine of inspiration grows out of that of revelation, and can only be made intelligible through the latter."

39. Orr, *Revelation*, p. 199.

40. Orr, *Revelation*, p. 209. He notes that, "Hodge and Warfield defend the word 'verbal,' but with careful explanation." At a later point in the book, (p. 214) Orr comments: "Even on the assumption of a 'verbal' inspiration, it has been seen in how wide a sense

literal accuracy in the Biblical records has to be interpreted. The theory may be stretched, moreover, by qualifications, admissions, and explanations, till there is *practically* little difference between the opposite views."

41. Orr, *Revelation*, p. 210.
42. Ibid. See also *HS*, pp. 157–158, for a discussion of Orr's views.
43. Orr, *Revelation*, pp. 210–211.
44. See Orr's comments in *The Fundamentals*, cited in Barr, p. 359, n. 12.
45. Orr, *Revelation*, pp. 102–103. See Carnell, pp. 52–53, where he adopts Orr's position. Carnell states: "The concept of 'progressive revelation' is the key to Biblical hermeneutics," p. 52. He comments ruefully: "This is clear enough. But apparently it is not clear enough for the cultic mind. Cultic thinking tends to impose a uniformity on Scripture that Scripture itself disavows. Since the Bible is plenarily inspired, the cultic mind assumes that all verses in the Bible are equally normative," p. 53.
46. Orr, *Revelation*, p. 218. Barr, pp. 269–270, compares Orr's position to that of Warfield and comments:

"It is scarcely to be doubted that Orr's doctrine comes closer than Warfield's to what most evangelicals in fact believe. As we have seen, biblical authority is far more central to their faith than can be represented by any doctrine that derives it solely and exclusively from that Bible's own claim to inspiration. For them, its roots lie in personal faith, in the experience of salvation, in what seems to be confirmation by the Holy Spirit. They do not for a moment believe that the Bible is in any way in error; but they do not express this in so exclusive a way as to suggest that errors in the figures in Chronicles, or even substantial differences between one gospel and another would mean the total destruction of all biblical authority and thereby of their faith (p. 270).

47. Translated by William Hendriksen (Grand Rapids: Eerdmans, 1951). For another treatment of the material in this section see Jack B. Rogers, "A Third Alternative: Scripture, Tradition and Interpretation in the theology of G. C. Berkouwer in *Scripture, Tradition and Interpretation: Essays Presented to Everett F. Harrison*, ed. W. Ward Gasque and William Sanford LaSor

(Grand Rapids, Mich.: Wm. B. Eerdmans, 1978), pp. 70–91.
48. John H. Gerstner, "Warfield's Case for Biblical Inerrancy" (hereafter cited as Gerstner, "Warfield"), in *God's Inerrant Word*, ed. John Warwick Montgomery (Minneapolis: Bethany Fellowship, 1974), pp. 121–122.
49. Abraham Kuyper, *Principles of Sacred Theology*, trans. J. Hendrik De Vries (Grand Rapids, Mich.: Wm. B. Eerdmans, 1965; reprint 1954), pp. 556–557. (Hereafter cited as *PST*.)
50. *PST*, p. 558.
51. Herman Bavinck, *Gereformeerde Dogmatiek*, vol. 1, p. 414. (Hereafter cited as *GD*.) All translations are by Jack Rogers from the fourth Dutch edition published by J. H. Kok in Kampen, The Netherlands in 1928. *GD*, p. 414.
52. *GD*, pp. 564–565.
53. *GD*, p. 564.
54. *GD*, p. 569, cited in *HS*, p. 241.
55. *HS*, p. 26, citing *GD*, p. 415.
56. *GD*, p. 416.
57. *GD*, p. 416.
58. *GD*, p. 417.
59. *Encyclopaedie der Heilige Godgeleerdheid*, Vol. II (Amsterdam: J. Wormser, 1894), p. 499. Interestingly, this is the only statement of Kuyper's that Bavinck quotes in *GD*. See p. 415.
60. *GD*, p. 420.
61. *GD*, p. 419. This was further developed in Bavinck's principle of "organic inspiration." See the next section and also Jack B. Rogers, "The Concept of Organic Inspiration in the *Gereformeerde Dogmatiek* of Dr. Herman Bavinck" (Th.M. thesis, Pittsburgh Theological Seminary, 1961).
62. See *PST*, p. 478–479.
63. *PST*, p. 479.
64. *GD*, pp. 409–410.
65. *GD*, p. 410. Bavinck wrote: "The hair of the head participates in the same life as heart and hand.... It is one Spirit, out of whom the whole of Scripture has come forth through the consciousness of the writers. But there is a difference in the way in which the same life is immanent and active in the various parts of the body. There are varieties of gifts, also in Scripture, but it is the same Spirit."
66. *GD*, p. 409.
67. *GD*, p. 409.
68. *GD*, p. 405.
69. *PST*, p. 596.
70. *PST*, p. 597.

71. *HS*, pp. 112–113.

72. *GD*, p. 447, cited in *HS*, p. 274.

73. *GD*, p. 428, cited in *HS*, p. 191.

74. *GD*, p. 416.

75. On Forsyth see Robert McAfee Brown, *P. T. Forsyth: Prophet for Today* (Philadelphia: Westminster Press, 1952) (hereafter cited as R. A. Brown, *Prophet*); John H. Rodgers, *The Theology of P. T. Forsyth* (London: Independent Press, 1965); and the articles by Robert McAfee Brown, "P. T. Forsyth," in *A Handbook of Christian Theologians*, eds. D. G. Peerman and Martin E. Marty (Cleveland: World Publishing, 1965), pp. 144–165, and Samuel J. Mikolaski, "P. T. Forsyth," in *Creative Minds in Contemporary Theology*, ed. Philip E. Hughes, 2d rev. ed. (Grand Rapids, Mich.: Wm. B. Eerdmans, 1969), pp. 307–340. Cf. Samuel J. Mikolaski, *The Creative Theology of P. T. Forsyth* (Grand Rapids, Mich.: Wm. B. Eerdmans, 1969). Marvin W. Anderson has collected and edited eight of Forsyth's essays in *The Gospel and Authority: P. T. Forsyth Reader* (Minneapolis: Augsburg Publishing House, 1971). (Hereafter cited as Anderson, *Gospel*.) See also A. M. Hunter, *P. T. Forsyth* (Philadelphia: Westminster Press, 1974).

76. These include: *The Cruciality of the Cross; The Work of Christ;* and *The Person and Place of Jesus Christ.*

77. See P. T. Forsyth, "The Evangelical Churches and Higher Criticism," *Contemporary Review* 88 (1905):574 (hereafter cited as "Evangelical Churches") and "Authority and Theology," *Hibbert Journal* 4 (October 1905):63. These essays are found in Anderson, *Gospel*, pp. 16ff. and 130ff.

78. P. T. Forsyth, *Positive Preaching and the Modern Mind* (Grand Rapids, Mich.: Wm. B. Eerdmans, 1966), p. 227. (Cited hereafter as *Preaching*.)

79. Robert Clyde Johnson, *Authority in Protestant Theology*, (Philadelphia: Westminster Press, 1959), p. 63.

80. R. C. Johnson, pp. 100–101.

81. *Preaching*, p. 43.

82. *Preaching*, p. 32.

83. *Preaching*, p. 32.

84. *Preaching*, p. 239. See his essay "Revelation and the Bible" (hereafter cited as "Revelation") *Hibbert Journal*, 10 (1911):240, in Anderson, *Gospel*, pp. 76ff.

85. *Preaching*, p. 10.

86. "Revelation," pp. 240, 242–243, in Anderson, *Gospel*, pp. 82, 84.

87. P. T. Forsyth, *The Person and Place of Jesus*

Christ, 6th ed. (London: Independent Press, 1948), p. 159. (Hereafter cited as *Person.*)

88. *Person*, p. 152.

89. *Person*, p. 154. He writes: "The Bible is not merely a record of the revelation; it is part of the revelation." See "Evangelical Churches," pp. 579–580, in Anderson, *Gospel*, p. 25.

90. *Person*, p. 172. Cf. p. 154.

91. *Person*, p. 159.

92. *Preaching*, p. 5. Cf. p. 176.

93. P. T. Forsyth, *The Work of Christ* (London: Collins, 1965), p. 61. (Hereafter cited as *Work of Christ.*) See also "Evangelical Churches," p. 592, in Anderson, *Gospel*, p. 43.

94. P. T. Forsyth, *The Principle of Authority*, 2d ed. (London: Independent Press, 1952), p. 328. (Hereafter cited as *Principle.*)

95. *Preaching*, p. 10.

96. See "Evangelical Churches," pp. 574, 578, cited in Anderson, *Gospel*, pp. 17, 23. Forsyth writes: "The Bible exists for the Gospel which created it," *Preaching*, p. 11, and "the Bible is there for the sake of the gospel within it," p. 245, "Revelation," in Anderson, *Gospel*, p. 87.

97. "Evangelical Churches," p. 594, in Anderson, *Gospel*, p. 45. "Revelation," p. 245, in Anderson, p. 87. See also Forsyth, *The Church and the Sacraments* (London, 1953), p. 276. Revelation, then, "is not merely the Bible. It is what gives value to the Bible; it is the gospel in the Bible," in "Revelation," p. 240, cited in Anderson, *Gospel*, p. 81. And thus for Forsyth, "The Word of God is the gospel, which is *in* the Bible, but it is not identical with the Bible."

A contemporary evangelical, Donald G. Bloesch, uses Forsyth's terms and identifies three basic approaches to Scripture in the history of the church. These are: the sacramental, the scholastic, and revelation as inner enlightenment or self-discovery. Among those he lists as holding the sacramental view, which he defines as seeing revelation as "God in action and regards Scripture as the primary channel or medium of revelation," are Augustine, Calvin, Luther, Forsyth, Bavinck, Kuyper, and G. C. Berkouwer. Bloesch himself holds to the sacramental view and writes: "We go astray if we base the authority of Scripture on the inerrancy of the writing and then try to demonstrate this according to the canons of scientific rationality. The authority of the Bible is based on the One whom it attests and the One who speaks through it in every age with the word of regenerating power.... This by no means implies that the biblical witness is fallible or untrustworthy. Instead we hold that this witness does not carry the force of infallible authority apart from the Holy Spirit who acts in and through it. Whenever the Bible functions as the sword of the Spirit in the community of believers, it wields indisputable divine authority in all areas pertaining to faith and practice," *Essentials of Evangelical Theology*, Vol. 2 (New York: Harper & Row, 1979), pp. 270, 271.

98. *Person*, p. 139.

99. *Person*, p. 160. The apostles were "organs of Christ himself," *Person*, p. 155. "The essence of Christianity is not in the bare fact, but in the fact and its interpretation," p. 168.

100. *Person*, p. 167. "The New Testament was the unfolding of this gospel; but it was an unfolding due to the free growth and power of God's saving act in the experience of certain men, and not their examination of it and their conclusions," in "Evangelical Churches," p. 583, cited in Anderson, *Gospel*, p. 30.

101. "Evangelical Churches," p. 581, in Anderson, *Gospel*, p. 27.

102. *Preaching*, p. 9. Forsyth argues from the Incarnation that "if the pure and perfect act of God when it entered human history was mixed with human sin in a way that baffles our thought, need we be surprised that the Word of that act, as *it* entered human vehicles and human story (by speech or writing), should also be mixed with foreign and imperfect elements in a perplexing way, and a way we cannot mark off with scientific exactness? If the *act* of salvation was bound up with a crime, need we be startled if its *Word* is mingled with error?" in "Revelation," pp. 244, 245, cited in Anderson, *Gospel*, pp. 86–87.

103. "Evangelical Churches," p. 594, in Anderson, *Gospel*, p. 46. He had argued that "*The Bible is at its highest as the preacher. And it does not preach itself, or its inerrancy, but the grace of God*," in "Evangelical Churches," p. 579, cited in Anderson, *Gospel*, p. 24.

104. "Evangelical Churches," p. 594, in Anderson, *Gospel*, p. 46. Forsyth believed that in relation to the Old Testament and everything else, "that in all matters of science, literary or other, Jesus was the child of his time. He never claimed omni-science in that region. His reading of the Old Testament was certainly uncritical by the standards of our time and knowledge. In this respect he took it as he found it—like everybody round him. It was not his knowledge that was perfect. He found God in nature, but did [he] escape the current belief that the sun went round the earth? ... It was not his knowledge that was perfect, but his judgment. And on the composition of the Old Testament he never passed a judgment. It never occurred to him. If it had, it would not have interested him. Historic sequences were naught to him. What was infallible was not the views he inherited, but his grasp of the Father and the Father's purpose in him. It was in regard to his own work and gospel that he could not err. And no contemporary errors as to nature or the past affect the truth of his witness to God, or the power of his gracious saving work for men," in "Evangelical Churches," p. 585, cited in Anderson, *Gospel*, p. 33.

105. See *Preaching*, pp. 26 and 19. "So we come back, enriched by all we have learned from repudiating a verbal inspiration and accepting an inspiration of men and souls, to a better way of understanding the authority than there is in the inspiration of a book, a canon," *Person*, p. 171.

106. *Person*, p. 155.

107. *Preaching*, p. 26.

108. *Work of Christ*, p. 56.

109. *Preaching*, pp. 169, 184.

110. *Preaching*, p. 169.

111. *Person*, p. 179.

112. *Preaching*, p. 184.

113. *Preaching*, p. 195.

114. "Evangelical Churches," p. 579, in Anderson, *Gospel*, p. 24.

115. *Preaching*, p. 11.

116. Quoted in R. A. Brown, *Prophet*, p. 100.

117. P. T. Forsyth, "The Cross as the Final Seat of Authority," *Contemporary Review*, 76 (October 1899):604. (Hereafter cited as "Cross.") Cited in Anderson, *Gospel*, p. 171. Here Forsyth reiterates about the Bible's authority: "Its authority is due to its place and function in the service of the gospel. The final authority is the redeemer. The Bible is authoritative only in so far as it conveys and serves his redeeming work and purpose. It is regulative neither for science nor history, but for the soul. Its key and goal is the gospel, as God's forgiving act in Christ. And the varying value of each part is

proportionate to its nearness and directness to this central aim."
118. *Preaching*, p. 14. See also "Cross," p. 604, in Anderson, *Gospel*, p. 171.
119. *Preaching*, p. 6.
120. "Evangelical Churches," p. 588, in Anderson, *Gospel*, p. 37.
121. "Evangelical Churches," pp. 594–595, in Anderson, *Gospel*, p. 47; see also p. 35. "Revelation," p. 246, in Anderson, *Gospel*, p. 87. See also *Preaching*, p. 19.
122. *Principle*, p. 59.
123. *Preaching*, p. 31.
124. *Principle*, p. 65.
125. *Principle*, p. 328.
126. *Principle*, p. 75.
127. *Principle*, pp. 333–334.
128. *Principle*, p. 365. See also pp. 302, 419.

129. See the section on Forsyth in R. C. Johnson, "Prophetic Reaction," pp. 100–107.
130. See Robert S. Paul, *The Church in Search of Its Self* (Grand Rapids, Mich.: Wm. B. Eerdmans, 1972), p. 374, citing Forsyth, *The Church and the Sacraments*, p. 32.
131. These relationships are developed more fully in Donald K. McKim, "The Authority of Scripture in P. T. Forsyth" (Pittsburgh Theological Seminary, 1973).
132. "Evangelical Churches," p. 595, in Anderson, *Gospel*, p. 47.
133. "Evangelical Churches," p. 598, in Anderson, *Gospel*, p. 51.
134. "Evangelical Churches," pp. 589–590, in Anderson, *Gospel*, p. 40.

f. Selected Bibliography

Barr, James, *Fundamentalism*. Westminster Press, 1977, 1978.

Berkouwer, G. C. *Holy Scripture*, trans. Jack B. Rogers. Wm. B. Eerdmans, 1975.

Bloesch, Donald G., *Essentials of Evangelical Theology*, vols. 1 and 2. Harper & Row, 1978, 1979.

Carnell, Edward J. *The Case for Orthodox Theology*. Westminster Press, 1959.

Hunter, A. M. *P. T. Forsyth*. Westminster Press, 1974.

Johnson, Robert Clyde. *Authority in Protestant Theology*. Westminster Press, 1959.

Rogers, Jack B. "The Concept of Organic Inspiration in the *Gereformeerd Dogmatiek* of Dr. Herman Bavinck." Th.M. thesis. Pittsburgh Theological Seminary, 1961.

CHAPTER 8

Recent Efforts to Recover the Reformed Tradition

a. Reaction to Liberalism: Karl Barth

Karl Barth (1886–1968) was born in Basel, Switzerland, the first son of Fritz Barth. His father was a minister of the Swiss Reformed Church and at that time lecturer at the Evangelical School of Preachers in Basel. Later Fritz Barth moved to Bern where he was professor of New Testament and church history.[1]

Barth began his theological training under his father and others at Bern. These early teachers gave him a thorough grounding in the historical-critical school, but he said, "They were incapable of interesting me more deeply and to any lasting effect."[2] At Berne, Barth learned all that could be said against "the old orthodoxy ... and that all God's ways begin with Kant and, if possible, must also end there."[3]

The first book to affect Barth powerfully was Immanuel Kant's *Critique of Practical Reason.* Gradually he began to diverge from his father's conservative theology. Reading Kant led him to want to study under a leading Kantian, Wilhelm Herrmann (1846–1922), at Marburg. But Fritz Barth distrusted Herrmann's theology and Karl Barth went instead to Berlin. There he was a pupil of the great liberal historian, Adolf von Harnack (1851–1930), who lectured on the history of dogma.[4] By this time Barth had also read Kant's *Critique of Pure Reason* and discovered the theology of Friedrich Schleiermacher (1768–1834). Schleiermacher became a dominant influence on Barth's theology and remained so for many years.

But during that year in Berlin in 1906, Barth also read Herrmann's *Ethik* published five years before. This too, deeply influenced him and he said in 1925: "Herrmann was *the* theological teacher of my student years. The day twenty years ago in Berlin when I first read his *Ethik* I remember as if it were today.... I can say that on that day I believe my own deep interest in theology began."[5] Only after a year at Tübingen at his father's insistence (where young Karl had been sent to imbibe the conservative theology of Adolf Schlatter) was Barth finally allowed to go to Herrmann's Marburg, "my Zion."[6] There he studied for three semesters under Herrmann as well as with leading neo-Kantian philosophers Hermann Cohen and Paul Natorp, and New Testament specialists Johannes Weiss, Wilhelm Heitmüller, and Adolf Jülicher.

Nineteenth-Century Liberalism

The understanding of God's revelation that Barth learned from Herrmann was in the tradition of Schleiermacher and Albrecht Ritschl (1822–1889). It stressed the continuity between God and human beings. In philosophy G. W. F. Hegel (1770–1831) had asserted a fundamental unity between human and divine and asserted also that the divine (ultimate reality) was rational. Therefore, God could be comprehended through human reason.[7] Hegel's contemporary in the field of religion, Schleiermacher, worked by the method of introspection. He proclaimed that the immediate awareness of God through an experience of the universe or by the human "feeling of absolute dependence" was the basis of true religion.[8] Thus both men asserted a "point of contact" between God and humans that was always accessible to human beings.[9]

Ritschl sought to establish Christian theology as a systematic and autonomous discipline. He rejected the speculative rationalism of Hegel and the subjectivism of Schleiermacher.[10] But he followed in their tradition by conceiving of the relationship of God to humans in terms of historical and positive religions.[11] The continuity between God and His creatures took expression for Ritschl in God's reveation of Himself in various religions and, supremely, in Jesus at the beginning of the Christian movement.[12] Ritschl approached the New Testament via the Reformation. His historical studies sought to show an historical continuity between the Reformers' doctrine of reconciliation and that of the earliest Christian communities to which the Gospel was initially committed.[13] This stress on history led Ritschl to emphasize the objective character of the Christian faith. Faith's object for him was the historical Jesus in whom God revealed Himself.[14]

The doctrine of revelation Barth learned from Herrmann was modified, however. For Herrmann, this objective faith worshipped and revered the mystery of God in Christ.[15] While Herrmann adopted Schleier-macher's starting point for theology, he moved beyond even Ritschl when Barth heard him say:

> The religious knowledge of the Christian begins with the group of obvious facts establishing religion's power to affect conscience, but it ends with the confession that the God whose innermost nature has become revealed to us as love, still remains for us a God enthroned in unapproachable light (1 Timothy 6.16). The doctrine of the Trinity has therefore supreme signifi-cance because it reminds us that God who gives us eternal life through himself must be inexhaustible and therefore an unfathomable mystery.[16]

The "hiddenness" of God was preserved, even in the midst of His revela-tion.[17]

World War I and a Return to the Bible

With this theology Barth began his work as an assistant pastor in Geneva after a brief stint as an editorial assistant on the *Christliche Welt* (*Christian World*). As he wrote later: "At the end of my student days I was second to none among my contemporaries in credulous approval of the 'modern theology' of the time."[18]

In 1911 Barth became pastor of the Reformed Church in Safenwil, a village in northcentral Switzerland. For the first three years Barth's ser-mons drew little attention. They emphasized "life" or "experience," terms used often in Marburg. He lamented: "I always seemed to be beating my head against a brick wall."[19] But in August 1914 World War I broke out. On the day it began, an event occurred that had far-reaching consequences for Barth's theological views. He said:

> One day at the beginning of August of that year stamped itself as the *dies alter* [this age]. It was that on which 93 German intellectuals came out with a manifesto supporting the war policy of Kaiser William II and his counsel-lors, and among them I found to my horror the names of nearly all my theological teachers whom up to then I had religiously honoured. Disillu-sioned by their conduct, I perceived that I should not be able any longer to accept their ethics and dogmatics, their biblical exegesis, their interpreta-tion of history, that at least for me the theology of the 19th century had no future.[20]

For Barth "a whole world of exegesis, ethics, dogmatics and preaching, which I had hitherto held to be essentially trustworthy, was shaken to the foundations, and with it, all the other writings of the German theolo-gians."[21] Among the names in support of the Kaiser were Harnack, Reinhold Seeberg, Schlatter, and most painful of all, Wilhelm Herrmann, professor of theology in the University of Marburg.

The outbreak of the world war was an indictment to Barth not only of his theological training but also of European politics in general. Through the influence of his close friend and now neighboring pastor Eduard Thurneysen in Leutwil, Barth was introduced to the eschatological theology of Johann Christoph Blumhardt (1805–1880). Blumhardt was a Lutheran pietist pastor who had founded a retreat center at Bad Boll in Germany. His son Christoph took the lead in the development of the Swiss religious-socialist movement, which stressed that one's commitment to the Kingdom of God made necessary a deep concern for all areas of individual and social needs. Barth had joined the Social-Democratic Party at the beginning of 1915 and sided with the workers of Safenwil and of his congregation in a labor dispute over a just wage. He had long conversations with Christoph Blumhardt at Bad Boll and was much influenced by his eager pursuits of signs of the "breakthrough" of the Kingdom of God while at the same time patiently "waiting" for God and performing whatever actions one could. Barth wrote: "The new element, the New Testament element, which appeared again in Boll can be summed up in the one word: hope."[22]

Barth's theology was going through profound changes at this time. Through long conversations and correspondence with Thurneysen the two men soon became aware that a new understanding of their Christian faith had developed. The theology in which they had been trained and which so stressed "ethics" was found to be ethically bankrupt.[23] At last Barth discovered that he could not go along with Schleiermacher.[24] The training he had received, which stressed the acquisition of knowledge by the mastery of certain theological disciplines, had not equipped Barth even to preach a meaningful Sunday sermon.[25]

> Barth and Thurneysen turned to the Bible. Barth wrote: We tried to learn our theological ABC all over again, beginning by reading and interpreting the writing of the Old and New Testaments, more thoughtfully than before. And lo and behold they began to speak to us—but not as we thought we must have heard them in the school of what was then 'modern theology'.[26]

In a 1916 address, "The Strange New World Within the Bible," Barth urged his hearers to approach the Bible in faith and with the confidence that "the Holy Scriptures will interpret themselves in spite of all our human limitations ... the Bible unfolds to us as we are met, guided, drawn on, and made to grow by the grace of God."[27] He continued:

> It is not the right human thoughts about God which form the content of the Bible, but the right divine thoughts about men. The Bible tells us not how we should talk with God but what he says to us; not how we find the way to him, but how he has sought and found the way to us; not the right relation in which we must place ourselves to him, but the covenant which he has made

with all who are Abraham's spiritual children and which he has sealed once and for all in Jesus Christ. It is this which is within the Bible. The word of God is within the Bible.[28]

Barth's break with Schleiermacher was complete when he shifted the focus on theological reflection from humans back to God:

> We have found in the Bible a new world, God, God's sovereignty, God's glory, God's incomprehensible love. Not the history of man but the history of him who hath called us out of darkness into his marvelous light! Not human standpoints but the standpoint of God.![29]

The Epistle to the Romans and Kierkegaard

Barth turned his attention to Paul's *Epistle to the Romans*. By 1919 he had produced a commentary (*Der Romerbrief*) in which he boldly announced:

> Paul, as a child of his age, addressed his contemporaries. It is, however, far more important that, as Prophet and Apostle of the Kingdom of God, he veritably speaks to all men of every age. The differences between then and now, there and here, no doubt require careful investigation and consideration. But the purpose of such investigation can only be to demonstrate that these differences are, in fact, purely trivial. The historical-critical method of Biblical investigation has its rightful place: it is concerned with the preparation of the intelligence—and this can never be superfluous. But, were I driven to choose between it and the venerable doctrine of Inspiration, I should without hesitation adopt the latter, which has a broader, deeper, more important justification.[30]

Barth said his concern was "to see through and beyond history into the spirit of the Bible, which is the Eternal Spirit."[31] Thus Barth broke with the tradition of modern liberalism, which concentrated on the philosophical and historical study of the biblical text. Barth's book received mixed reviews. Some heralded him for his prophetic powers. Others, including his former teacher Schlatter and the New Testament scholar Adolf Jülicher, found it unthinkable that anyone—especially a scholar—should disparage scientific exegetical procedures.[32]

In October 1920 Barth had several conversations with a fellow minister, the Lutheran, Friedrich Gogarten (1887–1967).[33] After this, Barth announced that he would completely rework the second edition of *Romans*. In eleven months he produced 521 pages and sent them off to the publisher as they were written. During that time Barth studied Plato, Kant, Kierkegaard, and Dostoevsky.[34] The influence of these studies appeared plainly in the second edition.

Barth wrote in his preface:

> If I have a system, it is limited to a recognition of what Kierkegaard called the 'infinite qualitative distinction' between time and eternity, and to my regarding this as possessing negative as well as positive significance: 'God is in heaven, and thou art on earth.' The relation between such a God and such a man, and the relation between such a man and such a God, is for me the theme of the Bible and the essence of philosophy. Philosophers name this KRISIS of human perception—the Prime Cause: the Bible beholds at the same cross-roads—the figure of Jesus Christ.[35]

The emphases Barth caught from Kierkegaard were his attacks on the objectivism of the historical method in favor of the approach of radical faith and this stress on the *dis-continuity* of God and humans.[36] The negative side of this latter point was the bane of nineteenth-century theology: God and humans were confused, God's spirit and the human spirit, God's revelation and human religion were blurred. Faith in the nineteenth century was only "a realisation of one of the forms of man's spiritual life and self-consciousness."[37] Now Barth emphasized God's transcendence and majesty: "The Gospel proclaims a God utterly distinct from men." The "Godness of God," God the "Wholly Other," the "Hidden One" was the God of the Bible.[38] On the positive side, God had revealed Himself as the Reconciler and Lord in Jesus Christ the Son of God and Son of Man who is the point at which heaven and earth meet: "In this name [Jesus Christ] two worlds meet and go apart, two planes intersect, the one known and the other unknown."[39] This was Barth's "crisis theology." For Barth, all of history and all of humankind stood under the "crisis" that had been brought to the world by Jesus Christ. In Him God rendered His judgment.[40] "Crisis" was both a moment of danger but also a "turning point" or change of direction. In Christ, God's judgment was "both negation and affirmation, both death and life."[41]

Jesus Christ as both "judgment" and "grace" to humankind was the ultimate source of all "dialectical thinking." Barth's "dialectical theology" as it was called, with its movement between question and answer, word and response ("yes" and "no") stressed that all theology was a dialogue between God and humankind.[42] Barth claimed this was the way of "Paul and the Reformers, and intrinsically it is by far the best.[43] It acknowledged that all theology was human expression by the sinner. All the Christian (or the preacher) could do was but witness to the incredible event that the "hidden God" (*Deus absconditus*) was also the revealed God (*Deus revelatus*) in Jesus Christ. God was always the "Subject" who must reveal Himself. All that humans could do was witness to this wonder.[44]

Göttingen and a Rediscovery of the Reformers

As early as 1921, before his second edition of *Romans* was published, Barth was offered the newly instituted chair for Reformed theology at Göttingen (this chair was founded with help from American Presbyterians).[45] By this time Barth was self-consciously tracing his theological ancestry back "through *Kierkegaard* to *Luther* and *Calvin,* and so to *Paul* and *Jeremiah.*" At the same time he carefully pointed out that it did *not* run back through Martensen or Erasmus, or Schleiermacher. Kierkegaard had replaced Schleiermacher, whom Barth had considered in 1912 as having renewed the theological tradition broken by the death of the Reformers but stretching back through the apostles and prophets.[46]

The beginning of 1922 brought Barth an honorary doctorate of theology from the University of Münster but also the daily pressures of preparing lectures. He immersed himself in the Reformed tradition, offering courses on the Heidelberg Catechism, Calvin, Zwingli, and Schleiermacher. His long admiration for Calvin's *Commentaries* on Scripture was now supplemented by an appreciation for his theology as a whole.[47] So powerful was the inspiration from the Reformers that Barth spoke of it in terms of a conversion. His previous theological views were really pre-Reformation, "somehow in a corner along with nominalism, Augustinianism, mysticism, Wycliffe, etc. It was not itself the Reformation, but nevertheless the Reformation later sprang out of it."[48]

Barth's theological work led him, "as it had to, to the Reformers' understanding of the Bible and of God."[49] Because of the great stress on "the Word of God," Barth's increasingly well-known theology was often labeled a "theology of the Word." The magazine *Zwischen den Zeiten* (*Between the Times*) was founded by Barth and a number of others. Its purpose was to reject "the positive-liberal or liberal-positive theology of neo-Protestantism from the beginning of the century," and "the man-God we thought we had recognized as its sanctuary." Barth declared:

> What we wanted was a theology of the Word of God. The Bible had gradually convinced us young pastors that something of this kind was absolutely necessary and we found a model among the Reformers.[50]

Barth's study of Calvin led him to become a systematic theologian. He wished to begin a course on dogmatics and read widely in the early church fathers, Aquinas, and the Protestant scholastics. But still he did not know what direction to take. He recollected:

> I shall never forget the spring vacation of 1924. I sat in my study at Göttingen, faced with the task of giving lectures on dogmatics for the first time. No one can ever have been more plagued than I then was with the problem, Could I do it? And how? ... That Holy Scripture must be the

controlling element in an evangelical dogmatics I also realised to the full. I was equally quite clear that the right thing was, in particular, to link up again with the Reformed. . . . But how to do it, without a guide?[51]

Barth's help came when he obtained a copy of Heinrich Heppe's *Reformed Dogmatics*, a compilation of theological *loci* drawn from the works of the Reformed scholastics. Barth described the work as "out of date, dusty, unattractive, almost like a table of logarithms, dreary to read, stiff and eccentric on almost every page I opened." But, he continued:

> I had the grace not to be slack. I read, I studied, I reflected; and found that I was rewarded with the discovery that here at last I was in the atmosphere in which the road, by way of the Reformers to Holy Scriptures, was a more sensible and natural one to tread than the atmosphere, now only too familiar to me, of the theological literature determined by Schleiermacher and Ritschl. I found a dogmatics which had both form and substance, oriented upon the central indication of the Biblical evidences for revelation, which it also managed to follow out in detail with astonishing richness.[52]

Barth was not an uncritical reader, however. His dogmatics proved to be neither "orthodox" nor "scholastic." But this acquaintance with the seventeenth century showed him that "Protestant dogmatics was once a careful, orderly business" and sparked "the hope that it might perhaps become so again."[53]

Münster and the Christian Dogmatics

In 1925 Barth moved to the University of Münster in Westphalia where he became professor of dogmatics and New Testament exegesis. He remained in that post until 1930. His *Christian Dogmatics in Outline* appeared in 1927 (*Die Christliche Dogmatik im Entwurf*). In this work he began by defining dogmatics as "reflection on the Word of God as revelation, holy scripture *and Christian preaching*. . . . Its primary object, therefore, is neither biblical theology nor church doctrine, nor faith, nor religious awareness, but Christian preaching as it is actually given."[54] Barth joined the battle against liberalism by grounding his theology on the threefold Word of God. He conceived of the "Word of God" as the speech or act of God in which God was always the Subject. The Word never became a human possession because God was the Lord of His Word. God and his Word had priority over human faith. God and his revelation were seen in light of the doctrine of the Trinity. Any anthropocentric or natural theology had to show that its reference was to the triune God.[55]

But Barth's concept of the "Word of God" also left a place for the human reception of that Word. He taught that God the Holy Spirit made hearing and response to God's Word possible. But revelation did not take place in a vacuum. It occurred in concrete situations, existentially.[56] Barth was saying here that part of the task of dogmatics at its foundation was the examination and explanation of the human experience of the Word of God.[57] In time Barth revised his Prologomena to Dogmatics when he came to a better understanding and when he saw the difficulties involved in existential philosophy. His thought was being misunderstood because of its close involvement with the writings of Kierkegaard. As he wrote: "In this second draft I have excluded to the very best of my ability anything that might appear to find for theology a foundation, support, or justification in philosophical existentialism."[58] For Barth this meant a complete rethinking of the relationship between philosophy and theology and in particular his own use of Kierkegaard. In short, Barth's whole theological methodology needed to be reworked. The question was how to keep God's self-revelation alone as the basis of theology and yet preserve the character of this revelation as an historical event. He wished to write of the knowledge of God, faith, belief, and experience without permitting them to be an independent basis for theological thinking.[59]

Bonn and Anselm: Faith Seeking Understanding

The key for Barth came with the seminar he gave in the summer of 1930 on Anselm's *Cur Deus Homo* (*Why God Became Man*). Barth had moved to the University of Bonn where he was Professor of Systematic Theology. By 1931 he had published the book *Fides quaerens intellectum: Anselm's Beweis der Existenz Gottes* translated as *Anselm: Fides quaerens intellectum: Anselm's Proof of the Existence of God in the Context of his Theological Scheme.* [60] Barth wrote: "In this book on Anselm I am working with a vital key, if not the key, to an understanding of that whole process of thought that has impressed me more and more in my *Church Dogmatics* as the only one proper to theology."[61] Nine years later in 1940 Barth still saw Anselm's importance: "I believe I learned the fundamental attitude to the problem of the knowledge and existence of God ... at the feet of Anselm of Canterbury, and in particular from his proofs of God set out in *Pros.* 2–4."[62]

"Faith seeking understanding" was Anselm's concept of theology. The sequence ran: revelation, faith, and *then* "*ut intelligam*" ("in order to understand").[63] To Barth the phrase "*Credo ut intelligam* meant: It is my very faith itself that summons me to knowledge."[64] Theology was the quest for understanding. Its purpose was not to create faith, to confirm it, or to overcome doubt, whether for the theologian or for anyone else. Faith itself was not touched by whether theological investigations failed or succeeded. The phrase was "faith seeking understanding," not "understanding seeking faith." One must begin with faith in the Word of God: "Faith is related to the 'Word of Christ' and is not faith if it is not conceived, that is acknowledged and affirmed by the Word of Chirst."[65] And "the Word of Christ is identical with the 'Word of those who preach Christ' . . . it is legitimately represented by particular human words." This meant that faith itself was not irrational or blind. This "faith comes by hearing and hearing comes by preaching." Thus, if faith was never "illogical, irrational and, in respect of knowledge wholly deficient," it followed that at the start faith had a certain understanding.[66] In other words faith was never without knowledge.

At first this knowledge was merely an understanding of the message of Christ as human speech. It was an understanding unbelievers could also share. But faith moved beyond this logical understanding to an understanding of the reality behind the words. The truth was the goal for faith from the very start. The end was contained in the beginning. In faith, the Christ who was proclaimed was now acknowledged.[67] The movement was from faith toward sight.

This was what made theology possible for Barth.[68] Because faith involved knowledge and because the object of faith was the true Word of Christ in the proclamation of the church, theology could be done. Theology was not a purely intellectual exercise. It began in faith and moved throughout in faith—*faith* seeking understanding. Where faith was lacking or false, the scientific nature of theology was damaged just as it would have been by wrong conclusions or a faulty method. A genuine faith directed toward the unique object of faith, Jesus Christ, was the essential requirement for the theologian. As Barth put it: "What is required is a pure heart, eyes that have been opened, child-like obedience, a life in the Spirit, rich nourishment from Holy Scripture to make him capable of finding these answers."[69]

For Barth reading Anselm, the "understanding" faith seeks was to be sought from Holy Scripture, which was the center of the church's confession or *Credo*. The Latin word used by Anselm, *intelligere* ("to understand") came from two words *intus legere* which meant literally "to read within." Thus the "understanding" faith sought from the Bible was not merely superficial. A reading of Scripture that did not pass beyond merely the understanding of its words, paragraphs, and histories was not enough. By grace, in faith, "understanding" moved to find the meaning of the Bible and to reflect on that meaning. On one level the Bible spoke in its words and histories. On the second level the truth of its message was revealed. It was this second level that demanded a "reading-within," an "understanding" according to Barth. This second level was experienced when one read the outward text. But it was found only as God illumined the text.

Merely quoting a text as a "proof text" would therefore not do. For it was precisely this verse or text that must be reflected upon and interpreted theologically. The text was what was to be understood. How then could it stand as proof for the *result* of understanding? To quote proof texts was only to state the problem again, not to clinch the argument.[70] Thus Anselm himself did not cite many "authorities." That was no substitute for scientific inquiry. Understanding came from God as one meditated upon Scripture or the church's confession, seeking its meaning, comparing and connecting it with other parts of God's revelation.

This was the difference between theology and philosophy for Barth. Philosophy had for its authority certain laws of logic and demanded a thinking that proceeded on that basis. If a theologian introduced philosophy into his attempt to understand, he diverted himself from the proper theological path. Barth perceived this as his mistake in his *Christian Dogmatics.* His understanding of faith was couched in terms of existential philosophy. This type of language and these concepts had controlled his understanding of faith's object.[71]

What Barth learned from Anselm was that theology must be carried on in faith from inside the circle of faith which was the church. The presupposition from which the theologian worked was that God had acted and revealed Himself.[72] Barth pointed out that, above all, if theology was faith seeking to understand, any understanding that came would be as an answer to prayer, which was the practice of faith. He pointed out that Anselm's work was theology in the form of a prayer. It was not an introductory textbook for philosophy.[73]

The Church Dogmatics

The lessons Karl Barth learned from Anselm were first used in the project that was to consume Barth's time for the next thirty-five years, until death—his *Church Dogmatics.* His dissatisfaction with the *Christian Dogmatics* because of its ties with existential philosophy, as well as the discoveries made from Anselm, led him to rewrite his Prologomena. Barth said:

> The positive factor in the new development was this; in these years I had to learn that Christian doctrine, if it is to merit its name, and if it is to build up the Christian church in the world as it needs to be build up, has to be exclusively and consistently the doctrine of Jesus Christ. Jesus Christ is the living Word of God spoken to us men. If I look back from this point on my earlier stages, I can now ask myself why I did not learn this and give expression to it much sooner. How slow man is, especially when the most important things are at stake! ... My new task was to rethink everything that

I had said before and to put it quite differently once again, as a theology of the grace of God in Jesus Christ.[74]

This position of Barth's reflected a move away from some of the more radical statements of his "dialectical theology." Faith seeking understanding could result in a true (though not complete) knowledge of God. Human statements and language about God might be analogous to their object.[75] This was a major shift in Barth's thought. It was a concern that was now present through successive volumes of the *Dogmatics*.[76] Barth wished to hold to the "analogy of faith." To him this meant "the likeness of the known in the knowing, of the object in thought, of the Word of God in the word that is thought and spoken by man" (Rom. 12:6).[77] The possibility of this "analogy" or "correspondence" came only *in* faith, *in* the relationship of faith. It came "not as an inborn or acquired property of man but only as the work of the actual grace of God."[78] For "one can never look back on the human, even the Christian act of knowledge as such as on a successful work corresponding to its object." Even in the context of faith, "there is only similarity, analogy. To see God 'face to face' without dissimilarity must await the eternal consummation even in the case of Christians (1 Cor. 13:12)." But it was "in virtue of this similarity the Church, Church proclamation and dogmatics are possible."[79]

With the rewriting of his Prologomena came also the change in titles from *Christian Dogmatics* to *Church Dogmatics*. Barth explained that he "tried to show that from the very outset dogmatics is not a free science. It is bound to the sphere of the Church, where alone it is possible and meaningful."[80] This also gave expression to Barth's awareness that he was working in a long tradition.

Barth's declaration of independence from philosophy meant that his own reliance on Kierkegaard had to be tempered. After 1931 Barth began mentioning him less and less.[81] But the distance between God and humankind remained a constant theme in his work.[82] In the 1960s Barth said of Kierkegaard:

> What attracted us particularly to him, what we rejoiced in, and what we learned, was the criticism, so unrelenting in its incisiveness, with which he attacked so much: all the speculation that blurred the infinite qualitative difference between God and man. . . . In the second phase of the revolution in which we were then involved he became one of the cocks whose crowing seemed to proclaim from near and far the dawn of a really new day. . . . I believe that throughout my theological life I have remained faithful to Kierkegaard's reveille as we heard it then, and that I am still faithful to it today. Going back to Hegel or even Bishop Mynster has been out of the question ever since.[83]

The Doctrine of the Word of God

Barth developed his new Prologomena to the *Church Dogmatics* in two large volumes called "The Doctrine of the Word of God." For Barth the "Word of God" was synonymous with God's self-revelation.[84] At its simplest, "God's Word means that God speaks."[85] According to Barth, "revelation in fact does not differ from the person of Jesus Christ nor from the reconciliation accomplished in Him. To say revelation is to say 'The Word became flesh.' "[86]

For Barth the "form" of the Word of God was threefold: the Word proclaimed, the Word written, and the Word revealed.[87] This did not mean, however, that there were three different Words of God—there was but one Word of God, God speaking to humankind in Jesus Christ.[88] Yet none of the three forms should be viewed in isolation from each other.[89]

The content of Christian preaching was Jesus Christ.[90] God took human language and it was in and through language that "God speaks about Himself."[91] True preaching occurred only when the church's proclamation was subservient to the Word of God as attested in Holy Scripture.[92]

Holy Scripture as a form of the Word of God was "written proclamation." It was "the deposit of what was once proclamation by human lips." In this sense Scripture was of the same genus as church proclamation: "Scripture as the commencement and present-day preaching as the continuation of one and the same event, Jeremiah and Paul at the beginning and the modern preaching of the Gospel at the end of one and the same series."[93]

For Barth it was the canon of the church (Holy Scripture) that prevented the church from merely reflecting upon itself.[94] The canon of Scripture in its written form was "a concrete authority with its own vitality, an authority whose pronoucement is not the Church's dialogue with itself but an address to the Church."[95] No proofs or reasons created the canon. It was self-authenticating: "The Bible is the Canon just because it is so. It is so by imposing itself as such."[96]

Barth concluded from this: "Revelation is originally and directly what the Bible and Church proclamation are derivatively and indirectly, i.e., God's Word."[97] There was a process of "becoming" at work here in Barth.[98] Both the church's proclamation and the Bible "must continually become God's Word." This happens through the freedom of God's grace. Yet Barth was careful to caution that the same could not be said about the other form of the word of God—Jesus Christ, God's revelation. For "when we speak about revelation we are confronted by the divine act itself and as such . . . [is] the basis and boundary, the presupposition and proviso, of what had to be said about the Bible and proclamation."[99]

Revelation was God's free grace. Inasmuch as preaching and Scripture witnessed and attested to revelation, "one may thus say of proclamation and the Bible that they are God's Word, that they continually become God's Word."[100] Yet, of revelation itself,

> one has to say the exact opposite, namely, that revelation becomes God's Word, i.e., in the Bible and proclamation, because it is this Word in itself. . . . Revelation is itself the divine decision which is taken in the Bible and proclamation, which makes use of them, which thus confirms, ratifies and fulfills them. It is itself the Word of God which the Bible and proclamation are as they become it (John 3:34–36).[101]

The Authority and Inspiration of Scripture

Barth used the theological approach he learned from Anselm, "I believe that I may understand" when he approached the authority of Scripture. Barth wrote: "Scripture is recognised as the Word of God by the fact that it *is* the Word of God. This is what we are told by the doctrine of the witness of the Holy Spirit."[102] The Bible as the Word of God was self-attesting for Barth. No propositions or principles or reasons led to this conclusion. The Bible was like no other book. It was the Word of God because God had made it so.[103] "Scripture is holy and the Word of God, because by the Holy Spirit it became and will become to the Church a witness to divine revelation."[104] The canonical Scriptures of the church derived their authority from their character as witnesses to the Word of God "whose image and echo they [the Christian community who recognized the canon in the fourth century] perceived in them."[105]

For Barth the Bible had to be approached by faith if its authority was to be realized. He rejected external proofs by which some sixteenth- and seventeenth-century theologians sought to prove the divinity and thus authority of Scripture through "human considerations."[106] For Barth the statement:

> We believe that the Bible is the Word of God . . . must first emphasize and consider the word 'believe.'

Barth declared:

> Believing is not something arbitrary. It does not control its object. It is a recognising, knowing, hearing, apperceiving, thinking, speaking and doing which is overmastered by its object. Belief that the Bible is the Word of God presupposes, therefore, that this over-mastering has already taken place, that the Bible has already proved itself to be the Word of God, so that we can and must recognise it to be such.[107]

The witness of the Scripture to itself was that it was a witness to Jesus

Christ, the incarnate Son of God.[108] But this revelation in Christ came to humanity through witnesses whose nature and function were crucial to the right understanding of this revelation.[109]

Barth's view of inspiration considered biblical passages from 2 Timothy 3:14–17 and 2 Peter 1:19–21.[110] His conclusion was that "the decisive centre to which the two passages point is in both instances indicated by a reference to the Holy Spirit, and indeed in such a way that He is described as the real author of what is stated or written in Scripture."[111] With this in view he discussed 2 Corinthians 3:4–18 and 1 Corinthians 2:6–16.[112]

Barth's emphasis was that the biblical writers were "called" or "elected" to this obedience, by God's Spirit. This was not a general call or election. But it was specially given to them in that through their obedient actions they were in a direct relationship to God's revelation. Barth contended:

> The special element in this attitude of obedience lay in the particularity, i.e., the immediacy of its relationship to the revelation which is unique by restriction in time, and therefore in the particular nature of what they had to say and write as eye-witnesses and ear-witnesses, the first-fruits of the Church.[113]

Barth found three negative tendencies in the early church's view of inspiration.[114] There was "a striking inclination to concentrate interest in the inspiration of Scripture upon one particular point in that circle, and to limit it to it: namely, to the work of the Spirit in the emergence of the spoken or written prophetic and apostolic word as such."[115] Second, there was "a tendency to insist that the operation of the Holy Spirit in the inspiration of the biblical writers extended to the individual phraseology used by them in the grammatical sense of the concept." And third, there was

> a tendency to explain the event of the inspiration of the biblical authors in a way which suggests that there is a secret desire to evade the asserted mystery of this matter: that here a real human word is the real Word of God, the real humanity of it being more or less compromised by a foolish conception of its diversity.[116]

The Reformers restored the authority and lordship of the Bible but did not develop either a "mantico-mechanical nor a docetic conception of biblical inspiration" and refused to make inspiration by the Holy Spirit into any kind of miracle or in order to compare it to any other inspiration. Instead they rested inspiration squarely on the relationship of the biblical witnesses to the definite content of their witness.[117] Barth lamented, however, that in the post-Reformation the "newly opened road to the meaning of the statement" that the Word of God descended to become flesh for us was lost. The Reformers knew that the prophets and apostles spoke a human word in witness to Christ's incarnation. In later scholastic orthodoxy "a statement about the free grace of God" was turned into a statement about "the nature of the Bible as exposed to human inquiry brought under human control. The Bible as the Word of God surreptitiously became a part of natural knowledge of God, i.e., of that knowledge of God which man can have without the free grace of God, by his own power."[118] When the post-Reformation scholastics called the biblical writers *amanuenses* [clerks, secretaries] (W. Bucan), *librarii* [copyists, scribes] (A. Hyperius) or *actuarii* [shorthand writers] (*Syn. pur. Theol.* Leiden 1624), Barth saw a departure from Calvin's description of them as *ministres* [servants, helpers]. Barth asked rhetorically: "Is there already a return to the idea that they are mere flutes in the mouth of the Holy Spirit?"[119] In addition, theologians in the post-Reformation period separated the doctrine of the internal testimony of the Spirit from the witness of the Spirit in Scripture or sought to bring it into relationship with other convincing qualities of the Bible.[120] The desire for "certainty" among the post-Reformation scholastics was for a tangible, human certainty of the Bible's inspiration rather than for a divine certainty brought about by faith. This was why the "modern" doctrine of inspiration, which stressed the overwhelming of the human element in inspiration (a "docetic" theory), arose in the seventeenth century. Barth saw that "the Bible was now grounded upon itself apart from the mystery of Christ and the Holy Ghost." The Bible was made a "paper Pope" and "was no longer a free and spiritual force, but an instrument of human power."[121] This opened the road to the historical relativism of the eighteenth- and nineteenth-century theologians. The further legacy of the Protestant scholastic view of inspiration according to Barth was that:

> Once the doctrine arose it was believed for only a short time, but it remained for many ages, and still is to some extent at the present time, a kind of theological bogeyman, the logically necessary interpretation of the statement that the Bible is the Word of God, which has prevented whole generations and innumerable individual theologians and believers from seeing the true, spiritual biblical and Reformation meaning of the statement, causing them to go past Luther and Calvin and even Paul in order to accompany Voetius and Calov.[122]

Verbal Inspiration

While Barth rejected the method and presuppositions of the scholastics, he did pay very close attention to the text of Scripture. He sought a reorientation of the biblical scholarship of the previous century which emphasized that "in the reading and understanding and expounding of the Bible the main concern can and must be to penetrate past the biblical texts to the facts which lie behind the texts."[123] This meant that revelation was to be found "in these facts as such (which in their factuality are independent of the texts).... The Bible is to be read as a collection of sources."[124]

Instead, Barth wanted to recognize that "the biblical texts must be investigated for their own sake to the extent that the revelation which they attest does not stand or occur, and is not to be sought, behind or above them but in them."[125] Revelation "in itself" had not been given by God. There was no revelation by God except through the biblical witness, that is, through the biblical witnesses. The "enlightening and empowering" of prophets and apostles was "indissolubly linked" with their expounding of their witness. Thus, "in this question of revelation we cannot, therefore, free ourselves from the texts in which its expectation and recollection is attested to us. We are tied to these texts."[126] "Strangely enough," Barth wrote, "Christianity has always been and only been a living religion when it is not ashamed to be actually and seriously a book-religion."[127] For Barth only in the words of Scripture could the Word of God be found: "The Word ought to be exposed in the words."[128]

Since God took and used "the concrete form of the biblical word" there was a real sense for Barth in which it was proper to speak of "verbal inspiration." God through his Spirit spoke his divine Word in human words:

> If God speaks to man, He really speaks the language of this concrete human word of man. That is the right and necessary truth in the concept of verbal inspiration. If the word is not to be separated from the matter, if there is no such thing as verbal inspiredness, the matter is not to be separated from the word, and there is real inspiration, the hearing of the Word of God, only in the form of verbal inspiration, the hearing of the Word of God only in the concrete form of the biblical word.[129]

Barth saw this understanding as following in the footsteps of the Reformers who

> took over unquestioningly and unreservedly the statement on the inspiration, and indeed the verbal inspiration, of the Bible, as it is explicitly and implicitly contained in those Pauline passages which we have taken as our basis, even including the formula that God is the author of the Bible, and occasionally making use of the idea of a dictation through the Biblical writers.[130]

Yet, claimed Barth, "the literally inspired Bible was not at all a revealed book of oracles, but a witness to revelation, to be interpreted from the standpoint of and with a view of its theme, and in conformity with that theme."[131]

The words the biblical witnesses spoke and wrote were human words. They were words that belonged to the created order and that therefore were limited to all the conditions of time and space:

> The witnesses of the Old and New Testaments were men like all others, men who had heard the Word and witnessed to it in a human way—in speech, vision, and thought that were human and conditioned by time and space."[132]

Because of the creatureliness of human language the biblical writers "can be at fault in any word, and have been at fault in every word." Yet "according to the same scriptural witness, being justified and sanctified by grace alone, they have still spoken the Word of God in their fallible and erring human word."[133] To be unwilling to acknowledge this was very serious for Barth:

> Every time we turn the Word of God into an infallible biblical word of man or the biblical word of man into an infallible Word of God we resist that which we ought never to resist, i.e., the truth of the miracle that here fallible men speak the Word of God in fallible human words—and we therefore resist the sovereignty of grace, in which God Himself became man in Christ, to glorify Himself in His humanity.[134]

"Verbal inspiration" for Barth

> does not mean the infallibility of the biblical word in its linguistic, historical and theological character as a human word. It means that the fallible and faulty human word is as such used by God and has to be received and heard in spite of its human fallibility.[135]

The Capacity for Error

In this regard Barth spoke of "the vulnerability of the Bible." This meant that "its capacity for error, also extends to its religious or theological content."[136] He did not wish to speak of "errors" *per se.* Rather, Barth wrote: "Instead of talking about the 'errors' of the biblical authors in this sphere, if we want to go to the heart of things it is better to speak only about their 'capacity for errors.' "[137] Barth realized that knowledge in the twentieth century was "neither divine nor even solomonic."[138] No one had the right to specify what was "error" and what was not. Since there was no "absolute standpoint" from which to judge "error" and since all the writers had the "capacity for error" and thus God could use *any* portion of Scripture through which to speak his Word, Barth denied anyone's right to pronounce on what was more fallible or less fallible in Scripture:

> We are absolved from differentiating the Word of God in the Bible from other contents, infallible portions and expressions from the erroneous ones, the infallible from the fallible, and from imagining that by means of such discoveries we can create for ourselves encounters with the genuine Word of God in the Bible.[139]

Such capricious choices led to a neglect of certain parts of Scripture and to the possibility that in "overlooking" something that was "written," one might have "really missed the one thing which Scripture as a whole attests."[140]

Biblical Interpretation

Barth's view of Scripture and its authority, inspiration, and human form had definite implications for his interpretation of it. For Barth, "in order to be proclaimed and heard again and again both in the Church and the world, Holy Scripture requires to be explained."[141] The form that scriptural exegesis or biblical interpretation should take, Barth said, was the subordinating of "all human concepts, ideas and convictions to the witness of revelation supplied to us in Scripture."[142] Scriptural interpretation had to begin in faith and proceed with "fidelity in all circumstances to the object reflected in the words of the prophets and apostles. This is the fidelity which this object in itself requires."[143] As a dogmatician he felt a responsibility to do exegetical work just as the exegetes had a duty to do dogmatic work.[144]

Barth's *Commentary on Romans* drew heavy fire from many European biblical scholars when it was published.[145] Barth's methods of exegesis were offensive to them. During the years his *Commentary* was developing, Barth expressed his evaluation of contemporary historical methods as applied to Scripture. He agreed with the view of J. A. Ernesti (1707–1781), who, in 1732, argued that the Bible should be studied like any other human document. Barth said: "It can lay no *a priori* dogmatic claim to special attention."[146] Yet on the other hand, in practice, Barth challenged the adequacy of this principle. He announced that "intelligent and fruitful discussion of the Bible begins when the judgement as to its human, its historical and psychological character has been made and *put behind* us."[147] Barth's attitude was decisively affected by his reaction to liberalism. His answer to the historian was that the "battle against 'stark orthodoxy' " was over and that this "human document" the Bible had a "special *content*" that mandated a special treatment.[148] Barth assaulted the whole concept of history associated with the "historical method" when he claimed that the "strange new world within the Bible" was where true and proper "history" went on—in the activity of God in Christ.[149] This view led Barth into dialogue and disagreement with biblical scholars through the years.[150]

Barth did not wish to annul "the results of biblical scholarship in the last centuries" or to break them off or neglect them.[151] He wanted criticism to stop serving "the foolish end of mediating an historical truth lying behind the texts" and examine Scripture instead "as it actually is before us."[152] He wanted to turn with "all the more attentiveness, accuracy and love to the texts as such."[153]

Barth wished his exegesis to be "theological exegesis." This meant that he did all his interpretation with the presupposition that the Bible was the book through which the church "has up to now heard God's Word." Secondly, Barth worked with the full expectation that he himself would also hear God's Word as it applied to his time.[154] In other terms, Barth's was "confessional exegesis." He undertook all his interpretative work on the basis of the church's primary confession: "Jesus Christ is Lord."[155] There was no single hermeneutical pattern in his work. Through the course of time his exegesis in general, and even occasionally that of the same passage, changed.[156] Because the biblical authors "shared the outlook and spoke the language of their own day," there were many "parallels" and points at which they seemed to echo their contemporaries. This did not weaken or rob the Bible of its character as a witness to revelation for Barth.[157] But he recognized too that some parts of the Bible functioned differently from other parts. For him "there are distinctions of higher and lower, of utterances which are more central and peripheral, of witnesses which have to be understood literally and symbolically."[158]

Barth's Influence

Karl Barth developed an appreciation for and approach to the Bible that was a viable alternative in the 1930s to both scholastic rationalism and liberal subjectivism, which had come to a standoff in America. Barth accepted the Bible as an authority for salvation and the life of faith. That salvation and life came through Jesus Christ to whom the Scripture bore witness: Barth insisted that God was Sovereign and initiated His gracious relationship to humankind. It was God's Holy Spirit who brought people to trust in Christ and have confidence in the authority of Scripture. Barth rediscovered, in Anselm, the Augustinian theological method of "faith seeking understanding." Barth thus founded the authority of the Bible on its divine function rather than its human form.

In all of these ways Barth provided a way back to the Reformation focus. That way had been essentially cut off both by the liberals' preoccupation with religious experience and equally by the fundamentalists' defense of post-Reformation scholastic systematizing. Barth's neo-orthodoxy was also something genuinely new because he responded to the influences and movements that affected his times. In a world where optimism in human progress had been shattered by two world wars and a worldwide economic depression, Barth spoke in the pessimistic language of existential philosophy. Kierkegaard's categories enabled Barth to develop a theology of crisis in which individuals could encounter a "wholly other" God despite the social and political problems of their environment. He later dropped existentialist language and deemphasized its role, but never wholly became free of its influence.

Barth was avowedly antiscientific in an era when science and technology had contributed to the devastation of the world by war. In his interpretation of Scripture, Barth's neo-orthodoxy again provided a fresh approach. He did not oppose biblical criticism in principle as the Princeton theologians had. At the same time he did not, in practice, use biblical criticism seriously as the liberals had. Barth's "theological exegesis" allowed him to affirm much of Reformed confessional doctrine. It also permitted him to exercise some rather strained allegorical exegesis in developing his Christological perspective throughout Scripture. Barth's theology was a theology for preachers. Those who followed him were helped to proclaim God's Word with confidence in a world that wanted certainty. And yet they were allowed to be modern persons, not confined to philosophical obscurantisms or constricting systems from the past.

b. A Reaction to Scholasticism: G. C. Berkouwer

A brief detour from the Reformation stance at the Free University in Amsterdam occurred when Herman Bavinck was succeeded in the Chair of Dogmatics by Valentine Hepp in 1922. Hepp shifted the emphasis to apologetics and adopted the Princeton model for doing theology. For Kuyper and Bavinck, apologetics had been the last theological discipline. For Warfield, it was the first.[159] Hepp agreed with Warfield and attempted to develop a distinctively Reformed apologetics. In his Stone Lectures at Princeton, *Calvinism and the Philosophy of Nature,* Hepp expressed an affinity with the theology of the First Vatican Council (1870) that God could be known from the world of created reality through the natural light of reason.[160]

One of Hepp's doctoral students was Gerrit Cornelis Berkouwer (b.1903). Berkouwer grew up in a devoutly Reformed home and a Reformed community committed to subjecting all of life and culture to the authority of the Bible.[161] Berkouwer went to the university intending to study mathematics, but the preachers in his home church had so captivated his interest that he switched his course of study to theology—an unusual and difficult decision in the Dutch educational system.[162] During Berkouwer's years of study, his denomination, the Gereformeerde Kerken, was rent with strife over the doctrine of Scripture. In 1926 a prominent minister was ejected for denying that the serpent had literally spoken to Eve in the garden. Berkouwer and his fellow students were deeply involved in discussion of these matters.

Hepp wanted Berkouwer to write his dissertation on Karl Heim, a German theologian who had devoted himself to the apologetic confrontation between faith and modern science and philosophy. Berkouwer corresponded with Heim, but became convinced that theological attention in Germany was shifting to dialectical theology.[163] Berkouwer received his doctorate in 1932, shortly after beginning his second pastorate. His subject was *Faith and Revelation in the Newer German Theologie.* He treated the views of Ritschl, Herrmann, Wobbermin, Troeltsch, Rudolf Otto, Barth and Brunner.[164] In 1938, after an early book on Karl Barth, Berkouwer wrote a work in defense of the divinity of Scripture, *The Problem of Biblical Criticism.*[165] It expressed in part the apologetic concerns of Hepp. In a speech Berkouwer gave to a minister's conference at this time he stressed the radical commitment of the Reformed view of Scripture to "It Stands Written." One preacher remarked to him that another dimension should be added to this theme, namely the work of the Holy Spirit in connection with scriptural authority and biblical faith. Berkouwer later commented: "The minister's remark had more to it than I realized when I first heard it, though I certainly was ready then to admit its truth."[166] A deepening awareness that for the Reformers, the Holy Spirit convinces us of the authority of Scripture was part of Berkouwer's finding his way back to his own tradition.

In 1941 Berkouwer began lecturing at the Free University in modern theology, interacting especially with the developing theology of Barth and the "crisis theologians," and Roman Catholicism. When Berkouwer succeeded Hepp as Professor of Dogmatics after the war years, he reaffirmed the theological tradition of Kuyper and Bavinck and began writing a series of monographs designed to bring that tradition into relationship with ongoing discussions in contemporary theology. Beginning with *Faith and Justification* in 1949, his series of Dogma Studies extended to fourteen volumes, the last four of which were published in Dutch as two-volume works.[167] Berkouwer's work *Heilige Schrift* was published in two volumes in 1966 and 1967, and the edited English translation appeared as *Holy Scripture* in 1975. This work received criticism from some evangelicals who had previously lauded Berkouwer's theology. The question arose: Had Berkouwer changed? In actuality he had simply described the approach to Scripture that had enriched his volumes on other doctrines for twenty-five years. The continuing power of the scholastic theory of inspiration bequeathed to American evangelicals from the Hodge/Warfield school was demonstrated in reviews of *Holy Scripture.* Authors who had for years praised Berkouwer's evangelical theology felt obligated to dismiss his doctrine of Scripture because it critiqued the old Princeton slogan of "inerrancy."[168]

Authority and Salvation

Berkouwer's theological method in *Holy Scripture* was rooted in the Augustinian tradition that accepted Scripture in faith and then sought further understanding of the Bible through a regenerated reason. Berkouwer was convinced that the purpose or function of Scripture was to bring people to salvation in Christ. Scripture was not given to satisfy our curiosity about philosophical questions. Therefore, Berkouwer, with Calvin, was concerned with Scripture in a functional, not a philosophical, way. The primary issue was: Are people rightly related to the Christ of Scripture?

Berkouwer declared that it was not theologically appropriate "to discuss Scripture apart from a personal relationship of belief in it."[169] Berkouwer expanded this view, saying:

> Faith is not and cannot be based on a theoretical reflection on what, according to our insight, must be the nature of the divine revelation and on which ways and forms it must have come to us in order to be a guarantee of certainty. The way of Christian faith is . . . a subjection to the gospel, to the Christ of the Scriptures; and from this alone can a reflection on Holy Scripture proceed.[170]

Berkouwer thus reflected Bavinck's attitude that no formal theological method guaranteed faith in Scripture.

The authority of Scripture, in Berkouwer's tradition, was affirmed to us by the internal testimony of the Holy Spirit. Berkouwer positioned himself with Calvin and the Reformed confessions saying that according to them, "faith in Scripture is possible and real only in connection with the witness of the Spirit to Christ and his salvation."[171]

The purpose or function of Scripture was a central concern for Berkouwer. He cited Bavinck's point that biblical criticism became a problem when the critics lost sight of the purpose of Scripture.[172] Berkouwer commented: "Scripture itself in a very explicit way speaks about its intention and directedness." That goal, he noted is salvation (John 20:31) which yields hope (Rom. 15:4) and equipment for every good work (2 Tim. 3:16).[173]

Because of his conviction that the purpose of Scripture was to bring us to salvation in Christ, Berkouwer, like Kuyper and Bavinck, was open to the results of critical scholarship in a way that the Princeton theology was not. Berkouwer rejected "an artificial view of revelation" that forgot "that Scripture is written in human words and consequently offers men legitimate freedom to examine these words and try to understand them."[174] Berkouwer expressed concern that humans not dictate God's methods to Him by declaring that Scripture had to come in what seems to us a perfect form. Such a demand on our part was impious according to Berkouwer. He said: "We may not risk tarnishing the mystery of Scripture by disqualifying the God-ordained way in which it came to us."[175] A fundamentalism that denies the human form of Scripture as prophetic-apostolic testimony and wants to substitute a divine form may be well intentioned, but presents serious problems "for it is God's way with and in Scripture that is at stake."[176] Just as serious for Berkouwer was Bultmann's view, for example, which also focused on the form of Scripture although in a different way than fundamentalism. Bultmann believed that an ancient world view was presupposed in the very heart of the gospel. Thus Bultmann's demythologization meant the "content of the *kerygma* is continually at stake."[177]

For Berkouwer the central concern of theology had to be hearing and obeying the divine message of salvation, rather than deifying or demythologizing the human milieu in which that message came. The New Testament writers had this focus on Scripture's saving purpose as they dealt with the Old Testament. Berkouwer commented: "We find a unique kind of Scripture proof in the New Testament, alien to our standards of exactness."[178] That should be instructive for us in our use of Scripture because "the background of this large freedom is an unprecedented concentration on the matter, the *content* of the gospel."[179] Berkouwer found this same ability to distinguish between the human form and the divine content in Calvin. The Reformer

> evidently did not worry very much about the different methods of quotation in the New Testament, and he underlined the freedom which the apostles displayed in their quotations. He merely wished to stress that the 'main point' was decisive for them.[180]

The findings of science, therefore, posed no threat to Berkouwer. He commented that "certain results of science, be it natural science or historical research, can provide the 'occasion' for understanding various aspects of Scripture in a different way than before."[181] Science was not an authority superior to Scripture, but an "occasion" to suggest the real questions theologians should be asking of Scripture. It also might be the "occasion" for questioning the validity of some traditional exegesis. The Word of God remained for Berkouwer authoritative, with science properly used as an aid in enabling persons to approach Scripture with a new openness to what God was saying in it.[182]

Scripture Its Own Interpreter

Berkouwer saw his hermeneutics, or principles of biblical interpretation, as clearly in harmony with the Reformers. He rejected allegorical exegesis and adhered to the grammatical-historical interpretation of the text. According to Berkouwer, the problem with allegory was that it lost the "sense" of Scripture in a multiplicity of meanings.[183] At the same time, appeal to a single sense of Scripture "is not a level literalism devoid of all reliefs, designed to rob Scripture of its depth and riches."[184] Berkouwer assumed the validity of Bavinck's concept of "organic inspiration," which drew attention to the fact that there is a center and a periphery to Scripture.

For Berkouwer and his tradition from Kuyper and Bavinck, the Reformation concept that Scripture is its own interpreter did not take away the need for interpretation, but focused on the way in which interpretation must be done. The Reformation rule "is its own interpreter," according to Berkouwer, "is mostly seen as concerning the intention of the author whom one seeks to know in every text."[185] Historical criticism was, at its best, a protest "against every form of Scripture exposition which went to work with *a priori* and external standards. It wanted to proceed from the Scripture as it actually existed."[186] Berkouwer, following Kuyper and Bavinck, did not fear scholarly investigation but considered it an essential aspect of a responsible faith. Berkouwer spoke sharply: "One can indeed say that those who, because of hesitancy and wariness, abandon new hermeneutical questions contribute to the relativizing of scriptural authority."[187]

The clarity of Scripture was, for Berkouwer, related to its central saving message, not to the particular words and sentences. Berkouwer noted that for the Reformers the doctrine of perspicuity "did not aim at the clarity of the words as such, but at the message, the content of Scripture."[188] The problem came in a later twist in history. Berkouwer commented:

> It is not until the post-Reformation theology that a shift occurred: for the idea of perspicuity is then applied to the *words* of Scripture.... In this manner Scripture is isolated from its context of salvation.[189]

For the Reformers, wrote Berkouwer, "behind this connection of message and words is the power of the Spirit." He concluded:

> For that reason the confession of perspicuity is not a statement in general

concerning the human language of Scripture, but a confession concerning the perspicuity of the gospel *in* Scripture.[190]

A Biblical Definition of Error

In this context then, Berkouwer confronted the question of error in Scripture. He first defined "error" in a biblical manner. When error in the sense of incorrectness was used on the same level as error in the biblical sense of sin and deception, Berkouwer lamented:

> Thus we are quite far removed from the serious manner in which error is dealt with in Scripture. For there what is meant is not the result of a limited degree of knowledge, but it is a swerving from the truth and upsetting the faith (2 Timothy 2:18).[191]

He continued:

> The supposition that limited human knowledge and time-boundness of any kind would cause someone to err and that Holy Scripture would no longer be the lamp for our feet unless every time-bound conception could be corrected is a denial of the significance of historical development and of searching out as the 'unhappy business that God has given to the sons of men to be busy with' (Ecclesiastes 1:13).[192]

Berkouwer acknowledged the "serious motivation" of advocates of scientific and historical inerrancy, but concluded: "In the end it will damage reverence for Scripture more than it will further it."[193] Berkouwer affirmed: "It is not that Scripture offers us no information but that the nature of this information is unique. It is governed by the *purpose* of God's revelation."[194]

Accommodation

Berkouwer emphasized that Chrysostom and Calvin adhered to the concept that God accommodated himself to our human forms of thought and speech.[195] He noted a similar acknowledgement "in Scripture itself, such as the wording of John 16:12 'I have yet many things to say to you, but you cannot bear them now.' "[196] For Berkouwer, the essential fact to remember was:

> For the purpose of the God-breathed Scripture is not at all to provide a scientific *gnosis* [knowledge] in order to convey and increase human knowledge and wisdom, but to witness of the salvation of God unto faith.[197]

In the context of Scripture's saving purpose, Berkouwer found interpretative principles that allowed him to take seriously the cultural context into which the Word came. It was the saving message of Christ that was normative, not the cultural milieu. Berkouwer, for example, dealt in this way with the issue of Paul's statements regarding women. He said:

> Paul ... did not in the least render timeless propositions concerning womanhood. Rather, he wrote various testimonies and prescriptions applicable to particular—and to a certain degree transparent—situations against a background of specific morals and customs of that period.[198]

Berkouwer was intent on finding the *meaning* of biblical statements. He commented that: "One must ... take note of the cultural context and intent of the words within that period precisely *in order* to hear the Word of God."[199] He said: "Obedience to the Word of God is impossible, even an illusion, if it is not a listening discovery of the *meaning* of the words, of their essential goal."[200] Berkouwer concluded that one must "walk the road of biblical research in the way of the Spirit," the way of continued association with Scripture—"Scripture that is *time-related* and has *universal* authority."[201] Berkouwer could thus freely acknowledge that Paul used arguments drawn from his culture.[202] Sometimes Paul interpreted the Old Testament by constructing a midrash like that used in the synagogue. But Berkouwer's conclusion was significant:

> The schism between church and synagogue is not found in the technique or the methods of scriptural usage in itself, but in the total and central understanding of the Old Testament as witness to the promise of Israel's God and in the reality of Jesus as Messiah.[203]

Berkouwer pointed warningly to the example of the Pharisees, who illustrated that one could know the words of Scripture and claim to believe all of them, and still miss their saving purpose. Berkouwer cautioned:

> When Christ accuses the Pharisees of not knowing Scripture (Matthew 22:29), he is not saying that they are strangers to it. For he asks, 'Have you not read?' (Matthew 22:31), and they in turn appeal to Moses. But they do not know or understand Scripture and do not discern its deep intent. They err (Matthew 22:29) and miss the message of Scripture.[204]

Berkouwer's Reformed tradition freely acknowledged that Scripture came in the form of a servant "as a human phenomenon of language."[205] Berkouwer affirmed that not only Scripture but preaching was the Word of God, as stated in the Second Helvetic Confession.[206] He noted that Paul did not make the preaching of the Word a problem, "yet he does not forget the nature of this weak medium, the weakness of man."[207] Human words may be imperfect, but the divine message is communicated when the preacher submits to the apostolic norm of the gospel.

Similarly, translation of Scripture from one language to another involves interpretation. Translation is not a simple matter of matching the word in one language with its exact equivalent in another.[208] The translator must be willing to change the form of words and expressions precisely in order that the message of the gospel may be communicated. According to Berkouwer: "One may exhaust every aspect of Scripture study in the expectation that limited and inadequate words will not undermine the secret of Scripture."[209]

Berkouwer offered encouragement to scholars. Further, he provided all people an incentive to take study seriously because, he contended, it was "for a good reason," that "God's Word was given to us in a form that called for research."[210] The necessity of scholarship for a full understanding of God's Word, for Berkouwer, was coupled with the priority of faith in understanding its central message. Berkouwer thus exemplified the Reformed tradition that can be traced back through Bavinck and Kuyper to Calvin and Augustine. That tradition accepted the saving message of Scripture in faith and then proceeded to a scholarly understanding of the details. Berkouwer noted that "Christians throughout the centuries acknowledged Scripture to be God's Word, and thus one does not need to wait until all questions are answered and all difficulties solved."[211]

The Function of Scripture

In Berkouwer's Reformed tradition, Scripture was not a book designed to answer human philosophical questions. The Bible was a book that answered people's basic need for salvation. That was its purpose, or function. Berkouwer stated emphatically: "It is possible to live with Scripture only when the message of Scripture is understood and is not considered 'a metaphysical document,' but a living instrument serving God for the proclamation of the message of salvation."[212] Scripture's function, for him, was not to give technical philosophical information to solve epistemological problems. Rather, it provided a message of salvation in Christ to meet the deepest human need—the need to be rightly related to God.

For Berkouwer, the model by which we understand Scripture should be functional, not philosophical. The Bible was not meant simply to communicate objective information about God's essence, but to tell people how to be related to God. Berkouwer was quite clear about the functional character of Scripture. While speaking of the central text usually used to develop a doctrine of Scripture, 2 Timothy 3:16, 17, he pointed to Paul's accent on the "usefulness" of Scripture: "One may well speak of the 'functional character' of the God-breathed writing in both translations of Paul's words." He continued: "The Scriptures of the Old Testament which Paul had in mind are holy and thus 'functional' and of utmost importance."[213] Berkouwer noted that "It is good to remember the unconcerned way in which the New Testament writers speak of the Scripture as 'profitable' without anxiety about pragmatism and functionalism." He pointed as well to the Heidelberg Catechism, questions 49 and 59, for the same emphasis.[214]

In his recent reflections on theology in the last fifty years, Berkouwer commented further on the growing awareness in the Christian community of the functional character of Scripture. He said:

> The gospels, it was discerned, were not cool reports of facts, but reports in which the purpose of writing played and sounded through the story in all sorts of ways. Thus we could speak of a 'religious pragmatic,' an expression that has been used in reference to the way the historical accounts of the Old Testament were influenced by the purpose for which they were written.[215]

Berkouwer expressed confidence that the Reformers had a "functional" view of Scripture. In discussing Calvin's view of faith, he declared:

> Faith, for Calvin, was not a leap in the dark; it was a form of knowledge, the knowledge of God's benevolence toward us. It was not an assent to something pressed on us, nor a mere believing *that* something is true; it was a personal trust that negates blind obedience (cf. INST III.ii.1,2).[216]

For Berkouwer, as for Calvin, faith involved knowledge. The crucial issue was: What kind of knowledge? Religious knowledge was either personal, relational knowledge, or it was not considered worthy of the name knowledge. Berkouwer again cited Calvin:

> Calvin used the word *cognitio,* but did not reduce faith to intellectual knowledge with it because he insisted that this *cognitio* was directed to 'the benevolence of God toward us' and was more an affair of the heart than the head.[217]

If a functional view of Scripture can be found in the New Testament and was held by the Reformers, why have evangelicals been so committed to a philosophical view of Scripture? Berkouwer pointed to the historical cause:

> In our time, the central point at issue has again become the post-Reformation theology in connection with the emerging Aristotelianism in theology, which has also begun to influence the doctrine of Scripture. This faulty view has occurred as theologians, in immediate relation to affirmation and certainty, began to interpret the word *est* in the expression *Sacra Scriptura est Verbum Dei* in such a manner that Scripture's divinity was thought to be found in its inner substantial form and had become an essential predicate of Holy Scripture as an inspired book that was elevated to the level of a source of supernatural truths.[218]

Unfortunately the desire of Christians often was to find religious certainty prior to and apart from the message of Scripture. The post-Reformation theology provided a system of so-called proofs that promised such certainty. Berkouwer noted:

> They saw this whole system of philosophical concepts and theoretical objectification as the result of an establishing of a basis of certainty whereby the inspiration already guaranteed certainty quite apart from the witness—the message—of Scripture, whose certainty could rest only on a preceding certainty regarding the source of this witness—Holy Scripture.[219]

Berkouwer rejected this search for *a priori* certainty as unbiblical and false to the Reformation tradition regarding Scripture. He stood with Kuyper in saying that: "Experiencing the *divinitas* of Scripture takes place through experiencing God's *benevolentia.*"[220] Berkouwer emphasized that in the Reformed tradition neither reasons nor the witness of the Holy Spirit authenticated Scripture *prior* to our encountering the message of Scripture. He stated:

> It is important that both Bavinck and Kuyper reject the idea that Scripture is the object of the *testimonium* apart from its message, for as Kuyper points out, such a view is contrary to the way in which faith works, which excludes such a formalization. . . . To formalize Holy Scripture in this way is as non-sensical as to praise a book without reading it; to do so violates the word-character of Holy Scripture.[221]

It was also possible to change the function, the meaning, the message of the gospel, according to Berkouwer. For him, that change is wrong. Berkouwer declared:

> There is another kind of preaching in which the gospel itself is at stake and whereby a different gospel comes forward as a threat to salvation and the way of Christ (Phil. 3:2f.). This preaching is judged according to its content, for it blurs the gospel message and can no longer be approached in terms of motivation alone.[222]

A true doctrine of Scripture must be developed in human interaction with the saving message of Christ in Scripture, not with some other theme or function supposedly found in Scripture, nor with some external proofs for Scripture derived from philosophical arguments about its form.

This meant for Berkouwer that human beings should not construct a philosophical theory about what Scripture ought to be and then expect Christian experience to conform itself to this abstract model. A true doctrine of Scripture for Berkouwer cannot be built in the abstract, using "logical inference" from a few verses. Christian interaction with the Word of God in faith must precede and shape every theory about Scripture. This was the appropriate approach according to Berkouwer since it took into account the nature of Scripture. Scripture, according to the Reformers, had a practical, not a theoretical purpose. "Scripture has not been given to the church primarily as a study book for 'theology' as such," Berkouwer said.[223]

For Berkouwer, therefore, people's experience of God's authority in their lives, mediated through the Scripture, should precede and shape any theory about Scripture that they developed. He commented on the last page of his book, *Holy Scripture:*

> It may seem like a roundabout way to go from the message of Scripture to its unique authority. In reality, it is the true and only way to obedience.[224]

Berkouwer urged that people not fear that they would fall into subjectivism if they moved away from the model of Scripture created by scholastic rationalism. That fear was always used as the defensive fortress of the rationalists. Berkouwer demonstrated that there was another alternative—a third alternative between rationalism and subjectivism. For him, it was the way of Augustine, Calvin, and Luther. It was the way of beginning in faith, but proceeding with a regenerate mind, through scholarly study to understanding. It was a way that distinguished between the central saving message of Scripture and all of the difficult surrounding material that supports that message. It was a way that held in balance the objective and the subjective, the Word and the hearing of the Word. The union, for Berkouwer, was a personal one. According to the Augustinian tradition, God was known in his Word in a personal relationship that God initiated.

Berkouwer specifically rejected any notion that "Scripture *becomes* God's Word 'through its use.'" He knew that Scripture "does not and cannot derive its authority from the fact that *we* use it, not even when we use Scripture in faith."[225] The Augustinian stance of faith seeking understanding was, for him, not spiritualism, subjectivism, blind submission, or a sacrifice of the intellect.[226] Berkouwer plainly declared: "Faith in terms of a sacrifice of the intellect is a perversion of Christian faith and obedience."[227] A sacrifice of the intellect was a bowing before external authority. Christian faith in Scripture was rather "an inner conviction regarding the object and content of the faith to which man is called."[228] The object was Jesus Christ as Savior. This conviction was wrought by the Spirit as a person encountered Christ in the Word. Berkouwer affirmed: "In this way the Spirit conquers the dangers of an objectivism that misunderstands the Spirit and of a subjectivism that loses perspective on the reality of Christ."[229] For Berkouwer, "These dangers are overcome in the relationship between the heart and Scripture."[230] Berkouwer concluded *Holy Scripture* by citing one of his favorite biblical texts. He wrote:

> In spite of all differences, this road for the church is the same as that of the walkers to Emmaus. After they had recognized the stranger and encountered the living Lord just prior to the dispensation of the Spirit, they came to themselves and said to each other: 'Did not our hearts burn within us while he talked to us on the road, while he opened to us the Scriptures?' (Luke 24:32)."[231]

Berkouwer thus offered twentieth-century evangelicals the Reformation stance as an alternative between scholastic rationalism and liberal subjectivism. He proposed a Reformed doctrine of Scripture that was neither rationalistic nor subjectivistic. It was rather a view that correlated the divine message of Scripture with human faith in it. It was not a philosophical fideism, but a Reformation focus on the Bible's saving function.[232]

c. The Search for a Confessional Consensus in the United Presbyterian Church in the U.S.A.

A Neo-Orthodox Consensus in the 1940s and 1950s

Presbyterians were spared the full consequences of their 1927 moratorium on confessional interpretation by the rise to dominance of neo-orthodoxy in the 1930s, 1940s and 1950s. The theology of Karl Barth provided a core of consensus in the Presbyterian Church that guided the teaching, preaching, and even church school curriculum of the denomination. Conservatives, who still held to the old Princeton position, rejected Barth as simply another and more dangerous form of liberalism and ignored denominational literature.[233]

After a 1958 merger of the Presbyterian Church, U.S.A., with the smaller and more conservative United Presbyterian Church in North America, a move to create a new confessional position was launched.[234] A committee, headed by "new Princeton" professor Edward A. Dowey, Jr., proposed a Book of Confessions, adding some representative Reformed documents to Westminster, and a new, contemporary confession of faith, named The Confession of 1967.

The neo-orthodox view of Scripture was offered as a new theological consensus to the United Presbyterian Church in the U.S.A. in the original draft of the Confession of 1967. The still strong reaction against the Princeton theology and its view of inerrant autographs pushed the authors of the Confession of 1967 to the extreme of denying that the text of Scripture was the Word of God. Pressures to amend the original document came both from scholars desiring to make the statement harmonize with the sixteenth-century Reformation confessions and from conservatives who still held the Hodge-Warfield position.[235]

Reactions to Confessional Revision

Following the presentation of the proposed confessional changes to the church in 1965, a year of discussion with opportunity to offer amendments was declared. A special committee of fifteen ministers and laypersons was established by the General Assembly to receive and consider amendments. Two organizations of conservatives—one largely of clergy and the other of laypersons—were created, fought the new confessional stance, and continued to exert significant pressure in the church.

The primarily clerical conservative group was called Presbyterians United for Biblical Confession (PUBC). It numbered several thousand adherents. PUBC leaders insisted on change in five areas. The first area was clearer affirmation of the inspiration and authority of the Bible. In addition the group desired; affirmation of the deity of Christ equal to that of his humanity; stronger emphasis on the need for repentance and faith in the reconciliation between God and people; revision and the addition of other areas of concern in the section "Reconciliation in Society"; change and strengthening of the requirement of subscription to Scripture and confessions.

The revision committee of the church recognized and the General Assembly in 1966 approved fundamental changes in the areas suggested, with the exception of the subscription questions. The Bible was recognized not only as the words of humans, but equally as the word of God. Both the humanity and the deity of Christ were affirmed. The necessity for individual repentance was acknowledged along with the stress on the objective accomplishment of reconciliation through Christ's work. A greater emphasis on the Holy Spirit offered an implied correction of the social philosophy in Part II of the confession, which had seemed to imply that the Church could effect reconciliation simply by following Christ's example. Throughout, a greater balance was achieved and closer harmony with the other Reformed confessions was accomplished.[236]

The phrasing of the sections on the Bible and on international relations were cited by the lay conservative group, the Presbyterian Lay Committee, Inc., as reasons for urging Presbyterians to vote against the new confession. The committee, whose directors included prominent business and professional people, purchased full-page advertisements in leading American daily newspapers. Among other objections, the advertisements alleged a "humanizing" of the Bible in the new confession.[237] They appealed to laypersons to work for rejection of the proposed confessional change.

The few years preceding confessional revision saw widespread discussion of confessional matters in both the church and the secular press. One hundred and forty thousand copies of *The Proposal to Revise the Confessional Position of The United Presbyterian Church in the United States of America* were sold. Public debates were held, and extra days were set aside for presbyteries' consideration of the confessional proposals. The revision committee received over 1,100 letters, from two to twenty pages in length of proposed amendments to the confession.

Scripture in the Confession of 1967

Out of all the discussion a revised statement on the doctrine of Scripture was prepared.[238] The Reformation focus on Christ as the content of Scripture was restored. An interpretative balance was again achieved between the importance of the written record and the witness of the Holy Spirit. Both the divine saving message and the human cultural context were taken seriously. Unfortunately, however, the sources of the polarization engendered during the 1920s and 1930s were not really faced or overcome.

The General Assembly in 1966 submitted the revised "Confession of 1967" as part of the *Book of Confessions* to the vote of the 188 presbyteries of the denomination. Presbyterians United for Biblical Confession publicly supported the amended proposal for confessional change. Denominational leaders did so too, even though George Hendry of Princeton Seminary, one of the principal authors of the original draft of the "Confession of 1967," referred to the revised document as "a hodgepodge which attempts to combine the view-points of 1967 and 1647."[239] Hendry objected especially to statements about the Bible as a "rule of faith," which in his opinion distorted the original intention to represent the Bible only as a "means of grace."[240] Hendry contended in the October 1966, *Princeton Seminary Bulletin:* "It is plain that the revisions which have been introduced in this section of the Confession have been made for the purpose of conciliating those for whom the authority of the Bible is still bound up with the traditional view of the inspiration of the written word, and so of avoiding a revival of the controversy of which the Church had more than enough in the nineteen-twenties." He concluded ominously: "Division in the Church has been avoided at the cost of an unstable theological compromise."[241]

Substantially more than the required two-thirds of the presbyteries of the United Presbyterian Church voted approval of the confessional change. An unsuccessful last-minute attempt was made to bar the change as unconstitutional because the Westminster Larger Catechism had been deleted from the confessional standards of the church. After a ruling that the deletion was constitutional, the delegates to the 1967 General Assembly voted approximately four to one for this confessional change in the church's constitution.

Theological Shifts in the 1960s and 1970s

The revival of interest in and discussion of confessional theology was encouraging to many. Edward A. Dowey, chairperson of the revision committee, commented after the presbyteries approved confessional revision:

> Now we can look forward. Writing the confession, studying it, and moving through the slow work of adoption were laborious processes. But they made us talk together, even fight together for the first time in decades about what we believe and what we must do. We discovered that the bitterness of the 1920s is practically gone. Fundamentalism is as dead as the merely social gospel.[242]

Unfortunately for the denomination, subsequent events failed to confirm Dowey's optimistic assessment. Neither Fundamentalism, nor the social gospel were dead, and both showed renewed vitality in the 1960s and 1970s. In the 1960s concern for particular social problems made theology issue-oriented.[243] In the 1970s, liberation theology became a framework through which social concerns were dealt with theologically in the Presbyterian Church.[244] Among professional theologians, the neo-orthodox consensus, on which the Confession of 1967 was built, was declared dead by the mid-sixties.[245] Process theology, with its concern to correlate theology with modern science and human experience, rose to prominence.[246] Presbyterian seminaries began to be sensitized to the themes of liberation theology. Some also sought process-oriented faculty members. Liberation and process theologies increasingly were used as resources in discussion of denominational problems. Significant consideration of confessional matters nearly ceased soon after acceptance of the Confession of 1967. Rarely was the Book of Confessions invoked in denominational literature or public controversy in the church.

In the 1970s, the United Presbyterian Church was rent by disagreement over social issues and the effects of bureaucratic reorganization. Ironically, the Confession of 1967 was blamed for the restructuring and retreat from social involvement by former denominational bureaucrat John R. Fry in *The Trivialization of the United Presbyterian Church,* published in 1975. Fry contended that the choice of "reconciliation" as the central theme of the Confession of 1967 was the call of timid liberals for peace-at-any-price rather than theological confrontation of issues.[247] Fry's thesis was not widely accepted in the denomination. It was, nevertheless, symptomatic of the lack of a confessional consensus in the UPCUSA. Later events of the seventies evidenced the lack of any working agreement on theological method of biblical interpretation in the denomination. Controversies over ordination of women and the ordination of homosexuals found church people who were in opposition still holding positions very similar to those of the fundamentalist-modernist controversy of the early decades of this century.[248] Documents prepared in studying ordination of homosexuals identified four methods of biblical interpretation being used in the church. They corresponded roughly to: (A.) Old Princeton; (B.) Barthian; (C.) Liberation; (D.) Process methodologies.[249]

In 1978 two different task force reports to the denomination declared that the basic problem in the church was a lack of consensus on theological method and interpretation of the Bible. A Task Force on Theological Reflection reported to the General Assembly Mission Council that no theological consensus existed in the church and that church members felt that the situation "is one of tension and inability to respond to or deal with pressing questions and issues." The report continued, however, that seeking immediately to reestablish a consensus "is both unnecessary and impossible."[250] A second group, the Committee on Pluralism, formed two years earlier to study the sources of conflict in the church, offered its conclusions to the Advisory Council on Discipleship and Worship. The report asserted: "Of all the factors that contribute to divisiveness within our denomination, none is as pervasive or fundamental as the question of how the Scriptures are to be interpreted. . . . Widely differing views on the ways the Old and New Testaments are accepted, interpreted, and applied were repeatedly cited to us by lay people, clergy, and theologians as the most prevalent cause of conflict within our denomination today."[251]

Commissioners to the 1978 General Assembly of the United Presbyterian Church repeatedly expressed concern that there was no identifiable confessional position in the church. The phrase "the center of the church has collapsed" was often used. Delegates desired guidance in the effort to restore a confessional centrist position. The Assembly ultimately adopted a recommendation to establish a "theologically balanced" task force to study the diverse understandings of the authority and interpretation of the Bible now prevalent in the denomination.[252] A component of the study was to be an exploration of the "theological heritage in the Reformed tradition," and an analysis of the denomination's confessional standards. The task force was given three years to develop recommended guidelines for "a positive and not a restrictive use of Scripture in theological controversies."

The situation described in the United Presbyterian Church in the

U.S.A. had analogues in the late 1970s in most denominations in the country. Confusion and polarization over questions of biblical authority and interpretation were the order of the day.

d. Summary

Karl Barth was trained in liberalism, which stressed the continuity between God and mankind. He reacted against this because of his experience in the pastorate and a renewed study of the Bible. The writings of Kierkegaard helped him formulate the notion of an infinite qualitative difference between God and humankind. Through Kierkegaard he worked his way back to the Reformers, especially Calvin. The Bible was unified for Barth because all of it told the story of Christ. Barth accepted biblical criticism, but he did not make much use of it. He could use the texts just as they stood because their function was to provide a catalyst whereby a person, through reading or hearing the written Word, might experience an encounter with the living Word, Jesus Christ.

G. C. Berkouwer was trained in scholasticism, which stressed apologetics as the foundation of theology. He reacted against this as a result of his pastoral experience and a rediscovery of the Reformation tradition mediated by his Dutch Reformed predecessors Kuyper and Bavinck. Berkouwer stressed that the clarity of Scripture was in the message, not in the inerrancy of the individual words. He took seriously the biblical notion of error as deliberate intent to deceive. That was quite different from the biblical writers having a limited degree of knowledge, which did not limit God's ability to communicate his saving Word. For Berkouwer, as for the Reformers, the authority of the Bible was functional, not philosophical. Its purpose was not to provide a superior scientific knowledge for some theologians. The Bible was "useful" to bring persons into a saving relationship with God.

The Confession of 1967 in the United Presbyterian Church in the U.S.A. was an attempt at consensus by those committed to a Barthian approach to the Bible. Their aversion to the memory of the Princeton theology led the original authors of C'67 to the ahistorical position of denying that the text of Scripture was the Word of God. Pressures to amend that original document came both from scholars desiring to make the statement harmonize with the sixteenth-century Reformed confessions and from conservatives who still held the Hodge-Warfield position. The final document was a worthy modern version of the Reformation vision of the Bible.

But the Barthian synthesis was not a resolution, but an evasion of the historical issues of 1927 and before. The authors assumed that fundamentalism and liberalism were dead. Unfortunately that was not the case. The Confession of 1967 did not function significantly in the United Presbyterian Church. The conservatives distrusted it because it did not breathe the atmosphere of the Hodge-Warfield definitions. And the academic world of professional theologians concluded by 1967 that the Barthian era was over. New liberalisms in contemporary forms were already engaging major theological attention. The Presbyterians, confronted with an amorphous pluralism of theologies regarding the Bible, began in 1978 to seek confessional guidelines for interpretation. Tensions and confusion in the Presbyterian Church over issues rooted in questions of the authority and interpretation of the Bible had analogues in most denominations in the United States.

e. Notes

1. The outstanding biography of Barth is Eberhard Busch, *Karl Barth: His Life from Letters and Autobiographical Texts*, trans. John Bowden (Philadelphia: Fortress Press, 1976). Also of interest are the collected pieces from *The Christian Century*, published as *How I Changed My Mind* (Edinburgh: The Saint Andrew Press, 1969).
2. Cited in Busch, p. 34.
3. Cited in Busch, p. 34.
4. On Harnack see Wilhelm Pauck, "Adolf von Harnack," in *A Handbook of Christian Theologians* (Cleveland: World Publishing, 1965), pp. 86–111 and the specialized study by G. Wayne Glick, *The Reality of Christianity: A Study of Adolf von Harnack as Historian and Theologian*, Makers of Modern Theology, ed. Jaroslav Pelikan (New York: Harper & Row, 1967).
5. Karl Barth, *Theology and Church: Shorter Writings, 1920–1928*, trans. Louise Pettibone Smith (New York: Harper & Row, 1962), p. 238. (Hereafter, cited as Barth, *Theology and Church*.)
6. See Busch, pp. 44ff. On Herrmann's thought see T. H. L. Parker, *Karl Barth* (Grand Rapids, Mich.: Wm. B. Eerdmans, 1970), pp. 13ff. (Hereafter cited as Parker, *Barth*.)
7. On Hegel see *EP*, s.v. "Georg Wilhelm Friedrich Hegel"; Karl Lowith, *From Hegel to Nietzsche*, trans. David E. Green (New York: Doubleday, 1967); H. R. Mackintosh, *Types*

of Modern Theology: Schleiermacher to Barth (London: Collins, 1964; rep. 1937); and Barth's own chapter on Hegel in his *Protestant Theology in the Nineteenth Century* (Valley Forge: Judson Press), pp. 384–421. (Hereafter cited as Barth, *Protestant Theology.*) William W. Wells refers to this "Identity Principle" in an unpublished paper, "The Reveille That Awakened Karl Barth," pp. 1, 8. He cites Hans W. Frei, "The Doctrine of Revelation in the Thought of Karl Barth, 1909–1922: The Nature of Barth's Break with Liberalism" (Ph.D. dissertation, Yale University, 1956).
8. On Schleiermacher see *EP*, s.v. "Friedrich Daniel Ernst Schleiermacher"; Richard R. Neibuhr, "Friedrich Schleiermacher" in *A Handbook of Christian Theologians*, pp. 17–35; Mackintosh, pp. 64–101; Barth, *Protestant Theology*, pp. 425–473. For the phrase used in Schleiermacher see his *The Christian Faith*, ed. H. R. Mackintosh and J. S. Stewart, 2 vols. (New York: Harper & Row, 1963), pp. 12ff., 19ff., and *passim*. Though Barth spent most of his theological life trying to set theology back on a better footing than Schleiermacher, he still kept a picture of "the father of modern liberal Protestantism" hanging on his wall. When asked why, Barth replied, "Why not? He was a good Christian." See Arthur C. Cochrane, "The Karl Barth I Knew," in *Footnotes to a Theology: The Karl Barth Colloquium of 1972,*

ed. with an introduction by Martin Rumscheidt (n.p.: Corporation for the Publication of Academic Studies in Religion in
Canada, 1974), (hereafter cited as Rumscheidt, ed. *Footnotes*), p. 145.
9. See Wells, p. 1.
10. Mackintosh, p. 140. On Ritschl see *EP*,
s.v. "Albrecht Benjamin Ritschl"; A. Dur-
wood Foster, "Albrecht Ritschl," in *A Handbook of Christian Theologians*, pp. 49–67;
Barth, *Protestant Theology*, pp. 654–661; David L. Mueller, *An Introduction to the Theology
of Albrecht Ritschl* (Philadelphia: Westminster Press, 1969) (hereafter cited as Mueller, *Ritschl*); and Philip Hefner, *Faith and the
Vitalities of History: A Theological Study Based on
the Work of Albrecht Ritschl*, Makers of Modern Theology, ed. Jaroslav Pelikan (New
York: Harper & Row, 1966). (Hereafter cited as Hefner, *Faith and Vitalities*.)
11. Mueller, *Ritschl*, p. 35. The influence of
Hegel was mediated to Ritschl via Ferdinand Christian Baur (1792–1860), founder
of the Tübingen school of New Testament
scholarship. Applying the Hegelian dialectic to history, Baur saw the history of the
early church as continuing "the career of an
'essence,' or '*Grundprincip*,' of Christianity
(or of the church) which is simultaneously
the principle of being and of history, their
unity lying in the fact that the principle of
being drives towards actualization in and
through history, and consummately in
Christianity because in Christ (and in the
church) spirit and matter are perfectly
united," Hefner, *Faith and Vitalities*, p. 26.
Ritschl accepted this basic framework for
his historical investigations. Baur was "the
dominant key to Ritschl's intellectual development." See Hefner, *Faith and Vitalities*,
pp. 26 and 14. On Baur see Peter C. Hodg-
son, *The Formation of Historical Theology: A
Study of Ferdinand Christian Baur*, Makers of
Modern Theology, ed. Jaroslav Pelikan
(New York: Harper & Row, 1966).
12. Mueller, *Ritschl*, p. 35. See Hefner, *Faith
and Vitalities* chap. 1.
13. See Hefner, *Faith and Vitalities*, chap. 2,
and Mueller, *Ritschl*, p. 35.
14. See Mueller, *Ritschl*, pp. 57ff. For the
relation of Harnack to Ritschl's and Baur's
views see Glick, pp. 82ff. and 42ff. See also
Dan L. Deegan, "Albrecht Ritschl on the
Historical Jesus," *SJT* 15 (1962): 133–150
and Philip Hefner, "The Role of Church
History in the Theology of Albrecht
Ritschl," *CH* 33 (September 1964): 338–

355. In 1857 Ritschl announced his break
with the Tübingen School. He criticized
Baur for adopting Hegelian philosophical
categories, claiming that these depersonalized man and failed to take history in all its
full concreteness. What Ritschl (and Harnack who followed Ritschl's "new mediating
theology," which rejected not only Hegelian
speculation but all forms of speculation) did
not jettison was Baur's historical-critical
method. See Glick, pp. 43 and 46–47.
15. Parker, *Barth*, p. 15. Barth wrote: "Although Herrmann was surrounded by so
much Kant and Schleiermacher, the decisive thing for him was the christocentric impulse, and I learnt that from him," in Busch,
p. 45.
16. Barth, *Theology and Church*, p. 253f.
Ritschl turned to a strictly historical method
after he rejected Baur, partly because Baur
underestimated the historical importance
of Jesus for the beginning of Christianity.
God's revelation in Jesus to Ritschl was ethical and the experience of faith and salvation was a dynamic impulse leading to a
final "kingdom of ends." This served as the
hope and motivation for religious living.
See Glick, p. 48, and Mackintosh's chap. 5
on Ritschl, especially p. 149.
17. Parker, *Barth*, p. 15. The nature of revelation in the Schleiermacher-Ritschl-Herr-
mann tradition is well summarized by Frei:
that "God has indeed revealed himself to
man and that the relationship established in
his self-revelation is a given, indissoluble
state or condition, a sort of *nexus* of divine-
human contact. On the one hand one must
not endeavor to go beyond this *nexus* for
knowledge of God; on the other hand one
may rely altogether and unquestioningly
upon it as a point of departure, objective
and enduring through time, for all Christian life and for the inquiries of theology,"
p. 18, as cited by Wells, p. 7.
18. Cited in Busch, p. 51. Yet Barth was
uneasy about the work of Ernst Troeltsch
(1865–1923) of whom he later said that
"with him the doctrine of faith was on the
point of dissolution into endless and use-
less talk," *CD*, IV/1, 387. Thus Barth wrote:
"To the prevailing tendency of about 1910
among the younger followers of Albrecht
Ritschl I attached myself with passable conviction. Yet it was not without a certain
alienation in view of the issue of this school
in the philosophy of Ernst Troeltsch, in
which I found myself disappointed in re-

gard to what interested me in theology, although for the time being I did not see a better way before me," Karl Barth, "On Systematic Theology," *SJT* 14 (September 1961):225f.

19. See Busch, pp. 62–63.

20. Karl Barth, "Evangelical Theology in the Nineteenth Century" (hereafter cited as Barth, "Evangelical Theology") in *God, Grace and Gospel*, trans. James Strathearn McNab, *SJT* Occasional Papers, No. 8 (London: Oliver and Boyd, 1959), p. 58.

21. Cited in Busch, p. 81.

22. Cited in Busch, p. 85. See pp. 83ff. See also *The Beginnings of Dialectical Theology*, volume 1, ed. James M. Robinson, trans. Keith R. Crim and Louis De Grazia (Richmond: John Knox Press, 1968), p.41. (Hereafter cited as Robinson, ed., *Beginnings*.)

23. A few minutes before Barth stepped into the pulpit to deliver his first sermon in Geneva the postman brought him a gift from Herrmann—the fourth edition of his *Ethik*. Parker, *Barth*, p. 16.

24. See the short autobiographical section in *CD* II/1, 634 ff.

25. In a 1909 article Barth blamed "religious individualism" and "historical relativism" for the fact that theological graduates of the more liberal faculties of German universities—Heidelberg and Marburg—were less willing to enter fields of practical Christian service than were graduates of the more orthodox and pietistic schools: "It is far more difficult to undertake activity in the pulpit, at the sick-bed or in the clubhouse, if you are an alumnus of Marburg or Heidelberg rather than of Halle or Greifswald." Parker, *Barth*, p. 20. David L. Mueller explains: "Because liberalism accepted the tenet of the prevailing historiography that there were no absolutes in history and therefore none in the realm of revelation or religion, it became necessary to treat the biblical witness to revelation in the same manner as all other similar phenomena in the history of religion. Barth summed up the outcome of this approach as follows: 'Religion knows only individual values; history knows only general truths,' " *Karl Barth*, Makers of the Modern Theological Mind, ed. Bob E. Patterson (Waco, Tex.: Word Books, 1975; rep. 1972), p. 18. Hereafter cited as Mueller, *Barth*.) Barth's article was "Moderne Theologie und Reichsgottesarbeit," *Zeitschrift für Theologie und Kirche* 19, no. 4 (1909): 319.

26. Cited in Busch, p. 97.

27. Reprinted in Karl Barth, *The Word of God and the Word of Man*, trans. Douglas Horton (New York: Harper & Row, 1957), p. 34. (Hereafter cited as *WGWM*.)

28. *WGWM*, p. 43.

29. *WGWM*, p. 45. Barth commented on Schleiermacher: "In the very places where the theology of the Reformation had said 'the Gospel' or 'the Word of God' or 'Christ' Schleiermacher, three hundred years after the Reformation, now says, religion or piety.... Schleiermacher reversed the order of this [the Reformers'] thought. What interests him is the question of man's action in regard to God," *Protestant Theology*, pp. 458, 459.

30. Karl Barth, *The Epistle to the Romans*, trans. Edwyn C. Hoskyns (London: Oxford University Press, 1968; rep. 1933), "The Preface to the First Edition," p. 1. (Hereafter cited as Barth, *Romans*.) Also translated by Keith R. Crim in Robinson, ed., *Beginnings*, p. 61. Cf. H. Bouillard, *Karl Barth*, 3 vols. (Paris: Aubier, 1957), 1: 90–95.

31. Barth, *Romans*, p. 1.

32. See the reactions and reviews of Barth, *Romans* in Robinson, ed., *Beginnings*, chap. 2. Cf. Parker, *Barth*, pp. 35ff.; Busch, pp. 92–109; and Hans Urs von Balthasar's discussion of the first edition in his *The Theology of Karl Barth*, trans. John Drury (New York: Doubleday, 1972; rep. 1971), pp. 48–52. The debate on the historical-critical method was the focus of the 1923 debates between Barth and Harnack. See H. Martin Rumscheidt, *Revelation and Theology: An Analysis of the Barth-Harnack Correspondence of 1923* (Cambridge: Cambridge University Press, 1972). Also in Robinson, ed., *Beginnings*, chap. 4 (selected parts). In 1879 Harnack had given his *Habilitationsschrift* (inaugural address) at Leipzig in defense of the thesis: "There is no other method for the exegesis of Holy Scripture than the grammatical-historical." See Glick, p. 80.

33. See Parker, *Barth*, p. 38. On Gogarten see Theodore Runyon, Jr., "Friedrich Gogarten," in *A Handbook of Christian Theologians*, pp. 427–444.

34. Barth, *Romans*, "Preface to the Second Edition," p. 4. See also Karl Barth, *Credo* (New York: Charles Scribner's Sons, 1962), p. 185. (Hereafter cited as Barth, *Credo*.) Barth, commenting in his preface, compares the exegesis of Jülicher with Calvin (p. 7) and laments over the inadequacy of prevailing university training in equipping young men to understand the Bible that they might preach (p. 9). See also Busch, pp. 117–125 and von Balthasar, pp. 52–57.

35. Barth, *Romans*, p. 10. See also Bouillard, 1:107–113; and Arthur C. Cochrane, *The Existentialists and God* (Dubuque, Iowa: University of Dubuque Press, 1950), pp. 31ff.

36. See Parker, *Barth*, p. 42. On Barth and Kierkegaard see Egon Brinkschmidt, *Søren Kierkegaard und Karl Barth* (Neukirchen: Neukirchener Verlag, 1971), especially pp. 64ff.

37. Barth, "Evangelical Theology," p. 68.

38. See for example, Barth, *Romans*, p. 49. See Busch, pp. 119ff.

39. Barth, *Romans*, p. 29. See Parker, *Barth*, p. 44.

40. See Barth, *Romans*, pp. 36, 57, 69, 91ff., 225, and *passim*. See also Parker, *Barth*, p. 46. On Barth's "crisis" or "dialectical" theology see Mackintosh, pp. 266ff.; T. F. Torrance, in the "Introduction" to Barth, *Theology and Church*, p. 22, and his *Karl Barth: An Introduction to His Early Theology, 1910–1930* (London: SCM Press, 1962); von Balthasar, pp. 57ff. Herbert Hartwell writes: "Since in Jesus Christ God has said to man both Yes and No, Barth then felt that, to interpret this Yes and this No and further the No by the Yes, the divine truth, which in itself is not divided, had to be expressed dialectically," *The Theology of Karl Barth: An Introduction* (Philadelphia: Westminster Press, 1964), p. 12.

41. Barth, *Romans*, p. 69.

42. See Mueller, *Barth*, pp. 25ff. See Busch, pp. 138ff. Barth said the term *Dialectical theology* was used to describe him and the developing school as early as 1922 (Busch, p. 144). Barth with Gogarten, Thurneysen, and Georg Merz established the periodical *Zwischen den Zeiten* (Between the Times) in 1922 to express their views. The name was from an article of Gogarten partially reprinted in Robinson, ed., *Beginnings*, pp. 277–282.

43. *WGWM*, p. 206.

44. Barth, *Romans*, p. 422. Barth frequently made reference to John the Baptist as "witness" and especially to the painting of the Crucifixion by Matthias Grunewald in which John the Baptist stands off to the right pointing at the Crucified with his "prodigious index finger." See *CD* I/1, 112, 262 (all references to I/1 are to the recent translation by G. W. Bromiley); I/2, 125; "The

Humanity of God" (1956) in *God, Grace and Gospel*, p. 31. This picture hung above Barth's desk. It is reproduced as the frontispiece in Busch's biography.

45. See Busch, p. 123.

46. See *WGWM*, p. 195f. and James D. Smart, *The Divided Mind of Modern Theology: Karl Barth and Rudolf Bultmann, 1908–1933* (Philadelphia: Westminster Press, 1967), p. 49. Wells traces the implications of this in terms of the "identity principle" inherited from the "rational theology" of the liberals, pp. 10–15.

47. James D. Smart, trans., *Revolutionary Theology in the Making Barth-Thurneysen Correspondence, 1914–1925* (Richmond: John Knox Press, 1964), (Hereafter cited as Smart, *Revolutionary Theology.*) In a letter to Eduard Thurneysen, June 8, 1922, Barth wrote: "Calvin is a cataract, a primeval forest, a demonic power, something directly drawn from Himalaya, absolutely Chinese, strange, mythological.... I could gladly and profitably set myself down and spend all the rest of my life just with Calvin," p. 101.

48. Cited in Busch, p. 143 (also in Smart, *Revolutionary Theology*, p. 82, from a letter to Thurneysen on January 22, 1922).

49. Cited in Busch, p. 143.

50. Cited in Busch, pp. 145–146. Illuminating in this regard are the letters between Barth and his colleague in the quest, Eduard Thurneysen. See their correspondence in Smart, *Revolutionary Theology*.

51. See Barth's Introduction to Heinrich Heppe, *Reformed Dogmatics*, trans. G. T. Thomson (London: George Allen & Unwin, Ltd., 1950), p. v.

52. Heppe, p.v.

53. Heppe, p. vi.

54. Cited in Busch, p. 155. See also Bouillard, 1:120–133.

55. See Mueller, *Barth*, pp. 33–34. Parker points out, however, that the section "The Word of God as Revelation" made no reference to Jesus Christ. Instead Barth dealt with a study of the sixteenth-century Reformation view of the relationship between revelation and the words of Scripture. See *Barth*, p. 66.

56. See Barth's statement: "The Word of God is not only speech, but address," as translated in Mueller, *Barth*, p. 35.

57. Parker, *Barth*, p. 67.

58. *CD* I/1, xiii. See also Mueller, *Barth*, pp. 35–37; Wells, p. 15.

59. Parker, *Barth,* p. 69.

60. Now reprinted in the Pittsburgh Reprint Series No. 2, ed. Dikran Y. Hadidian (Pittsburgh: Pickwick Press, 1975), being the translation of Ian W. Robertson (London: SCM Press, 1960). The reprint has a preface by Arthur C. Cochrane. (Hereafter cited as *Anselm.*)

61. *Anselm,* p. 11.

62. *CD* II/1, 4. See also *How I Changed My Mind,* p. 43; Busch, pp. 205–209.

63. See G. C. Berkouwer, *The Triumph of Grace in the Theology of Karl Barth,* trans. Harry R. Boer (Grand Rapids, Mich.: Wm. B. Eerdmans, 1956), p. 42, note 50, and Cochrane's "Preface," in *Anselm,* p. 128. (Hereafter cited as Berkouwer, *Triumph of Grace.*)

64. *Anselm,* p. 18. See also Bouillard, 1:134–148.

65. *Anselm,* p. 22; cf. p. 34.

66. *Anselm,* p. 22.

67. See Parker, *Barth,* pp. 71–72; Mueller, *Barth,* p. 39.

68. As Parker puts it, the tract of country between faith and understanding "lies between two events which have occurred—the grammatical comprehension of the message and the grasp and affirmation of its truth. This tract of country is the realm of theology, of faith seeking understanding. And because faith itself also has the character of knowledge and its object is the true Word of Christ in the proclamation of the Church, the search is a practicable proposition, theology is possible," pp. 72–73. Barth saw the task of theology as asking about the nature of the truth believed. See *Anselm,* pp. 27ff.

69. *Anselm,* p. 34.

70. See Parker, *Barth,* pp. 76–77.

71. See Parker, *Barth,* p. 78. Barth criticized Reformed orthodoxy because its dogmatics were "too closely bound up with a form not taken from the thing itself but from contemporary philosophies." Dogmatics for Barth must learn not from orthodoxy but from "biblical exegesis in the actual Reformers' school," Heppe, p. vi.

72. See *CD* I/1, 12.

73. See *Anselm,* pp. 35ff. On Barth and philosophy see Joseph C. McLelland, "Philosophy and Theology—A Family Affair (Karl and Heinrich Barth)" in Rumscheidt, ed., *Footnotes,* pp. 30–52. McLelland argues that the Platonic-Kantian base of Barth's thought (in the first edition of *Romans*)

"provides a constant, a permanent element in Barth's thought," p. 32.

74. Cited in Busch, p. 210.

75. Mueller, *Barth,* p. 40. Barth wrote: "Between our views, concepts and words, and God as their object, there exists, on the basis of the revelation of God, the relationship of analogy, or similarity, of partial correspondence and agreement. On the basis of this similarity there is a true human knowledge of God and therefore the human knowledge of God reaches its goal," *CD,* II/I, 227. See 225ff.

76. von Balthasar sees the concept of analogy growing stronger throughout the *Church Dogmatics* and becoming the "central theme in his treatment of creation (1945), human nature (1948), and providence (1950)," p. 88. von Balthasar concludes that Barth has finally come to a complete acceptance of the *analogia entis,* G. C. Berkouwer objected to this analysis. See *Triumph of Grace,* pp. 186ff.

77. *CD* I/1, 243–244. See Berkouwer, *Triumph of Grace,* p. 181. In *CD* I/1, 241, Barth wrote: "In faith and confession the Word of God becomes a human thought and a human word, certainly in infinite dissimilarity and inadequacy, yet not in total alienation from its real prototype, but a true copy for all its human and sinful perversion, an unveiling of it even as its veiling."

78. *CD* I/1, 244. For "men can know the Word of God because and insofar as God wills that they know it. . . ." I/1, 196. To Barth for both "man generally" and "religious man," the "epistemological order" must be from God to human. Without "preceding revelation there can be no faith," I/1, 213.

79. *CD* I/1, 244. The "analogy of faith" for Barth stood in strong contrast to the Roman Catholic *analogia entis*—the "analogy of being"—which Barth referred to as "the invention of Antichrist" (*CD* I/1, xiii.) and as "the cardinal dogma of Roman Catholicism" (*CD* II/1, 243). Barth was vehement against all such "natural theology" that sought to provide any natural knowledge of God outside God's revelation in Jesus Christ. For Barth, only through God can God be known. See II/1, 47–48, 85, 129ff. This was at the heart of his controversy with Emil Brunner (1889–1966). See *Natural Theology,* trans. P. Fraenkel (London: Geoffrey Bless, Centenary Press, 1946). His Gifford Lectures at the University of Aberdeen in

1937 and 1938 on John Knox's Confession of Faith (The Scots Confession, 1560) were to remind "natural theology" of its absolute opponent—"the knowledge of God and the service of God according to the teaching of the Reformation," See *The Knowledge of God and the Service of God According to the Teaching of the Reformation*, trans. J. L. M. Haire and Ian Henderson (London: Hodder and Stoughton, 1938), Lecture I, p. 8. Barth's use of terms such as *analogia fidei, relationis, attributionis, extrinseca*, and *operationis*—"all these expressions are for Barth antithetical to the idea of *analogia entis*," Berkouwer, *Triumph of Grace*, p. 193. See also Horst Georg Pohlmann, *Analogia entis oder Analogia Fidei?* (Göttingen: Vandenhoeck & Ruprecht, 1965) and Mueller, *Barth*, pp. 86–91; Hartwell, pp. 48–53.

80. *CD* I/1, xiii.

81. Wells, p. 16. Barth pointed this out himself in his speech upon being awarded the Sonning Prize: "A Thank-You and a Bow—Kierkegaard's Reveille," trans. Eric Mosbacher, in *Fragments Grave and Gay*, ed. Martin Rumscheidt (London: William Collins & Sons, 1971), p. 98. (Hereafter cited as Barth, *Fragments*.)

82. See Gustaf Wingren, *Theology in Conflict: Nygren, Barth, Bultmann*, trans. Eric H. Wahlstron (Philadelphia: Muhlenberg Press, 1958), p. 23, and J. Heywood Thomas, "Christology of Søren Kierkegaard and Karl Barth," *Hibbert Journal* 53 (April 1955):281, as cited in Wells, p. 16.

83. Barth, *Fragments*, p. 98.

84. *CD* I/1, 295, 117ff.

85. *CD* I/1, 132. This speaking is not a "symbol" (vs. Tillich). Barth also contrasts this understanding of the Word with Schleiermacher's "divine Word," which was "the spirit in all men, i.e., in all those united in the Church," I/1, 62; see also 136, 141, 150, and Barth's statement: "The Word of God is the word that God spoke, speaks, and will speak, in the midst of all men." See Karl Barth, *Evangelical Theology: An Introduction*, trans. Grover Foley (London: Collins, 1969); rep. 1963), pp. 22–23. (Hereafter cited as Barth, *Evangelical Theology*.)

86. *CD* I/1, 119; cf. 137, 157. See also Karl Barth, *Dogmatics in Outline*, trans G. T. Thompson (New York: Harper & Brothers, 1959), p. 17. In the face of Adolf Hitler's National Socialist State and the errors of the "German Christians," the German Evangelical Church adopted the Barmen Declaration in May, 1934. Barth was responsible for its theses, one of which read: "Jesus Christ, as he is attested for us in Holy Scripture, is the one Word of God which we have to hear and which we have to trust and obey in life and death." It rejected as "false doctrine" any other source of the Church's proclamation "apart from and besides this one Word of God, still other events and powers, figures and truths, as God's revelation." See the text in Arthur C. Cochrane, *The Church's Confession under Hitler* (Philadelphia: Westminster Press, 1962), pp. 238ff. See also Busch, pp. 245–248.

87. *CD* I/1, 88–124.

88. *CD* I/1, 120.

89. *CD* I/1, 121. The three forms were mutually interrelated. This was the Unity of the Word of God. Barth claimed that this threefold form is the only analogy to the doctrine of the triunity of God: "In the fact that we can substitute for revelation, Scripture and proclamation the names of the divine persons Father, Son and Holy Spirit and *vice versa.*"

90. *CD* I/1, 91. For Barth's views on preaching see *CD* I/1, 51f., 56, 69f.; I/2, 743–58. He comments on the impossibility of preaching in *WGWM* (cf. *CD* I/2, 750). His later views are found in *Prayer and Preaching* (London: SCM Press, 1964), pp. 67–98.

91. *CD* I/1, 95. In this context Barth quotes Luther: "We rightly call the pastor's or preacher's word God's Word," I/1, 96. Yet the sovereign decision about preaching is always God's. Of the human word "when and where it pleases God, it is God's own Word," I/1, 72. Barth said: "When the Gospel is preached God speaks: there is no question of the preacher revealing anything by means of preaching . . . is due to its divine subject," *Prayer and Preaching*, (London: SCM Press, 1964), p. 67. When there was success in preaching it was not human success but a "divine victory" through the work of the Holy Spirit. See *CD* I/2, 751; *CD* I/2, 248. See 247ff. The Spirit is "the subjective reality of revelation," I/2, 203ff. See also *CD* I/2, 239.

92. See *CD* I/1, 47ff. The task of dogmatics is "to investigate and say at each given point how we may best speak of God, revelation and faith to the extent that human talk about these things is to count as Church proclamation," I/1, 85.

93. *CD* I/1, 102.

94. *CD* I/1, 101. Barth points out that *canon* means "rod, then ruler, standard, model, assigned district." In the church's first three hundred years it was used for "that which stands fast as normative"—the *regula fidei*, the church's doctrine of faith. From the fourth century onwards it became specialized to mean Holy Scripture or the list of biblical books the Church recognized as normative.

95. *CD* I/1, 106.

96. *CD* I/1, 107. This it did by virtue of its content. See *CD* I/1, 108. God's Word dramatically confronted the hearer in Scripture, I/1, 109.

97. *CD* I/1, 117. The biblical writers witness to a "fixed event," which is identical with Jesus Christ, *CD* I/1, 116.

98. See *CD* I/1, 110. Barth contrasts his view with that of the orthodox Lutherans, who developed "a doctrine of the *efficacia Verbi divini etiam ante et extra usum*. The Word of God preached and written has its own divine power no matter what may be its effect on those who hear or read." David Hollaz (1648–1713) said the Bible is God's saving Word "in the same way as the sun gives warmth even behind clouds, or as a seed of grain has force even in the unfruitful earth, or as the hand of a sleeping man is a living hand."

99. *CD* I/1, 117. The interrelatedness of preaching and Scripture is stressed again when Barth reminds that: "(1) proclamation is real proclamation, i.e., the promise of future revelation, only as the repetition of the biblical witness to past revelation, and (2) the Bible is real witness, i.e., the factual recollection of past revelation, only in its relation to this past revelation attested in it," I/1, 117.

100. *CD* I/1, 118.

101. *CD* I/1, 118.

102. *CD* I/2, 537.

103. *CD* I/2, 535.

104. *CD* I/2, 457.

105. Barth, *Evangelical Theology*, p. 45. On the Canon see I/2, 473ff. Barth makes the point that "when we adopt the Canon of the Church we do not say that the Church itself, but that the revelation which underlies and controls the Church, attests these witnesses and not others as the witnesses of revelation and therefore as canonical for the Church," p. 474.

106. *CD* I/2, 536. Barth saw the Reformers as stressing not only inspiration in the writing of Scripture by the Holy Spirit but also the Spirit's work of illumination in certifying Scripture for the reader: "As Luther insisted in innumerable passages the word of Scripture given by the Spirit can be recognised as God's Word only because the work of the Spirit which has taken place in it takes place again and goes a step further, i.e., becomes an event for its hearers or readers. How else will God be recognised except by God Himself?" I/2, 521.

107. *CD* I/2, 506. See also I/2, 535.

108. *CD* I/2, 485.

109. *CD* I/2, 492, Cf. 487. Cf. Barth's *Evangelical Theology*, p. 29. On the unity of the Old and New Testament witness see pp. 30ff. The biblical witnesses differ from others in the history of the church solely because of the function of their divinely given office. See I/2, 491, 486. We have been helped throughout this section by the thorough study of Howard John Loewen, "Karl Barth and the Church Doctrine of Inspiration (An Appraisal for Evangelical Theology)," 2 vols. (Ph.D. dissertation, Fuller Theological Seminary, 1976). See p. 562.

110. *CD* I/2, 504ff. See Loewen's extensive examination of these passages, pp. 124–182.

111. *CD* I/2, 505.

112. *CD* I/2, 514ff. See Loewen's discussion, pp. 186–273.

113. *CD* I/2, 505.

114. *CD* I/2, 517. See 517–518.

115. *CD* I/2, 517. Barth saw the Reformers as restoring a more proper biblical emphasis that the work of the Spirit "goes a step further, i.e., becomes an event for its hearers or readers." See *CD* I/2, 521.

116. See *CD* I/2, 517, 518.

117. *CD* I/2, 520.

118. *CD* I/2, 522–523.

119. *CD* I/2, 523. The reference is to Calvin's sermon on 1 Timothy 4:1f. in *CR* 53, 338.

120. *CD* I/2, 523. Cf. 524.

121. *CD* I/2, 525.

122. *CD* I/2, 526.

123. *CD* I/2, 492. See Barth's comments on the historical-critical approach in the preface to his second edition of the *Romans* commentary, pp. 6ff.

124. *CD* I/2, 492.

125. *CD* I/2, 494.

126. *CD* I/2, 492. Barth continued: "And we can only ask about revelation when we

surrender to the expectation and recollection attested in these texts."
127. *CD* I/2, 495.
128. In the preface to the second edition of *Romans*, p. 8.
129. *CD* I/2, 532–533.
130. *CD* I/2, 520. Barth was careful to make clear, however, that in Calvin "neither a mantico-mechanical nor a docetic conception of biblical inspiration is in the actual sphere of Calvin's thinking." Like Luther's statements, Calvin's suffered from a loss of their context and were thus distorted in the period of Protestant orthodoxy. The seventeenth-century doctrine of inspiration Barth labels "false doctrine," I/2, 525.
131. *CD* I/2, 521.
132. Barth, *Evangelical Theology*, p. 33. Cf. p. 30: "Each prophet also spoke within the limits and horizons of his time, its problems, culture, and language." See also Loewen, p. 570.
Barth spoke of a "twofold indirectness" of "creatureliness" and "secularity." These refer to Luther's view that the indirectness in God's communicating with humans is caused by human (1) creatureliness and (2) sinfulness (*WA* 18, 633 line 7; see *The Bondage of the Will*, trans. J. I. Packer and O. R. Johnston, p. 101.) I/1, 167. For Barth "the incarnation means entry into this secularity. We are in this world and are through and through secular. If God did not speak to us in secular form, He would not speak to us at all. To evade the secularity of His Word is to evade Christ." *CD* I/1, 192.
133. *CD* I/2, 530. In this sense Scripture stands as a witness to Christ. The written Word directs its readers to the living Word. Therefore scriptural statements must not be directly equated with the reality of the revelation in Jesus Christ. See *CD* I/1, 165–66; I/2, 457, 499ff., 530, etc.
134. *CD* I/2, 529. Cf. I/2, 532: "This text in all its humanity, including all the fallibility which belongs to it, is the object of this work and miracle." Colin Brown writes "The idea that the coming to us of the revealing Word in fallible human words appears to be a parallel to Barth's contention that, in order to be a true incarnation, Christ must assume *fallen* human nature (I/2, 147–155)," *Karl Barth and the Christian Message* (London: Tyndale Press, 1967), p. 559.
135. *CD* I/2, 533. Barth was very pointed in his wish to carry through his "distinction

between inspiration and therefore the divine infallibility of the Bible and its human fallibility." He continued:

"We cannot expect or demand a compendium of solomonic or even divine knowledge of all things in heaven and earth, natural, historical and human, to be mediated to the prophets and apostles in and with their encounter with the divine revelation, possessing which they have to be differentiated not only from their own but from every age as the bearers and representatives of an ideal culture and therefore as the inerrant proclaimers of all and every truth. They did not in fact possess any such compendium. Each in his own way and degree, they shared the culture of their age and environment, whose form and content could be contested by other ages and environments, and at certain points can still appear debatable to us." CD I/2, 508.

136. *CD* I/2, 509. Barth attacked the seventeenth-century doctrine of inspiration because he said

"its supranaturalism is not radical enough. The intention behind it was ultimately only a single and in its own way very 'naturalistic' postulate: that the Bible must offer us a *divina et infallibilis historia;* that it must not contain human error in any of its verses; that in all its parts and the totality of its words and letters as they are before us it must express divine truth in a form in which it can be established and understood; that under the human words it must speak to us the Word of God in such a way that we can at once hear and read it as such with the same formal dignity as those of philosophy and mathematics. The secular nature of this postulate showed itself plainly in the assumption that we may freely reproach the good God if it is not fulfilled, threatening Him with distrust, scepticism and atheism—a threat which was no less freely carried out in the following generations, which men became convinced that the postulate could not be fulfilled." (I/2, 525).

137. *CD* I/2, 508. See also George H. Kehm, "The Bible, Orthodoxy, and Karl Barth," *Pittsburgh Perspective* 4, no. 1 (March 1963):25.
138. *CD* I/2, 509. James Barr relates John

Baillie's account of a discussion he had with Barth. For several hours in his study Baillie had pressed Barth to admit that Methuselah had not actually lived 969 years. As Barr relates it: "Barth was, as always, contemptuous of the conservative approach which would have sought to 'prove' the biblical figure 'right' by arguing from evidences, internal or external. But this did not mean that he would admit that Methuselah had not lived for 969 years. What possible valid theological reason could there be for anyone to want to know that this figure was not correct? What use could it be to theology to declare that this figure was a legendary one? At the end of several hours of conversation, Baillie told me, Barth had still not been persuaded to admit that Methuselah had not in fact lived for 969 years," *Fundamentalism* (Philadelphia: Westminster Press, 1978; rep. 1977), pp. 218–219.

139. *CD* I/2, 531.

140. *CD* I/2, 485. See also Loewen, p. 574. It is God in the sovereignty of his Spirit who freely and miraculously causes fallible human words to become again the Word of God, I/2, 502ff. See also I/2, 506, 514 and his chapter "Freedom in the Church," 661–740.

141. *CD* I/2, 712. For Barth Scripture even in "its apparently most debatable and least assimilable parts, is in all circumstances truer and more important than the best and most necessary things that we ourselves have said or can say." *CD* I/2, 719.

142. *CD* I/2, 715. Barth was well aware, however, that there was no such thing as exegesis without presuppositions. See *Credo*, p. 177. For this " 'freedom from presuppositions' is a presupposition exactly like any other," p. 178. See "The Problem of Subjectivity in Interpretation" among Bultmann, Fuchs and Barth in James D. Smart, *The Interpretation of Scripture* (London: SCM Press, 1961), pp. 44–53. (Hereafter cited as Smart, *Interpretation.*)

143. *CD* I/2, 725. See above on Anselm and the object of faith.

144. *CD* III/2, ix. In 1948 Barth felt that "the time does not yet seem to have arrived when the dogmatician can accept with a good conscience and confidence the findings of his colleagues in Old and New Testament studies."

Barth's extensive and intensive exegetical labors are obvious throughout his works. The *Registerband* of the German edition of his *Dogmatik* isolates approximately 15,000 biblical references and over 2,000 instances of exegetical discussions. This was only a fraction of Barth's total exegetical production when all of his commentaries, sermons, articles, etc. are considered. See James A. Wharton, "Karl Barth as Exegete and His Influence on Biblical Interpretation," *Union Seminary Quarterly Review* 28, no. 1 (Fall 1972):6.

145. See above note 32.

146. In "Biblical Questions, Insights, and Vistas," *WGWM*, p. 60. Johann August Ernesti was a German Lutheran who taught in Leipzig first as a classicist, then as a theologian. See M&S, and *ODC*, s.v. "Johann August Ernesti."

147. *WGWM*, pp. 60–61. Italics are Barth's.

148. *WGWM*, pp. 60–61. Barth's italics.

149. Parker, *Barth*, p. 33. See Paul Minear, "Barth's Commentary on the Romans, 1922–1972, or Karl Barth vs. The Exegetes," in Rumscheidt, ed., *Footnotes*, pp. 11ff. Barth wrote: "Biblical religious history has the distinction of being in its essence, in its inmost character, neither religion nor history —not religion but reality, not history but truth," *WGWM*, p. 66.

Barth was influenced at this time (the above address was delivered in April, 1920) by the work of Franz Overbeck (1837–1905), a New Testament scholar and church historian at the University of Basel (1870–1897) who was also a friend of the philosopher Friedrich Nietzsche (1844–1900). In reviewing Overbeck's *Christentum und Kultur*, Barth summarized Overbeck's point: "Relentlessly he puts us before the choice: If Christianity, then not history; if history, then not Christianity." See Thomas W. Ogletree, *Christian Faith and History: A Critical Comparison of Ernst Troeltsch and Karl Barth* (Nashville: Abingdon Press, 1965), pp. 84–87. See Barth *Theology and Church*, p. 61. See also Hans Schindler, *Barth und Overbeck; ein Beitrag zur Genesis der dialektischen Theologie im Lichte der gegenwartigen theologischen Situation* (Gotha: Leopold Klotz, 1936); Busch, p. 115f.; and Barth, *Romans, passim.*

Barth's early views are at the base of his later thoughts on "history" as *"Geschichte"* —"the reality of history christologically understood, history as determined by the sequence of encounters between God and man which has come to a decisive climax in the person of Jesus Christ" and *"Historie"*— "the notion of history which is characteristic of modern historical thinking—history in the 'historicist' sense," Ogletree, p. 192. See his whole chap. 11.

150. See Minear, p. 8. See for example Barth's discussions of Bultmann's "demythologizing" in III/2, 443ff. and Cullmann's view of Christ and time in III/2, 481f., 443. James Wharton acknowledges that Barth's exegesis has often been found "offensive, in virtually the full range of meanings that word can have," p. 5. Brevard Childs mentions Barth's relation to the biblical theology movement and reports that usually biblical theologians as well as the older liberals dismissed Barth's exegesis as "precritical," *Biblical Theology in Crisis* (Philadelphia: Westminster Press, 1970), p. 110. (Hereafter cited as Childs, *Crisis.*) James Barr's comments typify this assessment when he describes "the great theologian's alienation from the world of biblical scholarship" as "painful" and speaks of Barth's "embarrassment with historical criticism," *Old and New in Interpretation* (London: SCM Press, 1966), pp. 96, 92. Childs claims this is a misunderstanding of Barth, however—see *Crisis,* p. 110 and his "Karl Barth as Interpreter of Scripture," in *Karl Barth and the Future of Theology: A Memorial Colloquium Held at the Yale Divinity School January 28, 1969,* ed. David L. Dickerman (New Haven: Yale Divinity School Association, 1969), p. 34.

151. *CD* I/2, 494. Barth said, "All relevant, historical questions must be put to the biblical texts, considered as witnesses in accordance with their literary form." See also Walter Lindemann, *Karl Barth und die Kritische Schriftauslegung* (Hamburg: Herbert Reich Evangelischer Verlag, 1973).

152. David H. Kelsey notes that throughout Barth's discussion of reconciliation and "The Royal Man" (IV/2) "as Barth expressly and repeatedly points out, he authorizes his theological proposals by appeal to the New Testament narratives just as they stand in the received texts. He takes them as the expressions of a tradition having a particular point of view and not as the sources for historical reconstruction either of earlier traditions out of which the final tradition may have been fashioned or of 'what really happened,'" *The Uses of Scripture in Recent Theology* (Philadelphia: Fortress Press, 1975), p. 45.

153. *CD* I/2, 494. To approach the canon "critically as a collection of sources," to

probe "what is perhaps behind the texts" was to miss "the true nature and character of the writings" in Barth's eyes. This was what had been missed "for over a hundred years," *CD* I/2, 493. See also Barth's discussion "Exegesis and the Science of History" in *Credo,* pp. 189–191. There Barth says that since the Bible is a human document the scientific method of history can be of service in the investigation and exposition of Scripture texts "except that it must not raise the claim to be *the* method for true exegesis! It can be no more than a definite procedure which can be applied to the Bible among other methods, and which, precisely in its 'atheistic' character, can perform the service of removing impurities," p. 188.

154. Barth, *Credo,* p. 177.

155. See Wharton, p. 6. This meant that the two Testaments were an inseparable unity for Barth. Jesus Christ was the center of God's revelation in both Testaments. See *CD,* I/2, 481ff., 103, 72, 119. Barth claimed that theology was "threatened by a cancer in its very bones" when it preferred to neglect the classic rule: *Novum Testamentum in Vetere latet, Vetus in Novo patet:* the New Testament is concealed within the Old, and the Old Testament is revealed by the New," *Evangelical Theology,* p. 31. This led Barth to some rather strained allegorical interpretations. See Smart, *Interpretation,* pp. 125ff.

156. See Wharton, pp. 6–7, quoting a personal letter from Barth's son Professor Markus Barth. Examples of Barth's changes in exegesis can be seen in his treatments of John 1:14, 2 Corinthians 3, Ephesians 5:32 (the Greek term *mysterion*), and in his interpretations of the sacraments, especially baptism.

157. See *CD* I/2, 509. Because the biblical authors wrote with all their limitations, there was no "more or less complete and thoroughgoing theological system" in the Scriptures. The Bible was not a "systematic" book. Barth believed that a valid biblical theology could never be a "system in the sense of Platonic, Aristotelian or Hegelian philosophy," I/2, 483.

158. *CD* I/2, 509.

159. John H. Gerstner, "Warfield's Case for Biblical Inerrancy," (hereafter cited as Gerstner, "Warfield"), in *God's Inerrant Word,* ed. John Warwick Montgomery (Minneapolis: Bethany Fellowship, 1974), p. 122.

160. G. C. Berkouwer, *Een Halve Eeuw Theologie: Motieven en Stomingen van 1920 tot* *heden* (Kampen: J. H. Kok, 1974), p. 31. See the English translation by Lewis B. Smedes under the title, *A Half Century of Theology: Movements and Motives* (Grand Rapids, Mich,: Wm. B. Eerdmans, 1977), pp. 26–27 (hereafter cited as Berkouwer, *Half Century*).

161. The only introduction to Berkouwer's life and thought available in English is Lewis B. Smedes's article, "G. C. Berkouwer," in Philip Edgcumbe Hughes, ed., *Creative Minds in Contemporary Theology* (Grand Rapids, Mich.: Wm. B. Eerdmans, 1966), pp. 63–97.

162. An excellent interview with Berkouwer is found in the volume *Gesprekken Over Rome-Reformatie*, ed. G. Puchinger (Delft: W. D. Meinema, 1965), pp. 299–319. (Hereafter cited as Puchinger, ed. *Gesprekken*).

163. Berkouwer, *Half Century*, p. 32.
164. Puchinger, ed., *Gesprekken*, p. 303.
165. *Het Probleem der Schriftcritiek* (Kampen: J. H. Kok, 1938).
166. Berkouwer, *Half Century*, pp. 137–138.
167. All of them have been published in English by Eerdmans as one-volume works with some of the more recent larger works being abridged.
168. *HS.* See, e.g., reviews by J. I. Packer, *Eternity* (December 1975), pp. 45–46, and C. C. Ryrie, *Bibliotheca Sacra* (January 1976), pp. 64–65.
169. *HS*, p. 9.
170. *HS*, p. 33.
171. *HS*, pp. 54–55 and 46.
172. *HS*, p. 26, citing *GD*, p. 415.
173. *HS*, p. 125.
174. *HS*, pp. 19–20.
175. *HS*, p. 19.
176. *HS*, p. 22.
177. *HS*, p. 258.
178. *HS*, p. 228.
179. *HS*, p. 228.
180. *HS*, p. 227.
181. *HS*, p. 133.
182. *HS*, pp. 294–295. For the Reformed tradition that Berkouwer continued, the Bible was a functional, not a philosophical book. Its function was to present Christ as humanity's Savior. Human conversion to Christ and commitment to Scripture were caused, not by human reason, but by the Holy Spirit. Not a rational grasp of evidences, but a personal response to God in Christ moved people to accept Scripture as authoritative. The focus of Christian theologians, for Berkouwer, should remain the divine content of Scripture, not its hu-

man form. The Bible's function, for him, was to give people encouragement in salvation not information about science. Therefore, the human forms in which Scripture's message came could be examined by scholarship. Scientific findings were not considered by Berkouwer to be an obstruction to faith, but an occasion for understanding more fully the ways in which God had revealed himself through human means.

183. *HS*, p. 129.
184. *HS*, p. 129.
185. *HS*, p. 128.
186. *HS*, p. 130.
187. *HS*, p. 137. At the same time, Berkouwer stated firmly his Augustinian faith-commitment to Scripture's authority: "The discussion about Scripture, its God-breathed character and authority, cannot take place via a coerced concession to a new hermeneutical method and the 'occasion' of science. It can only take place in the perspective of that trustworthiness of Scripture which enables us to abandon ourselves in complete trust to its authority and to preach its message." *HS*, p. 138.
188. *HS*, p. 274.
189. *HS*, p. 275.
190. *HS*, p. 275.
191. *HS*, p. 181.
192. *HS*, p. 182.
193. *HS*, p. 183.
194. *HS*, p. 183.
195. *HS*, pp. 175–176.
196. *HS*, p. 176.
197. *HS*, p. 180.
198. *HS*, p. 187.
199. *HS*, p. 187.
200. *HS*, p. 188.
201. *HS*, p. 194.
202. *HS*, pp. 187–188.
203. *HS*, p. 234.
204. *HS*, p. 109.
205. *HS*, p. 205.
206. *HS*, pp. 335–336.
207. *HS*, p. 207.
208. *HS*, p. 216.
209. *HS*, p. 237.
210. *HS*, p. 238.
211. *HS*, p. 347.
212. *HS*, p. 333.
213. *HS*, p. 142.
214. *HS*, p. 142, note 9.
215. Berkouwer, *Half Century*, pp. 120–121.
216. Ibid., p. 157.
217. Ibid., p. 175. Berkouwer comments: "The reformers never talked as if one first

accepted and agreed to something and thereafter believed and trusted."

218. *HS*, p. 32.
219. *HS*, p. 32.
220. *HS*, p. 45.
221. *HS*, p. 45.
222. *HS*, p. 339.
223. *HS*, p. 11. Indeed, according to Berkouwer: "Faith is not and cannot be based on a theoretical reflection on what, according to our insight, must be the nature of the divine revelation and on which ways and forms it must have come to us in order to be the guarantee of certainty. The way of Christian faith is not one of a possibility becoming more clear on its way to the reality of certainty, but a subjection to the gospel, to the Christ of the Scriptures; and from this alone can a reflection on Holy Scripture proceed," *HS*, p. 33.
224. *HS*, p. 366.
225. *HS*, pp. 317–318.
226. *HS*, pp. 349–351.
227. *HS*, p. 351.
228. *HS*, p. 352.
229. *HS*, p. 366.
230. *HS*, p. 366.
231. *HS*, p. 366.
232. Even before the publication of Berkouwer's *Holy Scripture,* John Timmer, an American Christian Reformed pastor, had noted the transition from ontological to functional thinking in Berkouwer's theology: "Berkouwer's theology, in other words, is functional; it is relational. It is this that makes Berkouwer an influential theologian." See John Timmer, "G. C. Berkouwer: Theologian of Confrontation and Co-Relation," *The Reformed Journal* (December 1969):19.
233. Examples of treatments of Barth by those who defended the essential correctness of the Old Princeton position include Cornelius Van Til, *The New Modernism* (Philadelphia: Presbyterian and Reformed Publishing, 1947); and Gordon H. Clark, *Karl Barth's Theological Method* (Philadelphia: Presbyterian and Reformed Publishing, 1963). Conservatives who stayed within the Presbyterian Church, U.S.A., often looked, for theological leadership, to those who had separated from the denomination and had become associated with Westminster Seminary and the Orthodox Presbyterian Church.
234. See *Report of the Special Committee on a Brief Contemporary Statement of Faith: To the* *177th General Assembly (of) The United Presbyterian Church in the United States of America, May, 1965* (Philadelphia: Office of the General Assembly, 1965), p. 7.
235. For background on the scholarly concerns see Brian A. Gerrish, "The Confessional Heritage of the Reformed Church," *McCormick Quarterly* 19 (January 1966): 120–134; and, Arthur C. Cochrane, *Reformed Confessions of the 16th Century: Edited, with Historical Introductions* (Philadelphia: Westminster Press, 1966), pp. 11–31.
236. For further analysis of the changes and their significance see Thomas M. Gregory, "The Confession of 1967 as Revised," *The Presbyterian Outlook,* (November 21, 1966): 6–7.
237. "Lay Committee Advertisements Assail Proposed Confession," *Presbyterian Life* (February 1, 1967), p. 23, quotes the advertisement: "How far the authors would go in humanizing the Bible can be realized in this excerpt from the new Confession: 'The Scriptures given under the guidance of The Holy Spirit, are nevertheless the words of men, conditioned by the language, thought forms, and literary fashions of the places and times in which they were written.'"
238. *The Constitution of the United Presbyterian Church in the United States of America, Part I: Book of Confessions* (Philadelphia: Office of the General Assembly, 1967), 9.22–9.30.
239. George S. Hendry, "The Bible in the Confession of 1967," *Princeton Seminary Bulletin* 60 (October, 1966):24. (Hereafter cited as Hendry, "Bible.")
240. Hendry, "Bible," p. 21. See also Edward A. Dowey, Jr. *A Commentary on the Confession of 1967 and an Introduction to "The Book of Confessions"* (Philadelphia: Westminster Press, 1968), p. 103.
241. Hendry, "Bible," p. 24.
242. "Now We Can Look Forward," *Presbyterian Life* (April 1, 1967), p. 24.
243. For recent assessments of theological change see: Deane William Ferm, "American Protestant Theology, 1900–1970," *Religion in Life* 44, no. 1 (Spring 1975):59–72; Kenneth Cauthen, "The Present and Future of Theology," *Religion in Life* 45 (Autumn 1976):308–317; Thor Hall, "Does Systematic Theology have a Future?" *The Christian Century* (March 17, 1976), pp. 253–256; and Jack Rogers, "The Search for System: Theology in the 1980s" (Fuller Theological Seminary, 1978).

244. The first book in English to attract significant attention for Latin American liberation theology was Rubem Alves's Princeton Theological Seminary dissertation, *A Theology of Human Hope* (Washington, D.C.: Corpus Publications, 1969). Perhaps the best brief introduction to the movement is Jose Miguez Bonino, *Doing Theology in a Revolutionary Situation* (Philadelphia: Fortress Press, 1975). See also: Gustavo Gutierrez, *A Theology of Liberation: History, Politics and Salvation*, trans. and ed. by Sister Caridad Inda and John Eagleson (Maryknoll, N.Y.: Orbis Books, 1973); and Juan Luis Segundo S.J., *The Liberation of Theology*, trans. John Drury (Maryknoll, N.Y.: Orbis Books, 1976). On relating Latin American liberation theology to the situation in the United States see: John C. Bennett, "Fitting the Liberation Theme into Our Theological Agenda," *Christianity and Crisis* 37, no. 12 (July 18, 1977):164–169; Robert McAfee Brown, "The Rootedness of All Theology," *Christianity and Crisis* 37, no. 12 (July 18, 1977);170–174; and Beverly Wildung Harrison, "The 'Theology in the Americas' Conference," *Christianity and Crisis* 35 (October 27, 1975):251–254.

Regarding emphases in the United Presbyterian Church, see, e.g., *Minutes of the General Assembly of the United Presbyterian Church in the United States of America, Part I: Journal* New York: Office of the General Assembly, 1976), p. 584: "It is *recommended* that the 188th General Assembly (1976) direct its committee on Theology of Liberation and Renewal to enter into discussions with the Council of Theological Seminaries as to the best methods of introducing programs on liberation theology in each of the United Presbyterian Seminaries."

245. Robert H. King, in a review of *Ernst Troeltsch and the Future of Theology*, ed. John P. Clayton (Cambridge: Cambridge University Press, 1976) in *The Christian Century* (March 9, 1977), p. 234, remarked: "The appearance of a book linking the name of Ernst Troeltsch with 'the future of theology' is yet one more indication of the breakdown of a theological consensus that prevailed in academic circles from the early '40s to the mid-'60s. No longer is the theology of revelation in one form or another setting the terms for discussion. Instead issues which this theology sought to circumvent—social relativism, religious pluralism, the role of tradition, the place of metaphysics in theol-

ogy—have once more come to the fore." See also Ferm, p. 69.

246. A helpful and concise discussion of the development of process theology in the U.S.A. is found in John B. Cobb, Jr. and David Ray Griffen, *Process Theology: An Introductory Exposition* (Philadelphia: Westminster Press, 1976). See also Randolph Crump Miller, *The American Spirit in Theology* (Philadelphia: United Church Press, 1974). For recent changes see the articles in *John Cobb's Theology in Process*, eds. David Ray Griffen and Thomas J. J. Altizer (Philadelphia: Westminster Press, 1977). David Tracy, who identifies his own methodology, which he calls "revisionist," with the methodology or process theology notes that this theology is a continuation of "the critical task of the classical liberals and modernists in a genuinely post-liberal situation," *Blessed Rage for Order* (New York: Seabury Press, 1975), p. 32. See also David Tracy, "John Cobb's Theological Method: Interpretation and Reflections," in Griffen and Altizer, pp. 25–26.

247. John R. Fry, *The Trivialization of The United Presbyterian Church* (New York: Harper & Row, 1975), p. 3.

248. See case studies on these denominational issues written by Jack Rogers, "The Kenyon Case" and "Should the United Presbyterian Church Ordain Homosexuals?" available through Intercollegiate Case Clearing House, Boston, Massachusetts 02163.

249. See *Blue Book, Part I, 190th General Assembly (1978) of the United Presbyterian Church in the United States of America* (New York: Office of the General Assembly, 1978), "The Church and Homosexuality," pp. D–59 to D–100. The report tended to mix liberation and process literature together in support of (C) and (D) but the principal motifs were discernible. (Hereafter cited as *Blue Book.*)

250. *Blue Book*, C–49 and C–50.

251. *Blue Book*, E–10. The committee stated further: "It is our opinion that until our denomination examines this problem, we will continue to be impeded in our mission and ministry, or we will spiral into a destructive schism."

252. *Minutes of the General Assembly of the United Presbyterian Church in the United States of America, Part I: Journal* (New York: Office of the General Assembly, 1978), p. 40. The mandate reads

"That the General Assembly ... authorize the Advisory Council on Discipleship and Worship to engage in a study of the diverse ways of understanding biblical authority and interpreting the Scripture, which are now prevalent in our denomination; that components of the study include an exploration of our theological heritage in the Reformed tradition and an analysis of the confessional standards that guide our interpretation of Scripture; and that a result be recommended guidelines for a positive and not a restrictive use of Scripture in theological controversies.

"That the Advisory Council on Discipleship and Worship make an interim report to the 192nd General Assembly (1980) and final report with recommendations to the 193rd General Assembly (1981)."

f. Selected Bibliography

Busch, Eberhard. *Karl Barth: His Life from Letters and Autobiographical Texts,* translated by John Bowden. Fortress Press, 1976.

Hartwell, Herbert. *The Theology of Karl Barth: An Introduction.* Westminster Press, 1964.

Kelsey, David H. *The Uses of Scripture in Recent Theology.* Fortress Press, 1975.

Loewen, Howard John. "Karl Barth and the Church Doctrine of Inspiration." Ph.D. dissertation. Fuller Theological Seminary, 1976.

Mueller, David L. *Karl Barth.* Makers of the Modern Theological Mind, edited by Bob. E. Patterson. Word Books, 1975 (rep. 1972).

Parker, T. H. L. *Karl Barth.* Wm. B. Eerdmans, 1970.

Rogers, Jack B. "A Third Alternative: Scripture, Tradition and Interpretation in the Theology of G. C. Berkouwer." In *Scripture, Tradition, and Interpretation: Essays Presented to Everett F. Harrison,* edited by W. Ward Gasque and William Sanford LaSor. Wm. B. Eerdmans, 1978.

Smart, James D. *The Interpretation of Scripture.* SCM Press, 1961.

Smedes, Lewis B. "G. C. Berkouwer." In *Creative Minds in Contemporary Theology,* edited by Philip Edgcumbe Hughes. Wm. B. Eerdmans, 1966.

Torrance, Thomas F. *Karl Barth: An Introduction to His Early Theology, 1910–1930.* SCM Press, 1962.

Wharton, James A. "Karl Barth as Exegete and His Influence on Biblical Interpretation." *Union Seminary Quarterly Review* 28 no. 1 (Fall 1972):5–13.

Conclusions: Recovering the Foundations of the Central Christian Tradition

The church doctrine of Scripture has a different foundation and focus than that depicted in much of American theology during the last one hundred years. Twin facts that have distorted our vision are: (1) that Scottish realism was philosophical orthodoxy when American academia began; and (2) that Turretin was chosen as the text in theology at Princeton in 1812. Those realities symbolize the way in which American conservatives' view of the authority and interpretation of the Bible has been skewed in a post-Reformation, scholastic direction. Conservatives were unable to meet the rise of scientific criticism of the Bible constructively. They had located Scripture's authority in scientifically inerrant words. And they believed they could interpret the Bible without taking seriously its historical and cultural context. The result was a fundamentalist-modernist controversy from the 1890s to 1930s that scarred every denomination. Unfortunately, we still live with the implications of that era. Major denominations such as the United Presbyterian and the Missouri Synod Lutheran have been polarized by factions still taking sides on the debates of the twenties. And that large, vaguely defined group of Americans known as evangelicals are continually in controversy over the nature of the Bible and the methods of its interpretation.

The foundation of the doctrine of Scripture in the early church needs to be recovered. For early Christian teachers, Scripture was wholly authoritative as a means of bringing people to salvation and guiding them in the life of faith. This authority was affirmed to them by the Holy Spirit working in their hearts. With that faith as a sure foundation, they proceeded to understand the Bible by using the best scholarly tools available to them. The interpretation of the Bible was influenced by the understanding of its saving purpose. Scripture was not used as a sourcebook for science. Early theologians accepted God's accommodated style of communication. God, like a good father or mother, adopted the thought and speech of children in order to relate to them. Theology was meant to be a practical discipline, enabling people to understand God's relationship to them.

Teachers sometimes misused the Bible in the attempt to erect a speculative synthesis of all knowledge. The allegorical method, for example, was designed to ensure the unity of the Bible as a Christian book. But when each verse was treated independently, the exegete could go into flights of fancy. Gradually, the church moved to the more sober grammatical-historical method. Again, an atomistic treatment of biblical texts sometimes led to literalism and legalism. Both allegorism and literalism, however, were significantly modified in the early church by the understanding of accommodation and the context provided by the early creeds, which centered Scripture in its saving message.

These common foundations on which early interpretation of the Bible rested experienced certain modifications at the Middle Ages. Thomas Aquinas, using the rediscovered Aristotle, attempted a synthesis of reason and faith. His followers developed theology as a speculative, highly technical science. Theology now claimed to be the Queen of the Sciences, laying the basis on which all human knowledge was to be built. This Scholasticism became the official theology of the medieval church. In reaction to this academic approach some monks in the Middle Ages took refuge in mysticism. They urged faith alone and decried all but a devotional study of the Bible. Faith, stimulated by Scripture, was intended to lead to an experience of mystical union with God.

Between the extremes of rationalism and mysticism lay the common tradition from the early church. Developed by Augustine and reasserted by Anselm, this tradition argued that the Bible could be approached directly. One needed neither rational demonstration nor mystical experience as a foundation for certitude. The Bible evidenced its own authority, and the Holy Spirit affirmed that authority in people's hearts. With that innate faith, theologians proceeded to understanding using scholarship.

The Protestant Reformers, Luther and Calvin, adopted this Augustinian method. In interpreting the Bible, they used the scholarly resources of Renaissance humanism, including printed editions of the church fathers. They rejected the excesses of allegorism and embraced the grammatical-historical method for finding the natural meaning of the biblical author. They did not expect the Bible to inform them about current science. They knew that Scripture's center was Christ and his salvation, and that theology was a practical discipline, teaching about the life of faith. Like the early church theologians, Luther and Calvin acknowledged that God had condescended to use imperfect human forms of communication, infallibly to accomplish God's perfect purpose of bringing salvation. The historical and cultural context of God's revelation needed to be investigated for insights into the particular applications of God's saving actions. But the message, not the milieu, was normative for later generations.

Luther and Calvin tried to recover the common foundation for biblical authority and interpretation laid in the early church. They sought an Augustinian middle way between rationalistic scholasticism on the one hand and spiritualistic sectarianism on the other. They attempted to hold the Word and the Spirit together. But their immediate followers, under pressure from Roman Catholics and Unitarians, could not maintain the balance of their Reformation mentors. Melanchthon and Beza imposed a medieval, Aristotelian mold on their master's work as they rigidified the Reformers' insights into a system. An era of post-Reformation scholasticism followed in the seventeenth century and has been carried on into the present.

For post-Reformation scholasticism, the authority of Scripture was no longer located in its function of mediating salvation, but rather in its asserted form of scientifically inerrant words. Theology was increasingly a technical, theoretical science. The concept of accommodation was lost. Theological propositions now claimed a one-to-one correspondence with the thoughts of God. The historical and cultural context of biblical statements faded in importance as Scripture was treated as a compendium of logical propositions.

The impact of revolutions in science and philosophy pushed seventeenth-century Reformed scholastics into increasingly rigid positions. They reacted with fear to the rise of biblical criticism. Francis Turretin exemplified these attitudes in Geneva.

The Princeton theologians in nineteenth-century America adopted Turretin's method as their model of a theological system. They further buttressed their conservative stance with the interpretative principles of Scottish common sense philosophy. Thus armed, they hoped to hold an impregnable fortress against every new thought that might invade theology. They intended to preserve the Christian and the Reformation mainstream—what they actually did was divert a large segment of American Protestantism into a static and stagnant tributary.

Until the historical record is straightened out, we will continue to repeat the mistakes of the past. Major American denominations like the Missouri Synod Lutherans and the United Presbyterians have a critical need to clarify their theological roots. Presbyterians need to go back and rethink the decision of 1927 which left the Princeton theology's interpretation of history unchallenged, but asked the denomination to look in other directions. A church, if it is to be vital, must define what its "essential and necessary doctrines" are. And it must identify the range of acceptable principles of interpretation. Presbyterians should reaffirm their commitment to the foundations of the central Christian tradition regarding the authority and interpretation of the Bible. And they should recover the focus of their distinctive Reformed heritage. Presbyterians need to do theology in a flexible, responsible, contemporary style in a pluralistic church and world. But they should also do it under the guidance of their confessions. Not every theological method, from either the right or the left, should be able to call itself Reformed. Neither should one narrow theological method be able to claim exclusive rights to be called Presbyterian. There should be some middle ground, some spectrum on which there is consensus.

Presbyterians need a confessional centrist theology that takes the authority of the Bible as seriously as did the Princeton theologians and Barth. They equally need a method of interpreting Scripture that takes scholarly study of the Bible's historical context and our own cultural setting as seriously as do, for example, liberation and process theologies.

The same tensions that have confronted denominations like the Presbyterians have especially affected those persons in all denominations who think of themselves as evangelicals. The vast multitude of forty million evangelicals often invoked by the media represent a wide variety of theological traditions from Pentecostalism to scholasticism. If evangelicalism is to be a creative and renewing force in American life, it must come to historical clarity concerning the authority and interpretation of the Bible. Until now, the still heavy hand of the Princeton theology has prevented that from happening. Because of its pervasive influence in American evangelical theology, few have dared to challenge the Princeton theology's post-Reformation scholastic theory concerning the Bible. Those who self-consciously hold to the old Princeton position continue to assert that it is the historic Christian, and Reformed approach. The large majority of evangelicals are far from the Princeton position in their actual use of Scripture. Most thoughtful evangelicals, for example, accept the usefulness of responsible biblical criticism.* But because they have

---

*John R. W. Stott, "Are Evangelicals Fundamentalists?" *Christianity Today* (September 8, 1978), p. 45, comments: "My personal belief is that, in the original meaning of these terms, every true evangelical should be both a fundamentalist and a higher critic. In fact I wrote that very thing in a small book as long ago as 1954." On page 46, Stott goes on to distinguish fundamentalist and evangelical by saying: "The fundamentalist emphasizes so strongly the divine origin of Scripture that he tends to forget that it also had human authors who used sources, syntax, and words to convey their message, whereas the evangelical remembers the double authorship of Scripture."

no alternative theory, they continue to hold to the Hodge-Warfield apologetic, which was designed to deny any scholarly contextual study. Evangelicals are often reminded of the dangers of liberal subjectivism. In a sincere desire to avoid that extreme, they claim the rationalistic scholasticism of old Princeton as their theory, even though their practice is far from it.

The purpose of this study has been to document the fact that an historically accurate and biblically sound alternative exists. There is a middle way between rationalism and subjectivism. There is a third alternative that has been practiced by Origen and Chrysostom, by Augustine and Anselm, by Luther and Calvin, by the Westminster Divines and many nineteenth-century Reformed evangelicals. It is the way of accepting the Bible in faith, but proceeding through scholarly study to understanding. It is a way that distinguishes between the central saving message of Scripture and all of the difficult surrounding material that supports that message. It is a way that holds in balance the objective and the subjective, the Word and the Spirit.

The Reformation denominations and evangelicals everywhere need to begin to apply this Augustinian alternative to modern issues. Then we can avoid the unacceptable alternatives of being merely reactionary or just following fads. We can move forward by utilizing insights from our past. Commitment to the authority of the Bible's content, and sensitivity to the accommodated character of its language used by the early church theologians and Protestant Reformers offers a positive direction. Ancient principles must be applied using all that we can learn about language and cultures from the human and social sciences of the twentieth century. The authority and applicability of the Bible is not enhanced by defending inadequate theories from past sciences and philosophies. We can begin to do theology creatively, constructively, and in accord with the ancient creeds and the Reformation confessions. But most of all, we can be assured of a doctrine of Scripture that is faithful to the function or purpose of Scripture—"that you may believe that Jesus is the Christ, the Son of God, and that believing you may have life in his name" (John 20:31).

Appendix: Reformed Confessions on Scripture

The texts of the Reformed Confessions are from *Reformed Confessions of the 16th Century*, edited with Historical introductions, by Arthur C. Cochrane (Philadelphia: Westminster Press, 1966). Used by permission.

The text of the Westminster Confession of Faith is from *The Confession of Faith of the Assembly of Divines at Westminster: From the Original Manuscript Written by Cornelius Burges in 1646*, edited by S. W. Carruthers. Published by the Presbyterian Church of England in 1946. Used by permission.

The Text of The Confession of 1967 is taken from *The Constitution of The United Presbyterian Church in the United States of America, Part I: Book of Confessions*, 2d ed. (New York: Office of the General Assembly, 1970). Used by permission.

Zwingli's Sixty-Seven Articles of 1523

The following sixty-seven articles and opinions, I, Huldreich Zwingli, confess that I preached in the venerable city of Zurich on the basis of the Scripture which is called *theopneustos* [i.e. inspired by God], and I offer to debate and defend them; and where I have not now correctly understood the said Scripture, I am ready to be instructed and corrected, but only from the aforesaid Scripture.

I. All who say that the Gospel is nothing without the approbation of the Church err and slander God.

XV. For our salvation is based on faith in the Gospel and our damnation on unbelief; for all truth is clear in Him.

The Ten Theses of Berne, 1528

I. The holy, Christian Church, whose only Head is Christ, is born of the Word of God, abides in the same, and does not listen to the voice of a stranger.

II. The Church of Christ makes no laws or commandments without God's Word. Hence all human traditions, which are called ecclesiastical commandments, are binding upon us only in so far as they are based on and commanded by God's Word.

The Tetrapolitan Confession of 1530

Chapter I. Of the Subject-Matter of Sermons

And hence, as was necessary, while Satan was undoubtedly plying his work, so that the people were very dangerously divided by conflicting sermons, considering what St. Paul writes, that "divinely inspired Scripture is profitable for doctrine, that where there is sin it may be detected and corrected, and every one may be instructed in righteousness, that the man of God may be perfect, furnished for every good work," — we also, influenced and induced to avoid all delay, not only from the fear of God, but from the certain peril to the state, at length enjoined our preachers to teach from the pulpit nothing else than is either contained in the Holy Scriptures or hath sure ground therein. For it seemed to us not improper to resort in such a crisis whither of old and always not only the most holy fathers, bishops and princes, but also the children of God everywhere, have always resorted—viz., to the authority of the Holy Scriptures.

The First Confession of Basel, 1534

XII. Against the Error of the Anabaptists

Finally, we desire to submit this our confession to the judgment of the divine Biblical Scriptures. And should we be informed from the same Holy Scriptures of a better one, we have thereby expressed our readiness to be willing at any time to obey God and His holy Word with great thanksgiving.

The First Helvetic Confession of 1536

1. Concerning Holy Scripture

The holy, divine, Biblical Scripture, which is the Word of God inspired by the Holy Spirit and delivered to the world by the prophets and apostles, is the most ancient, most perfect and loftiest teaching and alone deals with everything that serves the true knowledge, love and honor of God, as well as true piety and the making of a godly, honest and blessed life.

2. Concerning the Interpretation of Scripture

This holy, divine Scripture is to be interpreted in no other way than out of itself and is to be explained by the rule of faith and love.

5. The Purpose of Holy Scripture and That to Which It Finally Points.

The entire Biblical Scripture is solely concerned that man understand that God is kind and gracious to him and that He has publicly exhibited and demonstrated this His kindness to the whole human race through Christ His Son. However, it comes to us and is received by faith alone, and is manifested and demonstrated by love for our neighbor.

The Lausanne Articles of 1536

I. Holy Scripture teaches only one way of justification, which is by faith in Jesus Christ once for all offered, and holds as nothing but a destroyer of all the virtue of Christ anyone who makes another satisfaction, oblation, or cleansing for the remission of sins.

V. The said Church acknowledges no ministry except that which preaches the Word of God and administers the sacraments.

VII. Further this same Church denies all other ways and means of serving God beyond that which is spiritually ordained by the Word of God, which consists in the love of himself and of one's neighbour. . . .

The Geneva Confession of 1536

1. The Word of God

First we affirm that we desire to follow Scripture alone as rule of faith and religion, without mixing with it any other thing which might be devised by the opinion of men apart from the Word of God, and without wishing to accept for our spiritual government any other doctrine than what is conveyed to us by the same Word without addition or diminution, according to the command of our Lord.

The Confession of Faith Used in the English Congregation at Geneva, 1556

IV. But this Church which is visible and seen by the eye has three tokens or marks whereby it may be known. First, the Word of God contained in the Old and New Testament which, since it is above the authority of the same Church and alone is sufficient to instruct us in all things concerning salvation, it is left for all degrees of men to read and understand, for without this Word no Church, council or decree can establish any point concerning salvation.

The French Confession of Faith, 1559

Art. II. As such this God reveals himself to men; firstly, in his works, in their creation, as well as in their preservation and control. Secondly, and more clearly, in his Word, which was in the beginning revealed through oracles, and which was afterward committed to writing in the books which we call the Holy Scriptures.

Art. IV. We know these books to be canonical, and the sure rule of our faith, not so much by the common accord and consent of the Church, as by the testimony and inward illumination of the Holy Spirit, which enables us to distinguish them from other ecclesiastical books upon which, however useful, we can not found any articles of faith.

Art. V. We believe that the Word contained in these books has proceeded from God, and receives its authority from him alone, and not from men. And inasmuch as it is the rule of all truth, containing all that is necessary for the service of God and for our salvation, it is not lawful for men, nor even for angels, to add to it, to take away from it, or to change it. Whence it follows that no authority, whether of antiquity, or custom, or numbers, or human wisdom, or judgments, or proclamations, or edicts, or decrees, or councils, or visions, or miracles, should be opposed to these Holy Scriptures, but, on the contrary, all things should be examined, regulated, and reformed according to them. And therefore we confess the three creeds, to wit: the Apostles', the Nicene, and the Athanasian, because they are in accordance with the Word of God.

The Scots Confession, 1560

Chapter XIX. The Authority of the Scriptures

As we believe and confess the Scriptures of God sufficient to instruct and make perfect the man of God, so do we affirm and avow their authority to be from God, and not to depend on men or angels. We affirm, therefore, that those who say the Scriptures have no other authority save that which they have received from the Kirk are blasphemous against God and injurious to the true Kirk, which always hears and obeys the voice of her own Spouse and Pastor, but takes not upon her to be mistress over the same.

The Belgic Confession of Faith, 1561

Art. III. Of the Written Word of God

We confess that this Word of God was not sent nor delivered by the will of man, but that *holy men of God spake as they were moved by the Holy Ghost,* as the Apostle Peter saith. And that afterwards God, from a special care which he has for us and our salvation, commanded his servants, the Prophets and Apostles, to commit his revealed Word to writing; and he himself wrote with his own finger the two tables of the law. Therefore we call such writings holy and divine Scriptures.

Art. V. Whence Do the Holy Scriptures Derive Their Dignity and Authority

We receive all these books, and these only, as holy and canonical, for the regulation, foundation, and confirmation of our faith; believing, without any doubt, all things contained in them, not so much because the Church receives and approves them as such, but more especially because the Holy Ghost witnesseth in our hearts that they are from God, whereof they carry the evidence in themselves. For the very blind are able to perceive that the things foretold in them are fulfilling.

Art. VII. The Sufficiency of the Holy Scriptures to Be the Only Rule of Faith

We believe that these Holy Scriptures fully contain the will of God, and that whatsoever man ought to believe unto salvation, is sufficiently taught therein. For since the whole manner of worship which God requires of us is written in them at large, it is unlawful for any one, though an Apostle, to each otherwise than we are now taught in the Holy Scriptures: *nay, though it were an angel from heaven,* as the Apostle Paul saith. For since it is forbidden *to add unto or take away any thing from the Word of God,* it doth thereby evidently appear that the doctrine thereof is most perfect and complete in all respects. Neither may we compare any writings of men, though ever so holy, with those divine Scriptures; nor ought we to compare custom, or the great multitude, or antiquity, or succession of times or persons, or councils, decrees, or statutes, with the truth of God, for the truth is above all: for all men are of themselves liars, and more vain than vanity itself. Therefore we reject with all our hearts whatsoever doth not agree with this infallible rule, which the Apostles have taught us, saying, Try the spirits whether they are of God; likewise, *If there come any unto you, and bring not this doctrine, receive him not into your house.*

The Second Helvetic Confession, 1566

Chapter I. Of The Holy Scripture Being The True Word of God

CANONICAL SCRIPTURE. We believe and confess the canonical Scriptures of the holy prophets and apostles of both Testaments to be the true Word of God, and to have sufficient authority of themselves, not of men. For God himself spoke to the fathers, prophets, apostles, and still speaks to us through the Holy Scriptures.

And in this Holy Scripture, the universal Church of Christ has the most complete exposition of all that pertains to a saving faith, and also to the framing of a life acceptable to God; and in this respect it is expressly commanded by God that nothing be either added to or taken from the same.

SCRIPTURE TEACHES FULLY ALL GODLINESS. We judge, therefore, that from these Scriptures are to be derived true wisdom and godliness, the reformation and government of churches; as also instruction in all duties of piety; and, to be short, the confirmation of doctrines, and the rejection of all errors, moreover, all exhortations according to that word of the apostle, "All Scripture is inspired by God and profitable for teaching, for reproof," etc. (II Tim. 3:16–17). Again, "I am writing these instructions to you," says the apostle to Timothy, "so that you may know how one ought to behave in the household of God," etc. (I Tim. 3:14–15). SCRIPTURE IS THE WORD OF GOD. Again, the selfsame apostle to the Thessalonians: "When," says he, "you received the Word of God which you heard from us, you accepted it, not as the word of men but as what it really is, the Word of God," etc. (I Thess. 2:13.) For the Lord himself has said in the Gospel, "It is not you who speak, but the Spirit of my Father speaking through you"; therefore "he who hears you hears me, and he who rejects me rejects him who sent me" (Matt. 10:20; Luke 10:16; John 13:20).

THE PREACHING OF THE WORD OF GOD IS THE WORD OF GOD. Wherefore when this Word of God is now preached in the church by preachers lawfully called, we believe that the very Word of God is proclaimed, and received by the faithful; and that neither any other Word of God is to be invented nor is to be expected from heaven: and that now the Word itself which is preached is to be regarded, not the minister that preaches; for even if he be evil and a sinner, nevertheless the Word of God remains still true and good.

Neither do we think that therefore the outward preaching is to be thought as fruitless because the instruction in true religion depends on the inward illumination of the Spirit, or because it is written "And no longer shall each man teach his neighbor . . ., for they shall all know me" (Jer. 31:34), and "Neither he who plants nor he who waters is anything, but only God who gives the growth" (I Cor.

3:7). For although "no one can come to Christ unless he be drawn by the Father" (John 6:44), and unless the Holy Spirit inwardly illumines him, yet we know that it is surely the will of God that his Word should be preached outwardly also. God could indeed, by his Holy Spirit, or by the ministry of an angel, without the ministry of St. Peter, have taught Cornelius in the Acts; but, nevertheless, he refers him to Peter, of whom the angel speaking says, "He shall tell you what you ought to do."

INWARD ILLUMINATION DOES NOT ELIMINATE EXTERNAL PREACHING. For he that illuminates inwardly by giving men the Holy Spirit, the same one, by way of commandment, said unto his disciples, "Go into all the world, and preach the Gospel to the whole creation" (Mark 16:15). And so in Philippi, Paul preached the Word outwardly to Lydia, a seller of purple goods; but the Lord inwardly opened the woman's heart (Acts 16:14). And the same Paul, after a beautiful development of his thought, in Rom. 10:17 at length comes to the conclusion, "So faith comes from hearing, and hearing from the Word of God by the preaching of Christ."

At the same time we recognize that God can illuminate whom and when he will, even without the external ministry, for that is in his power; but we speak of the usual way of instructing men, delivered unto us from God, both by commandment and examples.

HERESIES. We therefore detest all the heresies of Artemon, the Manichaeans, the Valentinians, of Cerdon, and the Marcionites, who denied that the Scriptures proceeded from the Holy Spirit; or did not accept some parts of them, or interpolated and corrupted them.

APOCRYPHA. And yet we do not conceal the fact that certain books of the Old Testament were by the ancient authors called *Apocryphal,* and by others *Ecclesiastical;* inasmuch as some would have them read in the churches, but not advanced as an authority from which the faith is to be established. As Augustine also, in his *De Civitate Dei,* book 18, ch. 38, remarks that "in the books of the Kings, the names and books of certain prophets are cited"; but he adds that "they are not in the canon"; and that "those books which we have suffice unto godliness."

Chapter II. Of Interpreting The Holy Scriptures; and of Fathers, Councils, and Traditions

THE TRUE INTERPRETATION OF SCRIPTURE. The apostle Peter has said that the Holy Scriptures are not of private interpretation (II Peter 1:20), and thus we do not allow all possible interpretations. Nor consequently do we acknowledge as the true or genuine interpretation of the Scriptures what is called the conception of the Roman Church, that is, what the defenders of the Roman Church plainly maintain should be thrust upon all for acceptance. But we hold that interpretation of the Scripture to be orthodox and genuine which is gleaned from the Scriptures themselves (from the nature of the language in which they were written, likewise according to the circumstances in which they were set down, and expounded in the light of like and unlike passages and of many and clearer passages) and which agree with the rule of faith and love, and contributes much to the glory of God and man's salvation.

INTERPRETATIONS OF THE HOLY FATHERS. Wherefore we do not despise the interpretations of the holy Greek and Latin fathers, nor reject their disputations and treatises concerning sacred matters as far as they agree with the Scriptures; but we modestly dissent from them when they are found to set down things differing from, or altogether contrary to, the Scriptures. Neither do we think that we do them any wrong in this matter; seeing that they all, with one consent, will not have their writings equated with the canonical Scriptures, but command us to prove how far they agree or disagree with them, and to accept what is in agreement and to reject what is in disagreement.

COUNCILS. And in the same order also we place the decrees and canons of councils.

Wherefore we do not permit ourselves, in controversies about religion or matters of faith, to urge our case with only the opinions of the fathers or decrees of councils; much less by received customs, or by the large number of those who share the same opinion, or by the prescription of a long time. WHO IS THE JUDGE? Therefore, we do not admit any other judge than God himself, who proclaims by the Holy Scriptures what is true, what is false, what is to be followed, or what to be avoided. So we do assent to the judgments of spiritual men which are drawn from the Word of God. Certainly Jeremiah and other prophets vehemently condemned the assemblies of priests which were set up against the law of God; and diligently admonished us that we should not listen to the fathers, or tread in their path who, walking in their own inventions, swerved from the law of God.

TRADITIONS OF MEN. Likewise we reject human traditions, even if they be adorned with high-sounding titles, as though they were divine and apostolical, delivered to the Church by the living voice of the apostles, and, as it were, through the hands of apostolical men to succeeding bishops which, when compared with the Scriptures, disagree with them; and by their disagreement show that they are not apostolic at all. For as the apostles did not contradict themselves in doctrine, so the apostolic men did not set forth things contrary to the apostles. On the contrary, it would be wicked to assert that the apostles by a living voice delivered anything contrary to their writings. Paul affirms expressly that he taught the same things in all churches (I Cor. 4:17). And, again, "For we write you nothing but what you can read and understand." (II Cor. 1:13). Also, in another place, he testifies that he and his disciples—that is, apostolic men— walked in the same way, and jointly by the same Spirit did all things (II Cor. 12:18). Moreover, the Jews in former times had the traditions of their elders; but these traditions were severely rejected by the Lord, indicating that the keeping of them hinders God's law, and that God is worshipped in vain by such traditions (Matt. 15:1 ff.; Mark 7:1 ff.).

The Confession of Faith of the Westminster Assembly of Divines, 1646

Chapter I. Of the Holy Scripture.

ALTHOUGH the light of nature, and the works of creation and providence do so far manifest the goodness, wisdom, and power of God, as to leave men unexcusable; yet are they not sufficient to give that knowledge of God, and of His will, which is necessary unto salvation. Therefore it pleased the Lord, at sundry times, and in divers manners, to reveal Himself, and to declare that His will unto His Church; and afterwards, for the better preserving and propagating of the truth, and for the more sure establishment and comfort of the Church against the corruption of the flesh, and the malice of Satan and of the world, to commit the same wholly unto writing: which maketh the Holy Scripture to be most necessary; those former ways of God's revealing His will unto His people being now ceased.

II. Under the name of Holy Scripture, or the Word of God written, are now contained all the books of the Old and New Testament, which are these.

Of the Old Testament.

Genesis	*II. Chronicles*	*Daniel*
Exodus	*Ezra*	*Hosea*
Leviticus	*Nehemiah*	*Joel*
Numbers	*Esther*	*Amos*
Deuteronomy	*Job*	*Obadiah*
Joshua	*Psalms*	*Jonah*
Judges	*Proverbs*	*Micah*
Ruth	*Ecclesiastes*	*Nahum*
I. Samuel	*The Song of Songs*	*Habakkuk*
II. Samuel	*Isaiah*	*Zephaniah*
I. Kings	*Jeremiah*	*Haggai*
II. Kings	*Lamentations*	*Zechariah*
I. Chronicles	*Ezekiel*	*Malachi;*

Of the New Testament:

The Gospels according to	*Galatians*	*The Epistle to the*
Matthew	*Ephesians*	*Hebrews*
Mark	*Philippians*	*The Epistle of James*
Luke	*Colossians*	*The first and second*
John	*Thessalonians I.*	*Epistles of Peter*
The Acts of the Apostles	*Thessalonians II.*	*The first, second, and*
Paul's Epistles to the	*To Timothy I.*	*third Epistles of John*
Romans	*To Timothy II.*	*The Epistle of Jude*
Corinthians I.	*To Titus*	*The Revelation of John.*
Corinthians II.		

All which are given by inspiration of God to be the rule of faith and life.

III. The books commonly called Apocrypha, not being of divine inspiration, are no part of the canon of the Scripture, and therefore are of no authority in the Church of God, nor to be any otherwise approved, or made use of, than other human writings.

IV. The authority of the Holy Scripture, for which it ought to be believed, and obeyed, dependeth not upon the testimony of any man, or Church; but wholly upon God (who is truth itself) the author thereof: and therefore it is to be received, because it is the Word of God.

V. We may be moved and induced by the testimony of the church to an high and reverent esteem of the Holy Scripture. And the heavenliness of the matter, the efficacy of the doctrine, the majesty of the style, the consent of all the parts, the scope of the whole (which is, to give all glory to God), the full discovery it makes of the only way of man's salvation, the many other incomparable excellencies, and the entire perfection thereof, are arguments whereby it doth abundantly evidence itself to be the Word of God; yet notwithstanding, our full persuasion and assurance of the infallible truth and divine authority thereof, is from the inward work of the Holy Spirit bearing witness by and with the Word in our hearts.

VI. The whole counsel of God concerning all things necessary for His own glory, man's salvation, faith and life, is either expressly set down in Scripture, or by good and necessary consequence may be deduced from Scripture: unto which nothing at any time is to be added, whether by new revelations of the Spirit or traditions of men. Nevertheless, we acknowledge the inward illumination of the Spirit of God to be necessary for the saving understanding of such things as are revealed in the Word: and that there are some circumstances concerning the worship of God, and government of the Church, common to human actions and societies, which are to be ordered by the light of nature, and Christian prudence, according to the general rules of the Word, which are always to be observed.

VII. All things in Scripture are not alike plain in themselves, nor alike clear unto all: yet those things which are necessary to be known, believed, and observed for salvation, are so clearly propounded, and opened in some place of Scripture or other, that not only the learned, but the unlearned, in a due use of the ordinary means, may attain unto a sufficient understanding of them.

VIII. The Old Testament in Hebrew (which was the native language of the people of God of old), and the New Testament in Greek (which, at the time of the writing of it, was most generally known to the nations), being immediately inspired by God, and, by His singular care and providence, kept pure in all ages, are therefore authentical; so as, in all controversies of religion, the Church is finally to appeal unto them. But, because these original tongues are not known to all the people of God, who have right unto, and interest in the Scriptures, and are commanded, in the fear of God, to read and search them, therefore they are to be translated into the vulgar language of every nation unto which they come, that, the Word of God dwelling plentifully in all, they may worship Him in an acceptable manner; and, through patience and comfort of the Scriptures, may have hope.

IX. The infallible rule of interpretation of Scripture is the Scripture itself: and therefore, when there is a question about the true and full sense of any Scripture (which is not manifold, but one), it must be searched and known by other places that speak more clearly.

X. The supreme judge by which all controversies of religion are to be determined, and all decrees of councils, opinions of ancient writers, doctrines of men, and private spirits, are to be examined, and in whose sentence we are to rest, can be no other but the Holy Spirit speaking in the Scripture.

The Confession of 1967

2. The Bible

The one sufficient revelation of God is Jesus Christ, the Word of God incarnate, to whom the Holy Spirit bears unique and authoritative witness through the Holy Scriptures, which are received and obeyed as the word of God written. The Scriptures are not a witness among others, but the witness without parallel. The church has received the books of the Old and New Testaments as prophetic and apostolic testimony in which it hears the word of God and by which its faith and obedience are nourished and regulated.

The New Testament is the recorded testimony of apostles to the coming of the Messiah, Jesus of Nazareth, and the sending of the Holy Spirit to the Church. The Old Testament bears witness to God's faithfulness in his covenant with Israel and points the way to the fulfillment of his purpose in Christ. The Old Testament is indispensable to understanding the New, and is not itself fully understood without the New.

The Bible is to be interpreted in the light of its witness to God's work of reconciliation in Christ. The Scriptures, given under the guidance of the Holy Spirit, are nevertheless the words of men, conditioned by the language, thought forms, and literary fashions of the places and times at which they were written. They reflect views of life, history, and the cosmos which were then current. The church, therefore, has an obligation to approach the Scriptures with literary and historical understanding. As God has spoken his word in diverse cultural situations, the church is confident that he will continue to speak through the Scriptures in a changing world and in every form of human culture.

God's word is spoken to his church today where the Scriptures are faithfully preached and attentively read in dependence on the illumination of the Holy Spirit and with readiness to receive their truth and direction.

Names Index

Subject Index